SPECIFIC MODELS AND SYSTEMS

Financial Planning and Control 12
**Presentations of Financial Information Systems for Use
by Financial Management** 13
Financial Reports for Use by Nonfinancial Management 14
Computer-Based Financial Modeling 15
**Design, Development, and Implementation of Decision
Support Systems** 16

INSTALLATION AND ADMINISTRATION OF A FINANCIAL INFORMATION SYSTEM

**Selection and Implementation of a Financial
Information System** 17
User Participation 18
The Information Center 19
Training of Personnel 20
Office Automation 21
**Security Implications for On-Line Financial
Information Systems** 22
Disaster Recovery 23

Financial Information Systems Manual

Editors

JAMES D. WILLSON
Senior Vice-President, Finance
Northrop Corporation

JACK F. DUSTON
Principal, Information Systems Consulting
Ernst & Whinney

WARREN, GORHAM & LAMONT
Boston • New York

Copyright © 1986 by
WARREN, GORHAM & LAMONT, INC.
210 SOUTH STREET
BOSTON, MASSACHUSETTS 02111

ALL RIGHTS RESERVED

No part of this book may be reproduced in any form, by photostat, microfilm, xerography, or any other means, or incorporated into any information retrieval system, electronic or mechanical, without the written permission of the copyright owner.

ISBN 0-88712-476-3

Library of Congress Catalog Card No. 85-63680

This publication is designed to provide accurate and authoritative information in regard to the subject matter covered. In publishing this book, neither the authors nor the publisher is engaged in rendering legal, accounting, or other professional service. If legal advice or other expert assistance is required, the services of a competent professional should be sought.

Contributors

Dwight Catherwood
Partner, Information Systems, and Member, National Information Systems Committee, Ernst & Whinney, Los Angeles
(Chapter 22)

James M. Conerly
Senior Manager, Office Automation, Ernst & Whinney, Los Angeles
(Chapter 5)

Jack F. Duston
Principal, Information Systems Consulting, Ernst & Whinney, Los Angeles
(Chapter 7)

Faith Goodland
Manager, Information Systems, The Warner Group, Woodland Hills, California
(Chapters 18 and 23)

Janice Hartman
Senior Analyst, Rand Corporation, Santa Monica, California
(Chapter 15)

Philip N. James
Chief, Strategic Information Systems Planning, Data Processing Department, County of Los Angeles, Los Angeles
(Chapter 21)

Harry Kraushaar
Vice-President and Manager, Management Consulting, Union Bank, Los Angeles
(Chapter 6)

Allen McMillen
Senior Consultant, Information Systems, Ernst & Whinney, Los Angeles
(Chapters 9 and 16)

Paul McNulty
Senior Manager, Information Systems, Ernst & Whinney, Los Angeles
(Chapter 20)

William O'Malley
Technical Support Staff, Office Automation, Ernst & Whinney, Los Angeles
(Chapter 23)

Douglas Potter
Data Systems Consultant, Newport Beach, California
(Chapters 8 and 11)

Keith L. Robinett
Corporate Vice-President, Information Resource Management (retired), Northrop Corporation, Los Angeles
(Chapters 4 and 19)

Janice M. Roehl
Manager, Information and Financial Systems Consulting, Ernst & Whinney, Los Angeles
(Chapter 17)

Steven J. Root
Director, Corporate Audit, Northrop Corporation, Los Angeles
(Chapters 1, 2, and 10)

Dane Sullivan
Manager, Information Systems, Ernst & Whinney, Los Angeles
(Chapter 6)

James D. Willson
Senior Vice-President, Finance (retired), Northrop Corporation, Los Angeles
(Chapters 3, 12, 13, and 14)

Preface

COMPUTER TECHNOLOGY, more broadly defined as "information technology," has undergone rapid change and has become a powerful, significant force in the economy. Businesses and other institutions depend increasingly on adequate, readily available information that is dispensed in a usable form.

A major segment of the information used by those who guide private enterprise is of a financial nature. These data are used not only by the financial executive but by other corporate executives as well. For example, the chief executive officer needs to know, in terms of profit, how actual results compare to the business plan and the direction in which the business is moving. The sales executive must know, from understandable figures, what products or services are selling best and how profitable they are. The chief manufacturing executive should know the actual costs of production as compared with expectations or standards and the trend of those costs. The research and development officer might want to know how much has been spent, by product, on R&D, and the estimated costs of completing each task. Of course, the chief financial officer must be continually aware of the financial health of the corporation, the operating results versus plan, the funds required over the short and long term, the most economical way of securing the capital, and the most beneficial uses of assets or shareholders' equity.

Financial Information Systems Manual, written in direct, nontechnical language, is designed for those business executives who assume primary responsibility for the development and dissemination of financial information, including information resource management officers, chief financial officers and their staffs, treasurers, controllers, chief accountants, and budget directors. The masculine pronoun is used for convenience only. It is intended to refer equally to men and women.

The *Manual* explains what should be done to provide reliable information, the types of information that are practical and useful, and the administrative and operational pitfalls to be avoided. The *Manual* is divided into four parts, which cover the key subjects of concern to executives responsible for FISs.

1 An overview of how an effective FIS should assist in managing a business, and a survey of the trends in technology.

2 Basic systems concepts: what makes up a system; the role of microcomputers, telecommunications, and networks; and the need for systems auditability and long-range systems planning.

3 Basic financial models and key points in the design of decision support systems, and examples of financial reports (including graphs) found useful in planning and control for financial and nonfinancial executives.

4 Key points to be observed in installing and administering a system—including system selection, user participation, personnel training, organization structure, and security.

The many illustrations and examples provided in the *Manual* explain the potentials of a good FIS—with emphasis on management uses of data. Such important, but sometimes unrecognized, subjects as systems auditability, systems security, and disaster recovery are also examined.

The design, installation, and operation of an effective FIS are affected by rapidly changing technology. Not only is hardware constantly evolving, but the application software written to perform specific functions and the programs that control the internal workings of a computer are changing as well. To keep the reader as up-to-date as possible, supplements will be issued annually to discuss emerging trends, review new technologies and applications, and provide further useful illustrations.

The contributing authors to the *Manual* are experts in their areas of computer technology and methodology, and have had personal exposure to the applications and practices about which they have written. The *Manual* blends the viewpoints of capable management consultants from the public accounting firm of Ernst & Whinney, whose day-to-day efforts include the design and installation of FISs, with those of experienced executives from the Northrop Corporation, a major aerospace firm, who are experienced in the use, development, and auditing of FISs. This collaboration has produced some very practical ideas and suggestions.

Of course, a quality publication is not developed solely by the contributing authors and editors. Much credit is due to the guidance, diligence, and patience of the publisher. We wish to thank the staff of Warren, Gorham & Lamont that participated in this project.

JAMES D. WILLSON
JACK F. DUSTON

Los Angeles
April 1986

Summary of Contents

TABLE OF CONTENTS ix

GLOSSARY xxvii

PART I – OVERVIEW

1. Perspectives on Financial Information Systems 1-1
2. Systems Technology Trends 2-1
3. The Financial Information System as Related to Management of a Business 3-1
4. Alternative Organization Structures for the Data Processing Function 4-1

PART II – BASIC SYSTEMS CONCEPTS

5. Ingredients of an Effective Financial Information System 5-1
6. Financial Accounting Systems 6-1
7. Role and Impact of Microcomputers 7-1
8. Database Management 8-1
9. Telecommunications and Networking 9-1
10. Systems Control and Auditability 10-1
11. Long-Range Systems Planning 11-1

PART III – SPECIFIC MODELS AND SYSTEMS

12. Financial Planning and Control 12-1
13. Presentations of Financial Information Systems for Use by Financial Management 13-1
14. Financial Reports for Use by Nonfinancial Management 14-1
15. Computer-Based Financial Modeling 15-1
16. Design, Development, and Implementation of Decision Support Systems 16-1

PART IV – INSTALLATION AND ADMINISTRATION OF A FINANCIAL INFORMATION SYSTEM

17. Selection and Implementation of a Financial Information System **17**-1
18. User Participation **18**-1
19. The Information Center **19**-1
20. Training of Personnel **20**-1
21. Office Automation **21**-1
22. Security Implications for On-Line Financial Information Systems **22**-1
23. Disaster Recovery **23**-1

INDEX I-1

Table of Contents

Glossary xxvii

PART I — OVERVIEW

1 Perspectives on Financial Information Systems

Overview 1	Management as a Barometer for Success 12
Some Useful Definitions 3	
Management Information Systems 3	**FISs: Some Implications** 15
Information Systems 4	Exposure to Systems Technology 15
Financial Information Systems 6	Effect on Traditional Roles of Functional Disciplines 16
Accounting Information Systems 7	Trend Toward Pooling Databases 16
A Perspective of FISs 8	Transition to More Costly Integrated Information Systems 16
Historical Perspective 9	Beneficial Impact on Systems Users 17
Forces of Evolution 9	
The Current Environment 10	**References** 17
Quality of Information as a Barometer for Success 12	

Fig. 1-1 An MIS 5
Fig. 1-2 A Typical FIS for a Manufacturing Company 7
Fig. 1-3 Evolution of ROI Analysis 13
Fig. 1-4 Selected Financial Reporting Milestones 14
Fig. 1-5 Payroll Calculation: 1945–1965, Compared With 1965–1985 15

2 Systems Technology Trends

Overview 2	Fiber Optics Technology 4
Application of Systems Technology to FISs 2	Network Technology 4
	Application Technology 5
	Security Technology 5
What Is Systems Technology? 2	Systems Technology Defined 5
Components Technologies 3	
Microprocessor Technology 3	**Systems Technology Trends** 6
Integration Technology 3	A Brief History 6
Advanced Materials Technology 4	**Systems Technology Trends Affecting FISs** 8
Memory Technology 4	
Disk-Storage Technology 4	The Current Scene 8

ix

TABLE OF CONTENTS

Stand-Alone Applications	8
Centralized Processing	8
Inefficient Processing	9
Costly Systems Maintenance	9
Informal Compensating Factors	10
Undue Risk	10
Computer Illiteracy	11
Trends Affecting Future FISs	11
Systems Integration and Interaction	11
Database Orientation	12
Ease of Development, Change, and Maintenance	12
Wider Application	13
Risk Reduction	13
The Future Scene	14
Organizational Trends	15
Effect on MISs	15
Effect on Finance Functions	16
Effect on Other Management Functions	17
Office Trends	18
References	19

Fig. 2-1 Systems Technology Evolution ... 7

3 The Financial Information System as Related to Management of a Business

Introduction ... 2

The Business Purpose ... 2

Management's Leadership Task ... 3

The Management Process ... 3
Planning to Meet Business Objectives ... 5
Coordinating/Organizing to Meet Company Goals ... 5
Directing to Implement Company Goals ... 6
Measuring and Controlling to Ensure Success of the Plan ... 6

The Managerial Decision-Making Process ... 6
Types of Management Decisions ... 7

Information Flows ... 9
Informal Information Flows ... 10
Formal Information Flows ... 11
Formal Vertical Flows ... 11
Formal Horizontal Flows ... 11

Information Needs of Managers ... 12
Types of Information ... 12

Managerial Activities as a Factor in Information Needs ... 13
The Managerial Level ... 13
Organization Structure ... 14
Nature of the Managerial Activities ... 14
Nature of Functional Operations ... 15

Reports for Decision Making and Information Gathering ... 15
Classifying Reports by Purpose ... 16
Classifying Reports by Conciseness ... 17
Classifying Reports by Occurrence ... 17
Classifying Reports by Format or Style ... 19

Reporting Systems ... 22

Responsibility Reporting ... 23

References ... 25

Fig. 3-1 The Management Process ... 4
Fig. 3-2 Categories of Management Decisions ... 8
Fig. 3-3 Management Levels and Primary Types of Decisions ... 10
Fig. 3-4 Profile of Information Needs ... 14
Fig. 3-5 Classification of Reports ... 16
Fig. 3-6 Summary Plan Report ... 17
Fig. 3-7 Summary Control Report—Corporate Headquarters Expense ... 18
Fig. 3-8 Budget Report—Exception Basis ... 19
Fig. 3-9 Alternative Report Formats ... 21
Fig. 3-10 The Flash Report ... 22
Fig. 3-11 Responsibility Reporting—Flow of Information ... 24

4 Alternative Organization Structures for the Data Processing Function

Introduction 2
Organization Concepts 2
Alternative Structures 3
Centralized Data Processing 3
Decentralized Data Processing 4
Distributed Data Processing 4
Federated Data Processing 7
Chief Information Officer's Relationship
to the Chief Financial Officer 9

Enterprise Factors 10
Nature of the Business Organization . . . 10
Form of the Business Organization 11
Location of Knowledgeable People 11
    Data Processing 11
    Office Automation 11
    Telecommunications 11
Stage of Systems Development 12
Knowledge and Interest of Senior
Management 12

Economic Factors 13
Hardware 13
Software 13
People 13
Facilities 13

Cultural/Political Factors 13
Historical Precedents 14
Organizational Independence 14
Service History 14
Power Bases 14

Departmental Organization 15
Systems Group 15
Operations Group 17
Technical Support Group 17
Administration Group 17
Management Staff 17

References 18

Fig. 4-1 Centralized Organization as a Major Department 4
Fig. 4-2 Centralized Organization Within a Major User Department 5
Fig. 4-3 Centralized Organization Within a Services Department 5
Fig. 4-4 Decentralized Organization 6
Fig. 4-5 Distributed Data Processing Network 7
Fig. 4-6 Federated Data Processing Network 8
Fig. 4-7 Internal Structure of the Chief Information Officer's Department 16

PART II — BASIC SYSTEMS CONCEPTS

5 Ingredients of an Effective Financial Information System

Introduction 1

The Enterprise Model 2
Organizational Factors 3
Rules of the Game 3
Critical Success Factors 4
Key Indicators 4
Executive Support Needs 5

Data Management 5

Relevant Data 5
Data Sources 7
Organization 7
Accuracy 9
Maintenance 10

Performance Management 10
Establishing Performance Criteria 11
Responsibility Management 11
Performance Feedback Reporting 11

Exception Reporting 13	**Distribution Management** 18
	Selection of Data for Distribution 18
Data Security Administration 14	Means for Data Distribution 19
The Security Program 15	Timeliness of Data Distribution 19
Access Restrictions 15	
Version Control 16	**Summary** 20
Protection of Data in Circulation 17	

6 Financial Accounting Systems

Introduction 2	Open Item System 23
	Features 24
The General Ledger 4	Interface to Billing 24
Features 4	Interface to General Ledger 24
Database 4	Reporting 24
Chart-of-Accounts Structuring 6	Cash Flow 25
Data Entry, Inquiry, and Update . . . 8	
Audit Trails 10	**Payroll** 25
Reporting 11	Features 26
Budgeting 13	Multistate Capabilities 26
Cost Allocation 15	Labor Distribution 26
Cost Accounting 16	Personnel Functions 27
Security 17	
	Fixed Assets 27
Accounts Payable 18	Features 27
Features 20	Asset Control 27
Integration With Purchasing/Receiving 20	Book Depreciation 29
Check Reconciliation 21	Tax Depreciation 29
Reporting 21	Multiple Records 30
	Reporting 30
Accounts Receivable 22	Other Features 30
Balance Only System 23	
Balance Forward System 23	**Current Developments** 30

Fig. 6-1   Core Accounting Systems Interrelationships 3
Fig. 6-2   General Ledger Processing Flow 5
Fig. 6-3   Account Coding Scheme 7
Fig. 6-4   Overlapping Reporting Relationships 8
Fig. 6-5   Trial Balance for the Cash Account 11
Fig. 6-6   Comparative Income Statement 12
Fig. 6-7   Custom Report Developed by a Report Writer 13
Fig. 6-8   Initial Budget Creation Feature 14
Fig. 6-9   Flexible Budget for Direct Materials 15
Fig. 6-10 Financial Accounting Cost Accumulation 17
Fig. 6-11 Cost Accounting Cost Accumulation 18
Fig. 6-12 Feature Comparison of Small and Large General Ledger Systems 19
Fig. 6-13 Standard Features and Reports in Small and Large Accounts Payable Systems . . 22
Fig. 6-14 Standard Features and Reports in Small and Large Accounts Receivable Systems 25
Fig. 6-15 Standard Features in Small and Large Payroll Systems 27
Fig. 6-16 Fixed Assets Processing Flow 28
Fig. 6-17 Feature Comparison of Small and Large Fixed Asset Systems 31

TABLE OF CONTENTS xiii

7 Role and Impact of Microcomputers

Introduction 2	Application Software 11
Effect of Microcomputers on Small	Spreadsheet Programs 11
Businesses 2	Database Management Programs . . . 11
Effect of Microcomputers on	Integrated Programs 12
Corporations 2	Software Favorites 12
	Accounting Packages; Getting Started . . 13
Microcomputer Hardware 3	Selected Key Features 14
Microprocessor 4	
Disk Storage 5	**Microcomputers and FISs** 15
Keyboards 5	Basic Microcomputer FISs 15
Monitors 6	Local Area Networks 16
Printers 6	Microcomputer/Mainframe FISs 17
Dot Matrix 7	
Near Letter Quality 7	**Security Management** 19
Letter Quality 8	
Laser 8	**Physical Security** 19
Boards 8	Software Security 20
Microcomputer Software 9	
Systems Software 10	**Training** 21

Fig. 7-1 The Microcomputer Configuration 4
Fig. 7-2 Type Styles of Printers 7
Fig. 7-3 Basic Logic Boards 9
Fig. 7-4 Top Twenty Independent Microcomputer Software Suppliers 10
Fig. 7-5 A Typical LAN Business Installation 16
Fig. 7-6 Diagram of EIS 18
Fig. 7-7 The Three-Generation Backup System 20

8 Database Management

Introduction 2	Record 9
	Key 9
Background 2	File 9
	Data Dictionary 9
Why Database Management Is Useful . . . 3	Schema 9
Advantages 3	Subschema 10
Information Needs 3	Data Base Administrator 10
Control and Standardization 4	
Fourth-Generation Languages 4	**The Database Environment** 10
User Department Programming 4	
Programmer Productivity 4	**Design and Implementation** 12
Disadvantages 5	Relationship to the Long-Range Planning
	Process 13
Allin Industries: A Database Management	Database Design 14
Example 6	Generic Classification of Databases 15
	Hierarchical Databases 15
Definition of Terms 8	Network Databases 16
Corporate Financial Database 8	Relational Databases 17
Database 8	Relationship to Fourth-Generation
Data Base Management Systems 8	Language Productivity Tools 19
Data Definition Language 8	
Data Element 9	**Database Software Selection** 20
Data 9	

Three Classifications of Database
  Software 20
    Information Center Database Software 22
    Large-Scale Development Software .. 23
    Programmer Productivity Software .. 23
Other Considerations in Selecting
  Database Software 24
    Database Management Systems 26
Software Product Costs 26

Maintaining Database Integrity 26
Managing the Sources of Financial Data—
  The FIS 27
    Controls 27
    User Training 28

Management Imperative 29
Security 29
  Role of the DBMS and the Operating
    System 29
  Use of a Separate Security Package .. 30
  Role of Application Software 30
  Test Database 32
Backup and Recovery 32
  Systems Backup 32
  Transaction Audit and Rollback 33

Future Trends in Database Management 33

References 34

Fig. 8-1 Sample Costs for Implementing IBM's IMS DBMS 5
Fig. 8-2 Major Elements of a Database Environment 11
Fig. 8-3 Corporate Financial Database Implementation Plan 14
Fig. 8-4 Selected Database Software and Costs 21
Fig. 8-5 Sources of Financial Data 27
Fig. 8-6 Typical Security Functions of a Database Environment 31

9 Telecommunications and Networking

Telecommunications Technologies 1
Telecommunications Today: An Overview 1
The New AT&T 3
VANs 3
Digital Private Branch Exchange: The
  PBX Explosion 6
Office Automation 7
  Word Processing 9
  Electronic Mail and Information
    Utilities 9
  Facsimile Systems 9
  Computer-Based Telephones 9
  Voice Messaging 9
  Electronic Document Handling 10
  Data Communications Networks 10
**Local Area Networks for Personal
  Computers** 12

Fig. 9-1 VANs 6

Overview 12
LAN Characteristics 14
Signalling Schemes 15
LAN Topologies 15
LAN Access Methods 16
Planning for an LAN 17

Case Study 18
Ernst & Whinney National Systems
  Group 18
History of the NSG Network 18
Researching LANs 19
The Evaluation Network 20
Evaluation Results 20
Installation Checklist 22

References 23

10 Systems Control and Auditability

Overview 2

Definitions 4

Systems Control Concepts 6
The FCPA 7

General Provisions 7
Accounting Standards 8
Variability of Control Systems 9
Authorization 10
Execution, Processing, and Recording ... 11
Accountability 11

TABLE OF CONTENTS

Security and Safeguarding 12
Reasonable Assurance 13
Auditability 14

EDP and Internal Control 15
Distinguishing Features 15
    Dynamic Environment 15
    Uniform Processing 15
    Error Correction 15
    Storage 15
    Auditability 16
    Security 16

Risks in EDP 16
Risk Analysis: A Useful Tool 16
Computer Fraud and Mischievous Acts 20
Violations of Laws and Regulations 20
Negligent or Ineffective Information
  Systems Management 21
Computer Dependence 22

Proliferation of Minicomputers and
  Microcomputers 22

Control Objectives and Techniques 23
Authorization 25
Execution, Processing, and Recording . . . 26
Accountability 29
Security 30
Internal Auditing 33
    Detailed Functional Auditing 34
    Installation Reviews 35
    Application Auditing 35
    Developing Systems Auditing 35
    Concurrent Auditing 35
Personal Computers 37
    Authorization 39
    Accountability 39
    Security 39

References 40

Fig. 10-1 Phases of EDP Organizational Growth 3
Fig. 10-2 Types of Security Exposure 17
Fig. 10-3 Preventive, Limiting, and Recovery Controls for Selected Exposures 19
Fig. 10-4 EDP Auditing Chronology 34
Fig. 10-5 Depiction of Embedded Audit Routines 36
Fig. 10-6 Tabulation of Generalized Audit Software Packages and Their Vendors 38

11 Long-Range Systems Planning

Introduction 2
Problems of the Non-LRSP Organization 2
Organizations That Should Use LRSP . . 3
    Size 3
    Amount of Change 3

Getting Started 4
Assembling the Project Team 4
Determining the Planning Horizon 5
Components of the Plan 6

Developing the LRSP 6
Step 1: Hold the Initial Kickoff Meeting 8
Step 2: Review the Corporate Strategic
  Plan, Including Goals and Objectives . . 9
    Examples of Corporate Goals and
      Objectives 9
Step 3: Define the Application Projects 11
    Application Status Summary 11
    Application Projects 14
    Tying the Application Projects Back to
      the Corporate Strategic Plan 14
    Software Architecture 15
Step 4: Define the Systems Software
  Projects 16

    Examples of Systems Software Projects 17
Step 5: Define the Hardware and
  Communications Projects 17
    Define Current and Future Man-
      Machine Interfaces 19
    Alternatives Analysis 20
    Define Hardware and
      Communications Projects 20
    Define Hardware and
      Communications Architecture 21
Step 6: Define the Personnel and Staffing
  Projects 23
Step 7: Review All Projects With the
  Project Team 24
Step 8: Develop the Implementation Plan 26
    Project Sequencing 26
    Totaling Resource Requirements by
      Time Period 28
Step 9: Final Review and Preparation . . 28
    Project Team Review 29
    Final Preparation 29
    Management Review 29

Implementing the LRSP 30
Assignment of Responsibility 30

Monitoring the Schedule 30
Holding Periodic Update Meetings 31
Being Flexible 31

Revising the LRSP 31

Steps to Updating the Plan 32

Summary 32

References 33

Fig. 11-1 Relationship of Organizational Size to Cost/Benefit Provided by LRSP 4
Fig. 11-2 Steps Involved in Developing the LRSP 7
Fig. 11-3 Example of an LRSP Table of Contents 8
Fig. 11-4 Illustrative Statement of Corporate Purpose, Strategy, and Goals 10
Fig. 11-5 Examples of Application Projects 12
Fig. 11-6 Example of an Application Status Summary 13
Fig. 11-7 Relationship Between Corporate Goals and Objectives and LRSP Projects 15
Fig. 11-8 Diagram of Software Architecture 16
Fig. 11-9 Systems Software Projects 18
Fig. 11-10 Man-Machine Interfaces 19
Fig. 11-11 Hardware and Communications Projects 22
Fig. 11-12 Hardware and Communications Architecture 24
Fig. 11-13 Personnel and Staffing Projects 25
Fig. 11-14 Planned Organization Chart 26
Fig. 11-15 Implementation Plan 27

PART III — SPECIFIC MODELS AND SYSTEMS

12 Financial Planning and Control

Introduction 2

**Some Practical Observations About
Financial Planning** 2
Two Principal Types of Planning 2
Different Information Input 3

Cost Classifications and Behavior 6
Different Types of Costs 6

Costs for Planning Purposes 8
Costs in Relation to Volume 9
Incremental Costs; Contribution Margin 10

Costs for Control Purposes 11
Responsibility Accounting and Reporting 12
Applying the Responsibility Concept . . . 12

Segregating Costs Into Their Components 14
Fixed Costs 14
Variable Costs and Measures of Activity 15
Determining Semivariable Costs 15
Direct Estimates 16

Calculation of Fixed and Variable
 Elements 20
Graphic Determination 22
The Least Squares Method 24
Allowing for Extraordinary Costs 24
Procedure Applicable to Most
 Departments 24

**Standard Costs in Relation to Plan or
Budget** 25

A Definition of Budgeting 25

Types of Budgets 26
Project Budgets 26
Fixed Budgets 28
Flexible or Variable Budgets 28

**Applicability of Planning and Control to
the Balance Sheet** 31

References 38

TABLE OF CONTENTS

Fig. 12-1 The System of Business Plans 4
Fig. 12-2 Relationship of Annual Plan to Strategic Plan 5
Fig. 12-3 Cost Classifications for Planning Decisions 8
Fig. 12-4 Costs in Relation to Volume 9
Fig. 12-5 A Realistic Cost Pattern 10
Fig. 12-6 Statement of Marginal and Operating Income 11
Fig. 12-7 Cost Classifications for Control and Analysis 12
Fig. 12-8 Manufacturing Expense Budget at Selected Levels of Activity 18
Fig. 12-9 Graphic Determination of Fixed and Variable Costs 23
Fig. 12-10 Actual and Budget Performance 27
Fig. 12-11 Distribution Cost Budget 29
Fig. 12-12 Budget Report 30
Fig. 12-13 Example of Flexible Budget 32
Fig. 12-14 Illustrative Monthly Budget Report 33
Fig. 12-15 Summary Marketing Division Budget 34
Fig. 12-16 Planned Cash Receipts and Disbursements 35
Fig. 12-17 Accounts Receivable Budget 36
Fig. 12-18 Materials Inventory Budget 37
Fig. 12-19 Comparative Working Capital Requirements 38

13 Presentations of Financial Information Systems for Use by Financial Management

Introduction 3
Functional Outline—CFO 3

Broad Scope of Financial Data 6
Financial Reporting Systems—Selected Report Structure 6

The Long-Range Financial Plan 8
Basic Financial Assumptions 9
Financial Highlights 10
Consolidated Net Sales 10
Net Sales 10
Consolidated Sales Backlog by Strategic Business Unit 14
Consolidated Net Income 14
Net Income by Strategic Business Unit 14
Earnings per Share 17
Cash Sources and Uses 17
Consolidated Financial Position 18
Percentage Return on Assets 18
Percentage Return on Shareholder's Equity 18
Ratio of Long-Term Debt to Net Worth 18
Current Ratio 18

The Annual Business Plan 23
Annual Business Plan Highlights 24
Sales by Business Group 24
Activity Summary by Business Group 25
Net Income by Business Group 25
Annual Changes in Net Income 25
Comparative Statement of Planned Income and Expense 25
Statement of Planned Sources and Uses of Cash 28
Statement of Consolidated Financial Position 28
Return on Average Assets by Profit Center 28
Trend in Operating Results 30
Return on Assets—Trend and Composition 30
Comparative Return on Shareholders' Equity 30
Borrowing Capacity 33
Debt to Equity Ratios 33
Other Data 33

Company/Segment Overall Performance 35
Some Manufacturing Companies 35
A Services Company 54

Daily Conditions Report 59

Other Financial Management Reports 59

Special Analyses 62

Fig. 13-1 Functional Outline for CFO	4
Fig. 13-2 Financial Reporting Systems—Selected Report Structure	7
Fig. 13-3 Basic Financial Assumptions	10
Fig. 13-4 Financial Highlights	11
Fig. 13-5 Consolidated Net Sales	12
Fig. 13-6 Net Sales by Strategic Business Unit	12
Fig. 13-7 Net Sales vs. U.S. Government Sales	13
Fig. 13-8 Net Sales—Percentage Nongovernment	13
Fig. 13-9 Consolidated Sales Backlog by Strategic Business Unit	14
Fig. 13-10 Consolidated Net Income	15
Fig. 13-11 Net Income by Strategic Business Unit	15
Fig. 13-12 Earnings per Share	16
Fig. 13-13 Earnings per Share—Various Scenarios	16
Fig. 13-14 Cash Sources and Uses	17
Fig. 13-15 Consolidated Financial Position (Assets)	19
Fig. 13-16 Consolidated Financial Position (Liabilities and Net Worth)	20
Fig. 13-17 Percentage Return on Average Assets	21
Fig. 13-18 Percentage Return on Average Shareholders' Equity	21
Fig. 13-19 Ratio of Long-Term Debt to Net Worth	22
Fig. 13-20 Current Ratio	22
Fig. 13-21 Annual Business Plan Highlights	24
Fig. 13-22 Sales by Business Group	25
Fig. 13-23 Activity Summary by Business Group	26
Fig. 13-24 Net Income by Business Group	26
Fig. 13-25 Annual Changes in Net Income	27
Fig. 13-26 Comparative Statement of Planned Income and Expense	27
Fig. 13-27 Statement of Planned Sources and Uses of Cash	28
Fig. 13-28 Statement of Consolidated Financial Position	29
Fig. 13-29 Return on Average Assets by Profit Center	30
Fig. 13-30 Trends in Operating Results	31
Fig. 13-31 Return on Assets: Trends and Composition	32
Fig. 13-32 Comparative Return on Shareholders' Equity	34
Fig. 13-33 Borrowing Capacity	34
Fig. 13-34 Debt-to-Equity Ratios	35
Fig. 13-35 Summary Financial Report for Management	36
Fig. 13-36 Summary Performance by Profit Center	37
Fig. 13-37 Comparative Statement of Income and Expense	38
Fig. 13-38 Summary of Operations	40
Fig. 13-39 Summary of Acquisitions (New Orders) by Organization	41
Fig. 13-40 Comparative New Orders Received	42
Fig. 13-41 Contract Acquisitions—Explanation of Variances	43
Fig. 13-42 Comparative Consolidated Sales	44
Fig. 13-43 Consolidated Net Sales by Organization	45
Fig. 13-44 Consolidated Net Sales—Explanation of Variances	46
Fig. 13-45 Consolidated Order Backlog	47
Fig. 13-46 Consolidated Order Backlog by Organization	48
Fig. 13-47 Comparative Consolidated Operating Margin	49
Fig. 13-48 Operating Margin by Organization	50

Fig. 13-49 Consolidated Operating Margin—Explanation of Variances 51
Fig. 13-50 Comparative Consolidated Net Income 52
Fig. 13-51 Comparative Consolidated Net Income and Expense 53
Fig. 13-52 Comparative Condensed Balance Sheet 55
Fig. 13-53 Comparative Income Statement 56
Fig. 13-54 Comparative Statement of Changes in Financial Position 57
Fig. 13-55 CFO's Commentary on Period Earnings 58
Fig. 13-56 Daily Conditions Report for Top Management 60
Fig. 13-57 Weekly Cash Activity 61
Fig. 13-58 Summary of Short-Term Investments 62

14 Financial Reports for Use by Nonfinancial Management

Introduction 2

Reports for the Marketing Manager 2
Marketing Objectives 3
Typical Reports 3
Illustrative Report Examples 5

Reports for the Manufacturing Manager . . 15

Illustrative Report Examples 15

Reports for the R&D Manager 29
Illustrative Report Examples 29

General and Administrative Activities . . . 31
Illustrative Report Examples 33

Special Analyses 33

Fig. 14-1 Typical Marketing Management Information Needs 4
Fig. 14-2 Statement of Income and Expense by Territory 6
Fig. 14-3 Statement of Income and Expense (and Contribution Margin) by Product Line 7
Fig. 14-4 Summary Marketing Division Budget 8
Fig. 14-5 Graphic Display—Sales Performance 9
Fig. 14-6 Graph and Table of Net Sales 10
Fig. 14-7 Summary Sales Performance by Division 11
Fig. 14-8 Project Budget Report—Market Research Division 12
Fig. 14-9 Exception Sales Performance Report 13
Fig. 14-10 Sales and Expenses by Salesperson 14
Fig. 14-11 Selling Expenses by District 16
Fig. 14-12 District Selling Expenses by Type of Expenditure 17
Fig. 14-13 Typical Manufacturing Manager's Information Needs 18
Fig. 14-14 Actual vs. Budget Performance by Department 20
Fig. 14-15 Departmental Budget Report 21
Fig. 14-16 Graph of Labor Efficiency Trend 22
Fig. 14-17 Graph of Material Usage Trend 22
Fig. 14-18 Manufacturing Overhead Summary by Department 23
Fig. 14-19 Material Price Variance (Monthly) by Material Classification 24
Fig. 14-20 Daily Excess Material Usage by Type of Material 25
Fig. 14-21 Changes in Unit Material Standard Cost 26
Fig. 14-22 Daily Labor Report 26
Fig. 14-23 Exception Report 27
Fig. 14-24 Capital Budget Status Report—Manufacturing Division 28
Fig. 14-25 R&D Expense Budget by Department 30

Fig. 14-26 R&D Expense Report by Department 31
Fig. 14-27 R&D Project Budget Report 32
Fig. 14-28 Summary of General and Administrative Expense—Planning Budget 34
Fig. 14-29 Budget Summary—Finance Department 35
Fig. 14-30 Budget Performance Report—Administrative Department 36

15 Computer-Based Financial Modeling

Definition of Financial Modeling 2

The Need for Financial Modeling 2
Planning and Scheduling Business
  Resources 2
Interrelated Impact of Poor Decisions on
  an Organization 3
External Regulations and Requirements . 3

**The Process of Designing a Financial
  Model** 3
Identify Key Issues to Be Addressed by
  the Model 4
Establish Report and Data Requirements 4
Develop Model Specifications 4
Select the Appropriate Financial Planning
  Software 5
Develop and Implement the Model 5
Prepare Documentation 6
Execute Model and Analyze Key Factors 6

**Overview of Selected Modeling
  Techniques** 6
"What-If" Analysis 6
Naïve Forecasting 6
Univariate Analysis 9
Multiple Regression 9
Sensitivity Analysis 9
Goal-Seeking Analysis 10
Optimization 10
Risk Analysis 10

**Selection of Financial Modeling Software
  Packages** 11

Fig. 15-1 Modeling Technique Overview 7

Microcomputer-Based Financial Modeling
  Packages 11
  Micro DSS/F 12
  Lotus 1-2-3 12
  Symphony 12
  Multiplan 13
  Context MBA 13
  Corporate MBA 14
  MicroFCS 14
  IFPS/Personal 14
  Encore! 15
  SuperCalc^3 15
  T/Maker III 15
Mainframe or Minicomputer-Based
  Financial Modeling Packages ... 16
  FCS-EPS 16
  IFPS (Interactive Financial Planning
    System) 16
  Focus Financial Modeling Language 17
  Impact 17
  MSA/Forecasting and Modeling
    System 17
  Summary 17

**Design and Documentation Guidelines for
  Financial Models** 18

**Future Developments for Computer-Based
  Financial Modeling** 19

References 19

16 Design, Development, and Implementation of Decision Support Systems

Overview and Definition 2
DSS Building Blocks and Applications . . 2

Framework for Designing DSS 3
Three Technology Levels for DSS 4
An Adaptive Approach for Developing a
  DSS 4

Individual Roles in the Development and
  Use of DSS 5

Design Objectives for Decision Support .. 7
Types and Levels of Decision Support . . 7
Specific Design Criteria 8
Factors In Design 8

TABLE OF CONTENTS

DSS Development	9	**Implementation Strategies**	14
The Four Major Components of a DSS	9	Steps Toward DSS Integration	14
		Phased Implementation	16
Database Management	11	Software Selection Criteria	17
Model Development	11	**Evaluation of DSS**	17
General Purpose Models	11		
Specific DSS Models	12	**Benefits**	18
DSS Model Generators	12		
Building DSS Through Interactive Design	12	**DSS Today and Tomorrow**	18
Levels of Flexibility	13	**References**	20
Development of a Prototype	13		

Fig. 16-1 DSS Building Blocks 3
Fig. 16-2 The Four Major Components of a DSS 10
Fig. 16-3 Evaluation Criteria for DSS 19
Fig. 16-4 Cited Benefits of a DSS 20

PART IV — INSTALLATION AND ADMINISTRATION OF A FINANCIAL INFORMATION SYSTEM

17 Selection and Implementation of a Financial Information System

Overview	2	**Cost of the System**	22
Reasons to Buy Software	2	**Final Selection**	23
Defining Systems Requirements	4	**Contract Negotiations**	23
Questionnaires	5	**Implementation Steps**	26
Interviews	5		
Document Reviews	7	**Postimplementation Review**	28
Outside Sources	7	**Appendix 17-1: Hardware Selection Criteria**	31
Preparing the RFP	10	Central Processing Unit	31
Cover Letter	11	Peripherals	31
General Information/Proposal Guidelines	11	Remote Devices	31
Background Material	11	Environmental Considerations	32
Vendor Questionnaire	11	Flexibility and Expandability	32
Vendor Cost Summary	12	Systems Reliability	32
Information Requirements	12		
Distribution of the RFP	12	**Appendix 17-2: Vendor Evaluation Criteria**	33
		Product Support	33
Review of the Completed RFP	15	Reputation and Stability	33
		Experience	34
Reference Calls	20	Product Availability	34
Site Visits	21	**References**	34

Fig. 17-1 Comparison of Software Packages With Software Developed In House 4
Fig. 17-2 Sample Questionnaire for Defining Systems Requirements 6

Fig. 17-3 Accounts Receivable System Requirements 9
Fig. 17-4 RFP Sections 11
Fig. 17-5 Vendor Cost Summary 13
Fig. 17-6 Accounts Payable System Requirements 14
Fig. 17-7 Completed Accounts Payable System Requirements 14
Fig. 17-8 Guidelines for Rating Application Software 17
Fig. 17-9 Application Software Rating Sheet 17
Fig. 17-10 Scoring for Systems Software 19
Fig. 17-11 Topics to Be Covered During Reference Calls 21
Fig. 17-12 The Implementation Process 29

18 User Participation

Introduction 2

The User: A Definition 3

Necessity for a User 4

Needs of a User and User Satisfaction 5
Design Considerations 7
Operational Considerations 7
Systems Flexibility Considerations 8
User Satisfaction 8
Systems Dependability 9
User Training 10
User Documentation 10

The Most Common User Complaints 11

Main Reasons for Failure of an FIS 12
System Does Not Meet User Needs 13
    Unrealistic Expectations 13
    Making People Fit the System 13
    Poor Systems Definition 13
    User Involvement Too Late in the Cycle 14
Implementation Was Poorly Planned, Managed, or Controlled 14
    Underestimation of Project Manager's Role 14
    Unrealistic and Rushed Schedules 14
    Implementing Too Many Systems Together 14
    Single-Person Dependency 15
    No Interim Reviews and Approvals 15
System Created Negative Impact on the Organization 16
    Resistance to Change 16
    Poor-Quality User Involvement 16
    Lack of Management Commitment 16
    Political Environment 16

Then and Now: Different User Roles 17

Traditional Role of Users 17

Inability of Data Processing to Respond to User Needs 18
    Formal Development Life Cycle 18
    Application Backlog 18
    Programming Languages and Techniques 18
    User Documentation 18
    Errors in the System 19

Users vs. Data Processing: The Gap 19

Current Direction of User Participation 20
Use of Decision Support Tools 20
Applications Built by the End User 21
Evolution of User-Driven Computing 21
Introduction of Fourth-Generation Languages 21
Use of Information Centers 21

How to Resolve and Make User Participation Work 22

What Constitutes a Good User 23

The Role of Management 24
Goals and Objectives 25
Commitment to the Investment 25
Political Perspective 25
Keeping Informed 26
Policy Statements 26
Selection of Key Personnel 26

What to Consider When Selecting a Project Manager 26
Communication Skills 27
Selling Ability 27
Decision Making 27
Good Time and Resource Management 27
Political Astuteness 27
Credibility 28
Open Mindedness 28

What It Takes to Get Users Involved 29
User-Friendly Software 29

TABLE OF CONTENTS

Good Training Courses 30	Preparing or Evaluating Cost/Benefit
High-Level User Languages 30	Analysis 33
Strong Project Management 30	Becoming Project Manager 34
How Users Should Be Involved in the	**How Users Should Be Involved in Testing**
Planning and Development Stages 31	**and Implementation** 34
Establishing a Design Team 31	Training 34
Defining Systems Requirements 32	Testing 35
Validating Systems Requirements and	Implementation 35
Conceptual Design 32	**Looking to the Future** 36
Attending Structured Walk-Throughs . . . 32	
Providing Approval to Proceed 33	**References** 38
Participating in Steering Committees . . . 33	

Fig. 18-1 Systems Development Life Cycle 5
Fig. 18-2 User's vs. Data Processing's Concept of Systems Design 6
Fig. 18-3 Quality Factors Researched for the U.S. Department of Defense 8
Fig. 18-4 Project Levels 28

19 The Information Center

Introduction 1	Northrop Corporation 4
	Security Pacific National Bank 5
History of the Concept 1	Kidder, Peabody, & Co. 6
	Bechtel Power 6
Growth 2	Exxon 6
Crwth Computer Coursewares	Bank of America 6
Information Center Survey 2	Other Organizations 6
Diebold Survey 3	
INPUT Planning Presentation 3	**Future Status of the Information Center** . . 7
Information Center Examples 4	**References** 8

Fig. 19-1 Information Center Growth, 1983–1985 3
Fig. 19-2 Typical Information Center Applications 4

20 Training of Personnel

The Importance of Proper Training 1	Internal Training 12
Levels of Training 2	**Determining the Time for Training** 13
Advanced User Management Training 3	When Something Is New 13
Operator Training 4	When Something Is Old 13
Systems Training 5	
User Training 6	**Effective Training** 14
Hardware Training 6	Location and Layout 14
Microcomputer Training 7	Effective Use of Visual Aids 15
	Class Session Format 15
Efficient Computer Use: Controls 7	Exercises, Examples, and Case Studies . . 16
Methods of Training 8	Exercises 16
Classroom Training 9	Examples 16
When to Use Classroom Training . . . 9	Case Studies 17
Optimum Classroom Conditions 9	What to Teach, When 17
Programmed Training 11	Beginning Classes 17
In-House Training 11	Intermediate Classes 18

Advanced Classes 18
Time Spent on Training 18
On-Going Professional Education 18

Fig. 20-1 Model Classroom 10

One-Time Training 18
Effects of Not Training 19

21 Office Automation

Introduction 2

Office Automation Defined 2
A Collection of Technologies 4
Support for Intellectual Work 5
Support for Both Group and Individual
  Work 6
Communication Among Groups and
  Individuals 7
The Competitive Edge 7

Office Productivity 8
Strategic Planning 9
Systems Engineering 9
Nominal Group Technique 10
The Sociotechnical Approach 11

Kinds of Office Technologies 11
Word Processing 11
Electronic Filing and Retrieval 12
Administrative Augmentation 13
Telecommunications 14
  Electronic Mail 14
  Voice Mail 15
  Teleconferencing 15
  Public Databases 17
  Telecommuting 18
Personal Computing 18

Key Issues 19
People Issues 19
Connectivity 19
Revisability 19
Support Infrastructure 20
Ease of Access to Information 20
Systems Availability, Reliability,
  Usability 20
Security and Privacy 21

Cost Justification for Office Systems . . . 21

**Common Pitfalls of Office Automation
  Implementation** 22
Failing to Plan 22
Waiting to Plan 25
Office Automation as a Political Issue . . 27
Failure to Sell Office Automation to Top
  Management 27
Picking the Wrong Client for a Pilot . . . 29
Automating Production Personnel 31
Focusing on Features 31
Insisting on Hard-Dollar Savings 32
Equating Office Automation With Word
  Processing 33
Ignoring Other Office Disciplines 34

References 35

Fig. 21-1 Graph of Investment vs. Productivity 2
Fig. 21-2 Human Resources Investments 3
Fig. 21-3 Pilot Project Planning Questions 25
Fig. 21-4 Sample Strategic Objectives 26
Fig. 21-5 Taxonomy of People Issues 28
Fig. 21-6 Office Technologies 33
Fig. 21-7 Office Disciplines 35

22 Security Implications for On-Line Financial Information Systems

Introduction 1
Computer Security 2

Controlling Systems Access 3

User Identification and Accountability . . 3
  Terminal Identification 4
  User Authentication 4
    Something the User Has 4

TABLE OF CONTENTS

Something the User Knows 4
Something Known About the User .. 5
Password Guidelines 5
   Confidentiality 5
   Password Content and Origination .. 6
   Frequency of Change 6
Authorization and Data Access 7
   Defining Systems Resources 7
   Defining User Capability 8
   Authorization Maintenance 8

Surveillance 9
Real-Time Surveillance Functions 9

Detection 9
Security Response 10
Reporting and Logging 10
Contents of a Security Audit Log 10
User's Role in Surveillance 11

On-Line Security Physical Checkup 12
User Identification and Accountability .. 12
Authentication 12
Authorization and Data Access 13
Surveillance 13

References 14

23 Disaster Recovery

Introduction 2

Background on Disaster Recovery 2

Why Disaster Recovery Is Important ... 4

Objectives of Disaster Recovery and Contingency Planning 5

Disaster Recovery Methodology 7
Step 1: Getting Started 9
   Task 1: Establish the Contingency Planning Team 9
   Task 2: Develop the Detailed Work Plan and Schedule 9
   Task 3: Evaluate Existing Backup Procedures and Insurance Provisions 9
   Task 4: Identify Short-Term Recovery Options 10
Step 2: Establishing Priorities 10
   Task 1: Interview Selected Company Personnel 10
   Task 2: Develop Evaluation Criteria 11
   Task 3: Prioritize and Select Critical Applications 11
   Task 4: Prepare Step 1 and 2 Project Summary 11
Step 3: Determining the Resources Required 12
   Task 1: Define Operating Requirements for Each Critical Application 12

   Task 2: Define the Minimum Operating Requirements for Each Critical Application 13
   Task 3: Develop Operating Requirements 13
   Task 4: Identify Scheduling Requirements 13
   Task 5: Prepare Step 3 Project Summary 13
Step 4: Analyzing Risks and Alternatives 14
   Task 1: Analyze Risk and Rank Resources 14
   Task 2: Identify Data Processing Resource-Loss Situations 14
   Task 3: Identify Recovery Alternatives 14
   Task 4: Evaluate Recovery Alternatives 14
   Task 5: Prepare Step 4 Summary ... 15
Step 5: Developing the Plan 15
   Salvage Team 16
   Facilities Administration Team 17
   Systems Software Team 17
   Application Software Team 18
   Operations Team 18
   Hardware Team 19
   Communications Team 19
   Logistics Team 19
   Data Preparation Team 20
   Data Control Team 20
Step 6: Making Sure the Plan Works ... 21
Step 7: Training Personnel 22

References 23

Index I-1

Glossary

access time The length of time required to store or retrieve data between main memory and an external storage device.

accounting information system A management information subsystem that accumulates, classifies, processes, analyzes, and communicates relevant financial data.

ADCCP Advanced Data Communication Control Protocol, a standard, bit-oriented protocol developed by the American National Standards Institute.

American Standard Code for Information Interchange (ASCII) A standard 7-bit code almost always transmitted with a parity bit (for a total of 8 bits per character). ASCII was established by the American National Standards Institute to achieve compatibility between various types of data processing and data communications equipment. ASCII is the most commonly used code for non-IBM equipment.

analyst A computer specialist who defines a problem and develops algorithms for its solution.

application program A program designed to solve a particular problem for an application, such as a payroll program.

architecture The composite of specific components and the way in which they interact, forming a computer system.

array A group of two or more logically related elements identified by a single name; generally stored in consecutive locations in main memory.

ASCII *See* American Standard Code for Information Interchange

asynchronous transmission A method of data transmission that allows data to be sent at irregular intervals by preceding each character with a start bit and following it with a stop bit.

auditability Features that allow verification of controls and of accuracy of data processing results.

automatic data processing Data processing in which machines are used to perform a series of operations on data, thus reducing the need for human intervention.

auxiliary storage On-line storage, other than in main memory, such as on a disk or tape.

baseband A transport facility used by LANs to support data transmission at high throughput rates. Baseband cable is less expensive and less complex than broadband cable. Its narrow bandwidth makes it unsuitable for voice or video transmission.

battery backup system A system, generally used with minicomputers or microcomputers having volatile memory, that goes into effect to protect data during a power failure.

baud A unit of measurement that denotes the number of discrete signal elements, such as bits, that can be transmitted per second. For example, a device that transmits 300 bps can also be said to transmit at 300 baud.

bit A digit in the binary system represented by a zero or a one. A bit is the smallest unit of storage in the computer. Groups of bits form other units of storage, such as a byte or word.

bps Bits per second, a measurement of the number of bits transmitted per second.

broadband channel In data communications, a channel with a relatively large bandwidth that can transmit data at approximately 10,000 to 50,000 bps to and from higher-speed devices, such as disk and tape drives, local terminals, and printers.

budget A goal to be reached; a short-term plan.

bug (1) An error or mistake in a program; (2) any hardware malfunction in a computer system.

byte A group of consecutive bits forming a unit of storage in the computer and used to represent one alphanumeric character. A byte usually consists of 8 bits but may contain more or fewer bits, depending on the model of computer.

Cathode ray tube (CRT) A screen similar to a television screen, used in computer systems for viewing data. A CRT may be used in place of a printer, and, with an attached keyboard, forms a terminal.

centralized data processing Data processing in an organization that is performed at one central location. The data may be obtained from all areas within the organization, including field office operations.

Central processing unit (CPU) A microprocessor included in a personal computer, where instructions are fetched, decoded, and executed and the overall activity of the computer is controlled.

character An alphabetic letter, digit, or special symbol.

character printer A printer that prints only one character at a time.

checkpoint A designated place in a program where normal execution is interrupted and data concerning the status of the program, such as the contents of registers and the storage locations used by the program, are stored temporarily on an external storage device. A checkpoint is used to avoid the repeated execution of the entire program if an error or malfunction should occur. If one does occur, it can be corrected, and execution of the program can be resumed from the last checkpoint.

chip An integrated circuit created on a tiny silicon flake upon which a large number of gates and the paths connecting them are formed by very thin films of metal acting as wires. The chip can be used as main memory or as a CPU.

coaxial cable A cable used for the transmission of data in a communications system. Coaxial cable is capable of carrying more messages at higher rates of speed than conventional telephone lines.

COBOL Acronym for Common Business Oriented Language. A high-level programming language capable of performing all the calculations most often used in business. It is specifically designed to handle highly structured records, which are stored in a wide variety of data structures and storage devices. COBOL is the primary language

GLOSSARY

used in administrative data processing, since its use of English terms makes programs easy to read, modify, and maintain.

compiler A program that translates a source program written in a high-level language into its equivalent machine language.

computer An electronic device for performing high-speed arithmetic and logical operations. A computer is composed of five basic components: (1) an arithmetic-logic unit; (2) a control unit; (3) input devices; (4) output devices; and (5) memory. Data are received, transmitted, stored, processed, and output by these components with minimal human intervention. The three general classifications of computers are (1) the microcomputer, (2) the minicomputer, and (3) the mainframe. The classifications are determined by the type of processor, size of memory, and input/output devices used. Because of rapid advances in technology, the boundaries between these classifications are not clearly defined.

computer-assisted instruction The use of a computer to provide educational exercises, such as drills, practice sessions, and tutorial lessons for a student. A terminal is used to respond to exercises that have been programmed to assist students at their individual levels of ability and speeds of learning.

computer center An office that provides computer services, such as the operation of a computer and peripheral equipment and the writing of application programs and computer reports, to a wide variety of people in an organization.

contribution margin Excess of sales revenue over direct costs, available to meet allocated expenses and profit.

control The act of keeping an activity or condition within predetermined limits.

control, accounting Organization and procedures to safeguard assets and ensure proper recording of transactions.

control, internal Plan of organization and methods of safeguarding assets and reliability of accounting data.

controls, application Regulation of individual computerized accounting applications.

controls, general (EDP) Those controls relating to all or many computerized accounting activities.

core memory A type of memory composed of storage units, called magnetic cores, made from a ferromagnetic material and magnetized in either of two directions to store a bit. Core memory is the earliest type of memory used in computers.

CPU *See* central processing unit.

CRT *See* cathode ray tube.

Data Base Management System (DBMS) A collection of software that handles the storage, retrieval, and updating of records in a database. A DBMS controls redundancy of records and provides the security, integrity, and data independence of a database.

data management system A group of programs that provide for the creation and maintenance of files, the production of reports from them, and the handling of a wide variety of different types of data structures.

DBMS *See* Data Base Management System.

decentralized data processing Data processing in an organization where the processing and storage of data are provided independently at various locations throughout the organization.

direct access storage device A storage device, such as a magnetic disk or drum, that provides direct access to the data stored on it and with an access time not dependent on the location of the data.

direct costs Those costs directly associated with a selected segment (and not allocated).

disk A magnetic disk. This is a platter resembling a phonograph record, coated with a material capable of being magnetized to store bits in concentric circular paths, called tracks, on either side of its surfaces. Each disk commonly has 200 or more tracks and is arranged with a number of other disks into a stack. When so grouped, the disks are called a disk pack. A disk is the most common type of direct access storage device.

dot matrix character A printed character formed of dots so close that they give the impression that the character was printed by uninterrupted strokes. The dots are formed by wire ends, jets of ink, electrical charges, or laser beams.

downtime The period during which a computer, a component of a computer system, or a software system is inoperable.

electronic mail Letters, memoranda, or text typed into a terminal and transmitted to a receiving terminal or terminals where the material can be displayed at the viewer's choice of time or at some prearranged time.

emulator A set of microprograms that can be used in a computer to perform the functions of, or execute programs designed for, another, different type of computer. A computer with an emulator can run programs in its own or another computer's machine language.

exception report A report that presents only significant, nonstandard results.

fiber optics The technology of transmitting data over communication lines made from flexible strands of glass or plastic through which laser beams or light from LEDs are passed to transfer data. The strands are formed into cables, and can carry many more times the amount of data than traditional copper wire.

FIS Financial information system. A system that provides information, largely financial in nature, and that is used to assist in the direction of a business.

fixed costs Costs that do not change as volume changes.

floppy disk A disk, usually 5¼ or 8 inches in diameter, made of a flexible piece of Mylar and coated with a material that can be magnetized to store bits. Floppy disks are inserted into a small disk drive, called a floppy disk drive (some systems can use up to four disk drives in series), and can be used to read or write data with any size of computer, although they are most commonly used with microcomputers and minicomputers. The 5¼-inch disk can store approximately 100,000 bytes, whereas the 8-inch disk can store approximately 300,000 bytes.

font A complete assortment of type characters of a given size and style.

hardware The physical equipment and components in a computer system.

GLOSSARY

information center A walk-in facility where the user can obtain data processing help.

information management system A system designed to create, update, and maintain a file or database.

information retrieval system A system designed to retrieve data from a storage device, usually a disk, and display it quickly to the requesting person in the proper form and format.

initialization The process of setting various counters, addresses, or variables in a program to their starting value.

job A unit of work for a computer, such as a program or a group of programs and the related data.

keyboard An arrangement of keys like that on a typewriter, used to enter data manually into a terminal or keypunch.

LAN *See* local area network.

leased line A permanent communication line between a computer and a terminal that provides private, full-time access to the connection by a subscriber for a fixed fee.

letter-quality printing Printed output from a computer that appears to have been typewritten.

local area network (LAN) A system linking together computers, word processors, and other electronic office machines to create an interoffice or intersite network. These networks usually provide access to external networks—for example, public telephone and data transmission networks and information retrieval systems.

machine Computer.

macro Macroinstruction. A single instruction that represents a given sequence of instructions. The macro is defined at the beginning of a program to represent a set of instructions. It can then be used throughout the rest of the program whenever that set of instructions is needed.

mainframe A CPU or, more precisely, the piece of equipment that contains the CPU. Applied chiefly to a larger computer, as distinguished from a minicomputer or microcomputer. Mainframe computers most commonly have a word length of 32 bites and operate at speeds 100 to 1,000 times faster than smaller computers. They have a memory capacity ranging from approximately 512K to 16 megabytes, and are used where large volumes of data are processed, as in large corporations, universities, and government offices.

main memory Storage locations in the computer that are used for programs, along with their data, while the programs are being executed. Main memory is composed of a number of locations, each of which has a unique address and is capable of storing a specified number of bits, such as a byte or a word. Main memory is a read/write memory allowing random access. The storage capacity of a main memory varies among computers.

management information system (MIS)   An information system designed to provide the information used to assist in decision making to all levels of management. The system should provide for quick retrieval of data, hold comprehensive files, be able to answer questions about the data, and present the data in a form that has meaning for the decision maker.

megabyte   One million bytes.

memory   A device that can store data recorded in it and from which the data can be retrieved. The term usually refers to the main memory of a computer.

memory technology   Technique for increasing the amount of data stored in a chip's memory section.

menu   A displayed list of the various functions a user can select to perform on a terminal.

message switching   In data communications, a technique by which the computer collects data from and distributes data to various terminals or computers in the system. The destination of the data is indicated by an address contained in it. The data are stored until the terminal or computer is ready to receive them.

microcomputer   A small, low-cost computer containing a microprocessor. It has an RAM for storing programs during their execution and, commonly, an ROM for permanent storage of required programs, such as language processors. Microcomputers have a word length of 4, 8, 12, or 16 bits, with 8 and 16 being the most popular, and a memory size ranging generally from 4K to 64K.

minicomputer   An intermediate-sized computer with a word length of 8, 12, 16, 18, 24, or, most commonly, 32 bits, and a memory size ranging from approximately 4K to 256K. It generally operates at about twice the speed of a microcomputer and supports many high-level programming languages, such as COBOL and FORTRAN.

MIS   *See* management information system.

modem   Modulator-demodulator. This device converts digital data output from another device, such as a computer or a terminal, into analog data that can be transmitted over communication lines. It also converts analog data into digital data that can be accepted by another device, such as a computer or a terminal.

network   A system consisting of a computer or computers and the connected terminals and related devices, such as modems and input/output channels.

network technology   Activities integrating communication of voice, data, and image in single localized systems called LANs.

operating system   A collection of systems programs that control the overall operation of a computer system. An operating system is normally composed of three basic types of programs: (1) the job control program; (2) the input/output control system; and (3) the processing program. An operation can rarely, if ever, be performed in a computer without the assistance of an operating system.

optimize   A procedure used to obtain the best solution to a problem, as by arranging the data and instructions in such a way as to use a minimal amount of computer time in executing the program.

GLOSSARY

packaged program *See* software package.

password A group of characters by which a user is uniquely identified when logging on to a terminal or when submitting a program for execution.

period costs Costs associated with the passage of time.

plan A predetermined course of action.

planning The act of developing a plan.

point-of-sale terminal A terminal in a retail operation that is connected to a computer in order to collect and store data when a sale is made. The terminal has a keyboard, a display area for prices, a printer for customer receipts, a display panel that guides the user through the purchase, and, optionally, a wand or scanner that can read universal product codes. These terminals are used throughout large stores (or a chain of stores) to maintain inventory control.

protocol A set of rules governing the communication and transfer of data between two or more devices in a communications system. The rules define the handling of certain communications problems, such as framing, error control, sequence control, transparency, line control, and start-up control. There are three basic types of protocol: (1) character-oriented; (2) byte-count-oriented; and (3) bit-oriented.

RAM Random access memory.

random access method Method in which records are directly accessed in any order by using their known addresses.

real-time processing The immediate entering, processing by the computer, and distribution of data as the event occurs in order to rapidly influence decisions, physical processes, or events.

record A group of logically related fields treated as a unit. A record contains all the information related to one subject that is needed for a given purpose, and a group of records make up a file. For example, an employee's name, address, Social Security number, rate of pay, hours worked, and deductions form a record in a payroll file.

record length The number of bytes (or characters) contained in a record.

recovery The process of resuming processing without irreparable loss of the data in the system after an error in a program or a malfunction in equipment has occurred.

remote devices Devices that are connected to the computer through a communications link and are physically located away from the central computer site.

Report program generator (RPG) A high-level programming language in which the specifications for a program, such as the files and the description of the records to be used, the arithmetic and/or logic operations to be performed, and the format of the printed report, are entered by the programmer. The computer generates a program that prepares the report to be printed. RPG is commonly used in businesses for simple (especially one-time) reports that do not require complex programs and that are needed quickly.

responsibility reporting A system for reporting data to identify results of individual performance. An individual is assigned responsibility for specific goals.

Request for Proposal (RFP) A formal request by an organization for a proposal to be submitted to meet specified needs.

restart The process of resuming the execution of a job at a checkpoint or at a specified step.

RFP *See* Request for Proposal.

ROM Read-only memory.

routine A set of instructions for solving a specified problem, such as finding the square root of a number.

RS-232-C In data communications, a set of standards specifying various electrical and mechanical characteristics for interfaces between computers, terminals, and modems. They include an interface consisting of 25 pins or leads, each of which is lettered and provides a function, such as timing, control, or the sending of data. Adopted by the Electronics Industries Association, this set of standards is widely followed by hardware manufacturers.

run book A list of the materials needed for a specific computer run, including a statement of the problem, controls, and operating instructions.

security The protection of data from unauthorized use or intentional destruction. Security measures are typically built into a computer's operating system and include the checking of passwords, identification numbers, and reading and writing privileges associated with each file.

semivariable costs Costs that change as volume varies, but not in direct proportion.

sequential access The type of access provided to data on a storage device in a serial order determined by the physical location of the data in the file. *Compare* direct access storage device.

short-term plan Course of action for a short term, usually one year or less.

software Programs, languages, and/or routines that control the operations of a computer in solving a given problem. Software is composed of two major types of programs, called systems programs and application programs.

software package A set of prewritten programs that can be purchased for use with a specified computer to perform various duties, such as accounting, payroll, statistical analysis, inventory control, spelling, and syllabification.

stand-alone operation An operation performed by a device, program, or system independently of another.

standard interface An interface designed according to standards so that different types of hardware and software can be interchanged.

storage The process of placing data into a device capable of retaining them for long periods and from which the data can be retrieved as needed.

strategic plan Long-range plan to guide a company toward its goals or objectives.

synchronous transmission The transmission of data from one location to another at regular, timed intervals. One device requests data from another, waits a specified length of time, and then reads the data.

system An aggregate of hardware, software, and personnel organized to perform a function or functions.

systems analyst A computer professional who is responsible for the systems analysis and design of programs for various applications.

GLOSSARY

systems generation The process of implementing a basic software system on a specific computer. Such a system is supplied by the computer manufacturer or a software vendor. A program, called a systems generator, processes the basic system and parameters that describe a specific installation to produce a system tailored to it. Systems generation is used to implement new operating systems and language processors or to update the existing versions.

systems library A collection of programs used by the operating system, and the various assemblers, compilers, linkage editors, and loaders.

systems overhead The percentage of time that a computer system functions in supervising rather than in performing an actual program.

systems programmer A programmer who creates, maintains, and controls the use of an operating system in order to increase productivity in a computer system.

systems software A collection of programs that enable the computer system for which they were prepared to be used more efficiently by a wide variety of people in an organization.

systems technology Complete range of disciplines operating directly and indirectly to evolve useful techniques in the development of information systems.

teleprocessing Data processing in which terminals and communication lines are used for sending and receiving data between distant locations and a data processing center.

terminal A device used to send and receive data from a computer system, especially one with a keyboard and an attached CRT and/or printer. Terminals can be located at great distances from the computer and connected by any of various communication lines.

test data A small sample of data, taken from a file or artificially created, used in the test run of a program.

throughput The amount of processing performed in a given amount of time by a computer or a component of the computer system.

timesharing A system of computer operation in which the rapid alternation in execution of programs allows two or more programs to be entered and processed in a way that appears simultaneous to humans.

transfer rate The rate at which data are transferred between a storage device and main memory. Transfer rate is expressed in bits, bytes, or characters per second.

utility program A program provided by a computer center or vendor to perform a task that is required by many of the programs using the system. Common utility programs are those that copy data from one storage medium to another and sort and merge programs. Other utility programs may provide text editing, initiate the execution of programs, and perform other functions not directly related to the processing of data in a program.

value added A term used to refer to those networks that add value to basic telephone services by offering speed, code, and protocol conversions that provide the user with enhanced data communications services.

variable costs Costs that vary in more-or-less direct proportion to volume.

videotex An information network service that links computers with telecommunications facilities to transmit text and graphics information. This information can be transmitted via cable, radio, or microwave to a display terminal, which may be a television set equipped with a decoder, a dedicated videotex terminal, or a personal computer.

virtual storage A direct access storage device used to store a program that requires more space than is available in main memory while it is being executed. Although the program appears to be held entirely in main memory, only those segments that are currently being used are so held.

word A storage unit, consisting of a number of bits usually determined when the machine is designed, that comprises one storage location in main memory. Many minicomputers have 16-bit words, whereas a larger computer may have 32, 48, or 64 bits in each word.

word processor An automated, computerized system that usually incorporates an electronic typewriter, CRT terminal, memory, and printer. It is used to prepare, edit, store, transmit, or duplicate letters, reports, and records, as for a business. Many programs now have spelling and syllabification verifiers.

PART **I**

Overview

CHAPTER 1

Perspectives on Financial Information Systems

Steven J. Root

Overview	1	Management as a Barometer for Success	12
Some Useful Definitions	3	**FISs: Some Implications**	15
Management Information Systems	3	Exposure to Systems Technology	15
Information Systems	4	Effect on Traditional Roles of Functional	
Financial Information Systems	6	Disciplines	16
Accounting Information Systems	7	Trend Toward Pooling Databases	16
A Perspective of FISs	8	Transition to More Costly Integrated	
Historical Perspective	9	Information Systems	16
Forces of Evolution	9	Beneficial Impact on Systems Users	17
The Current Environment	10	**References**	17
Quality of Information as a Barometer for Success	12		

Fig. 1-1 An MIS 5
Fig. 1-2 A Typical FIS for a Manufacturing Company 7
Fig. 1-3 Evolution of ROI Analysis 13
Fig. 1-4 Selected Financial Reporting Milestones 14
Fig. 1-5 Payroll Calculation: 1945–1965, Compared With 1965–1985 15

OVERVIEW

This chapter discusses the concept of financial information systems (FISs) and how they have evolved from simple accounting records to sophisticated financial analyses.

The purpose of this Manual is to provide a practical guide for those responsible for developing, improving, maintaining, operating, or using an effective FIS, which is defined in this chapter; the chapters that follow are devoted to considering these basic concepts:

1-1

- The role of FISs in managing a business and in meeting business objectives.
- Changing information needs of business—quicker information, better information, more analytical data.
- The rapid evolution of FISs as a result of such new technology as electronic data processing (EDP) hardware, software, and telecommunications.
- Illustrative examples of some modern FIS reports.
- Desirable procedures and techniques.
- Changes or potential changes in organization structure and responsibilities in relation to information resource management and the duties of the financial executive.

In the dynamic environment in which FISs exist, decisions regarding the who, what, where, when, and whys of systems change must be made constantly. Those who make the decisions must be knowledgeable about such topics as:

- Computer hardware
- Telecommunications/networking
- Software
- Systems development concepts
- Databases
- Distributed processing
- Decision support systems
- Personal computers

In the past, these topics, if they existed at all, were pretty much the purview of the EDP community. Those outside the community looked to EDP to master the technology and apply it to their benefit. More often than not, the function reported to the CFO or to the controller. However, some of these executives did not fully understand the function. In other cases, the reporting relationships bypassed the finance function. Huge centralized control and management of systems, resources, and processing of data arose.

This has changed dramatically. Advances in all phases of computer technology have enabled the power of the computer to be controlled more directly by the user. This change has come about so fast that most users have not prepared for it. Today, financial managers and executives must gain the necessary knowledge of FIS technology if they wish to minimize the chance of making poor systems decisions. Financial managers do not have to become technicians, programmers, or computer operators, but they must become more familiar with systems technology, its concepts, and its capabilities. In addition, they must be knowledgeable about the control implications of such technology, particularly as they apply to FISs.

Financial executives and FIS executives must develop a close working relationship, because it is likely that the latter will become increasingly involved in the development and maintenance of integrated, relational financial databases as part of the overall FIS. The financial executive will find that his systems needs will be more economically met by resources within his own control, as opposed to development by a centralized data processing group. In fact, all members of management are facing this same challenge. Managers of purchasing, marketing, engineering, and many other areas can apply these techniques to their functions. To some degree, each of these managers is interested in some type of financial data. A purchasing manager, for example, may be interested in purchase order preparation cost, change order preparation cost, savings resulting from competitive bidding practices, cost trends in various commodities, and buyers' performance measurement data. In most companies, it is not likely that such financial data will be developed by, or considered part of, the FIS. It is more likely that a manager needing such information will have to get it on his own. Probably each manager will perform his own analyses and interpretation of financial data, because he is better positioned to know what the information means than are financial managers. Thus, his reports to organizational superiors are apt to contain financial information and interpretations developed completely independently of the FIS.

Current systems technology makes the development of these support systems possible. All that is needed is for the manager to be aware of it and to make use of the necessary guidelines and techniques suggested in the following chapters.

SOME USEFUL DEFINITIONS

As with most human efforts, time and experience clarify and change definitions. Although some ambiguity still exists, an explanation of these closely related terms may prove helpful:

- Management information systems (MISs)
- Information systems (ISs)
- Financial information systems (FISs)
- Accounting information systems (AISs)

Management Information Systems

"MIS" is the term applied most frequently to the system used to provide management—at all levels—with sufficient information about transactions, activities or functions, events, and incidents affecting the area of interest. The data provide the basis for making necessary decisions. Of course, the information needs and the format in which they are presented vary as to management level and type of decisions made.

For our purposes, the term "MIS" means the entire spectrum of information used by management in organizing, planning, directing, and controlling an entity's business activities.[1] The term may also be used, however, where referring to an information system of a particular functional management segment, albeit in general terms. The goal of MISs is to support a company's operations and to contribute to the quality of decision making.

The "system" by which management information is furnished is a combination of formal and informal processes. It includes both financial and nonfinancial data, produced by both automated and manual means. The information may be summarized, as in the case of overall internal financial reports, or it may be specific, as in the case of major acquisition analysis.

Figure 1-1 presents a conceptual view of an MIS. In Figure 1-1, it should be noted that an MIS embodies a variety of information and information sources and techniques. In addition to the combinations described in the preceding paragraph, an MIS includes recurring and nonrecurring information. Also, controls play a critical role insofar as the utility and effectiveness of an MIS is concerned.

Finally, the preponderance with which financial data pervade the MIS is important to note. To be sure, the finance function supplies financial information; however, other functions and disciplines also supply a significant amount.

Information Systems

Information systems are the procedures, techniques, and facilities employed in each and every function of an enterprise to gather, file, process, and analyze data for use in the operation and management of an enterprise.

As systems technology evolved, all management disciplines were affected. EDP applications were developed for several disciplines, each having its own databases, processing programs, and report structures. Systems that were built around these applications began to be identified with the management discipline primarily affected. Thus, at this stage, the following terms came into use:

- Human resource or personnel information system
- Material system
- Production ordering, scheduling, and control system
- Engineering information system

---

[1] These widely quoted functions of management were first described by Harold Koontz and Cyril O'Donnell in *Principles of Management* (New York: McGraw-Hill, 1959), pp. 1–59.

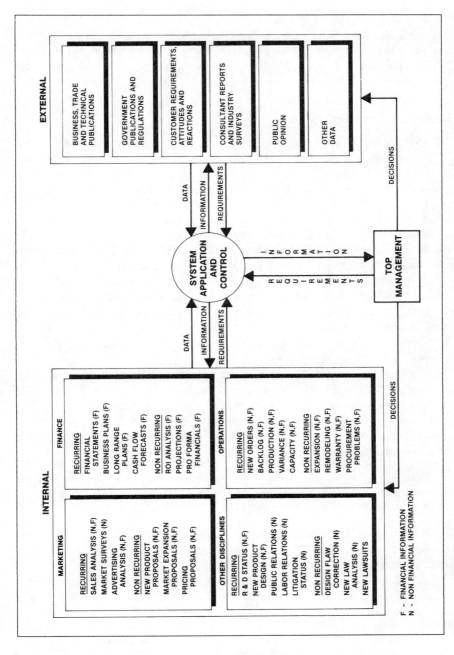

FIG. 1-1 An MIS

In time, further developments in systems technology permitted integration of systems and data simply and economically. The concept of integrated systems was envisioned, which brought forth the term "information systems."

IS is gaining widespread use. With the integration of the various subsystems, it is regarded as being substantially similar to the MIS discussed earlier.

Financial Information Systems

While MIS is indeed broad in scope and covers the entire spectrum of business activity, FIS, for our purposes, relates to information that is largely of a financial nature and is supplied in order to assist in the direction of the enterprise. It includes the financial information needed by the financial officers in analyzing and preserving the financial health of the business and in measuring financial trends and relationships of functions, business segments, product lines, and such. It deals with both historical and future conditions or events. An FIS extends beyond the financial manager's needs to senior management and operating management, as well as to certain interested third parties.

Its requirements encompass the needs of internal management, and extend to a large body of external users, such as the Securities and Exchange Commission (SEC), the Internal Revenue Service, shareholders (e.g., in annual and quarterly reports), creditors (e.g., commercial banks, long-term lenders, investment bankers), security analysts, suppliers, other federal and state agencies, and employees, to name but a few.

The National Association of Accountants (NAA) prepares and publishes Statements of Management Accounting. Statement No. 2 of that series, called *Management Accounting Terminology*, was issued in 1983. It consists of a glossary that serves as a guide for understanding terms used in the practice of management accounting. The glossary provides a broader definition for the related term, "financial information":

> That information, monetary or nonmonetary, necessary to interpret the cause and effect of actual or planned business and economic actions, activities, or asset and liability valuations.

This definition of financial information includes monetary and nonmonetary information. It also introduces the notion that the information is used to interpret cause and effect.

A combination of the NAA definition of financial information with a recognition of how systems must be developed (see Chapters 5 and 6) produces this enlarged description, which may be useful:

> A financial information system is an integrated combination of subsystems designed and operated to provide largely financial information to internal and external users with a need to know, enabling them to appraise the financial effects of transactions, activities, and events in which they have an interest.

PERSPECTIVES ON FIS

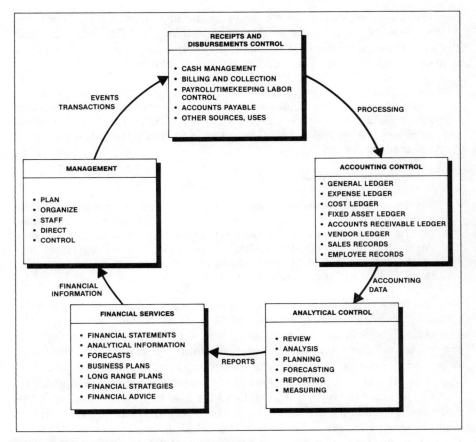

FIG. 1-2 A Typical FIS for a Manufacturing Company

This definition encompasses and conveys the notions that (1) multiple subsystems are involved, (2) the FIS is user- or service-oriented, and (3) appraising financial effects is an important and common goal. While the definition is broad, it is less so than that stated for MIS. Figure 1-2 is a flowchart presenting a typical FIS.

Those designing an effective FIS should consider the responsibilities of the chief financial officer (CFO) (as illustrated in Figure 13-1), of other financial officers, and, of course, of any executive who needs financial information.

Accounting Information Systems

AISs have been defined in many ways. One source considers the accounting subsystem as one of several subsystems in the MIS; the others are the production subsystem, the personnel subsystem, the finance subsystem (the chief responsibility of which is to secure resources and then monitor the efficient use by the other subsystems), the marketing subsystem, the EDP subsystem, and the production subsystem.[2] The accounting subsystem is referred to as the accounting information system and is defined as follows:

> An organizational component which accumulates, classifies, processes, analyzes, and communicates relevant financial-oriented, decision-making information to a company's external parties (such as federal and state tax agencies, current and potential investors, and creditors) and internal parties (principally management).[3]

Another source provides this definition:

> An accounting information system is a formal system in every sense of the word: that is, it collects, processes and stores data and provides formal reports ... embraces ... purposes, resources, tasks, elements, and users. An accounting information system ... is marked by distinguishing features—features that stem from accounting's concern with the economic impact of events upon a firm's activities.[4]

In earlier times, the AIS was considerably involved with historical data-gathering translated into accounting terms, such as "debit" or "credit." The first versions were largely financial accounting systems; however, these evolved into the second segment of management accounting systems. In the 1980s, decision support systems, using powerful microcomputers, sophisticated modeling, and "what-if" analyses, further clouded the distinction between AIS and FIS.

In this Manual, however, FIS and AIS are used interchangeably, with AIS being interpreted in the broadest manner—involving and effecting management decision making as well as traditional (historical) financial accounting. Thus, for clarity, the term "FIS" is used to represent AIS as well as MIS and IS throughout the Manual.

A PERSPECTIVE OF FISs

This Manual provides those responsible for developing, maintaining, disseminating, and using financial information with (1) an understanding of the principles and concepts involved, (2) an insight into specific models, and (3) systems, tools, and techniques for administering an FIS. Why this is important can be best understood by providing the reader with a brief historical view, an identification of the forces that effect FIS changes, and a picture of the current scene.

---

[2] Stephen A. Moscove and Mark G. Simkin, *Accounting Information Systems* (New York: Wiley, 1981), p. 3.

[3] Moscove and Simkin, p. 60.

[4] Joseph W. Wilkinson, *Accounting and Information Systems* (New York: Wiley, 1982), p. 9.

With that background, it is easier to see why understanding and applying the methodologies available for effective FIS management is important.

Historical Perspective

The use of financial information no doubt goes back to the time when money was first used as a means of exchanging property and other items of value. However, until the early 1970s, the needs of financial information users were such that simple manual ledger systems sufficed. History credits Pacioli, an Italian mathematician, with the innovation of double entry accounting near the end of the fifteenth century. The technique remains to this day. The frequently portrayed nineteenth-century image of stern-faced bookkeepers, hunched over large, bound books, steadfastly engaged in posting neat rows of accounting data onto pages in pen and ink instantly springs to mind.

Times were much simpler then. Companies were mostly privately owned, single-product, or service affairs that were geographically concentrated. The process of designing, manufacturing, and marketing a product or service was straightforward and uncomplicated. All activities usually occurred under the owner's close supervision. In fact, he was probably the product's designer, quality control expert, and salesperson. Companies of this era required small numbers of employees, most of whom were semiskilled and were directly engaged in one way or another with making the company product. Few had as many as 100 employees or more than a single plant or principal place of business activity. Government regulation was practically nonexistent. Investments in new products, plant, and equipment were relatively low.

In those days, management (the owners) obtained information the easy way. For the most part, the MIS consisted of techniques such as looking out the office window and directly observing what was going on. Financial information was obtained by walking over to the counting room and "going over the books," often a daily occurrence.

This MIS, although primitive, was very effective. It provided the owner with instant, accurate information upon which he could confidently base decisions. Such decisions were made quickly, since there was little to consider beyond satisfying the customer's need at a profit to the owner.

Forces of Evolution

The supposed comfort of the nineteenth century came to a rapid, although not abrupt, end in the twentieth century. Those forces that brought about change are still at work today and they continue to significantly affect how information upon which decisions are based is developed and disseminated:

- *The concept of free enterprise.* This is closely allied to the concept of private ownership of property. The chance to make (and retain) sizeable gains by using entrepreneurial skills in an unrestricted marketplace has produced a reliable growth-oriented economic environment.

- *The rise of large-scale business.* There are many reasons for the trend toward "bigness." Producing complex products for many customers dispersed over wide areas requires large investments in management, labor, facilities, and capital. Growth and competition forced bigness because of the economics of scale.

- *An independent skilled labor force.* The growth in the United States and much of the free world, despite continuing struggles and conflicts, of a knowledgeable, affluent, and independent labor force has effectively counterbalanced the global threat of communism as an alternative to the free enterprise system.

- *Technological innovation.* In a free enterprise society that is relatively free from predatory practices, competitive advantage is best assured by offering the best product or service at the lowest cost. This requires considerable continuing investment in technology, research, and development.

The Current Environment

The forces discussed previously have produced a business environment with effects that go far beyond FISs. They have a major effect on our culture, value system, and standard of living. Nevertheless, they are the pacing factors that have generated a myriad of changes, transforming the nineteenth-century scene of relative simplicity into a twentieth-century scene of dynamism, uncertainty, and complexity.

To paraphrase John Naisbitt in *Megatrends*,[5] although we live in an industrial society, we have become an information society. Of course, he cited nine other new directions that he sees as transforming our lives, but Naisbitt believes the megashift from an industrial society to an informational one to be the most subtle and explosive. There is much evidence to support that view. The profile of a typical manufacturing or service company of the 1980s is that:

- *It is large in comparison to its nineteenth-century predecessors.* In this context, "large" does not mean only the multinational corporate giants but also includes any company with more than one operating location and over $1 million in assets. Not only is it large in terms of business volume, assets owned, and number of employees, it is also likely to be involved in several related businesses.

---

[5] John Naisbitt, *Megatrends* (New York: Warner Books, 1982), p. 11.

- *It is likely to be publicly owned.* The management structure is apt to be decentralized, increasingly so with increasing size and number of businesses.

- *It is likely to experience formidable foreign competition.* Foreign-based companies are pushing ahead of their U.S. counterparts in many business areas.

- *It is probably involved in international operations.* These may range from issuing product licenses to maintaining foreign-based operations.

- *It is subjected to extensive reporting requirements.* This extends from internal needs to legal compliance reports, strategic requirements, and needs of creditors and owners.

- *Management members are not the sole owners.* They may be new to the company and their stock is probably small as a percentage of total stock outstanding.

- *Organized labor often is a factor.* The company probably has been the subject of, or is affected by, the collective bargaining process with one or more unions.

- *For every factory worker, there are three to four office workers.* This has given rise to many administrative bureaucratic empires that seem to exist independently from the company.

- *It has been accused of acting illegally.* Perhaps it has even been found guilty of some sort of regulatory wrongdoing such as violating Occupational Safety and Health Act (or OSHA) rules.

- *The management structure is decentralized.* Senior management spends much time developing long-term strategies that seldom succeed, creating much internal pressure on lower management levels.

Against this backdrop, top management's decisions affect much more than satisfaction of customer needs and return of a profit, as was the case a century ago. The interests of shareholders, employees, former employees, retired employees, suppliers, creditors, educators, politicians, government regulators, the general public, and other special interest groups (depending on the issues involved) are affected as well.

Today's senior management can no longer simply "size up" the status of business by walking into the next room and opening the accounting ledgers. Instead, it must depend on costly, elaborate systems very often involving multiple levels and layers of lower management. These systems gather financial and nonfinancial data from a vast array of sources. Often the FISs tend to "purify" the information so that much of it becomes useless or worse, capable of inducing misleading action. Although not the prevailing opinion, many believe that the risk of making the wrong decision in this environment is uncomfortably high.

Quality of Information as a Barometer for Success. Some experts believe that the level of success achievable by a given company is in direct proportion to the quality of information available to top management. For example, in the highly popular *In Search of Excellence*, authors Thomas J. Peters and Robert H. Waterman, Jr., write: "We are struck by the importance of available information as the basis for peer comparison. Surprisingly, this is the basic control mechanism in the excellent companies."[6]

Peters and Waterman go on to point out that the companies meeting their criteria for excellence not only have the information, but share it so widely that "people know quickly whether or not the job is getting done—and who's doing it well or poorly."

Put another way, companies with above-average FISs tend to produce above-average performances. The measures of performance may be growth rate in revenue or earnings, compounded return on investment (ROI), or some other yardstick.

Management as a Barometer for Success. On the other hand, there are those who do not completely subscribe to this view, who point to management itself as the primary key to success. Good managers can and do compensate, where necessary, when information does not go far enough. Decision making and risk taking go hand in hand. Over the long run, even good managers make mistakes. The frequency and impact of bad decisions may best be minimized by increasing the quality of the information base upon which the decisions are made.

It seems inescapable that the most important and sought after information is financial information. This was probably as true in the nineteenth century as it is today. However, since today's business environment is so much more complex, and since the modern financial manager is more technically sophisticated, so too are the FIS needs of the various interest groups. Thus, the types of financial information produced by FISs have undergone constant change.

Figure 1-3 illustrates the evolution of one of the more important types of financial information, ROI analysis, over a forty-year period. The graph depicts increasingly sophisticated ROI calculations springing from simple concepts such as the payback period (i.e., the period of time required for the earnings flow of an investment to return the full principal to the investor). The longer the period, the riskier the investment. Payback calculations are not

---

[6] Thomas J. Peters and Robert H. Waterman, Jr., *In Search of Excellence* (New York: Harper & Row, 1982).

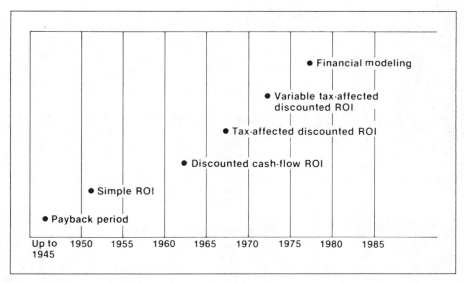

FIG. 1-3 Evolution of ROI Analysis

measures of ROI, but more the forerunners of ROI analysis. By 1965, simple ROI computations were made more informative by discounting the ROI for the time value of money.

Although ROI was usually calculated on an after-tax basis, the tax effects were relatively simple and consistent from one investment to another. Then in time, existing and emerging tax laws providing credit for investments, carrybacks and carryovers of net operating losses, and a myriad of other effects began to affect the investment alternatives to a significant degree. Thus, the tax effects of ROI calculations became a much more critical aspect of determining ROI.

Often it became necessary, for tax or other reasons, to display ROI calculations over a range of assumptions or possibilities. In this way, the effect of varying assumptions on ROI could be considered.

For the most part, all these calculations were done manually. With the development of computer timesharing, it was not long before the power of the computer enabled ROI calculations to be made under a variety of assumptions and conditions. Microcomputers now enable financial modeling to occur on a plane unimaginable only a few years ago.

Even more dramatic than the evolution in ROI analysis is the evolution in the form and content of financial statements and supplemental data included in published annual reports. As Figure 1-4 shows, the period from 1965 through 1985 was marked with numerous new disclosure requirements. These requirements add considerably to the effort needed to produce annual financial reports. Such production has developed into a highly technical and specialized

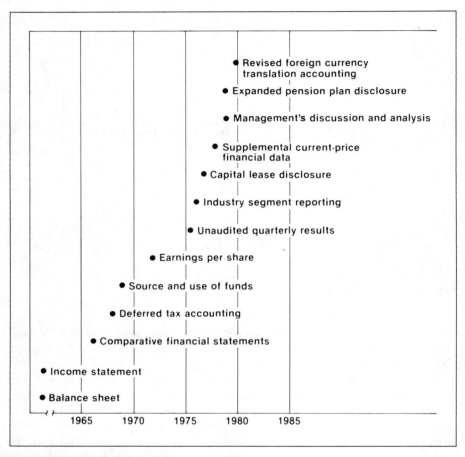

FIG. 1-4 Selected Financial Reporting Milestones

financial function and requires considerable planning, coordination, and systems assistance.

Furthering this picture of the current environment is the variety and volume of financial data, which has also undergone a colossal change, owing to the forces described earlier. Figure 1-5, using the example of payroll information, is an apt illustration. Of the 100 million-or-so employed workers in the United States, there are many old enough to remember when payrolls were distributed in cash. In those days, what you earned was, for the most part, what you received. Record-keeping requirements were minimal.

By contrast, the payroll calculation of the 1980s is an intricate maze of additions and subtractions used to arrive at net pay, as demonstrated by Figure 1-5. Several additional payroll-related transactions that were not formerly present could be added to this illustration, which must be accounted for. These

	1945–1965	1965–1985
Basic employee identification data	X	X
Regular earnings	X	X
Overtime		X
Sick pay		X
Holiday pay		X
Special award pay		X
Federal withholding		X
State withholding		X
Social Security		X
State disability		X
Voluntary contributions		X
Voluntary savings		X
Contributory life insurance		X
Contributory medical insurance		X
Union dues		X
Credit union transactions		X

FIG. 1-5 Payroll Calculation: 1945–1965, Compared With 1965–1985

include all the pension plan record-keeping requirements, employee taxes (e.g., unemployment insurance and Social Security), worker's compensation insurance, and many more. When these requirements are considered along with the fact that a great many companies employ several hundred to several thousand persons, the magnitude of payroll records can begin to be appreciated.

Thus, FISs required in today's environment are vastly greater, more sophisticated, and more complex than was the case even a generation ago. The prevailing forces keep the pressure on for more and more change. It has been said that comparing the controller of the 1980s to his counterpart in the 1940s would be like comparing Neil Armstrong to Charles Lindbergh.[7] So it is with FISs. There is every reason to expect that the FISs of the early twenty-first century will differ considerably from those of today.

FISs: SOME IMPLICATIONS

Exposure to Systems Technology

To repeat briefly: The most obvious implication is that both financial and nonfinancial managers are becoming exposed to systems technology much faster than they ever realized. The technology offers each type of manager an oppor-

---
[7] Robert M. Donnelly, "The Changing Role of the Controller," *Financial Executive* (Apr. 1982), p. 21.

tunity to greatly improve the quality and worth of the information he can develop, maintain, and distribute. Information can afford competitive advantage.[8] Those who are quickest to take advantage of the opportunity will gain competitively. To maximize this opportunity, sufficient knowledge is necessary. Financial and nonfinancial managers do not have to become EDP experts. However, they must improve their awareness of FIS technology so as to adopt it to their areas of responsibility in beneficial ways.

Effect on Traditional Roles of Functional Disciplines

Another implication is that, as systems technology is applied to more and more functions, the traditional roles of functional disciplines may be affected to some extent. Operational and financial information are likely to become more integrated, thus becoming even more difficult to distinguish. One authority foresees the possibility that future accounting systems could accept and report much nonfinancial information. This might include information regarding employee productivity and managerial effectiveness.[9]

Trend Toward Pooling Databases

The trend toward pooling databases into large integrated bases from which a specific user extracts, analyzes, and summarizes information into needed formats using powerful computer software packages poses another implication: It may directly challenge the accounting function, which has traditionally served management by performing data analysis and interpretive tasks. Also, as data become centralized, major questions of access arise. Information translates into power. Therefore, those permitted access to the most data are likely to be, or become, quite influential.

Transition to More Costly Integrated Information Systems

Another implication is that the transition to more integrated information systems is costly. Also, the transition is likely to result in decentralization of large computer centers. As a result, company management will find that it is more important and critical to control transition activities properly and adequately. Corporate-based information officers will become increasingly valuable, and

---

[8] See M.H. Notowidigdo, "Information Systems: Weapons to Gain the Competitive Edge," *Financial Executive* (Feb. 1984), p. 20. Several examples are cited; for instance, the case of the joint venture between two airlines, Eastern and TWA. Here, a joint venture between the two offered the frequent flyers of each free flights on either carrier based on accumulated paid-for-trip mileage. The success of the program demanded information sharing about customers, mileage, and such almost instantly. Not all of the other carriers were able to respond immediately. Thus, information systems capability translated into competitive advantage. Other cases cited involved a bank, an industrial company, a distributor, and a service company.

[9] Joseph W. Wilkinson, p. 12.

perhaps vulnerable too. The spotlight will be on them to oversee activities and provide guidelines. Those who are effective can expect to be well rewarded; those who are not can expect trouble and frustration—even new careers.

Beneficial Impact on Systems Users

The last implication discussed herein may be the most consequential. An effective application of systems technology to FISs should have a profound beneficial impact on the users of those systems. With the advent of real-time interactive systems, the timeliness of information is effectively optimized. Advances in office automation and gains in telecommunications will enable vast quantities of data to be transmitted anywhere in the office or the world with equal speed. With improving software technology, user information needs can be precisely met easily and simply. In effect, the managers who use such systems will be virtually restored to the position of their predecessors of a century earlier. They will be able to get accurate, relevant information quickly and simply.

Whether FISs actually achieve such a goal is less open to question than how soon it will happen. The rate of attainment will vary from company to company as a result of management style, competitive pressure, nature of the business, and other factors. Some companies may never achieve the ideal; however, even these are bound to be affected by developments in systems technology in a positive way. The important point is to recognize that the technology is here to stay and that it represents an opportunity whose potential benefits are limited only by the capacity of those responsible for applying it.

REFERENCES

Donnelly, Robert M. "The Changing Role of the Controller." *Financial Executive* (Apr. 1982), pp. 20–24.

———. "Keep Up With Decision Support Systems." *Financial Executive* (Aug. 1983), pp. 44–46.

Friend, David. "The New Promise of Graphic Information Systems." *Financial Executive* (Oct. 1982), pp. 20–26.

Hall, James A. "Decision Support Systems Arrive." *Management Accounting* (Dec. 1983), p. 69.

Maagd, Gerald R. "The Usefulness of Information to Management." *Management Accounting* (Jan. 1984), p. 31.

Mautz, Robert K., Alan G. Merten, and Dennis G. Severance. *Senior Management Control of Computer-Based Information Systems.* Morristown, N.J.: Financial Executives Research Foundation, 1983.

Moscove, Stephen A., and Mark G. Simkin. *Accounting Information Systems.* New York: John Wiley & Sons, 1981, ch. 1.

Naisbett, John, *Megatrends.* New York: Warner Books, 1982, ch. 1.

Notowidigdo, M.H. "Information Systems: Weapons to Gain the Competitive Edge." *Financial Executive* (Feb. 1984).

Peters, Thomas J., and Robert H. Waterman, Jr. *In Search of Excellence.* New York: Harper & Row, 1982.

Wilkinson, Joseph W. *Accounting and Information Systems.* New York: John Wiley & Sons, 1982, ch. 1.

CHAPTER 2

Systems Technology Trends

Steven J. Root

Overview	2	Centralized Processing	8
Application of Systems Technology to FISs	2	Inefficient Processing	9
		Costly Systems Maintenance	9
What Is Systems Technology?	2	Informal Compensating Factors	10
Components Technologies	3	Undue Risk	10
Microprocessor Technology	3	Computer Illiteracy	11
Integration Technology	3	Trends Affecting Future FISs	11
Advanced Materials Technology	4	Systems Integration and Interaction	11
Memory Technology	4	Database Orientation	12
Disk-Storage Technology	4	Ease of Development, Change, and Maintenance	12
Fiber Optics Technology	4	Wider Application	13
Network Technology	4	Risk Reduction	13
Application Technology	5	The Future Scene	14
Security Technology	5		
Systems Technology Defined	5	**Organizational Trends**	15
Systems Technology Trends	6	Effect on MISs	15
A Brief History	6	Effect on Finance Functions	16
		Effect on Other Management Functions	17
Systems Technology Trends Affecting FISs	8	**Office Trends**	18
The Current Scene	8	**References**	19
Stand-Alone Applications	8		
Fig. 2-1 Systems Technology Evolution			7

OVERVIEW

As noted in Chapter 1, the level of success achievable by any given company is in direct proportion to the quality of information available to its management. More and more, that quality and information are the result of applying systems technology to specific circumstances. Routines once not even possible are now performed easily, courtesy of the modern marvel of electronic data processing (EDP).

To be sure, individual company successes occur because of more obvious reasons, such as better products, marketing know-how, management competence, and financing wizardry. Less obvious is the profound effect systems technology, specifically financial systems technology, has had on promoting this success. It is the primary source of the vastly improving information being delivered to the user because of systems technology. Further, more timely information improves decision makers' productivity and effectiveness, which translates into a competitive advantage. With that concept in mind, it is worthwhile to develop a perspective of the systems technology that produces such an effect.

In this chapter, the focus is on systems technology, including the technical terminology, and the analysis of the historical basis of the current trends in systems technology that affect an FIS.

Application of Systems Technology to FISs

The FISs currently in general use are a key factor in enabling modern business to deliver products and services on a scale unimaginable a few decades ago, a trend that is examined throughout this Manual. Unfortunately, these systems are plagued with shortcomings and weaknesses. As a result, many of the systems, despite their improvements, are inefficient and present unnecessary risks. Current systems technology can be applied to produce new FISs that reduce inefficiencies and risks. In fact, many companies already allocate considerable resources toward such application; many more are cautiously waiting and watching these developments, and perhaps running the greatest risk of all: unknowingly endangering their very existence by failing to make the necessary commitment and investment to take advantage of new opportunities in the application of systems technology to FISs.

WHAT IS SYSTEMS TECHNOLOGY?

"Systems technology" is one of those recognizable terms that are used frequently in technical literature. When certain terms gain broad usage, actual definitions seem to get blurred; so it is with systems technology. Even technical dictionaries of computer and data processing terminology omit the term. Thus, a practical definition must evolve from related terms and usage patterns. The term "computer science" is somewhat synonymous with systems technology. Sippi and Sippi define computer science as follows: "The entire spectrum of theoretical and applied disciplines connected with the development and application of computers. Contributions have come mostly from such fields as mathematics, logic, language analysis, programming, computer design, systems engineering, and information systems."[1]

In this definition, the focus is almost exclusively on computers. To be sure, computers play a dominant role in systems technology, but the term seems to imply that more than computers are involved, at least for the present and near future.

When the forces reshaping the computer industry are discussed, the field of telecommunications, among other things, keeps coming up. According to a recent *Business Week* article, this reshaping is being driven by "the rapid convergence of computer and communications technologies—inexorably intertwining these once-separate industries."[2] Since computers and communications are becoming linked, the term "computer science" seems virtually obsolete. However, systems technology implies even more than computers and communication. Otherwise, the term would only encompass engineers, programmers, and technical people in related fields.

Components Technologies

Developments are occurring so rapidly and from such a variety of fields that it is impossible to categorize them using traditional terminology. There are many branches of this technology. Following are examples of its components.

Microprocessor Technology. Developments here include the migration from microprocessor chips that process 16 bits of data at a time to 32 and 64 bits. In addition, developers are designing microchips that are specially dedicated to performing routine tasks such as displaying graphics. The objective of these developments, of course, is to increase processing speed. With faster speeds come lower costs of processing and expanded capacity, among other things.

Integration Technology. Developments here are aimed not only at packing larger numbers of circuits on a single chip but also at introducing wafer-scale integration. This entails designing and developing the equivalent of approximately 200 integrated chips in a single process on silicon wafers the size of a man's hand. Efforts along these lines are commonly characterized as large-scale integration and very large scale integration. The former has resulted in

---

[1] Charles J. Sippi and Roger J. Sippi, *Computer Dictionary*, 3d ed. (Indianapolis: Howard W. Sams, 1980), p. 102.

[2] "Reshaping the Computer Industry," *Business Week* (July 16, 1984), p. 84.

packing 1,000 or more circuits on a single chip. The latter aims at putting more than 10,000 curcuits on the chip. As storage capacity increases, the relative investment required in semiconductor memory declines.

Advanced Materials Technology. Also related to chip technology, this field explores alternatives to silicon as the basic chip material. Recent attention has focused on gallium arsenide, a chemical compound that carries signals faster than silicon.

Memory Technology. Developments here focus on increasing the amount of data that can be stored in a chip's memory. Advances include using lasers to trace circuits so fine that memory is tripled. These advances also contribute to declining costs.

Disk-Storage Technology. Activity in this field is directed at increasing storage density within disks. This density now exceeds 10 million bits per square inch.[3] Improvements in the size of film heads, plated media, and other engineering advances promise to increase densities further.

Fiber Optics Technology. Developments here are aimed at increasing transmission speeds and the quantity of data that can be transmitted over lines while simultaneously lowering the cost. This technology uses light as the transmitting medium through hair-thin glass fibers. These fibers allow the light to be bent and reflected with little light loss. Since the glass fibers are nonmetallic, they are not susceptible to electromagnetic interference, a problem for wire transmitted messages. Data are transmitted in fiber optics systems by modulating light emitted from lasers.

Network Technology. Activities here are directed toward integrating the communication of voice, data, and image in single localized systems of equipment, lines, switches, and stations called local area networks (LANs). Developments include digital switches that enable interconnecting microcomputers, word processors, and other devices. LAN software packages capable of linking personal computers and word processors already exist. It will not be long before large mainframe processors, minicomputers, personal computers, and word processors will become linked, enabling the development of extremely flexible low-cost information management opportunities.

---

[3] Frederic G. Withington, "Winners and Losers in the Fifth Generation," *Datamation* (Dec. 1983), p. 198.

Application Technology. Advances in this area are directed toward reducing the obstacles and barriers to applying the computer's advantages effectively to specific user requirements. The aim is to make computers and their systems more useful. Developments range from enhancements in operating systems that permit computers to operate on more than one job at a time to improvements in programming languages and database designs that make it easier to instruct computers on what to do and, at the same time, make carrying out these instructions faster, easier, and more efficient. The third generation of programming languages is already in use. These languages use data abstraction and are capable of controlling asynchronous processes.[4] Although the distinctions in language generations are becoming difficult to discern, many believe that the fourth generation of languages, characterized by further control abstraction, is evolving. On the horizon looms the fascinating field of artificial intelligence (AI), which some refer to as the fifth generation, predicting that its emergence from the laboratory is almost at hand. AI is the process of embuing computers with powers to think like humans.

Security Technology. Although this area is not often thought of as a separate technology, it is fast becoming so. The amount and types of data that can be stored, processed, and disseminated and the speed with which each activity can be accomplished raise many security issues. Many developments are occurring with respect to hardware design, facilities layout, access control, software and file protection, and backup and recovery techniques. The products of these efforts reduce the chances of theft, destruction, and other irregularities, which could cause considerable damage and loss.

The kinds of activities that are joining or being joined together by the converging and emerging technologies are only briefly exemplified in the preceding sections. If technologies are being linked, then there must be a unifying term by which the related aspects may be perceived—systems technology.

Systems Technology Defined

For purposes of this Manual, "systems technology" is defined as the complete range of disciplines operating in direct and indirect ways in order to evolve techniques that present new opportunities or that eliminate obstacles pertaining to the effective development and use of information systems.

Systems technology can be thought of as being analogous to a giant diesel locomotive pulling a long string of railroad cars along a track, heading toward a predetermined destination. The locomotive is comprised of numerous subassemblies (wheels, engines, tanks, gears, and rods) directly and indirectly linked together and supported by various control mechanisms. Some are internal to the locomotive; others are external. If the locomotive operates properly, it

---

[4] Richard L. Wexelblat, "*N*th Generation Languages," *Datamation* (Sept. 1, 1984), p. 112.

moves the train along the track as intended, thus benefiting the passengers and cargo on board.

Similarly, systems technology can be thought of as a facilitating vehicle that, through its own movement, causes intended motion, through change, in organizations, functions, disciplines, procedures, and techniques. Like the locomotive, systems technology must be controlled to be sure that the changes occur for the better. Of course, the converse can result. In Part II of this Manual, basic systems concepts are described. Chapter 10, in particular, describes how controls are instituted to harness the power of systems technology to achieve the desired, auditable results.

SYSTEMS TECHNOLOGY TRENDS

A Brief History

The growth and development of systems technology are essentially twentieth-century phenomena of considerable proportions. Few events in recorded history can claim to surpass in impact the advent of EDP and its associated technologies.

Most accounts of computer history begin with the origin of the abacus in the Orient more than 5,000 years ago.[5] The first mechanical calculating machine was invented in Europe in 1642 by Blaise Pascal, the French scientist and philosopher, who used it as an aid in computing his father's business accounts. Today, a popular programming language bears his name. The device he invented carried out its arithmetic functions by a mechanical gear system with as many as eight columns of digits.

The first automatic digital computer was conceived in England in the 1830s by Charles Babbage. Limitations in manufacturing technology, however, prevented the design from becoming a working reality.

It was not until the late nineteenth century that an American, Herman Hollerith, invented the first machine that used punched cards. This invention was used in compiling census results and foreran the computer peripheral equipment in use today.

The first electromechanical computer was developed in 1944 and was known as the Mark I. In 1946, the first fully electronic computer, called ENIAC (Electronic Numerical Integrator and Calculator), was devised. Since that time, computer-related developments have occurred at a very rapid rate. Figure 2-1 summarizes only a few of those that have occurred since ENIAC. Today, systems technology is a massive, worldwide, $150-billion-plus industry.

---

[5] See "Origin of Computer Instruments," *Encyclopaedia Britannica*, Volume 4, *Knowledge in Depth* (Encyclopaedia Britannica 1984), pp. 1046–1048.

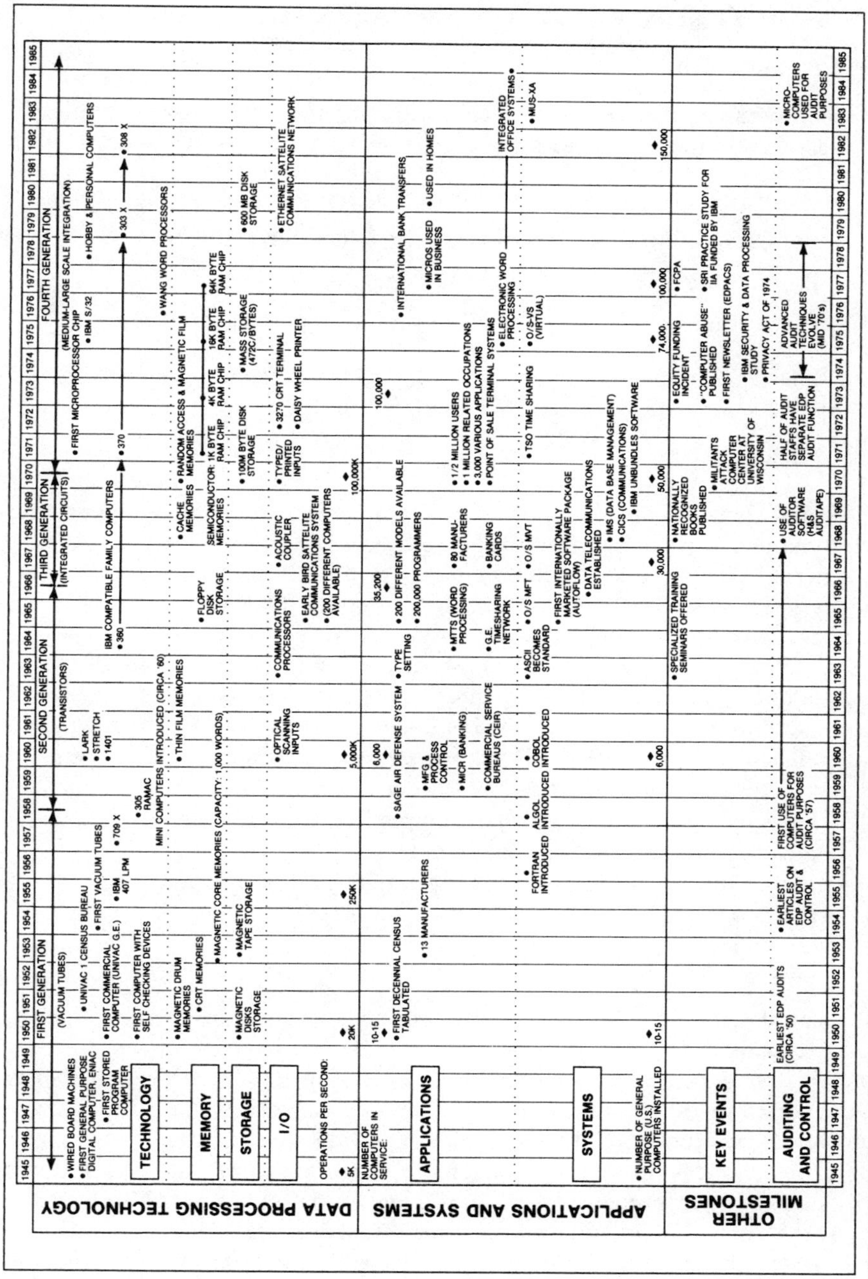

SYSTEMS TECHNOLOGY TRENDS

FIG. 2-1 Systems Technology Evolution

SYSTEMS TECHNOLOGY TRENDS AFFECTING FISs

The Current Scene

Financial organizations in medium to large companies are almost completely dependent upon the data processing department for such activities as:

- Processing payrolls and other disbursements
- Preparing billings and maintaining customer accounts
- Posting journal entries to general ledgers
- Generating financial statements and other reports for management

While the environment is changing rapidly, these supporting systems invariably have some or all of the characteristics described in the following sections.

Stand-Alone Applications. In most companies, applications supporting such functions as payroll, accounts payable, cost accounting, fixed assets, and the general ledger were developed, perhaps one at a time, over a period of several years. These systems came into being during the 1960s and 1970s and used the then-current technology.

Such systems tend to be batch oriented (largely independent, hence "stand-alone," applications), and require sequential processing. Each is apt to involve second-generation programming languages such as COBOL. Also, each system usually requires that all data necessary to execute the system be designed into, and made a part of, the system. Thus, any given system, particularly a complex one, requires much programming or coding merely to keep all the data accurate, complete, and up-to-date.

It is not unusual to find systems supported by dozens, even hundreds, of supportive programs. Each of these may contain several thousand lines of programming code.

Centralized Processing. Like other business applications, financial applications usually are run on very large mainframe computers in a central location, which may be located near the finance department. The large mainframes are supported by peripheral equipment including disk drives, tape drives, communications equipment, and printing devices. Data are submitted usually over coaxial telephone lines, often from remote terminals. Other communications methods ranging from mail systems to microwave data links may also be used.

These central processing centers are often operated for two (and even three) shifts, up to seven days a week. Successful operation of these complex installations requires a considerable investment in management, technical personnel, and special facilities, equipment, and supplies. It is not unusual for these centers to experience seemingly constant struggles to provide satisfactory

SYSTEMS TECHNOLOGY TRENDS 2-9

processing services while continually expanding their capability to meet the increasing demand for such services. Demand is most acute for on-line processing services as more and more systems are designed to use that capability. Users may experience periods of time when the quality of processed data suffers as expansion and conversions occur.

Inefficient Processing. Systems technology of the 1960s and 1970s seemed miraculous at the time. It is no exaggeration to assert that technology was the principal factor in enabling finance functions to provide management with modern financial services.

However, viewed from the perspective of current technology, such systems seem as limited and inefficient as a Model T Ford might be when compared to present-day automobiles. Systems design technology required massive and often redundant investments in manpower, space, equipment, and data in order to serve the users' common needs. Since processing often occurred sequentially and by batches, processing times and data storage requirements were often wasted because of the necessity of performing stored routines on all records in a given file, including those that remained unchanged.

Further, because both simple and complex applications were submitted to the large data center for processing, the small user consumed a portion of resources intended for much larger users, creating unnecessarily high costs.

Costly Systems Maintenance. Financial systems that were developed in the period up to about 1975 or 1980 still dominate the business environment. These systems are expensive to maintain, primarily due to their design. Many of these systems were originated by individuals or teams that developed unique systems solutions to specific circumstances. Documentation of these solutions, even of the systems themselves, often was (and is) lacking. If the programmer did not grow up with these systems, he found it difficult to gain the necessary knowledge to keep the systems operational. Changes were often accomplished over a longer time span than necessary. Because systems were comprised of multiple programs, a change in one area had an undetected effect on another area. Debugging systems during periods of change usually required considerable effort.

Although program utilities exist that make the task of changing these systems much more efficient than in the past, there is still a tendency to minimize the extent to which changes are made. Some systems are touched only rarely because they are unusually difficult to change; every company probably has one or two of these. Because of these and other factors, systems maintenance activity can consume as much as 60 to 80 percent of a programming group's budget. Users, such as finance managers, are often unfamiliar with the difficulties involved in effecting systems changes and become frustrated when maintenance efforts of the MIS group cause them such problems as delays in effecting changes and error-filled reports.

Informal Compensating Factors. Among other things, the limitations of many existing financial systems cause them to fail in meeting the needs of their user groups. The following are symptomatic of this condition:

- Information is not timely due to the batch-oriented nature of processing or some similar factor.
- Information is not complete or accurate due to high transaction rejection rates or insufficient controls to identify all errors.
- Report formats make it difficult to sift out relevant information.

Where these situations are present, the user is forced to develop means to compensate for the systems' limitations. In some companies, information such as cash collected, invoices to be paid, or orders received is too important to wait for batch systems to process. To avoid problems, direct telephone contact, morning briefings, or other similar techniques may be used. In other instances, the user may spend considerable time checking the accuracy of critical reports. For example, stock status reports, even if distributed daily, may be subjected to verification by physical counts of key items.

These techniques are informal to the degree that they were not designed into the original system. They came about usually because of unforeseeable limitations during the systems design phase. To some extent, nearly every application has them.

Undue Risk. For the most part, systems developed in earlier technological generations did not receive adequate attention from the standpoint of security. Users often were, and still are, unaware of the dangers inherent in these systems. Although the risks vary from system to system, the following are somewhat typical overall:

- Inability to recover effectively from interruptions in processing capability.
- Loss of data due to inadequate backup procedures.
- Theft of sensitive company files because of unauthorized access to computers, either from inside or outside the computer area.
- Damage to computer facilities and equipment as a result of insufficient physical protection.
- Fraud or other similar irregularities due to improper segregation of duties.

As more and more functions became dependent on the computer, more data became concentrated in its electronic files; the risks and their ramifications grew. Much has been done in recent years to improve security. Yet, the pace of technological advances and the rate at which computer use is expanding combine to keep the risks of computer use at an uncomfortably high level. See Chapter 12 for in-depth coverage of security aspects.

Computer Illiteracy. Computer illiteracy is vanishing quickly. Still, many financial managers are quite unfamiliar with systems technology. More important, they lack the necessary knowledge of the specific systems that have been developed for their organizations. Many are unaware of the risks to which they are exposed.

Some recognize their limitations and try to compensate by hiring one or more "computer literates" to represent them in relations with information systems groups. While some action is better than none, this still does not constitute an adequate solution to the literacy problem.

The FIS environment, although functioning largely as intended, is capable of considerable improvement. The advances in systems technology described earlier make that improvement not only possible but inevitable. It is well to consider next how these technological developments will affect future FISs.

Trends Affecting Future FISs

As noted, many companies have already begun to apply new systems technology to replace FISs developed in the 1960s and 1970s. These new systems are characterized by the following trends:

- Systems integration and interaction
- Database orientation
- Ease of development, change, and maintenance
- Wider application
- Risk reduction

Systems Integration and Interaction. Systems development activity in the 1980s is apt to occur in an integrated fashion: The development of one system (e.g., payroll) is likely to be coordinated with the development of another (e.g., personnel). Integration is desirable for a variety of reasons. Chief among these are the savings that result from eliminating data redundancy among systems that use the same data elements. The memory and storage capacities of CPUs, disk drives, and magnetic tape units make integration efforts virtually unlimited. Moreover, advances in telecommunications enables data to be transmitted and processed faster and more cheaply than ever before. Thus, geographic separation of component functions or elements is no longer a limiting factor in an FIS. Systems that once varied by geographic area may now be standardized or consolidated. It is now possible to centralize such treasury functions as accounts payable, accounts receivable, cash receipts, and disbursements and payroll for even the largest, most diversified company. Of course, not all new systems will consolidate or integrate the divergent requirements of users. For example, data security considerations of certain applications may be so sensitive that they will dictate other courses of action. Nevertheless, the trend is unmistakenly toward greater systems integration. Systems integration necessitates increased involvement by, and interaction among, users and systems developers. Responsibilities for systems ownership, data ownership, and data custodial activities must be clearly drawn. Finally, systems technology now permits greater interaction between the systems and the users. The majority of new FISs are designed to permit on-line real-time interaction where necessary. Also, use of personal computers to download data from mainframes for separate analysis and manipulation is becoming widespread in modern FISs. As a result, rapid analysis of virtually up-to-the-minute data is possible. Such capability is most useful in preparing and/or changing financial reports, business plans, and financial models, whether for a department, a product line, a geographic area, a division, or an entire company. (Part III offers specific and practical examples of this trend.)

Database Orientation. This is somewhat related to systems integration. Advances in design technology, as well as in computer storage capacity and processing, now cause minimal redundancy in applicable equipment and programming, maintenance, and processing activities. Essentially, these advances center around the development of large databases that exist separately and independently from the specific applications that access, change, or make use of the resident data. The subject data are made available in an on-line fashion and are controlled by a Data Base Management System and one or more database administrators to preserve its integrity and utility. Ideally, systems applications developed in database environments are free of the complexities and costs of controlling the data relevant to the system. In practice, this ideal is seldom attained. Nevertheless, as in the case of systems integration, the trend toward database development is unmistakable.

Ease of Development, Change, and Maintenance. To a large degree, the trends toward systems integration and databases account for the increased ease of systems development and maintenance. The advent of higher-level, third- and fourth-generation programming languages also plays a major role. Further, computer manufacturers and software suppliers have developed powerful automated tools to aid in designing, coding, testing, and documenting new programs and making changes to existing ones.[6] The development of smart terminals and personal computers (PCs) also has benefited the systems designer and programmer, resulting in decreased development time and costs for systems and increased satisfaction of the user. The growing ease with which systems may be developed coupled with the increasing familiarity of some users with aspects of computers and systems technology is producing an interesting situation. It is almost commonplace now for the user to take complete responsibility for, and perform all aspects of, developing new systems. This situation, unheard of only a few years ago, has caused some concern in the EDP community.

Wider Application. Not long ago, applying systems technology to business needs meant that only the most significant candidates for application would be selected. The costs of systems development and the ongoing costs of processing imposed inescapable limitations on the march toward automation. Systems development projects had to be justified on the basis of ROI calculations and other cost/benefit considerations. Careful control had to be maintained during systems development so that original design objectives were not sacrificed to cost overruns. In spite of intentions and actions to the contrary, however, systems goals often were not achieved. Many times, a user had to live with systems that delivered much less than was originally promised. Thus, this limited the timeliness, accuracy, and usefulness of systems intended to help control purchasing, inventory, costs, sales, fixed assets, and other areas of management interest.

Today's systems technology makes most, if not at all, of these experiences obsolete and not likely to be repeated. The ease of systems development noted earlier makes it possible for almost any legitimate need to be met. A user's unique and specific requirements can be easily fulfilled. The result is that more and more financial functions are potential beneficiaries of systems technology. Analytical and graphics functions and the advent of personal computers and powerful software packages for performing word processing offer yet another exciting opportunity to extend the power of the computer into the financial arena. The efficiency and effectiveness of such financial functions as planning, forecasting, reporting, budgeting, and auditing are being greatly increased.

Risk Reduction. Because older FISs often were operated in a risky environment, exposure to systems malfunction, processing interruptions, and other similar irregularities was, and continues to be, unnecessarily high. Valuable company assets such as cash, inventory, customer lists, vendor lists, trade secrets, and product designs could be stolen, lost, or converted through acts of God or humans. In the latter case, the action might have been accidental or intentional. Most users, lacking familiarity with EDP, were unaware of the

---

[6] Howard Bromberg, "In Search of Productivity," *Datamation* (Aug. 15, 1984), p. 74.

risks involved. Those familiar with EDP, while aware of the risks, were usually more interested in satisfying user needs and holding down costs. They tended to believe that their own competence and the honesty and integrity of company employees would adequately compensate for the risks. However, a series of sensational computer-related frauds beginning with the Equity Funding scandal in the early 1970s changed those beliefs dramatically. As noted more fully in Chapter 12, the FIS of the 1980s is much less likely to suffer from its predecessors' security risks. Not only has systems technology improved the physical environment for computer processing, but software and data protection environments are also more secure. Another positive factor in this area has been the emergence of a professional body of EDP auditors,[7] which is growing both in size and competence and is helping to focus management attention on security risks in all phases and activities of FISs. Most management groups are now aware of the need to monitor security risks constantly and to act when necessary to keep them as low as possible.

The Future Scene. The foregoing trends will result in FISs considerably different from those that characterize the current scene. A profile of the typical FIS of the future might be as follows:

- On line, interactive as opposed to batch oriented.
- Processed either near the financial organization (even within it) or, at the user's option, at a remote facility, depending on resource availability and need.
- Fully integrated with other MISs in such a way that it will be nearly impossible to distinguish it.
- Supported by localized decision support systems of individuals or functions using linked personal computers or smart terminals.
- Developed and controlled via database management concepts, making it relatively easy to satisfy unique and often changing information requirements.
- Well documented and with adequate provisions for backup and recovery in the event of processing interruptions, including disasters.
- Operated in an environment where responsibility for ownership, access, and change of systems-related personnel, procedures, controls, data, and facilities is clear.

These future FIS characteristics may seem ideal, even foolishly simple, to "real-world" financial managers who have been coping with FISs born from 1960s and 1970s technology. To them, it can only be said that their negative

---

[7] James D. Willson and Steven J. Root, *Internal Auditing Manual* (Boston: Warren, Gorham & Lamont, 1983), p. 17-37.

experiences do not have to continue. Systems technology now permits the problem side of FISs to all but vanish. Such an environment is attainable under present technology, provided there is commitment toward that goal and awareness of what can be done by all members of the management team.

ORGANIZATIONAL TRENDS

Organizational trends are briefly noted in the following sections because they are likely to affect FISs. Organizational structure as it pertains to the MIS function is dealt with in detail in Chapter 4, which focuses on the structure of the MIS function in particular. The organization of that function as described in that chapter is likely to remain intact for the foreseeable future. Ultimately, however, systems technology promises to alter its role substantially.

Effect on MISs

Whether known as the EDP department, information systems, MISs, or information resource management, the function of providing EDP and related services to user organizations has existed almost since the invention of the first computers. The growth of that function has paralleled the growth of systems technology. It is not uncommon to find MIS organizations supported by hundreds of staff persons and consuming as much as one to 2 percent of annual company expenditures. For billion-dollar corporations, that can amount to quite a sum.

In addition to being organizationally large, these functions are pervasively involved in almost every phase of the company's business. For many of these organizations, daily life is a constant struggle to provide reliable EDP services in the face of ever-increasing demand and a changing technical environment. Even the best of MIS functions experience instances of failure to satisfy user needs.

A growing number of users are becoming more than just vocal about their perceptions of the quality and cost of MIS services. Fortified by such systems technology developments as mini- and microcomputers, English-oriented programming languages, and LANs, some users have developed entire systems without the involvement or knowledge of the MIS organization.

Early MIS reaction to these developments runs from active support to outright opposition. This trend, with or without MIS support, is likely to increase simply because the technology permits it. But there is a more important reason for this likelihood. More often than not, the user gets what he wants and probably gets it at less cost. Thus, in the early 1980s, there has been a migration of control of EDP and related activities from the large centralized MIS functions toward the user community. The rate of migration no doubt varies from company to company, but it does occur.

If that is so, what will become of the MIS organizations of the 1960s and 1970s? Some have suggested that they will become facilitators, coordinators, and strategists.[8] According to this view, MIS organizations will not be responsible for much systems design, implementation, and operation. End users will assume this responsibility. Of course, this is a matter of opinion. In any event, it seems likely that the MIS manager will become increasingly responsible for overall planning and guidance encompassing computers, communications, and office automation.

Effect on Finance Functions

The migration of EDP and related services from the MIS function has obvious implications for financial managers. Heretofore, financial managers have looked to the MIS function to handle their EDP needs. Soon this may no longer be desirable or even possible. Future financial managers will need to become increasingly responsible for satisfying their EDP needs with a minimum of outside assistance.

There are other implications for those financial managers who have traditionally been responsible for their companies' MIS functions, as many have been. They may perceive their managerial control and influence as becoming diminished. Care must be taken to resist this feeling. Instead, it must be replaced with a commitment to help aspiring user groups meet their EDP needs by taking maximum advantage of new technologies. Moreover, their skills can be devoted more to applications in the planning and control field.

One further implication for finance functions warrants mention. Finance departments utilize MIS organizations in order to help provide the financial information needed by management. In the past, finance functions have had near total control over who gets to see the financial data they prepare. Systems technology now permits other organizations to prepare and/or analyze their own financial data (see Chapter 1 for some examples of this). Further commentary is contained in Chapter 16 in the form of decision support systems (DSSs). Finance functions must adapt to this emerging environment in ways that facilitate its development. Financial managers should act, perhaps in a consulting fashion, to help make sure that financial information developed outside its control is as relevant and reliable as the financial information it does control.

Finally, systems technology, according to one expert, will dramatically change the financial reporting scene.[9] By the beginning of the twenty-first century, it is highly likely that database reporting will replace the financial reporting ritual as we know it today, both for internal and external purposes. This means that, rather than filing financial statements, registrants will instead make

---

[8] Theodore J. Freiser's remarks to journalists at the Howard City Club in New York City, as quoted in the *Journal of Accountancy* (Nov. 1984), p. 42.

[9] John C. Burton, "What Lies Ahead for SEC's Financial Reporting?" *Legal Times* (Oct. 8, 1984), p. A11.

available multilayered databases of financial and operational information. The organizational impact of this eventuality is apt to be profound.

Effect on Other Management Functions

The growth and expansion of applying systems technology to the business environment has changed all management functions. This trend will likely accelerate. As stated earlier, systems technology is causing the transfer of responsibility to end users for designing, implementing, and maintaining systems. This means that the heads of all management disciplines such as marketing, purchasing, manufacturing, and engineering will become increasingly responsible for data processing activities. As in the case of financial managers, some will be better prepared for this than others. This effect has already started in a few leading-edge companies.[10]

One organizational trend that began several years ago is virtually certain to become more widespread—the establishment of the EDP steering committee. This function is one whereby high-ranking executives representing key user groups, together with high-ranking MIS management, organize in committee fashion to provide managerial overview of the activities associated with managing the company's investment in information.

A variation on this technique has the same objective for companies that have decentralized the MIS function. In these situations, several MIS managers and their equivalents may organize into a committee. Activities are coordinated, experiences and ideas are shared, and policies are developed out of this effort. Many companies, however, will find the committee approach to be inadequate for their purposes, because managing information as a company has become too critical for a committee approach alone. Today, companies face a bewildering array of choices and decisions about how best to apply systems technology to their situations. Many of these decisions require careful analysis, research, and study, not to mention an awareness of the technical aspects involved. The following is only a partial list of policy questions in this area that every company must answer.

- Should the company standardize on hardware and software decisions?
- Who is responsible for controlling systems, data, and related equipment?
- Should the company standardize on such items as personal computers, word processing equipment, and copiers?
- What is the best approach for LANs?
- Which systems/applications should be centralized? Decentralized?

---

[10] "Office Automation Restructures Business," *Business Week* (Oct. 8, 1984), p. 118.

These and a host of related questions require the full-time attention of individuals with executive capabilities supported by a staff with sufficient technical expertise. Many forward looking companies are establishing high management positions for these individuals. Thus, the age of the chief information officer is upon us. These corporate executives are being given broad management responsibility for establishing companywide policies pertaining to information together with the investment in facilities, equipment, software, and personnel necessary to manage it effectively.

As noted earlier, these companies are finding that increased effectiveness and efficiency is attained by centralizing in this executive the policy-making authority for MISs, telecommunications, and office automation. Early indications of improved coordination and cooperation among these historically disparate disciplines are bound to accelerate this trend.

OFFICE TRENDS

Chapter 23 contains a detailed discussion of the revolution now occurring in business offices everywhere. It is, however, worthwhile to note some trends with a few comments here.

The most obvious and, at the same time, the most significant trend in office automation is the growth and widespread use of personal computers. Some claim that the office of the future will contain nothing more than a PC and a communications link.[11]

Managers and their staffs of every discipline are finding that much of their computing needs are satisfied with these small but powerful machines. As a result, their use is proliferating at an astounding rate. Corporations, educational institutions, and government units are finding PCs popping up everywhere.

This revolutionary event is changing the concept of the "office of the future" that once prevailed. That concept held that offices and managers would become linked somehow through a series of intelligent terminals connected to a large control mainframe that contained all the software and memory needed to make the network operational.

The personal computer revolution has changed that concept by enabling managers to move ahead with their own automation independently of any central control. The office of the future will have personal computers. However, they will not be linked together through a centralized mainframe, although mainframes no doubt will be part of the network. Instead, new communications equipment and software will evolve to link stand-alone PCs, word processors, and corporate databases together.

Related to this is the drive to link together voice, data, and facsimile communications. Intense competition toward that end is occurring between tele-

---

[11] "Computer Shock Hits the Office," *Business Week* (Aug. 8, 1983), p. 46.

communications companies and computer manufacturers. The lack of a single effective solution to the communications issues raised by the foregoing developments is causing widespread confusion.[12]

Although the choices may be difficult and the investments considerable, companies will probably continue to move quickly toward office automation. Companies that develop clear-cut policies regarding PCs seem to be in a better position to avoid wasting resources than those who do not.

REFERENCES

"Computer Shock Hits the Office." *Business Week* (Aug. 8, 1983), pp. 46–49.

Ferris, David. "The Micro-Mainframe Connection." *Datamation*.

Ferris, David, and John Cunningham. "Local Nets for Micros." *Datamation* (Aug. 11, 1984), pp. 104–109.

MacCallum, Jeff. "Local Area Networks: Putting It All Together." *Management Technology* (Aug. 1984), pp. 45–54.

"Office Automation Restructures Business." *Business Week* (Oct. 8, 1984), pp. 118–125.

"Reshaping the Computer Industry." *Business Week* (July 16, 1984), pp. 84–92.

Rosenberg, Jerry. *Dictionary of Computers, Data Processing & Telecommunications*. New York: John Wiley & Sons, 1984.

Sippi, Charles J., and Roger J. Sippi. *Computer Dictionary*, 3d ed. Indianapolis: Howard W. Sams & Co., Inc., 1980.

Wexeblat, Richard L. "*N*th Generation Languages." *Datamation* (Sept. 1, 1984), pp. 111–117.

Withington, Frederic G. "Winners and Losers in the Fifth Generation." *Datamation* (Dec. 1983), pp. 193–208.

Wolf, Carl, and Jim Treleaven. "Decision Support Systems: Management Finally Gets its Hands on the Data." *Management Technology* (Nov. 1983), pp. 44–51.

---

[12] "Computer Shock Hits the Office," p. 47.

CHAPTER 3

The Financial Information System as Related to Management of a Business

James D. Willson

Introduction 2	**Information Needs of Managers** 12
The Business Purpose 2	Types of Information 12
Management's Leadership Task 3	**Managerial Activities as a Factor in Information Needs** 13
The Management Process 3	The Managerial Level 13
Planning to Meet Business Objectives ... 5	Organization Structure 14
Coordinating/Organizing to Meet Company Goals 5	Nature of the Managerial Activities 14
Directing to Implement Company Goals 6	Nature of Functional Operations 15
Measuring and Controlling to Ensure Success of the Plan 6	**Reports for Decision Making and Information Gathering** 15
The Managerial Decision-Making Process 6	Classifying Reports by Purpose 16
Types of Management Decisions 7	Classifying Reports by Conciseness 17
	Classifying Reports by Occurrence 17
Information Flows 9	Classifying Reports by Format or Style .. 19
Informal Information Flows 10	**Reporting Systems** 22
Formal Information Flows 11	**Responsibility Reporting** 23
Formal Vertical Flows 11	**References** 25
Formal Horizontal Flows 11	

Fig. 3-1 The Management Process 4
Fig. 3-2 Categories of Management Decisions 8
Fig. 3-3 Management Levels and Primary Types of Decisions 10
Fig. 3-4 Profile of Information Needs 14
Fig. 3-5 Classification of Reports 16
Fig. 3-6 Summary Plan Report 17
Fig. 3-7 Summary Control Report—Corporate Headquarters Expense 18

3-1

Fig. 3-8 Budget Report—Exception Basis 19
Fig. 3-9 Alternative Report Formats 21
Fig. 3-10 The Flash Report 22
Fig. 3-11 Responsibility Reporting—Flow of Information 24

INTRODUCTION

A business is an economic entity whose objective is to provide needed or desired goods or services in an economical manner. To meet this purpose, management uses several interrelated functions: planning, organizing, directing, and measuring. A well-conceived FIS is of key assistance in effectively executing these steps.

In considering exactly what constitutes a practical, results-oriented FIS—or, indeed, a sound MIS—it is helpful to review both the purpose of business and the management process. Included in such a review is a recognition of information sources as well as information needs of the successful business manager.

THE BUSINESS PURPOSE

The purpose of a business organization, under the private enterprise system as it operates in the United States, has long been characterized by the business sector as the earning of the highest possible return over an extended period of time.[1] In more sophisticated terms, it optimizes the return on assets or return on shareholders' equity, as the case may be, over the long term. The enlightened businessperson therefore looks to *continuity* of the enterprise and the efficient allocation of the firm's resources.

To be sure, the profit motive must remain dominant, but in a larger sense, a business organization is an economic institution. It must economically provide its customers with those goods and/or services they desire. There is no other basic reason for its existence. If it can efficiently and effectively supply this service on an economical basis, it will survive and prosper. If it cannot, then ultimately it will wither and die.

A business may pursue other collateral or supplemental objectives as its social responsibility. It may use corporate resources to further national goals or community welfare, improve employee benefits, or better environmental conditions. Yet, such purposes can be supported only if the business achieves its principal objective, which is the economical satisfaction of customer needs or desires.

---

[1] This and the next three sections are adapted from James D. Willson, *Budgeting and Profit Planning Manual* (Boston: Warren, Gorham & Lamont, 1983), ch. 1.

MANAGEMENT'S LEADERSHIP TASK

Management must guide or lead the business enterprise toward earning the highest possible return over time for the owners. This is not a simple undertaking. Management must take the broad objective, refine it, and carry it out by setting specific goals in a constantly changing environment. To begin with, management must perceive or determine the needs and desires of the prospective customers. Within its managerial and financial capabilities, it must assemble and organize the financial, technical, production, and distribution agencies to satisfy those needs. It must coordinate and direct its activities to meet the overall objective; goals must be intelligently conceived and activities efficiently planned and properly executed.

The task is continuous and challenging because customers' wants and needs change frequently. Further, the environmental constraints ebb and flow—whether they be governmental restrictions, competitive retaliation, economic pressures, or other factors. Management must successfully meet these challenges. New products, services, or processes must be developed continually. All the business functions of management, production, marketing, research, finance, and administration must be constantly reviewed and improved to effectively and efficiently meet the customer's needs and desires.

THE MANAGEMENT PROCESS

The management process by which business achieves its objectives may be divided into any number of functions. For purposes of discussion here, its activities are segregated into four functions, each with different information needs:

1 Planning
2 Coordinating
3 Directing
4 Measuring and controlling

Each function has several aspects, and the entire process may be regarded as an iterative one, with information being continually fed into the system for further action and reaction. Essentially, the flow of data and ideas is that depicted in Figure 3-1. Thus, as indicated at the top of the diagram, tentative objectives and goals are set for the enterprise, are tested and evaluated, and finally, perhaps with adjustments, become the approved ones. Plans are then developed by each department or function to achieve these goals and objectives. When the plans are analyzed, consolidated, and found acceptable, they are approved. They must then be executed. In so doing, actual performance is measured against plan, and any necessary corrective action is taken to bring the operations back on course. In a very definite sense, the management function depends on access to relevant information on a timely basis and in a usable format.

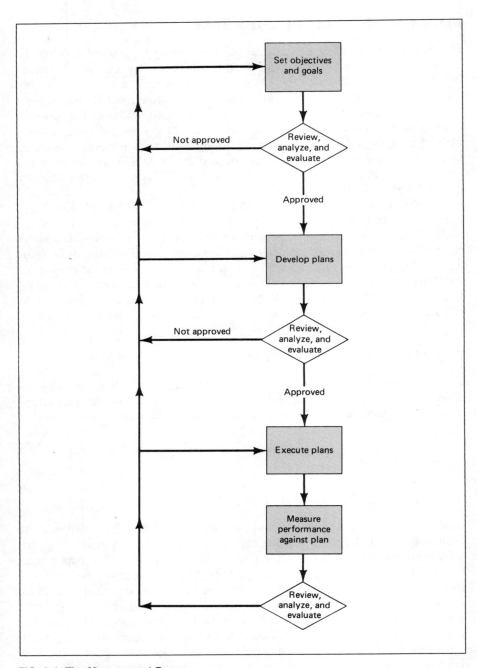

FIG. 3-1 The Management Process

THE FIS AS RELATED TO BUSINESS MANAGEMENT 3-5

Each of the four functions of management is discussed in order to provide background for use in planning and developing an FIS. Actually, all functions are interrelated and overlap and cannot be completely separated according to time sequence; that is, several activities may proceed at the same time.

Planning to Meet Business Objectives

In a general sense, planning simply determines what should be done and how and when it should be accomplished. From a total company or corporate viewpoint, planning involves two aspects:

1 Establishing the goals and objectives of the enterprise; and
2 Developing plans to achieve them.

Actually, planning is a very complex procedure. Setting goals and objectives involves judgments and decision making related to both the future environment and the future resources of the company. Conditions change, and management objectives may change. Hence, planning is by necessity an iterative process, as reflected in Figure 3-1, requiring constant, repeated communication on the present environment and resources, prospective changes in these factors, and progress toward meeting objectives. Planning is the continual process of making judgments about the events and activities essential to attaining stated goals and objectives and, as such, is closely linked to management's leadership task.

Coordinating/Organizing to Meet Company Goals

For practical purposes, "coordinating," or "organizing," may be defined as securing the necessary personnel, plant, equipment, and materials and arranging them to meet the business' objectives. This involves coordinating the firm's various subdivisions so that each works toward the accepted goals. An "organization" has been defined as a system of consciously coordinated activities, relationships, and people attempting to meet a common objective. The planning and budgeting process is integral to this coordinating activity. The MIS, the communication process, through which the business operates, should recognize these common characteristics of an effective organization:

- The willingness or desire to achieve a common objective or goal that a single individual cannot accomplish alone.
- The division or segregation of the various elements of the total task according to the skills, knowledge, or facilities required.
- Assignment of responsibility to specific organizational units for accomplishing specified functions.

- Coordination of personnel, resources, and facilities in an effective, smoothly working manner.
- A sensitivity to the need for change, as circumstances change, in organization, procedures, or objectives.

Directing to Implement Company Goals

The third basic management function is directing. Directing involves seeing that the tasks involved in implementing or executing the plan or activity (the doing) are performed efficiently and economically. Work must be carried out under time and cost constraints. Obviously, directing or implementing implicitly assumes that the plans have been communicated to all levels of management and that the expected results are known.

Measuring and Controlling to Ensure Success of the Plan

Measuring, sometimes referred to as the control function, is the last of the business management functions. It is an evaluative activity, which involves a comparison of actual activity with planned performance. This comparison may be in monetary terms, man-hours, quantity, or value. The process involves making such a comparison and then acting to bring substandard performance into line with expectations. Decisions are made concerning the unacceptable results, and the information is fed back into the management cycle.

Differences between plan and actual performance may occur for either or a combination of the following two reasons:

1 Execution or implementation of the plan was faulty.

2 The plan was inadequate or not suitable to existing conditions.

Consequently, as a result of the differences reported, new plans or strategies must be pursued, or new actions taken, to bring actual performance up to the plan.

THE MANAGERIAL DECISION-MAKING PROCESS

An essential ingredient of an effective business organization is sound decision making by its managers. To be sure, the process by which decisions are reached varies greatly from one individual to another. Some decisions are made on an emotional basis whereby personal bias, personal ambition, or company political considerations are paramount factors in the decision-making process. Here, we are concerned with decisions that are characterized by a more reasoned approach, although intuition and experience are often relevant as well. However, the process is generally systematic and logical; information is needed to make a sound decision. Because the FIS is influenced by, among other things, sensitivity to the steps in the decision-making process, as well as the kinds of business decisions to be made, we focus on these considerations.

The steps in the decision-making process are as follows:

1 *Recognize and define the problem.* The initial step is recognizing that a problem exists and that a decision about it must be made. For example, the chief executive officer (CEO) may observe from a long-range sales analysis that the sale of electric typewriters is falling off; or he may observe at a trade show that tremendous strides are being made in developing personal computers that can handle word processing efficiently; therefore, he must take steps to revise his business plan to accommodate new product development.

However, the problem must be properly defined as to the key factors and such elements as the time horizon, constraints, or assumptions (e.g., competitive activity). Information (mostly financial) that will aid in solving the problem must be made available.

2 *Consider alternative courses of action.* These alternatives may call for more information, perhaps about costs, revenues, and profit. Further, the process may be iterative, whereby newly discovered alternatives require further data.

3 *Analyze alternatives and select the best course of action.* This requires arranging the data to make the elements comparable. In some instances, a decision model might be developed to describe the relevant relationships and their behavior. The model should assist in comparing the alternatives according to pertinent criteria (e.g., return on investment (ROI), risk/reward rating, probability of occurrence).

4 *Begin implementation of the decision and provide for appropriate follow-up.* The necessary planning, organizing, directing, and measuring or controlling of the affected activities should be accomplished.

Types of Management Decisions

To many in business, especially those schooled in finance or science, the decision-making process is almost intuitive or automatic because of their training in problem solving. The process is essentially the same, although varying in complexity, whether considering a strategic problem at the chief executive level (e.g., the direction the firm should take) or at the operating level (e.g., correcting defects in the manufacture of semiconductor chips).

Types of business decisions may be classified in any number of ways. Figure 3-2 illustrates some possible groupings and various types of decisions. One of the most useful categories is by level or type of managerial activity. As discussed in Chapter 12, strategic planning ordinarily involves a long-time planning horizon, perhaps of three, five, or ten years. Strategic planning tends to be

Classification	Type of Decision	Example
A. Level or type of managerial activity	■ Strategic planning ■ Tactical planning ■ Managerial control ■ Operational control	■ Acquire major supplier ■ Initiate advertising and sales promotion program in City L ■ Institute "quality assurance" circle ■ Replace type of adhesive
B. Resource	■ Financial ■ Manpower ■ Facilities ■ Information	■ Use long-term debt ■ Subcontract finishing ■ Subcontract Product X ■ Install personal computers at vice-president and manager level
C. Problem-solving apparatus	■ Programmed ■ Semiautomatic ■ Nonprogrammed	■ Approve credit terms ■ Make selection of temporary investment type ■ Sell Eastern subsidiary
D. Nature of problem	■ One-time ■ Recurring ■ Routine ■ Complex ■ Strategic ■ Short-term	■ Divest French subsidiary ■ Approve credit limit ■ Approve credit limit ■ Establish company's long-term objectives ■ Decide on Japanese joint venture ■ Reduce inventory level
E. Operational	■ Marketing ■ Manufacturing ■ Research ■ Finance ■ Information resource management	■ Replace Salesperson Jones ■ Rearrange final assembly line ■ Use outside pressure testing ■ Recheck internal controls ■ Replace existing computers in Eastern region

FIG. 3-2 Categories of Management Decisions

general in nature, and may depend significantly on outside information. In contrast, tactical planning is usually for a relatively short period, is more detailed, and relies more on in-house data. Quite different are control decisions, which ordinarily involve comparing actual with planned or standard performance, that should follow organizational lines quite closely. Tactical planning decisions are of short range, and the relationship among the relevant factors is well known and may be amendable to the use of decision models.

Another useful way of classifying business decisions is according to the problem-solving apparatus used. Thus, well-structured (and recurring) problems may be handled largely on a programmed or formula basis. In some other situations, part of the decision may be handled on a programmed basis (such as the amount allowable for 30-day certificate-of-deposit investments) and the segment of the decision relating to which institution's paper would be considered handled on a nonprogrammed (judgmental) basis.

As shown in Figure 3-2, other decision classifications include those relating to resources involved, nature of the problem, or functional operation.

Any given type of decision may be included under most or all classifications. Thus, a strategic planning decision under Classification A (level of managerial activity) is also listed under Classifications B through D. The nature of the decision helps to determine the kinds of information needed by the decision makers. Those involved in information systems design and operation should be aware of the kinds of information needed for various types of business decisions. After all, the basic purposes of the FIS are to provide adequate data for decision making on a timely basis, in an appropriate format, and at a reasonable cost.

INFORMATION FLOWS

Before reviewing management's information needs, it is useful to recognize the network of information flow in a typical enterprise. This flow, of course, recognizes the various management and functional levels and the kinds of decisions made at each level. A useful matrix is that shown in Figure 3-3. Each management segment should have (and needs) different management and financial information for different types of decisions. For example, top management is, or should be, concerned with setting objectives and goals for the overall enterprise, planning strategy, and guiding the entity. It is concerned with the "big picture" and certain critical factors. Middle management is concerned with carrying out plans, reaching the objectives and goals set by top management, developing the tactical plans for their operations, and exercising managerial control over lower management. Middle management needs more detailed planning and control. The lower echelon of management requires detailed control data relating to its operating control decisions.

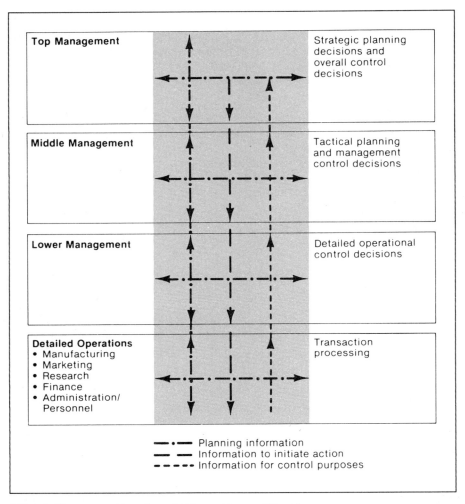

FIG. 3-3 Management Levels and Primary Types of Decisions

Informal Information Flows

Within most organizations, there are formal flows of information (discussed in the next section). However, not all information is received from this stream. Managers also use data acquired through informal communication channels. These sources are varied: colleagues, friends, subordinates within the firm itself, contacts in other companies, and industry organs, perhaps company-generated newspapers and trade journals. Cocktail parties are often a fountain of information. How often has the chairman asked the financial vice-president, "Why aren't we doing so and so?" His understanding of the supposed action is often substantially different from the reality.

Informal flows do exist, and are listened to; quite often, however, the information is incorrect or undependable. It may be biased at the original source or the transmitter. In any event, there will be instances where the formal information system must refute or rebut the "rumor," or perhaps encompass the data. This is not to say that the informal system should not exist. Very often, useful factual data may be secured through this source.

Formal Information Flows

The formal information flow consists of (1) vertical information transmitted both upward and downward among the various echelons of management and (2) the horizontal flows between the various functional activities, which are roughly at the same management level. Both formal and informal data flow along these lines. However, in the real world, flows are not merely vertical and horizontal, but diagonal, circular, or of another kind. The more formal type of flow is described in the next section.

Formal Vertical Flows. In most business entities, and certainly in medium to large firms, information flows both upward and downward. The upward flow consists of data needed to plan, as well as to control decisions or actions. That is, much of the short-term planning data needed at higher echelons are based on internal company information found at the lower levels. Thus, the sales data by product, territory, or salesperson are essential in developing the overall sales plan. Again, control data, such as actual sales performance compared to plan, may be forwarded upward to the appropriate level to facilitate control decisions, such as action needed to bring actual performance in line with plan.

The downward vertical flow relates to decisions to initiate actions in controlling operations (also depicted in Figure 3-3). As vertical information proceeds from echelon to echelon, it usually changes in extent of detail and sometimes in frequency.

Formal Horizontal Flows. Horizontal information flows connect "action centers," such as manufacturing and marketing, within the same management level. Thus, the manufacturing vice-president must be attuned to the plans and activity levels of the marketing vice-president, since goods must be available for sale when needed by the salesperson. In addition, the financial vice-president must be aware of the activities of both the manufacturing and marketing executive so that the requisite funds are available for investment in such areas as receivables, inventory, or plant and equipment. Similarly at a lower echelon, the sales manager for Territory Y must be apprised of activity by the manufacturing department and know that his planned product is available for delivery to the customer.

In addition to the horizontal contacts between different functions, there are contacts between the information processing centers (e.g., between the controller of the company and the controller of the division activity, the budget department and the related operational department, or the corporate informaton resource management center and the division center).

INFORMATION NEEDS OF MANAGERS
Types of Information

Before evaluating whether an FIS is effective, it is helpful to review some general concepts about management information. It is not always practical to identify the kinds of data that will be most useful to a particular manager. Based on his unique background, experience, interests, and style of management, one executive will find certain kinds of information more helpful than others. For example, he might find graphics much easier to understand than tabulations. He may consider certain types of information to be more significant than others (e.g., trends instead of comparison with standard, comparisons with competitors rather than simply with internal measurements, percentages as opposed to absolute numbers, summarized data instead of a multitude of detail).

However, certain fundamental criteria ought to be considered when weighing any information system. If data are to be used, they must be communicated to the recipient; that is, they must be received and understood. There are any number of key properties that data should possess, among which are the following:

- *Relevance* — the property of relating to, or bearing upon, the matter at hand. For example, the rate of return on shareholders' equity for the past year may be germane to setting a new target for the next plan year; or a comparison of actual sales to planned sales, by product, in Territory *Y* may be relevant to motivational or stimulation activity of the salespeople in that territory.

- *Timeliness* — related to two factors: frequency and delay. Frequency indicates how often information is updated (i.e., the interval between two or more reportings). Information may be made available on a real-time basis, or every hour or day or month. Delay relates to the span of time between the occurrence of the event and when the user receives the relevant data.

- *Accuracy* — simply freedom from error. It is derived from precision and reliability. This is more important for certain business decisions than for others.

- *Conciseness* — the brevity of expression or the elimination of superfluous detail. It can be achieved by summarizing transactions (e.g., individual labor costs, departmental data) or through the use of statistical measures (mean, median, mode), by sampling, or by drawing inferences from a body of opinion.

Conciseness is desired in some circumstances (e.g., division sales performance), but it may be highly undesirable in others, since it conceals individual events.

- *Quantifiability* — the ability to assign numeric values to objects or events. Obviously, this is one of the principal characteristics of financial data.

  This quality is particularly important in the measurement aspects of performance—actual versus planned. Information that cannot be measured usually is categorized as qualitative.[2]

MANAGERIAL ACTIVITIES AS A FACTOR IN INFORMATION NEEDS

Those who are interested in an effective FIS should be aware not only of the significant characteristics of information but also of the impact of managerial activities on the types of data needed. There are at least four facets to any such consideration:

1 The managerial level;

2 The organization structure;

3 The nature of the managerial activities; and

4 The technical nature of the function.

The Managerial Level

Managers at different levels have varying information needs. For example, those at the highest level are (or should be) concerned with strategic and long-range planning decisions that involve the enterprise's survival and growth. Their information needs cover a long time horizon and may require data from both internal and external sources (e.g., markets, economic cycles, competitive actions, foreign exchange matters, industry trends, new product developments, financial markets). Moreover, extreme accuracy and timeliness are not important. Much of the data may be qualitative rather than quantitative. The control activities of this group tend to be broader and less detailed than those at a lower level.

In contrast, lower-level managers are more involved with planning daily, weekly, or monthly operations. Moreover, much of their attention is directed to

---

[2] For a detailed discussion of information theory and properties, see Joseph W. Wilkinson, *Accounting and Information Systems* (New York: Wiley, 1982), ch. 5, Appendix C, pp. 195–198.

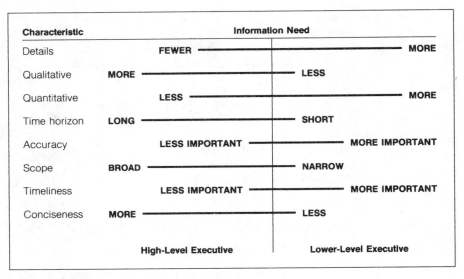

FIG. 3-4 Profile of Information Needs

detailed control problems. Much of the information they need tends to be more detailed, more timely, more accurate than for a higher level, and generally of an internal nature.

Middle-management executive information needs are somewhere in between the two. Figure 3-4 gives a sense of the contrasting information needs of two levels of managers.

Organization Structure

Organization structure is, of course, closely related to management activities. Although generalizations can be dangerous, by and large, executives in centralized organizations have different information needs from those in a decentralized structure. For example, the middle-level executive (e.g., the division manager) in a decentralized company, may have profit and investment responsibilities and requires data related to these facets of his activities. In contrast, his counterpart in a centralized firm may only need cost information, but, to a greater degree than in a decentralized operation, may want information showing, for example, the comparative manufacturing costs in different factories, comparative selling costs in difficult territories, or advertising costs for varying products.

Nature of the Managerial Activities

From an information standpoint, the two important managerial activities are planning and control (more detail is given about these functions in Chapter 12), but, basically, the information needs for each of these functions are dissimilar.

THE FIS AS RELATED TO BUSINESS MANAGEMENT   3-15

but, basically, the information needs for each of these functions are dissimilar. Thus, planning is related to future events and emphasizes alternative courses of action and the probable results. Accordingly, in the potential allocation of resources, the relative probable contribution margin, or return on assets used, of Product A versus Product B or Territory Y versus Territory X is weighed. For many planning phases, organization structure or responsiblity is temporarily ignored.

In contrast, control decisions basically consist of comparing actual results with a standard (plan, standard cost, variable budget). Such data must be accumulated by responsibility (i.e., the person responsible), and often information needs are more time related and detailed in nature than for other types of decisions.

Thus, the broad type of managerial activity has a bearing on the financial information to be gathered or provided.

Nature of Functional Operations

Those experienced in business know that different functions have different information needs. To be sure, some operational functions share data—for example, the manufacturing function shares sales expectations or results in scheduling production. However, by and large, each operational function has its own unique requirements—the data required to carry out its assigned responsibilities. Thus, the marketing manager needs operating margins or contribution margins by product, territory, channel of distribution, or salesperson. The production manager requires data on scrap, material costs, labor hours, machine-hours, and machine productivity. The research manager requires estimates to complete specific research projects as well as the accumulated costs to date. The financial manager may require an aging of accounts receivable or past-due accounts, comparative costs of financing, and relative returns from different types of investments, as well as return on assets.

REPORTS FOR DECISION MAKING AND INFORMATION GATHERING

Given the various managerial levels and certain report characteristics, what types of reports, or information, might a business manager want? Inevitably, those responsible for a good FIS must have some idea about the information each manager wants, perhaps the data he should want, so that they can provide the necessary knowledge.

The types of reports provided for the various echelons of management may be grouped in several ways, as shown in Figure 3-5. For discussion purposes here, comments or illustrations relate only to the following classifications: purpose, conciseness, occurrence, and format. Throughout many sections of this Manual, however, the commentary relates to most categories.

Purpose	Format	Time frame
■ Planning	■ Oral	■ Long range
■ Control	■ Written	■ Short term
—Broad	—Narrative	
—Detailed	(interpretive)	**Function**
■ Legal compliance	—Graphic	■ General and
■ Stewardship	—Tabular	administrative
■ Informational	—"Hard" copy	■ Financial
	—Computer display	■ Marketing
Conciseness	(soft copy)	■ Manufacturing
■ Summary	—"Flash" reports	■ Research or
■ Exception		engineering
■ Detailed	**Organizational scope**	■ Personnel
	■ Consolidated	
Occurrence	■ Division	
■ Scheduled or periodic	■ Department or	
■ Event-triggered	subdivision	
■ On demand	■ Detailed operations	

FIG. 3-5 Classification of Reports

Classifying Reports by Purpose

A most useful way to classify reports is by their purposes (the most typical of which are planning, control, legal compliance, stewardship, and informational (see Figure 3-5)). The purpose is a powerful influence on content, conciseness, frequency of need, and format, to say the least. Thus, a planning report may provide data on total planned results without regard for specific accountability by specific executives. An example of an overall plan summary for a profit center is illustrated in Figure 3-6, which illustrates the plan summary of income and expense as compared with prior-year results. In contrast, a control report compares actual results with the standard (plan) and should identify particular performance, as shown in Figure 3-7. From these two figures, it is apparent that purpose may be a determinant in content, as in providing marginal costs or variable costs in lieu of total costs. These illustrations should not lead to the conclusion that planning reports are never by responsibilities.

A legal compliance report is a mandatory one that meets legal requirements, such as a report needed to comply with the terms of a loan and credit agreement, or perhaps a financial statement required by a governmental body such as the Securities and Exchange Commission.

The annual report to shareholders is one of the most common financial reports in the stewardship category, providing as it does a report on operations for a year.

An informational report is intended merely to inform the reader, with no action contemplated on his part.

THE FIS AS RELATED TO BUSINESS MANAGEMENT

THE JOHNSON COMPANY
ANNUAL BUSINESS PLAN FOR 19X6
Summary of Operations

	Plan	Prior Year	Increase/(Decrease) Amount	Increase/(Decrease) Percentage
Net sales ($000)	$340,000	$302,000	$38,000	13.0
Net income ($000)	$34,000	$27,180	$6,820	25.0
Percentage of sales	10.0%	9.0%	—	11.1%
Per share	$3.40	$2.72	$.68	25.0
Percentage return on shareholders' equity	16.5%	14.0%	—	18.0%

FIG. 3-6 Summary Plan Report

Of course, some reports may be multipurpose. Thus, a document intended for planning purposes to the board of directors may be informational to large creditors or consultants. A control report on sales performance to the marketing manager may be informational to the chief internal auditor.

Classifying Reports by Conciseness

There are occasions where specifics by individual performer, or for each hour, product, or transaction, are important; thus, a detailed report is called for. In other instances, data may be summarized, inasmuch as overall performance for a period is perfectly adequate for control purposes. A summary report of each salesperson's total sales for the month may therefore serve the sales manager's purpose. Another type of report is the exception report, which presents only nonstandard results. If a department or worker is on plan or on standard, or within a reasonable tolerance, then why report unnecessary detail? A form of exception report is depicted in Figure 3-8.

Classifying Reports by Occurrence

When the subject of reports comes to mind, the financial manager usually thinks of scheduled reports—those issued on a predetermined periodic basis such as a daily cash report, a weekly inventory report, or a monthly statement of income and expense. The largest category of reports is probably comprised of scheduled reports, yet reports need not be issued at a predetermined period.

Event-triggered reports may well be used in the computer world of today. Such reports are set in motion by a given event (e.g., a hurricane, a power outage, an inventory shortage, a failure to meet plan, or an unusual performance).

THE JONES COMPANY
CORPORATE HEADQUARTERS OVERHEAD
Month of June 19X4
(dollars in thousands)

Department	Month			Year to Date		
	Actual	Budget	(Over)Under Budget	Actual	Budget	(Over)Under Budget
Chairman	$242	$250	$ 8	$1,483	$1,600	$117
President	156	155	(1)	901	940	39
Senior vice-president marketing	93	90	(3)	574	560	(14)
Senior vice-president manufacturing	71	75	4	419	440	21
Senior vice-president finance	79	80	1	462	480	18
Senior vice-president administration	40	40	—	247	240	(7)
Senior vice-president research	62	65	3	416	390	(26)
Vice-president and general counsel	112	115	3	690	700	10
Vice-president public relations	33	30	(3)	182	190	8
Vice-president personnel	69	70	1	397	410	13
Total	$957	$970	$13	$5,771	$5,950	$179
Percentage (over)/under budget			1%			3%

FIG. 3-7 Summary Control Report—Corporate Headquarters Expense

THE FIS AS RELATED TO BUSINESS MANAGEMENT 3-19

THE MANHATTAN CORPORATION
DEPARTMENTAL BUDGET REPORT
March 19X5

DEPARTMENT 204
DEPARTMENT MANAGER Johnson

	Month		Year to Date	
Item	Actual	(Over) Under Budget	Actual	(Over) Under Budget
*Better than budget**				
Direct labor	$ 146,200	$ 8,940	$ 441,600	$ 17,700
Direct material	89,760	4,510	271,280	8,140
Supplies	12,310	370	31,930	170
Total	$ 248,270	$13,820	$ 744,810	$ 26,010
*Worse than budget**				
Power	$ 103,400	$ (3,100)	$ 301,600	$(12,100)
Maintenance	12,610	(570)	35,840	1,010
Tooling	71,400	(4,300)	115,400	(3,140)
Total	$ 187,410	$ (7,970)	$ 452,900	$(14,230)
All other costs	$ 961,400	$ 6,240	$2,981,500	$ 41,620
Total costs	$1,397,080	$12,090	$4,179,210	$ 53,400
Percentage (over)under budget		1%		1%

*By 2 percent or more for month

FIG. 3-8 Budget Report—Exception Basis

On-demand reports, as the name implies, usually are prepared only when requested. They are often analytical reports used to assist the manager in making a decision about a special problem or situation.

To the extent possible, information systems must anticipate and provide the bases for preparing any of these types of reports.

Classifying Reports by Format or Style

The purpose of a management report is to communicate and secure action—in other words, to motivate. To this end, there are several corollaries to selecting the report format, some of which were briefly discussed in terms of report properties.

1 Adapt the form of presentation as much as possible to the style or preference of the user. If a reader prefers graphs over tabulations,

then an attempt should be made to provide the data in such a form. With the advent of the microcomputer, several software packages are available that can quickly prepare graphs, and hard copy can be made. More variety and special graphs can be secured on a custom basis.

2. Make financial reports either self-explanatory or include a narrative section to properly interpret the information—particularly where the recipient may not truly understand the figures. This principle is called interpretive reporting.

3. Use terms and language familiar to the manager. If relationships are more meaningful, these, rather than raw or summarized data, should be shown. If man-hours or tons are more expressive than monetary units or percentages, these should be used.

4. Supplement oral reports by graphs (e.g., colored slides or transparencies) can be in order to get a message across. For example, the financial vice-president may make an oral presentation to the board of directors on the monthly or quarterly financial results, supported by meaningful charts and graphs. With this format, he may answer questions more easily and make more effective explanations.

5. Make reports simple and clear. Reports should be designed so that the recipient can grasp all the essential facts in a minimum amount of time. For example, technical accounting language should not be used when addressing nonaccountants.

Thought should be given to every possible manner in which the report can be made simple—from short words and phrases to the numbers themselves, a procedure that can be accomplished without a loss in the data's value. Consider the three alternatives, X, Y, and Z, shown in Figure 3-9. Which is the easiest to understand?

6. Present the data in a logical sequence. In some instances, it is best to present the data from general to specific; in other instances, logic dictates the reverse. For example, if each current asset is to be discussed, it might be helpful to proceed from the most liquid to the least liquid. If labor costs are being reviewed, perhaps the best sequence would either be from the greatest problem to the smallest, or in the order in which the product is manufactured.

7. Make reports timely. Data should be issued while it is "hot" and useful. Quite often, it is far better to make available information that, although largely complete, uses estimates and sacrifices some accuracy. This could influence format and procedures in that:

- The information tends to be highly summarized.
- The report may be handwritten rather than typewritten or computer-generated.

THE FIS AS RELATED TO BUSINESS MANAGEMENT   3-21

THE JONES CORPORATION
SUMMARY SALES REPORT
month of June

[Alternative X — Full dollars and cents]

Territory	Month	Year to Date
Pacific Northwest	$127,389.26	$ 752,335.57
Southwest	92,411.26	592,467.56
Midwest	76,800.10	472,800.60
South	25,437.96	159,627.76
East	96,841.47	591,048.82
Total	$418,880.05	$2,568,280.31

[Alternative Y — Nearest dollars only]

Territory	Month	Year to Date
Pacific Northwest	$127,389	$ 752,336
Southwest	92,411	592,468
Midwest	76,800	472,801
South	25,438	159,628
East	96,841	591,049
Total	$418,879	$2,568,282

[Alternative Z — Nearest thousands of dollars]

Territory	Month	Year to Date
Pacific Northwest	$127	$ 752
Southwest	92	592
Midwest	77	473
South	25	160
East	97	591
Total	$418	$2,568

FIG. 3-9 Alternative Report Formats

	Month	Year to Date This Year	Year to Date Last Year

THE JOHNSON COMPANY
FLASH REPORT
Consolidated Operating Results
March 1985
CONFIDENTIAL

	Month	This Year	Last Year
Net sales ($000)	$47,869	$136,380	$121,520
Operating income ($000)	$4,308	$12,001	$10,205
Percentage	9%	8.8%	8.4%
Net income ($000)	$1,982	$5,521	$4,695
Per share	$.20	$.46	$.39

*Element of estimate: 5 percent; the computer division is the primary reason for the year-to-date improvement over the prior year.

FIG. 3-10 The Flash Report

- Qualifications or limitations in the data may be noted.
- Subsequently, if needed, a more accurate report may be published.

Such quick reports are sometimes called flash reports and may be used in a number of instances where management needs fast, albeit not complete, information. One such application could be the flash report on operating results, as in Figure 3-10. This report for a decentralized operation is issued on the second working day of the month, about three days before the official financial performance is known. Other flash applications might show the results of a special sales promotion or estimate a probable unfavorable litigation outcome. In summary, to meet the needs of top management, the information system often must provide timely and less accurate data before the usual checks and cross-checks are made.

Other suggestions on management reports appear in some of the recent literature.[3]

REPORTING SYSTEMS

A discussion of the management process, types of decisions to be made, and information needs should readily lead to this conclusion: Each business enterprise should have an FIS that permits it to record the various transactions and

---

[3] See, for example, James D. Willson and John B. Campbell, *Controllership, The Work of the Managerial Accountant* (New York: Wiley, 1983), ch. 29.

THE FIS AS RELATED TO BUSINESS MANAGEMENT 3-23

data concerning operations and, from this input, to provide a variety of financial reports. Fundamentally, the system permits the information to be reported in a variety of ways to suit different needs. Some data are detailed, perhaps by each transaction or event (e.g., each sale). Other data are summarized for another purpose. In most instances, the same informaton must be rearranged to fit several needs. Thus, one report may show only the total cost of the product, whereas another, for other purposes, segregates such total costs into their direct, or variable, and indirect elements. Obviously, the information systems designers must be aware of the range and type of data needed to fit the diverse purposes to which the data may be put.

RESPONSIBILITY REPORTING

As previously stated, the FIS must meet managers' needs. Knowledge of the purpose, types of reports, and some principles regarding content and format are important in designing and operating an effective information system. These matters and other related subjects are covered in considerable detail throughout this Manual. One overriding point should be understood, however, particularly with respect to control reports: The financial information should incorporate the concept of responsibility reporting. This means that transactions and events should be recorded and reported, where applicable, so that revenues and costs, and often assets and liabilities, may be identified with the person who controls the activity and is held accountable for it. By implication, the system avoids such items as allocation of expenses for control purposes if the organizational segment to be reported upon does not control such transactions and cannot be held accountable.

An overly simplified diagram of responsibility reporting is shown in Figure 3-11.[4] This illustration concerns expense reporting, wherein the reporting system follows the organizational chart. Inasmuch as the president is responsible for the entire company, he is provided with an expense summary of actual expenses and over- or under-budget conditions segregated by the individuals he holds responsible (Item A). This segregates the expenses for which he personally is accountable, as well as the functional costs indicated for which each vice-president is responsible.

In turn, each responsibility center manager receives a summary of performance of each department manager reporting to him. Illustrated is the manufacturing division summary (Item B). In the example, the production superintendent receives a next-lower-echelon report on the three cost centers for which he is held accountable (Item C). Finally, at the lowest management level, the detail of types of expenses is illustrated for the cost center. Item D reflects the assembly department expenses, but comparable data should also be made

---

[4] Willson, p. 2-6.

3-24 OVERVIEW

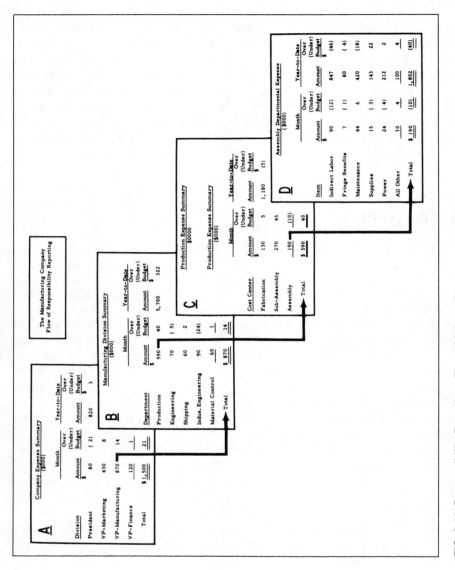

FIG. 3-11 Responsibility Reporting—Flow of Information

available for each of the cost centers reporting to the production superintendent.

Typically, the cost center summary by types of expenses is supported by a computer run reflecting the individual transactions making up each expense account balance. Thus, the engineer can check the details to learn the composition of the charges and verify the fact that he is the manager responsible for these particular charges.

A more detailed explanation of responsibility reporting is provided in Chapter 12. It is important to recognize this principle of responsibility reporting before considering other, more detailed aspects of a financial reporting system.

REFERENCES

Moscove, Stephen A., and Mark G. Simkin. *Accounting Information Systems*. New York: John Wiley, 1981, chs. 1 and 2.

Robinson, Leonard A., James R. Davis, and C. Wayne Alderman. *Accounting Information Systems*. New York: Harper & Row, 1982, ch. 1.

Wilkinson, Joseph W. *Accounting and Information Systems*. New York: John Wiley, 1981, chs. 5 and 6.

CHAPTER 4

Alternative Organization Structures for the Data Processing Function

Keith L. Robinett

Introduction 2	**Economic Factors** 13
	Hardware 13
Organization Concepts 2	Software 13
	People 13
Alternative Structures 3	Facilities 13
Centralized Data Processing 3	
Decentralized Data Processing 4	**Cultural/Political Factors** 13
Distributed Data Processing 4	Historical Precedents 14
Federated Data Processing 7	Organizational Independence 14
Chief Information Officer's Relationship	Service History 14
to the Chief Financial Officer 9	Power Bases 14
Enterprise Factors 10	**Departmental Organization** 15
Nature of the Business Organization ... 10	Systems Group 15
Form of the Business Organization 11	Operations Group 17
Location of Knowledgeable People 11	Technical Support Group 17
Data Processing 11	Administration Group 17
Office Automation 11	Management Staff 17
Telecommunications 11	**References** 18
Stage of Systems Development 12	
Knowledge and Interest of Senior	
Management 12	

Fig. 4-1 Centralized Organization as a Major Department 4
Fig. 4-2 Centralized Organization Within a Major User Department 5
Fig. 4-3 Centralized Organization Within a Services Department 5
Fig. 4-4 Decentralized Organization 6
Fig. 4-5 Distributed Data Processing Network 7
Fig. 4-6 Federated Data Processing Network 8
Fig. 4-7 Internal Structure of the Chief Information Officer's Department 16

4-1

INTRODUCTION

In this chapter, we discuss the organization of business information functions, which include data processing and the related areas of telecommunications and office automation. For simplicity, this method of organization is referred to as data processing. Data processing managers, executives to whom they report, the chief financial officer, and the chief executive officer should all be concerned with, and be knowledgeable about, data processing.

We first examine the data processing department's location in the larger organization, and discuss basic concepts applicable to most organizational situations. We also offer alternative approaches to the problem of location, using sample charts as illustrations.

Next, we discuss the enterprise and the economic and cultural/political factors that influence the organizational placement decision.

Finally, we analyze the internal organization of a data processing department in order to encompass all aspects of the data processing function.

ORGANIZATION CONCEPTS

As with other organizations, the data processing function should include the following:

- A clear definition of lines of authority, responsibility, and reporting relationships;
- Spans of control that are not so wide that they overwhelm a manager or make him unavailable when needed by his subordinates, yet not so narrow that they are wasteful; and
- The grouping of like functions in order to use manpower and equipment resources most effectively.

In addition, special emphasis should be given to the following organizational concepts:

- Locate the data processing function in the organization to provide good and equitable service to all of its "customers."
- Provide for effective two-way communication with the users of the service.
- Institute a system of checks and balances. No individual or small unit should have complete control over the information being processed. The opportunity to manipulate results or cover fraudulent activity must be avoided.
- Provide for specialized facilities and equipment planning within the data processing organization.

ALTERNATIVE STRUCTURES

Before discussing the factors that influence the location of data processing within the larger organization, it is useful to define and review four generalized alternatives:

1 Centralized structure
2 Decentralized structure
3 Distributed structure
4 Federated structure

Centralized Data Processing

In its purest form, centralized data processing houses the activity in a single location under one management. This approach is observed frequently in small- and medium-sized companies as well as in large companies where there is much sharing of databases, where one department interacts frequently with other departments, and where standardization of equipment and/or systems is highly desirable. Some advantages of centralization are that:

- There are economies of scale for the computer and support staff.
- All departments are equally considered in selecting priorities.
- Information systems planning and development are well integrated.
- Management understanding of data processing uses and costs is simplified.

Disadvantages are that:

- A centralized staff may not keep up-to-date with the needs of the operating organizations.
- Establishing priorities can become complicated. Suspicious users may feel slighted, and a "no-win" situation can develop.
- Computing and programming resources may be out of step with organizational plans unless excellent communication with users is maintained.

Figures 4-1 through 4-3 illustrate alternatives using a centralized structure. Figure 4-1 illustrates a centralized organization as a major department on the same level as other functional departments. This type of organization is appropriate where the enterprise is highly dependent upon data processing for all or most of its departments. Figure 4-2 depicts an alternative whereby the centralized data processing organization is located within a principal user department (in this case, finance). Services to other departments are provided from this centralized department. This type of organization is appropriate where one depart-

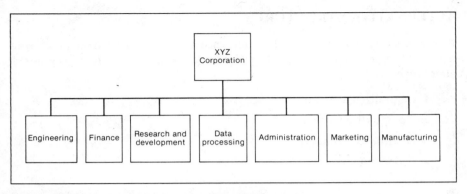

FIG. 4-1 Centralized Organization as a Major Department

ment accounts for a majority of the demand for computer time. Figure 4-3 depicts the centralized organization as part of a service department (e.g., administration). This approach can be used where data processing services are used by most, if not all, departments, but not in a highly dependent manner.

Decentralized Data Processing

The decentralized structure permits each operating entity with a need for data processing services to establish its own organization.

Some advantages of decentralization are that:

- Each department is in control of its own data processing operation.
- The size and type of equipment are tailored to the user's specific needs.
- Interdepartmental priority conflicts are eliminated.

Disadvantages are that:

- Integration of various departments' applications becomes very difficult.
- Control over data integrity is scattered, thereby increasing the opportunity for compromise or error.
- The total cost of data processing is almost certain to be greater.

Figure 4-4 shows a typical decentralized organization structure.

Distributed Data Processing

The distributed structure is a form of centralized data processing. Control of data processing activities remains centralized, but a network of computing cen-

ALTERNATIVE STRUCTURES FOR DATA PROCESSING   4-5

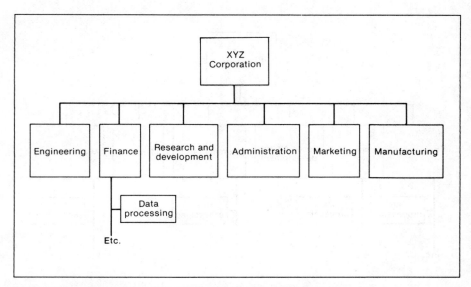

FIG. 4-2 Centralized Organization Within a Major User Department

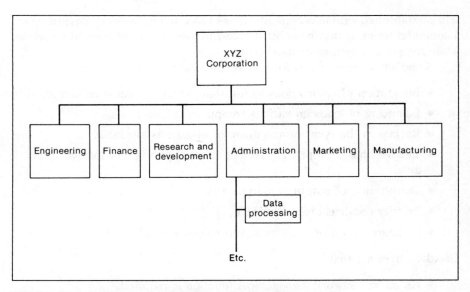

FIG. 4-3 Centralized Organization Within a Services Department

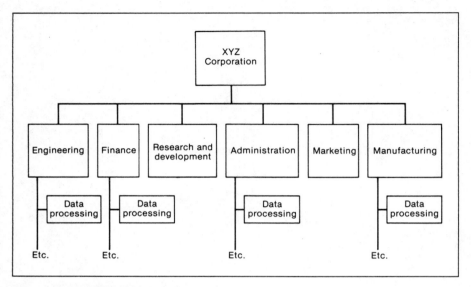

FIG. 4-4 Decentralized Organization

ters is established with telecommunications links. In an "on-line" environment, a computer terminal may be granted access to more than one computing center while receiving output at its local center.

Some advantages of this form of organization are that:

- Integration of applications to form an overall system is enhanced.
- Balancing of loads on various computers is easier.
- Backup in the event of an outage or disaster is available.
- The user has a proprietary feeling about the computer located in his area.
- Distribution of output is more timely.
- Priority conflicts are diminished.
- Standardization of equipment and software is achieved.

Disadvantages are that:

- An added network management function is required.
- Telecommunications costs may rise.
- More people are required to operate multiple centers than would be needed in a central location to provide the same amount of computing power.

Figure 4-5 illustrates a distributed data processing network, showing the centralized location and the telecommunications links.

ALTERNATIVE STRUCTURES FOR DATA PROCESSING

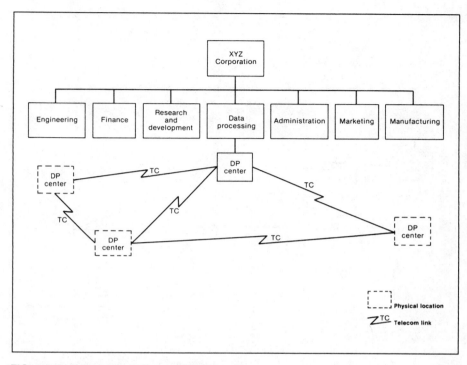

FIG. 4-5 Distributed Data Processing Network

Federated Data Processing

Federated data processing combines centralized, decentralized, and distributed structures. Under this alternative, a corporate executive is charged with the direct line responsibility for overseeing the company's information resources. Decentralized data processing centers are then established under local management with a "dotted line" relationship to the corporate center. The centers are linked by telecommunications, as in the distributed data processing model. A corporate data center is established to take care of corporate office needs and serves as the network hub. Some advantages of the federated approach are:

- Planning is integrated while preserving local control.
- There are economies of volume purchases through corporate agreements.
- Hardware and software are standardized to facilitate communications.
- Sharing of knowledge is enhanced.
- There is high-level corporate visibility in a major resource area.

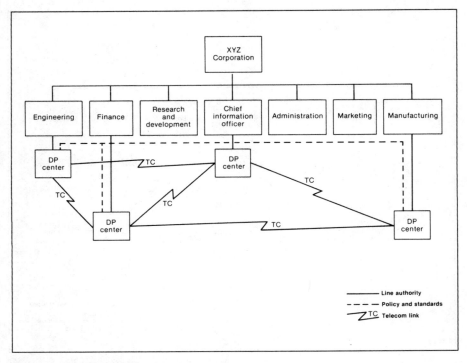

FIG. 4-6 Federated Data Processing Network

Some disadvantages are that:

- Local company segments may see the corporate information executive as an unwanted czar.
- Some limitation of hardware and software choices is bound to occur.

Figure 4-6 illustrates the federated data processing organization.

Note that Figure 4-6 introduces the concept of chief information officer into the federated organization. To better understand the concept, its philosophy and the specific duties of this executive are described as follows:

1 *General philosophy*
- Information generated or acquired by a company is regarded as an asset akin to financial, material, facility, and people resources.
- Information is used by all levels of a company and must be made available rapidly and efficiently to all locations where it is needed.
- Overall management of the information resource is the responsibility of the chief information officer.

ALTERNATIVE STRUCTURES FOR DATA PROCESSING

2 *Specific functions of the chief information officer*
- Overall planning for information systems, telecommunications, and office automation.
- Integrating data processing, telecommunications, and office automation for the company.
- Coordinating information resource planning activities of the various company segments.
- Making sure that appropriate internal security controls and disaster recovery plans are in place.
- Establishing "preferred" hardware and software lists.
- Establishing technical standards for telecommunications, including network protocols and data formats.
- Providing for corporate agreements with suppliers of hardware, software, and data processing supplies.
- Providing consulting services to the various company segments as required.
- Operating the data processing center at company headquarters.
- Publishing a manual containing standards, best practices, and planning guidelines.
- Chairing a corporate information resource management committee to ensure free interchange of knowledge among the various company segments.

Companies that have implemented the chief information officer concept include the FMC Corp. As reported in the October 8, 1984 issue of *Business Week*, FMC has appointed a director of information resources, who reports directly to the president of the company. Other companies with some form of this position include the Northrop Corporation and the McDonnell-Douglas Corporation.

Since the trend toward an information society is apparently very strong, the position of a chief information officer within an organization may be appropriate and beneficial in many instances.

Chief Information Officer's Relationship to the Chief Financial Officer

If any alternative other than a decentralized one is instituted, there is always a principal executive who, even though he may not be known as chief information officer, is responsible for the information resource. His relationship to the chief financial officer therefore merits some comment.

Since there is a universal need for financial information in all companies, and a virtual certainty that this information will be automated in companies of significant size, the chief financial officer has a vested interest in the chief information officer's activities. In fact, in many companies, the data processing function first appears as part of the financial organization.

It is essential that a close relationship be maintained between the chief financial officer and the chief information officer for the following reasons:

- Equipment and information systems proposals should be subjected to rigorous return on investment analyses. The chief information officer should look to the chief financial officer for support in this area.
- Operating budgets for the chief information officer's department are usually coordinated through the chief financial officer's department.
- Integration of financial and nonfinancial systems often generates substantial economies.
- Protection of information against compromise or disaster is a concern shared by both company officers.

Because of these factors, the chief information officer must consult with the chief financial officer on a regular and frequent basis. It is not uncommon for the chief information officer to report to the chief financial officer. However, even if this is not the case, the obligation to consult is in no way diminished.

ENTERPRISE FACTORS

Nature of the Business Organization

A careful consideration of the nature of the business and its information needs should precede the selection of the organizational alternative. For example, airlines, financial institutions, retail chains, and manufacturers have very diverse information needs that impact on the organization structure. Some related observations are as follows.

- An airline cannot operate its reservation system on a completely decentralized basis.
- Financial institutions deal almost exclusively in information. A bank with many branches is likely to have a form of centralized or distributed data processing.
- A national retail chain could operate under a distributed or federated approach. Regional data centers associated with distribution warehouses could be one scenario.
- Manufacturers probably have the largest number of options. A single-plant manufacturer of modest size probably would be centralized. At the other extreme, a nationally dispersed multiproduct conglomerate

ALTERNATIVE STRUCTURES FOR DATA PROCESSING 4-11

might be completely decentralized, with only sales, financial, and personnel information flowing to headquarters.

Form of the Business Organization

The approach to organizing the data processing function should somewhat parallel the organization of the business. Based on many years of experience, the following observations seem valid:

- If the business is highly centralized, it should lean toward a centralized data processing department.
- If the venture is organized into profit centers—that is, is decentralized—profit-center managers need more authority over the data processing functions. If there is no need for information to flow between profit centers, then either the decentralized or federated approach may be used.
- If a hybrid organization exists, under which certain major functions are centralized while others are decentralized (e.g., manufacturing), then the distributed or federated concepts may apply.

Location of Knowledgeable People

Location of personnel may influence the organizational alternative in data processing as follows:

Data Processing. Many information systems depend on a handful of programmers. These people are difficult to clone. It often makes sense to centralize a family of applications while decentralizing others.

Systems programmers (who deal with the computer's operating software) are in short supply. The same applies to network software people; only in a very large organization can they be centralized. Even then, consideration should be given to retaining a small central cadre to consult with decentralized segments.

Office Automation. Office automation experts frequently develop their talents outside of the data processing organization. Although the trend is toward integration of the two, adversarial relationships may have developed. Care must be taken to avoid losing good talent by using heavy-handed reorganization methods.

Telecommunications. Most companies find that they have two groups of telecommunications people. One group is in data processing and is expert in the movement of data in digital form by microwaves, fiber optics, and coaxial cables. A second group is concerned with voice communications in which analog signals are moved over traditional twisted-pair copper telephone lines. Current technology permits the movement of voice and data over the same lines through the use of digital switches. A number of companies now sell digital switches to private companies. With proper communications engineering, the same outlet can be used to service voice and data simultaneously.

The savings potential in this combination is quite large. The objective is to get the two telecommunications groups to work toward a common goal. In the long run, it is desirable to combine them into one organization. Since the new digital switches are computer based, the trend is toward merging the voice communications group into the data processing group.

Stage of Systems Development

In the early stages of systems development, the tendency is to implement stand-alone applications. As the portfolio of applications grows, however, it soon becomes apparent that there is a lot of duplication of data between systems. In addition, input errors and timing differences cause data that are supposed to be the same from system to system to be, in fact, very different.

Because of this, integrated systems are proposed in order to eliminate redundancy, errors, and lack of synchronization. With the growth in computer terminals, these integrated systems rely heavily on direct access storage devices. With common data for multiple systems stored together, some degree of centralized management is required. Thus, companies in later stages of systems development cannot operate effectively on a completely decentralized basis.

Knowledge and Interest of Senior Management

Top management's involvement often influences the chief information officer's reporting level. With the growing importance and cost of computer-based information systems, most senior managers are very aware of their data processing organizations. The executive who performs the chief information officer's function in a large company is often a vice-president.

Where he reports in the organization structure often depends on the knowledge and interest of senior management. If the company's president has a good knowledge of computing and sees the effective use of information as a means of improving his company's competitive position, he may decide to have the chief information officer report to him.

Lacking knowledge, interest, or both, he may decide to make a senior vice-president responsible for the position. This could be the senior vice-president of finance, services, administration, or operations. Again, knowledge and interest influence the choice. In any event, if the chief information officer is important to the company, the position must report high enough to attract top talent, either from inside or outside the company.

ALTERNATIVE STRUCTURES FOR DATA PROCESSING

ECONOMIC FACTORS

Hardware

From the late 1940s through most of the 1960s, the conventional wisdom was that computer power was approximately proportional to the square of computer cost (Grosch's Law). However, with the advent of modern solid state electronics, this is no longer true. Although there can still be some economies of scale in the hardware area, it is not the decisive factor favoring centralization that it once was.

Software

The cost of software definitely increases for any alternative other than a centralized computer. Multiple computers require multiple operating systems. Extra copies of computer-room software aids for such activities as scheduling, tape handling, or data security add to the cost.

Special purpose software packages (often known as program products) usually cost more when run on multiple computers. To prevent unauthorized multiple use, some software packages erase themselves if installed on a computer other than the one for which they were purchased.

People

The cost of computer operations personnel increases if multiple computer centers are provided. Each center must have a minimum cadre of operators for each shift.

Facilities

Multiple computer centers require increased facility costs to cover other necessities, such as special air conditioning, power, fire protection, and raised floors. Taken together, the overt costs of alternatives other than centralization are generally greater. However, the less tangible costs incurred by degraded service, perceived priority problems, disaster recovery risk, and general user dissatisfaction may be greater than the economies of scale provided by centralization. Thus, careful consideration must be given to all of the complexities.

CULTURAL/POLITICAL FACTORS

Those attempting to install an effective data processing or information system should be sensitive to a number of cultural or political factors that may influence the organization structure.

Historical Precedents

If a company has a long history of computer use, some important precedents will exist. For example:

- If the engineering department pioneered scientific computing in a company using Brand A computers, it will resist any organizational move that would require it to switch to Brand B.
- If the finance department has always run the business applications, it will resist a change to an independent data processing organization reporting somewhere else, despite the advantages that might accrue.
- If the services group has always been in charge of the telephone system, it will fight any attempt to merge its telecommunications personnel into data processing.

Those concerned with the proper functioning of an information system should carefully examine the firm's historical precedents before making organizational proposals. It may be wise to appoint a broad-based organizational task force to study all the problems and possibilities and to make recommendations.

Organizational Independence

A significant number of managers take pride in their own self-sufficiency. They do not want to depend on others for service if they can avoid it. The presence or absence of this factor should be determined when contemplating organization changes.

Service History

If the data processing department has a poor record of meeting schedules or if errors are common, pressures for organization change often emerge. Some companies have found that service improves where distributed or federated approaches are implemented.

Power Bases

It is quite common for many managers to view the importance of their organizations in terms of size. They see any organizational proposal that would diminish the number of people under them as a threat. This factor can lead to political infighting. Once again, there is merit in the use of an organizational task force to make recommendations.

ALTERNATIVE STRUCTURES FOR DATA PROCESSING 4-15

DEPARTMENTAL ORGANIZATION

Organizing the internal functions of a data processing department follows the same basic principles that apply to any organization. As noted earlier, the most important are:

1 Clear definition of authority and responsibility;
2 Proper span of control; and
3 Grouping of like functions.

When filling management positions created by the basic structure, it may be necessary to modify the organization to fit the available talent. Within limits, this is acceptable. The basic functions of a data processing department may be grouped as follows:

- Systems group
- Operations group
- Technical support group
- Administration group
- Management staff

A model structure of these functions is shown in Figure 4-7. Following is a precise explanation of each.

Systems Group

The systems group is responsible for:

- Systems analysis and design
- Application programming
- Systems testing and installation
- Systems maintenance

Where major systems development is undertaken, a project leader should be named from this group. He manages all resources provided to the project by the data processing department. Because such projects nearly always involve user departments, many companies select an overall project manager from outside the data processing department, usually from the primary user department. This approach assures the high degree of user involvement and cooperation required for a smooth and successful installation.

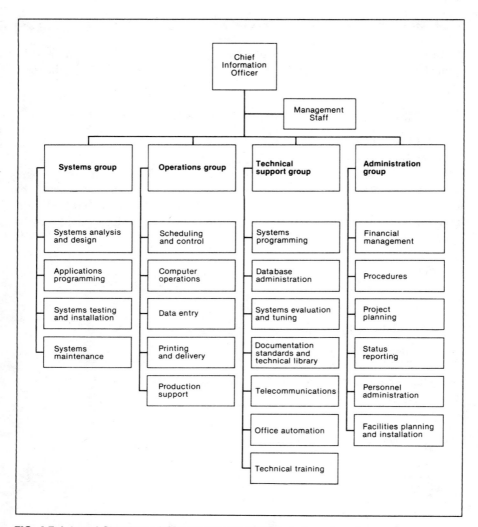

FIG. 4-7 Internal Structure of Chief Information Officer's Department

ALTERNATIVE STRUCTURES FOR DATA PROCESSING 4-17

Operations Group

The operations group is responsible for:

- Scheduling and control of data processing jobs
- Setup and operation of the data processing equipment (e.g., computers, data entry, printers)
- Production support (e.g., maintaining the tape library, documentation, supplies, and computer-room security)

Technical Support Group

The technical support group is responsible for:

- Systems programming (operating systems software and purchased software packages)
- Database administration
- Systems evaluation and tuning
- Documentation, standards, and the technical library
- Telecommunications (e.g., hardware, software, and protocols)
- Office automation
- Technical training

Administration Group

The administration group is responsible for:

- Financial management
- Departmental procedures
- Project planning support
- Status reporting
- Personnel administration
- Facilities planning and installation

Management Staff

The management staff includes people who are free of day-to-day operational demands and can consider such important subjects as:

- Strategic and long-range planning
- Overall security
- Liaison with industry groups and professional societies

In companies that are heavily involved in use of computers for engineering analysis, computer-aided design, and computer-aided manufacturing, an additional organizational group is required. This group is often called scientific programming. Its purpose is to provide programming support in the aforementioned areas, and it reports to the chief information officer.

The alternative organization structures to consider when developing, installing, and implementing an effective information system, as well as some factors that influence the organization, form the basis for reviewing the ingredients of an effective FIS, as presented in Chapter 5.

REFERENCES

"An Information Guru in FMC's Executive Suite." *Business Week* (Oct. 8, 1984), p. 124.

Emery, James C. "Managerial and Economic Issues in Distributed Computing." *Data Processing Management.* New York: Auerbach Publishers (1978), pp. 1–17.

Fried, Louis. "Managing Distributed Data Processing." *Data Processing Management.* New York: Auerbach Publishers (1979), pp. 1–8.

Richard, Robert H. "Computer Federalism." *Datamation* (Nov. 1982), pp. 147–148, 150.

Shirey, Robert W. "What Managers Should Know About Distributed Computing." *MITRE Technical Report.* McLean, VA: The Mitre Corporation, Metrek Division (June 1980).

PART **II**

Basic Systems Concepts

CHAPTER 5

Ingredients of an Effective Financial Information System

James M. Conerly

Introduction	1	Establishing Performance Criteria	11
		Responsibility Management	11
The Enterprise Model	2	Performance Feedback Reporting	11
Organizational Factors	3	Exception Reporting	13
Rules of the Game	3		
Critical Success Factors	4	**Data Security Administration**	14
Key Indicators	4	The Security Program	15
Executive Support Needs	5	Access Restrictions	15
		Version Control	16
Data Management	5	Protection of Data in Circulation	17
Relevant Data	5		
Data Sources	7	**Distribution Management**	18
Organization	7	Selection of Data for Distribution	18
Accuracy	9	Means for Data Distribution	19
Maintenance	10	Timeliness of Data Distribution	19
Performance Management	10	**Summary**	20

INTRODUCTION

Building an effective information system for financial management is a challenging and difficult task. Most financial managers appreciate its difficulty and are reluctant to assume the responsibility for implementing an FIS, which is understandable. The literature provides numerous examples of large, expensive information systems that, for all practical purposes, have failed to achieve their design objectives. In most of these cases, a major reason for the projects' failure to achieve their objectives was that a senior financial executive did not accept the responsibility, challenge, and risks associated with the project. Thus, without a financial executive's active leadership, the chance of achieving a truly effective FIS is extremely low.

In lieu of leadership from a financial executive, a person not immediately involved with the financial management of the enterprise is frequently given the responsibility for the information systems project. The typical result is an information system that yields financial data but provides very little data that can be used to produce information. "Information" is defined as what results where raw data are translated by the application of intelligence, reasoning, or intuition. The extent to which the information has value to the management of an enterprise is one measure of the effectiveness of the FIS.

Traditionally, FISs have been oriented to basic operational and accounting applications. At one time, those responsible for systems development were primarily concerned with capturing basic transaction-oriented data. These data formed the basis for producing detailed reports, such as transaction journals for auditing purposes. The reports presented very little information that directly aided financial executives. Many of the reports failed to have totals to aid management in determining the completeness or accuracy of the transactions being reported. These original FISs focused on the efficiency of transaction processing, but offered very little to improve the effectiveness of financial management.

Today, enterprises are increasingly affected by external environmental factors. Competition, government regulation, and social responsibility have increased to the point where businesses must take active steps to improve their organizational effectiveness. One way is through its information systems.

In addition to the leadership requirement, there are additional ingredients that contribute to an effective FIS, as follows:

- The enterprise model
- Data management
- Performance management
- Data security administration
- Distribution management

Each of these ingredients is discussed in detail in this chapter. Together with proper leadership and management commitment from senior executives, an effective FIS can be successfully implemented at reasonable costs, within an acceptable time frame, and at manageable levels of risk.

THE ENTERPRISE MODEL

A model of the enterprise is important in developing any significant information system. It is a representation of the organization that facilitates communication and provides a base for analysis. The modeling process results in a document that narratively and pictorially describes the organization. Although it may be desirable to computerize the enterprise model at a future time, it does not need to be automated during the early stage in the systems development process. The model forms the basis for preparing an information systems plan, which should be accomplished before initiating any large-scale systems development effort. Following are the major components of the modeling process:

- Organizational factors
- Rules of the game
- Critical success factors
- Key indicators
- Executive support needs

Organizational Factors

Each enterprise must perform certain functions to sustain its existence. These functions include such activities as marketing, manufacturing, personnel administration, finance, and accounting. Each enterprise organizes these functions and establishes relationships among them. The process may be very conscious, or may happen quite naturally and without specific effort as the enterprise expands. This organizational process results in an enterprise that takes a unique form. Where combined with the personality and management style of key leaders, the enterprise then develops its own culture. The structure and culture of the organization provide the initial form of an enterprise model.

Rules of the Game

Given an organization's structural and cultural aspects, each major function establishes policies and procedures to guide the actions of its functional units and their assigned personnel. Frequently, these policies are not formally written down. Personnel new to the enterprise, or who have transferred into a new functional unit, typically learn the "rules of the game" through verbal communication or close observation. In the accounting function, for example, rules explain how a transaction such as a back order for a part is processed and posted as revenue. During an audit, it is not unusual to discover that certain rules, whether written or not, are not always followed consistently. Over time, each enterprise develops its own set of rules of conduct. It is rare for any two enterprises to have similar rules, even if the companies provide very similar products or services. Even in highly regulated industries, there are differences between organizations. Rules define how the various components of the enterprise work individually and how they relate to one another. Thus, rules are an important aspect of the enterprise model.

Critical Success Factors

Certain factors are extremely important to an organization's survival. These are commonly known as critical success factors. Although a few of the critical success factors are shared by many organizations, they typically vary by industry, by company within an industry, and by situation. For example:

1. Almost all enterprises require positive cash flow in order to remain in operation.
2. Product companies in an industry built upon the immediate delivery of products after receiving and order must carry inventory on hand or they cannot provide the same necessary level of customer service as their competitors, in which case, the organization's ability to survive in the marketplace for any length of time is highly suspect.
3. A critical success factor that is situational is composed of the covenants associated with a line of credit. In this situation, an external entity imposes various conditions on an enterprise that affect the normal rules of conduct over a period of time. If the organization is unable to comply with the rules imposed by the covenants of the contract, doubt may arise about the organization's future as a going concern.

An organization's continued success depends on these critical factors, thus making them an important component of an enterprise model.

Key Indicators

It is sometimes difficult to measure an organization in performance relative to these critical success factors until it is too late to reverse adverse trends. It is therefore necessary to develop formal reporting procedures and informal communications channels that provide management with periodic feedback on key indicators of the enterprise that act as early warning signals to management that critical operations are not going as planned.

Key indicators are statistical in nature, in that they are usually presented as ratios or trend lines. In product-oriented companies, for example, the inventory-to-sales ratio is a key indicator that informs management when current stocking levels are not in balance with short-term sales projections. Key indicators alert management to potential business problems before they actually develop. Except for highly regulated industries, key indicators may vary by company within an industry due to differing organizational structures, policies, and procedures. In addition, within a company, the choice of indicators used to monitor organizational activities and achievements is very personal. A manager's education, experience, organizational level, and managerial style determine which indicators are key to his approach to management. Thus, because of their information value, key indicators are vital components to the enterprise model.

Executive Support Needs

The term "executive support system" is quite prevalent in a wide variety of management literature. It broadly defines those systems that aid executives to be both more efficient and more effective. It encompasses such technologies as office automation, executive information systems, decision support systems, and expert systems. With respect to the enterprise model, the concept of expert systems as an executive support tool has much merit. An "expert" system is one in which the essence of the problem-solving thought process of one or more experts in a given area is codified within a system and made available to others.

This systems design concept can be seen in many present-day systems. For example, blood analysis now requires that a technician operate a piece of specialized equipment rather than having a trained clinician spend hours performing a chemical evaluation. The newer approach is feasible because it is possible to design a machine that mimics the intelligence and analytical process of one or more experts in the field.

Expert systems are rapidly making their way into the business world. Not only do these systems allow the true experts to work more efficiently, they enable the people who are yet to be experts to work more effectively. Considering the potential impact of this technology on overall organizational effectiveness, the design concept and the experts' "rules of thumb" and logical thought processes should be incorporated into the enterprise model.

DATA MANAGEMENT

Few organizations know the real costs associated with the data they collect and maintain. Most information systems in use by organizations were designed in a vacuum, without the benefit of the enterprise model discussed in the previous section. Systems designers typically focused on the operational aspects of the business functions that were being computerized, and gave little thought to the managerial data requirements necessary to monitor the system and to manage the organization more effectively. Thus, too many operational data were designed into these older systems and too few useful managerial data were provided. Systems designed in this manner may have improved organizational efficiency, but rarely did they improve, or have the potential to improve, its effectiveness.

To deal with issues of managerial and organizational effectiveness, a formal and active data management function is needed. Data, when transferred into information, are a true organizational asset. Because of their value to an organization, data should be as actively managed as cash, capital resources, and time.

Relevant Data

It is easy to either under- and/or over-design an information system relative to its database. A "database" is the collection, organization, and interrelationship of individual pieces of data necessary to achieve an information system's objectives. Building databases that contain data relevant for the organization's intended use is the primary goal of data management. Reaching this goal is difficult because the intended use for data is not always known when databases are initially developed. The need for different types of data and the use of these data changes as an organization evolves and becomes more knowledgeable about how best to conduct its operations in an ever-increasingly competitive environment.

"Relevant" data are data needed to describe, analyze, or forecast a specific business situation. Simply stated, data are relevant when they have an immediate and direct bearing on the matter at hand. All other data are useless in that they may lead managers to make incorrect decisions. In addition, the real costs of maintaining such irrelevant data can be quite high.

Data may be obtained from a variety of internal and external sources. They may be current or historical in nature. They may also be divided into detail data or aggregated data. The degree of accuracy may vary depending on the intended use of the data. Audit trail data, for example, must be detailed and very accurate and are typically historical in nature. In contrast, data for use in long-range planning are typically aggregated, based on averaged or trended data, and are of relative (as opposed to absolute) accuracy.

Maintaining a database of relevant data is a challenging task because data needed to facilitate decision-making may change in one of two ways. First, entirely different data elements may be needed each time a decision is to be made. This occurs frequently at middle- and upper-management levels because different managers have varying decision-making styles and because an executive gets smarter each time he makes a decision. When decision-making styles change, so do the data requirements. It is difficult to anticipate the overall data requirements to support decision making within an organization. Therefore, maintaining relevant data is an ongoing and dynamic process rather than a design activity that can be accomplished once and then forgotten.

Second, specific data elements may be valid and usable for current purposes, but in the wrong form. "Data relevance" has different meanings to people at various organizational levels. For an auditor who is performing tests of transactions, aggregate data are next to useless. However, these same data may be invaluable to upper management when making strategic business decisions. Therefore, the form in which the data are presented contributes to data relevance. Large amounts of data or very complex data relationships should be presented in graphic form wherever possible. Numerous studies have shown that executives are better able to assimilate and understand the meaning of data presented pictorially, thus helping to improve the data's information value. As Marshall McLuhan aptly stated, "The medium *is* the message." (See also Chapter 3 for a discussion of relevant data.)

Data Sources

There are many sources of data relevant to an enterprise's operations. The business environment is rife with data. All too often, these data are referred to as information and assumed to have value. In search of the supposed value, an executive can, with little effort, become inundated by all the data at his disposal. Most executives frequently experience this condition of "information overload." To avoid this condition, an organization must take steps to actively manage its data resources.

There are two primary data sources: internally produced data pertaining to normal operations and external data obtained through a variety of communications channels. At one time, the traditional data model for an organization suggested that the data source that provided the most relevant data for the matter at hand varied by organization level. Internally produced data were more appropriate for lower organizational levels; data from external sources were more relevant for upper-management levels. That model, however, was too simplistic. Although the model held true fairly well at lower organizational levels, it failed to describe the needs of upper management. Recent behaviorial studies on the decision-making process have determined that less than one percent of the data used by executives when making strategic business decisions come from external sources, implying that the other 99 percent come from internal sources. On closer inspection, one finds that the data, whether from internal or external sources, are presented in their original form. The data are routinely manipulated and reformatted by staff analysts who act as decision support agents to upper management. In fact, the most valuable source of decision-oriented data is provided in staff-produced materials. These types of data account for less than 5 percent of the information that bombards an executive, but they have the highest informational value relative to organizational success. Since executives receive over 50 percent of their data from external sources, but only one percent of the data have value to the organization, much opportunity exists for improving managerial effectiveness by filtering the mass of irrelevant data that executives receive from external sources.

Organization

How an enterprise organizes its data is vitally important. Managerial effectiveness depends on having timely access to relevant data. Poorly organized data, whether in electronic or physical (e.g., paper) form, lead to inefficiencies that can affect both the operational and financial effectiveness of an organization.

A typical situation often found in both large and small organizations is one where the desired data are available but not accessible. Bank of America, for example, recently made public the fact that it maintains a lot of information about its customers. Yet, to date, the bank has no way of determining the total portfolio of financial services a given customer maintains at the bank. The bank's management team believes that this situation contributes to the high cost of operations, affecting overall corporate effectiveness and adversely affecting the bank's competitive position in the financial services marketplace. The primary reason for this situation is the inadequacy of the design of the system for data storage. Much thought should be given to how data are stored in an organization's data banks; otherwise, it is highly likely that they will not be retrievable at reasonable cost in the future.

Analysis of data structure should begin at the top of an organization. One very successful analytical approach for determining the needs for, and uses of, data is the top-down method of analysis. This method starts with the organization's leaders and progresses downward through the various managerial and organizational levels. By adopting this method of analysis, the information requirements critical to organizational management are uncovered. This method of analysis helps ensure early identification of the organization's critical success factors and key management indicators. Once these significant information requirements are identified, it is possible to determine the basic types of data that must be collected and stored to support the information needs of the organization's leaders. Knowledge of the ultimate use of key data elements is critical to the design of effective and efficient data structures.

There are numerous methods available for organizing and storing data. The trend is toward the use of database management technology for organizing, storing, and managing the masses of data required to run an organization. The use of this technology has matured to the point where numerous articles are appearing in the literature that describe how an organization can use the data it captures to make better strategic decisions. These articles almost always discuss the advantages of using database approaches to data organization and management. In summary, the database approach provides better data structures for supporting the day-to-day operational data needs as well as management's decision-oriented information needs. In addition, database approaches improve data accessibility to support unplanned-for uses of the data, such as that required by special business analysis and strategic planning projects.

Many organizations have found that a single approach to data management is frequently not sufficient, and are implementing two or more methods for organizing and managing data banks, as different data storage methods are appropriate for different purposes. For example, the adoption of decision support systems within an organization requires an extremely flexible data management system. It is next to impossible to anticipate all the data requirements needed to support decision processing within an organization. As a result, many data processing organizations have adopted the "relational" method of database management for these decision-oriented systems that provide the flexibility and adaptability needed by end users responsible for decision support. Organizational effectiveness can be improved upon by using this approach to data management.

In contrast, relational database management technology is not the most efficient approach to data organization and management from a data processing resource perspective. Therefore, many companies have adopted one database approach for capturing, storing, and day-to-day operational data and another approach for satisfying all other uses. The necessity for this multiple approach to data management will disappear over time as computer hardware performance is improved and newer database management systems are introduced. For now, however, the multiple approach to data management appears to be the best way to satisfy organizational hunger for relevant and timely access to critical business information.

Accuracy

In most organizations, data accuracy is a major issue. Obviously, from an auditor's perspective, data are either accurate and therefore valuable or they are useless. However, this perspective applies to the data's intended use. For another use, the absolute accuracy of the data may not be as important. The situations described in the following paragraphs illustrate where the degree of data accuracy varies.

The operational or financial auditor, the customer support representative, the payroll clerk, and the accounts payable clerk require data that are absolutely accurate. In general, day-to-day operational data must be very accurate. Inaccurate data can destroy the organization's credibility in the eyes of its customers, shareholders, and creditors. On the other hand, absolute data accuracy is not necessary for most planning projects. Data that are generally accurate relative to other data used in the planning process are typically adequate. In most cases, the planning function, which is so important to an organization, does not have very accurate planning-oriented data. This is particularly true for long-range, strategic planning projects. In fact, accurate data are frequently not available from any source. The further the planning project looks into the future, the poorer the absolute data accuracy. At best, one can hope that planning assumptions and forecasting methodologies can be adopted to provide a reasonable degree of relative data accuracy.

An organization should make every attempt to maintain a high degree of accuracy for day-to-day operational data. These types of data are typically captured as a result of the processing of normal business transactions. If these data are not accurately maintained, poor operational decisions will be made and people will act in inappropriate ways that lead to overall organizational inefficiency. Data accuracy can be guaranteed with some assurance by establishing data administration and internal audit functions.

The data administration function is responsible for maintaining critical control-oriented data and key data relationships. This function is typically a user department function and is separate and distinct from the database management function, traditionally a more technical function within the data processing department. For example, the data administration function maintains the organization's vendor and inventory item master databases as well as critical table files that contain keys to data accuracy and organization. It frequently prepares special reports that compare data elements that are related to one another to make sure that proper relationships are being maintained. It then develops programs aimed at correcting erroneous data or data relationships.

The internal audit function is responsible for identifying data problems and erroneous transaction processing that could lead to significant control problems. These problems could either be operational or financial. Typically, internal audit functions are more concerned with the prudent use of organizational resources than with specific control issues. On the other hand, independent auditors are more interested in matters pertaining to financial control.

Maintenance

It is difficult to keep an organization's databases at an acceptable level of accuracy. However, for FISs to be usable at all, the data must be available when needed, as well as accurate. These goals of data management are achieved through active data maintenance, a function well suited for the data administration function mentioned in the previous discussion.

Data maintenance is important because it concentrates on historical data that form the basis for comparative financial analysis and projections of business activity. The ability to perform these types of financial activities readily is a significant way to enhance the effectiveness of an organization's financial management. Yet, most organizations find that historical data become almost insignificant because they are not maintained at an acceptable level of accuracy. Thus, data relevant to financial analysis and planning are frequently maintained by individuals in their own financial databases.

In a typical organization, the same data are kept in several places and, frequently, the same data are not similar in every location, a fact that can cause serious problems. First, some of the data are erroneous and can lead to inappropriate recommendations, depending on how accurate the data must be relative to the type of analysis being performed. Second, the cost of storing and maintaining the same data in multiple locations is high, unless the specific uses of the data require such a database design.

PERFORMANCE MANAGEMENT

The effectiveness of FISs is greatly aided by adopting appropriate performance goals and frequently reporting on actual performance. The issues involved in establishing performance reporting are:

- Establishing performance criteria
- Assigning responsibility for specific performance
- Determining appropriate feedback reporting cycles
- Implementing focused exception reporting

Establishing Performance Criteria

Organizational performance does not generally improve by itself, but is improved one step at a time through conscious effort. Such managerial approaches as management by objectives (or MBO), responsibility accounting, and quality circles have been instituted in many organizations to improve employees' effectiveness and performance. These approaches have one thing in common: They establish literal goals of performance for individuals to achieve that are normally aimed at attaining a higher level of organizational performance than currently exists. Even if an organization wants to make improvements, the only way to effect them is to develop a well-conceived plan of action where key members of the organization lead the way.

When establishing performance criteria, an organization should assure itself that the performance is achievable. If the performance goals are not "doable," the effect of the program can be just the opposite of what is desired. It is a good idea to seek small, but continuous, improvements in performance. Programs, specifically those in financial management, that hope to improve the accuracy or consistency of financial data can have a significant impact on effectiveness. Another valuable program with far-reaching effects is the consolidation of key financial data into shared databases suitable for decision processing.

Responsibility Management

Defining a performance improvement program and the criteria for its success is one thing; making the program successful is quite another. In most organizations, performance improvement programs take a great deal of time away from normal activities that have very real deadlines. A conscious effort needs to be made to allocate precious time to an extra program, especially where that program is not instrumental to daily short-term operations. Therefore, the responsibility for making performance improvement goals must be assigned to specific individuals, who must be made aware that these added responsibilities are just as important as any other activity assigned to them. In addition, management must be careful to define and to assign responsibilities so that there is minimal overlap and so that no dependencies give rise to internal politics, which may impede progress.

Performance Feedback Reporting

A solid performance reporting system should be a major goal of all organizations that want to improve internal effectiveness. For many organizations, however, this is very difficult because of internal politics and corporate culture. Management personnel may not be too receptive about receiving feedback where their performance has not been as expected. They may feel threatened and sometimes even fear the ramifications of feedback reporting. Such feelings are akin to those of a child who brings home a less-than-perfect report card. The child knows that his parents expect excellence and that any degree of poor performance is not very acceptable. Needless to say, the child is placed under tremendous emotional stress, even though at that point, he cannot do much to rectify the situation. Managers may also have some of these feelings if a performance feedback reporting system is not properly designed and administered.

The best approach to implementing a performance feedback system is to start with an analysis of the organization. Both its structure and its operations should be well understood. From a purely business perspective, the organization's critical success factors and key management indicators should be identified and agreed to by all key management personnel. Then the organizational structure should be studied to ensure its appropriateness for success at those business functions critical to the organization's very existence. The main structural aspect to be dealt with is overlapping responsibility. Although everyone must work together to be successful, the major activities necessary to perform well on a factor critical to success should be assigned to a single individual. If this rule of organizational structure is not adhered to, success is much more difficult to achieve.

To summarize, the significant aspects of such a reporting system are as follows:

1 Performance measures should be clearly defined and understood by those persons who are to receive the feedback.

2 As a minimum, feedback should be provided on those factors critical to the organization's success. All key management personnel should receive this feedback, since success cannot be achieved and sustained in these critical areas unless the entire management team is pushing in the same direction.

3 Organizational units primarily responsible for critical success factors should be the first to receive feedback reporting on their achievements. Feedback to other organizational units is also important to the achievement of overall excellence within a company, but only if the company has been successful enough at factors critical to its existence.

4 Feedback on key indicators should be provided to each functional manager. Analysis should be performed in advance to determine the information or statistical measures needed to indicate the performance of each major functional unit within the organization.

5 Specific and realistic performance goals should be established for the organization as a whole, for each major functional unit, and, in some cases, for specific individuals. These goals should be communicated to all management personnel who are directly involved in making the organization successful.

6 Feedback reporting should be frequent enough for corrective actions to be formulated and taken before the close of a major reporting period. For example, if maintaining high market share is a critical success factor to an organization, it does not help to report market share only on an annual basis. By that time, it is too late to do anything about declining market share. All that can be done is to accept the discouraging feedback and formulate a program to improve the situation during the next reporting period. It is far better to report on critical factors of success at least quarterly, and more often if possible.

7 Every key management person should support the overall performance plan. Bonuses should be based only partially on individual achievements. They should also be based on the achievement of overall organizational goals of performance.

8 Performance should be openly discussed at management meetings held specifically for such purposes. The tone of the meeting should be positive. Where performance is less than expected, the management team should attempt to understand why the situation occurred. More important, its members should focus as a group on how to correct the situation in the future.

9 Performance reports should be closely circulated within the organization because of their sensitivity. In the hands of the wrong person, good feedback reporting can be misused, which can have a dramatic impact on organization morale. In addition, the competition may be well positioned to use performance reports against the company if, through analysis, it can determine who the key personnel are or can discover the company's "Achilles' heel."

Once in place, performance feedback reporting is a major organizational asset. Of all the data that an organization collects, those associated with the performance reporting system are the most valuable to senior management. When used correctly, these are data that spur the organization to continued and greater success.

Exception Reporting

In an information society, it is easy to become overloaded with information that is provided or made readily available. Within an organization, this is frequently referred to as information overload. A manager in this situation finds it difficult to be effective. Most of the data necessary to perform a job are available somewhere in the piles of reports that make their way to a manager's office; the trick is to find the right information when it is needed. One solution to this problem is to adopt exception reporting as a design criterion for the organization's information systems.

Exception reporting is not new, yet it is not routinely observed in most organizations. Typically, exception reporting is designed for line management, to highlight operational conditions that deviate from a predetermined goal or standard of performance. Exception reporting resembles the performance feedback reporting discussed in the previous section, except that it focuses primarily on internal operations and deals with an organization's specific transactions rather than on its aggregate performance.

Establishing an effective exception reporting system correctly is difficult. If it were easier, surely more organizations would use this management reporting approach. The difficulty centers around the definition of "exceptions." Both positive and negative deviations from an expected level of performance must be defined. Negative deviations are reported so that conditions can be quickly changed to make sure that such performances are not repeated. Positive deviations are reported so that they can be capitalized on and possibly repeated. Typically, a range of performance is better than specific point estimates. This helps to limit the number of exceptions reported so that attention can be focused on the more important deviations.

Exceptions should be reported in a timely manner, and some should be reported immediately. This is frequently seen in on-line systems as part of the data entry process, where the data entered are edited and highlighted when they fail to satisfy tests of validity. In this same process environment, transactions that fail to meet certain criteria, such as minimum order profitability, are suspended until released after appropriate management review. Although these exceptions are reported very quickly because they need immediate action, other types of exceptions do not need such quick attention and can be reported at daily, weekly, or monthly intervals.

Each type of exception should have a defined course of corrective action. In addition, senior management should receive direct reporting on certain types of exceptions as well as a summary report on the number of exceptions by type during a reporting period. This is one way to monitor organizational effectiveness quickly. Management or the internal auditors should review the exception reporting system periodically to make sure that it is being used and that prompt corrective actions are being taken. (See also Chapter 3 for examples of exception reporting.)

DATA SECURITY ADMINISTRATION

A detailed discussion of data security is found in Chapter 22. However, because of its importance to the effectiveness of an organization's information system, a few main points regarding security and informational effectiveness are highlighted here.

The Security Program

Every organization should have some form of data security program. Countless hours are spent collecting, processing, storing, and maintaining organizational data. These hours translate into dollars. At the very minimum, an organization should have policies and procedures in place to protect this corporate asset from intentional or inadvertent destruction or misuse. Not to take a minimum level of precaution relative to data security is imprudent at best.

Data security becomes even more important as an organization's computerized information system becomes more sophisticated. There are several reasons for this situation. First, the more sophisticated the information systems, the more likely it is that types of data being captured and stored are critical to the organization's operations and management. Thus, it would be severely damaging to lose these data or to have them disclosed to someone without the organization's best interests at heart.

Second, it is very easy for vast quantities of data stored in a computer to be destroyed. A simple computer command can wipe out an entire database of vital information unless stringent steps are taken to positively ensure data security. If senior management realized how unsecure most of their data processing operations were, it would realize how easily primary databases and backup data files can be destroyed.

Third, typically larger, more developed databases indicate that data are more widely disseminated. If there are no adequate safeguards covering the distribution and use of this information, an organization opens itself up to many problems, since extraneous sources may have convenient access to sensitive data.

Last, the use of the personal computer is widely prevalent. Critical organizational information is routinely stored on these devices. All too often, there is no control over these resources or the information stored on them. It is easy to wipe out an entire database on a personal computer by issuing a simple, routinely used format command. Unfortunately, many managers have found out just how easy this is to do. It is also quite easy to destroy or walk off with information stored on a floppy disk. Managers should look around the company's offices to discover how secure the information resources and personal computing tools are.

In the business world, an active data security program is essential. Further, with the reported rise in corporate espionage in some industries, a data security program is the only way for an organization to establish measures to protect its valuable information from intentional or unintentional destruction or misuse.

Access Restrictions

An organization's information resources exist in physical and electronic forms. Access to each of these forms should be closely controlled. Restricting access to the electronic information resources should be an integral part of any information systems development element. Wherever critical data are maintained in computer databases, management should ensure the existence of proper hardware and software in the data processing environment to implement adequate levels of data security. Security measures within data processing should be strictly enforced. This applies to programmers as well as to visitors within the data processing center.

Restricting access to computer-based information is becoming more and more difficult, not because of the lack of good security tools for use within data processing operations, but because so many new decision support systems and micro- to mainframe link programs make security difficult to establish and maintain. Thus, a continuous ongoing effort must be taken to keep information security at reasonable levels. There is a fine line between being too controlled and too wide open to disclosure problems. Too much restriction leads to the availability, but inaccessibility, of information. There is no set solution to this problem. Every organization must deal with the issues and the level of security deemed necessary under the given circumstances. A general rule is that too much security is better than too little. If someone truly needs information that he cannot otherwise access, he should be required to justify his need. Data processing should have tools for effecting a one-time (or limited) access to sensitive information on an as-needed basis.

Restricting access to information that has been printed and circulated within an organization is next to impossible. However, one approach is to implement an application within data processing that creates reporting packages addressed to a specific individual. In this manner, individuals obtain only the information for which they are authorized, and they know immediately when they do not receive what they are supposed to receive. Management and data processing know exactly who receives what types of information and therefore know whom to contact if there has been a breach of security. A strict policy is needed to establish the fact that recipients of corporate information are directly responsible for the security of the information they receive. Individuals make security programs effective. A corporate awareness program must keep reinforcing this point.

Version Control

An organization's databases change over time. More changes are made to current data than to historical data. Some controls must be exercised over the various versions of the databases as they change. This is known as version control. In traditional data processing operations, version control is implemented by creating backup databases or data files at periodic intervals, such as daily or weekly. The type of database and the extent to which it is used determine the frequency of backup and therefore the degree of version control needed. A good example of where version control is important is reflected in the budget. The annual budget is typically cast in concrete, once approved. For purposes of this example, let's call this Version O. Since the budget is only a best guess of how the next year will progress financially, it will change as new information about the business becomes available. Most organizations modify the budget periodically to reflect the latest information. Each time the budget changes, a new version number is assigned and a new copy of the budget is archived. In this manner, several copies of the approved annual budget will be available for reporting and analysis. Thus, version control enables management to access the proper copy of the budget. Frequently, it is desirable to compare the year-to-date actual performance to the current (i.e., revised version) budget as well as to the original budget (i.e., Version O). Without version control, such comparison reports could not readily be produced by data processing.

Today, version control is becoming more of an issue in the business world because of the proliferation of personal computers. When a white-collar worker has a personal computer connected to the corporate computer, he can frequently access and download selected information needed for analysis. In some cases, data may be uploaded to the corporate computer from the personal computer. This capability poses some interesting questions regarding version control because, unlike most database updates, the database update coming from the personal computer did not result from a transaction. This is why most organizations are leery of allowing database updates to come from data uploaded from personal computers. The easiest way to pollute a database is to allow unstructured ways in which it can be updated.

There is another issue of version control related to personal computers. Within an organization, it is typical to find several people using the same data at the same version level on personal computers. However, it is normal to find that the data are not actually the same. This is particularly true in organizations where PCs are not connected to the corporate computer and therefore are incapable of downloading data. In these organizations, data are entered into the personal computers by rekeying them from reports produced from the corporate databases. Key entry errors are the primary cause for the discrepancies noted in data used by different people. However, other problems exist as well. People do not like to spend time updating data stored in personal computer databases. Therefore, the data are seldom, if ever, accurate. Although many of the decision support applications of personal computing do not require perfectly accurate data, the mere fact that a discrepancy can be found in raw data leads one to challenge the results obtained. There is no immediate, simple solution to the version control problem of data stored in personal computers. However, management should be aware of the potential problems and establish administrative guidelines for version control that are deemed appropriate for the type of personal computing performed within its organization.

Protection of Data in Circulation

In the normal course of business, an organization's information is provided to many people. At best, it is difficult to establish any kind of control over who actually has access to the data or how they use them. In such cases, the best defense is a good offense. A means of determining the importance of various types of data should be established. Then, circulation of the more sensitive information should be tightly controlled. Employees should be made aware of the sensitive nature of the information contained in various reports and should be held accountable for their use and for subsequent distribution of information. Reports containing sensitive information that are not being actively used should be stored in a secure place. Reports with outdated information should be destroyed (e.g., by shredding). Reports provided to third parties should be prepared specifically for the person to whom the data will be given. Standard reports providing third parties with more information than they ask for or need should be avoided. It may cost slightly more to produce customized reports, but the cost of disseminating sensitive information can be far higher in the long run.

DISTRIBUTION MANAGEMENT

As discussed earlier, the role of distribution management is critical to information security, and also key to the effectiveness of the organization's information system. The role of distribution management is to provide the right information in the right form to the right individuals at an appropriate time. Achieving this goal of information management requires constant attention because of the shifting roles of individuals within an organization and because the types of information that individuals need to perform their jobs change over time. Determining the what, how, and when for distributing information is a challenge that each organization must address.

Selection of Data for Distribution

There are several methods for distributing information. The two predominant forms of distribution are through the use of (1) hard-copy reports, which include media such as paper and microforms, and (2) electronic reports, such as through on-line inquiry or file download to a personal computer. Traditionally, information has been distributed most often in a hard-copy form. This has become expensive because of the time it takes to print the information as well as the cost of the paper used for printing. After all these costs are incurred to produce hard-copy output, the recipient of the reports typically does not use the information except for reference. In other words, it is not actively used to make running the organization more efficient. Realizing this fact helps management to determine what should be distributed in hard copy.

Deciding what information to distribute should be done on a need-to-know basis. If a person needs certain information, then it should be distributed to him. However, if that person's need to know is infrequent, then distribution should be by exception. This is implemented and controlled by establishing procedures for providing certain types of information on request only. Where

INGREDIENTS OF AN EFFECTIVE FIS

an individual has a routine need for data, the system should be able to make them available in suitable form.

Means for Data Distribution

Attempts to implement "paperless" offices have not been widely successful. Paper is convenient for communicating information, and, therefore, it is not likely to disappear in the near future. However, other options may be considered when designing an information delivery system. Microforms are now widely used to disseminate large volumes of data without the bulk associated with paper. Specialized equipment is needed to produce and retrieve the data in a usable form. The latest approaches to information distribution are quite exotic in that they are looking to incorporate the increasing numbers of personal computers into the distribution network. Under these newer approaches, personal computers are connected to the main organizational computers, which are then controlled under the same database security system as other on-line terminals in the network. Each personal computer user is assigned an appropriate level of security that allows him to access certain types of data and reports. Production reports are stored electronically in a report database, which is accessible by authorized users through the personal computers. Reports for which an individual has authorized access appear on a customized report menu that is part of the information distribution network. An individual can then select a report from the menu of available ones. These reports can be viewed on the video display, and selected pages of the reports can be printed on locally attached printers in the end user's department. Selected records from the available reports can be downloaded into the personal computer in a form that is immediately accessible by the end-user for modeling or special report creation. If the entire report is needed in hard-copy form, a print request can be submitted directly through the personal computer.

This new approach has tremendous possibilities in that it enables virtually customized reporting of only the needed information in the right form whenever necessary. No other form of information distribution management comes close to this approach. However, it is costly to implement in smaller organizations with limited information resources or in organizations where personal computers are not widely used. This situation is changing rapidly, as the cost of personal computers continues to drop to levels where it is more cost effective to purchase a personal computer with a terminal emulation capability than to purchase a terminal for access to information as well as a personal computer to perform the analytical work for decision support.

Timeliness of Data Distribution

The timeliness of information availability is a major design issue. Data can be classified by type so that certain classes of data are distributed immediately, while other classes are distributed only when requested. For example, process control data and error messages returned from editing entered on line should be immediately distributed. These types of data have an immediate impact on subsequent processing. Other types of data, such as month-to-date sales statistics, can be accumulated daily and made available (e.g., through on-line inquiry) where needed. This type of information is valuable; however, it is not necessary for immediate control of the organization's operations.

The exception reporting mentioned earlier should be distributed in a timely manner. If an order is on credit hold awaiting management review, it should be available immediately via on-line inquiry if the time from order booking until shipment is very short. On the other hand, if the time frame is a few days or more, it might be adequate to report credit holds daily via hard copy. The organization's characteristics and its business environment are critical in determining when information should be distributed.

If the distribution approach based on the inclusion of personal computers into the information network is adopted, the issue of when to distribute largely disappears. End users can access the needed information whenever they need it. In addition, many of the issues associated with version control disappear.

SUMMARY

Thus, the five key ingredients of an effective FIS are:

1 Having a model of the enterprise that reflects critical success factors and identifies key indicators;

2 Actively managing the organization's data as a valuable resource;

3 Implementing a performance measurement and reporting system;

4 Administering a data security program that covers the electronic and physical aspects of information storage, dissemination, and usage; and

5 Designing an information distribution system that facilitates providing the right information in the right form to the right individuals in a timely manner.

CHAPTER 6

Financial Accounting Systems

Harry Kraushaar and Dane Sullivan

Introduction	2
The General Ledger	4
Features	4
Database	4
Chart-of-Accounts Structuring	6
Data Entry, Inquiry, and Update ...	8
Audit Trails	10
Reporting	11
Budgeting	13
Cost Allocation	15
Cost Accounting	16
Security	17
Accounts Payable	18
Features	20
Integration With Purchasing/Receiving	20
Check Reconciliation	21
Reporting	21
Accounts Receivable	22
Balance Only System	23
Balance Forward System	23
Open Item System	23
Features	24
Interface to Billing	24
Interface to General Ledger	24
Reporting	24
Cash Flow	25
Payroll	25
Features	26
Multistate Capabilities	26
Labor Distribution	26
Personnel Functions	27
Fixed Assets	27
Features	27
Asset Control	27
Book Depreciation	29
Tax Depreciation	29
Multiple Records	30
Reporting	30
Other Features	30
Current Developments	30

Fig. 6-1 Core Accounting Systems Interrelationships 3
Fig. 6-2 General Ledger Processing Flow 5
Fig. 6-3 Account Coding Scheme 7
Fig. 6-4 Overlapping Reporting Relationships 8
Fig. 6-5 Trial Balance for the Cash Account 11
Fig. 6-6 Comparative Income Statement 12
Fig. 6-7 Custom Report Developed by a Report Writer 13
Fig. 6-8 Initial Budget Creation Feature 14
Fig. 6-9 Flexible Budget for Direct Materials 15
Fig. 6-10 Financial Accounting Cost Accumulation 17
Fig. 6-11 Cost Accounting Cost Accumulation 18

Fig. 6-12 Feature Comparison of Small and Large General Ledger Systems 19
Fig. 6-13 Standard Features and Reports in Small and Large Accounts Payable Systems . . 22
Fig. 6-14 Standard Features and Reports in Small and Large Accounts Receivable Systems 25
Fig. 6-15 Standard Features in Small and Large Payroll Systems 27
Fig. 6-16 Fixed Assets Processing Flow 28
Fig. 6-17 Feature Comparison of Small and Large Fixed Asset Systems 31

INTRODUCTION

Except for highly complex mathematical models, financial accounting systems were the first types of systems to be automated. Although the initial systems were very cumbersome and difficult to use, they gained acceptance because they performed repetitive tasks at high speeds and generally did not make as many errors as humans did. Most of these systems were designed in house by data processing departments and were custom designed to automate existing manual systems. Due to the constraints imposed by the hardware, the various components of a total financial system operated independently of each other—that is, they were not integrated. Also, they were batch oriented, and most input was card based.

As hardware technology evolved, however, it became feasible to develop financial accounting systems that allowed on-line input and simple systems integration. These systems were still primarily developed in house, but several firms began to develop packaged software solutions. A "packaged software solution" is one that is developed with the intent of licensing its use to other firms. These packaged systems typically offered more features than systems developed in house, but they did not necessarily meet all the needs of the businesses to which they were sold. However, for financial accounting systems applications, it became clear that most business needs could be met by a software package. As a result, software companies developed packaged systems to meet the financial accounting needs of businesses.

The basic or core systems that were developed as packages were generally classified as follows:

- General ledger
- Accounts payable
- Accounts receivable
- Payroll
- Fixed assets

To most businesspeople, these systems are referred to as the general ledger and the subsidiary ledgers that make up the accounting system. For the purposes of this Manual, each is referred to as a separate application or system, and the use of "subsidiary ledger" to describe any of them is omitted.

FINANCIAL ACCOUNTING SYSTEMS

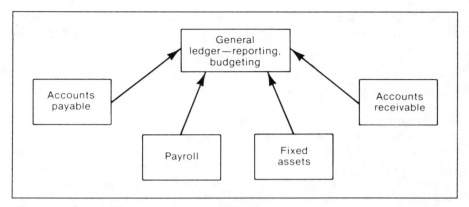

FIG. 6-1 Core Accounting Systems Interrelationships

These systems interact and combine to form the core of the FIS. Figure 6-1 depicts the interrelationships of the core financial systems. In most organizations, several other operational systems are also needed, such as inventory control and order entry. For the core financial systems to be useful to a company, they must contain many intricate and detailed features. This chapter examines and outlines the features a businessperson can expect from the core financial systems available on the market, as there is a proliferation of software companies selling an enormous number of packaged systems from which to choose.

Since the features contained in these core FISs are consistent and standard, the businessperson need only tailor and customize the system to his particular needs.

The main functions of the core financial systems provide management with the information required to manage a growing, complex business by accounting for, and reporting on, financial transactions. The systems also enable a business to define and alter a sophisticated financial and managerial accounting system, allowing management to:

- Perform business planning.
- Evaluate management performance.
- Control access to sensitive data.
- Maintain a base of data that are relevant to decision making.
- Produce financial statements for internal as well as external purposes.
- Compare planned with actual results.

Thus, FISs have evolved at an extraordinary pace during the 1970s through the mid-1980s. In this chapter, each system is described by developing a typical processing flow and by outlining the system's features and the data it stores. Finally, the chapter concludes with information on current developments in the core financial packages and what future financial systems will most likely contain.

THE GENERAL LEDGER

The general ledger is the backbone of a financial accounting system. If the financial accounting system's user is thought of as the brain, then the general ledger is the spinal cord, because it accepts inputs from the various transactional systems (e.g., payroll, accounts payable) and summarizes and reports them to the brain. The functions of the general ledger allow the user to acquire, summarize, store, and report data. Thus, the key general ledger features are those that allow a user to summarize and manipulate important data.

The general ledger produces reports that range from detail trial balance of postings to financial statements. The main sources of input to the general ledger are summarized transaction data from the other financial accounting systems and the correcting, adjusting, or other journal entries prepared by the accounting department.

The main processing flow used by the general ledger consists of entering journal entry transactions, editing and balancing the journal entries, and preparing financial transaction reports, including the trial balance, general ledger, and journal entry register. Figure 6-2 illustrates this typical processing flow. The basic data entry, edit, and reporting cycle can be repeated several times before the accounting period is closed. As far as the general ledger is concerned, summary input from other financial accounting systems is treated in the same way as journal entries entered individually.

The general ledger is also used for other business requirements, including budgeting, financial planning, and account analysis. These functions are performed on an as-needed basis, and they are considered to be outside the main processing flow. Thus, they are excluded from Figure 6-2.

The general ledger is not designed to handle all of a business' detailed transactions. Detail transactions are usually listed as part of the other financial systems discussed in this chapter. If the other systems are weak, then the general ledger is usually called upon to fill their voids. This can have disasterous side effects, which typically include long closing times and inordinately long journal entries.

Features

Database. As mentioned earlier, the general ledger mainly collects, summarizes, stores, and reports financial information. Therefore, it is a database of financial information and should be designed in a way that makes it easy for a user to perform these functions. However, this does not necessarily mean that the general ledger must be written in a database language.

FINANCIAL ACCOUNTING SYSTEMS

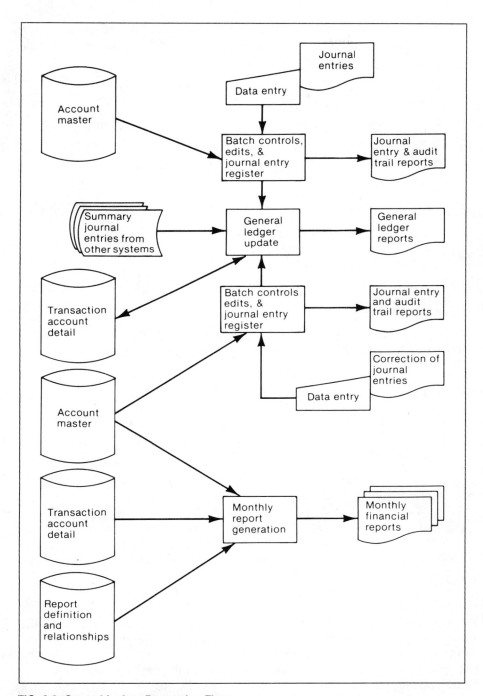

FIG. 6-2 General Ledger Processing Flow

The data stored by the general ledger is centered around the different accounts used to track financial transactions. At a minimum, the general ledger should store the following information for each account:

- Account master data including account number, account description, and type of account
- Current-period (month or year) actual transaction data in detail or summary form
- Current-period budget data
- Prior-year actual transaction data in detail or summary form

The general ledger may also store or maintain the following optional data:

- Balances for different accounting periods, including weekly, daily, monthly, or twelve-, thirteen-, or fourteen-period years
- Nonmonetary, or statistical, data
- Unlimited number of years of historical information
- Multiple budgets

In addition to the account data mentioned, the general ledger keeps several other optional data files that are used to perform specialized functions, including:

- Report specification files
- Account reporting relationships
- Allocation specifications
- Foreign currency translation specifications

A user should be able to access the data contained in the general ledger in an on-line fashion—that is, at a computer terminal with a screen where he can view the input data and correct them if they are in error. Almost all current systems offer on-line input. The general ledger should provide an on-line menu facility or have a command language that allows the user to easily view data. Optimally, the command language should consist of an English-like structure and work with key words or verbs, such as "extract," "compute," "if," "list," "analyze."

Chart-of-Accounts Structuring. The chart of accounts is a listing of all the accounts used in the accounting system with a number or character code attached. A considerable amount of thought should be put into determining the information that must be captured by the accounting system. If the chart of accounts does not capture enough detail, it will be difficult to develop reports at a detailed level. On the other hand, if the chart of accounts captures

FINANCIAL ACCOUNTING SYSTEMS

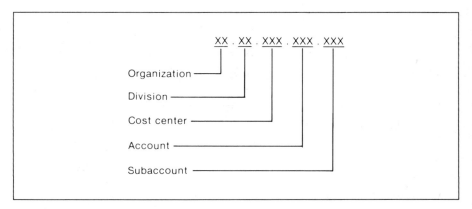

FIG. 6-3 Account Coding Scheme

too much detail and the detail is not used, the organization has unnecessarily burdened the accounting department. Thus, the effective chart-of-accounts structure allows an organization to record and to report data at the appropriate level of detail without being overly restrictive. The chart of accounts should not be designed until the business' reporting requirements have been determined. A chart of accounts can then be created that meets the business' particular needs.

There are two solutions to developing an effective chart of accounts. The first entails building logic into the account number. For example, the account coding scheme shown in Figure 6-3 may be used to record and report data at the organization, division, cost center, account, or subaccount level.

Each grouping of digits is used to code specific information. This solution is implemented by most of the smaller general ledger packages because it is the easiest to implement, and that method of account coding is usually the easiest for the accounting clerks to use. However, it does have some disadvantages. The number of digits in a grouping may not be sufficient; this method is not very flexible where new accounts are added or other changes are made. Some systems overcome the problem by allowing a user to define his own coding scheme and the number of digits in each field.

The other solution is not to place any logic into the account number. Accounts are related by account relationships, which are defined in a separate general ledger file. This approach requires more software, and is usually implemented in the larger mainframe packages. Since this approach is more flexible, it is easier to alter reporting relationships without losing major portions of account history. In addition, using this approach makes it easy for management to design overlapping reporting structures.

Figure 6-4 illustrates the overlapping reporting relationships that enable management to easily extract information in the form of an accounting report

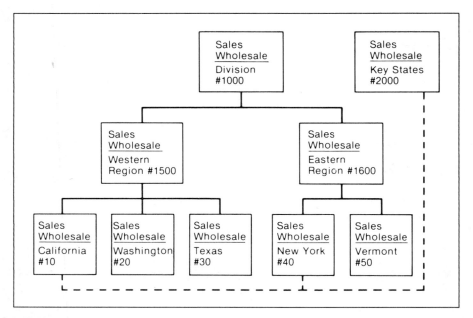

FIG. 6-4 Overlapping Reporting Relationships

without having to do a special sort of the database. The figure shows two ways of grouping sales: (1) by region or (2) by key states. Reports by region include all of the states and are the normal way of aggregating sales information. However, management has identified two states, California and New York, that are critical to the company. By using account relationships instead of account numbers, management is able to define another way of aggregating sales information.

Another advantageous feature of overlapping reporting relationships is the capability of including statistical or nonmonetary data in the same chart of accounts. These data are extremely useful for cost allocations or flexible budgeting. Most of the larger systems accept nonmonetary as well as monetary data.

Data Entry, Inquiry, and Update. The general ledger must be able to accept data and report them back to the user. Two main types of journal entries enter the general ledger. The first includes the automated journal entries that come from the other operational systems. Examples of these journal entries include:

- Expense account distribution debits and cash credits for the periodic payrolls from the payroll system

FINANCIAL ACCOUNTING SYSTEMS

- Expense and asset account distribution from the accounts payable system
- Depreciation entries from the fixed asset system

The second type includes journal entries that are made monthly by the accounting department.

Journal entries that summarize the activity from an operating system do so by general ledger account. Sometimes the detail by transaction is transferred to the general ledger. Usually, however, the data are transferred in summary form by account. The journal entry is usually made via disk file or tape file. The accounting department instructs the operating system to produce the journal entry; it also instructs the general ledger to accept the journal entry as input. It does not, however, have to create the journal entry manually. This feature is standard in most systems if the systems are all supplied by the same vendor. If systems from multiple vendors are used, then additional programming must be performed to obtain an automatic interface.

The accounting department makes journal entries each period to augment the standard transactions that are captured in the other systems. These entries can be one of three types:

1 Nonrecurring, nonreversing

2 Recurring, nonreversing

3 Reversing

The nonrecurring, nonreversing journal entries are the typical journal entries made each period. They may be created to adjust an account for an error or record a capital lease. The general ledger should provide an on-line method for making the journal entry. In addition, the general ledger should provide the user with on-line account editing and journal entry balancing. The user should have the option of posting the journal entry into any of the unclosed accounting periods. This feature is very useful at the beginning of a new accounting period when transactions need to be posted to the new period but the old period has not been closed.

The recurring, nonreversing journal entries are made the same way each period, and the accounts and amounts do not change. The general ledger should enable the user to schedule these recurring entries and have the system make them automatically. Posting should be controlled by accounting period or date.

The reversing entries are entries made at the end of a period but reversed during the next period. These entries typically represent accruals or estimates. The general ledger should provide a facility that allows the user to have the entry reversed automatically during the next accounting period.

In addition to making journal entries, the user must be able to inquire into the general ledger database in an on-line manner. Inquiries are usually made to review the status or postings into an account. Inquiries can also be made by date of transaction, accounting period, or account balance. The general ledger should provide all of these features.

Transactions do not affect the general ledger database until they are posted. In a manual system, posting occurs when the journal entry or transaction is written into the general ledger accounts. In an automated system, posting can occur in two forms, batch or on-line real time.

In a batch update system, all journal entries are entered and edited. Then they are stored in a file until the user decides to post them to the general ledger. Thus, all the journal entries are collected and posted in a batch. The batch posting can occur immediately or overnight. Small systems tend to allow immediate updating because the number of accounts in the system and the number of transactions are typically minimal. Also, the amounts of time and computer resources required to update the system are usually minimal. Until very recently, most large general ledger systems aggregated all the journal entries to be updated into one big batch and performed the update during the evening hours when the demand for computer time was typically lower.

In a real-time system, the update occurs as soon as the user has entered and validated the journal entry input.

For most organizations, a batch update in the general ledger is all that is required. The immediate batch update is useful at the end of the accounting period, but it is not generally required. Some organizations, such as financial institutions that close their books on a daily basis, will, however, find the immediate updating or real-time updating features useful.

If an error has been made in a journal entry and the computer edit facility can detect it, large systems offer two choices:

1 They do not post the entry.

2 They post the entry to a suspense account.

Smaller systems usually prevent the user from posting any journal entry with an inconsistency.

Audit Trails. The general ledger system should provide an adequate audit trail of all transactions entered into the system. The "audit trail" is a series of reports detailing the transactions that have been entered into the system. These reports are usually called "transaction registers" or "transaction logs" and are all-inclusive—that is, they include all transactions entered.

Another form of audit trail is the exception report, which assumes that most of the transactions entered into the system are correct. The user decides what criteria must be present before a transaction is classified as incorrect; he then instructs the system to look for that type of transaction. The system screens each transaction entered, but only reports those that are incorrect. Transactions can be flagged for being out of balance, having an amount that

FINANCIAL ACCOUNTING SYSTEMS

Date	Account	Description	Reference	DR	CR	Balance
1/31/XX	10101	Cash				$5,000.00
2/15/XX	10101	Cash	CR	$500.00		
2/28/XX	10101	Cash	CD		($750.00)	
2/28/XX	10101	Cash				4,750.00

FIG. 6-5 Trial Balance for the Cash Account

exceeds a specified amount, or being of the wrong sign. Exception reports are usually found only in larger systems.

The general ledger should also produce error listings where a transaction has been posted that is out of balance or that attempts to post to an undefined account. As previously discussed, transactions with errors can be posted to a suspense account or not posted at all. The larger systems allow the user to decide how the system should proceed.

Reporting. General ledger systems offer three types of reports: standard, semicustom, and custom. A "standard" report is one that comes with the system. The user has little option of what information the report contains or how it is printed. This type of report usually includes the basic posting journals, transaction registers, trial balances, and general ledger account reports. Figure 6-5 depicts a trial balance, one of the standard reports contained in a general ledger system.

Many column headings appearing on most reports are quite common to most businesses. These reports are typically balance sheets or income statements that most businesses use. The user customizes the report lines by telling the system the accounts to be included on each line and where the subtotals and totals should be entered. The system uses the standard column headings with the user's line items. For that reason, these reports are called "semicustom" reports. Following are some typical semicustom reports:

- Current-year balance sheet
- Current-year balance sheet compared with prior-year balance sheet
- Current-month and year-to-date income statement
- Current-month and year-to-date compared to prior-year month and year-to-date income statement
- Current-month and year-to-date compared to budgeted-month and year-to-date income statement

Figure 6-6 shows a comparative income statement, which is also a semicustom report. The column headings include the month-to-date actual, budget, and

COMPANY
INCOME STATEMENT
Three Months Ended 3/31/XX

Description	Month to Date			Year to Date		
	Actual	Budget	Variance	Actual	Budget	Variance
Sales	$2,000	$1,650	$350	$6,000	$5,900	$ 100
Cost of sales	1,500	1,400	–	4,700	4,600	(100)
Gross margin	$ 500	$ 250	$250	$1,300	$1,300	$ 0
G&A expenses						
Salaries	100	90	(10)	350	330	(20)
Rent	50	50	0	160	150	(10)
Miscellaneous	25	30	5	90	100	10
Total G&A	$ 175	$ 170	$ (5)	$ 600	$ 580	$ (20)
Income before taxes	$ 325	$ 80	$275	$ 700	$ 720	$ (20)

FIG. 6-6 Comparative Income Statement

variance, and the year-to-date actual, budget, and variance are fixed by the general ledger system. The user cannot alter these columns. The report headings, including sales, cost of sales, gross margin, and the other expenses, are all determined by the user, which enables him to customize the report to his specifications.

Most general ledger systems contain standard and semicustom reports, which, most of the time, are adequate to meet the user's needs. However, some general ledgers for smaller systems do not allow the user to customize the report lines. Instead, they create a set of reports with fixed columns and line items. Thus, before purchasing a general ledger system, the user must determine whether the system allows him to customize the report line items. If it does not, then he should spend considerable time reviewing the reports that come with the system to be sure that the reports will meet his needs.

For a general ledger system to really become a management tool and not just a financial reporting system, a "custom" reporting facility is required. These custom reporting facilities are called "report writers," and allow the user to specify report line items and column headings. They also permit the user to specify how the columns are related to each other. For example, the second column might be defined as two times the first column. The large general ledger systems offer the report-writer facilities described here. Unfortunately, every software vendor claims that its system contains a report writer. Before purchasing a general ledger system, the user should spend considerable time reviewing the features of its report writer, because not all report writers are equal. As a rule of thumb, the more expensive the system, the better the report writer.

YEAR-TO-DATE EXPENSE OF OVER $1 MILLION X 105%		
Account	Amount	Amount × 105%
Managers' salaries	$2,004,675	$2,104,909
Rent	1,000,000	1,050,000
Raw materials	5,675,240	5,959,002
Direct labor	3,006,250	3,156,563

FIG. 6-7 Custom Report Developed by a Report Writer

Figure 6-7 depicts a full custom report developed by a report writer. In this example, the user has asked the report writer to extract all expense accounts with year-to-date balances in excess of $1 million. He then asks the report writer to create a new column of information consisting of the extracted amounts multiplied by 105 percent, management's estimate for inflation for the following year. As can be seen by the example, the report writer allows the user to specify three things:

1 The column headings
2 The rules for extracting specific accounts
3 The ways in which the columns interrelate

Report-writer specifications should be entered in an on-line manner. The specifications can be formatted into transaction codes and data or they can be free format, English-like commands and data. Custom reports are typically used for responsibility reporting, exception reporting, special reporting restructures, and financial planning.

Budgeting. To be successful, most budgets must be developed at the account level. Thus, the general ledger is the most appropriate place in the financial accounting system to create, store, alter, and report budgeted data.

Most general ledger systems support a budget facility. At the lowest level, this means that room in the general ledger database has been reserved for budget data. Typically, these data are entered at the account level and used as is for the entire year.

Larger general ledgers offer several additional features that can be used in the budget creation and reporting process and allow the user to choose between top-down and bottom-up budget creation. Top-down budget creation means that an amount is budgeted for an entire department or division. It is then split into the various components that make up the department or the division. The general ledger facilitates this by offering the user various ways of allocating the amount to specific subdepartments or accounts. The most typical methods are percentage based.

Account	Year to Date (8 months)	Annualized	Next-Year Initial Budget Estimate
Sales			
Product 1	$3,000,000	$4,500,000	$4,950,000
Product 2	1,500,000	2,250,000	2,475,000

FIG. 6-8 Initial Budget Creation Feature

Larger general ledgers offer the user easier ways of creating the initial budget, by allowing him to automatically create a new budget based on the prior-year budget and actual data. For example, a user can create a budget based on prior-year actual data, current-year actual data multiplied by some factor, current-period actual data, or current year-to-date amounts plus the remaining budgeted amounts. The general ledger does not use any sophisticated fixed- and variable-cost analyses to prepare the initial budgets. Instead, it uses an amount and annualizes or multiplies it by a user-supplied factor. Figure 6-8 illustrates such a feature. In this example, management has decided to generate a first pass at the sales budget for the following year by:

- Extracting existing sales accounts (for eight months of activity);
- Annualizing the amounts (dividing by 8 and multiplying by 12); and
- Multiplying the annualized amounts by 110 percent, the planned sales increase.

All of these methods will produce a first pass at the new budget at the account level without requiring much management or clerical time. These features, however, are not designed to produce a company's final or approved budget. For a budget to be effective, management must use all of its resources and skills. However, these features do offer an excellent way to initiate the budget process cost effectively.

The larger general ledgers also let the user develop a budget that can be varied, based upon some level of activity, which is usually more appropriate for evaluating managerial performance. The general ledger system uses a nonmonetary amount stored in a statistical account to compute a variable budget. For example, the production department budget may be based upon the number of units produced and a standard cost for each unit. A sophisticated general ledger system allows a user to input the number and the standard cost of units produced in a period. Then the system computes the budget amount based on actual production. This is a good example of why it is important for the general ledger to allow statistical or nonmonetary accounts in the chart of accounts.

Figure 6-9 shows how the variable budget process works. The top section of the example contains three accounts from the chart of accounts:

FINANCIAL ACCOUNTING SYSTEMS

Account Number	Description	Amount
500201[a]	Number produced	$15
500202[a]	Material cost per unit	$350
500203[b]	Material costs actual	$5,500

	Actual	Budget	Variance
Material costs	$5,500	$5,250[c]	$(250)

(a) Statistical or nonmonetary account
(b) Normal or monetary account
(c) Amount equals number produced multiplied by the standard material cost per unit

FIG. 6-9 Flexible Budget for Direct Materials

1 500201 — Number produced
2 500202 — Material cost per unit
3 500203 — Material costs actual

The number produced and material cost per unit accounts are statistical, or nonmonetary, accounts—that is, amounts stored in these accounts do not enter the trial balance or the financial statements, and are used for such purposes as producing a variable budget. In the example shown in Figure 6-9, the actual number of units produced must be entered into the number produced account on a monthly basis. The standard cost per unit is entered at the beginning of the budget process and probably remains fixed throughout the year. The material costs actual account contains the actual materials costs that have been incurred.

When the comparative income statement is produced, the general ledger system computes the budgeted amount for material costs by multiplying the amount in the number produced account by the amount in the material costs per unit account.

The smaller general ledgers allow some budget revision. This usually means that the original budgeted amount is altered and the new amount is entered. The original amount is usually overwritten and lost. The larger general ledger systems allow the user to keep multiple versions of budgets; thus, budgets can be altered without losing the original budgeted information. Large and small general ledgers allow the user to revise the budgets in an on-line manner.

Cost Allocation. In many organizations, each department is charged with a portion of the company's overhead expenses. These allocations are usually based on what the department uses or controls. For accounting purposes, these costs are usually accumulated in a control account; for reporting purposes, they are allocated back to the individual department. The distribution of the amounts from one account to another is called "cost allocation." This feature is only found in the larger general ledger systems. Although it is possible to perform the allocation calculations manually and then develop and post the appropriate journal entries, it is often a very time-consuming and error-prone task.

The larger general ledger systems allow the user to develop a series of cost allocation rules; the system then uses the rules to automatically generate and post the appropriate journal entries. These journal entries allocate the costs as required by the user. Thus, the user omits the repetitive and time-consuming task of recreating the journal entries each month.

Allocation rules can be as simple as allocating all the dollars in Account X into Account Y. Allocation rules can also become much more complicated. Listed are five ways some of the larger systems can allocate costs.

1 Base them on fixed percentages.
2 Base them on ratios of amounts in other accounts.
3 Base them on statistical amounts (e.g., square feet).
4 Base them on a weighted percentage to the total.
5 Base them on a series of simultaneous equations where the amount to be allocated depends on the amount that will be allocated from another account.

In most organizations, managers are measured by the costs they can control. If an organization uses cost allocation from one department to another, a department should be charged at the budgeted amount, not at the actual amount, so that inefficiencies that occur in the allocating department are not passed on to the user department. This means that the general ledger system should also be able to allocate costs based on budgeted amounts.

General ledgers that allow cost allocation should also allow the user to create, inquire, and alter the allocation rules via on-line facilities. In addition, whenever an allocation entry has been created, it should be entered onto an allocation journal entry register and printed.

Cost Accounting. Cost accounting is difficult for most general ledgers because it involves accumulating the data in a different direction from that required by general financial reporting. Figure 6-10 depicts the typical summarization that occurs in normal financial reporting. The direction and summarization is upward, starting at the account level and accumulating costs at the department, division, and company levels. Because costs associated with producing a product or delivering a service include various accounts, departments,

FINANCIAL ACCOUNTING SYSTEMS 6-17

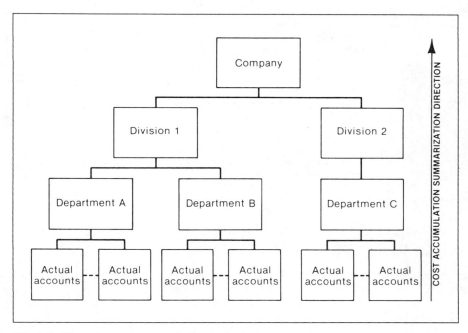

FIG. 6-10 Financial Accounting Cost Accumulation

or divisions, the direction in which they must be accumulated in order to obtain a total product or service cost is sideways. This is depicted in Figure 6-11.

General ledger systems implement cost accounting features by appending a product or job number onto the end of an account number. Actual costs are still posted into their normal accounts, but products or services can be costed by summarizing by product or job number. In this way, the general ledger can be used to develop product cost information. The general ledger, however, is not well suited to producing the detailed job costing variance reports usually required in a manufacturing accounting system.

That type of reporting is only found in the larger general ledgers. An alternative to using the general ledger system for cost accounting is to purchase a true job costing system, which enables the user to develop all the standard variance reports common to a job cost environment. The general ledger costing features may generate cost data, but they are not true cost accounting systems.

Security. The information stored in the general ledger system is private. Generating and updating journal entries must be limited to those who are authorized to do so. General ledger systems provide security features that can minimize the sort of problems mentioned previously. Security is provided by sign-on codes, restricted terminals, and passwords. Some systems also limit the

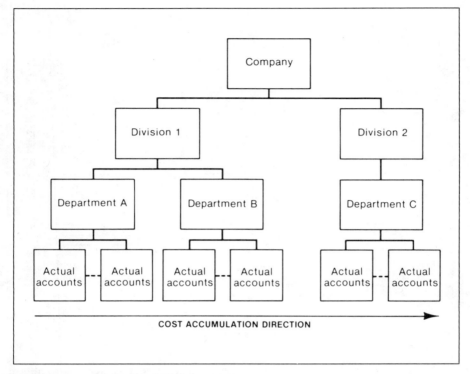

FIG. 6-11 Cost Accounting Cost Accumulation

user's ability to perform certain transactions based on the user's sign-on or password code. Security features are very important, and general ledgers should include them. (See Chapters 10 and 22 for a detailed discussion of this subject.)

The general ledger may contain many complex features. The user must decide which features are required and which are desired or not needed. Figure 6-12 is a chart of the features that are likely to be available on small and larger general ledger systems.

ACCOUNTS PAYABLE

The purpose of the accounts payable subsidiary ledger system is to provide a mechanism by which to pay on a timely basis, per contract, for merchandise or services received from vendors. In paying for merchandise or services, most companies seek to optimize their use of cash resources. This optimization process generally includes the consideration of any cash discounts offered and/or the scheduling of disbursements.

FINANCIAL ACCOUNTING SYSTEMS

Feature	Small Systems	Large Systems
Database		
Account master data	Yes	Yes
Historical data	1 year	Many years
Budget data	1 budget	Many budgets
Nonmonetary data	No	Yes
Multiple balances (e.g., weekly, monthly)	No	Yes
Report specifications	Yes	Yes
Account relationships	No	Yes
Foreign currency translation	No	Yes
Chart of accounts		
Size	8–12 digits	15–30 digits
User designated fields	Maybe	Yes
Flexible account relationships	No	Yes
Data entry, update, and inquiry		
On-line data entry	Yes	Yes
Recurring entries	Yes	Yes
Automatic reversing entries	No	Yes
Real-time update	Maybe	Maybe
On-line inquiry	Yes	Yes
Audit trails		
Standard transaction registers	Yes	Yes
Exception reporting	No	Yes
Reporting		
Standard reports	Yes	Yes
Semicustom reports	Yes	Yes
Custom reports	No	Yes
Financial modeling	No	Yes
Budgeting		
Single budget capability	Yes	Yes
Multiple budget capability	No	Yes
Budget creation assistance	No	Yes
Cost allocation		
Simple cost allocation (amount, %)	No	Yes
Complex cost allocation (simultaneous equations)	No	Yes
Cost accounting	No	Yes
Security	Yes	Yes

FIG. 6-12 Feature Comparison of Small and Large General Ledger Systems

The typical accounts payable application includes at least two major files:

1 *Vendor master file.* This file generally contains the following basic elements:
   - Vendor number
   - Vendor name
   - Vendor address
   - Usual terms
   - Contact
   - Year-to-date purchases

2 *Open item (unpaid invoice) file.* This file details each open invoice. An invoice record usually has the following basic components:
   - Vendor number
   - Vendor invoice number
   - Purchase order number
   - Invoice amount
   - Invoice due date
   - Discount amount

Depending on the size and sophistication of the accounts payable system used, additional data elements may be included.

As vendor invoices are received, the amounts are compared manually or automatically to purchase order and receiving information. Items within a certain tolerance are generally input to the accounts payable open item file. With the invoice due date serving as a key, most systems provide some type of open item or aged payables report, on the basis of which, items are selected for payment on the next scheduled disbursement date, which can be manual or automatic.

Prior to the cutting of a check, most systems generate a prepayment listing detailing invoices scheduled to be paid on the next check processing run. The listing allows for a final audit prior to check writing.

Once approved, the system generates disbursement checks, a check register, and a disbursements journal. Paid invoice records are then written to a history file and/or flagged as paid. In addition, summary journal entries are created for manual or automatic posting to the general ledger.

Features

Integration With Purchasing/Receiving. Typically, the accounts payable process begins with the letting of a purchase order. A purchase order form details the order items, quantities, prices, terms, and expected delivery date. This form is mailed to vendors; at the same time, a purchase order record is

FINANCIAL ACCOUNTING SYSTEMS   6-21

created. Although not usually considered a legal obligation for payment, the purchase order record provides an excellent method for auditing subsequent vendor invoices and automating the vouching (matching) process.

As merchandise is received, three additional receiving documents pertinent to the transaction are introduced: (1) the packing slip, (2) the bill of lading, and (3) the receiving report. The packing slip generally shows the items shipped and quantities included. The bill of lading details freight charges, if any. The receiving report is an internal document noting any inconsistencies between ordered and received quantities and/or damaged goods. The combination of the three documents can be input to create a receiving record.

As vendor invoices are received, more sophisticated systems may only require the entry of the invoice number, due date, vendor number, purchase order number, and total invoice amount. The system can then compare the invoice total dollar amount to that of the original purchase order. Those items within a predefined tolerance amount (e.g., $5), and also in order with respect to receiving, can automatically be written to the open item (pending invoice) file. Such a practice greatly reduces manual intervention. Items not meeting this test should be reported on an exception report and followed up by personnel in accounts payable.

Integrating purchasing/receiving is highly desirable in a large-fund accounting installation. Generally, the letting of a purchase order requires recording an encumbrance of fund balance. As a fund accounting installation may have many funds, automation of this recording function can greatly reduce manual bookkeeping and improve available fund balance reporting capabilities. However, not all systems contain fund accounting capabilities.

Check Reconciliation. During the check processing cycle, disbursement checks and remittances are generated for the items selected for payment. The typical system prepares a check register containing manual checks entered since the last check run and checks produced during the current cycle. These checks are maintained in an outstanding-check file for subsequent reconciliation.

Depending on the services provided by the disbursement bank, input of cleared checks can be provided on tape or else must be input manually. This cleared file is then compared to the outstanding-check file to relieve cleared, cancelled, or voided checks. If the reconciliation process is to be provided by the user's bank, many systems can generate a tape to be forwarded to the bank for processing.

Reporting. The reporting features of the accounts payable system are perhaps the most important ones to consider in the selection process. Generally, reporting falls into two major categories: current and historical. Current reporting includes such reports as:

Standard Features/Reports	Small Systems	Large Systems
Batch control balancing	X	X
Ability to accept manual checks	X	X
Automatic discount and due date calculation		X
Processing of both debit and credit memoranda automatically		X
Automatic selection of invoices to be paid		X
Automatic consolidation of multiple vendor invoices		X
Ability to distribute an invoice to multiple accounts	X	X
Automatic interface to general ledger	X	X
Automatic interface to purchasing/receiving		X
Vendor listings	X	X
Open reports	X	X
Purchases journal	X	X
Check register	X	X
Bank reconciliation		X
History reports (detail)		X

FIG. 6-13 Standard Features and Reports in Small and Large Accounts Payable Systems

- Open invoices by vendor
- Aged payables report
- Bank reconciliation reports
- Purchases journal

The availability of and flexibility in designing these reports are generally in direct proportion to the system's size and cost. Historical reporting most commonly includes purchases made, discounts taken/lost, and a period-to-period comparison of vendor activity.

Figure 6-13 lists some standard features and reports found in most accounts payable systems. It also shows the systems (small or large) that typically have the attributes listed.

ACCOUNTS RECEIVABLE

The purposes of any accounts receivable subsidiary ledger system are to provide detail of the investment in accounts receivable, to track amounts owed by customers, and to facilitate the posting of remittances as well as other adjustments. This information is used to prepare up-to-date customer statements (usually monthly) and collection reports.

There are three types of accounts receivable systems: balance only, balance forward, and open item.

Balance Only System

This type of accounts receivable system is the one encountered most often. Virtually all credit card and department store accounts are of this type. A monthly statement usually shows the amount due and details activity (purchases and payments) only for the current month. Any past due amount usually carries with it a late-payment fee or an interest charge. All payments to this type of account are posted on account as opposed to being applied to specific purchases.

Balance Forward System

The balance forward accounts receivable system is found in industries where customers pay their bills in total each month. The statement is much the same as that for the balance only system, except that aged past due balances are generally shown in addition to current activity. Payments to this type of account are usually posted on account or automatically applied to the oldest outstanding balance. The balance forward system was common in the late 1970s; in the mid-1980s, it has all but been replaced by the open item system.

Open Item System

The open item method of receivables processing is the most complex. In this type of system, the customer statement shows all open invoices, including particular open items. In this system, the customer usually specifies exactly which invoices are being paid. The open item method of accounts receivable processing is the most common in business. Because of the widespread use of the open item system, it is used as the basis for the following discussion.

An accounts receivable system generally consists of two major files: the customer master and the open item master.

   1 *Customer master file.* At a minimum, the customer master file usually contains the following elements:
   - Customer number
   - Customer name
   - Customer address
   - Year-to-date sales

2 *Open item file.* At a minimum, the accounts receivable open item file usually contains the following data for each invoice/payment:
- Customer number
- Invoice number
- Check number (for payments)
- Reference number
- Invoice date (payment date)
- Invoice amount
- Payment amount

In some systems, the invoice file is separate from the payment file.

Typically, an open invoice is posted automatically following billing processing. Using the open item file detail, monthly statements are produced and mailed to customers. As payments are received, they are posted to individual open items. These matched items are then posted to a history file for reporting purposes.

Features

Interface to Billing. Without a direct integration to the billing function, all invoices must be posted manually. This can be time consuming. As a result, virtually all accounts receivable systems are fully integrated with billing. Generally, new invoices are posted to the accounts receivable open item master directly following the regular billing cycle.

Interface to General Ledger. Most accounts receivable systems offer an interface to the general ledger. This interface basically involves the totalling and controlling of the accounts receivable control accounts with the subsidiary accounts. If the system does not directly post to the general ledger, then, at a minimum, most accounts receivable systems provide for journal entries to be posted manually on a periodic basis.

Reporting. Perhaps the most important feature to consider in selecting an accounts receivable system is its reporting capability. The most common accounts receivable report is the aged trial balance, which details all open invoices for all customers and ages them into periods. The most common aging periods are:

- Current
- Over thirty days
- Over sixty days
- Over ninety days

FINANCIAL ACCOUNTING SYSTEMS

Standard Features/Reports	Small Systems	Large Systems
Batch control	X	X
Interface to billing	X	X
Interface to general ledger	X	X
Cash forecasting feasibility		X
Variable aging periods		X
Receivables trend statistics		X
Customer payment history		X

FIG. 6-14 Standard Features and Reports in Small and Large Accounts Receivable Systems

However, the user may find that these standard periods are not applicable to his industry. For this reason, many systems have user defined aging periods. Many users employ the aging report as a collection tool. As a result, it may be useful to have a customer contact and telephone number printed on the aging report.

Cash Flow. Using data from the accounts payable (disbursements) system and accounts receivable (receipts) system, many vendors now offer cash-flow analysis reports. These reports vary widely in sophistication and application, but can be very useful to management in analyzing cash requirements. Usually, the cash-flow system is separate, but many vendors include it as a subsystem of their accounts payable or accounts receivable systems. Many systems allow a user to customize the type and level of detail of the cash-flow reports to his unique requirements.

Figure 6-14 shows the standard features and reports found in most accounts receivable systems. It also indicates the systems (small or large) that typically have these attributes.

PAYROLL

To many businesses, the processing of payroll is the most important accounting function. Accurate and timely payment of earned wages and salaries boosts employee morale, which many business leaders feel is the key to success.

Payroll processing is typically broken down into four major steps.

1 *Input.* In this step, the user inputs all current payroll data. These include hours worked by the employee, pay action data, and master file changes.

2 *Edit/validation.* In this step, the data entered are compared to, edited, and updated to the system's master files. Validation is important for guarding against errors in late payments. Most systems provide a means to correct rejected input easily.

3 *Processing.* The actual payroll is processed in this step. Many systems provide a prepayroll register that details the pay and deductions for each employee prior to actual process.

4 *Output.* The final step in payroll processing is the generation of paychecks, check registers, and journals. At this point, all relevant year-to-date information is updated.

Payroll applications generally consist of two major files: one containing employee data, the other containing tax data.

1 *Employee data.* This file generally contains the following basic elements:
- Employee number
- Employee name and address
- Employee birth date, sex, and hire date
- Tax exemptions claimed (W-4) data
- Voluntary deduction data
- Vacation data
- Current pay and tax data
- Year-to-date pay and tax data

2 *Tax data.* This file contains the necessary federal tax table and FICA and state and local tax-rate data to compute these taxes on a regular basis.

In addition to the two major files, the system maintains an input file for all current data generally used.

Features

Multistate Capabilities. For companies that operate in more than one state, a multistate payroll system is almost essential. Generally, this capability is found only in larger systems.

Labor Distribution. Labor distribution is a key expense consideration of virtually any company. Whether the goal is to assign labor costs to a specific job or merely to a department within the organization, responsibility accounting is the end result. Input to the labor distribution system comes almost uni-

Standard Features/Reports	Small Systems	Large Systems
Multistate payroll computations		X
Benefits administration		X
Direct deposit features		X
Paycheck reconciliation aids		X
Employee timecards	X	X
Payroll register	X	
Paychecks	X	
Integration with general ledger	X	X
Labor distribution	X	X

FIG. 6-15 Standard Features in Small and Large Payroll Systems

versally from the employee timecard, from which labor cost totals by job and/or department are generated.

Personnel Functions. All payroll application vendors market a complementary, closely interrelated personnel system. Many current personnel applications are quite sophisticated, allowing for the storage and reporting of myriad personnel data.

Figure 6-15 depicts the standard features and reports in small and large payroll systems.

FIXED ASSETS

The fixed asset system maintains the data necessary for the accounting department to provide the information used in planning and controlling the capital assets purchased by a business. It assists the user in recording the acquisition, depreciation, and disposition of a fixed asset in conformance with generally accepted accounting principles (or GAAP), the Internal Revenue Code (Code), or other guidelines. The fixed asset system interfaces with the general ledger for the recording and depreciating of fixed assets. The main processing flow in the fixed asset system is depicted in Figure 6-16. This processing flow is comprised of entering and editing fixed asset data.

Features

Asset Control. One of the fixed asset system's primary purposes is to provide a means of controlling information on fixed assets used by a business. Thus, the fixed asset system should maintain detailed data on asset purchases, dispositions, and transfers.

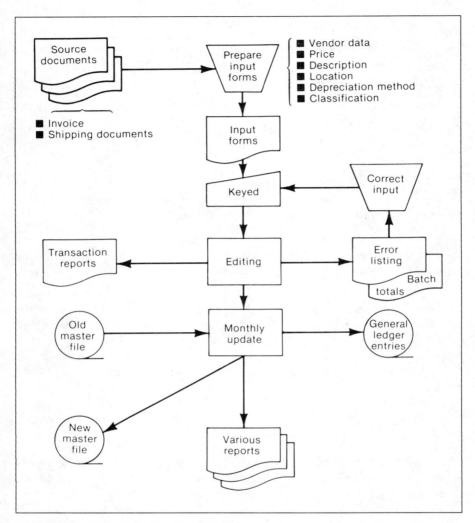

FIG. 6-16 Fixed Assets Processing Flow

FINANCIAL ACCOUNTING SYSTEMS

The data stored on each asset should include the following:

- Asset number
- Description
- Division
- Location
- Building
- Department
- Account
- Acquisition date
- Purchase order number
- Vendor name and model number
- Serial number
- Book depreciation data
- Tax-depreciation data
- Insurance data
- Optional area for user supplied data

The fixed asset system should produce a transaction register of all additions, dispositions, or transfers. In addition, an audit trail report should be produced that includes all before-and-after changes in the base data of any asset.

Input to the fixed asset system should be on line, and edits should be performed before allowing a new asset to be entered into the fixed asset system.

Book Depreciation. One of the primary functions of the fixed asset system is to compute the proper depreciation for a fixed asset. The system should be able to accommodate the various methods for computing depreciation, including:

- Straight line
- Sum of the year's digits
- Declining balance

The fixed asset system should also offer the feature of switching to the most advantageous method of depreciation at the optimum point.

Tax Depreciation. Because assets may be depreciated in one way for book purposes and in another for tax purposes, the fixed asset system must compute the depreciation of an asset based on various tax-depreciation and cost recovery methods, which include:

- All the book methods mentioned
- Accelerated cost recovery (ACR)
- Asset depreciation range (ADR)

The fixed asset system should also create the various tax forms that relate to fixed assets. These forms include the 4562 Tax Depreciation Report, the 3468 Investment Tax Credit Report, the 4255 Investment Tax Credit Recapture Report, and the 4797 Supplemental Gains and Losses Report.

Multiple Records. Because of the complexity of the tax laws and the differences between state and federal tax laws, the fixed asset system must be able to maintain at least three different depreciation calculations and balances for each asset. In addition, if an organization has any special regulatory requirements, additional calculations or records may be required. Most large fixed asset systems accommodate five to seven different records or bases of calculation for each asset, and most small fixed asset systems accommodate two or three different calculations.

Reporting. The fixed asset system should provide several standard reports that include the transaction registers, depreciation summaries, and tax reports. In addition, it should provide the user with a report writer that allows him to create custom reports detailing assets by account, amount, location, or any other feature that has been stored in the fixed asset database.

Other Features. The fixed asset system should be able to project depreciation in future periods. This feature is useful in budgeting or planning. In addition, the system should be able to provide cost replacement data that may be required by the Securities and Exchange Commission.

The user should also seek a vendor for the fixed asset system who can be expected to remain in business for several years. This is important because several features of the system may need modification as the tax code is changed.

The fixed asset system contains information about all of the company's fixed assets. Figure 6-17 lists the features usually available in small and large fixed asset systems. With the exception of the number of records and special features, the main difference between small and large fixed asset systems is the number of assets for which the system can account. That number is determined by the system's design and the storage capacity of the computer on which it operates.

CURRENT DEVELOPMENTS

As noted, many core financial systems were developed as automated versions of the manual systems that they replaced. That is, each application or system was designed and implemented individually. In order to integrate the applications, various interface files were developed. Thus, accounts payable transactions could be entered into the general ledger without having to reenter any data manually. The hardware available when the applications were first developed forced this type of design.

Over the years, hardware capabilities improved dramatically; in addition, major advances in the features offered by the core financial systems were made, aimed at enhancing what the systems could do. The advances, however, were not aimed at changing the concepts that provided the structure for the original core financial systems. Thus, the advanced core financial systems that we see

Feature	Small Systems	Large Systems
Fixed asset data	Minimal	Everything remotely necessary
Book depreciation		
Straight line	Yes	Yes
Sum of the years digits	Yes	Yes
Declining balance	Yes	Yes
Tax depreciation		
Accelerated cost recovery	Yes	Yes
Asset depreciation range	No	Yes
Multiple sets of books	2 or 3	4–6
Reporting		
Flexible report writer	Maybe	Yes
Other features		
Depreciation projection	Maybe	Yes

FIG. 6-17 Feature Comparison of Small and Large Fixed Asset Systems

are still automated versions of the manual systems they replaced. This occurred primarily because the marketplace asked for applications or systems that could be purchased individually. For example, a company purchases an accounts payable system. Two years later, it decides that it needs a general ledger system. At this point, the company has two choices: either buy a general ledger from the original vendor or buy a general ledger from another vendor and create an interface program to interface the general ledger and the accounts payable systems. Because many companies purchased systems in this fashion, software vendors responded by developing systems that could operate independently of each other. Even though the systems might have used advanced database concepts in their operation, each system had to have its own database. The result of this was a series of advanced systems with an incredible amount of data redundancy that continued to automate the manual systems they replaced.

Software vendors have begun to reevaluate the premises underlying core financial systems, and customers have begun to request accounting systems offering on-line and real-time transaction recording. The combination of these two trends has resulted in the design of accounting systems based on large databases and not on a series of independent applications or systems. The type of system whose design is based on these concepts is truly borderless and makes maximal use of the computer system's capabilities. It represents a real change in the concepts underlying core financial systems. These systems will soon be available.

CHAPTER 7

Role and Impact of Microcomputers

Jack F. Duston

Introduction 2	Application Software 11
Effect of Microcomputers on Small	Spreadsheet Programs 11
Businesses 2	Database Management Programs ... 11
Effect of Microcomputers on	Integrated Programs 12
Corporations 2	Software Favorites 12
	Accounting Packages; Getting Started .. 13
Microcomputer Hardware 3	Selected Key Features 14
Microprocessor 4	
Disk Storage 5	**Microcomputers and FISs** 15
Keyboards 5	Basic Microcomputer FISs 15
Monitors 6	Local Area Networks 16
Printers 6	Microcomputer/Mainframe FISs 17
Dot Matrix 7	
Near Letter Quality 7	**Security Management** 19
Letter Quality 8	Physical Security 19
Laser 8	Software Security 20
Boards 8	
	Training 21
Microcomputer Software 9	
Systems Software 10	

Fig. 7-1 The Microcomputer Configuration 4
Fig. 7-2 Type Styles of Printers 7
Fig. 7-3 Basic Logic Boards 9
Fig. 7-4 Top Twenty Independent Microcomputer Software Suppliers 10
Fig. 7-5 A Typical LAN Business Installation 16
Fig. 7-6 Diagram of EIS 18
Fig. 7-7 The Three-Generation Backup System 20

INTRODUCTION

The growth of personal computers (PCs) or microcomputers continues at a rate somewhat unprecedented in the history of computers. More important, their use is spreading rapidly throughout corporate offices. Initially, the growth within corporate offices was confined to the use of the microcomputers on an individual basis for specific purposes. Managers and staff who were self-motivated and who felt that the economics of microcomputers justified their use in their areas of responsibility were prolific. This was somewhat unplanned, particularly with respect to the total use of computers within the organization. These systems were initially designed for personal use; hence, the term "personal computer." However, the most rapid growth in microcomputers has been, and is forecasted to be, in the business environment.

A common question is, What is the difference between personal computers and microcomputers? Most would answer that none exists. The term "personal computer" was first used in anticipation of its use by individuals in the home. With the entrance into the microcomputer field of IBM, who named its system the IBM Personal Computer (IBM PC), the term will probably remain but will mostly be associated with IBM and IBM PC compatibles. The name "microcomputer" is based more on the technological makeup of the system and is used more when referring to its capabilities. For example, the words "microcommunications," "micro language," and "micro networks" are common in the marketplace. "Microcomputer" is the label generally being embraced and used more frequently by non-IBM suppliers and by those discussing more sophisticated systems.

Small businesses and large corporations at the departmental level first jumped on the microcomputer bandwagon when managers felt that they could finally computerize an application or business area without lengthy planning, waiting, and extensive cost justification. Of course, this initial use rapidly led to greater knowledge and use of the microcomputer. The resulting effects on small businesses and large corporations are discussed in the following sections.

Effect of Microcomputers on Small Businesses

As the small businessperson has become more comfortable with the use of computers because of their lower costs, increasing numbers of packaged programs, and comparative ease of operation, there have been attempts to do more with microcomputers than use them for only a few applications. In fact, many small businesses attempt as much with their microcomputers as they previously did with minicomputers. This has increased demand for additional storage, faster printers, and multiterminal capability.

Effect of Microcomputers on Corporations

Once microcomputers obtained a foothold within the corporate structure, the demand by other management groups, staff, and departments began. This created other needs within the corporate framework, such as for their use in corporatewide policy and planning. Demand was also generated for more sophisticated software and the ability of microcomputers to communicate with common databases.

These scenarios have created a need for knowledge and assistance in many areas related to microcomputers, such as:

- Understanding hardware and its capabilites
- Up-to-date knowledge of everything happening in the microcomputer software and production areas
- Planning for, and management of, microcomputers
- Interfacing microcomputers with mainframes and data processing departments
- Interfacing microcomputers with word processing and other office automation activities
- Networking and communicating with and between microcomputers
- Communicating with mainframes
- Understanding the role of microcomputers for executive information systems (or EISs) and in supporting FISs
- Instituting data security in the microcomputer environment
- Keeping up with the most up-to-date models and applications

MICROCOMPUTER HARDWARE

"Hardware" is usually easy to define, describe, and understand. In addition, it is usually easy to advertise. In fact, the marketing of microcomputer hardware led the way in the rapidly expanding microcomputer world. However, defining the use of microcomputers and selecting the software to do the job are more important than actually selecting the hardware equipment. Even in the earliest planning stages, knowledge of hardware components—that is, of the various equipment parts that make up a system—is still necessary. Many companies have entered the microcomputer hardware business. Some only produce or specialize in certain components such as printers, disk files, and internal circuit boards that accomplish specific tasks. These specialized companies are growing fast but primarily supply to microcomputer manufacturers (e.g., IBM) and not directly to the general public or business community. Most microcomputers are identified by their basic hardware (microprocessor, keyboard, and CRT) manufacturer (see Figure 7-1). Some of the top microcomputer companies, measured by revenue, are IBM, Apple Computer, Commodore, and Tandy Corp.[1] There

---

[1] "The Datamation 100," *Datamation* (June 1984); *PC World, Annual Hardware Review*, special ed. (1984).

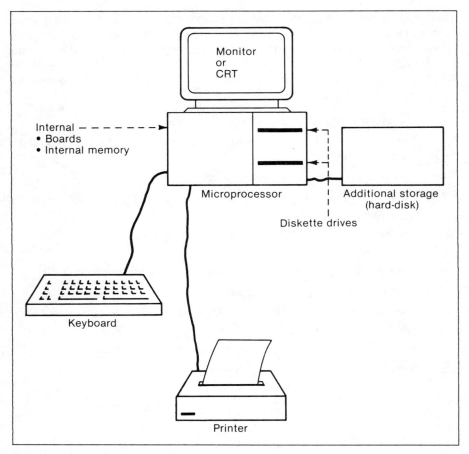

FIG. 7-1 The Microcomputer Configuration

are, of course, many others; any compilation of companies is subject to possible major change in the rapidly growing world of microcomputers. Several of the other smaller companies will probably grow and continue to be a force in the industry; some may not succeed at all or will be acquired by larger companies.

Microprocessor

The processor is the microcomputer's central unit and contains its memory and logic circuitry. The original PCs (sometimes called home computers) were fairly unsophisticated processors and were developed and sold for home use for games, personal budgets, and other comparatively simple applications. The original microprocessors, or internal memory, were made up of logic that processed data in 8-bit bytes. A byte is comparable to one character. These processors moved data around 8 bits at a time. Because of the very rapid growth of microcomputers during 1982 and 1983, most of the systems are 16-bit bytes, meaning that more data can be processed at one time. This does two things for a system:

1 It greatly increases the internal processing speed; and

2 It allows more data to be handled internally at one time.

IBM PCs, Apples, Commodores, and most other models are 16-bit systems. Software developed for a 16-bit system generally cannot run on an 8-bit or 32-bit system. Alpha Micro, originally one of the more powerful microcomputers, and Hewlett Packard's new microcomputers are 32-bit systems. "Power," in this context, is defined as the ability to process internally more data at a faster rate.

It is essential to stress the importance of first matching software to the job needs, then matching the selected software to the microprocessor and the processing speed needs. Typically, microprocessors are offered in 64K (64,000), 128K, 256K, and 516K bytes of internal memory. The IBM definition of a "byte," which is 8 bits to a "word," can be 1, 2, or 4 bytes. Whether the words in the system have 16 bits or 32 bits, it is a significant factor contributing to the software's efficiency.

Disk Storage

A typical system of internal 256K (256,000 bytes) represents the limit of the amount of data that can be handled internally at any one time. However, the system usually requires additional memory space to store operating systems software (discussed in a following section), the application software, and the data being processed. This generally means that extra storage is needed. With regard to microcomputers, this is typically accomplished by using diskettes, which provide data storage outside the main memory. Systems can have one diskette drive (where a diskette is inserted and processed) or use up to four or possibly more. The number of drives is determined by data storage needs. Many systems, instead of adding more diskette drives, offer either an internal fixed disk that is nonremovable and faster with more capacity or external hard disks (separate box), also with greater capacity.

Keyboards

Keyboards are the most common component used to communicate with the system. Most data are entered into the system through the keyboard. Unfortunately, the industry has not yet developed a true standard keyboard, except for the alphabetic keys that are arranged like typewriter keys. Most of the remaining keys are referred to as "function" keys, performing functions peculiar to that microcomputer system. Although the location and exact function of keys from one system to another are not standardized, there is usually enough similarity for a trained person on any one system to have little difficulty operating another system.

Keyboards come with the microprocessor and are used to operate the system. Usually, instructions on the display unit show the user what keys to depress to perform a particular function.

Monitors

As the term indicates, a monitor tells the operator what the system wants or is doing and is controlled by the software being used. Typical functions of the monitor are:

- Showing menus or lists of applications and functions the system can perform. The user makes a selection by using the keyboard or possibly by touching the screen or moving a "mouse."
- Questioning or asking for data that the user must complete or enter.
- Informing the operator of errors or providing other instructions, such as, "turn on the printer."
- Instructing the operator how to use the system, through tutorials, which are available in many systems.
- Displaying results of processing for review. Changes can be made to the data displayed. Graphs can be shown. Generally, all data are displayed on a screen for review prior to printing.

Systems almost always have a standard monitor (also referred to as CRT, VDT, or screen) as part of the system, but few are built in. Therefore, many systems are purchased with other manufacturers' monitors (to obtain another size, a color screen, or possibly a monitor that is already available or owned).

Printers

When data have been processed and results or analyses reviewed, it is often desirable to have these results printed on paper for later use. Most systems used for business purposes include one or more printers.

Printers are the one component where the widest choices are available and where, most often, a buyer will purchase a model other than one by the manufacturer of the microprocessor and the other components being used.

Printers can be classified into four categories (see Figure 7-2):[2]

---

[2] *Printers Buyers Guide, A Supplement to PC Week* (May 22, 1984).

ROLE AND IMPACT OF MICROCOMPUTERS

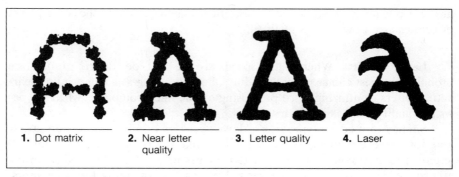

1. Dot matrix   2. Near letter quality   3. Letter quality   4. Laser

FIG. 7-2 Type Styles of Printers

1 Dot matrix
2 Near letter quality
3 Letter quality
4 Laser

Price, speed, quality, and use are considered in selecting a printer. The vendor or store can assist the purchaser greatly, but it is best to have a general knowledge of the different types of printers and the data needed for decisions prior to shopping.

Dot Matrix. The original printers supplied with microcomputers, and probably still the biggest sellers because of their price, are dot matrix types, from which there are dozens of models to choose.

All dot matrix printers form characters by striking a ribbon, much as a typewriter does. Unlike a typewriter, the dot matrix printer printhead is connected to an array of wires that, when struck together, create a collection of dots that form each letter.

A majority of these printers sell for less than $1,000, which accounts for their popularity among those whose needs are met by the dot matrix. They come in a variety of speeds (usually quoted in characters per second (cps)) and several carriage widths. Speed and width are two of the variables to be carefully considered in the specific application prior to making a purchase. Many buyers sacrifice speed for lower price only to find that printing out a spreadsheet, for example, can be a very slow process.

Near Letter Quality. These printers are also dot matrix, but various manufacturers have developed different techniques to improve quality and maintain speed. A great number of printers with varying speeds and features are available. Prices vary from under $1,000 to more than $4,000. A cost effectiveness exercise must be developed for specific needs to determine the correct level of printer at a price that is justified.

Letter Quality. When higher speeds are the goal, dot matrix printers are probably the best choice. There are times, however, such as when printing marketing letters or utilizing word processing on the microcomputer, when a typewriter quality print is necessary.

Similar to modern typewriters, daisy wheel or thimble printers are available for microcomputers. These processes strike the ribbon with fully formed letters. The most common type of letter quality printers are daisy wheel printers, where the character set is arranged on a wheel of thinly formed sectors, each with a fully formed character at its end.

Thimble printers use an interchangeable head similar to that used on IBM Selectric typewriters. This, of course, provides the user with several font types and styles. Usually, this type of printer only prints between 20 and 80 cps.

Laser. The laser is now readily available, offering nonimpact printing, which means "noiseless." There are other nonimpact printers, such as thermal and ink jet. However, recent technical innovations have reduced the cost and size of laser printers, making them the leader in nonimpact printers.

A laser printer works much like a copying machine. Resolution is very high and can print presentation quality documents and overheads. The cost of laser printers still varies greatly—as low as $2,000 and as high as $14,000.

Boards

The memory and logic of microprocessors are contained on circuit boards or boards (see Figure 7-3). The initial system comes with basic logic boards to handle the keyboard, monitor, and generally a diskette drive. As additional memory is desired, certain printers are added for special functions, such as clock calendar capability or a game adapter. Then, new circuit boards, or "cards," must be added internally to the system. Generally, specific boards are available and sold for specific use and expansion of the microcomputer. There are only so many slots available for boards inside a microcomputer's processing unit. To maximize the use of these slots, manufacturers are also marketing multifunction boards.

Some examples of board functions are:

- *Memory expansion* — enabling runs of larger spreadsheets and creating larger memory databases.
- *Parallel port* — for operating most printers.
- *Serial port* — for communications adapters (modems), plotters, and letter quality printers.

FIG. 7-3 Basic Logic Boards

MICROCOMPUTER SOFTWARE

Software is the program or the set of instructions that instructs the computer on what to do. Without software, a computer is little more than an inoperative futuristic looking box. Microcomputers allow the processing of larger amounts of data more economically than ever before, but not without the "soul" of the machine, which is software. It is estimated that there could now be up to 50,000 different programs available for microcomputers with at least 1,000 companies developing programs.[3] Although the major companies are contributing many programs, some of the most successful programs have come from small companies like Lotus (1-2-3) and Ashton-Tate (dBase II), as well as from companies such as Microsoft, Peachtree, CYMA, Micropro, and Digital Research. However, 80 percent of the revenue generated in 1983 by software product and service companies was done by forty companies. This represents companies supplying software to all computer systems, not just to microcomputers. There are only twenty-two microcomputer software companies ranked in the Top 200, according to *ICP Business Software Review*. Indications are that microcomputer software companies will continue to penetrate the Top 200 because of the growth of microcomputers, the tendency toward mergers, and the probable dominance of fewer companies. Some of the significant software distributions, as measured by their 1983 revenue, are illustrated in Figure 7-4.[4]

---

[3] "Computer Software–The Magic Inside the Machine," *Time* (Apr. 16, 1984).

[4] "The Top 22 Software Products for 1983," *ICP Business Software Review* (special issue (1984)).

Rank	Company	Total Microcomputer Software Revenue (in millions of dollars)
1	Softsel	$88
2	Lotus Development Corporation	53
3	Alpha Microsystems	52
4	Microsoft Corporation	50
5	MicroPro International Corporation	45
6	VisiCorp (NOW)	40
7	Digital Research, Inc.	38
8	Softeam, Inc.	27
9	Lifeboat Associates	22
10	Micro D, Inc.	22
11	Ashton-Tate	18
12	Broderbund Software	13
13	Sierra On-Line Inc.	13
14	Software Arts Inc.	12
15	Sorcim Corporation	12
16	Holland Automation	10
17	Software Publishing Corporation	10
18	Perfect Software Inc.	10
19	Multimate International Corporation	10
20	Software Knowledge Unlimited	10

FIG. 7-4 Top Twenty Independent Microcomputer Software Suppliers

When discussing software, it is best to distinguish the two general categories: (1) systems software and (2) application software.

Systems Software

Systems software consists of programs that control the parts of a computer (including the screen, the central processing unit, the disk drives, the printer) and make the parts work together. Systems software usually comes with the microcomputer under such obscure brand names as CP/M, MS-DOS, and UNIX. The most popular, Digital Research's CP/M, was used by Apple and most early microcomputers. Microsoft developed MS-DOS for the IBM PC. AT&T and others are now promoting UNIX as the most advanced systems software. To a great majority of users, however, the application software and the microcomputer selected dictate the systems software to be used. Application software is written to work through specific systems software, although some application software is available to operate under several types of systems software.

Application Software

The user interfaces most directly with application software or programs. It is used to perform specific jobs, such as those involving general ledger, payroll, and accounts payable. Not only does application software support common business functions, but more specific programs are available for use in manufacturing, construction, legal, banking, distribution, and almost any other type of industry. The availability of these programs is mostly through more than 7,000 stores in the United States that sell application software. As an example, Softsel, a large distributor to retail stores, has over 3,000 products in its catalog.

Falling into the application software category are products that are probably more accurately described as "user support systems." These are more generalized systems that provide the user with the framework for tailoring a program to his specific needs. The more successful examples are discussed in the following sections.

Spreadsheet Programs. Spreadsheet programs, Lotus 1-2-3, VisiCalc, and SuperCalc, let the user enter data into specific boxes (cells) of a matrix and then to develop formulas to process against these data. Once data have been entered and formulas defined, the microcomputer performs all the tedious mathematics. By changing the data in any one cell, the user can analyze the effect on other cells. Examples of the uses of spreadsheets include personal budgets, business plans, cash-flow forecasting, and sales forecasting. In effect, the user plays "what-if" games. If a matrix contains a personal budget, the user may change a cell representing monthly house payments by asking, "What if I refinance my home and my payments are X per month?" The computer then immediately recalculates the total monthly budget.

One reason for the electronic spreadsheet's popularity is that this type of program presents and works with data in a format similar to what most managers encounter in their daily work. The true success of the spreadsheet program is its ability to project and evaluate alternatives.

Although programs vary, most have common commands that allow the user to process, such as "format," "insert," "load," "file," "retrieve," "move," "print," and "save."

Database Management Programs. Like dBase II, database management programs allow the user to tailor a program to fit his needs where the requirement is not only to process information but to retain data and results, and to easily retrieve these data, update files, and further process. "Database" may be defined as any organized collection of information.

Integrated Programs.[5] Most spreadsheet programs have now been updated to provide database management capability. A newer product, Symphony, introduced by Lotus, includes five of the functions required by business computer users: spreadsheet, word processing, data management, business graphics, and data communications. These packages are sometimes referred to as integrated products. Of course, the more a program does, the more complex it becomes to learn how to use. It is probably better to start with more specific programs; however, it is inevitable that once a person or business begins using the powers of the microcomputer, he will eventually want to do more with it. Programs such as Symphony or Framework are referred to as integrated packages.[6]

Another kind of integration can best be illustrated by accounting software. In this other context, "integration" means that the various accounting applications (e.g., general ledger, accounts receivable, accounts payable, payroll) are tied in with each other. An entry into one automatically updates applications to the others.

Yet another kind of integration approach is software that enables the user to integrate different (i.e., not programmed together) applications from many software vendors. Examples of such software are Microsoft Windows, Visi On, and Des Q. An advantage of this type of integration program is that applications may be added as needed, and the user can conveniently move from one application to the next, as well as transfer data among applications.

On the surface, integration appears to be a technique that provides more efficient production. However, it is not necessarily appropriate to every situation. A potential user must look at the features, the data transfer difficulty, and, of course, the cost.

Software Favorites

With all the software now in the marketplace, various surveys and study results indicate that the most popular software during 1983 and early 1984 were these:[7]

1. *Word processing.* WordStar from MicroPro is far out in front, followed by Applewriter II from Apple and Multimate.

2. *Database management products.* The oldest, dBase II from Ashton-Tate, leads the way. Several PFS products—PFS: File and PFS: Report from Software Publishing Company—are also favorites.

---

[5] "Understanding Integrated Software," *PC World* (Oct. 1984).
[6] "Symphony," *PC World* (July 1984).
[7] "Favorite Personal Computer Software," *ICP Business Software Review* (Aug./Sept. 1984).

ROLE AND IMPACT OF MICROCOMPUTERS 7-13

3 *Financial package.* A category defined by ICP *Business Software Review* consists of the Calcs—the leader being VisiCalc. Others are Multiplan and SuperCalc.

4 *General business packages.* Lotus 1-2-3 dominates this category.

However, the rapidity of change in software popularity must be recognized.

Accounting Packages; Getting Started

Selecting the hardware and software for automating an accounting system is generally only the tip of the iceberg. The total cost of the new system far exceeds the tangible costs of hardware and software. During the rapid growth of microcomputer installations, it has become evident that smaller systems are not much different from larger systems with regard to the need for planning, consulting, implementation assistance, training, and conversion. Planning effort more than pays for itself if the installation is done well. User requirements may be such that there is a need for a hard disk, extra memory, program modification, or consulting guidance, all of which costs may be unanticipated. Installation should proceed only where the developers are confident that the correct requirements have been determined and that the required resources can be committed.

Generally, most microcomputer installations cost more than anticipated. However, significant savings are usually identifiable and can be quantified just as is done in larger installations where the capabilities of the system are tremendous.

Probably the key to a successful installation is getting the proper assistance. There are many new microcomputer sales and systems people who are weak in accounting and many accountants who have become very interested in microcomputers but are inexperienced in the total installation requirements or are familiar only with limited packages or systems. The best guideline for locating a consultant is to seek an individual with an accounting background combined with an occupation that demands that the person keep up with the most current information on the available packages. Actual implementation experience is also a must.

Searching for the proper assistance takes time, but the resulting improved system makes it worthwhile. Some areas to investigate might include:

- *A computer retail store.* Not all dealers have been able to obtain employees with the desirable accounting knowledge or a business background.

- *An accountant.* Again, precautions apply. Accountants vary in their understanding and depth of knowledge of computers. Their primary job is accounting. It is important to know how much time they have been able to devote to computers.

- *Computer vendors.* Vendors are appropriate if one can be located with accounting expertise in the type of business in which the system is to be used. Questions pertaining to what individual would be providing assistance, his implementation efforts, and amount of experience are appropriate.
- *Computer systems consultants.* This is a good approach if the consultant specializes in guiding business through conversion and is not primarily a computer programmer. Some consultants specialize in selection and implementation.

Selected Key Features

It is important for the buyer to spend some time thinking about his needs and then comparing some of these needs to various packages. He is then in a much better position to work with a consultant or vendor. Emphasis should not be on the bells and whistles of a software package but on the features that meet basic needs. Key features of general accounting software packages might be the following:

- *Accounts receivable or accounts payable*
  - Supports open-item and balance-forward billing of customers/clients.
  - Generates finance charges and suppresses charges for preferred customers.
  - Sets credit limits and discount rates for customers, if needed.
  - Provides for automatic posting of recurring charges.
  - Maintains historical information on each customer.
  - Supports zip code sorting and label printing and/or an interface to a mailing list program.
- *Payroll*
  - Calculates gross pay for all pay schedules.
  - Supports piecework and incentive pay, if needed.
  - Allows for immediate payoff against accumulated hours.
  - Handles local, state, and federal reporting requirements.
  - Permits multiple deductions and variations in type of deduction.
  - Assigns payroll expenses to general ledger accounts.
  - Assigns payroll expenses to cost centers.
- *Inventory*
  - Supports various methods of inventory costing.
  - Maintains multiple pricing and discount levels.
  - Maintains open orders and back orders.

- Allows user defined reorder points and minimum inventory levels.
- Generates reorder reports and purchase orders.
- Permits interfacing with accounts receivable and accounts payable programs.
- *General ledger*
  - Reports on activity for various cost centers.
  - Generates budgets and compares them to actual costs.
  - Compares performance among several accounting periods.
  - Permits customized income statements and balance sheets.
  - Accepts input of new period entries before closing old period entries.
  - Provides for automatic input of recurring entries.
- *Other features*
  - Maintains all data through common or connected database structure.
  - Supplies program source code and permits customization of program and/or database manager.
  - Provides a clear and consistent method of data entry and function selection.
  - Allows spooling reports.
  - Offers a comprehensive data backup and recover facility.
  - Includes a data security (password) facility.
  - Contains flexible reporting and query facility.

MICROCOMPUTERS AND FISs

There are many ways to define an FIS, and any system that provides financial management information can be truthfully called an FIS (see Chapter 1). The FIS can thus best be defined and classified by its size and approach. Today, FISs almost always include the use of microcomputers. The following three descriptions represent different configurations and uses of microcomputers in supporting an FIS.

Basic Microcomputer FISs

The previously defined stand-alone microcomputer with integrated software, the ability to inquire, and with good financial reports is an FIS. Systems such as Alpha Micro, Altos, the AT&T microcomputers, and the IBM-AT that provide for multiple terminals allow access to the FIS by operating management. An FIS that allows the user to inquire into areas such as budgets, accounts receivable status, and inventory status utilizing microcomputers is truly a

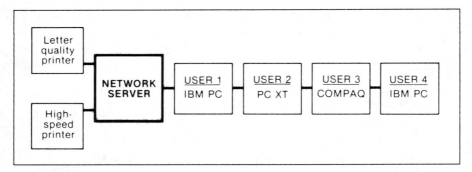

FIG. 7-5 A Typical LAN Business Installation

microcomputer FIS. A good microcomputer FIS also includes effective periodic financial management summary reports. These reports become more useful where microcomputer graphics capability is used to a great extent. Imagine how efficient management could be if it received the following:

- Current and year-to-date budget graphs by department and/or product
- Cash-flow graphs
- Total accounts receivable status graphs
- Various statistical graphs (e.g., units shipped, items changed, backlog)
- Profit and loss by period, illustrating trend

Local Area Networks

Where a company or department gets to the point of possessing four or more stand-alone PCs that exchange diskettes to share data and programs, it is probably time to consider a local area network (LAN).[8] In the case of an accounting system, a single master copy of accounting files can be maintained, but must be accessible to all department microcomputers, thereby avoiding many redundancy problems. An LAN also provides the capability of sharing printers.

An LAN consists of a master microcomputer that serves the other microcomputers and contains the appropriate LAN board, software, and files (usually a hard disk) to serve the other microcomputers. Figure 7-5 illustrates a typical LAN.

The LAN performs the following:

- Dynamically links to volumes on the network server hard disk.
- Prints documents on either of two printers.

---

[8] "Local Area Networks for Micros," *Datamation* (Aug. 1, 1984).

- Sends mail to other users or picks up the user's mail from the network server.
- Telephones in for program files from home.
- Creates and destroys new user names.
- Creates and destroys volumes on the server hard disk if the user is the owner.

Some of the original leaders in providing LAN products are Corvus, Nestar, 3COM, Orchid Technology, Sytek, Novell, and Ungerman-Bass. Other microcomputer manufacturers have been announcing LAN capabilities rapidly. The use of an LAN should be considered if:

- Security and accessibility may be a problem.
- The budget is small and a comparatively easy installation is desired.
- Problems exist keeping data and programs synchronized.
- Multiple files must be updated simultaneously.
- Several different types of printers are to be shared.

Use of an LAN does entail extra costs and installation effort. The master server must contain extra storage, LAN interface boards, and extra cabling. This extra equipment and software could be at least $15,000 over the cost of an average PC. In addition, extra effort in physical planning, cabling, program conversion, and training must be planned for. Nevertheless, if properly installed, an accounting LAN can contribute greatly to the efficiency of the departments it serves.

Microcomputer/Mainframe FISs

When FISs are discussed, most individuals assume the use of mainframes accessed by terminals. The arrival of PCs into an accounting environment creates new situations:

- PCs can act as terminals.
- These same microcomputers can collect and process data of their own outside the mainframe.
- New microcomputer professionals exist outside the structured data processing department.[9]

All of this has prodded data processing professionals and management to accept the PC and to develop software and management techniques to deal

---

[9] "Links Between Micros and Mainframes," *ICP Administration and Accounting Software* (Autumn 1984).

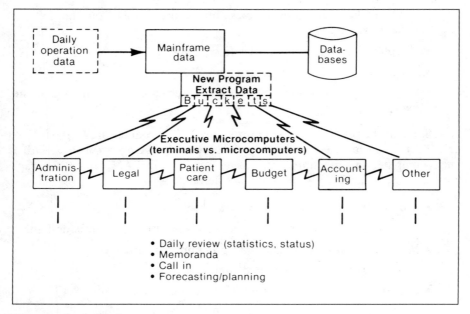

FIG. 7-6 Diagram of EIS

with it. Many sophisticated software products that link microcomputers to mainframes are now on the market. In general, these are fairly sophisticated programs, and the software vendors have taken many different approaches. Selecting "linkage" systems and software is definitely a job for the professional.

The exposure of financial executives to the PC has brought with it the desire to obtain current data in which to review, graph, and forecast. This requires integration of the PC into the FIS so that controlled data can be available to the microcomputer and to the executive.

Figure 7-6 illustrates a typical EIS using the following hypothetical situation: The administrator, accounting director, and budget manager each desires to work with data on his own microcomputer. It is absolutely necessary that the administrator, who might be creating a financial graph, work with the same data as the controller.

To minimize or prevent use of inconsistent information, the data processing system must provide for control of and access to the mainframe data. Each of the following would be a controlled approach:

- Develop data information requirements of each executive. Some will require detail data and others, summary information. Executives operate with different styles and manage with different types of information with regard to both format and context.

- Plan and develop a mainframe program that periodically updates a "data bucket" file for each microcomputer user.
- Modify the microcomputer screens to remind the user about the currency of his data and that new data are available in the bucket file.
- Make the microcomputer user responsible for downloading current data from the mainframe bucket file.

SECURITY MANAGEMENT

Many problems may arise that can endanger the data and the system. Those problems can be caused by carelessness, theft, unauthorized access to sensitive data, fire, accidental destruction of data, as well as many more potentially damaging exposures. The microcomputer is usually much more accessible (i.e., not located in a "dedicated" room), used by several people, and much of the data are stored on external media (diskettes). In short, microcomputers are usually found in the day-to-day business environment and are therefore exposed to all of the elements of an ordinary document, except that they are more visible and accessible.

Two categories of security should be addressed by the microcomputer user who processes financial information—physical security and software security.

Physical Security

Microcomputers are just as susceptible to physical danger as mainframes, and usually are more exposed. Many of the operating rules should be the same for both, such as the following:

- Install shelves for diskettes to prevent their being used as coasters or exposed to magnetic media.
- Provide the computer with a cover or storage cabinet.
- Post simple operating rules—for example: "Coffee and food do not mix with microcomputers." "Do not write on diskette labels with hard ball-point pen." "No smoking."
- Implement special antitheft arrangements (e.g., special locks for systems).
- Provide for static electricity and power surges, just as for other systems.

Probably the best all-around solution for physical security is initially to provide a special desk for the microcomputer. A proper desk contains space for all components and keeps it away from the dangers of daily activity, and it may

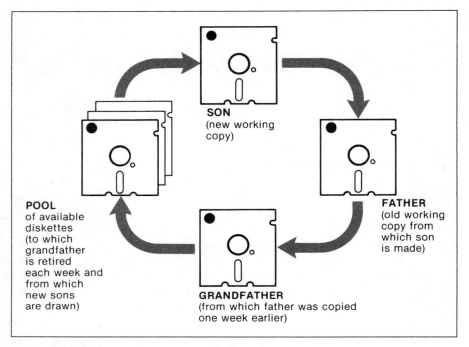

FIG. 7-7 The Three-Generation Backup System

have certain lockable shelves or security locks. In addition, it encourages a sense of organization in the operation of the system, and that, many times, can be the best security.

Software Security

When offering advice on software security, factors such as access problems, backup, communications security, and audit considerations are prominent. How do we protect data? For many years, the best insurance against the risk of losing confidential data and protecting databases has been to provide a backup copy in every instance. A standard policy is to maintain three copies of all computer information (see Figure 7-7).

Software systems are also available for protecting sensitive data from "snooping." The biggest problems with these programs are economic, in that most microcomputers are purchased to run only a limited number of programs at the same time and memory space may not be available. However, if a company needs to enhance data security beyond the normal "password" stage, it should consider some of the presently available programs such as:

CIPHER, from Software Development Corp.

SECRETS, from Balis Computing, Inc.
DATASAFE, from Trigram Systems

These systems are reasonably priced, so the principal cost results from the possible additional memory required. These programs use some form of data encryption, and many times are referred to as encryption programs. For more detailed information on security, see Chapter 22.

TRAINING

A general understanding and a knowledge of microcomputers are certainly desirable. However, many times a major problem is learning to use them or finding the time to learn.

Usually, everything initially done on a microcomputer takes much longer than anticipated. For most busy people, computer classes are the most efficient and the best bet. They are available through many sources: at the computer dealer; at a local junior college; at national training companies; and at many CPA firms. In addition, many self-teaching programs and videotapes can be purchased.

There are many reasons to consider a classroom approach as opposed to a self-study course.[10] A two-day class, for example, offers the following advantages:

- Provides a concentrated, uninterrupted environment.
- Enables questions to be more quickly explained than reading or self-teaching.
- Requires fewer man-hours than self-teaching over a period of time.
- May be tailored to specific needs and to a specific industry.

There are many kinds of classes: the one-day executive introduction, two-day Lotus or dBase classes, basic programming, and many others. On average, the cost runs between $200 to $300 per day for class instruction. This includes materials, use of a well-equipped classroom, and, in some cases, a class tailored to specific company needs if that has been arranged. Once a concentrated course of instruction has been followed, the many computer tutorials become more valuable and much easier to understand. Tutorials do exist on many specific programs and packages as well.

When selecting a class, there are certain questions to ask to make sure that the class will meet specific needs:

- Have previous students found the class worthwhile?

---

[10] "PC Training—Which Way to Go?" *PC World* (Sept. 1984).

- How many students are in the class? (Eight to sixteen is ideal, with two instructors.)
- May the student keep the reference material?
- What type of organization supports the course?
- Are the instructors familiar with student objectives and needs?

For the foreseeable future, microcomputers will probably be part of a modern or useful FIS. For smaller organizations, they may constitute the sole hardware. Software necessary for all financial applications is readily available. Integrated software systems combined with the appropriate equipment make an effective microcomputer-based FIS system available.

It is important to remember that basic requirements such as understanding, planning, learning, operating, and security are the same as for a mainframe system, although most certainly not to the same degree. There will undoubtedly be continuing rapid advances in the microcomputer world regarding equipment, software, and support of organizations' needs with respect to FISs. It is still the obligation of management to be aware of these rapid changes. It must plan or use materials, consultants, or classes to the extent that it remains aware and up-to-date on developments in the field of microcomputers. Today, microcomputers are making FISs more useful to many more financial managers than ever before. This portends well for the future.

CHAPTER 8

Database Management

Douglas Potter

Introduction 2	Hierarchical Databases 15
	Network Databases 16
Background 2	Relational Databases 17
Why Database Management Is Useful . . . 3	Relationship to Fourth-Generation
Advantages 3	Language Productivity Tools 19
Information Needs 3	**Database Software Selection** 20
Control and Standardization 4	Three Classifications of Database
Fourth-Generation Languages 4	Software 20
User Department Programming 4	Information Center Database Software 22
Programmer Productivity 4	Large-Scale Development Software . . 23
Disadvantages 5	Programmer Productivity Software . . 23
Allin Industries: A Database Management	Other Considerations in Selecting
Example 6	Database Software 24
	Database Management Systems 26
Definition of Terms 8	Software Product Costs 26
Corporate Financial Database 8	
Database 8	**Maintaining Database Integrity** 26
Data Base Management Systems 8	Managing the Sources of Financial Data—
Data Definition Language 8	The FIS 27
Data Element 9	Controls 27
Data 9	User Training 28
Record 9	Management Imperative 29
Key 9	Security 29
File 9	Role of the DBMS and the Operating
Data Dictionary 9	System 29
Schema 9	Use of a Separate Security Package . . 30
Subschema 10	Role of Application Software 30
Data Base Administrator 10	Test Database 32
The Database Environment 10	Backup and Recovery 32
	Systems Backup 32
Design and Implementation 12	Transaction Audit and Rollback 33
Relationship to the Long-Range Planning	
Process 13	**Future Trends in Database Management** 33
Database Design 14	
Generic Classification of Databases 15	**References** 34

Fig. 8-1 Sample Costs for Implementing IBM's IMS DBMS 5
Fig. 8-2 Major Elements of a Database Environment 11

8-1

Fig. 8-3 Corporate Financial Database Implementation Plan 14
Fig. 8-4 Selected Database Software and Costs 21
Fig. 8-5 Sources of Financial Data 27
Fig. 8-6 Typical Security Functions of a Database Environment 31

INTRODUCTION

In the early 1970s, the data processing industry began evolving away from the traditional disk-file organization of data that dominated third-generation computing. That evolution was fueled by the drawbacks associated with disk-file organizations (often referred to as flat files), as follows.

- Adding a new data element to a file required changing file definitions for all programs referencing the file and recompiling the programs.
- Keeping track of the various file generations proved to be a cumbersome task that, if done incorrectly, resulted in much effort to recover corrupted data.
- There was a large backlog of user requests for information on some files.
- There was a high level of data redundancy in which the same data occurred in several different files.

The database management approach overcomes these drawbacks. Intrinsic to database management is the concept of data independence: data need not (and, in fact, should not) be owned by application programs. Instead, they should reside as a collective set of files and tables with appropriate interrelationships, known as a database.

Database management is concerned with the human functions necessary to maintain and use a database as well as with the software functions that assist this human process. The focus of this chapter is, in large part, on the human, managerial issues that relate to database management. Often highly complex by nature, the software functions are addressed here from the nontechnical perspective with which a user or financial manager must be concerned.

Background

Database management first appeared when vendors began to offer software products and Data Base Management Systems (DBMS) to perform the independent management of data. Researchers began expanding the notion of database management to include many new concepts and features. In turn, vendors took the concepts and features and put them back into the marketplace in the form of new products, enhancements, and innovations. This continues, with products offering the following:

- Database management for personal computers (PCs) and personal computer links that access information from central computer databases.
- Rapid application systems development so dramatically different from past methodologies that these software products have been referred to as fourth-generation languages.
- Database management capabilities as an integral function of the overall hardware product rather than as a separate software product that is purchased and used optionally.

Because of these recent trends, financial managers are becoming increasingly affected by database management. Thus, it is important to gain a broad understanding of the concepts and features of database management in order to interface with data processing personnel, to help select appropriate hardware and software, and to support the corporate organization better. Understanding and utilizing the concepts presented in this chapter help to accomplish this.

WHY DATABASE MANAGEMENT IS USEFUL

The advantages of using database management over the more traditional (flat file) approach to storing data span a range of issues from technical to managerial. The disadvantages are almost exclusively concerned with cost issues. Thus, it is rare to find an organization justifying database management by using a cost/benefit comparison, at least on paper. Usually, the decision to adopt this approach stems from a decision made by a knowledgeable manager or committee. Typically, the decision is based on an analysis of considerations discussed in the following sections.

Advantages

Information Needs. An organization's information needs are in a constant state of flux and change. In some organizations, the change takes place over a period of years; in others, it may occur over a period of months. The latter type of organization is typically characterized by government regulation, fast growth, mergers and acquisitions, or rigorous industry competition. More static organizations can be fed with information from software packages or in-house-developed systems that change very slowly to meet new demands for information, but dynamic organizations constantly demand new and different forms of information: Diagnostic Related Group Systems for hospitals and advanced inventory control techniques for competitive manufacturers are both examples.

The use of database management tools (including fourth-generation languages, relational DBMS, ad hoc query, and reporting modules) satisfies the rapidly changing needs of these dynamic organizations much more quickly.

As a case in point, consider the example of a newly appointed data processing executive in a large public organization. He must make some quick successes in order to gain the confidence of his superiors and the user department managers. His first major project is to develop an employee benefits administration system. Using UNIVAC's MAPPER, a fourth-generation language within an integrated relational database, he completes the project in months. Using traditional programming methods, the project would have taken at least a year. His approach allows him to meet the organization's information needs for this type of system very quickly.

Control and Standardization. Database management offers a level of control over data that cannot be achieved by alternative methods. Consider the following:

- Using a data dictionary enables strict enforcement of standard data element and data file names that previously could only be achieved through written policies and policing.
- DBMS security is typically much stronger than the basic security offered by the operating system.
- By restricting the user's view of the database, sensitive data elements can be hidden so that certain users (and programmers) are not even aware of their existence.

Fourth-Generation Languages. Most fourth-generation languages (also called nonprocedural languages) use a database for storage and retrieval. Therefore, a database and a DBMS must be present to accomplish the rapid application development made possible by the fourth-generation language. As an example, consider Applied Data Research's fourth-generation language, IDEAL. This product uses the company's relational DBMS, DATACOM/DB, and its data dictionary, DATADICTIONARY, to construct fourth-generation language applications.

User Department Programming. With all the inquiry and reporting tools available for database users, many simple requests previously honored through the development of a special program by the data processing department are now honored by the user's direct query into the database. Typically, one or more technically oriented users in each department becomes skilled at using database inquiry tools and serves the requests from that department.

For the user departments, this approach offers much quicker turnaround. It also frees the central data processing department to work on larger projects.

Programmer Productivity. There is a mild controversy over whether database management increases programmer productivity. The controversy ex-

DATABASE MANAGEMENT

One-Time Implementation Costs		Monthly Maintenance Costs	
Database software purchase	$10,000	Database software maintenance	$4,800
Application conversion costs[1]	46,250	Personnel costs[3]	3,800
Programmer training classes	35,000	Monthly maintenance costs for	
User training classes	4,750	additional hardware	500
Manuals	2,200		
Additional hardware[2]	38,000		
Incremental one-time costs	$136,200	Incremental monthly costs	$8,100

(1)

Program Type and Number		Conversion Hours Required per Program	Application Hours
Simple programs	170	.5	85
Average programs	80	3	240
Complex programs	50	8	400
			725
File and job stream conversion			200
Total hours			925
Rate per hour			× $50
Cost estimate			$46,250

(2) 2MB memory, 10 terminals, 2 printers

(3) Data base administrator's salary and benefits

FIG. 8-1 Sample Costs for Implementing IBM's IMS DBMS

cludes fourth-generation development tools and relational databases, about which there is no question that there is improved productivity. A noted database management expert, James Martin,[1] claims that it does increase programmer productivity. Others claim that it merely standardizes certain functions in application development but produces no productivity gains.

Certainly, increased standardization is present with database management. However, if properly implemented, probably some programmer productivity would occur as well. The use of database file definitions rather than "copy library" or hard-coded file definitions, the ability to change the database without recompiling affected programs, and the use of a data dictionary to perform data editing are all examples of how programmers become slightly more productive because of the conveniences afforded by a DBMS.

Disadvantages

As previously mentioned, the disadvantages of using a DBMS are almost exclusively cost issues. These costs are fairly easy to estimate and should be quantified when considering the implementation of a DBMS. Figure 8-1 shows the

---

[1] James Martin, *Principles of Data-Base Management* (Englewood Cliffs, N.J.: Prentice-Hall, 1976), p. 47.

costs that should be considered in implementing an IMS database and converting an order entry and accounts receivable system to run it. The figure can serve as a guideline for estimating similar database implementation projects.

ALLIN INDUSTRIES: A DATABASE MANAGEMENT EXAMPLE

Allin Industries (a fictitious company) is a large manufacturer and distributor of consumer electronic products. Its annual revenues recently topped $200 million. However, competitive pressure in the industry has forced it to look for innovative ways to increase profitability. Allin's product lines consist of twenty-four household electronic products that are manufactured in five domestic locations, each location specializing in the manufacture of no more than six product lines. The distribution channels consist of three primary sources:

1 Foreign and domestic sales offices selling directly to small- and medium-sized retailers.
2 Authorized representatives who distribute to geographic locations not covered by the sales offices.
3 Direct sales to large retail chains.

Allin's chief financial officer (CFO) has been reading about innovations in FISs, and has decided to use the company's corporate financial database to generate some critical success factors. These, he feels, will better enable him to monitor the business' vital signs and perhaps to identify areas that, if better managed, can improve profitability.

He settles on three critical success factors:

1 Current and projected liquidity based on cash, receivables, payables, and the market value of investments in order to reduce short-term borrowings and better manage cash flows.
2 Inventory turns by product line, which will provide information on the effectiveness of both sales and inventory policies.
3 Profit by product line, broken out by distribution channel to help identify the effectiveness of the various distribution channels.

These data must be updated twice a week in order to be effective.

Management assigns the task of generating these indicators to an able financial analyst in the corporate finance group. This individual, after some thought, concludes that this is really a simple task:

"Liquidity can be computed from the general ledger, accounts payable, and accounts receivable systems using the financial report writer and perhaps some programming. I can use any of several financial market quota-

DATABASE MANAGEMENT 8-7

tion services to supply the market value of our investments in order to value our portfolio.

"Reporting inventory turns is quite simple. All five manufacturing locations have their perpetual inventory in various computers at each location. Surely they will have a breakdown by our twenty-four product lines. All I have to do is to consolidate the inventory balances across all manufacturing locations and compute ratios based on the sales reports by product line that come from our corporate sales system.

"The corporate sales system already prints a profit by product-line report. I just need a programmer to add a sales code designating the distribution channel to the order entry input screen—or should I tell him to use the customer number, or key off of the 'sold to' name and address to determine the distribution channel? I'd better get some help on this."

Six months later, the new system is in place and the CFO is receiving his critical ratios. The only problem is that the ratios are seven days' old by the time he receives them and they take half of a full-time equivalent to produce. Why?

- The investment portfolio is not automated, so market prices are extracted from published sources rather than from on-line linkage to a financial database of market prices. The resulting cash-flow computations are done with a microcomputer using keyed-in accounting systems information, portfolio information, and market prices.

- Inventory turns are computed by calling each of the five plants twice weekly to get twenty-four product-line inventory levels. These are then accumulated manually across all warehouses, and the ratios are generated manually from the sales by product-line report produced by the corporate sales system.

- The programmer made the changes so that the profit by product-line report would include a breakout by distribution channel. However, since the rest of the critical success factors are on various different media, the results are typewritten along with the previous two sets of results. (Soon, however, this will be done on a word processor.)

Having an inclination for automation, the CFO has his secretary key the resulting numbers into a microcomputer spreadsheet so that he can plot data and spot trends.

This hypothetical situation is true to life for many businesses. All the issues involved revolve around the correct development and use of a corporate financial database. The financial analyst may have made the correct decisions about preparing the data, given the limitations and tools of his environment, but a more appropriate solution can easily be obtained using database management.

DEFINITION OF TERMS

In most cases, the terminology used in this chapter is standard throughout the industry. Definitions are presented here to provide a clear understanding of their meaning in the context of database management.

Corporate Financial Database

This is not one but a collection of databases that, when viewed together, comprise all the automated financial information for the entire organization. Typically included in the corporate financial database are databases for the general ledger, accounts payable, accounts receivable, fixed assets, and payroll.

Database

"Database" is widely misused to mean computer-stored records or information (e.g., the production manager referring to his inventory stock status as his inventory database). The definition adopted here describes a shared collection of interrelated data that is defined and managed with a DBMS (see the next section).

Data Base Management System

This is systems software, which interfaces between any user (and application program) and the physical database. The DBMS is responsible for functions such as:

- Security
- Backup and recovery
- Maintenance of all pointers and links within the database as updates occur
- Provision for the capability to reorganize the database and optimize performance (Examples of DBMSs currently available are shown in Figure 8-4.)

Data Definition Language

This refers to a set of instructions used to define all data elements, files, file interrelationships, and other characteristics concerning a database. These instructions are used by the DBMS to create and maintain the database.

DATABASE MANAGEMENT

Data Element

A data element is the smallest unit of recorded information with a unique name and location in the database (e.g., Customer Address = CUSTADDR; Account Balance = ACCTBAL). Also the smallest piece of stored data that are recognized by an end user, sometimes called a field.

Data

The term "data" refers to the contents of data elements (e.g., "130 Henderson Street, Suite 1A").

Record

This is a collection of data elements that are logically related to one entity (e.g., "personnel record for employee No. 53192").

Key

A key is a data item used to identify a record in a unique manner (e.g., an employee's number).

File

A file is a collection of records containing data about similar entities (e.g., a personnel file).

Data Dictionary

This refers to a collection of information describing the qualities of an entire database, its files, records, and data elements. As an example, consider the following possible information describing a data element:

Name	Description	Length	Attribute	File	Security Code
CUSTADDR	Customer address	20	Alphanumeric	Customer master	12

Associated with a data dictionary is the data dictionary system. This is a software system that helps manage the data dictionary by providing reports, inquiry, update, and other capabilities.

Schema

The logical view of an entire database showing all files and data elements in the database is known as a schema.

Subschema

The logical view of the database, incorporating restricted views of data elements is known as a subschema.

Data Base Administrator

The data base administrator (DBA) is an individual who assumes responsibility for additions or deletions of data elements to the database and the data dictionary, assigning ownership of data to other individuals in the organization, and managing data security. The DBA interacts with both the user and technical systems personnel in order to accomplish these tasks.

THE DATABASE ENVIRONMENT

The preceding definitions can best be understood by looking at a practical example that ties all of them together. Figure 8-2 shows many of the components defined as they would function in a typical database environment, where the FISs, as well as other production systems, are automated using database management.
 Figure 8-2 shows various users accessing different databases to perform specific functions (e.g., order inquiry, a bill of material parts explosion). This accessing is accomplished in two cases by application programs and in one case by an ad hoc inquiry and reporting module. The actual databases are shown toward the bottom of the figure.
 The application programmers are responsible for developing and maintaining the applications. As in a nondatabase environment, the programmers must interact with the user to see that the latter's information needs are being adequately met. Programmers can design systems that update and change the database, but they have no authority to run the systems in a production environment. Programmers in a well-controlled environment are restricted to using a test database for all their development, testing, and maintenance. (See the section following Figure 8-5 on maintaining database integrity for additional information on test databases.)
 The DBA controls the data's safekeeping by administering database security and access privileges to the user and programmers. He may sometimes get involved in defining and modeling the data by setting up data relations and access paths. Although the bulk of this work is taken up by a technical individual, the database designer, the DBA is in constant communication with the user and programmers and is aware of changes and enhancements that may be needed. For example, he may be aware that, due to new requirements at the order desk, an alpha search feature is needed for the inventory file. The DBA may create a new key to the inventory file using the description field of the

DATABASE MANAGEMENT

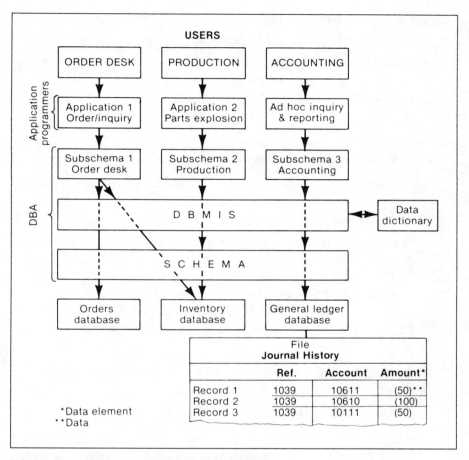

FIG. 8-2 Major Elements of a Database Environment

inventory items so that the programmer can use it to design the alpha search feature.

The user actually owns and is responsible for the data's accuracy through input and maintenance procedures. Typically, a well-controlled user department employs procedures for controlling total checking and balancing, timely input, and error correction and follow-up. These may be enhanced by application program features that help support accurate data entry; however, the burden for accurate data rests ultimately with the user.

The data dictionary plays an important role in the environment depicted in Figure 8-2. It contains the standardized data name, size, and type for all data elements in the database. The data dictionary has increased in importance over the years, due to the increasing functions it supports, as follows:

- Cataloging of all data elements
- Cataloging of all files and record types
- Editing of data to be added to the database by application programs
- Inquiry of data elements and access paths by the user
- Recording ownership and security information about the data elements

The ad hoc inquiry and reporting system shown in Figure 8-2 offers capabilities that are very valuable to any database environment, including:

- On-line structure of the database query with a response prepared either on a terminal or on hard copy
- The ability to update the database with the proper security
- The ability to structure a complex query (e.g., all customers who have bought Product A in the last six months and are located in California)
- The ability to design report formats by specifying such items as column headings, column locations, and page breaks
- The ability to perform computations with numeric data elements
- Counting records selected
- Sorting on one or more data elements
- Creating files of selected records for future use
- Storing queries for later rerunning

On-line inquiry of the database can use significant systems resources and easily create degraded response times to other users on the system. This is particularly true where several users are employing the database inquiry system. Because of this, it may be desirable to use an off-line query system if one is available. The obvious advantage of doing this is that inquiries that do not need to be answered immediately can be answered overnight in a batch environment, when processing resources are less in demand. Ideally, the ad hoc inquiry system allows the user to build the query on line, but defers execution of the query until later.

DESIGN AND IMPLEMENTATION

Financial managers must understand the concepts of database design and implementation and how they relate to FISs. With this understanding, they may:

- Communicate more effectively with data processing-oriented employees;

DATABASE MANAGEMENT 8-13

- Challenge software vendors and participate more actively in vendor discussions and presentations; and
- Better manage their portion of database design and implementation.

Detailed aspects of these areas require highly technical expertise (e.g., the database designer). However, just as in other technically oriented areas that relate to accounting, such as corporate tax accounting, a conceptual knowledge on the part of management can make the difference between success and failure.

Relationship to the Long-Range Planning Process

Database design begins with the long-range data processing plan. Database activity is best planned on a high level during this process to coordinate the timing of implementation with other major data processing projects. Typically, this process involves a joint project team of user department managers defining high-level action activities that will take place in the next three to five years. Examples of such action items include:

- Converting the fixed assets system to database;
- Implementing a personnel system to be integrated with the payroll database; or
- Expanding the general ledger database to include all subsidiary companies.

Scheduled tasks emanate from the plan and are assigned tentative start dates, stop dates, and resource commitments.

The advantages to this approach are inherent in the planning process itself. However, the most important advantage is that the corporate financial database is allowed to grow in a controlled, integrated manner. This avoids the costly mistake of planning the corporate financial database all at once.

Such a mistake was made by one of the largest school districts in the United States. It attempted to develop a single, integrated database to perform all the payroll, personnel, budgeting, and accounting needs for the district. These areas encompassed four of the five largest, most complex systems required by the district. The database and design implementation project lasted many years and resulted in the loss of millions of dollars. It was put to a halt by top management, who finally realized that development of the resulting database was extremely late and hopelessly over budget.

Thus, large databases must be implemented in manageable pieces. An organization seeking to improve its corporate financial database may follow an implementation plan similar to the one shown in Figure 8-3. The time estimates vary with the organization's size, resources, and staff level; however, the important points to note here are that:

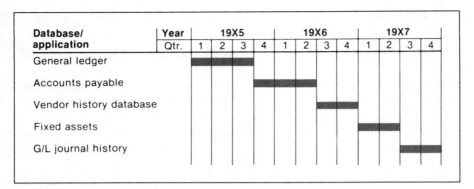

FIG. 8-3 Corporate Financial Database Implementation Plan

1 The individual databases should be implemented piecemeal as manageable projects; and
2 The correct priorities should be assigned to each implementation task.

Database Design

Once a database application project is approved for implementation, a project team of users, analysts, programmers, and database technicians is formed. If the project does not involve the selection of a packaged software application, one of the database technician's first tasks is to design the database. This individual becomes the database designer. In a large organization, the database designer is typically a technical individual who works closely with the other members of the project team to translate their requirements into functions that the new database will accommodate. In smaller organizations, where the database is designed on a minicomputer, the database designer is usually the data processing manager (who is also typically the DBA).

The database designer must define various characteristics about the database that relate to performance, storage requirements, and processing, including:

- Proper access paths to the data, so that the user and on-line database programs can retrieve records in a fast, efficient manner within a reasonable response time.
- Transaction volumes, so that necessary batch database processing can be completed within a reasonable amount of time.
- Efficient utilization of disk storage.
- Achievement of optimal good performance by periodically fine tuning the database.

Naturally, if packaged software is used for any particular database project (as opposed to in-house development), this individual's role changes. Any application package that uses a database has an inherent design built into the application. As a member of the selection and evaluation team, the database designer should be assigned to assess technical strong and weak points of any package being evaluated. During implementation, he will also be responsible for any database design changes to the selected package.

All DBMSs provide the designer with a language to work with in describing the design of the database, called the data definition language. This language and the data dictionary are the tools that the designer uses to accomplish his work.

As an example of poor design, consider one database designer who was requested by the order entry department to add a description search feature to the inventory database. This was needed to find inventory part numbers so that orders could be placed quickly for customers requesting "ten of those coiled cables with the 6-inch adapter on each end."

The designer developed a search feature using a sequential search of the entire inventory file based on a partial description of the part entered by the operator. The search took up to four minutes if the part was near the end of the file; thus, the operators never used it. The designer should have created an access path, or index, into the file, using a key constructed from the partial description field.

Generic Classification of Databases

Databases fall into one of several generic categories according to their design. These categories are explained here by way of example with a brief introduction explaining the pros and cons. A good, flexible DBMS supports the design of any of these types of databases. However, this is not true in all cases. Some DBMSs are designed specifically to support one type of database. For example, IBM's DBMS, manufactured for its mainframe computer, IMS, is primarily intended to create hierarchical data models.

Hierarchical Databases. In a hierarchical database, a hierarchy exists among the various files. In this hierarchy, one master record in a particular file owns one or more slave records in another file. This relationship can continue, if necessary, to create a multilevel hierarchy in which records in all other files are "owned" by the records in a single file. The relationships between the records in a hierarchical database are usually maintained via pointers that indicate the displacement of the record being pointed to from the beginning of the file. The file containing the master records and files containing slave records are determined in the data definition language.

Consider the following example of a hierarchical organization between customer records and open invoice records:

CUSTOMERS					OPEN INVOICES		
Customer No.	Name				Invoice No.	Amount	Next Invoice
D300	Smith	01	→	01	221	$135.00	02
P201	Jones	00		02	225	$95.30	00
S450	Brown	03	→	03	230	$75.25	04
				04	231	$290.10	05
				05	237	$100.00	00

The example shows that Smith has two outstanding invoices, invoice numbers 221 and 225; Jones has no open invoices; and Brown has invoices 230, 231, and 237 outstanding.

The main advantage to hierarchical databases is that access to slave records is extremely fast[2] where the slave records are accessed through the master (e.g., accessing open invoice records through the customer record, as opposed to using the invoice number). However, this data model has some important disadvantages.

- The design is fairly inflexible and only works well in environments where a "one to many" relationship exists between the records.
- Due to this inflexibility and to other processing considerations, database designers may be constrained to designing hierarchical databases that store much redundant data and thus make poor use of available disk space.

Network Databases. Network databases allow much better treatment of "many to many" relationships among database files than do the hierarchical databases. Unlike hierarchical databases, network databases require no master record and do allow relationships among any of the files. Because of this, one characteristic of network databases is that many pointers may be needed to ultimately reach data stored in a record in a particular file.

To expand on the previous example, suppose that each invoice had one inventory record associated with it. In a network database, this relationship would be shown in this manner:

---

[2] The speed of data access is generally measured by the number of records and keys fetched in order to retrieve the requested record. This, of course, has a direct effect on response time in an on-line environment.

DATABASE MANAGEMENT

OPEN INVOICES

	Invoice No.	Amount	Next Invoice	Inventory Record
01	221	$135.00	02	02
02	225	$95.30	00	01
03	230	$75.25	04	02
04	231	$290.10	05	04
05	237	$100.00	00	04

INVENTORY FILE

	Item No.	Description
01	375-60	60" cable
02	375-72	72" cable
03	410	Adapter plug
04	410X	Extended adapter

A hierarchical database would not allow multiple master (open invoice) records to own a single slave record; however, as seen in the example, this relationship is allowed in the network databases. Also, network databases are more generalized and are a superset of hierarchical databases. It is, however, possible to create hierarchical databases using a network-oriented DBMS.

The advantages of network databases are that:

- They can be used to establish access paths between records on any files.
- Data redundancy can be minimized by using pointers to original data rather than by storing the data a second time.

Their disadvantages are that:

- They are good for well-established relationships among files, but adding or changing relationships can be cumbersome.
- In order to access a particular piece of information stored in the database, the user must know and name all pointers and files that link to the file that stores the ultimately requested data. For example, to get the inventory record associated with an invoice, the user must know that a link through the invoice record exists and, therefore, must ask for the inventory record via that link. This can become somewhat cumbersome in a large, complex database.

Relational Databases. Relational databases are receiving much publicity regarding their role with fourth-generation languages. An understanding of the power and capabilities of relational databases helps support the appreciation for this recent acclaim. A relational database is one in which the records in any two files are, or can be, associated with one another by the use of a third file, which establishes a relation between records in the original two files. This third file, called a "relation" or "relational" file, takes the place of pointers in hierarchical or network databases.

In a relational database, the first example, showing customers and open invoices, looks as follows:

CUSTOMERS

Customer No.	Name
D300	Smith
P201	Jones
S450	Brown

CUSTOMER INVOICES

Customer No.	Invoice No.
D300	221
D300	225
S450	230
S450	231
S450	237

OPEN INVOICES

Invoice No.	Amount
221	$135.00
225	$95.30
230	$75.25
231	$290.10
237	$100.00

The customer invoice file is a relation associating customer number with invoice number. The second example, showing open invoices and the inventory file, looks like this in a relational database:

OPEN INVOICES

Invoice No.	Amount
221	$135.00
225	$95.30
230	$75.25
231	$290.10
237	$100.00

INVOICE ITEM

Invoice No.	Item No.
221	375-72
225	375-60
230	375-72
231	410X
237	410X

INVENTORY FILE

Item No.	Description
375-60	60" cable
375-72	72" cable
410	Adapter plug
410X	Extended adapter

The invoice item table is used to associate invoices with inventory items. No pointers to associated records are necessary.

The very nature of this approach affords distinct advantages over hierarchical and network databases.

- The user is not restricted to accessing data via preestablished pointers; if a path to a record does not exist, the DBMS can create it by setting up a relation.
- In a properly designed database, these relations can be created for any data elements in the database.

Despite their advantages, there are some significant disadvantages to relational databases.

DATABASE MANAGEMENT 8-19

- Performance problems created by a large number of users simultaneously accessing the database can make response time and turnaround time far more excessive than the other kinds of databases discussed; this is because of the large number of disk accesses required to process relational database files.
- Relational databases require more storage space because relational files contain completely redundant data.
- The nature of relational databases typically requires that the files in a relational database be constructed in a special way, called "third normal" form. This process is complex and is an issue of database design.

The biggest drawback, however, is the performance problems that are often so significant that they severely limit the number of users allowed into the database at any one time. This is probably the most significant reason for the inhibition of widespread acceptance of relational databases.

Relationship to Fourth-Generation Language Productivity Tools

The process of freely accessing data in the database by using new or existing relations is a feature of relational databases that fourth-generation languages take advantage of. Key verbs in the fourth-generation language enable file-oriented commands to process one file at a time, whereas conventional programming techniques, such as a COBOL program, require record-by-record processing. Even hierarchical or network databases require this type of record by record processing.

Consider, for example, what would be needed to write an open invoice report by customer, first using conventional programming and the hierarchical database and second, the relational database. The first report would be printed by a program that would:

1 Read a customer record.

2 Obtain the invoice record for that customer and print it.

3 Repeat Step 2 until no more invoices exist for that customer.

4 Repeat Steps 1 through 3 until no more customer records exist.

The same report could be printed in a relational environment by the command: "Select customer number, name, invoice number, and amount from customer invoice." This is a fourth-generation language command to print the indicated data elements using the relation "customer invoice."

Another term for a fourth-generation language is "nonprocedural language" because the system needs only to be told *what* information is needed, rather than *how* to go about getting it. The above example shows this clearly.

Although many products on the market are called "fourth-generation," only those with certain qualities deserve recognition as such. Those qualities usually include, but are not limited to, the following:

- A relational or relational-like DBMS
- An on-line query and reporting facility
- An integrated data dictionary accompanying the DBMS
- Screen formatting for terminal input and output screens
- Formatting of output reports
- The ability to accommodate traditional programming constructs (e.g., "if, then, else")

Examples of such products include:

    IDEAL from Applied Data Research
    MANTIS from Cincom
    ADS/OnLine from Cullinet

DATABASE SOFTWARE SELECTION

Because there are so many choices of database software, it is important to consider the business or data processing needs that will be served and to carefully select software based on these needs. It is dangerous to approach vendors without giving appropriate thought to the selection criteria. Salesmen generally represent their database software as being the best for a user's needs because of an unrelated issue—for example, "It works great for the guy down the street," or "It was designed specifically for your hardware."

Figure 8-4 lists just a small sample of the available DBMSs. A brief examination of these DBMSs reveals that each system is designed for vastly different purposes. When selecting database software, it is important to understand the differences among products as well as the various reasons for purchasing them.

The view of database software can be expanded to include any software using or enhancing the capabilities of a DBMS, and thus to include DBMS-related products such as fourth-generation languages, database inquiry software, and data dictionaries.

Three Classifications of Database Software

Database software may be classified into three general categories depending on its features: (1) it either appeals to the user-oriented environment of the corporate information center; (2) it appeals to the data processing environment for use in supporting large-scale systems development; or (3) it is a productivity tool for the data processing environment.

DATABASE MANAGEMENT

Product	Vendor	Operating Environment	Features	Current Price Range	Number Installed
TIS	Cincom Systems	IBM mainframe, DEC VAX	Successor to TOTAL; many integrated components for query, reporting, and program generation	$240,000–$300,000	80
IDMS/R	Cullinet Software, Inc.	IBM mainframe	Supports relational, hierarchical, and network databases; offered with full range of application software	$75,000–$350,000	1,400
IMS/VS	IBM Corporation	IBM mainframe	Supports hierarchical databases	$400–$4,000 (lease only)	5,000 (est.)
MAPPER	Sperry Corporation	Univac 1100 series	Combined relational DBMS and nonprocedural language; used for application systems development	Not available	Not available
TOTAL/MINIS	Cincom Systems	Most minicomputers	Simple to use and learn	$20,000–$40,000	3,500
IMAGE 3000	Hewlett Packard	HP 3000 series	Integrated data dictionary, query, and reporting components available	Included with hardware	30,000
System/38 Data Base	IBM Corporation	System/38	Integrated with operating system and hardware	Included with hardware	Not available

FIG. 8-4 Selected Database Software and Costs

Information Center Database Software. Corporate information centers typically have three elements:

1 A mainframe computer
2 A copy of the corporate financial database (as well as copies of other databases)
3 Database software and related software tools

In the information center environment, the user employs the software tools available to massage the data and produce the information he wants. Following are several characteristics unique to this environment:

- The user controls the format and frequency of the information produced.
- All software tools are controlled predominantly by the user, with installation and consulting support provided by data processing personnel.
- The environment is output oriented, where most use is centered around reporting and query.

Naturally, database software packages used in this environment have some unique features.

- They emphasize user friendliness and ease of use by unsophisticated personnel.
- They are largely oriented around producing information (output) from the database.
- They usually consume a large amount of hardware resources for the amount of useful information they are used to produce.
- They often interface with other systems that perform statistical analysis.
- They commonly feature a graphics output system.

Relational database software is common in the information center environment. However, network and hierarchical database systems also adapt well to this environment when they are equipped with the features mentioned.

Following are some excellent examples of information center database software presently available:

FOCUS, from Information Builders, Inc.
NOMAD2, from D&B Computing Services
RAMIS II, from Mathematica Products Group

DATABASE MANAGEMENT   8-23

Large-Scale Development Software. On the other end of the spectrum from the user-friendly information center database software lies database software designed to support the development of large-scale corporate information systems.

These software products are the heart of large database environments found in today's corporate computer centers. Typical software includes:

- A DBMS, most often hierarchical or network oriented
- Other integrated software for the data dictionary and ad hoc query and reporting
- Several application systems written to run under this environment (see Figure 8-2)

The characteristics of the large database software are quite opposite to those of the information center database software in that:

- Its use requires a large central support staff for programming, application development, database design, and database administration.
- Programmer friendliness is more important than user friendliness.
- The database software is highly capable of both input (transaction) and output processing.
- The software is much more efficient with hardware resources than is information center database software.

Relational DBMSs are less popular than the network and hierarchical DBMSs that have traditionally dominated the large database environment because relational DBMSs are not efficient enough to support the huge processing load and transaction volumes the environment requires.

Sample DBMSs (see Figure 8-4) include:

IDMS/R, from Cullinet Software, Inc.
IMS/VS, from IBM Corporation
TIS, from Cincom Systems

And running on smaller machines:

IMAGE/3000, from Hewlett-Packard
System/38 Data Base, from IBM Corporation

Programmer Productivity Software. Database software often has been adapted to aid the data processing department in developing new systems quickly and meeting the demand for requested services. Software used for this purpose:

- Works with a large-scale development DBMS and/or performs DBMS-like functions with flat files (e.g., the cataloging of data elements from flat files in a data dictionary).
- May use relational or relational-like views of the database.
- Has a facility for screen formatting and output report formatting.
- Has the ability to accommodate interfaces to traditional programs (COBOL) and/or use procedural programming constructs such as "if, then, else."

As is evident from these functions, the programmer-productivity software is somewhat of a hybrid between the user-oriented database software of the information center and the large-scale development software used by the data processing department. Productivity software is used predominantly by data processing personnel because of the technical requirement for understanding the detailed features of these tools.

Fourth-generation languages are indeed such productivity tools. Their functions make them a subject of the software productivity tools, whose capabilities are described herein: fourth-generation languages require a relational DBMS; productivity tools generally do not. See the preceding discussion of relationship to fourth-generation language productivity tools for examples of programmer productivity tools.

Other Considerations in Selecting Database Software

Of course, there is much more to consider when selecting database software than the function it will serve. Other considerations are often equally important to the selection process:

1 *Application software selection.* Very often, the decision to purchase a DBMS is made in conjunction with an application software package using that DBMS. Application software vendors typically provide a version of their application software that will run with a DBMS; some may only offer software that uses a DBMS (although obviously it is to their advantage to offer a variety). Businesses may take the opportunity to select a DBMS when purchasing application software. This is often because of the relative advantages of installing and maintaining a database application over installing and maintaining one that uses flat files.

Thus, the decision to purchase database software is sometimes secondary to the decision to purchase application software because the application software vendors such as MSA and McCormack and Dodge offer products that can run under databases. This traditional approach may be changing, however. Database software vendors are beginning to provide application software that runs with their DBMS.

DATABASE MANAGEMENT

8-25

Cullinet appears to be pioneering this role with various integrated application systems, which they offer under IDMS/R. Companies seeking application software are looking to companies like Cullinet for these application systems.

It will be interesting to see how this affects the software marketplace in the future.

- Will the database software vendors prove to be viable application software vendors?
- Will application software vendors begin marketing database software?

2 *Hardware.* Selecting a DBMS is much easier if there is a requirement that the DBMS run on specific hardware. If a decision on the kind of hardware and operating system has not been made, it is desirable to evaluate combinations of hardware and DBMSs concurrently. Most often, however, the hardware has already been installed, and it is therefore not appropriate to examine DBMSs that run on another vendor's hardware.

3 *Size.* The number of users (and applications) and the size of the database affects the size of the hardware selected and consequently the DBMS used. Certainly, Hewlett-Packard's IMAGE (see Figure 8-4) is not appropriate for environments of more than 300 users, simply because Hewlett-Packard minicomputers are best suited for smaller systems.

As mentioned earlier, hierarchical and network databases support a larger number of users at a given level of performance than do relational databases. Thus, the issue of hierarchical versus network versus relational is one of both selecting database software and of design.

4 *The personal computer link.* Many DBMSs offer personal computer links that allow data to be stored locally in a microcomputer. This typically includes downloading the data into a spreadsheet. If a large number of microcomputers are available, this may be a desirable feature to consider in selecting database software. Certainly, more database software vendors will be offering and expanding this capability—the popularity of the personal computer almost ensures it.

5 *Distributed data.* Some vendors now offer the capability to manage data at multiple computer locations with a single (distributed) DBMS. An example of this is Applied Data Research's DATA-COM/D-Net product, which manages multiple location databases under their DBMS, DATACOM/DB. The need for this type of DBMS is rare, and only occurs in distributed environments where the user must concurrently access databases at several different computer locations.

In most cases, each local database is only accessed by local users, and a standard DBMS is sufficient, even though the database is distributed.

6 *Database machines.* Today, products that offload the central computer of the entire responsibility of database management are available. These products are called "database machines." They include both software (for the DBMS and related functions) and hardware (for storage, processing, and interfacing with the host computer). Database machines offer a unique feature, in that they are highly modular—that is, the hardware can be purchased in increments. Thus, they adapt easily to different-sized databases.

Although database machines have not yet been proved in the marketplace, it should be realized that they are new and have not yet had a chance to be adequately tested. Two prominent vendors of database machines are:

Britton Lee, Inc. of Los Gatos, California
Teradata of Los Angeles

When selecting database software, it is advisable to create a list of specific requirements for evaluation purposes. For example, regarding the functionality of the database software, if it is to support a corporate information center, some requirements might be that:

- The software must provide a "help" function for database inquiries.
- A clerk or secretary must be able to learn the basic inquiry functions with no more than two hours of training.
- The vendor must provide a "hotline" for users to call with questions.

Database Management Systems. This book contains a list of primary evaluation elements to use in selecting a DBMS. This text also provides additional information about organizing and managing a database selection project.

Software Product Costs

Figure 8-4 shows sample costs for several common DBMSs. It is only intended to give a sample of relative costs, rather than a cost comparison of related products. Obviously, the products shown differ widely in their applicability and functionality.

MAINTAINING DATABASE INTEGRITY

Selecting database software and designing a database only take place once in a great while. Maintenance is an ongoing process that involves many responsibil-

DATABASE MANAGEMENT 8-27

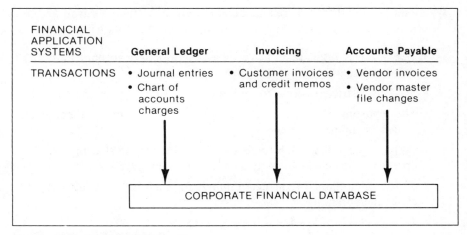

FIG. 8-5 Sources of Financial Data

ities and techniques. The following sections examine how database integrity is maintained from a management standpoint, and also analyze technical considerations and capabilities about which management should be aware.

Managing the Sources of Financial Data—The FIS

Financial databases are constantly being fed with data in the form of transactions: journal entries, customer invoices, vendor invoices, and all the other routine transactions generated from the financial application systems (e.g., general ledger, invoicing, accounts payable). Figure 8-5 represents that financial data on a conceptual level.

With the constant bombardment of data going into the database, it is easy to see why managing these transaction systems is important to maintaining the integrity of the database. Financial managers should focus on several basic areas in order to effectively manage financial application systems, such as:

- Controls
- User training
- Management imperative

These areas address both the software and the people who routinely affect the database.

Controls. One important purpose of controls is to help maintain database integrity. A detailed discussion about controls is not pertinent here, but there are several controls that, where properly used, do effectively increase the integrity of data in a database. These include both built-in systems controls and user procedures. Among the built-in systems controls are the following:

- Use of check digits (e.g., to verify a general ledger account number that has been keyed in for a journal transaction).
- Systems-restricted access to updating key fields (e.g., product prices).
- The reporting of record totals so that the user can match them against counts of input documents.
- Systems-generated batch totals of dollar amounts so that input operators can match them against manually prepared totals.
- Systems-maintained sequence numbers for such items as invoices and credit memoranda.
- An edit check of key fields.
- Limit and reasonableness testing of certain fields (e.g., hours worked per pay period).

User procedures include:

- Maintaining logs of data-entry batches.
- Review of edit reports.
- Independent accrual of systems-generated totals (e.g., batch or dollar totals).

The importance of these basic controls cannot be overstated. A billion-dollar manufacturer of computer peripheral products had failed to build sufficient software edit checks into its billing applications. The result: a database of billing information full of inaccuracies. A two-year effort to redesign the database and all major billing applications finally ended the database integrity problems. However, the company filed for reorganization under the bankruptcy laws a month before the new system was implemented. Said one employee, "Well, at least we can get accurate invoices out now."

Naturally, there is much more to controls than what is presented here. (For more details on how controls may be applied to each application, see Chapters 6 and 10.) The point here is that effective controls have a positive effect on financial database integrity.

User Training. A foolproof way to degrade database integrity is to allow untrained or poorly trained users to become data entry operators. Of course, training is more of a procedure than a control, but it deserves special mention with regard to database integrity. All the procedures and actions needed to control transactions updating the database effectively are worthless if data entry operators are not trained in using them.

DATABASE MANAGEMENT 8-29

Key points of good user training are:

- Clear and complete user documentation for every application
- Use of a test system for training new operators
- Written training guides using either programmed instruction or videotapes

Low turnover of key personnel is also critical. Knowledgeable supervisors and seasoned operators who have worked with the application systems and database inquiry software for at least a year are a valuable asset, especially if they participated in designing the application when it was under development.

Management Imperative. Like many other aspects of directing a corporation, the correct ongoing operations of the FIS and high accuracy of data in the corporate financial database are best achieved where there is a clear management imperative to do so. At a minimum, the organization must be aware that attaining this goal is expected of all affected departments and individuals. Where employees are aware that their superiors expect them to meet goals, they work much more consciously toward achieving them. Many organizations structure this imperative by tracking one or more key indicators and keeping a running record posted for all employees to see. Examples of these indicators are:

- The number of rejects from a financial institution's item processing system
- The number of items appearing on an edit reject report
- The number of customer billing errors
- The amount of unapplied cash in accounts receivable

Security

Maintaining appropriate security among the FISs and the corporate financial database is of paramount importance in maintaining database integrity. Following is an overview of database security, which includes a few guidelines that should be followed in its administration (see Chapters 10 and 22).

Role of the DBMS and the Operating System. In a database environment, the DBMS and the operating system work closely together in controlling security. The operating system is generally responsible for validating the user's user ID and password. In some environments, this is the responsibility either of a separate piece of systems software that performs transaction processing or of a portion of the DBMS that manages this function. From there, systems access may be granted to running database applications or the other database functions (e.g., using ad hoc inquiry or reading the data dictionary). Thus, it is the job of these secondary levels of software to restrict user actions once general systems access has been granted by the operating system.

Menu-level security, which restricts the user from accessing different options on the menu, is an application function. The application system itself must check for a user's authorization to process a particular transaction through the use of internal tables built into the application system.

The DBMS has security tables (which often exist in the data dictionary) where detailed user ID access rights may be defined. The security tables contain user ID (and possibly password) information to control:

- Access to various subschema (i.e., views of the database)
- Access and update authorization for the ad hoc inquiry system
- Access and update authorization for data elements in the database

These security tables should be under exclusive control of the DBA (and perhaps another individual for backup). An additional DBMS function is to protect data from concurrent updating by two or more users or applications. However, this is more of an integrity feature than a security feature, and is not controlled by the DBA or anyone else.

Figure 8-6 is an adaptation of Figure 8-2, with an explanation of how the various security features interrelate. It is only a generalization; specific systems may offer different implementations of the same concept.

Use of a Separate Security Package. Figure 8-6 represents only one of the many different tables where a user ID and password must be maintained. Some security packages are available that centralize the entire security function protecting all on-line and database file access through one source. Examples of such packages include:

> RACF from IBM
> ACF2 from The Cambridge Systems Group, Inc.
> Top Secret from CGA Software Products Group

The packages are not database software, and care must be taken to ensure the integration of any security package with the DBMS already being used. Through this integration, the DBMS must be able to look to the security package for on-line log-on authorization and file access privileges.

Role of Application Software. Each set of users should be able to view only the portions of the corporate financial database they need to accomplish their jobs. There is no reason for anyone in the accounts receivable department to view general ledger account balances. Restricting a user to appropriate data, views, transactions, and functions needed for his job is accomplished predominantly at the application level. (The DBA contributes to this process by defining what is contained in each subschema; however, the application program

DATABASE MANAGEMENT

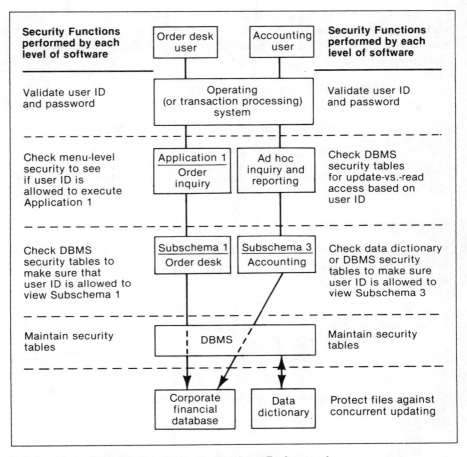

FIG. 8-6 Typical Security Functions of a Database Environment

ultimately controls the part of the subschema that is displayed on a screen and allowed to be updated.)

Thus, the issue of database security should be addressed during the design of each financial application that uses the database. The systems analyst, DBA, and user should agree on:

- The contents of each subschema
- Each menu, menu option, and associated restrictions
- Restrictions for using the ad hoc inquiry and reporting system

It is then the systems analyst's responsibility to implement these features into the new application. It is the DBA's responsibility to update the DBMS's security tables and implement the new subschema (created by the database designer).

Test Database. During development of any new database application and throughout its life, the systems and programming department should have a test database available that is separate from the production database. The test database should be used for:

- Developing initial application systems
- Maintaining sample test data
- Testing any new application features to produce known results
- Testing out new versions of packaged application software

Although programmers are denied general access to the production database, they may use the test database to serve their needs.

Backup and Recovery

One of the main advantages to using a DBMS is the protection afforded by the backup and recovery features for protecting the integrity of the database against:

- Hardware failure resulting in physical damage to the database;
- Batch jobs that were discontinued in the middle of a database update due to programming errors;
- On-line update transactions that updated the database that should not have been processed; and
- The effect of batch jobs that were run by mistake.

These features are:

- Systems backup
- Transaction audit, rollback, and checkpoint/restart

Systems Backup. Backing up a database onto tape may be done either by using utilities provided with the DBMS or by using an operating systems command to dump the entire contents of disk to tape. The net effect is the same: a copy of the database is created at a certain point in time. In the event of the physical damage to the database (static electricity on the disk, a head crash, or an operator dropping the disk pack), this copy may be used to recreate the database and resume processing from that point.

There are a few rules to follow to make sure that this process is safe and smooth.

- An audit trail of source documents should be maintained to allow all financial transactions to be reprocessed from the time the backup was created. This means that source documents must be stored so that the user can determine which ones were processed before and which ones

after the backup. This is one reason for the use of serial numbers and data entry logs to record source documents of data entry activity.
- Operators must retain good records so that batch jobs can be rerun from the time the backup was created. The systems log maintained by the operating system can help determine this. However, it is not always true that a log is available both from the backup made earlier and from the current system. Therefore, good manual operator schedules and logs should be maintained.
- Systems backup should occur at least daily for the entire database.
- At least once each week, a copy of the backup tape(s) should be rotated off site in case of a fire or flood in the tape storage area.

Transaction Audit and Rollback. Audit and rollback functions enable the database to erase the effect of one or more (batch or on-line) jobs against the database. They are very useful integrity features and are available in most DBMSs.

Those features all involve using a special audit trail of database activity called a transaction audit—actually a tape file logging all changes to the database by recording both the before-and-after images of each updated database record. Each record stored on this audit log also contains identification of the job that caused the change.

All information on the transaction audit can be used to reverse the effect of any job that was run to update the database. In fact, when a database update job aborts, the DBMS can automatically initiate a cleanup job that reads the audit trail and reverses all transactions made by the job. This leaves the database as if the job were never run. This reversal process is called database rollback.

FUTURE TRENDS IN DATABASE MANAGEMENT

The various database software products offered are functionally fairly distinct. That is, the software package purchased for a specific purpose, such as serving a corporate information center, probably will not be used for the DBMS that supports the transaction processing systems. As database software vendors learn to survive and grow, they will offer a more complete product line to their customers. This may mean a mild shakeout or consolidation of database software vendors as the industry matures. (Granted, this is a long-term effect; a shakeout is likely to take ten years or so.)

This fuller product line will blur the distinction between functionally different systems so that a single vendor's product line will offer all possible functions, such as security, corporate database management, fourth-generation application development, and graphics. Currently, most companies whose software serves all these functions have purchased it from several vendors.

Database software vendors will push for the presence of software in the home, front office, and general user communities and will try to shake off its image of being a technical database designer's tool that requires a shelf of documentation to use.

Vendors and theoreticians will push to develop more efficient database software that will improve performance. Overcoming performance problems is a key to widespread acceptance of software for relational database management.

Technology changes in software, however, are produced less frequently and less effectively than technology changes in hardware. Thus, as the trend of decreasing hardware cost/performance, which has fueled the data processing industry's growth over the past three decades, continues, there will be more widespread use of performance-constrained database software such as relational databases systems and information center software systems.

The PC or microcomputer will undoubtedly have an increasing role in future database management. When microcomputers first gained popular acceptance in the early 1980s, many industry analysts talked about using them as an extension of the central computer. In this capacity, they could "off load" the central computer by allowing a portion of the database to be stored locally on the microcomputer, updated by the user, and returned to the central database.

These ideas have not yet been put into practice—not because of a lack of hardware technology but because the software to manage these functions easily was not available. This software needs to be part of a DBMS or a similar database-related software that runs on both the central computer and the PC. Only now are these capabilities being made available as part of the overall software products offered in the marketplace.

REFERENCES

Auerbach Publishers, Inc. *Data Base Management*. Pennsauken, N.J.: Auerbach Publishers, 1984.

Curtice, Robert M., and Paul E. Jones, Jr. "Database: The Bedrock of Business." *Datamation* (June 15, 1984).

Martin, James. *Principles of Data-Base Management*. Englewood Cliffs, N.J.: Prentice-Hall, 1976.

Mimno, Peter. "Power to the Users." *Computerworld* (Apr. 8, 1985), p. ID/19.

———. "Power from the Products." *Computerworld* (Apr. 15, 1985), p. ID/1.

Sweet, Frank. "What, if Anything, Is a Relational Database?" *Datamation* (July 15, 1984).

CHAPTER 9

Telecommunications and Networking

Allen D. McMillen

Telecommunications Technologies	1	Overview		12
Telecommunications Today: An Overview	1	LAN Characteristics		14
The New AT&T	3	Signalling Schemes		15
VANs	3	LAN Topologies		15
Digital Private Branch Exchange: The PBX Explosion	6	LAN Access Methods		16
		Planning for an LAN		17
Office Automation	7			
Word Processing	9	**Case Study**		18
Electronic Mail and Information Utilities	9	Ernst & Whinney National Systems Group		18
Facsimile Systems	9	History of the NSG Network		18
Computer-Based Telephones	9	Researching LANs		19
Voice Messaging	9	The Evaluation Network		20
Electronic Document Handling	10	Evaluation Results		20
Data Communications Networks	10	Installation Checklist		22
Local Area Networks for Personal Computers	12	**References**		23

Fig. 9-1 VANs 6

TELECOMMUNICATIONS TECHNOLOGIES

Telecommunications Today: An Overview

How effective and efficient a corporation becomes is heavily influenced by the corporate body's ability to communicate. Making things happen, producing results, and meeting and maintaining objectives are the signs of achievement in a company's ongoing pursuit toward corporate excellence and success. Telecommunications are providing increasingly important tools to aid in the process of communications. Emphasis on communications is of significant corporate strategic and operational importance. Communications systems are the key link between the corporation and its environment; between senior executives, management, and staff; and between planning and performance.

From the onset of the industrial revolution to the present, automation has swept over the business world. Batch processing gave way to on-line processing, and applications, tools, and reports were requested daily. Terminals of all shapes and sizes multiplied in great abundance, appearing in every imaginable place, including corporate and branch offices, airport countertops, fast-food chains, supermarkets, warehouses, and even at home. Data communications have become a critical and necessary element in our day-to-day activities.

The age of information networks has arrived and is here to stay. Information is at our fingertips, with information networks providing access to public and private databases. Consider the East Coast clothes manufacturer who picks up his telephone, dials a number connecting him to a database in California, and types in a few key words on his portable terminal. Within seconds, the California-based computer displays the latest retail activity data, while the terminal device prints out summaries that will assist him in his planning. Consider also the financial executive who can tap into the Dow Jones stock quotations with just the touch of a few buttons, or the housewife who shops and pays bills from home with the use of new videotex services.

During the mid-1970s to mid-1980s, major technological advances have been made in computer, microwave, microelectronics, and photonics technologies. The combination of telephone and computer technologies has expanded information into national networks and, with the use of satellites, into world telecommunications. Telecommunications capabilities can transfer information electronically and even integrate voice, data, and image transmission into an efficient stream of information. Telecommunications and information networks can tie intelligent devices, terminals, computers, and databases to one another through shared communications links within the office or at home. State-of-the-art technologies process and transmit information throughout the world. As information networks continue to evolve from AT&T's public switched networks (i.e., the telephone system), as well as from value-added networks (VANS), extensive benefits and new, economical information services will continue to become available to users. Current telecommunications and information services available include office automation, electronic mail, high-speed digital services, teleconferencing, and videotex.

Advanced telecommunications technologies offer the opportunity for greatly improved corporate effectiveness and achievements. The applications of telecommunications, as well as the environment in which the tools are applied, influence productivity improvement. It becomes important for corporate financial executives to understand more clearly what telecommunications tools are and how they can be used to benefit their businesses, as well as to understand the environment in which they are applied. To capitalize on the benefits and opportunities of telecommunications, companies must begin to plan their communications in much the same way they plan for product development, financing, sales, or marketing—that is, by developing a long-range plan with top-management support. Developing a corporate communications plan allows a company to take advantage of the cost savings to be had by sharing resources such as private lines, terminals, and peripherals.

The New AT&T

After more than 100 years of working toward becoming the world's largest industrial corporation, AT&T announced on January 8, 1982 its full divestiture of the twenty-two Bell operating companies. A new, much leaner structure would facilitate AT&T's entry into the worldwide information industry but the company would still maintain its manufacturing and research operations, Western Electric and Bell Laboratories.

Advances in microcircuitry, which spawned tremendous growth in the computer industry, are also taking a stronghold in the area of telephony. Fiber optic links are providing tremendous point-to-point bandwidths, thus permitting the transmission of far more information than standard wire or cable. Microwave and satellite transmission have ended the distance sensitivity of communications and introduced new carriers in competition with AT&T. As a result of these technological advances, increased economies of scale and reduced message-unit costs are making possible the tremendous growth of new options in information networks, such as value-added information services and voice/data PBXs.

VANs

A powerful new generation of value-added services such as routing, error checking, and high-speed transmission to protocol conversion provide the user with enhanced data communications services. VANs add value to basic telephone services by bundling data in packets for efficient data transmission. Through the lease of underlying transmission facilities from AT&T and other common carriers, value-added carriers offer the structural foundation of information networks for cost-effective data transmission.

Fortune 500 companies in the financial, real estate, and insurance professions have been the major data communications users since the mid-1970s through distribution of their services to customers via global networks. As early contenders in the data communications market, Fortune 500 companies were willing to assume the risks of the new technology in order to be among the first to benefit from it. These companies typically preferred to own and control their own private networks of dedicated leased lines, satellite earth stations, and/or microwave links.

On the other hand, small and medium-sized companies have generally resisted using any data communications application more sophisticated than electronic mail or on-line databases. These technologically conservative companies are now taking advantage of the VANs' benefits, as vendors continually push them toward networking. Thus, they are compelled to remain competitive in their own industries. Unlike some Fortune 500 companies, small and medium-sized companies have neither enough data intensive networking traffic nor sufficient internal resources to justify the cost of implementing a private network. Smaller businesses, therefore, turn to VANs for help in transmitting data in a much more cost-effective manner than that provided by private networks.

Most VANs have hundreds of user access nodes around the country for local dial-up access to their networks. For example, GTE's subsidiary Telenet now serves an estimated 150,000 terminal users in 290 U.S. cities, who may also access 1,200 remote computer systems and interconnect with information networks in 50 other countries. Also, Tymshare's subsidiary Tymnet, Telenet's T-net twin, services over 400 cities and 41 countries. Both networks are experiencing an annualized growth rate of approximately 50 percent and are working at continually enhancing their network services. VAN carriers have been quick to respond with new services to maximize the use of personal computers. Telenet has introduced a new communications protocol developed by Microcom, Inc., in order to support direct transmissions between personal computers and host computers or other systems. Tymnet will use the X.PC protocol (which permits microcomputers to communicate with mainframe computers) to support a wide range of personal computers in addition to the IBM PC. Most VANs also sell X.25 packet assemblers/disassemblers and dedicated leased-line interfaces for users who want their data to travel at 9,600 bits per second (bps) (instead of 1,200 bps) over dial-up telephone lines. UNINET entered the VAN market in 1981 and, as of 1985, charges an installation fee of $500 plus a monthly connection fee of $900 for a synchronous network connection. Installation of a leased line runs approximately $450, plus an additional $400 for up to fifteen miles of line. United Telecom, the parent company of UNINET, has acquired controlling interest in ISACOMM, a resale communications carrier offering integrated voice, data, and image services over Satellite Business Systems' satellite network. United Telecom is investing heavily to integrate its UNINET VAN with its satellite-based ISACOMM network for future expansion of its network services.

In addition, RCA has acquired Cylix Communications as another value-added carrier offering satellite-based services. Cylix's nationwide communications network combines satellite links and terrestrial communications facilities for long-distance data transmission. Cylix offers the business community an economical alternative to the much more expensive private networks.

Network service charges are considerably lower than either dial-up or WATS. While AT&T charges according to the distance data travel, network services charge according to user connection time and by the amount of data transmitted. They generally offer discounts for transmissions during nonpeak hours and to high-volume users.

TELECOMMUNICATIONS AND NETWORKING 9-5

Unfortunately, the faster data travel by public telephone lines, the more prone they are to distortion and outside interference. Data transmission across AT&T lines cannot transmit faster than 1200 baud (data transmission speed) without losing some information along the way. High-speed dedicated land lines and satellite links transmit at speeds of 1.544 megabytes per second, and VANs typically can transmit at 2.4K to 9.6K bps.

VANs are also capable of resolving the incompatibilities between their customers' host mainframes and different terminals. They also support the use of common protocols such as asynchronous, IBM SNA/SDLC, and 3270 terminal-emulation. An increasing number of vendors are offering microcomputer file-transfer protocols.

AT&T moved in a similar direction on June 15, 1982, when it introduced its first enhanced service, Advanced Information Systems (AIS)/NET 1000. Net 1000 translates codes, converts protocols, and monitors the speed of different terminals and host computers to permit the business user to communicate effectively with other computer systems manufactured by different vendors.

IBM's Information Network (IBM/IN) offers customers remote interactive processing. Information Network is based on IBM's System Network Architecture (SNA), permitting users to perform their own tasks from terminals linked through the network to IBM's centralized computer facility in Tampa. IBM/IN currently provides services to over 200 customers in 13 cities with a combined total of 2,500 terminals. As a result of a recent agreement with GTE Telenet, IBM/IN will extend its services overseas.

The competition within the VAN arena continues. To date, at least six VAN vendors exist (see Figure 9-1). Contenders in this competitive market for value-added services are companies from four related fields:

1. Value-added carriers such as MCI and Western Union plan to offer data communications services such as terminal-to-host links as a means to expand their telecommunications services. Both have been successful competitors in electronic mail services and have been equally successful in capturing some of the market serviced by AT&T.

2. Computer companies, having helped their customers design, purchase, and install long-range networks, are now offering interfaces between customers' local facilities and long-distance networks.

3. Fortune 500 companies now offer their network services for a price. As early major data communications users, these companies offer their own expertise, databases, and networking facilities to other companies.

4. Bell operating companies are doing their best to install direct fiber optic links between their business customers and central switching facilities as a means to discourage business customers from bypassing their dial-up lines in favor of private leased-line and microwave links.

Network/Company	Communications Facilities	Major Customers/Allies
Telenet (GTE)	■ Data only ■ Terrestrial pocket service	■ Physicians, banks
Tymnet (Tymshare)	■ Data only ■ Terrestrial pocket service	■ Alascom, Chase Manhattan, Hong Kong, and Shanghai Banking Corp.
Uninet (United Telecom)	■ Data only ■ Terrestrial	■ Travelhost (reservation system)/Control Data Corp.
Cylix (RCA)	■ Data only ■ Satellite/terrestrial	■ Republic Airlines/Burroughs
AIS/NET 1000 (AT&T)	■ Data only ■ Terrestrial/satellite pocket service	■ Ford Motor Co., Northwest Industries, Roadway Express, Inc.
Information Network (IBM)	■ Data only ■ Terrestrial/satellite	■ Insurance agents

FIG. 9-1 VANs

Competition in this market will continue to be fierce as more entrants arrive. However, as evidenced in the microcomputer marketplace, only those companies with a large market share and flexible product lines will survive.

Digital Private Branch Exchange: The PBX Explosion

Digital private branch exchange (PBX) technology has experienced recent growth as well as market penetration. Contenders in this competitive market of information services include AT&T, Northern Telecom, Rolm Corporation, IBM, and Exxon Enterprises. PBXs are compact electronic switchboards that can be programmed with software to provide advanced telephone functions such as speed dialing, least-cost routing, and call forwarding. PBXs can handle large volumes of data generated from a variety of intelligent devices, communicating word processors and multifunction electronic copiers, mainframe computers, and personal computers. In addition, PBXs are capable of combining voice and data as well as serving as "gateways" to information networks.

AT&T's Dimension System 85 PBX uses digital communications protocols to combine or "multiplex" voice and data for transmission at high speeds. Northern Telecom, a hefty competitor of AT&T, with its own SL line of switching systems, introduced the first digital switch in the United States and has grown to be second only to Western Electric as a full-line telecommunications manufacturer. Northern's SL-100 PBX is targeted for the large-line-sized PBX market, and services up to 30,000 lines. Another tough competitor in the PBX market is Rolm Corporation with its Computerized Branch Exchange (CBX) product line. The CBX is a fully digital computer-controlled telephone system designed to integrate voice, data, and text with advanced data communications features. Rolm took a very significant step last year when it introduced software enhancements allowing asynchronous data communications devices, such as terminals, host mainframes, and personal computers, to be interconnected over long-distance data networks, as well as to interconnect with value-added data networks such as Tymshare's Tymnet, GTE Telenet, and AT&T's AIS/NET 1000. Rolm's current IBM gateway allows most ANCII (American National Code for Information Interchange) devices, personal computers, and communicating word processors to emulate IBM 3270 computer terminals and thus be able to communicate with IBM host mainframe computers.

Creative ways of offering information networks and information services continue as PBX manufacturers tie in with computer makers. IBM has become a 15 percent owner of Rolm Corporation, and will continue to develop additional ways to connect IBM computers with Rolm CBXs. Both Rolm and Northern Telecom are working with Data General and Hewlett-Packard to increase their networking capabilities. Although not yet officially announced, GTE is pursuing opportunities with DEC; also, NCR has acquired interest in Ztel, which will be marketing an advanced PBX.

Office Automation

Various computer and telecommunications technologies used to manage and communicate information effectively are at the heart of office automation. Office automation comprises a wide range of modern technology that offers financial and business managers significant opportunities to improve office operating efficiency by uniting computer equipment in one companywide information system. The high-stakes players in the field of office automation (OA) include IBM, Digital, Wang, and Data General, whose strategies have been to sell microcomputer customers minicomputers and minicomputer customers microcomputers. However, competition is unfolding with smaller OA systems vendors such as Xerox, NBI, NEC, and Computer Consoles Inc., who are entering the OA market by offering their own host-based systems and value-added work stations for the big vendors' computers.

Today's computer and telecommunications technologies provide an increasing variety of alternatives for automating office tasks. Office systems range from word processors and microcomputers to computer-based telephones and voice-messaging systems. More sophisticated systems combine the functions of microcomputers with word processing and data processing capabilities in addition to linking shared resources through a local area network. Microcomputers usually do not have any inherent communications capabilities, but they hold the promise of greatly enhancing all types of communications by providing communications links to mainframe computers.[1] A mainframe computer can be characterized as any computer large enough to require one or more full-time operators, large disk-storage requirements capable of storing megabytes of data, and the ability to be automatically answered from a remote terminal via a telephone link or modem. New-generation microcomputers, dominated by the IBM PC and its many clones, are being equipped with modems.

Communications occupy much of the financial manager's time, which is spent recording and summarizing transactions, meeting with associates, accessing corporate data, making inquiries to vendors, controlling inventories, and preparing mandatory reports and financial statements. As such, a financial manager's time is spent among four broad areas:

1 Meetings/telephone calls
2 Administration
3 Analysis/other
4 Document creation

To assist with his daily, time-consuming activities, the financial manager seeks alternatives to automate these tasks. Within most companies, the financial executive starts with a personal computer or workstation to generate spreadsheets and graphics with Lotus 1-2-3. He then moves on to creating memoranda with a simple word processor or text editor. Soon, he outgrows the services of the small microcomputer and depends on larger ones for producing high-resolution graphics or making several copies of a long report. He wants to tap into the corporate mainframe for his department's latest expense figures and sales data without always having to go through the MIS department. Also, he would like his microcomputer to handle his more time-consuming tasks, such as dispensing interdepartmental mail or sending a report, with comments appended, to his division head on the East Coast, or scheduling a meeting with members of his department without having to play telephone tag all day. His single-user, single-tasking microcomputer needs to be hooked up to a multitasking local area network server before it can send electronic mail, share a database, or even schedule meetings. Smaller companies typically start with just a few microcomputers, and gradually add more as the need arises. In time, they progress to a local area network and "server" to perform multitasking/multiuser access to expensive peripherals such as high-speed, letter-quality printers and large fixed or hard disk drives capable of storing large amounts of data and programs. The network server functions as an electronic mailman and meeting scheduler for system users.

---

[1] Roger W. Berger, "Telecommunications Today," *Small Business Computers* (Jan./Feb. 1984), p. 18.

The much acclaimed "office of the future" conjures up the vision of word processing, voice processing, electronic mail, electronic file cabinets, information services, and more. Consider the following:

Word Processing. Word processing is computerized typing. Documents are created and stored electronically, enabling easy modification and editing. Where documents need to be revised, only the changes are entered as the system reformats the document. An obvious benefit is the significant reduction in time spent typing and proofreading.

Electronic Mail and Information Utilities. Electronic mail uses low-cost software and inexpensive modems for transmitting and receiving typed communications electronically over telephone lines. A user can access an information utility (e.g., The Source or CompuServ) to receive the latest corporate news, price trends, schedules, stock information, and much more.

Facsimile Systems. Facsimile systems send printed pages, drawings, or handwritten notes to other facsimile systems over telephone lines at rates of from twenty seconds to three minutes per page, depending on the equipment. This enables an organization to communicate visually with other locations very quickly.

Computer-Based Telephones. Telephone systems can establish private networks that manage the cost of long-distance calls by routing them along the least costly service. These systems can provide detailed reports itemizing calls made from each extension, which helps to isolate expenses by department, detects and prevents long-distance abuses, and verifies long-distance charges. Other features include custom calling, speed calling, and call redialing.

Voice Messaging. Voice messaging systems are a new technology that allows tone dialing telephones to (1) activate sophisticated voice answering devices to maintain continuous communications regardless of differences in time zones and (2) eliminate human errors in message taking. The voice messaging systems currently available include stand-alone systems and integrated systems. Stand-alone systems, such as those offered by VMX, IBM, Wang, and Commterm, allow for voice store-and-forward applications, but they do not support telephone answering or message notification. An integrated message system, such as Rolm's PhoneMail System, ties directly to a PBX and enables automatic telephone answering and message notification. Market research, predicting that voice messaging systems will account for $500 million to $1 billion in industry sales by 1990, indicates that the turn to voice messaging is not merely a trend but a solution to business communications problems.[2]

Electronic Document Handling. Electronic document management is the electronic storage and retrieval of documents. Database operations permit easy access to memoranda, correspondence, and reports, eliminating the need to search through a file cabinet. Such systems require sufficient storage capacity to handle daily operations, along with reference data and documents.

Data Communications Networks. Data networks allow a group of word and data processing systems, microcomputers and mainframes, printers, or other related communicating devices to be linked so that information can be exchanged or shared among all users connected to a network. Data are transferred via telephone, microwave, or satellite transmissions.

Although office automation needs depend on the nature and volume of the information and paperwork an organization handles, how fast it needs it, and how and where it uses it, office automation can help an organization do the following:

- Reduce time spent typing and revising letters and reports, thus improving turnaround time.
- Communicate more quickly and effectively with other office locations, customers, and suppliers.
- Manage customer orders and become more responsive to customer requests.
- Improve access to more information, enabling managers and staff to do their jobs better.
- Control inventory more efficiently by tracking items as they are ordered and used in production.
- Improve cash flow by monitoring outstanding customer invoices more easily.
- Record and summarize financial transactions more efficiently.
- Reduce paper storage requirements.
- Reduce time spent on such activities as internal mail distribution.
- Keep pace with business growth.[3]

---

[2] Laura Livingston, "Leaving Your Voice," *Infosystems* (Sept. 1984), p. 102.

[3] Mathew D. Shedd and Myrna U. Furlong, "How Office Automation Can Benefit Your Business," *Ernst & Whinney Ideas* (Winter 1984–1985), p. 12.

TELECOMMUNICATIONS AND NETWORKING 9-11

Whatever an organization's office automation needs may be, it is important to assess them thoroughly. Failure to do so may result in the purchase of equipment and systems that are (1) too large or too small, (2) not compatible with other equipment used, or (3) cannot expand as the organization's needs change. Good planning is essential to an organization's approach to office automation and communications. The following steps should help.[4]

1. *Commit the right people and adequate management time.* Select people who not only understand management's needs and options but who can help ensure the successful implementation of the plan. These people must have the time to commit to the project and must be capable of challenging management's needs as well as vendors' recommendations.

2. *Assess company needs.* Review present office equipment and procedures to determine the company's needs and identify problem areas. Discuss the equipment and procedures with people in the organization who know them best. Analyze the work flow. Before investing in new systems, find out whether the company's present arrangement adequately and effectively meets the company's needs. Perhaps only procedural changes are needed.

3. *Establish objectives.* Based on the assessment of the company's needs, develop specific objectives to address areas that need improvement. For example, office automation objectives may include development of a system that provides faster turnaround time on documents, increases communications while reducing telephone expense, records and summarizes financial transactions, or speeds mail delivery while reducing mailing costs.

4. *Find out what is available.* Talk to vendors and investigate several systems or brands of equipment thoroughly. Learn what products are available and their specific capabilities. Focusing on only five or six vendors out of the hundreds in the marketplace makes the process manageable. Inform the vendors of the company's immediate and long-term needs. Make sure each vendor offers the range of equipment to meet those needs now and in the future. Compare vendors' recommendations not only on the basis of price but also on their ability to service the organization over the long term.

5. *Take an integrated approach.* To the extent possible, select equipment and systems capable of handling multiple functions and ones that are compatible with others in use in the organization. Particularly if the organization plans to phase in different office automation functions

---

[4] Shedd and Furlong, p. 13.

over an extended period, this will maximize efficiency and may minimize the company's long-range office automation investment.

6 *Challenge the company's office automation plan.* Determine the worth of benefits to be gained against total cost. For example, quick turnaround time on important documents may justify an investment in a word processing system, even if the volume of typing does not.

7 *Implement in stages.* The complexity and cost of the company's office automation plan dictate the number of stages required for implementing it. Phase-in periods should be long enough to allow for adequate training of personnel and testing of equipment and systems. This should be coordinated to minimize disruption of operations.

8 *Consider the human factors.* New equipment and systems result in new procedures and may change job responsibilities. Some of the organization's employees will view this change positively, while others may be negative and feel intimidated. Yet, office automation can boost employee morale significantly by eliminating much of the monotony of routine office tasks. The amount of time it takes individuals to become comfortable and productive with the new equipment and systems varies greatly; however, a well-thought-out plan can maximize employee acceptance and minimize transition problems.

Computer and telecommunications technology allows companies of all sizes significant opportunities to improve office operating and communicating efficiency. By carefully planning an organization's communications needs and implementing an appropriate office automation plan, significant benefits can be realized in increasing administrative productivity.

LOCAL AREA NETWORKS FOR PERSONAL COMPUTERS

Overview

Long ago, people cried to be freed from their dependence on data processing shops. Requests for reports were queued for months, or the programmers just never prepared them. Executives wanted their own tools for accessing information and producing reports. In time, the personal computer age was upon us. Personal computers popped up in financial executives' offices in response to their demands for independence from their data processing (DP) departments and a chance to control their information. This led to sharing software programs and altering data for individual purposes. Soon, the need for communicating between personal computers became apparent.

Many businesses face the time when their microcomputers will not meet their needs for flexibility and effectiveness. They will have outgrown the functions and limitations of a stand-alone microcomputer environment and will seek alternatives that permit communications and peripherals sharing between microcomputers. One such alternative is called a "local area network" (LAN). LANs provide a very flexible alternative to interconnect microcomputers, share costly computer resources such as high-speed printers, access central data files, and communicate from one personal computer to another.

Although LANs have been around for some time, only in the last year or two have the number of customers and vendors grown to a critical mass. The burst of interest in LAN products has obscured the fact that very little software exists in the marketplace to manage these networks. LAN application products are primarily single-user application products that have been retrofitted to run in a multiuser environment. The market awaits the arrival of application software optimized for an LAN environment.

One of the simplest ways to share a resource such as a printer is to use a switch box to connect the printer to several computers. Each computer has a wire cable that plugs into the switch box and another cable that runs from the box to the printer. The switch box checks each computer for data to print. Stopping at the first computer with data to print, the switch box gives the computer access to the printer. When the computer has finished printing, the switch continues to search for the next computer with data to print. Devices called "spoolers" combine switching ability with memory storage. Spoolers store data to be printed from high-speed computer processors, thus freeing the computer for other tasks and processing while the printer slowly prints the information.

Several computers can be multiplexed to share a single disk-storage unit. A multiplexer unit allows personal computers to share a single disk-storage unit and software. This tends to be more complex and expensive than simple printer sharing switches. Connecting more than one computer to a hard disk unit requires methods or software for controlling access to records and sharing files.

Although LAN technology has been around for some time, only recently has the hardware been available at a reasonable cost, making it more cost effective to tie many users together than to have them swap floppy diskettes. From a hardware standpoint, there are four principal components to an LAN: (1) the personal computer, (2) the network interface cards that plug into a computer to connect it to the network, (3) the cabling that physically links the cards, and (4) the network control hardware such as file or print servers that allow users to share peripheral devices.

Software must be considered as well, because, without the right software, the network cannot function. There are two considerations for software: (1) the application programs that run on the network (e.g., word processing, spreadsheets, and accounting applications) and (2) the network software for controlling the network operations and equipment.

LAN Characteristics

LANs consist of communications nodes linking computers and other communicating devices into a functional whole. Information travels between nodes over wires or cables under the control of network servers and procedures. An LAN has the following characteristics and features:

- LANs service a limited geographic area such as an office, building, or a cluster of buildings.
- Communication can be visual through the use of display terminals.
- Communication may be either conversational or nonconversational.
- Communication can involve more than two people.
- The entire LAN entity and accompanying processing environment is generally owned and operated by a single organization.
- The complete LAN configuration is self-contained.
- Transmission speed for local networks is usually one million bps, but actual transmission rates sometimes only approach 20 to 25 percent of this figure, due to the impact of real-life constraints.
- Error rates are low, thereby reducing the level of transmissions.
- LANs have a flexible means of connecting equipment of different manufacturers, which is met by existing products with varying degrees of success.
- LANs contain support functions such as electronic mail, file transfer, word processing, graphics, and database operations.

One of the most significant advantages of LANs is the capability to share critical systems resources. Network stations are capable of sharing communications paths and expensive peripherals (e.g., large capacity disk storage and high-speed printers). As such, a typical configuration may only have one of each of this type of device, rather than several divided among a few end users. In addition, LANs generally offer lower communications costs over the long run.

A key aspect of a local network is the wire or cable over which information travels. Cables represent the electronic glue that holds the pieces of the network together. The most economical type of wire for a network is a simple paired wire; one wire carries the signals, the other acts as a return or ground. To help eliminate electrical noise, the cable is twisted together. Twisted-pair wires accommodate a maximum data rate of about one million bps over a maximum wire distance of about 4,000 feet. Coaxial cable is a single wire surrounded by a mesh wire or solid cylinder of return conductors. Coaxial cable permits higher network speed and operation over longer distances. Installation costs for simple twisted-pair wires run about 40¢ per foot to over $2 per foot for shielded cable links, while coaxial cable costs about $2.50 to $4 per installed foot.

Signalling Schemes

Information flows over cable in either of two signalling schemes: baseband or broadband. Baseband is the preferred medium among available LAN products because it supports data transmission at high throughput rates, and is less expensive than broadband. A cable's information carrying ability is measured in hertz (Hz), and the cable's total carrying capacity can be divided into separate bands. Broadband LANs have several bands that can transport computer data, video images, voice transmissions, and other types of information simultaneously. For example, data travel in packet form over the band. Each packet includes an address or location so that the network processor knows where to send it. At one moment, the band could be carrying information packets from a desk-top microcomputer, whereas, at the next moment, it could be receiving other packets from a disk-storage unit. With broadband cable, different channels coexist to carry information and operate simultaneously. Broadband networks are more complex than baseband networks because they use radio frequency (RF) modems to convert computer signals from baseband to RF band. In a broadband system, information is sent over the network by a modulating process similar to the one used in ordinary modems. Although broadband networks are more complex and expensive than baseband, they do offer more channels of information flow in return.

There is growing support for broadband networks among LAN vendors because of their capability to manage data, voice, and image transfer. IBM's PC Network is a broadband network; for this reason, broadband networks will continue to become more popular.

On the other hand, baseband is a narrowband cable with much lower capacity and no provision for video. Baseband is inherently less complex than broadband because the digital signal does not require the modulation necessary with analog transmission. Most networks used in office and business applications use only packet transmission and have no provision for video communication or dedicated channels; therefore, they use a baseband signalling scheme. In a baseband network, the signals are sent between devices as digital pulses and are not modulated or converted from digital data to analog data. Omninet is a good example of a low-cost baseband system for local area networking. It uses twisted-pair wires to interconnect the nodes in the network, which can support up to sixty-four microcomputers.

LAN Topologies

LANs come in a variety of configurations or topologies. For example, networks with star topologies have a central controller (or host) and radiating spokes to other computers and peripherals; networks with ring topologies connect all computers and peripherals in a circle with no open ends; networks with backbone or bus topologies connect each station to a linear strip cable, called the "backbone."

In a star configuration, the computer at the center is vital. All centralized control is in one master unit. This can ensure flexible and well-regulated control, but if anything causes the control unit to go down, the whole network goes down with it. However, any computer or peripheral connected to the central unit can go down or be disconnected without affecting the others. With signal handling at the center, the individual devices or nodes connected to the system can be fairly simple and inexpensive. All communications with the controlling unit are point to point, and packets do not have to be used. A star system tends to use a lot more cabling than other network topologies, because a wire or cable must run from every device to the central unit.

In a ring configuration, all nodes are equally vital, and failure or disconnection of any computer or peripheral on the ring interrupts the flow of data around the circle. However, if broken at any spot, it may be able to become a bus-connected network, and all connected devices still operating can continue to communicate with one another.

By contrast, bus-connected networks distribute control of the network among the nodes. Control is needed so that only one computer or peripheral at a time uses the network and messages from one connected device do not interfere with those from another. In a bus, any node can go down or be disconnected at any time without affecting the network's operation. As such, bus configurations are more commonplace than rings or stars.

LAN Access Methods

There are two basic methods for controlling access to networks: (1) token passing and (2) carrier sense multiple access/collision detection (CSMA/CD). In token passing, a special data packet, called a "token," is handed from one node to another. The token is circulated around the network, stopping at each station. If the token is marked "empty," a station can latch to it, append it to a message packet, mark it "in use," and send it back onto the network. Only the node holding the token is allowed to send packets over the network. Other nodes on the network, seeing the token in use, will not transmit. When the receiving station receives the token, it reads the message packet, marks the token "empty," and sends it out to the network for yet another node to attach to it. Token passing is easily implemented on networks with ring topologies, in which all stations on the network are connected to one another.

Another widely used control method is called "carrier sense multiple access/collision detection" (CSMA/CD). With this method of network control, each node listens to network traffic (collision avoidance, CSMA/CA) and sends a packet message only when it cannot hear any other node's transmission. If it cannot, a station wanting to transmit can proceed. However, if two nodes happen to start transmitting simultaneously, there is a collision that destroys the data. Both nodes stop and send a jamming signal to tell everyone that a collision has occurred. They then try to retransmit the collision spoiled messages. Ethernet is a collision detection network, and is relatively inexpensive to set up. However, since each device on the network is in competition with every other device, collision detection networks can be relatively inefficient for a large number of users.

Although token passing is more inherently sophisticated and expensive than collision detection, it is also more efficient at carrying data and supporting larger volumes of data and users. This is so because, in collision detection networks, each node is unaware of the others' presence; each transmits a packet message whenever it has one to send, regardless of whether another node is trying to transmit at the same time. If two or more nodes attempt to send at once, none get through and they have to try again.

Planning for an LAN

For the financial manager contemplating installation of an LAN for his department, caution is well advised. Clearly defining needs and evaluating options prior to selecting a network are crucial for avoiding the misfortune, extra cost, and potential frustration of selecting inappropriate products.

Most businesses are overburdened to start, and the introduction of a network means training personnel, reorganizing procedures, and often learning several new programs. Thus, they cannot afford to encounter software incompatibility, printer problems, or a serious disaster (e.g., lost data). Careful planning can help to avoid these risks.

The financial manager should answer fundamental questions about an LAN's technical characteristics. The following[5] are a few of these questions.

- What is the provider's track record and experience level?
- What categories of IO devices can be connected to the network, both in terms of hardware and software compatibility?
- What plan for LAN management and control exists in the system?
- What types of systems services are provided to users of the network?
- What performance parameters can be expected from the network?
- What degree of flexibility prevails in the network?

With a properly planned LAN and procurement of the hardware and software, the financial manager can dramatically increase his staff's productivity and effectiveness. The network could be nothing more than a standard coaxial cable linking all microcomputers, office copiers, and the data processing mainframe computer. A properly planned and designed LAN enables a financial executive to more rapidly manipulate, edit, and retrieve data for financial anal-

---

[5] Jay McCoy, "A Cautionary Perspective on Local-Area Networks," *Small Business Computers* (Jan./Feb. 1984), p. 46.

ysis and document development. By extending the communications network to other functional areas, it speeds document transmission and decreases review times. An LAN system might operate in the following manner.[6]

- Financial analysts would be able to send, receive, and manipulate common financial information. Data could be sent between workstations using electronic mail technology. The analyst could access the database through his personal computer to perform large data calculations.
- Economies of scale could be realized for document development. With the LAN approach, all documents would be entered into the system once, with revisions keyed later.
- Interoffice communications would be greatly improved. Revisions to documents, memoranda, and reports could be distributed to all users.
- Operational economies of scale would also be realized. Financial documents and statements could be easily transmitted to LAN users for their review and edit changes.

The decision to implement an LAN requires careful planning and product selection. With careful planning, networks provide a flexible and effective alternative to bringing communications capabilities to personal computers.

CASE STUDY

Ernst & Whinney National Systems Group

The purpose here is to share the experience and knowledge gained from the installation of a 3Com Ethernet LAN for IBM personal computers by Ernst & Whinney's National Systems Group (NSG) in Cleveland.[7] Ernst & Whinney is one of the world's largest certified public accounting (CPA) firms, specializing in three major service areas: audit, tax, and management consulting.

The material presented should be valuable for financial executives who want to learn about local area networking. Businesses for which an LAN similar to the one described in this section is appropriate should find the following guideline extremely useful.

History of the NSG Network

Ernst & Whinney's National Systems Group had always used personal computers to develop and test software. As the number of personal computers in

---

[6] Jerry Cashin, "Local Area Networks: Still More Promise Than Action?" *Small Systems World* (Mar. 1984), p. 45.

[7] James H. Nestor, "Local Area Networks for Personal Computers," Ernst & Whinney, *Technical Report Series National Systems Group* (1984).

the group increased, several problems caused the group to turn to local area networking of personal computers. These problems included delayed backup of data, slow transfer of files between personal computers, and lack of source code security and control.

The introduction of the IBM PC XT added to these problems. The XT's 10MB (megabyte) hard disk required wasteful use of professional time to backup data using floppy diskettes. Since the data were stored on a hard disk, users became dependent on a particular machine for access to stored information. To add to the difficulty of backing up data, it was also very difficult and time consuming to transfer large files between computers. If a particular machine was not available, productivity decreased. Although hard disk machines proved to be faster and more efficient than the use of floppy diskettes, they were also more expensive.

Having recognized these problems, the group began to look for alternative solutions and soon realized that an LAN offered many benefits. In short, members of the group benefited by sharing expensive hard disks and printers, machine independence for programmers, rapid-file transfer between machines, rapid backups of data and programs, common source libraries and data files, and improved communications using electronic mail. By eliminating the duplication of programs and data from the disks of many users, the total amount of disk space used to store the information was reduced.

NSG researched the possibilities of networking in great detail. A cost/benefit analysis was prepared, and a small test network was installed and evaluated. Then a final design was developed, and the network was installed.

Researching LANs

NSG's principal research activities included reading textbooks and magazine articles, attending seminars and trade shows, and reviewing product literature. It was necessary to gain an understanding of LANs for personal computers. By primarily reading microcomputer magazines and by taking college courses, the group was able to gain a general knowledge of computer communications, networking technology, and packet protocols. Various trade shows (e.g., COMDEX and PC Faire) afforded the opportunity to examine vendors' products, ask questions, and collect product literature.

The group examined over fourteen different networks for IBM PCs. Networks were classified into standard networks (e.g., Ethernet) and PC-only networks (e.g., Corvus Omninet). The 3Com Ethernet Network for IBM PCs was selected because:

- It was compatible with other Ethernets for mainframes;
- Its 10MB transfer rate offered high performance; and
- It provided the level of security required for the installation.

The Evaluation Network

When the basic LAN research had been completed, there were still unanswered questions. The principal concern was that of acceptable performance in terms of speed and reliability. Because of the substantial investment required for a full-blown department network, the group decided to conduct a limited evaluation network.

For purposes of evaluation, the group tested and installed a four-unit 3Com Ethernet Network for approximately two months. The IBM PCs and Florida Data printer had already been purchased for development work and were borrowed for the evaluation. The following list shows the equipment purchased from 3Com.

Quantity	Description	Approximate Cost
4	EtherLink cards	$3,180
1	EtherShare software	500
1	EtherPrint software	500
1	EtherMail software	500
1	Cables and connectors for four units	200
	Total	$4,880

The personal computer components consisted of one IBM PC XT used as the network server and a pair of two-drive IBM PCs as network users. A COMPAQ portable computer was added as the third-user PC.

Evaluation Results

The following summarizes the results of testing the four-unit network for approximately two months. Conclusions are those drawn at that time and do not include additional information gained since then.

1 *Documentation, installation, configuration, and support*
   - 3Com documentation was good. The installation manuals and user's guides were complete and accurate.
   - Hardware installation was relatively simple.
   - Configuration of the systems software was the most complex task, since decisions had to be made regarding disk directories and user privileges. This part of the configuration could be modified easily without reinstalling the network software.
   - It took approximately two hours to install the network and make it operational.
   - 3Com support with technical questions was prompt.

TELECOMMUNICATIONS AND NETWORKING

2 *Description of the test configuration*
- A PC XT with 256KB was used as a dedicated file server, printer server, and mail server.
- The file server handled requests for access to the shared 10MB disk drive. The printer server controlled the Florida Data line printer by accepting print requests, storing them as files on the disk, and printing them from the queue. The mail server transferred messages and files between users.
- The three user machines on the network consisted of two IBM PCs and a COMPAQ portable, all with 256K. Each had access to a common read-only disk volume or program area, one or more private volumes or storage areas, and the line printer.

3 *Software compatibility tests.* Following is a list of software that had been installed and that operated satisfactorily on the network.

- IBM PC DOS 2.0 commands
- IBM PC BASIC (BASICA)
- COMPAQ BASIC
- IBM BASIC compiler (BASCOM)
- BDS extensions to IBM BASIC
- Lattice C compiler
- IBM Personal Editor (PE)
- WordStar word processing
- Multimate word processing
- dBASE II data base
- MDBS III data base
- SuperCalc ^{3}

All of the software operated exactly the same way on the network as it did on a single computer. Two copy-protected programs were tested: Lotus 1-2-3 and PFS File. These programs required that the user insert a key diskette in his drive A to operate the program. Otherwise, they operated correctly on the network, permitting program and data storage on the server disk and printouts via the network printer.

4 *Verification of network benefits*
Because of the network's 10 megabyte transfer rate, simulated backups took approximately ten minutes per week for each user. The previous method using floppy diskettes took about two hours per week for each user. The time savings were consistent with earlier projections.

5 *Summary and recommendations*
Evaluation of the four-unit 3Com LAN was a success. The system met or exceeded all expectations. The projected benefits of time savings during backup and file transfer were verified. The group recommended that the network be expanded to include all the IBM PCs, XTs, and COMPAQs in the NSG.

Installation Checklist

The following is an installation checklist used for the 3Com LAN.

- ☐ Meet with electrician to plan cable installation:
  - Which offices?
  - Order of installation
  - Location of repeater and terminators
  - Cable and connectors to be ordered
  - Tools to be ordered
- ☐ Supervise installation of cable.
- ☐ Order PCs for servers.
- ☐ Order hard disks and tape drives.
- ☐ Order Ethernet hardware:
  - EtherLink cards
  - Repeater
  - Terminators
  - Loopback plug
  - Transceivers and cable repeater
- ☐ Order Ethernet software:
  - EtherShare
  - EtherPrint
  - EtherMail
- ☐ Order accoustical cabinets for printers.
- ☐ Design physical layout for servers and printers.
- ☐ Set up, test, and "burn-in" the PCs.
- ☐ Install EtherLink cards.
- ☐ Test EtherLink cards.
- ☐ Install disk drives on the servers:
  - Install controller cards.
  - Make boot disks.
- ☐ Test the PCs with hard disks.
- ☐ Decide on the order in which to add PCs.
- ☐ Make a list of users assigned to each server.
- ☐ Connect printers to servers.

- [ ] Assemble printer accoustical cabinets.
- [ ] Install and test server units.
- [ ] Make server boot diskettes.
- [ ] Install a few users on test loop.
- [ ] Test the local loop network.
- [ ] Install and test office cables.
- [ ] Test first segment before adding users.
- [ ] Add users to first segment:
  - Connect cables.
  - Install cards in PCs.
  - Make boot diskettes.
  - Add user IDs and volumes.
  - Train users.
- [ ] Make temporary backup arrangements.

The purpose here has been to share the experience gained from the installation of a 3Com Ethernet LAN. The network described is a successful working example that other companies can use as a prototype.

REFERENCES

Berger, Roger W. "Telecommunications Today." *Small Business Computers* (Jan./Feb. 1984), pp. 18–25.

Cashin, Jerry. "Local Area Networks: Still More Promise Than Action?" *Small Systems World* (Mar. 1984), pp. 42–46.

Ferris, David and John Cunningham. "Local Nets for Micros." *Datamation* (Aug. 1, 1984), pp. 104–109.

Gabel, David. "Local Area Networks." *PC Week* (Mar. 19, 1985), pp. 3–5.

Gartner Group Inc. "Information Networks: Emerging Trends & Markets." Produced by Kenneth A. Smalheiser (1984).

Glatzer, Hal. "The Promise of LANs: MIS Back in Control." *Software News* (Mar. 1985), pp. 51–58.

_____. "Before Hooking Up, It Helps to Understand LAN Concepts." *Software News* (Mar. 1985), pp. 59–65.

Hillhouse, Joseph. "The New World of Telecomm." *Computer Decisions* (Sept. 15, 1983), pp. 95–118.

Horwitt, Elizabeth. "Confronting the Communications Quandry." *Business Computer Systems* (Sept. 1984), pp. 38–45.

———. "Long-Distance Networks." *Business Computer Systems* (Dec. 1984), pp. 36–43.

Jamison, J.F. "Computer Networks—The Ubiquitous Communication Medium." *Data Management* (Aug. 1984), pp. 18–21.

Jenkins, George A., Jr. "LAN Is the Answer to White-Collar Productivity." *Data Management* (Aug. 1984), pp. 14–17.

Johnson, Jan. "The Corporate Communications Conundrum." *Datamation* (June 1983), pp. 112–116.

Larson, Richard. "New Corporate Excellence Options Gained Through Telecommunications." *Communications News* (May 1984), pp. 38–40.

Livingston, Laura. "Leaving Your Voice." *Infosystems* (Sept. 1984), pp. 102–104.

McCoy, Jay. "A Cautionary Perspective on Local-Area Networks." *Small Business Computers* (Jan./Feb. 1984), pp. 46–47.

Nestor, James H. "Local Area Networks for Personal Computers." *Ernst & Whinney Technical Report Series* (1984).

Schedd, Mathew D., and Myrna U. Furlong. "How Office Automation Can Benefit Your Business." *Ernst & Whinney Ideas* (Winter 1984–1985), pp. 11–13.

CHAPTER **10**

Systems Control and Auditability

Steven J. Root

Overview	2	Risk Analysis: A Useful Tool	16
		Computer Fraud and Mischievous Acts	20
Definitions	4	Violations of Laws and Regulations	20
		Negligent or Ineffective Information	
Systems Control Concepts	6	Systems Management	21
The FCPA	7	Computer Dependence	22
General Provisions	7	Proliferation of Minicomputers and	
Accounting Standards	8	Microcomputers	22
Variability of Control Systems	9		
Authorization	10	**Control Objectives and Techniques**	23
Execution, Processing, and Recording	11	Authorization	25
Accountability	11	Execution, Processing, and Recording	26
Security and Safeguarding	12	Accountability	29
Reasonable Assurance	13	Security	30
Auditability	14	Internal Auditing	33
		Detailed Functional Auditing	34
EDP and Internal Control	15	Installation Reviews	35
Distinguishing Features	15	Application Auditing	35
Dynamic Environment	15	Developing Systems Auditing	35
Uniform Processing	15	Concurrent Auditing	35
Error Correction	15	Personal Computers	37
Storage	15	Authorization	39
Auditability	16	Accountability	39
Security	16	Security	39
Risks in EDP	16	**References**	40

Fig. 10-1 Phases of EDP Organizational Growth 3
Fig. 10-2 Types of Security Exposure 17
Fig. 10-3 Preventive, Limiting, and Recovery Controls for Selected Exposures 19
Fig. 10-4 EDP Auditing Chronology 34
Fig. 10-5 Depiction of Embedded Audit Routines 36
Fig. 10-6 Tabulation of Generalized Audit Software Packages and Their Vendors 38

10-1

OVERVIEW

Possibly the most critical topic involving systems concepts is systems control and auditability. It is through systems control and auditability features that management may be assured that systems will achieve their objectives. This is universally true for any system, financial or otherwise.

In the past the topic often received scant attention and consideration during the systems development phase. In part, the inattentiveness to control and auditability considerations may be explained as lack of awareness. The financial manager had long been considered to be an expert in internal controls; thus, the designation "controller." However, his expertise traditionally revolved around accounting controls in a nonEDP environment.

Controllers and other financial managers depended on the EDP department for ensuring the accuracy and completeness of information in their systems. The EDP community, although expert in systems designing, programming, testing, and implementing functions, was not knowledgeable about internal accounting control. Thus, although any accountant knows that the manually prepared general ledger and books of account must be properly protected and locked up at night, the general ledger automated system designed and installed by the MIS function may be accessible to anyone who has or knows the password.

Another reason often cited for the lack of attention to controls and auditability features was that they were costly. Both systems developers and the user wanted systems to be installed at the lowest possible cost. Sometimes it was hard to convince them, given their orientation toward frugality, that time and effort needed to be directed at defining control requirements. This was particularly true where actual costs overran budget.

Eventually, however, negative experiences with systems testing, and later with efforts to correct problems after installation, convinced users that controls and auditability were an indispensable part of systems development.

This evolutionary scenario has recurred so often that it has fostered a popular theory that depicts the phases of EDP growth. This theory is presented in Figure 10-1.[1]

The phases illustrated suggest that, as growth occurs in EDP activities, the structure changes from the simple processing of data (Phase I) to strategic managing of related resources (Phase V). After an EDP capability is installed, a period of rapid growth follows, during which the challenge is to meet the sharply increasing demand for EDP services. This usually involves considerable activity in new systems development, added hardware configurations, operating systems conversions, and staff expansion.

---

[1] International Business Machines, *Organizing the I/S Business* (White Plains, New York: IBM, 1983), p. 20.

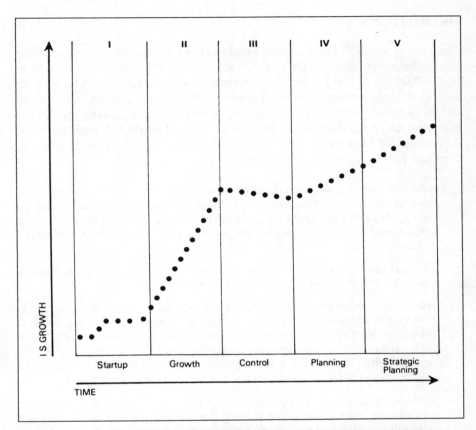

FIG. 10-1 Phases of EDP Organizational Growth (Source: James D. Willson and Steven J. Root, *Internal Auditing Manual* (Boston: Warren, Gorham & Lamont, 1984), p. 26A-3. Reprinted by permission.)

The growth phase is followed by the need to respond to user complaints of poor response time for existing applications, excessive errors, and computer malfunctions, as well as delays in developing new systems. Thus, control becomes paramount.

In the latter phases, management begins to realize that the investment in resources required to process information is considerable and must be managed in much the same way as other significant investments, such as those in capital facilities and inventory.

The discussion in this chapter is about the nature and types of controls and auditability features that modern FISs must use. Systems control and security concepts form the basis for understanding control objectives and techniques.

DEFINITIONS

Controls in an EDP environment simply cannot be explained without using terminology that may be alien to the reader. The glossary of terms at the front of this Manual should be used for reference. Familiar terms pertaining to the subject of control, such as "internal control," "accounting control," or "administrative control," warrant definition here, however. Understanding these terms is central to understanding the concept of internal control. Widely accepted definitions for these terms have been advanced by the American Institute of Certified Public Accountants (AICPA).[2]

> *Internal control* comprises the plan of organization and all of the coordinate methods and measures adopted within a business to safeguard its assets, check the accuracy and reliability of its accounting data, promote operational efficiency, and encourage adherence to prescribed managerial policies.[3]
>
> *Internal control*, in the broad sense includes ... controls which may be characterized as either accounting or administrative. ... [4]
>
> *Administrative control* includes, but is not limited to, the plan of organization and the procedures and records that are concerned with the decision processes leading to management's authorization of transactions. Such authorization is a management function directly associated with the responsibility for achieving the objectives of the organization and is the starting point for establishing accounting control of transactions.
>
> *Accounting control* comprises the plan of organization and the procedures and records that are concerned with the safeguarding of assets and the reliability of financial records and consequently is designed to provide reasonable assurance that:
>
> a. Transactions are executed in accordance with management's general or specific authorization.

---

[2] AICPA, *AICPA Professional Standards*, Vol. 1, *Statement on Auditing Standards* No. 1 (Nov. 1972) (hereinafter referred to and cited as AU), Section 320. The original definition of "internal control" was developed by the AICPA's Committee on Auditing Procedure and published in a special report entitled *Internal Control-Elements of a Coordinated System and Its Importance to Management and the Independent Public Accountant* in 1948. This definition was broad and not helpful in identifying the segment of internal control that is of particular interest to public accountants in conducting examinations of financials. Thus, definitions evolved for "accounting control" and "administrative control." Public accountants were primarily interested in the former. These definitions were somewhat deficient in that they permitted possible differing interpretations that affected the public accountant's scope of work. In 1973, the AICPA's Auditing Standards Executive Committee, a successor organization to the Committee on Auditing Procedure, revised the definitions of "administrative control" and "accounting control" into that shown in the text.

[3] AU Section 320.08.

[4] AU Section 320.09. (This was originally published in AICPA Committee on Audit Procedure, "Scope of the Independent Auditor's Review of Internal Control," *Statement on Auditing Procedure No. 29* (1958), paragraph .09.)

b. Transactions are recorded as necessary (1) to permit preparation of financial statements in conformity with generally accepted accounting principles or any other criteria applicable to such statements and (2) to maintain accountability for assets.

c. Access to assets is permitted only in accordance with management's authorization.

d. The recorded accountability for assets is compared with the existing assets at reasonable intervals and appropriate action is taken with respect to any differences.[5]

In subsequent paragraphs, the Auditing Standards Board points out that "where computer processing is used in significant accounting applications, internal accounting control procedures are sometimes defined into two types: general and application control procedures."[6]

General controls are those controls that relate to all or many computerized accounting activities and often include control over the development, modification, and maintenance of computer programs and control over the use of and changes to data maintained on computer files.[7]

Application controls relate to individual computerized accounting applications, for example, programmed edit controls for verifying customer account numbers and credit limits.[8]

The AICPA classification of EDP controls into either general or application controls, as subdivisions of internal accounting control, is intended to provide public accountants with guidance and understanding of the controls that are relevant in conducting a study of internal controls as required by generally accepted auditing standards (GAAS).

This classification may be useful to outside accountants in the context of examining their clients' financial statements, but it does not reflect management's thinking with regard to organizing, planning, staffing, and controlling EDP resources.

Furthermore, as database technology becomes more commonplace, systems technology makes the distinction between general and application controls less significant. As noted in Chapter 2 and elsewhere under discussions of database technology, data are maintained independently from their applica-

---

[5] AU Sections 320.26–320.27. (The definition for "administrative control" is intended only to provide a point of departure for distinguishing accounting control and, consequently, is not necessarily definitive for other purposes. This portion of AU Section 320 was originally published in AICPA, "Codification of Auditing Standards and Procedures," *Statement on Auditing Standards No. 1* (1972), paragraphs 26 and 27.) Reprinted by permission.

[6] AU Section 320.34. Reprinted by permission.

[7] AU Section 320.34, n. 6. Footnote added by issuance of AICPA, "The Effects of Computer Processing on the Examination of Financial Statements," *Statement on Auditing Standards No. 48* (1984), p. 6.

[8] *AU Section 320.34, n. 6. Reprinted by permission.*

tions. Thus, the number of procedures and controls that can be specifically associated with a given application is shrinking.

Finally, the section under EDP control concepts of the Foreign Corrupt Practices Act (FCPA) applies to all internal accounting control applications regardless of the method of processing. The Act uses terms related to authorization, execution, recording, accountability, and security in discussing internal control adequacy. However, it is not clear how general and application controls fit into the FCPA terminology. Since these terms are more consistent with the managerial viewpoint and contribute to a better understanding of the subject, terms consistent with FCPA terminology are used and defined in this chapter explaining EDP control concepts.

One final definition, that for "auditability," is provided here, since the title of this chapter includes the term. According to the Stanford Research Institute, a widely recognized source, auditability refers to "features and characteristics of an information system, either computer-based or manual, that allow verification of the adequacy and effectiveness of controls and verification of the accuracy and completeness of data processing results."[9]

An important point made in the foregoing definition is that auditability covers a set of controls designed as part of a system. It does not apply to techniques and procedures that an auditor might use in studying and testing a system. In discussing internal control concepts, objectives, and techniques, auditability controls are covered, but are not necessarily identified as such.

SYSTEMS CONTROL CONCEPTS

From a conceptual viewpoint, attaining adequate control in an EDP environment is fundamentally no different from adequately controlling non-EDP activities. This point is underscored by the standards of field work contained in the AICPA's *Professional Standards* in its discussion of accounting control objectives: "Since the definitions and related basic concepts of accounting control are expressed in terms of objectives they are independent of the method of data processing used; consequently, they apply equally to manual, mechanical and electronic data processing systems."[10]

Once the discussion moves beyond broad concepts, a very different picture emerges. To quote again from the AICPA's *Professional Standards*: "However, the organization and procedures required to accomplish those objectives may be influenced by the method of data processing used."[11]

For those familiar with non-EDP control techniques only, the degree of understatement inherent in that statement will soon be obvious.

---

[9] Stanford Research Institute, "Systems Auditability and Control," *Control Practices* (USA: Institute of Internal Auditors, Inc., 1977), p. 149.

[10] AU Section 330.32.

[11] AU Section 330.32.

Since the basic concepts listed below are the same regardless of how data are processed, only brief mention is made of them in the following paragraphs.

- The role of the FCPA
- Variability of control systems
- Authorization
- Execution, processing, and recording
- Accountability
- Security and safeguarding

The FCPA

Before approaching the specifics of internal control concepts, it is useful to add a reminder of the FCPA's role in internal control. Following is an insightful discussion along these lines.

Business management has long been responsible for reasonably assuring that an adequate system of controls was in place in the business organization, and was, in fact, operating. And, as later described, financial management had, and has, a particular role in establishing and maintaining adequate internal accounting controls. The role of independent accountants has been to review the system of internal controls primarily to determine the scope of examination considered necessary. Yet the business executive had a continuing interest, day after day, in the effective operation of the controls. It was through his day-to-day observations that he knew if his policies and procedures were adhered to and carried out efficiently. As the size and complexity of the enterprise grew, and he was further removed from the scene of activity, these controls became more important. They were a necessary vehicle in achieving the business objective. Thus, business involvement with the control system in fact has existed for many years. However, in December 1977 Congress enacted the Foreign Corrupt Practices Act (FCPA), which gave a new perspective to, and emphasis on, internal controls.[12]

General Provisions. The FCPA arose, among other reasons, from disclosures of unacceptable business practices and recommendations relating thereto from several sources:

1 *The investigative results of the Office of the Watergate Special Prosecutor and the Securities and Exchange Commission (SEC), showing the use of corporate resources for domestic political contributions and for bribery of foreign officials.* Some of the payments

---

[12] James D. Willson and Steven J. Root, *Internal Auditing Manual* (Boston: Warren, Gorham & Lamont, 1984), pp. 3-7–3-9. Reprinted by permission.

were illegal at the time, and others were at least questionable. Many were achieved through off-the-books funds or bank accounts and use of methods that circumvented the internal accounting control systems.

2 *The SEC's findings and recommendations as disclosed in* Report on Questionable and Illegal Corporate Payments and Practices, *submitted to the Senate Banking, Housing and Urban Affairs Committee on May 12, 1976.* In this document, the SEC recommended that Congress enact legislation to improve the accuracy of corporate books and records.

3 *Hearings on illegal and questionable business payments, conducted by the Senate Banking, Housing and Urban Affairs Committee.* This committee proposed legislation, part of which was incorporated into the FCPA.

Accounting Standards. The concern here is principally with the Act's accounting standards. In summary, if a company is subject to the Securities Exchange Act of 1934 (e.g., a company with publicly traded stock), the FCPA's accounting standards provision requires that the company keep in reasonable detail "books, records and accounts" that accurately and fairly reflect the company's transactions and disposition of assets and maintain a system of internal accounting controls. Specifically, every issuer covered by the law shall:

(A) make and keep books, records, and accounts, which, in reasonable detail, accurately and fairly reflect the transactions and dispositions of the assets of the issuer; and

(B) devise and maintain a system of internal accounting controls sufficient to provide reasonable assurances that—

    (i) transactions are executed in accordance with management's general or specific authorization;

    (ii) transactions are recorded as necessary (I) to permit preparation of financial statements in conformity with generally accepted accounting principles or any other criteria applicable to such statements, and (II) to maintain accountability for assets;

    (iii) access to assets is permitted only in accordance with management's general or specific authorization; and

    (iv) the recorded accountability for assets is compared with the existing assets at reasonable intervals and appropriate action is taken with respect to any differences.

Some feel that compliance with the accounting standards provisions is difficult in that the law is unclear. Interpretations of the law are being provided with the passage of time; future statutory actions may help to further clarify matters. In considering compliance with the law, both congressional intent and the concept of reasonableness should be applied in determining the appropriate action to be taken. Financial record keeping is not, in fact, separable from the internal accounting systems that generate the records. Therefore, in demonstrating compliance with the Act's accounting standards, a company is well advised "to consider the entire internal control system and especially the internal accounting controls."

As most seasoned financial managers know, the language of the FCPA, as it pertains to internal accounting control, is taken directly from the professional literature of the AICPA. As a result, compliance with the law must be measured by the degree to which compliance with this language is achieved. Since EDP controls are an integral part of internal accounting control, according to this literature, the FCPA applies to them as well.

The SEC is charged by law with administrative responsibility for internal accounting controls. In fact, the FCPA, upon enactment, amended the securities laws for which the SEC is administrator. In discharging its responsibility in this area, the SEC has chosen not to issue guidance as to what kinds of internal accounting controls meet FCPA requirements.

In the absence of such guidance, there is some uncertainty about what constitutes "books, records, and accounts, which, in reasonable detail, accurately and fairly reflect the transactions and dispositions of the assets of the issue." Moreover, the concept of reasonable assurance is built into the FCPA; the uncertainty here is equally great.

When the FCPA was passed, little attention was given to the fact that EDP controls would be covered. It soon became clear, however, that since internal accounting control involved the processing of transactions, and since the professional literature made no distinction regarding the method of processing in its fundamental definitions, EDP controls indeed were subject to the FCPA.

Variability of Control Systems

The nature and extent of controls present vary considerably from system to system. Among the factors that have been cited for this variability are:

- Overall size of company
- Geographic dispersion of operating units
- Degree of centralization or decentralization
- Style of management
- Type of industry
- Relative amount of foreign vs. domestic operations
- Management philosophy[13]

---

[13] Willson and Root, p. 3-9.

As noted in Chapter 1, the control environments of small, single-product, single-owner companies differ vastly from those of publicly held, multinational, conglomerated leviathans of the 1980s. The owner or manager of a small company or department is close enough to day-to-day activities to exercise managerial influence with little assistance. He can sense whether sales are lagging, inventory is building, or collections are dragging without having to depend on elaborate systems.

Yet, as a business (or operation) grows, much of the owner's or senior manager's personal involvement is lost. In an expanding company, the increasing volume of activities and the pace of events force delegation and division of duties, responsibilities, and authority. Thus, systems must emerge as replacements for this lost involvement.

As the systems emerge, it is incumbent upon top management, including the board of directors, to establish an appropriate control environment. The environment must be such that the rest of the management team and its support personnel sense the importance attached by top management to establishing and maintaining adequate internal controls. In the opinion of one public accounting firm, the following factors are involved in setting up a proper control environment:

- Code of business ethics
- Internal audit or monitoring function
- Formal, written control procedures surrounding transactions in areas of high business risk
- Written confirmation from executive and line management affirming compliance with policies and control procedures[14]

Authorization

In business, authority for the activities of any given enterprise ultimately rests with its owners by virtue of their rights and duties as owners. However, to achieve their business objectives, owners must delegate authority to act to competent and reliable employees. This delegation is dynamic and ongoing. When it functions properly, the desired results occur. When it does not, the consequences can be disastrous. Much mismanagement is attributable to the improper use of delegated authority.

Authority may be delegated generally or specifically. Thus, the board of directors or top management may generally authorize the performance of certain actions by establishing policies that the organization must follow. Examples include authority to enter into contracts, acquire or dispose of assets, open bank accounts, and incur debt. On the other hand, specific authority usually

---

[14] Joseph E. Connor and Burnell H. DeVos, eds., *Guide to Accounting Controls* (Boston: Warren, Gorham & Lamont, 1979), p. 1-15.

relates to specific undertakings, such as the acquisition or construction of specific assets, the development of a given system, or the production of a specific part.

Execution, Processing, and Recording

From a conceptual standpoint, execution, processing, and recording are the carrying out of instructions or orders generally or specifically authorized. Their meanings overlap considerably; thus, individual definitions are not advanced here.

Controls in these areas must be sufficient to make sure that the books of account accurately and fairly reflect the company's transactions and dispositions of assets. To accomplish this, certain characteristics are invariably present:

- Competent personnel
- Adequate allocation of resources
- Written policies and procedures
- Approved forms
- Recurring routines
- Segregation of duties
- Provision for error detection and correction
- Flexibility

In addition, executing, processing, and recording are sufficiently controllable only where the systems and routines provide for a set of checks and balances. These techniques come in a variety of forms, including edits, duplicate processing or reperformance, reconciling, reviewing, and scanning, to name but a few. Involved here is the notion that a certain amount of control redundancy is necessary for accuracy, completeness, and consistency.

Finally, the activities involved in executing, processing, and recording require supervisory or disciplinary controls to make sure that everything and everyone continue to function as intended.

Accountability

Accountability is closely related to the supervisory or disciplinary type of control just mentioned. It involves pinpointing responsibility for decisions, actions, and other events or occurrences with specific functions and individuals.

Accountability also involves certain types of control practices designed for verification or validation. For example, the periodic verification of physical assets and/or inventory by inspection with subsequent reconciliation to accounting records entails accountability. Other examples of accountability controls include:

- Periodic balancing between the general ledger control account and subsidiary ledgers (as for accounts receivable and payable)
- Periodic reports of actual vs. budgeted or planned performance for a project, department, division, or company
- Periodic reconciliations of labor distribution reports with payroll journals
- Periodic bank account reconciliations

Effective and adequate accountability controls tend to exhibit the following characteristics:

- Competent and involved supervisory personnel
- Segregation of duties
- Policies and procedures that clearly define responsibilities and duties in understandable terms
- Documentation sufficient to fix responsibility for any given decision or action and the reasons therefor

Security and Safeguarding

Any system of internal control is not complete unless the risks of loss, damage, destruction, alteration, pilferage, and/or theft of property are effectively minimized. Security or safeguarding (used synonymously throughout this Manual) are vital to any internal control system.

Thus, in every control environment, several control mechanisms are introduced to reduce the chance that some type of harmful event will come to pass, either intentionally or unintentionally. Security controls usually involve:

- Limiting access to records and assets
- Providing physical protective features such as secured buildings, fenced perimeters to facilities, badge control systems, security forces, lockable offices and files, and fire fighting equipment:
- Segregating duties
- Rotating personnel
- Maintaining adequate insurance

The nature and extent of security controls present in any given system are apt to vary considerably. Among the factors involved are:

SYSTEMS CONTROL AND AUDITABILITY   10-13

- Amount and type of assets at risk (the more liquid or convertible the asset, the greater the risk)
- The risks involved
- The complexity of the system
- The geographic location
- The cost of additional security
- The history of security incidents
- The overall management philosophy

Decisions regarding how much security to provide in any situation are far from simple to make. However, the decisions made are often critical to the organization's long-term well-being.

The technique of risk assessment has gained considerable popularity. This is probably because of the rapid growth in use-automated processing techniques. The resultant increased concentration of company records in computers has raised management's concern about "what could happen if. . . ." Perhaps for this reason, most risk analysis is performed in connection with automated systems, a subject discussed in greater detail in a following section.

Reasonable Assurance

Essential to an understanding of internal control is the concept of reasonable assurance. This concept recognizes the fact that there is no absolute way to prevent errors, omissions, and irregularities. For this reason, no system of internal controls can be considered 100 percent reliable. This is particularly true in terms of the accounting and financial information produced by these systems.

Knowing when a given system is sufficiently controlled to provide the degree of assurance inherent in the concept of "reasonable" is a matter of judgment. This determination is made by management, at times implicitly, by considering whether the estimated costs of a given control procedure are exceeded by the benefits derived. When this is the case, prudent management is expected to implement the control.

Considering costs and benefits for possible control alternatives is a subjective process. Since the passage of the FCPA, many companies have made cost/benefit analysis a staple in the exercise of their responsibility for maintaining adequate internal control systems.

Although the FCPA itself makes no direct reference to cost/benefit analysis, it specifically uses the term "reasonable assurances" in its internal control section. The FCPA left it to the SEC to decide, through administrative procedure, what further guidance might be necessary.

The SEC has chosen not to promulgate specific guidelines that might be used to measure internal control adequacy better, to the chagrin of thousands of companies affected. However, in proposed rules for a statement by management on the subject of internal accounting controls to be included in annual Form 10-K reports, the SEC explicity discusses cost/benefit considerations inherent in the concept of reasonable assurance. Although many registrants would have preferred the SEC to introduce the concept of materiality into this process, it has refused to do so. In addition, attempts to change the FCPA to recognize materiality have so far been unsuccessful.

Auditability

The term "auditability" was defined earlier as the features of a system that allow verification of the adequacy and effectiveness of controls. The term "audit trail" is often used by accountants and auditors when referring to these features.

Auditability is based on the premise that records of events, decisions, activities, and transactions should be kept in sufficient detail to permit independent verification. In this sense, auditability is related to accountability.

The concepts differ in purpose, however. Accountability implies leaving a record of the discharge of duties and responsibilities for superiors to monitor and review. Auditability would have that, and perhaps other records, periodically checked by someone not related to the function.

The entire concept of auditing is built, in part, on systems of internal control being auditable. Thus, it is important to:

- Maintain adequate records.
- Maintain a set of standards or criteria that may be used by the auditor as a measuring tool, in order to gauge the adequacy of the system or function under review.
- Employ persons sufficiently competent to be able to perform the measurement tasks.

Of the three, maintaining adequate records is probably the easiest. Next is attracting persons sufficiently competent to measure the task. The professional practice of auditing, whether by internal or external auditors, has come a very long way in the last fifty years. The set of standards or criteria used to measure adequacy is the most difficult to evolve. Internal control systems vary considerably. Thus, the extent to which these concepts of internal control are applied in any given system is a matter of management judgment.

It is unlikely that a single set of guidelines or criteria will evolve to cover all situations, which seems to be the point of view of the SEC. Ultimately, the criteria for determining adequacy of controls will be left for the courts to decide, since the FCPA has made adequacy of internal control a matter of law. Under these circumstances, it would seem desirable to apply criteria that follow the language of the FCPA as closely as practicable. The concepts, objectives, and techniques outlined in this chapter attempt to do just that.

EDP AND INTERNAL CONTROL

Distinguishing Features

The computer environment is vastly different from other environments. Most people are familiar with the fact that computers require special facilities, equipment, and personnel in order to function. However, the environment is characterized by other features that are equally important, but less well known.

Dynamic Environment. EDP is characterized by constant, significant change. From a control standpoint, this means that continual attention must be given to monitoring and evaluating controls in the EDP environment for purposes of adequacy. Computer processing must continue to meet standards of accuracy and reliability in the face of installing new equipment, modifying systems and programs, experiencing staff turnover, and meeting the ever-increasing demand for services.

Uniform Processing. Computers do exactly what they are instructed to do, eliminating the chance of random error in processing inherent in manual systems. However, this is not to say that computers are error free. Since computers must be instructed by humans, the accuracy and reliability of computer processed data is in direct proportion to the quality of the instructions fed into them.

Error Correction. Where errors occur in computer systems, correction routines are usually more complex than in manual situations. Input errors are usually anticipated, and correction routines are built into the system to take care of them. However, errors in the instructions are much more difficult to deal with. The nature and frequency of these cannot be reliably anticipated. Thus, considerable effort must be spent during systems design (and in subsequent change activities) to test systems thoroughly for flaws or bugs. Some programming bugs may escape detection of even the most intense testing; eventually, however, these surface at some point. When they do, the results can be disruptive, and fixing them can be costly.

Storage. Vast amounts of data may be economically stored in computers, one of the principal advantages of the computer age. The ease and speed with which information may be automatically filed and retrieved by computers is another advantage. One of the disadvantages is that the information in its stored state is readable only by the computer. Thus, unless a user's information needs are satisfied by routine report distributions, specialized knowledge is required to extract relevant information. Another potential difficulty is the fact that the data owners and users are usually not the custodians of the data, as is often the case in manual systems. Limiting access to authorized personnel can be much harder in an automated environment. Finally, the concentration of data in computers places a premium on backup and recovery, since data can be lost or destroyed in many unusual ways.

"Backup" refers to the process by which information stored in computer memory is duplicated. This is usually done on magnetic tape and stored outside the computer area. If the data in memory are somehow lost or destroyed, they can be reconstructed from the duplicates, known as recovery. Backup and recovery procedures are necessary not only for stored data but also for programs, documentation, forms, supplies, and even equipment.

Auditability. Transactions processed in manual systems are evidenced by some type of form or document. This is much less true in the case of computerized systems. Certain transactions may be automatically initiated, and certain procedures may be automatically performed. The record of these transactions may be retained only temporarily. For some on-line systems, this may be no longer than one or two days. Moreover, the record may exist only in machine-readable form.

Security. The concentration of data in automated memory, the size of the investment in facilities, equipment, personnel, and supplies, and the near total dependence of almost all important company elements on the continued operation of the EDP function pose many unique security requirements. Routines that might be considered incompatible in a manual environment become, when automated, concentrated so that programmers, computer operators, and others may be in positions to misappropriate assets or perform other irregularities with little fear of detection.

The internal controls present in automated systems must be responsive to the foregoing distinguishing features.

RISKS IN EDP

Risk Analysis: A Useful Tool

Gains in speed, efficiency, and accuracy do not come risk free. Although some risks are present in both EDP and non-EDP environments, many others are not. Examples of the former include acts of God (e.g., floods and earthquakes), which cause damage whether or not computers are present. Examples of the latter include hardware failures (e.g., a computer outage) or software failures (e.g., program errors that alter or delete valid data).

Because of the significance and uniqueness of EDP in most companies, it is desirable to assess inherent risks and their potential consequences. This assessment is often called risk analysis. Although risk analysis was rarely recognized as a formal technique as recently as ten years ago, it is much more widely practiced today. An illustration of how risk analysis might be performed is shown in Figure 10-2.

SYSTEMS CONTROL AND AUDITABILITY

Risks	Loss of Funds*	Records Loss Minor	Records Loss Major	File Loss Minor	File Loss Major	F — Damaged E — Intact P — Intact	F — Intact E — Damaged P — Lost	F — Intact E — Damaged P — Intact	F — Damaged E — Damaged P — Damaged
External:									
Earthquake	0	1–2	0–1	1–2	0–1	0	0	0–1	0
Fire	0	0–1	0	0–1	0–1	0–1	0–1	0–1	0
Flood from storms	0	0	0	0	0	0	0	0	0
Act of war	0	1–2	0–1	0–1	0–1	0–1	0	0	0
Lightning	0	1–2	0–1	0–1	0–1	0–1	0	1–2	0
Explosion	0	0–1	0–1	0–1	0	0	0–1	0–1	0
Water supply loss	0	0	0	0	0	0	0	0	0
Nuclear accident	0	2–3	1–2	0	1–2	0	0	1–2	0
Power supply interruption	0	0–1	0–1	0–1	0–1	0–1	0	0	0–1
Airliner crash	0								
Internal:									
Head crash	0	1–2	1–2	1–2	1–2	NA	NA	NA	NA
Program error	3–4	2–3	1–2	2–3	1–2	NA	NA	NA	NA
Operator error	3–4	2–3	1–2	2–3	1–2	NA	NA	NA	NA
Data control error	2–3	2–3	1–2	2–3	1–2	NA	NA	NA	NA
Magnetism	0	2–3	1–2	2–3	1–2	NA	NA	NA	NA
Criminal Acts:									
Vandalism	0	1–2	0–1	1–2	0–1	0–1	0	0–1	0
Espionage	1–2	1–2	1–2	1–2	1–2	0	0–1	0–1	0
Fraud	1–2	1–2	1–2	1–2	1–2	0	0	0	0
Theft	1–2	1–2	1–2	1–2	1–2	0–1	0	0–1	0
Terrorist activity	0–1	1–2	1–2	1–2	1–2	1–2	1–2	1–2	1–2
Sabotage	0–1	1–2	1–2	1–2	1–2	1–2	1–2	1–2	1–2

Key: Frequency of Occurrence

0 = Less than once in 100 years
1 = Less than once in 10 years
2 = Less than once a year
3 = Less than once a month
4 = Twice a week
5 = Several times daily

*Also other items of value such as negotiable instruments, supplies, and assets, by means other than damage.

F = Facilities
E = Equipment
P = Personnel

NA = Not Applicable

FIG. 10-2 Types of Security Exposure (Source: James D. Willson and Steven J. Root, *Internal Auditing Manual*, Boston: Warren, Gorham & Lamont, (1984), p. 16-9. Reprinted by permission.)

The first step in risk analysis is to identify all known risks or threats. In Figure 10-2, these are classified according to external, internal, and criminal acts. "External" refers to risks caused by an event outside the computer room; "internal" refers to those caused by an incident inside the computer area; "criminal" acts are self-explanatory.

The next step is to specify the kind of loss or exposure, as shown in several of the column headings. Note that loss exposure involves various combinations of assets. Figure 10-2 presents the typical situation in which the assets exposed are funds, records, files, as well as EDP personnel, equipment, and facilities.

Once the risks are listed and the assets at risk determined, the analysis may be performed in a matrix format. The lines and columns are completed by estimating the frequency of occurrence for each situation and posting each result in the appropriate space. Since these are educated guesses at best, ranges may be used. Estimates are selected from a graduated scale that reflects broad orders of magnitude. Any scale may be used. In Figure 10-2, the scale increases almost exponentially by multiples of ten (other multiples could have been applied as well). The results of this analysis display rough orders of magnitude and help isolate areas where the risk and exposures are greatest. This technique helps to pinpoint areas that need to be controlled.

Some security experts extend the risk analysis process to categorize the control alternatives. For example, controls may be categorized according to whether they prevent the exposure, limit the frequency of occurrence, or, failing that, help recovery in the event of occurrence. Figure 10-3 presents such a categorization for selected exposures. This aspect of risk analysis helps focus on the specific controls that might be implemented. Decisions may be further aided by preparing cost/benefit analysis where necessary.

The mechanics of risk analysis may vary with circumstances and the preferences of the analyzer. Regardless of form, some kind of documented approach should be used to identify risks, nature of exposures, frequency of occurrences, as well as possible preventive, limiting, or recovery controls.

But what are the risks? Figure 10-2 lists several external and internal risks and criminal acts. Another way to look at risk is through the eyes of senior management. The next sections provide a helpful discussion from that perspective, as taken from *Internal Auditing Manual*.[15] Most management groups are concerned with the possible adverse effects on the company of the following:

- Computer fraud and mischievous acts
- Violations of laws and regulations
- Negligent or ineffective information systems management
- Computer dependence
- Proliferation of minicomputers and microcomputers

---

[15] Willson and Root, pp. 26A-16–26A-20.

SYSTEMS CONTROL AND AUDITABILITY 10-19

Exposure	Preventive Controls	Limiting Controls	Recovery Controls
Fire	■ Fire-resistant facility ■ No-smoking rules ■ Prompt removal of combustibles ■ Frequent fire prevention inspections	■ Sprinklers ■ Fire extinguishers ■ Halon system ■ Nearby fire-fighting capability ■ Offsite back-up capability	■ Recovery plan ■ Duplicate records of vital data ■ System documentation ■ Back-up facility/equipment
Computer outage	■ Overall system design ■ Effective maintenance program ■ Constant power supply ■ Protection against other risks (fire, flood, etc.) ■ Restricted access	■ Solid vendor support ■ Distributed processing ■ Monitoring by operators ■ Detective controls	■ Recovery plan ■ Duplicate records of vital data ■ System documentation ■ Back-up facility/equipment
Malicious programmer	■ Effective employment screening ■ Strict segregation of duties ■ Review and approval of programmer activities ■ Formal programming routines ■ Protective software utilities	■ Segregation of duties ■ Automated logging of changes ■ Review and approval routines ■ Active EDP auditing ■ Application controls (e.g. limit checks, edits, and batch balancing)	■ Effective programming documentation ■ Duplicate program tapes ■ Duplicate vital records ■ Recovery plan
Embezzlement	■ Effective employee screening ■ Strict segregation of duties ■ Restricted access to blank negotiable instrument forms, programs, documentation, etc. ■ Formal procedures for effecting program changes ■ Protective software utilities	■ Segregation of duties ■ Automated logging ■ Active EDP auditing ■ Application controls ■ User controls	■ Pursuit of legal remedies including punitive damages ■ Recovery plan ■ Duplicate records

FIG. 10-3 Preventive, Limiting, and Recovery Controls for Selected Exposures (Source: James D. Willson and Steven J. Root, *Internal Auditing Manual* (Boston: Warren, Gorham and Lamont, 1984), p. 16-10. Reprinted by permission.)

Computer Fraud and Mischievous Acts

Computer fraud, despite its relatively rare incidence, is perhaps the risk that most concerns management because, when it does occur, significant sums of money or other assets such as valuable data are usually involved. Also, these events are often highly publicized in ways that sometimes suggest that the company involved has been lax in minimizing risk. Adverse publicity undermines the images of prudence and competence most companies try carefully to develop, usually at considerable expense.

Major frauds involving computers have been reported against government agencies, utilities, banks, insurance companies, and other institutions. With the advent of powerful personal computers with telecommunications capability, fraud through computer timesharing networks is becoming alarming. While many hackers take "innocent" intellectual sport in foiling expensive and intricate computer security systems, others have more damaging motives in mind. Theft of property and other valuables, such as trade secrets, special formulas, research data, and intelligence records, may be the aim. Successful hackers can alter or destroy data in ways that leave no trace or that can wrongfully implicate innocent parties. As more and more people gain computer knowledge, this risk is likely to increase. Fraud and hacking are not the only risks in this category. Computers have been, and will continue to be, the targets of saboteurs, terrorists, disgruntled employees, and others seeking to cause damage and injury.

To help curb the exposures, about one third of the states have enacted some type of legislation making fraud involving computers and other mischievous acts criminal. There have been various efforts at passing federal legislation along these lines, and the Institute of Internal Auditors, among others, has lent support. Whether making computer fraud and mischievous acts felonies will successfully deter would-be perpetrators remains to be seen. The best present defense seems to be a vigilant management and a working system of preventive security measures.

Violations of Laws and Regulations

Management universally intends to achieve its business objectives within the framework of all applicable laws and regulations. Computers are becoming a primary means to enable companies to comply with the innumerable record-keeping and reporting requirements of federal, state, and local information reporting, as well as other regulatory requirements. At the federal level alone, most business entities are subject to statutory and other regulations by the following agencies:

- Treasury Department
- Internal Revenue Service

SYSTEMS CONTROL AND AUDITABILITY

- Department of Labor
- Department of Health, Education, and Welfare
- Federal Commerce Commission
- Securities and Exchange Commission
- Department of Commerce
- Department of Defense
- Comptroller General

It is inconceivable that any information systems organization can monitor the innumerable changes in the vast array of rules with which the systems they maintain must comply. They must depend on the user to specify new and changing requirements; however, the user is not always able to judge whether the systems changes have preserved compliance as intended. Thus, exposure to filing erroneous, incomplete, or untimely information arises with attendant risks of fines, penalties, and extra legal costs.

Another risk of considerable concern to many companies is that posed by violations of federal laws such as the Privacy Act of 1974, aimed at securing the individual's right to privacy. Vast amounts of data pertaining to individuals are stored in many company computer files under such categories as employees, customers, prospective customers, or debtors. Unintended misuse of these data can bring about violations of the laws.

Negligent or Ineffective Information Systems Management

As stated earlier, information systems management consumes a significant and growing share of company budgets. Many executives are concerned with how efficient and effective information systems organizations are in spending these substantial sums and in managing allocated resources. Often the following questions arise:

- Are user needs for low-cost services being sacrificed to preserve information systems empires?
- Are future data processing requirements adequately anticipated?
- Are systems development budgetary goals achieved at the expense of necessary control and security measures?
- Are equipment and software decisions impacted more by the desire for keeping pace with technology than by cost/benefit factors?
- Is information systems management being overly optimistic in its assessment of risks?

- Are managers too permissive or restrictive regarding the conduct of technical staff?
- Is computer utilization too high or too low?

Management is usually able to evaluate the effectiveness of other functional unit performances. However, the information systems business involves unfamiliar technical factors and considerations, thus making it more difficult to appraise information systems managment performance.

Computer Dependence

Many executives express concern that their companies are becoming too dependent on computers to design, market, manufacture, and/or deliver products and services. Indeed, a significant number of business entities would have to cease operation within a few days if the functioning of their computers were interrupted.

Few computers are interrupted for long periods of time (in excess of one day). However, short interruptions of a few minutes to a few hours are not uncommon. As more operations and functions are automated, the effects of interruptions multiply, so that excessive computer downtime can delay designs, affect delivery schedules, cause unnecessary costs, as well as alter a company's competitive position. These risks can be minimized by techniques such as distributed processing and adequate backup practices and recovery arrangements.

Proliferation of Minicomputers and Microcomputers

The era of the minicomputer has enabled numerous companies to minimize the risks of loss by distributing the EDP load among several interconnected computers in network configurations. This evolvement has also reversed the long-term organizational direction of information systems away from centralization, moving control of EDP operations back to the user. This trend has been accelerated with the proliferation of small, inexpensive, powerful, and easy-to-use microcomputers. Management is concerned that if this occurs too rapidly, controls may be adversely affected.

Systems and methodologies nurtured by information systems units usually become reasonably controlled over time in centralized environments where adequate technical expertise exists. However, the user may not yet possess sufficient technical competence to ensure maintenance of the same level of control and security when decentralization occurs. His ability to evaluate hardware and software alternatives and to obtain suitable programming and other technical support is also less certain. Overall, costs of information systems management could increase due to gaps in coordination, leading to redundancies in data, software, facilities, personnel, and equipment. This could put unwanted pressure on pricing strategies, profitability, and a company's competitive posture.

CONTROL OBJECTIVES AND TECHNIQUES

The following discussion of objectives and control techniques is seen from the perspective of the financial manager as an application owner. An application owner is an individual or organization responsible for the given application. The responsibility involves decisions as to:

- Systems requirements
- Systems design
- Systems acceptance
- Systems change
- Accessibility
- Control and security features
- Systems testing

Until recently, many owners left decisions with respect to these factors to the information systems group. The methodology of this section requires the application owner to become much more involved in controlling the systems and data for which he bears ultimate responsibility. It also means that information systems groups must be willing to permit the owner to get involved to the extent necessary to effect satisfactory control decisions.

There are many authoritative discussions on the subject of EDP control objectives and techniques. Willson and Root address the subject in the following way:

> Over the years, much information has been published that defines EDP objectives and internal control techniques. A brief listing of these is as follows:
>
> - Statement on Auditing Standards No. 3, "The Effect of EDP on the Auditor's Study and Evaluation of Internal Control," American Institute of Certified Public Accountants, 1974.
> - Computer Control Guidelines, the Canadian Institute of Chartered Accountants, 1975.
> - Systems Auditability and Control, the Institute of Internal Auditors, Inc., 1977.
> - Control Objectives 1980, EDP Auditors Foundation.[16]

To these must be added the many texts authored by knowledgeable EDP experts that deal with the subject of controls. Although the terminology and descriptions vary, the general trend is to describe the control objectives and techniques in terms of overall management controls and specific applications.

---

[16] Willson and Root, pp. 16-13–16-14. Reprinted by permission.

A representative grouping of seemingly similar terminology drawn from these publications is shown in the following:

- *Management controls*
  - Administrative controls
  - Organizational controls
  - General controls
  - Management controls
  - Computer center controls

- *Application controls*
  - Input controls
  - Transaction entry controls
  - Data communications controls
  - Conversion controls
  - Processing controls
  - Hardware and software controls
  - Output controls
  - Output processing controls
  - Physical security controls

Even though the publications mentioned above provide excellent insight into EDP controls and objectives, taken together, they have provided redundant and overlapping concepts and terminology, resulting in an absence of any single generally accepted set of control classifications, definitions, and guidelines. In essence, the cited works identify objectives and controls according to EDP functions or processes and activities.

Many of the control objectives and techniques described in the cited works are directed at the information systems function, which, of course, must be well managed. That is, it must be properly organized; its activities adequately planned from strategic, tactical, and operational viewpoints; its functions suitably staffed; and, finally, its operations appropriately controlled. A discussion along these lines is unnecessary from the perspective of the financial manager, unless, of course, he is responsible for the information systems function. (In that case, the selected references at the end of this chapter should be consulted.)

In discussing instances where computer processing is used in significant accounting applications, the AICPA literature divides EDP controls into two classes: general controls and application controls.[17] The previously cited SAS No. 3 devotes considerable attention to this division. However, SAS No. 3 has been superceded by SAS No. 48, entitled "The Effects of Computer Processing on the Examination of Financial Statements." That pronouncement seems to discount the importance of such classifications. It states: "Whether the control procedures are classified by the auditor into general and application controls, the objective of the system of internal accounting control remains the same...."[18]

---

[17] AU Section 330.34.

[18] Auditing Standards Board, "Effects of EDP on Examination of Financial Statements," *SAS No. 48* (New York: AICPA, 1984), paragraph 34 (*Professional Standards*, AU Sections 1030.05 and 320.34, as amended).

The early AICPA distinction made between general and application controls is somewhat unnecessary for nonauditors. Little is gained by this distinction in terms of understanding control objectives and techniques in situations where computer processing is an important aspect of significant accounting applications.

The ensuing discussion omits such a classification for that reason. Financial managers, if they are application owners, must be concerned with all control aspects having a bearing on the applications they own. The presentation here is based on that premise.

For purposes of consistency, control objectives and techniques are discussed following the concepts of internal control described earlier in this chapter. This has the added advantage of consistency with the FCPA.

Authorization

Internal control of financial applications begins with the concept of authorization. The objective is to reasonably make sure that all activities pertaining to systems development, maintenance, and operation are generally or specifically authorized by appropriate management.

Establishing an environment in which this objective is realizable is critical to controlling EDP functions sufficiently, because successful EDP operations depend on the combined efforts of EDP organizations and those that use their services. The best chance for those combined efforts to produce the desired effect is to have clear-cut definitions of responsibility and authority for application owners, data owners, data users, and data custodians.

Other techniques for attaining the internal control objective for authorization are:

- Specifying authority for such systems-related activities as approving:
  - Systems development methodology
  - Systems requirements
  - Systems changes
  - Systems testing
  - Systems documentation
  - Systems security features
  - Systems accessibility (i.e., approving those permitted to read systems files and records or segments thereof)
  - Systems update (i.e., approving those permitted to change or update systems data)
  - Systems input forms and changes thereto
  - Systems operating procedures
  - Systems report formats and distribution
  - User manuals and changes thereto

- Formal policies and procedures that spell out levels of authority and the manner in which records evidencing the discharge of that authority are to be maintained
- A formal mechanism for approving deviations from established routines
- Formal organization charts depicting lines of authority

Execution, Processing, and Recording

As noted earlier, these functions tend to overlap, and therefore are treated here as essentially equal. Internal control objectives are twofold:

1 To reasonably ensure the performance of all activities pertaining to systems development and maintenance in accordance with general or specific authority and to make sure that they are accurately recorded in sufficient detail to permit effective review by management and/or other interested parties; and
2 To reasonably ensure the transmission, conversion, storage, processing, and reporting of applicable data in accordance with approved systems specifications.

These objectives imply quite correctly that two missions are involved. First, execution of instructions authorized either generally or specifically means that activities, transactions, and events follow the expression of the authority. To preserve control, records of these activities must be made so that supervisory or management personnel, by monitoring the records or summarized reports thereof, may be satisfied that the activities, transactions, and events occurred as intended.

These records may be manual, such as control logs, or also automated, such as systems logs, program listings, or systems measurement facilities. A systems measurement facility is a software product that enables the collection of information, such as paging activity and the use of the processor, input/output devices, and channels. Systems and programming documentation also count as records for this purpose.

The second mission entails controlling how the data are actually processed. This area of control is usually envisioned for application (as opposed to general) controls. "Input," "processing," and "output" are terms used for the functions affected. Although these are the commonly recognized terms, more is involved than what they suggest. More informative terms such as "transmission," "conversion," "storage," "processing," and "retransmission" are applicable.

Control techniques to achieve these objectives vary depending on the nature of the system. The principal variants are whether the system is batch oriented or on line, stand alone or integrated.

SYSTEMS CONTROL AND AUDITABILITY 10-27

Control techniques for batch-oriented systems (those in which data to be processed are accumulated into batches for later processing at a time convenient to the EDP operation but still meeting user needs) include:

- A written manual.
- Policies and procedures.
- Forms for all types of transactions.
- Batch control techniques (e.g., item counts, hash totals).
- Control logs.
- Conversion controls. (Note that controls here differ depending on how and where the data are converted. If conversion occurs at the EDP center and magnetic tape or punched cards are involved, some type of conversion verification may be used. If conversion occurs at the user's location before transmission, some type of editing may be involved.)
- Transmission controls. (These controls also vary depending on the mode of transmission.) Most common is the use of telephone lines, either on a shared or dedicated basis. Controls for telephone transmission include:[19]
  - Restricted access
  - Identification codes (passwords)
  - Validity checks
  - Echo checks
  - Automatic storing and switching
  - Routing controls
  - Line controls
  - Protocol verification
  - Detection and retransmission
  - Line usage records
  - Message logs
  - Error recording and correction techniques
- Encryption.
- Processing controls, which might include:
  - Program-run manuals
  - Transaction identification codes
  - Validity checks
  - Label checks

---

[19] Transmission of data by telephone invariably uses an established communications architecture such as SNA developed by IBM. Such architectures provide many of the transmission controls listed here.

- Control totals
- Run-to-run controls
- JCL standards
- Sysout messages
- Machine logs
- Error detection and correction controls, which might include:
  - Automated suspense files
  - Display messages
  - Batch balancing
  - Error listings
  - Discrepancy reports
  - Error reentry
  - Provisions for summary of transactions by location
  - Procedure for overprevention during systems failure
- File handling controls, which might include:
  - Logging of operating systems interruptions and processing halts
  - Written procedures for restarts
- Storage controls, which might include:
  - Written retention procedures
  - Records in adequate detail that account for tapes, disks, files, and other documentation
- Output or reporting controls, which might include:
  - Reconciliation of output control totals with input control totals
  - Recording all output reports and their disposition
  - User organization batch controls
  - Retransmission controls (similar to the transmission controls previously described)

Control techniques for on-line integrated systems include all of the controls for batch-oriented systems, where applicable, except possibly some of the batch control techniques. In addition to these, unique controls must be added by virtue of the nature of on-line systems. These control techniques are:

- Restricting access to terminals.
- Transaction edits or other means to identify and correct errors.
- Passwords to identify operators (users).
- Systems interaction/dialogue to prompt or guide operators in the proper sequence of events.
- Sequential logging of transactions.
- Dialogue designed to catch errors.

SYSTEMS CONTROL AND AUDITABILITY 10-29

- Self-checking operations.
- Passwords to control access and update capability.
- Data base administrator function.
- Data dictionary.
- Data Base Management System.
- Audit trails.
- Inquiry logging.
- Program change control and logging.
- Header/trailer label checks.
- Tape library custodial function.

Accountability

As stated earlier, accountability is closely related to supervisory or disciplinary controls. It involves pinpointing responsibility for decisions, actions, and other events. It is a force that helps ensure compliance with established policies and procedures. Accordingly, the objective, with respect to EDP application control, is to reasonably ensure review of pertinent activities involved in executing, processing, and recording application-related events in sufficient detail by designated management and the taking of appropriate action with respect to deviations.

"Pertinent activities" refer to those procedures that are important to execute processing and recording properly. "Reviewed in sufficient detail" means that the designated responsible person(s) gains enough knowledge about what is happening to be effective in stopping undesirable or unintended activity. This is accomplished chiefly by reconciling, comparing, monitoring, reviewing, and inquiring. Such actions depend on the existence of files, records, and, most importantly, reports. Control techniques in this area also vary depending on whether the system is batch oriented or on line interactive.

For batch-oriented systems, control techniques include:

- Reconciling output control totals with input control totals
- Reviewing and comparing independently produced transaction logs generated during processing
- Monitoring and resolving console messages and sysouts
- Reviewing machine logs
- Periodic auditing
- Reporting transactions processed to designated users for further checking

For on-line systems, the control techniques include most of the above controls. In addition, the following apply:

- Off-line file scanning and balancing
- Single-transaction checks
- Real time monitoring of terminal operator activities
- Real time investigation and resolution of reported errors and other problems by terminal operators

While this list is not all inclusive, it is sufficient to familiarize the reader with the more important control techniques involved in accountability.

Security

Security is discussed in detail in Chapter 22, but, in order to cover the subject of EDP internal control in all respects, it is also commented on here. The objectives of security in an EDP application are (1) to reasonably ensure restriction of access to EDP resources, including facilities, personnel, equipment, supplies, and records, to authorized personnel and (2) to reasonably ensure sufficient protection of EDP resources from exposure to loss, damage, or other unintended results due to security incidents that might otherwise occur, such as fraud, theft, and natural disasters.

A third objective arises in situations where the application entails processing negotiable instruments such as payroll checks or other sensitive forms. In these instances, the additional objective is (3) to reasonably ensure restriction of access to sensitive forms and documents to authorized personnel and protection from theft or other unintended activity.

Of the first two objectives, probably the one dealing with controlling access is the most critical. That is because so much data can be stored in computers that potentially can be accessed by unauthorized persons unless proper controls are introduced. The following, excerpted from *Internal Auditing Manual,* provides a useful perspective:

> The vast concentration of data in computer files makes critical the controlling of access to data. Before computers, information was generally stored by those who owned it. Limiting access in that environment was comparatively easy primarily because the information was physically visible. Locked desks, files, storage cabinets, vaults, and secure rooms usually offered sufficient protection. Controlling the availability of information in an automated environment is much more challenging because
>
> - The data are not physically visible to the custodian.
> - The data do not have to be removed to gain access.
> - The data may be accessed remotely.
> - The custodians (the DP group) invariably are not the originators or users of the data; therefore, they must be told who is to have access.

SYSTEMS CONTROL AND AUDITABILITY   10-31

- The originators or owners of the data stored in automated files often do not realize the extent to which their data may be accessed by others, because they do not possess sufficient technical awareness.
- The trend toward large data bases to eliminate redundancy means that a given file or record must be made available to more than one organization. Some types of payroll data, for example, probably must be made available to individuals from employee relations, accounting, law, insurance, and pension administration.
- Personal and small business computers are now able to be used to access potential to unprotected data.

The methodology usually employed to control the availability of information requires the development of a company-wide policy and involves:

- Defining responsibilities for data owners, users, and custodians
- Developing definitions for classes of information (secret, confidential, etc.)
- Classifying all information according to definitions
- Developing controls to apply within each information class
- Identifying a data security administrator

This methodology is based on the concept that data owners must accept the responsibility for determining the classifications of data owned by them as well as the level of control desired. Owners are usually also the primary users; they are never I/S personnel. Generally, the custodian of data is the I/S unit, which is responsible for complying with the owner's stipulations as to the level of control.

Also inherent in this methodology is the concept that the owners are involved in risk assessment and cost/benefit analysis. Custodians act in an advisory capacity where technical considerations beyond the capabilities of the owners are involved.

Until recent years, many owners have left the decisions regarding access control to the I/S group. Hence, the foregoing methodology requires these owners to become much more involved in controlling the systems and data for which they bear ultimate responsibility. It also means that I/S groups must be willing to permit the owners to get involved to the extent necessary to effect satisfactory control decisions. For some ISMs and some owner/users, this may prove to be difficult. Internal auditors should watch for any indications of problems in this area and promptly report them as appropriate.

While it is difficult to generalize about specific types of owner controls, the following are usually present in well-controlled systems where remote access is involved:

- *Secret codes.* A means known only to the accessor to identify him from all others. Passwords are the best and most often used technique, even in the most critical of systems (such as automated bank telling).
- *Verifications.* A means by which the identity of the accessor is verified. This might be a birthdate or some other personalized data. Some systems even have the capability to recognize fingerprints.
- *Confirmation.* This involves a procedure such as call back.
- *Audit trail.* This requires keeping sufficient records of all access attempts.
- *Restricted directories.* This means restricting access to the records or files of passwords, secret codes, etc.

In the past few years, many software products have been developed by computer manufacturers and others to aid in controlling access to data. In large installations where systems are interactive, software aids are a must.[20]

Equally important to controlling access is the requirement that employees involved in EDP functions be honest and trustworthy. Many companies have instituted procedures to help minimize the potential of loss by the dishonest acts of employees. Following are some of the more common techniques:

- Institute background checks prior to making job offers.
- Enforce vacation policies.
- Rotate duties periodically.
- Divide duties and responsibilities so that no single individual is in a position to perpetrate an irregularity and, at the same time, conceal it.

There are limits in the application of these techniques, however. In many EDP functions, certain employees must be given broad powers in order to keep everything functioning. Operating systems programmers, for example, usually are in a position to override most security controls. Some application programmers may be given authority to access production versions of application programs. This is done to enable timely fixes of program-run halts that computer operators are not able to resolve.

Because of these limitations, a number of companies have emphasized the need for recording all events that occur during processing. In addition, they stress the value of activity codes and identification codes where possible. The existence of these audit trails is believed to deter would-be wrongdoers, because the likelihood of their acts being discovered is, for them, uncomfortably high. Adequate fidelity insurance is also vital.

---

[20] Willson and Root, pp. 26A-34–26A-35. Reprinted by permission.

SYSTEMS CONTROL AND AUDITABILITY

Other control techniques for limiting access and/or effectively segregating duties are as follows:

- Prevent computer operators' access to programs and program documentation.
- Require program changes to be authorized in writing by management and tested by an independent group prior to implementation.
- Segregate systems development activities from computer operations.
- Restrict access to the computer area.

Measures that protect against physical damage and related security risks include some of the same control techniques as for access control. Others are uniquely designed to help guard against damage or loss to computer equipment, data, facilities, and personnel. The following list includes both types.

- Remote or disguised location of computer facility
- Specially constructed facility (e.g., environments that are temperature and humidity controlled, dust free, clean)
- Adequate physical design of facility
- Techniques to limit access (e.g., lockable doors, badge recognition system)
- Appropriate fire suppression equipment (e.g., fire extinguishers, sprinkler systems, halon systems)
- Alarm systems
- Periodic inspections by security force
- Backup power source
- Elimination of redundant hardware
- Published emergency procedures
- Disaster recovery plan
- Program of disaster recovery plan testing

Internal Auditing

Internal auditing acts as an overall control that tests and evaluates other controls as a service to management. Although internal auditing can trace its origins as far back as ancient Rome, the profession is largely a twentieth-century development. It owes its growth to the rapid changes occurring in the private sector. One of those changes, of course, is the development of computers.

Internal auditing in a computer environment, or EDP auditing, probably originated in the 1950s. However, it did not receive much attention or encouragement until the 1970s. The sensationalism of the Equity Funding fraud served as a

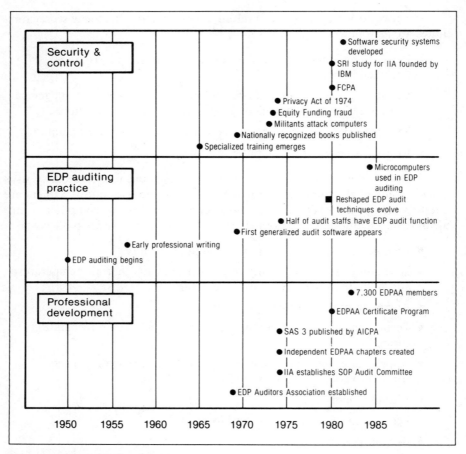

FIG. 10-4 EDP Auditing Chronology

watershed for this segment of internal auditing. That case dramatically drove home to management the importance of properly controlling EDP operations. It seemed evident to many that the EDP control environment at Equity Funding was not much different than it was in a lot of companies. One of the embarrassing deficiencies was the absence of any serious auditing, however.

Since that time, the growth in EDP auditing has been impressive. Figure 10-4 depicts a chronology of the events affecting this growth. Today, EDP auditing is a significant aspect of the practice of material auditing.

Although practice varies, the following reflects the type of auditing that is generally performed.

Detailed Functional Auditing. This type of auditing focuses on the internal controls of a single functional aspect of the EDP operation. Examples include audits of such functions as systems programming, database administration, telecommunications, and equipment strategy planning. The objective of these audits is to provide assurance and information to management regarding the internal controls of a particular function.

Installation Reviews. These audits review all important functions within a given EDP facility. They are similar to the reviews of general controls that external auditors perform under GAAS. Their objective is to provide assurance and information regarding internal controls for the installation taken as a whole. They are most effective for small- to medium-sized installations.

Application Auditing. These audits entail a comprehensive review of specific EDP applications. The nature and extent of this type of auditing are affected by the adequacy of controls over the systems development process. If systems are developed under a well-controlled cycle, the auditor may limit the extent of application auditing. On the other hand, a weak systems development process implies a need for more application auditing. The objective of this type of auditing is to determine whether the application controls are sufficient to result in the processing of accurate and complete data with adequate provision for security, backup, and recovery. In addition, the application's efficiency and effectiveness are also evaluated.

Developing Systems Auditing. These audits review not only the controls being designed for specific applications but also the techniques used in the process of developing the application. The objectives of developing systems auditing are threefold: (1) to provide information with respect to the adequacy of controls and appropriateness of the system for user purposes; (2) to determine whether systems development is occurring efficiently in accordance with prescribed procedures; and (3) to implement any devices needed to facilitate systems auditability.

Concurrent Auditing. The foregoing audit types are historical in nature. That is, the transactions or activities upon which they focus have already occurred. New techniques have emerged that permit the auditing of EDP controls to occur simultaneously with the operation of those controls. This type of auditing, known by various terms such as concurrent or continuous auditing, minimizes the potential for distortion that is inevitably present in after-the-fact auditing. In effect, the auditing occurs through the computer in a real-time fashion. Real-time auditing is accomplished by embedding audit routines in the application programs. These routines perform audit procedures designed by the auditor to test selected control features. Usually, a file of the results is accumu-

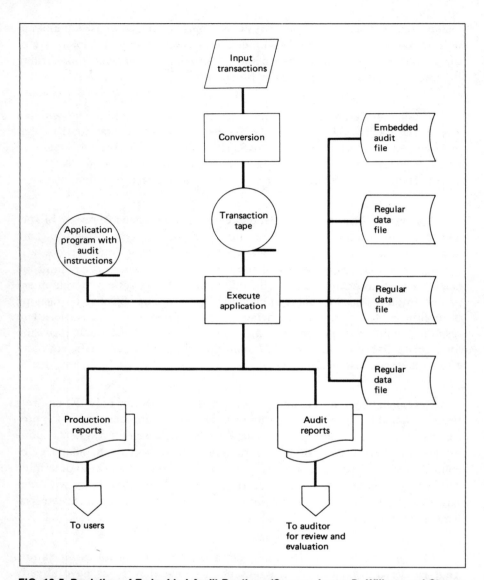

FIG. 10-5 Depiction of Embedded Audit Routines (Source: James D. Willson and Steven J. Root, *Internal Auditing Manual* (Boston: Warren, Gorham & Lamont, 1984), p. 18-25. Reprinted by permission.)

lated that is accessible only to the auditor or to others authorized by him. Figure 10-5[21] shows how such a routine operates.

In addition to concurrent auditing, many techniques have been designed to aid EDP auditing. In essence, they reflect efforts to use the power of the computer to audit the computer. These techniques have become known as computer-assisted audit techniques (CAATs). Examples include:

- Tracing
- Mapping
- Test data
- Integrated test facilities
- Parallel simulation

These techniques are designed for specific applications or circumstances; they are not designed to operate in a real-time fashion. Usually, they execute on duplicate versions of the applications under study. They are extremely useful in situations where embedded routines do not exist.

Another computer-assisted audit technique is widely used where specially designed CAATs are not present. These techniques, known as generalized audit software, offer powerful, easy-to-use, flexible tools for auditors. There are numerous versions, as indicated by Figure 10-6.[22] With these devices, auditors can extract selected data from files, make comparisons, perform statistical analyses, and test controls.

Although not all aspects of EDP auditing can be covered here, the foregoing discussion is sufficient to alert the reader to the basics. An active, on-going program of EDP auditing does much to help make sure that computer operations occur in the well-controlled environment that management intends.

Personal Computers

A discussion of internal control in the computer environment is incomplete without including the special control techniques for personal computers (PCs). A detailed discussion of PCs and their importance is covered in detail in Chapter 7.

It is enough to say here that PCs are revolutionizing the way information is created, processed, stored, and reported. They make possible the development and maintenance of entire information systems, sometimes called decision support systems (see Chapter 16), outside the auspices of the MIS function. When this occurs, the system is usually suspect from a control standpoint. As more and more of these systems proliferate, questions over control adequacy multiply.

---

[21] Willson and Root, p. 18-25. Reprinted by permission.
[22] Willson and Root, p. 18-29. Reprinted by permission.

Package	Vendor	Package	Vendor
ASI-ST	Applications Software, Inc. 21515 Hawthorne Boulevard Torrance, Calif. 90503	CARS	Cullinane Corporation Wellesley Office Park 20 William Street Wellesley, Mass. 02181
ASK-360	Whinney Murray 57 Chiswell Street London, ED1 4SY, England	COMPUTER FILE ANALYZER	Price Waterhouse & Co. 1251 Avenue of the Americas New York, N.Y. 10020
AUDASSIST	Alexander Grant & Co. One First National Plaza Chicago, Ill. 60670	DYL-AUDIT	Dylakor Software Systems, Inc. 16255 Ventura Boulevard Encino, Calif. 91436
(AUDEX (AUDEX 100	Arthur Andersen & Co. 69 West Washington Street Chicago, Ill. 60602	EDP-AUDITOR	Cullinane Corporation Wellesley Office Park 20 William Street Wellesley, Mass. 02181
AUDIT	U.S. Department of Commerce Springfield, Va. 22151		
AUDITAID	Seymour Schneidman & Associates 405 Park Avenue New York, N.Y. 10022	EDP-Auditor/3	Cullinane Corporation Wellesley Office Park 20 William St. Wellesley, Mass. 02181
AUDITAPE	Deloitte, Haskins & Sells 1114 Avenue of the Americas New York, N.Y. 10036	HEWCAS	Department of Health, Education & Welfare Audit Office of the Assistant Secretary, Comptroller 330 Independence Avenue Washington, D.C. 20201
AUDITEC	Carleton Corporation 44 Bromfield Street Boston, Mass. 02108		
AUDITFIND	Dataskil Reading Bridge House Reading, England	MARK IV AUDIT	Informatics, Inc. 21050 Vanowen Street Canoga Park, Calif. 91303
AUDITPAK II	Coopers & Lybrand 1251 Avenue of the Americas New York, N.Y. 10020	PANAUDIT	Pansophic Systems, Inc. 709 Enterprise Drive Oak Brook, Ill. 60521
AUDIT REPORTER	Burroughs Corporation World Headquarters 1 Burroughs Place P.O. Box 418 Detroit, Mich. 48232	SCORE-AUDIT	Programming Methods, Inc. 1301 Avenue of the Americas New York, N.Y. 10019
		STRATA	Touche Ross & Co. 1633 Broadway New York, N.Y. 10019
(AUTRONIC-16 (AUTRONIC-32	Ernst & Whinney 1300 Union Commerce Building Cleveland, Ohio, 44115	S/2170	Peat, Marwick, Mitchell & Co. 345 Park Avenue New York, N.Y. 10022
BASE	Computrol, Inc. 187 Baker Avenue St. Louis, Mo. 63119	THE AUDIT ANALYZER	Program Products, Inc. 95 Chestnut Ridge Road Montvale, N.J. 07645

FIG. 10-6 Tabulation of Generalized Audit Software Packages and Their Vendors (Source: James D. Willson and Steven J. Root, *Internal Auditing Manual* (Boston: Warren, Gorham & Lamont, 1984), p. 18-29. Reprinted by permission.)

SYSTEMS CONTROL AND AUDITABILITY 10-39

Internal control concepts and objectives do not change when PC-driven systems are present. The difference is the way in which these concepts and objectives are realized. The techniques are covered in the following sections.

Authorization. There are special control techniques for authorization.

- Statements should clearly identify authority and responsibility for personal computer
  - Acquisition
  - Software development
  - Standards for security and operation
  - Custodianship duties
  - Record keeping
  - Backup and recovery
  - Training and education
- There is a system of approval for deviating from established practices.
- For PCs, executing, processing, and recording occur in a very individualistic way. Since personal computers are used to expand people's capabilities or output, they are both flexible and easy to operate. The extent of controls in this area can range from only those built into the machine to controls one might encounter in an application run on a mainframe. A few basic procedures might be as follows:
  - Maintain up-to-date instruction manuals and/or booklets for hardware and software.
  - Keep logs of PC utilization (particularly important where multiple users are involved).
  - Require unique or original applications to be supported by adequate documentation including an application flow chart, a program listing, and instructions for operation.

Accountability. Accountability is much less of an issue in PC operation, since, in many instances, only one person is involved. However, there are situations where PCs are shared among two or more users. Also, some level of supervision over use may be desirable where use involves sensitive data or functions.

Security. PCs must be properly secured. Proper security requires the adoption of specific and unique control techniques. The exposure to physical accessibility risks and the absence of hardware security features normally encountered in mainframes such as multiple processing, privileged instructions, and memory protection together make the operation of PCs riskier. Some control techniques are as follows:

- Require removable diskettes to be locked in secure places.
- Obtain lockable enclosures for PCs. This is particularly desirable if the PC is equipped with a hard disk. In those situations, data can only be protected from unauthorized access by restricting access to the PC. (Some PCs may be located in isolated lockable rooms; others may not be. In some situations, exposure to after-hours access is an open risk.)
- Prevent company-sensitive data from being stored on PCs.
- Develop means to control data inadvertently left in memory.
- Use encryption techniques.
- Ensure the quality of power to the PC. Where the power source is unusually poor, the user may need to invest in power conditioning or uninterruptible power supply systems.
- Minimize the effect of contaminants (PCs attract charged particles in the air, such as smoke and dust).
- Minimize the effect of contaminants on magnetic devices (e.g., diskettes).
- Develop regular and systematic backup procedures for important files, and possibly equipment, if continued use is critical.

REFERENCES

AICPA. "Codification of Auditing Standards and Procedures." *Statement on Auditing Standards No. 1.* New York: AICPA, 1973.

———. "The Effects of EDP on the Auditor's Study and Evaluation of Internal Control." *Statement on Auditing Standards No. 3* (Dec. 1974) (New York: AICPA, *Professional Standards,* Vol. 1, AU Section 321).

Conner, Joseph E., and Burnell H. DeVos, Jr. *Guide to Accounting Controls.* Boston: Warren, Gorham & Lamont, Inc., 1979.

Coopers & Lybrand. *Computer Concepts and Controls.* New York: Coopers & Lybrand. Usage Restricted.

Davis, Gordon B., Donald L. Adams, and Carol A. Schaller. *Auditing & EDP.* New York: AICPA, 1983, ch. 3.

EDP Auditors Foundation for Education and Research. *Control Objectives, 1980.* USA: EDP Auditors Foundation for Education and Research, 1980.

Fitzgerald, Jerry. *Internal Controls for Computerized Systems.* San Leandro, Cal.: E.M. Underwood, 1978.

Stanford Research Institute. *Data Processing Control Practices Report.* New York: The Institute of Internal Auditors, Inc., 1977.

Study Group on Computer Control and Audit Guidelines, *Computer Control Guidelines.* The Canadian Institute of Chartered Accountants, 1970.

Willson, James D., and Steven J. Root. *Internal Auditing Manual.* Boston: Warren, Gorham & Lamont, Inc., 1979.

CHAPTER 11

Long-Range Systems Planning

Douglas Potter

Introduction	2	Alternatives Analysis	20
Problems of the Non-LRSP Organization	2	Define Hardware and Communications Projects	20
Organizations That Should Use LRSP	3	Define Hardware and Communications Architecture	21
Size	3	Step 6: Define the Personnel and Staffing Projects	23
Amount of Change	3		
Getting Started	4	Step 7: Review All Projects With the Project Team	24
Assembling the Project Team	4		
Determining the Planning Horizon	5	Step 8: Develop the Implementation Plan	26
Components of the Plan	6	Project Sequencing	26
Developing the LRSP	6	Totaling Resource Requirements by Time Period	28
Step 1: Hold the Initial Kickoff Meeting	8		
Step 2: Review the Corporate Strategic Plan, Including Goals and Objectives	9	Step 9: Final Review and Preparation	28
		Project Team Review	29
Examples of Corporate Goals and Objectives	9	Final Preparation	29
		Management Review	29
Step 3: Define the Application Projects	11		
Application Status Summary	11	**Implementing the LRSP**	30
Application Projects	14	Assignment of Responsibility	30
Tying the Application Projects Back to the Corporate Strategic Plan	14	Monitoring the Schedule	30
		Holding Periodic Update Meetings	31
Software Architecture	15	Being Flexible	31
Step 4: Define the Systems Software Projects	16	**Revising the LRSP**	31
Examples of Systems Software Projects	17	Steps to Updating the Plan	32
Step 5: Define the Hardware and Communications Projects	17	**Summary**	32
Define Current and Future Man-Machine Interfaces	19	**References**	33

Fig. 11-1 Relationship of Organizational Size to Cost/Benefit Provided by LRSP 4
Fig. 11-2 Steps Involved in Developing the LRSP 7
Fig. 11-3 Example of an LRSP Table of Contents 8
Fig. 11-4 Illustrative Statement of Corporate Purpose, Strategy, and Goals 10
Fig. 11-5 Examples of Application Projects 12

11-1

Fig. 11-6   Example of an Application Status Summary 13
Fig. 11-7   Relationship Between Corporate Goals and Objectives and LRSP Projects 15
Fig. 11-8   Diagram of Software Architecture 16
Fig. 11-9   Systems Software Projects 18
Fig. 11-10 Man-Machine Interfaces 19
Fig. 11-11 Hardware and Communications Projects 22
Fig. 11-12 Hardware and Communications Architecture 24
Fig. 11-13 Personnel and Staffing Projects 25
Fig. 11-14 Planned Organization Chart 26
Fig. 11-15 Implementation Plan 27

INTRODUCTION

Long-range systems planning (LRSP) is an important process that many organizations overlook. This is perhaps because its benefits are highly intangible. Also, LRSP is not a process that is traditionally associated with data processing. More and more, however, financial managers as well as data processing managers are becoming aware that the effects of not using LRSP are much more costly than the effort to produce and implement a good long-range systems plan.

Problems of the Non-LRSP Organization

Organizations that do not use LRSP often suffer from a variety of symptoms, such as:

- The use of extensive manual procedures to interface automated applications that do not share data, either because they run on different (incompatible) computers or because a programmer has not developed an interface.

- Duplication (often contradictory) of data being stored by two or more applications.

- Alienation of key user departments due to their perceived lack of participation in planning how data processing should support them.

- Scheduling conflicts over resources allocated to different data processing projects.

Taking a long-range view minimizes these problems because it plans and controls growth rather than letting growth take place and reacting to it after the fact. The benefit of LRSP is that it can negate these symptoms. Long-range planning allows an organization to achieve more highly integrated applications, more effective rapport with user departments, and more effective use of data processing resources.

LONG-RANGE SYSTEMS PLANNING

Improvements resulting from LRSP may appear only after several years of planning. A study by McKinsey & Company supports this.[1] That organization surveyed thirty-six major corporations and found a striking difference between those that used LRSP and those that did not. Those that planned EDP activities were much more likely to have successful data processing environments than those that did not. The survey measured success according to three components:

1 Return on computer investment
2 The usefulness of existing computer applications
3 The chief executive officer's (CEO) impressions of the company's data processing environment

It is clear from this study that LRSP provides some very desirable benefits. Also, LRSP can change a user's attitudes about data processing, a process that otherwise can take years. LRSP is defined as planning the use of data processing resources over a horizon of three to five years so that the allocation of resources can be coordinated to support the evolution of the organization.

Organizations That Should Use LRSP

Two characteristics of an organization determine the need to use LRSP: (1) its size and (2) the amount of change that is taking place.

Size. LRSP is most effective in large organizations where the computer hardware investment is over $250,000 or the annual data processing budget is over $250,000. The larger the organization, the more cost/beneficial LRSP becomes. Benefits increase in almost even proportion to the size of the organization (because of the proportionally larger size of the data processing budget); however, the cost and effort to develop the plan increase less proportionately.[2] Figure 11-1 shows this relationship.

Amount of Change. Change can have a detrimental effect on an organization. Because LRSP is intended to help an organization adapt to and plan for change, almost any organization experiencing rapid change should use LRSP. Examples of such change include:

- Rapid increase in business volumes (particularly revenues)
- Rapid decrease in business volumes

---

[1] F. Warren McFarlan, "Problems in Planning the Information System," *Harvard Business Review* (Mar.-Apr. 1971), p. 75.

[2] This can be proved empirically by using consulting fees to represent the cost of the plan. A plan developed for a company twice as large as another does not necessarily cost twice as much.

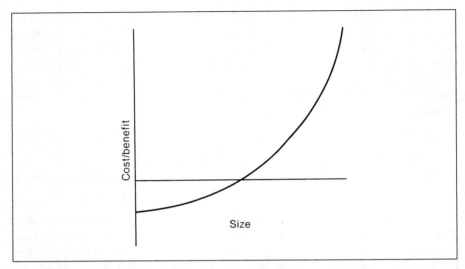

FIG. 11-1 Relationship of Organizational Size to Cost/Benefit Provided by LRSP

- Merger, acquisition, or divestiture
- Significant change in the makeup of an organization's products or services
- Redefinition of basic business policies and/or procedures

Even a small organization that is anticipating rapid expansion (e.g., from a merger) can benefit from LRSP.

GETTING STARTED

The sections that follow provide guidelines for developing a sound LRSP. First, the groundwork for the planning process is discussed. Second, the actual steps that must be followed in developing the plan are described.

Assembling the Project Team

Having an effective project team is critical both to the successful development of the plan and to an effective implementation. The team should be composed of managers from key accounting departments, functional departments, and the data processing department. A manager who is responsible for effective information systems should manage the project team, chair the meetings, and help approve the final product.

Typical team members from the financial and accounting areas may include the following:

- Vice-president, finance (often the project leader)
- Controller or chief accountant
- Accounts payable department manager
- Manager of credit and collections
- Treasurer and/or budget director

If the organization has a data processing steering committee, the project team should be comprised of some of the members of this committee, but it should have no more than six to ten members.

The most critical team member is the information officer or the data processing manager. He is responsible for coordinating the detailed data gathering for the plan, assembling its components, and coordinating changes necessary for the plan's ultimate approval. He is also the one individual most responsible for implementing the plan. The required characteristics of an effective information officer or data processing manager for accomplishing these functions are:

1 Commitment to the plan and its ultimate success
2 Knowledge of sound information management and data processing practices (e.g., knowing when it is beneficial to have applications running on separate computers and when it is not)
3 Sufficient time and personnel resources to develop the plan

With the correct leadership and a properly composed project team, the planning process is off to an excellent start.

Determining the Planning Horizon

The planning horizon is the time period used for planning future events. For many organizations, developing a long-range systems plan involves a planning horizon of three to five years. The reason for this is fairly obvious: A horizon of under three years makes the process less of a long-range plan and more like tactical planning (which is similar to planning one's day, as opposed to planning one's career), whereas a period of over five years is generally impractical because of the uncertainties of technology, events, and the organization itself.

Whether a three-, four-, or five-year time period is chosen for the planning horizon is not significant. What is significant is how long ahead it is useful to plan. However, any of the following factors tend to influence an organization toward a longer planning horizon:

- The probable amount of change is relatively constant and predictable.
- One or more long-term projects (over two years overall) are in the plan.
- The organization is generally slow in getting things done.

The planning horizon should be broken down into individual time intervals that will be used to plan the beginning and ending of various projects. These intervals may either be in weeks, months, or quarters, depending on the level of detail in the plan. Regardless of the intervals chosen, the first twelve to eighteen months of the plan should have shorter intervals than the remainder of the plan. (Figure 11-15 shows an implementation plan that initially uses months as intervals, and then later uses quarters.) It is usually much easier to control and monitor tasks taking place during a plan's first twelve to eighteen months. Also, it makes less sense to use the same level of detail for later events, since there is less certainty regarding events that are planned farther into the future.

Components of the Plan

The LRSP usually relates four areas of information systems:

1 Application systems
2 Hardware and communications
3 Systems software
4 Personnel

The plan itself addresses anticipated changes in each of these areas by defining each change as a project. Each project has associated with it a beginning time and an ending time, an amount of resources required for its execution, and an individual responsible for its execution. Large projects may also have checkpoints within the project itself with a specific time and possibly a specific output associated with the checkpoint.

The plan coordinates these projects so that they can be carried out with the financial and human resources available. This coordination is also necessary so that the projects defined in the plan can be implemented in the proper sequence.

DEVELOPING THE LRSP

The sequence of steps for the development of an LRSP is outlined in Figure 11-2. They are detailed in this section and should be followed rigidly, regardless of the size and nature of the organization. Ideally, the steps should all proceed in the sequence listed. In practice, however, Steps 4, 5, and 6 may be performed simultaneously, as long as the results of Step 5 are reviewed at the completion of the other two steps to make sure that enough hardware resources have been planned. The time period spanning Steps 2 through 9 should be from one to three months.

LONG-RANGE SYSTEMS PLANNING 11-7

Step		Person(s) Responsible	Outputs
1	Hold initial kickoff meeting	Project team	Project time line
2	Determine corporate goals and objectives	Assigned (managers)	Goals and objectives
3	Define application projects	All team members	Application projects
4	Define systems software projects	Data processing team members	Systems software projects
5	Define hardware and communications projects	Data processing team members	Hardware and communications projects
6	Define personnel and staffing projects	Assigned team members	Personnel and staffing projects
7	Review with project team	Project team	None
8	Define implementation plan	Data processing team members	Implementation plan
9	Perform final review and preparation	Project team and assigned managers	LRSP

FIG. 11-2 Steps Involved in Developing the LRSP

Depending on the project team's available time and the organization's desire to develop a detailed plan, the team may spend extra effort to define the projects in greater detail (e.g., for high-level projects).

Selecting the personnel and implementing the system may be broken down as follows:

1 *Selection:*
- Define requirements.
- Examine packages.
- Evaluate vendor bids.

2 *Implementation:*
- Purchase software.
- Train users.
- Gather data.
- Load files.
- Perform live run.

Naturally, this additional effort not only goes into defining the nature of these projects, but also provides more information about their timing and the amount of resources each will require.

Regardless of the level of detail that will generally prevail in defining the projects, there are certain circumstances under which one project should be defined in more detail than others in the LRSP. For example:

```
                    TABLE OF CONTENTS

              I  COVER LETTER

             II  EXECUTIVE SUMMARY

            III  BACKGROUND
                  A Progress on Previous Year's Plan
                  B Scope of Current Plan

             IV  APPLICATION PROJECTS

              V  SYSTEMS SOFTWARE PROJECTS

             VI  HARDWARE AND COMMUNICATIONS PROJECTS

            VII  PERSONNEL AND STAFFING PROJECTS

           VIII  APPENDIX
                  A Application Status Summary
                  B Projected Processor Utilization
                  C Software Architecture
                  D Man-Machine Interfaces
                  E Hardware and Communications Architecture
                  F Planned Organization Chart
```

FIG. 11-3 Example of an LRSP Table of Contents

- If the project falls within the first twelve or eighteen months of the planning horizon
- If the project is very large and must be defined as a set of subprojects or tasks in order to be planned effectively

An LRSP should not get into such detail as defining specific reports, screens, or detailed features needed in a particular application system. A sample table of contents of a complete LRSP is shown in Figure 11-3. Some comments on each step of preparing an LRSP follow.

Step 1: Hold the Initial Kickoff Meeting

The purpose of this meeting is to do the following:

1. Orient the project team.
2. Assign responsibilities.

LONG-RANGE SYSTEMS PLANNING   11-9

   3 Set deadlines for when the plan should be completed and sent to management.

   4 Decide on the criteria to be used for setting priorities.

The orientation introduces team members and provides a chance to answer any initial questions about the process. Responsibilities for at least Steps 2 through 4 should be assigned. Assignments for other steps can be made either at this time or at a later meeting.

The deadlines defined in the kickoff meeting determine when Steps 2 through 9 should be completed. As mentioned elsewhere in this chapter, this should span from one to three months. A result of this meeting would be a project timeline.

Step 2: Review the Corporate Strategic Plan, Including Goals and Objectives

One of the benefits of LRSP is that it builds an information systems environment that supports the development of the organization. In order to accomplish this properly, the LRSP process must be coordinated with the corporate strategic plan. Assigned executives from the project team (possibly the team leader) should review and understand the corporate goals and objectives as set out in the corporate strategic plan. These may, in fact, be restated as a relevant part of the LRSP.

Many organizations do not formally engage in corporate strategic planning. However, in almost all cases, a plan does exist, even if just in the minds of the key executives who run the company. If the corporate strategic plan does not exist on paper, executive-level managers should be interviewed to gain an understanding of the corporate goals and objectives. In the following section, we show some examples and explain their relationship to the plan.

Examples of Corporate Goals and Objectives. Most firms have long-term goals and objectives. Included are items critical to the ultimate success of the organization. Typically, they cover most areas of the business, such as marketing, personnel, production, finance, and research. In an effective corporate strategic plan, some of the objectives are quantified. The corporate strategic plan, extending as far into the future as is practical and useful (perhaps twenty or thirty years in a wood products concern, or only two seasons in the women's apparel business), may be composed of several segments, including:

- A statement of the company's basic purpose, mission, or objective
- A delineation of the strategy or factors to accomplish the basic purpose
- A list of specific, quantified goals, usually within a specific time frame, which must be accomplished to meet the long-term goal

PURPOSE

The company is engaged in the business of meeting customer needs in the Pacific Southwest for the electronic movement and management of information.

STRATEGY

To best meet the corporate purpose, these specific actions are planned:
- Build research competence in Product *N*.
- Diversify into related Product Line *L* by acquisition.
- Divest of Product *K*.
- Increase advertising coverage in San Diego territory.

GOALS

In accomplishing the corporate mission, these goals should be achieved by the time indicated:

	198X	199Y
1 *Net sales ($00,000)*	$75	$150
Net sales (percentage of present products)	80%	50%
2 *Rate of return*		
On shareholder's equity	20%	25%
On total assets	8	10
On net sales	10	12
3 *Earnings per share*	$2.25	$4.90

FIG. 11-4 Illustrative Statement of Corporate Purpose, Strategy, and Goals

A list of these three segments in the LRSP of a high technology company is shown in Figure 11-4.

Knowledge of the corporate strategic plan or LRSP is necessary for those developing an effective information system in that:

- The long-range financial plan should include provision for the required resources—manpower and finances—to develop and implement the LRSP.
- The systems plan must be consistent with, and supportive of, the corporate LRSP.

For example, if a certain company plans to divest itself of its toy business, systems resources probably should not be used to develop the special information requirements of this segment. Conversely, if the firm intends to enter a new, but related, product area, then those information needs must be incorporated into the planning.

Step 3: Define the Application Projects

A crucial part of developing the LRSP is defining the application projects within the plan. These are important because they represent the desired services that the information systems department should be providing to the organization. It is an important step and the only one in which every member of the project team participates individually.[3]

Examples of application projects are shown in Figure 11-5. Step 3 consists of defining all application projects that will take place over the planning horizon.

Application Status Summary. Prior to defining the application projects, a review of each existing and planned application system must be made. This systematic walk-through of each application system makes sure that all areas of current and potential automation are reviewed by the project team members. This task should produce an application status summary like the one shown in Figure 11-6 for each application system.

Sources of information for preparing the application status summary include:

- The previous LRSP if one exists
- The backlog of data processing requests
- Key application users and user department managers
- Any available literature or publications discussing the application being examined

As shown in Figure 11-3, the application status summary should appear in the plan's appendix. Normally, it ought to include the following information for each application:

1 *Definition* — a brief paragraph defining what each application does.

2 *Application status* — a statement about whether that application will have no change, major enhancements, or a completely new system over the course of the planning horizon.

3 *Costs and benefits* — a statement of the estimated costs and benefits that are anticipated for each major enhancement or an entire new system. (This is not necessary if no changes are anticipated for the application.) Because these costs and benefits are often intangible, the format should accommodate a verbal statement of costs and benefits, as well as a quantifiable one.

(continued on page 11-14)

---

[3] If a member has no functions relating to application systems, perhaps he should not be part of the project team.

Projects	Benefits	Related Goals and Objectives	Person Responsible	Priority	Estimated Hours	Estimated Cost	Beginning Date (Month or Quarter/ Year)	Ending Date (Month or Quarter/ Year)
A1 Develop accounts payable vendor history	Estimated tangible savings of $30,000/year due to improved purchasing.	6	Smith	High	100		3/X5	4/X5
A6 Select payroll/personnel system	Savings of 120 hours in programmer time. Intangible benefits of:	1,6	Jones	Medium				
a Define requirements	■ Automating manual personnel functions				60		10/X6	10/X6
b Examine packages	■ Improved personnel information				40		11/X6	11/X6
c Evaluate vendor bids	■ Fewer disrupted payroll processing cycles				40		11/X6	11/X6
A7 Implement payroll system	See Project A	1,6	Brown	Medium		$ 25,000		
a Purchase software					40		12/X6	12/X6
b Train users					20		Q1/X7	Q1/X7
c Clean up existing data					40		Q1/X7	Q1/X7
d Load files					32		Q1/X7	Q1/X7
e Perform parallel run							Q/X7	Q2/X7
f Perform live run							Q2/X7	
A8 Implement personnel system	See Project A	1,6	White	Low		$ 20,000		
a Purchase software					40		Q1/X8	Q1/X8
b Train users					80		Q1/X8	Q1/X8
c Gather data					40		Q2/X8	Q2/X8
d Load files							Q2/X8	Q2/X8
e Perform live run							Q3/X8	
			TOTALS		1,020	$410,000		

FIG. 11-5 Examples of Application Projects

LONG-RANGE SYSTEMS PLANNING

GENERAL LEDGER

The general ledger maintains the chart of accounts and all account balances. It is also used for preparing all financial reports based on these data. Primary financial reports currently produced are:

- Income statement
- Balance sheet
- Sources and uses of funds

Status. No major changes.

	Current	Three-Year Planned
Master File Sizes		
Chart of accounts	8,000	9,000
On-line journal history records	5,000	10,000
Financial reporting records	2,500	3,500
Transaction Volumes		
Manual journal entries/month	2,000	1,000
Automated journal entries/month	5,000	8,000
Account inquiry transactions/month	200	200

PAYROLL

The payroll application accepts hourly time input for hourly workers and produces paychecks and all other relevant reports for all hourly and salaried employees. It also maintains master file information containing employee payroll data.

Status. The current payroll system is eight years old. It needs enhancements to accommodate newly required deductions. In addition, the documentation is poor. The project team recommends replacing the existing system with a packaged payroll system. For security purposes, the project team recommends a stand-alone system running on a dedicated minicomputer. Savings are estimated at 120 hours annually in reduced program maintenance. Estimated costs are:

Software	$25,000	
Hardware	60,000	
Total	$85,000	

	Current	Three-Year Planned
Master File Sizes		
Employee master file	1,000	1,500
Average number of deductions per employee	5	8
Transaction Volumes		
Paychecks/month	2,000	3,000
Employee master file changes/month	100	150

(continued)

FIG. 11-6 Example of an Application Status Summary

PERSONNEL

Status. A new personnel system will be added in connection with the new payroll system. Functions planned for automation include:

- Reporting vacation, sick leave, and days worked
- Salary grade and promotional reporting
- Insurance benefits tracking

Benefits achieved will be the automation of manual tasks currently performed by three clerical personnel. It is expected that an automated personnel system will not eliminate any positions or provide any tangible cost savings. Cost estimates are as follows:

Software	$20,000
Hardware (included in previous estimate)	
Total	$20,000

	Current	Three-Year Planned
Master File Sizes		
Personnel master file	0	1,500
Transaction Volumes		
Personnel file inquiries and updates/month	500	550

FIG. 11-6 (*cont'd*)

4 *Transaction volumes and master file sizes* — an estimation of file sizes for all major files and application uses and an estimation of the monthly volumes for all important transactions input to the application. Two estimations should be made for every application: one for the current period; one for the end of the planning horizon.

Application Projects. Each application system that is identified as new or having major enhancements in this summary should have at least one application associated with it. These projects should define:

1 The nature of the work to be done
2 Estimated beginning and ending times of the project
3 Estimated resources in man-hours and dollars that the project will require.

Tying the Application Projects Back to the Corporate Strategic Plan. As mentioned elsewhere in this chapter, much credence is added to the plan if each application project is properly related to the corporate goals and objectives. This is especially important for top management, which will review the finished product and support its implementation. The only place where this association

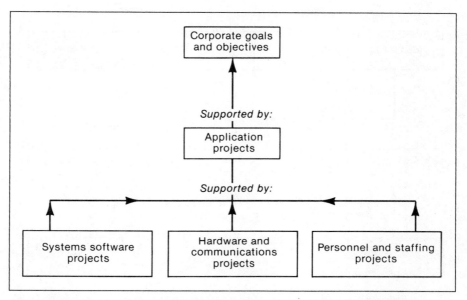

FIG. 11-7 Relationship Between Corporate Goals and Objectives and LRSP Projects

can be made directly between the long-range systems planning projects and the corporate goals and objectives is at the application level. Systems software, hardware, and organizational projects do not directly support the corporate goals and objectives, but are considered to be essential elements. Figure 11-7 illustrates this relationship.

Software Architecture. Once all the application projects have been defined, selected members of the project must define the software architecture. This is a crucial representation of all the application systems and their interfaces as they are expected to exist at the end of the planning horizon. Figure 11-8 shows an example of a software architecture. The applications are represented in boxes that are either shaded or all white, thus visually highlighting the planned activities for each application. Also, the architecture gives no indication of any hardware or communications. It merely shows applications and their interrelationships as they will exist irrespective of hardware and communications. This brings out an important point in the entire LRSP process: Application software (or information) needs drive the entire planning process. Only after the application projects and the software architecture have been defined does the LRSP process address hardware and other issues.

Although it is not shown as a step in Figure 11-2, it is advisable, as an interim step, for the project team to meet so that the group may review the application projects and the software architecture and agree that everything has been adequately defined up to this point.

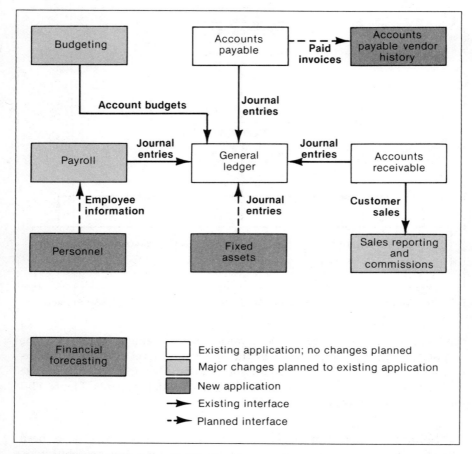

FIG. 11-8 Diagram of Software Architecture

Step 4: Define the Systems Software Projects

Once all application-related issues have been defined, selected data processing oriented members of the project team should identify the systems software projects. Systems software is computer software that serves general utility needs rather than specific application needs. Examples of systems software include:

- Spreadsheet software
- Graphics software
- Software for generating user-formatted reports from existing files

Systems software may also be software that very much affects the efficiency and operation of the data processing department. Examples of this type of systems software include:

LONG-RANGE SYSTEMS PLANNING

- Database management software
- Application development aids such as compilers or programmer productivity tools
- The operating system (software that controls the basic operation of the hardware)

Because of the technical nature of systems software, the data processing personnel involved in the planning process will be responsible for identifying most of the systems software projects. Even when a user initiates the idea of including such a project in the plan, data processing personnel will be heavily relied upon to assess the technical feasibility of each project.

Examples of Systems Software Projects. Several examples of systems software projects are shown in Figure 11-9. Information about timing and resource requirements is necessary for these projects just as it is for application projects. The project team members defining the systems software projects should place less emphasis on tangible benefits such as cost savings when justifying them, because most of the benefits will be intangible and difficult to quantify.

In many cases, the need for including these projects into the plan and their relative priority among other projects must be trusted to the good judgment of the data processing personnel involved in the planning process. Naturally, this leaves some exposure for the data processing manager to set his own needs above the needs of the rest of the organization. An objective way to assess the necessity and correct priorities of the systems software projects is through a technically competent outside consultant.

Step 5: Define the Hardware and Communications Projects

Once the application software and systems software projects have been defined, team members from the data processing department must define the hardware and communications projects that will be necessary over the planning horizon. Naturally, these projects reflect needs created by the application software and systems software projects, such as increased transaction volumes, new applications, and new systems software.

This step should be broken down into four separate tasks:

1 Define current and future man-machine interfaces.
2 Perform any necessary alternatives analysis.
3 Define hardware and communications projects.
4 Define hardware and communications architecture.

Projects	Benefits	Person Responsible	Priority	Estimated Hours	Estimated Cost	Beginning Date (Month or Quarter/ Year)	Ending Date (Month or Quarter/ Year)
S1 Select and implement word processing software	Estimated 30% productivity increase in letter and document preparation	Jones	Medium	80	$ 5,000	Q1/X7	Q2/X7
S2 Purchase and implement new editor	Improved productivity in programming staff	Jones	Low	40	8,000	Q4/X7	Q4/X7
			TOTALS	120	$13,000		

FIG. 11-9 Systems Software Projects

LONG-RANGE SYSTEMS PLANNING 11-19

Department	Devices		Uses
	Current	Three-Year Planned	
Corporate accounting	7 terminals 1 printer	12 terminals 2 printers 2 microcomputers	■ Financial forecasting ■ General ledger journal entries ■ Chart of account inquiry and maintenance ■ All financial reporting ■ Budget input and maintenance ■ Fixed-asset management ■ Word processing
Accounts payable	4 terminals 1 printer	6 terminals 1 printer	■ Invoice entry and payment selection ■ Vendor inquiry ■ Check printing
Accounts receivable	2 terminals 1 printer	3 terminals 1 printer	■ Customer account inquiry ■ Cash receipts posting ■ Sales reporting and commissions
Payroll/ personnel	2 terminals	4 terminals 1 printer	■ Payroll data entry ■ Personnel reporting and inquiry ■ Payroll reporting and check printing
Data processing	4 terminals 1 printer	6 terminals 1 printer	■ Programming
Totals	19 terminals 4 printers	31 terminals 6 printers 2 microcomputers	

FIG. 11-10 Man-Machine Interfaces

Define Current and Future Man-Machine Interfaces. Defining the man-machine interfaces refers to defining the functions and locations of all devices that will be used to get input to, and receive output from, the computer(s). Examples of these devices include:

- Terminals
- Microcomputers
- Printers
- Cash registers that generate point-of-sale data
- Optical scanners

Defining the current and future man-machine interfaces merely means tabulating a list of all such devices that are currently in place and projecting the requirements for these devices to the end of the planning horizon. Each department's requirements should be detailed by device, along with a brief description of the application functions the devices will be serving. This will result in a table similar to that shown in Figure 11-10.

This information originates from the user departments themselves. Users tend to overstate their future requirements for these devices; thus, the data processing manager or consultant must challenge and moderate this tendency.

Requiring a brief description of the application functions helps to reduce this tendency. The description also assists in tying these requests to specific application needs and thus indirectly to the overall corporate goals and objectives. That is why the last column shown in Figure 11-10 is necessary.

Alternatives Analysis. The alternatives analysis section provides a means of documenting the reasons for choosing a particular hardware or communications project over an alternative one, such as:

- A separate computer to automate a particular application instead of expanding the central computer
- A service bureau to automate a particular function instead of an in-house computer
- A packaged switching network (a particular kind of purchased computer network service) to handle data communications instead of leased telephone lines

Such an analysis is typically necessary when documenting any major expenditures for additional hardware. It is a means of documenting the research and thought that went into each decision. The format of the analysis can vary, but it should generally contain:

- An explanation of all the alternatives
- An analysis of the costs, risks, and benefits of each one
- The chosen alternative
- The reason for the chosen alternative

In the hardware projects shown as examples in this chapter, it would be appropriate to include an alternative analysis explaining why the payroll/personnel system is planned to run on a separate minicomputer.

Define Hardware and Communications Projects. Defining hardware and communications projects also heavily involves data processing technical personnel. These personnel are aided by the following:

- Projections of processor hours required over the planning horizon
- Vendor proposals for additional hardware
- Projections of increased data communications activity
- Communications vendor proposals for additional required communications lines and equipment

LONG-RANGE SYSTEMS PLANNING 11-21

These items may be included as exhibits supporting the final plan; in general, however, they should not be included in the body of the plan. (For example, Figure 11-3 shows a projected processor utilization chart included in Appendix B.)

Hardware and communications projects are also determined by reviewing the following:

- *Pending application projects.* They create demand for additional hardware.

- *Applications' transaction volumes and master file sizes as defined in the application status summaries.* These serve as a rough indicator of expected increase in demands for hardware.

- *Systems software projects.* They, too, create a (sometimes significant) demand for additional hardware.

- *Current and future man-machine interfaces.*

The hardware and communications projects should be defined with specific start and stop dates and estimated resource requirements just as are the other projects that are part of the plan. They should be defined in sufficient detail and with appropriate timing for their execution to support the application and other projects already defined for the plan. Figure 11-11 illustrates hardware and communications projects as the should appear in the plan.

Define Hardware and Communications Architecture. Hardware and communications architecture is the hardware analogy to software architecture. This architecture summarizes earlier portions of the plan relating to the software architecture, the man-machine interfaces, and the hardware and communications projects. It is a high-level, nontechnical depiction that defines the following at the end of the planning horizon:

- The computers (hardware) that will exist
- The applications that will run on each computer
- The communications capabilities that will exist
- The user departments and other remote locations that will be served

Defining what computers will exist is a way to summarize any new minicomputers and larger computers (mainframes) that will be installed. This is documented by the hardware projects. (Microcomputers are best addressed when defining the man-machine interfaces.)

Defining the applications that will run on each computer illustrates how each of the applications listed in the software architecture will eventually be distributed among the computer systems. This provides an opportunity to identify the following:

Projects	Benefits	Person Responsible	Priority	Estimated Hours	Estimated Cost	Beginning Date (Month or Quarter/ Year)	Ending Date (Month or Quarter/ Year)
H1 Order and install additional 512 Kb main memory	Response time expected to decrease by 5 seconds during peak periods.	Jones	High	0	$ 5,000	1/X6	1/X6
H2 Order 6 terminals, 1 printer, and 1 microcomputer	Supports: ■ Accounts payable ■ Word processing	Jones	Medium	0	16,000	9/X6	9/X6
H6 Purchase minicomputer and related hardware	Supports payroll/personnel department.	Brown	Medium	16	60,000	11/X6	12/X6
H7 Relocate terminals from payroll/personnel department	Deimplementation of current payroll system.	Jones	Low	0	0	Q2/X7	Q2/X7
			TOTALS	40	$220,000		

FIG. 11-11 Hardware and Communications Projects

LONG-RANGE SYSTEMS PLANNING 11-23

- Stand-alone applications that run on a completely dedicated computer
- Distributed applications that run on one computer but share data with an application that runs on another computer
- For applications that are planned to be converted, the computer on which they will eventually reside
- The results of phasing out any old hardware and applications

References to hardware should generally be generic and not refer to specific vendor products, particularly for new computers that have not been selected. At this time, it is not necessary to put this level of detail into hardware and communications architecture.

The communications capabilities that are planned to exist should also be indicated only in high-level, generic terms. The hardware and communications architecture should (graphically) indicate:

- Local departments tied directly into the computer system
- Remote locations that have terminals or printers
- The computer into which these locations are directly tied
- Communications capabilities that will exist between any two computers

Figure 11-12 illustrates hardware and communications architecture.

Step 6: Define the Personnel and Staffing Projects

The final set of projects that need to be defined for the plan are the personnel and staffing projects. This is an important step that cannot be neglected. Staffing often comprises the largest portion of a data processing department's budget.[4] This portion of the plan defines all anticipated changes to staffing resources and allows them to be planned to coincide with other related projects in the plan.

Changes to any personnel having responsibility for development, maintenance, and ongoing support of data processing within the organization should be included in the scope of this effort. In addition to data processing department personnel, this may include personnel reporting to a user department with responsibilities such as liasion to the data processing department or systems analysis. The scope of this planning should exclude data entry personnel, however.

---

[4] Larry Marion, "The DP Budget Survey: PCs Make Waves," *Datamation* (Apr. 15, 1984), p. 86.

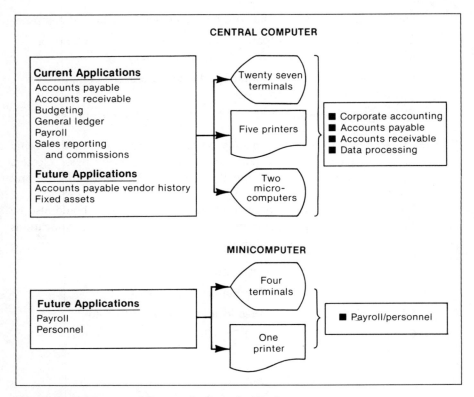

FIG. 11-12 Hardware and Communications Architecture

Figure 11-13 is an example of some personnel and staffing projects. The format used provides for a brief description of the staffing project, its timing, and the resources that it is expected to consume. After this has been completed, it may help to indicate graphically the changes that have been planned on an organization chart, as is depicted in Figure 11-14.

Step 7: Review All Projects With the Project Team

Once all projects have been defined, the project team should meet to discuss them. The objective of this meeting is to get an overall consensus on the definition, timing, and resources planned for these projects so that the planning process can proceed to the next step.

This is the first opportunity the team members will have to review all of the projects together. They often realize that they are asking the organization to commit too much and that some projects must be eliminated or postponed. Deciding which projects should be affected will probably cause some dissent;

LONG-RANGE SYSTEMS PLANNING

Projects	Benefits	Person Responsible	Priority	Estimated Hours	Monthly Estimated Cost	Beginning Date	Ending Date
P1 Hire administrative assistant	Assumes responsibility for all documentation. Sets up controls over program documentation updates.	Smith	Medium	40	$2,500	Q1	X7
P2 Create production systems specialist position	Is responsible for all nonaccounting systems. May fill internally.	Smith	Low	40	3,000	Q3	X7
P3 Hire technical support specialist	Is responsible for all systems software and all microcomputers.	Smith	Low	60	3,000	Q1	X8
			TOTALS	140	$8,500		

FIG. 11-13 Personnel and Staffing Projects

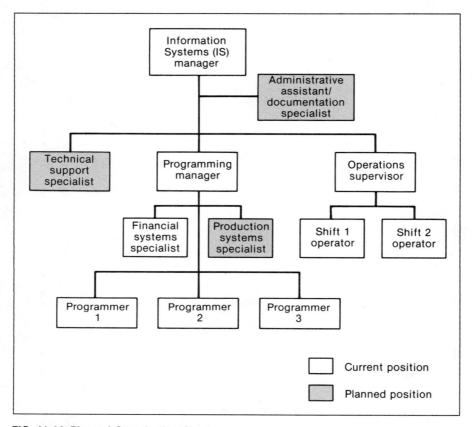

FIG. 11-14 Planned Organization Chart

however, this dissent and its resolution are valuable to the overall acceptance of the plan. It is the responsibility of the project team's leader, using the data processing manager as a technical resource, to resolve this and arrive at a tentative list of projects.

Step 8: Develop the Implementation Plan

Step 8 involves the final series of tasks that must be completed before assembling the finished product. The input to this step is formed by the projects that have been agreed upon earlier. The output is a Gantt chart showing the timing of all the projects and their costs in each time period, which is illustrated in Figure 11-15.

Project Sequencing. Based on each project's expected start and end dates and the criteria for setting priorities that were established in Step 1, each pro-

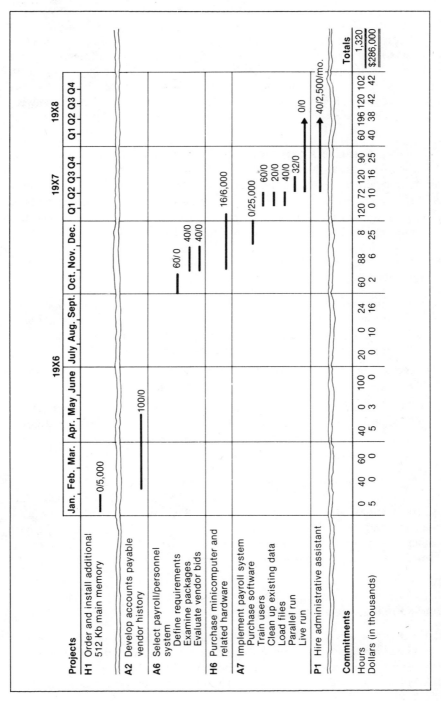

FIG. 11-15 Implementation Plan

ject needs to be scheduled in a sequence suitable for implementation. The information systems manager (or his designee) who has been assigned this task may have to change the beginning and ending dates of some projects, because many people initially tend to request all projects closer to the beginning of the planning horizon than to the end. If such changes are made, the sequence of project execution should still accommodate any interdependencies between projects.

Totaling Resource Requirements by Time Period. Other factors to consider when sequencing the tasks are the costs and hours expected to be incurred in each time period. As shown in Figure 11-15, the implementation plan identifies these resources by each time period throughout the planning horizon. These totals should not be unacceptably high in any timeframe. If so, certain tasks must be resequenced or even eliminated. (All of this is subject to final approval by the project team.)

The following general rules should be adhered to when totaling resource requirements.

1 Resource requirements for projects spanning several time periods should be prorated across those time periods. The purpose in doing this is so that the totals for each time period accurately reflect the resources that are expected to be consumed in that time period.

2 Recurring costs, such as salaries for new employees, should be added to each time period after they are initially incurred.

3 The use of additional resources (besides hours and dollars) may even be planned. For example, it may be advantageous to further define hours into hours committed among any of several key people responsible for executing the plan.

There are various microcomputer-based software products available to assist in developing the implementation plan. Project Manager's Workbench from Applied Business Technology, Inc., is one. Such products can aid in task sequencing and in totaling the resource requirements. They can even prepare graphics depiction of the implementation plan. The real value of such a tool is the time saved in updating where changes are made to the projects in the implementation plan.

Step 9: Final Review and Preparation

Finally, Step 9 involves first a review of the implementation plan by the project team. The completion of this review marks acceptance of all parts of the LRSP by the group. The completed document can then be compiled and sent to top management for review and approval. The process is described in more detail in the following discussion.

Project Team Review. Once the implementation plan has been completed, it is ready for an initial review by the project team. During this review, the team should determine the following:

- Have all projects been appropriately identified?
- Do the resource requirements in each time period and in total represent a commitment acceptable to top management?
- Have the criteria for setting priorities been respected when the task sequences were set in the implementation plan?

The project team often objects to the implementation plan, and perhaps objects as well to some of the projects, requiring another revision of part of the plan. This revision can frequently be outlined in the meeting, leaving the detail and cleanup work to be done under the direction of the staff.

During the process of changing the plan, some of the earlier steps may have to be followed to make sure that the right considerations have been made during this revision. For example, during the project team review, an accounting manager may convince the project team that the planned accounts payable vendor history system can produce the highest tangible savings of all the application projects by providing information that can reduce purchase costs by 4 percent. Having scheduled this project for two years out, it must now be rescheduled for execution in the first year of the plan. To ensure an even allocation of resources, other projects originally scheduled for earlier execution must be rescheduled. The hardware and communications projects must also be reviewed and possibly rescheduled to support the application projects that were moved.

Final Preparation. Once the project team has accepted the implementation plan and all the projects, it is necessary to prepare the final plan for submission to management. This consists of assembling all parts of the plan, attaching any supporting materials or exhibits, writing the necessary narratives such as the cover letter and the executive summary, and reviewing the finished product editorially for consistency. The table of contents illustrated in Figure 11-3 should closely outline the contents of the finished product.

The project team may want to review the final document before it is submitted for management's review. Although this is not unreasonable, it can be avoided. Since the team members have already approved all major portions of the plan, the only comments they could make are editorial ones. In the interests of efficiency, such comments can be communicated informally to the data processing manager (or to the primary author).

Management Review. The final review and approval of the plan should come from executive management, which may include corporate officers, the board of directors, or other executives not directly involved in the planning process but responsible for matters of budget and policy. This approval is vital for the plan's overall success.

The executive(s) reviewing the plan may decide that further work is necessary. Common points of concern often are as follows:

- Total resources required are too high.
- The plan is inconsistent with corporate goals and objectives.
- Project sequencing and priorities do not reflect the executive's perception of overall priorities.

Any additional revisions resulting from the executive review should go through the necessary sequence of steps outlined here. In a well-conceived plan, these revisions should be minimal.

IMPLEMENTING THE LRSP

Developing an LRSP is relatively easy compared to implementing the projects defined in the plan, controlling the resources expended on each project, and controlling the timing of the projects. In this section, we discuss some brief project control techniques that experience indicates may be helpful.

Assignment of Responsibility

Responsibility for the plan's overall execution should rest with a capable individual such as the information systems manager or his superior. Responsibilities for each of the initial projects should have been assigned to key individuals as part of the plan's development. These responsibilities should be flexible and may be changed as time progresses.

Once these assignments have been made, each individual should be held accountable for the timely completion of his affected segment. The most common reason for a plan failing is that no one is held accountable for its implementation (and, related to this, there is an overall lack of commitment to its execution). The plan will succeed much more easily when individuals are held accountable for implementing the projects defined in it.

Monitoring the Schedule

A well-thought-out plan has defined checkpoints for the larger projects and clearly defined beginning and ending points for each project. Outputs or deliverables should be defined at these junctures wherever possible. The information systems manager (or whoever is responsible for the plan's execution) should monitor the plan's progress against these events. This means frequent meetings and contact with the individuals responsible for each project. If it

LONG-RANGE SYSTEMS PLANNING 11-31

appears that project completion dates will be missed, the data processing manager should:

1 Determine the new project completion deadline.

2 Notify people affected that the deadline may be missed and assess the severity of the delay.

3 Depending on the severity, take action to recover and try to meet the deadline, such as by adding additional resources or authorizing staff overtime. If slippage is not severe, perhaps no action need be taken.

4 Determine the need to update the timing of other projects in the plan and present this at the update meetings, as explained in the following discussion.

Holding Periodic Update Meetings

The results of the plan's progress (or lack thereof) should be communicated to the project team in periodic update meetings. These meetings serve as a forum for approving timing changes as well as announcing project completions. The project team should meet quarterly or semiannually. It may also be helpful to circulate an update memorandum to the project team explaining progress made on the plan or reporting significant events.

Being Flexible

Unplanned events often take place and affect a plan's execution. For example, the information systems manager may resign, or a slump in business may cause funds to be cut sharply. These events may necessitate a change in the plan's progress; however, they should not cause its abandonment. Those managing the plan should be flexible enough to accommodate such disruptions without forsaking the plan. The plan should also be revised periodically—the best way to keep it current in light of such changes.

REVISING THE LRSP

The LRSP, as originally defined, should never become implemented in full over the complete planning horizon. Instead, a plan is typically revised periodically every twelve to eighteen months. In all likelihood, the projects defined over the first twelve to eighteen months are the only ones to become implemented from the original plan.

Revising the plan enables later versions to reflect the following:

- New priorities that have come about due to changes in the environment, marketplace, or organization

- New projects or changes to projects already defined in the plan
- Changes in the resources available for executing the plan

Obviously, these will change enough over time for the accuracy and utility of the original plan to diminish significantly after a year or so. The original plan should be updated approximately every twelve to eighteen months.

Steps to Updating the Plan

Each time the plan is revised, the new project team should retrace the nine steps originally outlined. However, revising a plan that was originally well thought out takes much less effort than was initially expended in developing it. The previous plan provides a good base for starting each step. For example, the application status summary in the revised plan will simply be an updated version of the current application status summary. Detailed data gathering need only be done for new applications. There is a good point to be made for saving detailed records and notes that were used to develop the previous plan. Having these available makes revising the plan much easier.

SUMMARY

An attempt has been made here to provide a workable approach to LRSP. Over years of practical application, refinements and revisions have been applied to this approach. The following is a brief reiteration of the major points presented herein.

LRSP supports the proper growth and development of the information systems by planning the deployment of data processing resources in their proper relationship to the strategic or LRSP of the enterprise itself. Organizations with information systems budgets above $250,000 probably should consider an LRSP. The larger the organization, the more cost beneficial LRSP is to the organization.

The nine steps outlined in Figure 11-2 present the approach to developing an LRSP. This plan is essentially a series of projects defined in a sequence that can be implemented within the organization's limited resources. The plan should be revised periodically to reflect changes in the organization's needs and resources.

If a long-range view of information systems planning is taken, rather than a piecemeal approach, the organization will notice benefits, such as:

- More fully integrated application systems
- Better utilization of information systems resources
- Increased user participation in information systems activities

REFERENCES

Babcock, Charles. "Put DP in Sync with Corporate Strategy, Execs Told." *Computerworld* (May 6, 1985), p. 24.

International Business Machines Corporation. *Information Planning Guide* (1981).

Levy, Joel D. "Bridging the Gap With Business Information Systems Planning." *Infosystems* (June 1982).

Systems Development Management. (Pennsauken, N.J.: Auerbach (1980)), sec. 31-01-16.

Vacca, John R. "Planning an Information System." *Infosystems* (June 1982).

PART **III**

Specific Models and Systems

CHAPTER **12**

Financial Planning and Control

James D. Willson

Introduction 2	Calculation of Fixed and Variable Elements 20
Some Practical Observations About Financial Planning 2	Graphic Determination 22
Two Principal Types of Planning 2	The Least Squares Method 24
Different Information Input 3	Allowing for Extraordinary Costs 24
Cost Classifications and Behavior 6	Procedure Applicable to Most Departments 24
Different Types of Costs 6	**Standard Costs in Relation to Plan or Budget** 25
Costs for Planning Purposes 8	
Costs in Relation to Volume 9	**A Definition of Budgeting** 25
Incremental Costs; Contribution Margin 10	
Costs for Control Purposes 11	**Types of Budgets** 26
Responsibility Accounting and Reporting 12	Project Budgets 26
Applying the Responsibility Concept ... 12	Fixed Budgets 28
	Flexible or Variable Budgets 28
Segregating Costs Into Their Components 14	
Fixed Costs 14	**Applicability of Planning and Control to the Balance Sheet** 31
Variable Costs and Measures of Activity 15	
Determining Semivariable Costs 15	**References** 38
Direct Estimates 16	

Fig. 12-1 The System of Business Plans 4
Fig. 12-2 Relationship of Annual Plan to Strategic Plan 5
Fig. 12-3 Cost Classifications for Planning Decisions 8
Fig. 12-4 Costs in Relation to Volume 9
Fig. 12-5 A Realistic Cost Pattern 10
Fig. 12-6 Statement of Marginal and Operating Income 11
Fig. 12-7 Cost Classifications for Control and Analysis 12
Fig. 12-8 Manufacturing Expense Budget at Selected Levels of Activity 18
Fig. 12-9 Graphic Determination of Fixed and Variable Costs 23
Fig. 12-10 Actual and Budget Performance 27
Fig. 12-11 Distribution Cost Budget 29

Fig. 12-12 Budget Report 30
Fig. 12-13 Example of Flexible Budget 32
Fig. 12-14 Illustrative Monthly Budget Report 33
Fig. 12-15 Summary Marketing Division Budget 34
Fig. 12-16 Planned Cash Receipts and Disbursements 35
Fig. 12-17 Accounts Receivable Budget 36
Fig. 12-18 Materials Inventory Budget 37
Fig. 12-19 Comparative Working Capital Requirements 38

INTRODUCTION

Of all the management functions involved in guiding an enterprise, two of the most important are planning and control. Yet, depending on the background of those primarily involved, there is a tendency in the development of an FIS to emphasize the traditional accounting functions—that is, the traditional types of financial statements, accounts payable procedures, accounts receivable, or payrolls, or perhaps the usual fixed asset accounting. Although these may be the core systems (see Chapter 6) and must be properly treated, the aggressive financial manager is simply not interested in the ordinary or traditional financial statements or routines. Most likely, he is concerned with forward-looking programs related to sound planning and effective controls that will help direct the business toward its goals and objectives. Certain important aspects of planning and control, each differentiated, do not surface in the usual financial accounting discussions; yet those concerned with the development and implementation of a useful FIS should be aware of them. The information in this chapter should prove useful in assisting that audience.

SOME PRACTICAL OBSERVATIONS ABOUT FINANCIAL PLANNING

A plan is a predetermined course of action. It involves thinking about the future, considering alternative courses of action, and deciding which one should be selected. The various parts of a plan are carried out by appropriate segments of the business organization.

Two Principal Types of Planning

Those concerned with developing an effective FIS should recognize two primary types of planning, each having its unique information needs:

1 *Strategic planning* — long range in nature
2 *Short-term planning* — often called "annual business planning" or "annual profit planning"

The purpose of a strategic plan is to guide the company toward its long-range mission, objective, or goals. It extends far into the future—or as far as it is practical to plan. A typical plan is for a period of five years; however, in some industries (e.g., forest products), the period might be fifty years. The strategic plan places heavy emphasis on new products and markets.

Thus, development plans are important. Included in that category are:

- Divestment plans
- Diversification plans
- Research and development plans

Operations plans must consider not only existing products and markets but also the impact of development plans. The interrelationship of such plans is shown in Figure 12-1.

Closely related to the strategic plan is the annual or short-term plan. This relationship is shown graphically in Figure 12-2. While the near-term plan emphasizes existing products and markets, the annual plan must consider actions that ought to be initiated during the short-term planning years as specified in the long-range plan. In fact, the short-term plan spells out many actions required in the first year or two of the long-range plan.

Different Information Input

The input and output data for the financial aspects of long-range planning differ considerably from the data for short-term planning. Under most circumstances, therefore, different planning models may be necessary, and different instructions govern.

The systems developer should keep in mind some of the following distinctions between strategic and long-range planning, on the one hand, and short-term planning, on the other.

> 1 *Extent of detail needed.* The long-range plan is broad and directional. Thus, it may project and consider the total cost of a product by year, or, at most, the total variable cost and total fixed cost. In contrast, the annual budget may consider each element of cost (direct labor, direct material, variable manufacturing expense, and fixed manufacturing expense) by cost center or department. Moreover, the applicable annual plan schedules probably require costs by element, department or cost center, or month.
>
> Depending on the problem or strategy being considered, overall ratios may be used. Thus, the model may provide for a constant ratio of cost of sales to sales for each product line. Annual sales volumes may be factored as a given percentage increase over the prior year for each product. Selling expenses may be determined as a fixed percentage of sales for each period. Capital expenditures may be

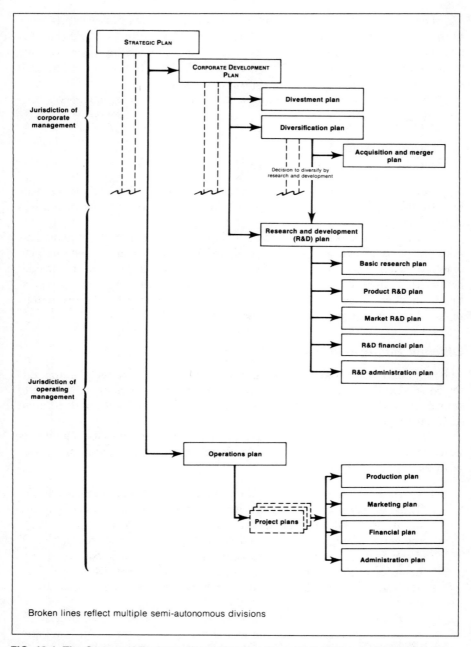

FIG. 12-1 The System of Business Plans (Source: Business Intelligence Programs, "A Framework for Business Planning," Research Report No. 162 (Menlo Park, Cal.: SRI International, 1963), p. 4. Reprinted by permission.)

FINANCIAL PLANNING AND CONTROL

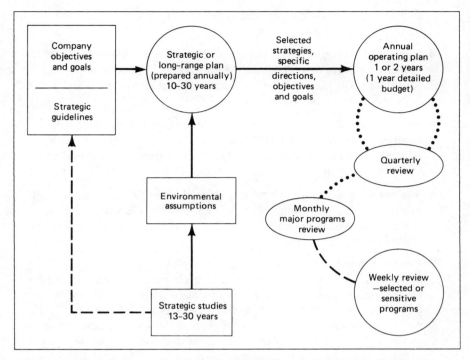

FIG. 12-2 Relationship of Annual Plan to Strategic Plan (Source: James D. Willson, *Budgeting and Profit Planning Manual* (Boston: Warren, Gorham & Lamont, 1983). Reprinted by permission.)

calculated as a percentage of internal cash flow. Depreciation may be estimated as an overall percentage of gross capital assets.

In contrast, the annual profit plan is specific with regard to each functional type of cost or expense, by month and by organization. Depreciation is determined on the basis of specific equipment lives.

Thus, long-range planning is more general in nature, with correspondingly less detailed information needed than in short-term planning.

2 *Information sources.* Generally, the bulk of the data used for the short-term planning process are internal in nature. In contrast, strategic planning may use a great deal of externally generated data. Thus, such items as industry growth rates, inflation rates, foreign exchange differentials, and wage rate increases may be based on information secured from industry, government, or other outside sources.

3 *Time horizons.* Tactical or short-term planning ordinarily covers a period of one or two years by months. Strategic planning may relate to a ten- or thirty-year time span by years—or even by five-year periods for many applications.

4 *Number of scenarios.* Alternatives or scenarios are likely to be quite numerous in strategic planning. Many "what-if" actions must be considered. On the other hand, substitution choices for the annual plan are likely to be few.

5 *Degree of accuracy.* By implication, the broad, general, directional nature of long-range planning indicates that a great deal of detail accuracy is simply not required. Attention is focused on broad trends and potentials, not unimportant details.

6 *Amount of uncertainty.* There is a large element of uncertainty (and subjectivity) in long-range planning. Perhaps that is why there are more condensed plans and fewer frequent plan revisions than in the annual planning process.

7 *Degree of regularity.* Finally, short-term planning is usually performed on a predictable or regular cycle basis. In contrast, a new strategic plan may be called for each time a major outside event (new threat, product breakthrough, major new opportunity) occurs. To be sure, there is usually a yearly strategic plan review and revision; however, the likelihood of other irregular calls for new plans is great.

In some ways, planning is a continuous process. Perhaps provision should be made in the FIS for frequent revisions as major events occur.

In any case, those designing the FIS should be aware of the different information needs for each type of plan. The user's proclivities should also be explored, even though the user may be unaware of the effect on FISs of the various alternatives in relation to input and output.

COST CLASSIFICATIONS AND BEHAVIOR

A knowledge of how costs and expenses should relate to various activity levels, what costs should be considered in making various types of decisions, and how individuals may relate to the responsibility for incurring specific costs is essential to proper planning or control. Only when these considerations are known can costs and expenses be properly planned; only then can specific individuals be held accountable and responsible for results; and only then can performance be properly judged.

Different Types of Costs

In order to classify costs properly, segregate them in a meaningful manner, and apply them properly to planning or control decisions, the following concepts should be understood:

FINANCIAL PLANNING AND CONTROL

- *Variable costs and expenses* — costs and expenses that vary in the aggregate more or less in direct proportion to production or sales volume, as applicable (e.g., direct labor, direct material, sales commissions).

- *Fixed costs and expenses* — costs and expenses that do not change as the level of output varies (within the limits of the planned activity). Examples are depreciation (other than unit variable depreciation methods), property taxes, rent (flat-period payments), and property insurance.

- *Semivariable costs and expenses* — costs and expenses that change as the volume factor varies, but not in direct proportion to that factor (e.g., supervisory salaries, power, maintenance, and perhaps supplies).

- *Direct costs* — costs that result from, are incurred by, or are directly traceable to the business segment being analyzed (i.e., a specific product, particular sales territory, identified research project, designated organization segment). This category represents costs that would not have been incurred without the operation of the segment (e.g., direct labor, direct material, various direct expenses).

- *Indirect costs* — costs that cannot be clearly identified with a cost objective, such as a particular product. Since this category of costs cannot be clearly associated with a particular cost objective, such costs must be allocated among the various objectives to which they apply (e.g., utilities, occupancy costs, maintenance).

- *Period costs or expenses* — costs or expenses associated with the passage of time, but not directly related to changing activity levels as incurred by management decision. For practical purposes, they are the same as fixed costs or expenses.

- *Programmed costs or expenses* — costs or expenses based on a definite program or project, such as advertising and sales promotion, or research and development. They are closely related to period costs and, once established by management, may be considered fixed; however, management may change the level of expenditure when it so chooses.

- *Marginal or incremental costs* — the increase in total costs resulting from the production of an additional quantity (e.g., one more unit, one month's production).

- *Sunk costs* — costs already incurred in plant and equipment or intangible assets (and on which the recovery may be limited if the product or process is discontinued).

- *Replacement costs* — costs associated with replacing existing facilities or products.
- *Standard costs* — what the costs should be if produced according to standard processes and with standard material and labor costs. (Certain variances of actual costs from the calculated, planned, or standard cost are ignored.)
- *Opportunity costs* — costs (and income) associated with alternative courses of action.
- *Actual costs* — Costs of manufacturing the product, or carrying out the process, including excess costs over standard or variances below standard. It may be determined on any one of several cost methods (e.g., first-in, first-out; last-in, first-out; moving average) over a specified period.

COSTS FOR PLANNING PURPOSES

Those experienced in financial planning and control know that different cost classifications are needed for different purposes. This is another way of recognizing that, for different decisions, certain cost characteristics cause some costs to be more important than others and require different treatment. For planning purposes, as illustrated in Figure 12-3, two factors are significant: (1) how the

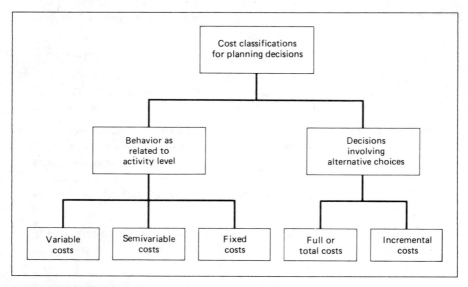

FIG 12-3 Cost Classifications for Planning Decisions (Source: James D. Willson, *Budgeting and Profit Planning Manual* (Boston: Warren, Gorham & Lamont, 1983). Reprinted by permission.)

FINANCIAL PLANNING AND CONTROL

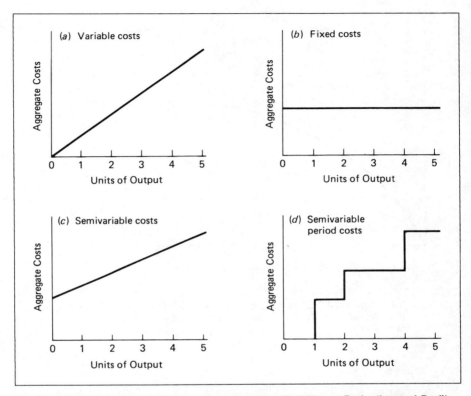

FIG 12-4 Cost in Relation to Volume (Source: James D. Willson, *Budgeting and Profit Planning Manual* (Boston: Warren, Gorham & Lamont, 1983). Reprinted by permission.)

costs should behave as related to the planned level of activity and (2) what the incremental costs, as distinguished from total costs, are that are associated with the decision under review.

In planning departmental costs or the costs for an entire function (such as marketing) or for an entire division or company, the expected costs must be determined for the planned level of activity. (It is also required knowledge for control purposes.)

Costs in Relation to Volume

The relationship of costs to volume may be illustrated graphically as shown in Figure 12-4. Thus, variable costs are in direct proportion to volume, as in (*a*). An example is the direct material content of a product. Fixed costs, or period costs, bear no immediate relationship to volume output, as reflected by the horizontal line in (*b*). Illustrative of this expense is depreciation expense, which is not determined on a unit-of-output basis. Semivariable costs may be graphi-

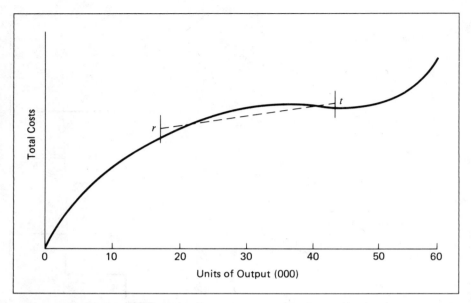

FIG. 12-5 A Realistic Cost Pattern (Source: James D. Willson, *Budgeting and Profit Planning Manual* (Boston: Warren, Gorham & Lamont, 1983). Reprinted by permission.)

cally depicted as in (*c*); or, if the movement is somewhat inclined to be in a series of steps, then (*d*) is representative. The supervisory costs in a factory are one category that may be considered in this classification.

As a practical matter, costs may not behave in the ways illustrated. Rather, the real pattern may be as shown by the curved line in Figure 12-5, caused, for example, by overtime penalties above a given amount. Within reasonable limits, the solution to this situation is to recognize the costs as variable or fixed within the limited range for the period of budgeted activity. See line *rt*.

How to segregate costs or expenses into their separate elements is discussed elsewhere in this chapter.

Incremental Costs; Contribution Margin

Knowing cost behavior is only one requirement in planning (or control). In certain types of planning decisions, incremental costs must be known. Thus, a product line may show a loss on a full-cost basis, as in Figure 12-6. However, when the variable or incremental costs are determined, it may be concluded that discontinuing Product *B* would increase the loss by $5,000, not reduce it by $500. Thus, the development and use of a practical FIS involves knowledge of cost behavior as related to volume, as well as marginal and incremental costs and income of the segment being analyzed. The contribution margin of the product illustrated in Figure 12-6 should be known in order to facilitate pru-

FINANCIAL PLANNING AND CONTROL

THE MARTIN COMPANY
STATEMENT OF CONTRIBUTION MARGIN AND OPERATING INCOME
AND EXPENSE BY PRODUCT LINES
For the month ended October 31, 19XX

		Products		
Description	Total	A	B	C
Net sales	$100,000	$50,000	$20,000	$30,000
Less variable cost of sales	43,000	20,000	13,000	10,000
Manufacturing margin	57,000	30,000	7,000	20,000
Less variable distribution costs	20,000	15,000	2,000	3,000
Contribution margin	$ 37,000	$15,000	$ 5,000	$17,000
Less fixed and allocated costs				
Manufacturing	$ 3,000	$ 1,000	$ 1,000	$ 1,000
Selling	5,000	2,000	2,000	1,000
Advertising	5,000	2,000	2,000	1,000
Administrative	2,200	1,000	500	700
Total	$ 15,200	$ 6,000	$ 5,500	$ 3,700
Operating income or (loss)	$ 21,800	$ 9,000	($ 500)	$13,300

FIG. 12-6 Statement of Marginal and Operating Income (Source: James D. Willson, *Budgeting and Profit Planning Manual* (Boston: Warren, Gorham & Lamont, 1983). Reprinted by permission.)

dent decision making. The contribution margin is calculated by deducting from the assumed sales income all of those costs and expenses that would not be incurred if the segment costed were not present. The result is a measure of what the segment (each product in the illustration) contributes to the company's fixed or continuing expenses and to its overall operating income. Thus, Product B, with sales of $20,000 and variable costs of $15,000 (cost of sales plus distribution costs), produces a margin of $5,000 toward the fixed costs and expenses of the company.

COSTS FOR CONTROL PURPOSES

In business, the planning function has as its objective the selection of the most profitable (or appropriate) course of action by which the enterprise may reach its goals. By contrast, control, or measurement, another basic business activity, involves comparing actual performance with planned or expected performance and taking action, if required, to bring actual performance in line with the overall plan.

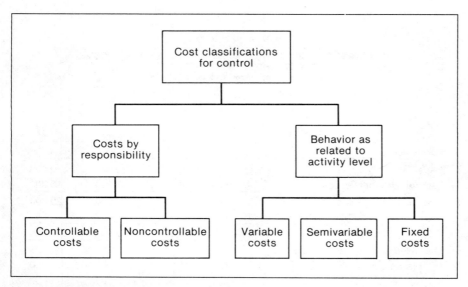

FIG. 12-7 Cost Classifications for Control and Analysis

In planning decisions, attention is focused on the level of expected costs, both variable or marginal (or total). *Who* is responsible for the incurred costs is therefore not germane. However, in control-type activities, costs must be segregated and accumulated according to those held responsible. So, for control purposes, both behavior as related to activity level and responsibility for incurring costs must be recognized. The significant cost segregations for control purposes are identified in Figure 12-7.

Responsibility Accounting and Reporting

As touched upon in Chapter 3, responsibility accounting involves the recording of transactions or events so that they are identified with the department or individual responsible. (The related responsibility reporting for certain corporate expenses is schematically presented in Figure 3-12.)

Applying the Responsibility Concept

The principle of accounting control involves four steps, each of which must be considered in developing and implementing a sound FIS, as follows:

1 Establish a budget or plan that is regarded by the person to be held responsible for achieving it as fair. Among other things, this means that he will participate in setting it. Under normal circumstances, it is not mandated from a higher echelon, although in certain cases, this action may be required.

FINANCIAL PLANNING AND CONTROL

2 Accumulate actual costs or expenses by responsibility center (but only those costs for which the executive is responsible and that he can control).

3 Compare actual and budgeted expenses.

4 Take action to bring actual expenses for the remainder of the budget period in line in order to achieve the cumulative budget level.

For most costs, there is no particular problem. Costs are accumulated properly by department. These actual costs are compared to budget. However, the budget report must be regarded as fair by the person to be evaluated or judged.

Following are examples of typical problems that should be addressed in any FIS project, along with some possible solutions, so that the budget report fairly presents budget performance.

1 *Department is charged with expenses unrelated to the activity.* For significant charges, perhaps the system could provide for a review of the cost document by the supervisor before the charge is made. Alternatively, large budget variances could be analyzed for errors before the budget reports are issued. In addition, a note could be included in the report indicating that the error will be corrected.

2 *Functional costs are charged to a department (that does not control them).* Normally, for example, all costs of professional tax counseling are charged to the tax department. However, the CEO may make extensive use of such services.

Perhaps the policy should be changed, and whatever department receives the services should be charged for their costs. If professional tax service charges are to be monitored by, and retained in, one department, then a special allowance could be made for any unplanned expenses incurred by another department.

3 *Actual service charges are allocated to using departments.* Assume actual maintenance expense is allocated monthly to all departments on a square footage basis (space occupied). In effect, that procedure allocates the inefficiencies of the maintenance department to the users.

Perhaps only the budgeted maintenance department expenses should be charged, not the variance. Alternatively, charges should be made based on the actual maintenance hours required (at the standard rate) and not on an arbitrary basis. Moreover, the using department budget should be determined on a comparable basis.

4 *Expected volume factor is not attained.* Normally, the department supervisor is expected to keep expenses within budget limits. For example, if the tonnage handled is running less than planned, then work crews are assigned to other tasks. If instances of severe interruption occur (such as a strike at another location), then a system of special allowances may be considered. Obviously (1) the variable budget would be based on normal conditions, not unusual circumstances, and some adjustment might be proper temporarily; but (2) a system of special allowances should not be the device for avoiding budgetry control.

SEGREGATING COSTS INTO THEIR COMPONENTS

For planning as well as for control purposes, costs ought to be segregated into their components, such as fixed costs, variable costs, and semivariable costs. But just how is this to be done?

The undertaking of any such determination in a business organization requires, first of all, an understanding of the various processes and functions in the business. With such a background, a review of the cost history and the application of common sense will help establish the cost behavior pattern.

The steps in the process may be outlined as follows:

1 A general review of costs by type of item, by department, and in total
2 The selection of the activity measure or factor of variability for each function and/or cost
3 The review of costs in relation to the measure of activity, and determination of the cost segments and rate of variability, if applicable

In classifying costs into the variable, fixed, and semivariable segments, such classification should be made within restricted volume ranges. For example, if the sales volume is not more than $1.5 million nor less than $1 million, certain costs will be fixed. The same costs might increase, however, were the volume to be extended beyond $1.5 million. As a rule, the volume ranges under consideration in any one budget period are sufficiently restricted to occasion no difficulty in setting such limits.

Although few costs are entirely fixed or 100 percent variable within a given volume range, a considerable number are so nearly so that, for all practical purposes, they can be thus classified. All others must be assigned to the semivariable group.

Fixed Costs

By definition, fixed costs are those that remain the same at each level of activity, either planned or experienced. There should be no particular difficulty in identifying and planning or controlling this category. Some illustrative fixed expenses include depreciation charged on a time basis (not a unit production basis); property taxes on plant and equipment; and fixed executive salaries, rent, and bond interest.

FINANCIAL PLANNING AND CONTROL

Variable Costs and Measures of Activity

Variable costs[1] are those that vary in direct ratio to some volume factor, such as direct material, direct labor on a piece-rate basis, and salespeople's or agents' commissions.

The selection of the proper measure of activity is an important step in assuring an effective budgetary control system. Four possible requirements of an acceptable base are as follows:

1 It should be a direct measure of cost-incurring activity.
2 It must be readily understood by those using the budget.
3 It must be generally unaffected by any factor other than volume.
4 It should be sufficiently sensitive to changes in activity, and be generally applicable to all products of the company.

The bases that seem plausible should be carefully studied in their application to the various departments, whether a sales activity, a direct production function, or a service.

Suggestive of acceptable bases are these popular applications:

- Standard man-hours
- Standard machine-hours
- Sales volume
- Actual man-hours
- Direct labor dollars
- Pounds of material consumed
- Units of output (i.e., finished product)
- Number of orders filled
- Number of deliveries

Many different measurements of volume must be used for the various functions and operations of the business. The characteristics of the industry or activity determine the bases, and special volume factors often must be used. For example, in hotels, the percentage of room occupancy is used; in office buildings, the floor space occupancy; and in parking garages, the units handled.

The measures of activity selected for the variable costs are often applicable to the semivariable costs.

Determining Semivariable Costs

Semivariable costs are those that vary with volume but do not vary in direct relationship to the volume changes. It is with this group that the chief difficulty

---

[1] For this and the following sections, see Willson, *Budgeting and Profit Planning Manual* (Boston: Warren, Gorham & Lamont, 1983), pp. 5-8–5-18.

12-16 SPECIFIC MODELS AND SYSTEMS

arises in determining what the costs should be at different volume levels. As in the case of the variable costs, these items must first be classified according to their relationship to various production or sales volume factors. Next, some methods must be found for determining what the relationship is between these cost items and the respective volume factors to which they are related.

There are at least three methods available for determining the expected cost at different volume levels:

1 Direct estimate or synthesis of the semivariable costs
2 Calculation of fixed and variable elements of costs, based on the minimum and maximum expected volume
3 Graphics determination of fixed and variable costs

Direct Estimates

One method of budgeting the semivariable costs for different volume levels is to make individual estimates and calculations of every semivariable cost item at each of several volume levels falling within the range of volume expectancy. The steps involved are as follows:

1 Select measurement factors of production or sales volume for the cost items under consideration.
2 Establish maximum and minimum limits of volume expectancy.
3 Establish various production or sales volume levels or brackets within the range of volume expectancy as a basis for the cost estimates.
4 Perform estimates and calculations for each cost item for each of the volume levels or brackets.

To illustrate this procedure, it may be assumed that production volume for any one month is not expected to be under 600 units or over 1,200 units and that sales are not expected to be under $1,200 or over $2,400. Here, the measure of production volume is physical units and the measure of sales volume is dollar sales. It may be further assumed that it is desirable to know what costs should be expected at each of the following volume levels:

Production Volume in Units	Sales Volume in Dollars
600	$1,200
800	1,600
1,000	2,000
1,200	2,400

It is further assumed that the semivariable costs relating to production volume include only supervision, and those relating to sales volume include

FINANCIAL PLANNING AND CONTROL

only sales salaries and accounting department salaries. The next step is to determine the amount of each of these semivariable costs that is justified at each volume level. Such calculations must be based upon estimates made by the various managers concerned. Once the calculations are made, they need not be changed until there is some change in conditions or circumstances affecting the cost items.

It may be assumed in this case that the estimates and calculations indicate that the semivariable costs should be as follows:

Costs Relating to Production Volume		Costs Relating to Sales Volume			
Production Volume in Units	Supervision Cost	Sales Volume in Dollars	Sales Salaries	Accounting Department Salaries	Total
600	$245	$1,200	$160	$ 80	$240
800	280	1,600	190	90	280
1,000	300	2,000	200	100	300
1,200	320	2,400	220	110	330

This procedure is the same regardless of the factors used for volume measurement. If direct labor hours were used for production volume, then the estimates and calculations of supervision would be made for different numbers of direct labor hours. Different measures may be used in different departments and for different operations; for example, labor hours may be used in some departments while machine-hours are used in other departments.

One objection to this method is that it does not indicate what costs should be expected at every volume point, but only at certain points established as a basis for calculation. For example, assume the production volume in January was actually 720 units. What should the supervision cost have been? In the preceding table, it is shown that a supervision cost of $245 may be expected at a volume of 600 units and $280 at a volume of 800 units, but no cost is shown for 720 units. Between the established points, costs can be determined by interpolation. In this case, the calculation would be as follows:

$$\left(\frac{\$280 - \$245}{800 - 600}\right) \times (720 - 600) + \$245 = \text{expected cost at 720 units}$$

or

$$\frac{\$35}{200} \times 120 + 245 =$$
$$\$26 + 245 = \$266$$

Another method is to perform calculations for a sufficient number of volume levels so that any actual volume is closely approximated by one of the calculations. This plan is illustrated in Figure 12-8. In this example, expenses

THE CONSOLIDATED CORPORATION
AIRCRAFT DIVISION
MANUFACTURING EXPENSE BUDGET
(dollars in thousands)

Department: Subassembly
Department Head: Ship

Year: _____
Normal Activity: 8,500,000
Base: Standard Labor Hours

Account	Percentage of Normal Activity							
	60%	70%	80%	90%	100% (N.A.)	110%	120%	130%
Salaries								
General Foremen	$ 700	$ 700	$ 700	$ 700	$ 700	$ 700	$ 700	$ 700
Foremen	1,100	1,500	1,900	2,200	2,200	2,200	2,600	2,600
Clerks, etc.	700	700	950	950	950	950	950	1,200
Subtotal	$ 2,500	$ 2,900	$ 3,550	$ 3,850	$ 3,850	$ 3,850	$ 4,250	$ 4,500
Hourly labor — Indirect	$ 1,500	$ 1,750	$ 2,000	$ 2,250	$ 2,500	$ 2,500	$ 2,750	$ 3,000
Fuel	350	400	430	470	510	530	570	620

FIG. 12-8 Manufacturing Expense Budget at Selected Levels of Activity (Source: James D. Willson, *Budgeting and Profit Planning Manual* (Boston: Warren, Gorham & Lamont, 1983). Reprinted by permission.)

Power	2,620	3,020	3,430	3,870	4,300	4,740	5,140	5,320
Water	210	220	230	240	250	260	270	280
Maintenance and repairs	1,630	1,875	2,050	2,250	2,500	2,790	3,070	3,660
Supplies	270	315	360	405	450	495	540	585
Meal expense	140	180	190	200	210	230	260	270
Traveling	70	70	100	100	100	100	120	120
Telephone and telegraph	70	80	90	100	100	100	110	120
Cartons and containers	150	175	200	225	250	275	300	325
Recreation and welfare	30	40	50	50	50	60	60	60
Miscellaneous	120	130	150	160	175	190	200	210
Subtotal	$ 9,660	$11,155	$12,830	$14,170	$15,245	$16,120	$17,640	$19,070
Depreciation — Building	$ 900	$ 900	$ 900	$ 900	$ 900	$ 900	$ 900	$ 900
Depreciation — Machinery and equipment	1,800	1,800	1,800	1,800	1,800	1,800	1,800	1,800
Property taxes	1,200	1,200	1,200	1,200	1,200	1,200	1,200	1,200
Insurance	350	350	400	400	400	400	400	450
Total	$13,910	$15,405	$17,130	$18,470	$19,545	$20,420	$21,940	$23,420

were calculated for selected volumes ranging from 5.1 million standard labor hours (60 percent of normal activity) to 11.05 million standard labor hours (130 percent of normal activity). It is to be noted that depreciation, property taxes, insurance, and the salaries of foremen (all fixed expenses in this case) were included in calculating the cost levels at the specified volumes. This chart was prepared for one production department; similar charts may be prepared for all other departments. Costs at actual production levels are compared with the nearest volume calculation on the chart.

This method seems to involve a vast amount of calculation. In practice, however, once a method of calculating individual cost items is established, much less work is involved than might appear. Moreover, it will be found that many semivariable costs bear a similar relationship to volume changes and may be grouped for purposes of calculation.

Calculation of Fixed and Variable Elements. Another method of budgeting semivariable costs at different volume levels is based on the theory that every semivariable cost item consists of a fixed and variable element; that, between certain volume limits, a cost item can be separated into these two elements; that the fixed element remains the same between these two limits; and that the variable element bears a constant relationship to volume between the two limits.

Under this method, an estimate is made of each semivariable cost at the maximum and minimum volume levels expected. A calculation is then made of the fixed and variable elements of these costs, and the two are separated. By this procedure, it is then possible to ascertain the cost justified at any volume level lying between the maximum and minimum volume limits.

Reverting to the previous figures, this method, sometimes called the high-low method, may be illustrated as follows:

Costs Relating to Production Volume

	Minimum	Maximum
Production volume limits (units)	600	1,200
Estimated costs		
Supervision	$245	$320

Costs Relating to Sales Volume

	Minimum	Maximum
Sales volume limits	$1,200	$2,400
Estimated costs		
Sales salaries	160	220
Accounting department salaries	80	110

The first problem is to find for each of these cost items (1) the percentage relationship between the variable portion and volume and (2) the portion that

FINANCIAL PLANNING AND CONTROL   12-21

is fixed. Taking supervision cost, for example: a difference of 600 units in volume makes a difference of $75 in supervision cost. This gives a variable relationship of 12.5 percent (75 ÷ 600), or 12.5 cents per unit. The fixed portion can be determined as follows:

	Minimum Volume	Maximum Volume
Total supervision cost	$245	$320
Variable portion of cost (12.5% of 600 and 1,200, respectively)	75	150
Fixed portion of cost	$170	$170

The variable percentage and the fixed portion of every semivariable cost item can be determined in this manner. For example, the calculations for the remaining costs in this illustration would be as follows:

	Variable Percentage	Fixed Portion of Cost
Sales salaries: $\dfrac{\$220 - \$160}{\$2{,}400 - \$1{,}200} =$	5.0%	
$\$160 - (5\% \text{ of } \$1{,}200) =$		$100
Accounting department salaries: $\dfrac{\$110 - \$80}{\$2{,}400 - \$1{,}200} =$	2.5%	
$\$80 - (2.5\% \text{ of } \$1{,}200) =$		$ 50

Assume that the actual volume for January consisted of production of 720 units and sales of $1,600. What costs should be expected at these volumes? These may be shown as follows:

Actual production volume = 720 units
Actual sales volume = $1,600

Costs	Variable Portion			Total Expected Cost	Actual Cost	Gain (Loss)
	Fixed Portion	Percentage	Amount			
Supervision	$170	12.5%	$90(a)	$260	$270	$(10)
Sales salaries	100	5.0	80(b)	180	190	(10)
Accounting department salaries	50	2.5	40(c)	90	90	None

(a) 12.5% of 720 (or actual production volume) = $90
(b) 5% of $1,600 (or actual sales volume) = $80
(c) 2.5% of $1,600 (or actual sales volume) = $40

By this method, it can readily be determined what costs should be expected at any volume, and such costs can then be compared with the actual costs to signal failure or success in adjusting costs to changes in volume. In this case, the production department used $10 more supervision, or 3.86 percent ($10 ÷ $260) more, than was justified by the production volume; the sales department used $10 more sales salaries, or 5.55 percent ($10 ÷ $180) more, than was justified by the sales volume. The accounting department, on the other hand, kept its salaries in line with the changes in sales volume.

This method may be criticized in that it assumes a constant relationship between the variable element of the costs and volume within the volume range under consideration; but the error is usually slight and not sufficient to affect the usefulness of the method.

It should be noted that this method can be applied to groups of costs as well as to individual cost items.

Graphic Determination. The use of only two or a few points, such as minimum and maximum limits only, to determine the fixed and variable cost segments is sometimes subject to a wider degree of error than may be desirable, because only a limited number of activity levels are considered. If more accuracy is desired, another convenient approach is the use of a scatter chart. Assume that data on production control department costs are available, adjusted for wage differences and similar factors as follows:

Month	Reference	Factory Standard Man-Hours	Total Departmental Costs
January	1	20,000	$6,100
February	2	16,000	5,300
March	3	13,000	4,700
April	4	14,000	4,900
May	5	17,000	5,200
June	6	19,000	6,000
July	7	21,000	6,200
August	8	23,000	6,300
September	9	25,000	6,800
October	10	22,000	6,100
November	11	18,000	5,900
December	12	19,000	5,800

These points are then plotted on a chart as shown in Figure 12-9, each point being numbered for reference purposes. The vertical axis represents the dollar costs, while the horizontal axis represents the factor of variability (standard man-hours in the illustration). After the points are plotted, a line of best fit may be drawn by inspection in such a manner that about one-half of the

FINANCIAL PLANNING AND CONTROL

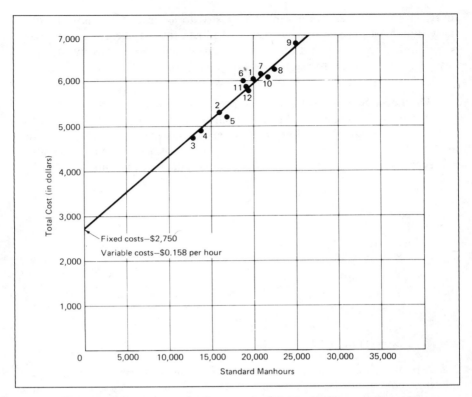

FIG. 12-9 Graphic Determination of Fixed and Variable Costs (Source: James D. Willson, *Budgeting and Profit Planning Manual* (Boston: Warren, Gorham & Lamont, 1983). Reprinted by permission.)

points are above it and the other half below. Any highly variant items should be disregarded. For a higher degree of refinement, the method of least squares may be used instead of inspection.

The point at which the line of best fit intersects the vertical axis indicates the fixed cost that might be expected if the plant were in an operating condition but producing nothing. The total cost at any level of activity is determined by reading the chart. For example, at a level of 25,000 standard man-hours, the budgeted expense is $6,700. This is made up of $2,750 fixed and $3,950 variable elements. The variable rate is $0.158 per standard man-hour.

In reviewing the chart, it can be seen that the slope of the line indicates the degree of variability. Thus, a horizontal line represents a fixed cost, whereas a line that goes through the point of origin indicates a completely variable cost. Sometimes, in constructing a chart, the points show no tendency to arrange themselves along a line. If this situation does exist, then either the control of costs has been absent or a poor choice has been made as to the factor of variability. Use of another factor should be tested to ascertain the cause. Incidentially, the chart may be used as a tool in illustrating the degree of success in controlling costs, the extent of accomplishment being measured by the closeness of actual expense to the line of budgeted expense.

The Least Squares Method. The previous graphic determination will be recognized by statisticians or those familiar with computer applications in this area as a rough approximation of the least squares method. A more accurate method of determining the regression line (the line of best fit) is by this statistical technique. It involves the use of two simultaneous equations:

$$\Sigma XY = a(\Sigma X) + b(\Sigma X^2)$$

and

$$\Sigma Y = Na + b(\Sigma X)$$

where
- N = Number of observations
- X = Units of volume
- Y = Total costs
- a = Total fixed costs
- b = Variable cost per unit
- Σ = Sum of

A book on statistical methods should be consulted for an understanding of this now commonly used procedure. Use of a computer, of course, permits accurate calculation rather quickly, using substantially larger samples.

Allowing for Extraordinary Costs

The preceding discussion of the methods of classifying costs into fixed, variable, and semivariable is related to the normally expected costs. Often, however, extraordinary or unanticipated expenditures of a manufacturing expense nature must be made. These may fall well outside the scope of the usual budget, even when the cumulative yearly condition is considered. In such instances, and if the expenditure is considered necessary and advisable, a special budget allowance may be made over and above the usual budget—something superimposed on the regular flexible budget structure.

It is to be emphasized that the important consideration is not necessarily *how* flexibility is introduced into the budget plan, but rather that it *is* made a part of planning, coordinating, and control techniques.

Procedure Applicable to Most Departments

In order to reveal clearly the principles involved, the examples in this chapter have been reduced to the simplest possible terms. Only a few cost items relating to production and sales have been considered. It should be emphasized, however, that the procedure must be extended throughout the full range of operations and to most departments and cost items involved. Many different measures of volume may be in use at the same time in different divisions or departments. Since volume does not necessarily run uniformly in different divisions, the maximum and minimum limits may differ in the various divisions. For example, the measures and volume limits for the purchasing department may be entirely different from and independent of those applicable to the maintenance or accounting departments.

STANDARD COSTS IN RELATION TO PLAN OR BUDGET

The reader may be familiar with the standard cost concept—that is, a predetermined cost or a determination of what a cost should be. A basic point to be clarified is the relationship of this standard cost to the operating plan or budget.

In line with the previous discussion, it is perhaps evident that the so-called standard cost must be segregated into its variable and fixed elements. The standard variable cost can be used to determine what the aggregate variable cost for the planned volume should be. In addition, if experience indicates that the standard variable cost cannot be attained, then the business plans must include a factor for this inefficiency.

The fixed element of the standard cost is, of course, recognized in arriving at the planned level of the total fixed expense.

A DEFINITION OF BUDGETING

In this chapter, we have discussed planning and control. However, we have also used the word "budget." Those involved with FISs must understand the various kinds of budgets that may be used in conjunction with the accumulation of the actual data for particular applications. Therefore, before discussing types of budgets, some definitions are necessary.

A budget is often thought of as a financial plan, but this alone is an inadequate definition. There are several names for a planning process that focuses on the near term (usually one or two years into the future): "annual profit plan," "short-term profit plan," "tactical plan," "operating plan," or "budget." Although "budgeting" is the commonly used term, some feel it has negative connotations of restraint. Of course, if certain expenditures must be limited, there are usually good management reasons for doing so—all directed to meeting a short-term profit objective.

The word "budget" and the term "budgeting" as used in this chapter mean the short-term or annual profit plan and its development, expressed largely in financial terms, consistent with the long-range or (strategic) plan together with the actions taken to meet the goals of the plan. It includes quantifying the operating plans and expectations. The process involves converting, usually month by month, the sales and revenue plans, the costs and expenses of doing business, the capital expenditures, and planned changes in financial position into an integrated financial model of the company. Finally, it involves taking the corrective actions necessary to bring substandard actual performance into line with the plan.

Thus, budgeting is composed of two phases: (1) the planning phase of determining what is to be done and when, where, and how it is to be done and (2) the control phase of bringing actual performance into line with the plan.

TYPES OF BUDGETS

For the purposes of this Manual, budgets for business enterprises may be classified into three principal types:

1 Project budgets
2 Fixed budgets (nonproject)
3 Flexible or variable budgets

Project Budgets

Under a project budgeting system, a particular sum, and perhaps the related man-hours, is approved to be spent toward the accomplishment of certain results. Actual expenditures, plus the estimated cost to complete the projects or programs, are periodically compared with the approved project budget to check cost performance.

Types of costs or expenses planned and controlled on a project basis include:

- Capital expenditures for plant and equipment
- Expenses for research and development projects
- Advertising and sales promotion expenses for particular programs
- Market research expenses for identified projects

These budgets are normally approved each year, based on the results to be obtained, the company's financial capability, and the expected profitability for the period, among other factors. They are fixed budgets; that is, they ordinarily do not change for the year, once they are approved. Such approval may or may not include a formal appropriation of funds by the board of directors.

A typical budget report for the planning and control of project budgets is shown in Figure 12-10 (see also Figure 14-27). Actual expenditures to date, both in man-hours and amounts, plus existing commitments and the estimated

FINANCIAL PLANNING AND CONTROL

THE MANUFACTURING COMPANY
STATUS REPORT—ADVERTISING AND SALES PROMOTION BUDGET
As at April 30, 19XX
(dollars in thousands)

Category	Project Budget	Actual to 4/30/XX Expenditures	Commitments	Total	Estimated Cost to Complete	Indicated Total Cost	Balance Available for Use or Transfer
Broadcast Media:							
Television							
National	$ 800	$270	$390	$ 660	$120	$ 780	$ 20
Local spots	200	40	60	100	100	200	—
Total	$1,000	$310	$450	$ 760	$220	$ 980	$ 20
Radio — Local	100	20	10	30	40	70	30
Total Broadcast	$1,100	$330	$460	$ 790	$260	$1,050	$ 50
Printed Media:							
Consumer magazines	140	70	20	90	40	130	10
Newspapers	90	20	10	30	20	50	40
Business publications	40	30	10	40	—	40	—
Total	$ 270	$120	$ 40	$ 160	$ 60	$ 220	$ 50
Direct mail	180	110	60	170	20	190	(10)
Catalogs	70	60	10	70	—	70	—
Displays and exhibits	80	—	70	70	30	100	(20)
Total Printed Media	$ 600	$290	$180	$ 470	$110	$ 580	$ 20
Advertising Administration	300	100	—	100	200	300	—
Grand Total	$2,000	$720	$640	$1,360	$570	$1,930	$ 70

FIG. 12-10 Actual and Budget Performance (Source: James D. Willson, *Budgeting and Profit Planning Manual* (Boston: Warren, Gorham & Lamont, 1983). Reprinted by permission.)

cost to complete each project are compared to the approved project budget. Figure 12-10 reflects treatment for an advertising and sales promotion budget. (Figure 14-27 shows the comparable application to research and development projects.)

Fixed Budgets

Under a fixed-budget concept, based on an expected sales volume and other expected conditions, budgets are set by time period (e.g., month or quarter) for each operation (e.g., each cost center, department, and division). This type of budget does not change during the annual budget period. Actual costs and expenses are measured against such a budget or plan, even though the actual volume level may change from that anticipated. This budgetary system is sometimes referred to as a planning budget, because it reflects the business plan for a stipulated span of time. All of its costs and expenses relate to the planned volume level.

There are types of operations or functions for which a fixed budget is practical. For example, it may be applied to functions that are not directly influenced by month-to-month changes in sales or production levels. Essentially, it relates to personnel who are engaged in the broad planning and management of the enterprise, where the output is subjective. Even these expenses, over a period of time, must bear a reasonable relationship to planned sales (i.e., income) volume. Because this type of budget often applies only at the top echelons of management and is largely related to "people" expenses (salaries, fringe benefits, travel, and communications expenses), it is sometimes referred to as an administrative type budget. Typical functions for which it may be practical to have an administrative fixed budget include:

- Chief executive officer
- Chief operating officer
- Chief sales executive
- Chief financial officer
- Chief research executive

A fixed budget for the general sales manager might be developed, based on the prior-year expense levels and expected increased sales activity, as shown in Figure 12-11. A monthly budget report comparing actual and budget expense might appear as shown in Figure 12-12.

Flexible or Variable Budgets

A flexible budget, sometimes called a variable budget, is one that permits revision of the level of planned, expected, or allowable expenses or costs (or prof-

THE SALES CORPORATION
ANNUAL BUDGET
GENERAL SALES MANAGER
(dollars in thousands)

	Prior Year			Plan Year				Increase (Decrease)
	Actual 10 mos.	Estimated 2 mos.	Total	1st Quarter	2nd Quarter	Second Half	Total	
Number of staff	7	7	7	7	8	8	8	1
Expenses								
Salaries — Exempt	$124.5	$25.5	$150.0	$ 40.5	$ 40.5	$ 81.0	$162.0	$12.0
Salaries — Other	25.0	7.0	32.0	8.5	11.8	23.6	43.9	11.9
Incentive pay	40.0	—	40.0	50.0	—	—	50.0	10.0
Fringe benefit costs	75.8	13.0	88.8	39.6	20.9	41.8	102.3	13.5
Travel	74.2	12.0	86.2	25.0	25.0	50.0	100.0	13.8
Occupancy	20.0	4.0	24.0	7.5	7.5	15.0	30.0	6.0
Entertainment	46.0	10.0	56.0	14.0	15.0	34.0	63.0	7.0
Communications	5.3	1.5	6.8	1.9	2.0	3.5	7.4	.6
Dues and subscriptions	4.0	1.0	5.0	1.0	2.0	2.0	5.0	—
Supplies	8.0	2.0	10.0	3.0	3.0	5.0	11.0	1.0
Depreciation	4.7	1.0	5.7	1.5	1.5	3.0	6.0	.3
Insurance	3.1	.6	3.7	1.0	1.0	2.0	4.0	.3
Miscellaneous	2.0	.2	2.2	.3	.5	1.6	2.4	.2
Total	$432.6	$77.8	$510.4	$193.8	$130.7	$262.5	$587.0	$76.6
Percentage net sales			1.4					1.2

FIG. 12-11 Distribution Cost Budget (Source: James D. Willson, *Budgeting and Profit Planning Manual* (Boston: Warren, Gorham & Lamont, 1983). Reprinted by permission.)

THE SALES CORPORATION
BUDGET REPORT
GENERAL SALES MANAGER
(dollars in thousands)

Month: March 19XX

	Current Month		Year-to-Date	
	Actual	(Over) Under Budget	Actual	(Over) Under Budget
Number of staff	7	—	7	—
Expenses				
Salaries — Exempt	$13.5	—	$ 40.5	$ —
Salaries — Other	2.8	—	8.5	—
Incentive pay	—	—	47.0	3.0
Fringe benefit costs	6.5	—	38.4	1.2(a)
Travel	8.0	.6	25.7	(.7)
Occupancy	2.5	—	7.5	—
Entertainment	4.4	.2	13.8	.2
Communications	.6	—	1.8	.1
Dues and subscriptions	—	—	1.0	—
Supplies	.9	.1	2.8	.2
Depreciation	.5	—	1.5	—
Insurance	.3	—	1.0	—
Miscellaneous	.1	—	.3	—
Total	$40.1	$.9	$189.8	$4.0
Percentage net sales	1.1		1.0	

(a) Fringe benefit costs under budget relate solely to incentive pay.

FIG. 12-12 Budget Report (Source: James D. Willson, *Budgeting and Profit Planning Manual* (Boston: Warren, Gorham & Lamont, 1983). Reprinted by permission.)

its), with changes in the sales, production volume, or other activity measure. It refines the fixed or static budget by adjusting for variation in the output rate.

A flexible-budget approach is inherently more valuable for both planning and control purposes than is a fixed budget. If the behavior of costs is known for any given activity level, the budget or plan can be readily determined. Thus, for a particular department, the expense budget may be the sum of the individual types of expenses, as follows:

- The proper level of fixed expenses for the planning horizon (perhaps a year) by month; plus
- The sum of prudent variable costs or expenses, by type of expense, for the planning period, by month. This is determined by multiplying

FINANCIAL PLANNING AND CONTROL

the planned activity level by the variable expense rate per factor of variability. Thus, if the proper variable rate for indirect wages is $0.50 per departmental productive hour, and the planned monthly level for January is 10,000 hours, then the allowable variable budget for that expense for the month is $5,000 ($0.50 × 10,000 hours). It is a convenient way to determine what the budget should be for the planned activity level.

By the same token, assume that actual departmental hours are only 9,000 for the month. Then, the supervisor is generally responsible for keeping the indirect wage expense at $4,500 (9,000 × $0.50).

Where flexible budgets are applicable, the supervisor should be provided with his planning budget (with which he has previously concurred) and the basis of its determination.

Figure 12-13 provides an example of a flexible budget. It shows the annual budget for a department by expense account, segregated into its fixed and variable components, and the variable rate per unit of variability.

This type of information, incorporated into the FIS, permits a rapid determination of an expense budget by type of expense for any reasonable level of activity. It also serves as a quick means of comparing actual expenses with expenses as they should have been at the level experienced for the time period under review. The application of this approach to the monthly budget report for a food terminal is shown in Figure 12-14.

The concept of identifying the fixed costs and expenses in the aggregate and the unit variable costs or expenses adds tremendous flexibility to the planning and control processes. It can be applied to departments, functions, divisions, product lines, and the company as a whole, depending on the segment being reviewed.

In any particular company, the FIS may have to accommodate all three types of budgets—project, fixed administrative, and variable. One type may represent the best planning and control tool for one category of expense, but not another. As an example, Figure 12-15 illustrates how the marketing activities of a West Coast company are directed by the three types of budgets.

APPLICABILITY OF PLANNING AND CONTROL TO THE BALANCE SHEET

This chapter's discussion centers largely on the planning and control of costs and expenses. It applies also to income-producing factors, such as product sales and other revenues. But planning and control should not be restricted to operations. They apply to every item in the statement of financial condition. Planning should extend to every significant asset: cash, accounts receivable, inven-

(continued on page 12-36)

THE MIDDLE MANUFACTURING COMPANY
ANNUAL BUDGET—FLEXIBLE TYPE
DEPARTMENT 12
Activity Level—160,000 Hours

Expense	Annual Budget			Fixed Amount Per Month	Variable Rate Per Hour[a]
	Total	Fixed	Variable		
Supervisory salaries	$ 48,000	$ 48,000	$ —	$ 4,000	$ —
Other salaries	72,000	60,000	12,000	5,000	.075
Indirect wages	160,000	80,000	80,000	6,667	.50
Fringe benefit costs	84,000	56,400	27,600	4,700	.1725
Power	120,000	60,000	60,000	5,000	.375
Supplies	12,000	2,400	9,600	200	.06
Repair and maintenance	80,000	20,000	60,000	1,666	.375
Depreciation	12,000	12,000	—	1,000	—
Other	12,000	—	12,000	—	.075
Total	$600,000	$338,800	$261,200	$28,233	$1.6325

(a) Variable amount ÷ 160,000 hours

FIG. 12-13 Example of Flexible Budget (Source: James D. Willson, *Budgeting and Profit Planning Manual* (Boston: Warren, Gorham & Lamont, 1983). Reprinted by permission.)

FINANCIAL PLANNING AND CONTROL

THE STANDARD FOOD DISTRIBUTING CORP.
SAN FRANCISCO TERMINAL
BUDGET REPORT

Month April, 19XX

Dept. _____
Dept. Head Roth
Units Handled 800,000

Perishables

	Budget				(Over) or	Year-to-Date		(Over) or Under Budget	
Description	Fixed	Variable	Total	Actual	Under Budget	Budget (Adj.)	Actual	Amount	Percent*
Salaries	$2,000	$ 800	$ 2,800	$ 2,770	$ 30	$ 11,500	$ 11,300	$ 200	—
Wages	1,000	24,000	25,000	24,800	200	102,000	105,300	(3,300)	(3.2%)
Fringe benefits	600	4,960	5,560	5,510	50	22,700	23,320	(620)	—
Subtotal	$3,600	$29,760	$33,360	$33,080	$280	$136,200	$139,920	($3,720)	(2.7%)
Supplies	$ 200	$ 800	$ 1,000	$ 1,240	($240)	$ 4,800	$ 4,680	$ 120	—
Gasoline and oil	340	1,600	1,940	1,860	80	7,360	7,810	(450)	(6.1%)
Repairs — Regular — Labor	120	800	920	950	(30)	3,480	3,220	260	7.5
Repairs — Regular — Material	120	800	920	900	20	3,480	3,100	380	10.9
Repairs — Major — Labor	—	—	—	—	—	12,300	12,000	300	2.4
Repairs — Major — Material	—	—	—	—	—	15,700	16,800	(1,100)	(7.0)
Heat, light, and power	420	200	620	600	20	2,280	2,090	190	8.3
Miscellaneous	60	20	80	80	—	320	310	10	3.1
Depreciation	900	—	900	900	—	3,600	3,600	—	—
Property taxes and insurance	250	—	250	250	—	1,000	1,000	—	—
Total	$6,010	$33,980	$39,990	$39,860	$130	$190,520	$194,530	($4,010)	(2.1%)
Percent					.003				

Comments:
* Only if significant (2 percent or more).
Issued by Budget Dept. 5/10/XX

FIG. 12-14 Illustrative Monthly Budget Report (Source: James D. Willson, *Budgeting and Profit Planning Manual* (Boston: Warren, Gorham & Lamont, 1983). Reprinted by permission.)

THE WEST COAST CORPORATION
MARKETING DIVISION BUDGET
For the Plan Year Ending 12/31/XX
(dollars in thousands)

Department	Type of Budget	Plan Year 19XX Quarter 1	2	3	4	Total	Prior Year	Increase (Decrease)
Direct selling								
East	Administrative	$ 5,310	$ 5,420	$ 5,440	$ 5,530	$ 21,700	$ 20,840	$ 860
Middle West	"	3,100	3,140	3,190	3,220	12,650	11,060	1,590
Far West	"	5,820	5,910	6,180	6,270	24,180	22,810	1,370
Canada	"	1,700	1,770	1,790	1,820	7,080	6,700	380
Total		$15,930	$16,240	$16,600	$16,840	$ 65,610	$ 61,410	$4,200
Advertising and sales promotion	Project	$ 8,820	$ 9,210	$ 9,400	$ 9,610	$ 37,040	$ 35,100	$1,940
Warehousing	Standard							
Camden, N.J.	(fixed	$ 1,600	$ 1,640	$ 1,730	$ 1,790	$ 6,760	$ 6,300	$ 460
Chicago, Ill.	and	1,120	1,100	1,210	1,240	4,670	4,400	270
Los Angeles, Cal.	variable)	2,630	2,720	2,540	2,560	10,450	10,300	150
Vancouver, B.C.		470	480	460	490	1,900	2,000	(100)
Total		$ 5,820	$ 5,940	$ 5,940	$ 6,080	$ 23,780	$ 23,000	$ 780
Administrative								
General and administrative	Administrative	2,100	2,100	2,100	2,210	8,510	8,300	210
Market research	Project	470	490	490	510	1,960	1,900	60
Customer relations	Administrative	100	100	100	110	410	410	—
Branch offices								
New York, N.Y.	Administrative	$ 340	$ 340	$ 350	$ 360	$ 1,390	$ 1,320	$ 70
Chicago, Ill.	"	220	230	230	230	910	880	30
Los Angeles, Cal.		440	440	450	460	1,790	1,700	90
Total		1,000	1,010	1,030	1,050	4,090	3,900	190
Total administrative		3,670	3,700	3,720	3,880	14,970	14,510	460
Grand Total — Division Budget		$34,240	$35,090	$35,660	$36,410	$141,400	$134,020	$7,380
Percentage of net sales						9.6%	9.4%	(.2%)

FIG. 12-15 Summary Marketing Division Budget (Source: James D. Willson, *Budgeting and Profit Planning Manual* (Boston: Warren, Gorham & Lamont, 1983). Reprinted by permission.)

THE JOHNSON COMPANY
STATEMENT OF ESTIMATED CASH RECEIPTS AND DISBURSEMENTS
For the Year Ending 12/31/XX
(dollars in thousands)

Item	January	February	March	1st Qtr. Total	December	4th Qtr. Total	Year Total
Cash at beginning of period	$ 2,300	$ 4,000	$ 700	$ 2,300	$ 6,100	$ 5,000	$ 2,300
Cash receipts:							
Regular							
Collections on account	$ 8,400	$ 7,200	$ 9,100	$24,700	$ 7,000	$21,300	$ 96,300
Cash sales	300	100	400	800	100	200	1,900
Dividends	1,400	700	1,400	3,500	800	2,700	12,100
Interest income	700	1,000	600	2,300	1,000	3,200	10,200
Subtotal	$10,800	$ 9,000	$11,500	$31,300	$ 8,900	$27,400	$120,500
Special							
Sale of fixed assets	3,100	—	—	3,100	—	3,500	6,600
Bank loans	—	—	4,000	4,000	—	2,000	6,000
Sale of subsidiary	2,200	—	—	2,200	—	—	2,200
Total cash receipts	16,100	9,000	15,500	40,600	8,900	29,400	135,300
Total cash available	$18,400	$13,000	$16,200	$42,900	$15,000	$37,900	$137,600
Cash disbursements:							
Accounts payable	$ 3,200	$ 4,000	$ 2,700	$ 9,900	$ 3,100	$ 8,700	$ 24,600
Payrolls — Net	8,600	7,100	8,800	24,500	7,400	22,900	82,400
Dividends on common stock	—	—	900	900	900	900	3,600
Interest expense	900	—	100	1,000	100	100	2,200
Capital expenditures	700	300	800	1,800	800	1,100	4,100
Retirement plan	900	800	900	2,600	800	2,200	13,000
Other	100	100	200	400	600	700	1,700
Payments on indebtedness	—	—	—	—	—	—	4,700
Total cash disbursements	14,400	12,300	14,400	41,100	13,700	36,600	136,300
Cash at end of period	$ 4,000	$ 700	$ 1,800	$ 1,800	$ 1,300	$ 1,300	$ 1,300

FIG. 12-16 Planned Cash Receipts and Disbursements (Source: James D. Willson, *Budgeting and Profit Planning Manual* (Boston: Warren, Gorham & Lamont, 1983). Reprinted by permission.)

THE ILLUSTRATIVE COMPANY
BUILD-UP OF THE ACCOUNTS RECEIVABLE BUDGET
For the Year Ending December 31, 19XX
(dollars in thousands)

Month	Beginning Balance	Sales	Cash Collections	Other Adjustments (Credit)	Ending Balance
January	$12,210	$ 9,400	$ 8,450	—	$13,160
February	13,160	9,900	10,240	—	12,820
March	12,820	10,300	12,560	—	10,560
April	10,560	10,700	11,600	$110	9,550
May	9,550	9,400	9,400	—	9,550
June	9,550	8,760	8,300	—	10,010
July	10,010	9,100	8,960	20	10,130
August	10,130	10,700	10,240	—	10,590
September	10,590	13,430	10,870	—	13,150
October	13,150	12,400	12,510	—	13,040
November	13,040	11,040	13,100	—	10,980
December	10,980	10,800	12,330	80	9,370
Total	$12,210	$125,930	$128,560	$210	$ 9,370

FIG. 12-17 Accounts Receivable Budget (Source: James D. Willson, *Budgeting and Profit Planning Manual* (Boston: Warren, Gorham & Lamont, 1983). Reprinted by permission.)

tories, current liabilities, long-term debt, and shareholders' equity. Just as these items should be planned, so also should they be held within acceptable limits.

The reader should consult some of the current literature covering the planning and control of assets, liabilities, and net worth. Certainly, budgetary concepts of these balance sheet items should be incorporated into the FIS. However, some sample or illustrative summary budget reports are included herein as samples of possible information outputs.

Planned Cash Receipts and Disbursements—Figure 12-16
Accounts Receivable Budget—Figure 12-17
Materials Inventory Budget—Figure 12-18
Comparative Working Capital Requirements—Figure 12-19

These types of plannning or budgeting documents are often supporting documents for an annual business plan, or possibly for the long-range financial plan (see Chapter 13).

FINANCIAL PLANNING AND CONTROL

THE GENUINE COMPANY
MATERIALS INVENTORY BUDGET
For the Plan Year 19XX
(dollars in thousands)

Month	Beginning Inventory	Purchases	Usage	Ending Inventory
January	$42,610	$ 21,840	$ 21,040	$43,410
February	43,410	20,460	21,500	42,370
March	42,370	22,400	21,910	42,860
Total	$42,610	$ 64,700	$ 64,450	$42,860
April	42,860	21,540	20,870	43,530
May	43,530	20,760	21,600	42,690
June	42,690	21,870	21,930	42,630
Total	$42,860	$ 64,170	$ 64,400	$42,630
July	42,630	22,870	22,450	43,050
August	43,050	24,500	22,670	44,880
September	44,880	22,040	23,100	43,820
Total	$42,630	$ 69,410	$ 68,220	$43,820
October	43,820	18,120	20,160	41,780
November	41,780	17,800	19,700	39,880
December	39,880	18,210	19,000	39,090
Total	$43,820	$ 54,130	$ 58,860	$39,090
Grand Total	$42,610	$252,410	$255,930	$39,090

FIG. 12-18 Materials Inventory Budget (Source: James D. Willson, *Budgeting and Profit Planning Manual* (Boston: Warren, Gorham & Lamont, 1983). Reprinted by permission.)

THE JEFFREY COMPANY
SCHEDULE OF WORKING CAPITAL REQUIREMENTS
AT SELECTED SALES LEVELS
(dollars in thousands)

Annual sales volume	$20,000	$40,000	$80,000
Current Assets			
Cash — Fixed	$ 500	$ 500	$ 500
Cash — Fluctuating	500	800	1,400
Total	$ 1,000	$ 1,300	$ 1,900
Receivables	$ 1,800	$ 3,900	$ 6,800
Inventories — Minimum	$ 1,000	$ 1,000	$ 1,000
Inventories — Fluctuating	600	1,400	2,700
Total	$ 1,600	$ 2,400	$ 3,700
Total current assets	$ 4,400	$ 7,600	$12,400
Current Liabilities			
Notes payable	—	$ 1,000	$ 2,000
Accounts payable	$ 1,400	1,800	2,600
Accrued items	900	1,200	1,700
Accrued income taxes	700	900	1,400
Total current liabilities	$ 2,000	$ 4,900	$ 7,700
Total Working Capital Requirements	$ 2,400	$ 2,700	$ 4,700
Current ratio	2.2 : 1	1.55 : 1	1.61 : 1

FIG. 12-19 Comparative Working Capital Requirements (Source: James D. Willson, *Budgeting and Profit Planning Manual* (Boston: Warren, Gorham & Lamont, 1983). Reprinted by permission.)

REFERENCES

Sweeny, H.W. Allen, and Robert Rachlin. *Handbook of Budgeting.* New York: John Wiley & Sons, 1981.

Wilkinson, Joseph W. *Accounting and Information Systems.* New York: John Wiley & Sons, 1982.

Willson, James D. *Budgeting and Profit Planning Manual.* Boston: Warren, Gorham & Lamont, Inc., 1983.

CHAPTER **13**

Presentations of Financial Information Systems for Use by Financial Management

James D. Willson

Introduction 3	Activity Summary by Business Group . . . 25
Functional Outline–CFO 3	Net Income by Business Group 25
	Annual Changes in Net Income 25
Broad Scope of Financial Data 6	Comparative Statement of Planned
Financial Reporting Systems–Selected	Income and Expense 25
Report Structure 6	Statement of Planned Sources and Uses of
	Cash 28
The Long-Range Financial Plan 8	Statement of Consolidated Financial
Basic Financial Assumptions 9	Position 28
Financial Highlights 10	Return on Average Assets by Profit
Consolidated Net Sales 10	Center 28
Net Sales 10	Trend in Operating Results 30
Consolidated Sales Backlog by Strategic	Return on Assets–Trend and
Business Unit 14	Composition 30
Consolidated Net Income 14	Comparative Return on Shareholders'
Net Income by Strategic Business Unit . . 14	Equity 30
Earnings per Share 17	Borrowing Capacity 33
Cash Sources and Uses 17	Debt to Equity Ratios 33
Consolidated Financial Position 18	Other Data 33
Percentage Return on Assets 18	
Percentage Return on Shareholder's	**Company/Segment Overall Performance** 35
Equity 18	Some Manufacturing Companies 35
Ratio of Long-Term Debt to Net Worth 18	A Services Company 54
Current Ratio 18	
	Daily Conditions Report 59
The Annual Business Plan 23	**Other Financial Management Reports** . . . 59
Annual Business Plan Highlights 24	
Sales by Business Group 24	**Special Analyses** 62

The author acknowledges the assistance of William G. Dudley, partner, Ernst & Whinney, in securing some of the illustrative material from clients, with permission to use it in this Manual.

13-1

Fig. 13-1 Functional Outline for CFO	4
Fig. 13-2 Financial Reporting Systems—Selected Report Structure	7
Fig. 13-3 Basic Financial Assumptions	10
Fig. 13-4 Financial Highlights	11
Fig. 13-5 Consolidated Net Sales	12
Fig. 13-6 Net Sales by Strategic Business Unit	12
Fig. 13-7 Net Sales vs. U.S. Government Sales	13
Fig. 13-8 Net Sales—Percentage Nongovernment	13
Fig. 13-9 Consolidated Sales Backlog by Strategic Business Unit	14
Fig. 13-10 Consolidated Net Income	15
Fig. 13-11 Net Income by Strategic Business Unit	15
Fig. 13-12 Earnings per Share	16
Fig. 13-13 Earnings per Share—Various Scenarios	16
Fig. 13-14 Cash Sources and Uses	17
Fig. 13-15 Consolidated Financial Position (Assets)	19
Fig. 13-16 Consolidated Financial Position (Liabilities and Net Worth)	20
Fig. 13-17 Percentage Return on Average Assets	21
Fig. 13-18 Percentage Return on Average Shareholders' Equity	21
Fig. 13-19 Ratio of Long-Term Debt to Net Worth	22
Fig. 13-20 Current Ratio	22
Fig. 13-21 Annual Business Plan Highlights	24
Fig. 13-22 Sales by Business Group	25
Fig. 13-23 Activity Summary by Business Group	26
Fig. 13-24 Net Income by Business Group	26
Fig. 13-25 Annual Changes in Net Income	27
Fig. 13-26 Comparative Statement of Planned Income and Expense	27
Fig. 13-27 Statement of Planned Sources and Uses of Cash	28
Fig. 13-28 Statement of Consolidated Financial Position	29
Fig. 13-29 Return on Average Assets by Profit Center	30
Fig. 13-30 Trends in Operating Results	31
Fig. 13-31 Return on Assets: Trends and Composition	32
Fig. 13-32 Comparative Return on Shareholders' Equity	34
Fig. 13-33 Borrowing Capacity	34
Fig. 13-34 Debt-to-Equity Ratios	35
Fig. 13-35 Summary Financial Report for Management	36
Fig. 13-36 Summary Performance by Profit Center	37
Fig. 13-37 Comparative Statement of Income and Expense	38
Fig. 13-38 Summary of Operations	40
Fig. 13-39 Summary of Acquisitions (New Orders) by Organization	41
Fig. 13-40 Comparative New Orders Received	42
Fig. 13-41 Contract Acquisitions—Explanation of Variances	43
Fig. 13-42 Comparative Consolidated Sales	44
Fig. 13-43 Consolidated Net Sales by Organization	45
Fig. 13-44 Consolidated Net Sales—Explanation of Variances	46
Fig. 13-45 Consolidated Order Backlog	47
Fig. 13-46 Consolidated Order Backlog by Organization	48
Fig. 13-47 Comparative Consolidated Operating Margin	49
Fig. 13-48 Operating Margin by Organization	50

PRESENTATIONS FOR FINANCIAL MANAGEMENT 13-3

Fig. 13-49 Consolidated Operating Margin—Explanation of Variances 51
Fig. 13-50 Comparative Consolidated Net Income 52
Fig. 13-51 Comparative Consolidated Net Income and Expense 53
Fig. 13-52 Comparative Condensed Balance Sheet 55
Fig. 13-53 Comparative Income Statement 56
Fig. 13-54 Comparative Statement of Changes in Financial Position 57
Fig. 13-55 CFO's Commentary on Period Earnings 58
Fig. 13-56 Daily Conditions Report for Top Management 60
Fig. 13-57 Weekly Cash Activity 61
Fig. 13-58 Summary of Short-Term Investments 62

INTRODUCTION

One of the objectives of a good FIS—and of an MIS—is to support a firm's operations and therefore contribute to sound decision making. In most companies, the chief financial officer (CFO), typically reporting to the chief executive officer (CEO), is responsible for the financial management program, including the related reporting and analysis. (See Chapter 1 for some of the principal duties of the CFO.) Figure 13-1[1] depicts a detailed functional outline of the CFO of an advanced technology company.

Functional Outline—CFO

Two observations may be made regarding the functional outline of the senior vice-president, finance, as shown in Figure 13-1.

1. Most of the specific functions depend for execution on the availability of a significant database consisting largely of internal data, but also of some external information.

2. The data requirements may be segregated into two types:
   - Those needed by the CFO to perform the basic primary functions of analyzing the financial information, making recommendations where appropriate, and taking action to keep the company in sound financial health, thereby promoting the continued growth and stability of the concern; and
   - Those required for the important service function, as mentioned in Item 12 of the functional outline, of "determining that all members of top management are provided with operating and financial data as required and on a timely basis to enable them to control their individual areas of responsibility and meet established budgets and goals."

---

[1] James D. Willson and Steven J. Root, *Internal Auditing Manual* (Boston: Warren, Gorham & Lamont, 1983), pp. 22-14, 22-15.

SENIOR VICE-PRESIDENT, FINANCE

Summary

The senior vice-president, finance, as the principal financial officer of the corporation, is responsible to the chairman and chief executive officer for creating and maintaining an effective financial management program. Financial management activities include accounting, budgeting, financial planning, reporting and analysis, internal auditing, insurance, taxes, property administration, financing, cash management, renegotiation, financial aspects of employee group insurance and retirement and savings plans, and such other related financial matters as may be necessary to provide for the continued growth and stability of the company.

Specific Responsibilities

1. Analyzes the financial and economic aspects of all company business activities as they relate to current, near-term, and long-term financial requirements.

2. Directs regular analyses of the current financial position of the corporation to identify any significant deviations from sound financial planning or the sound allocation of capital funds; develops and recommends corrective action where necessary.

3. Analyzes the financial and economic impact of proposals for the acquisition of other companies and/or the sale or lease of major properties and makes recommendations in relation thereto.

4. As specified by the executive office, takes the actions necessary to ensure fulfillment of company objectives with respect to acquisitions, joint ventures, licenses, and divestitures.

5. Formulates or reviews and approves the principal financial policies of the corporation.

6. Develops and recommends short- and long-term cash, financing, investment, pension plan, and dividend policies and plans for approval by the board of directors.

7. Represents the company in establishing and maintaining sound relationships with banks, investment bankers, and other financial institutions and groups.

8. Maintains relations with existing and potential professional financial community investors on all financial matters.

9. Provides for appropriate liaison with regulating bodies at local, state, and national levels.

10. Directs the preparation or authorizes the release of all financial data and reports developed for the board of directors, shareholders, or lending institutions.

11. Develops and conducts an internal audit program to assist all members of management in the effective discharge of their responsibilities by furnishing them with objective analyses, appraisals, recommendations, and pertinent comments concerning the activities reviewed.

12. Determines that all members of top management are provided with operating and financial data as required and on a timely basis to enable them to control their individual areas of responsibility and meet established budgets and goals.

FIG. 13-1 Functional Outline for CFO

> **13** Furnishes policy direction to members of division and subsidiary management with regard to overall financial matters and advises and assists them in the fulfillment of their functions.
>
> **14** Directs the administration of the financial aspects of the company's insurance, employee group insurance, retirement, and savings plans.
>
> **15** Reviews for concurrence the organizational structure of division and subsidiary financial groups, including proposed changes thereto, and the selection, transfer, or termination of key employees.
>
> **16** Reviews and evaluates the effectiveness of division and subsidiary financial activities. Makes recommendations to the general managers, subsidiary presidents, or the executive office, as appropriate.
>
> **17** Consults with and advises the executive office with regard to corporate long-range, worldwide, financial objectives.
>
> **18** Keeps the executive office and the board of directors informed regarding operating results and the financial position of the corporation.

FIG. 13-1 (cont'd)

The discussion in this chapter concerns reports the CFO needs to keep the board of directors, and top management and other related groups with a need to know, informed about the financial status of the company, as well as the information needed to maintain the company in sound financial health. (Chapter 14 deals with information provided as a service to other executives to assist them in carrying out their duties and responsibilities.) Obviously, for a subject as extensive as this, not all applications can be illustrated.

When an enterprise is small, planning and control are usually exercised by the owner or manager, based on personal observation and experience. Most of the time, he knows which products are selling well, which items are the most profitable, whether inventories are too high, if the receivables are being collected on a timely basis, and which workers are the best performers. As the business grows, however, that personal contact is lost to some degree; thus, financial reports become more important as a basis of planning and control.

As reports replace other forms of communication, attempts are made to minimize management deficiencies. However, excessive reliance on written reports may discourage initiative and cause people to avoid responsibility and risk taking. To be sure, medium- to large-sized companies require control systems. Those who design and use them must learn how to combine good financial reporting, which motivates the executive and employee, with the right amount of personal contact. Initiative must be encouraged; the personal equation cannot be ignored.[2]

---

[2] For a commentary on reporting, see John F. Lawrence, "It's What You Do, Not How You Report It," *Los Angeles Times* (Nov. 25, 1984), Part V, p. 1.

BROAD SCOPE OF FINANCIAL DATA

Financial Reporting Systems—Selected Report Structure

Most companies have a financial reporting system that, in varying degrees, summarizes, analyzes, and presents financial as well as some operating data (often in several different cuts or configurations) in order to meet the needs of the customer—in this case, the myriad of managers at different levels of authority. No tabulation of reports as made here can be complete for any one firm, because the reporting system must be adapted to the specific needs of an enterprise; thus, changes are required according to the particular circumstances. However, some indication of the types of data typically provided for medium- to large-sized manufacturing or service firms, by board management level, are depicted in Figure 13-2.

A great deal of the material in this chapter is devoted largely to illustrating some of the reporting formats and content that have been found useful for internal management purposes. The FIS should produce the needed data on a timely and economical basis. The data may be prepared by computer, manually, or by a combination of the two.

It is important to reiterate that the FIS should provide a broad range of data for individuals in and outside the management chain. The CFO is responsible for communicating effectively with a significant number of people who have an interest in the firm, such as:

- *Management* — internal management reports
  - Board of directors
  - Top-level management
  - Middle-level management
  - Segment management
  - Department managers
  - Lower-echelon management
- *Shareholders* — annual and quarterly financial statements and related commentary
- *Financial analysts and prospective shareholders* — financial status, trends, and relationships
- *Creditors* — including present and prospective financial status and operating results for:
  - Commercial bankers (required financial reports, financial plans)
  - Long-term lenders (present and prospective financial status and operating results)
- *Credit agencies (e.g., Dun & Bradstreet)* — financial status and historical operating results

SELECTED REPORT STRUCTURE

Board of Directors

1 Long-range plan (financial aspects)

2 Annual business plan—in financial terms

3 Monthly comparison of actual and planned performance, and perhaps update for remainder of year, including consolidated and segment data, as follows:
- Statement of income and expense
- Statement of financial position
- Statement of sources and uses of cash
- Capital commitments and expenditures
- Supporting analyses, as appropriate

4 Selected financial analyses of problem areas or fields of special interest—for example:
- R&D expenditures
- Debt composition
- Refinancing or financing plans
- Operating margin trends
- Acquisition analyses
- Sales trends
- Impact of particular product lines or programs

Top-Management and Division Managers

1 Comparable data as presented to the board of directors, but in somewhat more detail and as related to the company as a whole or as applicable to each major organizational segment

2 Flash reports on the company as a whole or organization segments as to operating results, including:
- New orders
- Net sales (partially estimated)
- Net income (partially estimated)

3 Daily report on financial position, where appropriate

4 Special analyses showing probable results of alternative scenarios

5 Comparative reports showing actual and budget or plan by function or department

Functional Managers

1 Comparative annual summary of plans—long-range and annual business plan

2 Comparison of actual and planned, or budgeted, performance by month or selected time period, showing summarized functional performance and that of each subordinate management segment as applicable, covering as may be appropriate:
- Net sales
- Manufacturing output
- Costs and expenses

(continued)

FIG. 13-2 Financial Reporting Systems

> - Cash collections
> - Asset status (accounts receivable)
> - Current liability status
>
> 3 Daily operating reports, as needed
> 4 Special analyses to highlight trouble spots
>
> **Lower Management**
>
> 1 Operating reports as needed—hourly, daily, weekly, monthly—showing actual and planned performance
>   These control reports could relate to:
> - Sales
> - Output (efficiency)
> - Direct costs (labor and/or material)
> - Expenses
> - Product/operating margin
> - Variance analysis

FIG. 13-2 (cont'd)

- *Government agencies (federal, state, and local)* — mandatory reports, including reports for:
  - Internal Revenue Service
  - Securities and Exchange Commission
  - Department of Labor
- *Employees*
  - Reports on the company's financial status and on their stake in it
  - Reports to participants in such benefits as savings plans, retirement plans, and stock options

THE LONG-RANGE FINANCIAL PLAN

Rapid change, increasing competition, and growing internationalism are causing medium- to large-sized businesses to give more consideration to formal long-range and strategic planning. To be sure, product planning and marketing are the primary focal points. Nevertheless, long-range financial planning is important for making sure that the firm has the necessary financial resources when needed, the financial wherewithal with which to grow, and the ability to live within its financial means.

The CFO must translate the plan into financial terms, analyze it, consider alternative scenarios, and summarize it in a manner that indicates its critical elements. The final plan must be communicated to the board of directors and top management so that each group understands its underlying assumptions

PRESENTATIONS FOR FINANCIAL MANAGEMENT 13-9

and becomes aware of the company's more important strengths, weaknesses, risks, and potential.

The objectives of a good financial report or presentation on the long-range outlook to the upper echelons of management include the following:

- To make known, in financial terms, the results of the planning process for the company and its segments. For example:
  - Income and expense
  - Financial position
  - Sources and uses of cash
  - Capital expenditures
  - Commitments
- To provide reasonable assurance that funds will be available, as needed, on a satisfactory basis.
- To provide evidence that the company will remain in an acceptable financial condition for meeting the needs for stability and growth.
- To demonstrate that the plan will enable the corporation to attain selected financial goals (e.g., return on shareholders' equity, return on assets, percentage gross margin on sales) and that each operating segment probably will reach its goals.
- To test financial results and conditions to make sure that the terms and conditions of loan agreements can be met.

One way to communicate these points is through a graphics or slide presentation, accompanied by appropriate oral commentary. In addition, of course, the information may be conveyed by a written report with appropriate interpretive remarks. Some illustrative charts for a manufacturing company's presentation to its board of directors are shown in Figures 13-3 through 13-20. The method of presenting financial data must be modified to fit the recipient. In the illustrative case shown in the figures, the objective is to communicate the significant facts or opinions so that the board of directors may be fully informed. To achieve that purpose, the charts are largely graphic and intentionally simple in order to convey only a limited number of ideas. The subjects covered are those the CEO and the CFO consider crucial or important to the board's understanding, and include some subjects in which particular members have expressed special interest. It should be kept in mind that long-range plans, quite in contrast to short-term plans, are very general and contain few details. Concern is focused on the direction the company is going vis-à-vis its mission or purpose and whether it is likely to reach certain goals. Following are some brief comments about each figure.

Basic Financial Assumptions

Basic assumptions (see Figure 13-3), or underlying assumed conditions, are crucial to the reasonableness of the plan. The board of directors and top man-

---

BASIC FINANCIAL ASSUMPTIONS
198X–199Y

- Increase in inflation rates from 6 percent in 198X to 9 percent in 199Y
- Increase in long-term interest rates for new funds from 10¾ percent to 14 percent
- Increase in prime interest rates for new funds from 11 percent to 14 percent
- Capital expenditures 28 percent of net income
- R&D expenditures 2 percent of net sales
- Minor recession in 198Y–198Z
- No major corporate acquisitions or mergers
- Increase in defense budget to 8 percent above inflation
- Reduction of federal income taxes by 15 percent
- Expiration of foreign tax credits

FIG. 13-3 Basic Financial Assumptions (Source: James D. Willson, *Budgeting and Profit Planning Manual,* 1984 Supplement (Boston: Warren, Gorham & Lamont, 1984), pp. 1B-9–1B-27. Reprinted by permission.)

agement should be aware of them and, in some instances, should have participated in their development, each person in his field of expertise.

Financial Highlights

The intent of the financial highlights (see Figure 13-4) is to convey to the board the trend of some significant financial measures that are important factors in the industry, such as new orders received, order backlog, net sales, net income, return on assets, and return on shareholders' equity.

Consolidated Net Sales

The graph shown in Figure 13-5 very simply indicates the trend in net sales. Oral commentary may be made on the annual percentage increase and how it is expected to compare with the industry or selected competitors.

Net Sales

Three aspects of net sales (see Figures 13-6 through 13-8) are considered important vis-à-vis corporate goals:

1. The growth (or lack of growth) of each strategic business unit
2. The amount of sales to the U.S. government (more subject to cancellation, or at a lesser margin, than other sales)
3. Percentage of nongovernment sales (degree of company dependence on U.S. government)

(continued on page 13-14)

198X–199Y LONG-RANGE PLAN
(dollars in millions, except per share)

	Past Year	Present Year	198X	198Y	Plan 198Z	199X	199Y
New orders	$6,600	$4,002	$3,200	$4,200	$4,000	$4,600	$5,600
Sales backlog	6,408	7,130	6,760	7,130	6,830	6,790	7,340
Net sales	2,500	3,280	3,570	3,830	4,300	4,640	5,050
Net income							
Amount	78	165	190	210	240	270	300
Percentage of sales	3.1%	5.0%	5.0%	5.0%	6.0%	6.0%	5.1%
Capital expenditures	165	352	285	151	180	180	200
Earnings per share	$5.21	$11.00	$12.69	$13.76	$16.06	$17.70	$19.40
Book value per share	$37.62	$46.92	$57.94	$69.75	$83.89	$99.48	$116.92
Turnover on average assets	1.8	1.9	1.8	1.7	1.7	1.6	1.6
Return on average assets	5.6%	9.7%	9.5%	9.4%	9.7%	9.3%	9.5%
Return on average equity	14.6%	26.0%	24.2%	21.5%	20.9%	19.3%	17.9%

FIG. 13-4 Financial Highlights (Source: James D. Willson, *Budgeting and Profit Planning Manual, 1984 Supplement* (Boston: Warren, Gorham & Lamont, 1984), pp. 1B-9–1B-27. Reprinted by permission.)

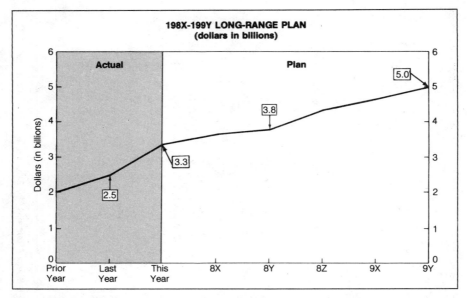

FIG. 13-5 Consolidated Net Sales (Source: James D. Willson, *Budgeting and Profit Planning Manual,* 1984 Supplement (Boston: Warren, Gorham & Lamont, 1984), pp. 1B-9–1B-27. Reprinted by permission.)

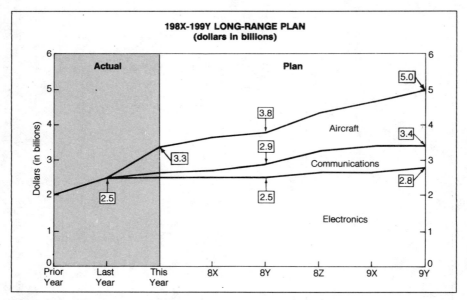

FIG. 13-6 Net Sales by Strategic Business Unit (Source: James D. Willson, *Budgeting and Profit Planning Manual,* 1984 Supplement (Boston: Warren, Gorham & Lamont, 1984), pp. 1B-9–1B-27. Reprinted by permission.)

PRESENTATIONS FOR FINANCIAL MANAGEMENT 13-13

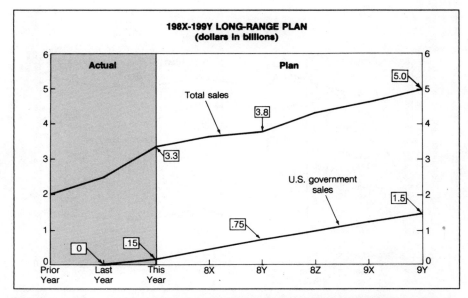

FIG. 13-7 Net Sales vs. U.S. Government Sales (Source: James D. Willson, *Budgeting and Profit Planning Manual,* 1984 Supplement (Boston: Warren, Gorham & Lamont, 1984), pp. 1B-9–1B-27. Reprinted by permission.)

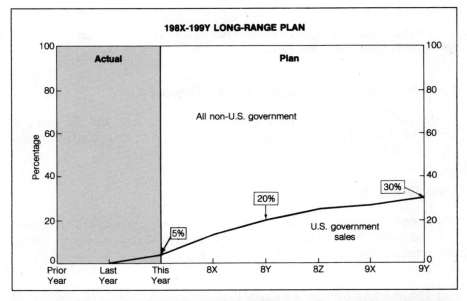

FIG. 13-8 Net Sales—Percentage Nongovernment (Source: James D. Willson, *Budgeting and Profit Planning Manual,* 1984 Supplement (Boston: Warren, Gorham & Lamont, 1984), pp. 1B-9–1B-27. Reprinted by permission.)

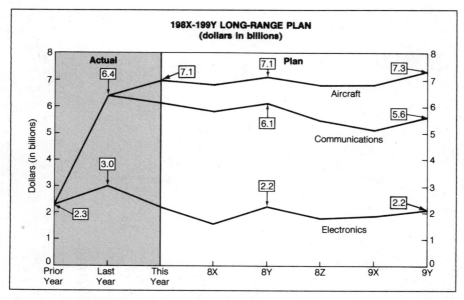

FIG. 13-9 Consolidated Sales Backlog by Strategic Business Unit (Source: James D. Willson, *Budgeting and Profit Planning Manual*, 1984 Supplement (Boston: Warren, Gorham & Lamont, 1984), pp. 1B-9–1B-27. Reprinted by permission.)

Oral commentary expands on the reasons for the condition and actions to be taken to reach the levels indicated.

Consolidated Sales Backlog by Strategic Business Unit

In this particular industry, the amount of unfilled orders, and the trend, is important. Limited commentary on the trend by strategic unit should be made. (See Figure 13-9.)

Consolidated Net Income

The trend of net income in the absolute and as a percentage of sales is important and should be commented on as it relates both to corporate goals and to competitive performance. (See Figure 13-10.)

Net Income by Strategic Business Unit

The sources of net income should be made known (see Figure 13-11), together with comments on strategy and resource allocation resulting therefrom.

PRESENTATIONS FOR FINANCIAL MANAGEMENT

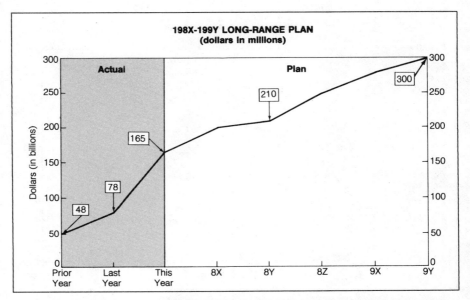

FIG. 13-10 Consolidated Net Income (Source: James D. Willson, *Budgeting and Profit Planning Manual*, 1984 Supplement (Boston: Warren, Gorham & Lamont, 1984), pp. 1B-9–1B-27. Reprinted by permission.)

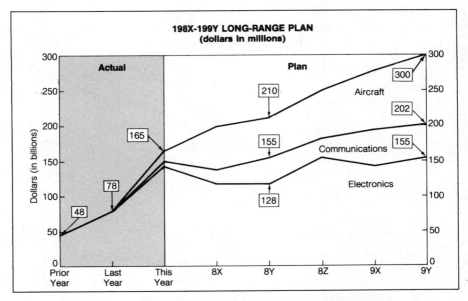

FIG. 13-11 Net Income by Strategic Business Unit (Source: James D. Willson, *Budgeting and Profit Planning Manual*, 1984 Supplement (Boston: Warren, Gorham & Lamont, 1984), pp. 1B-9–1B-27. Reprinted by permission.)

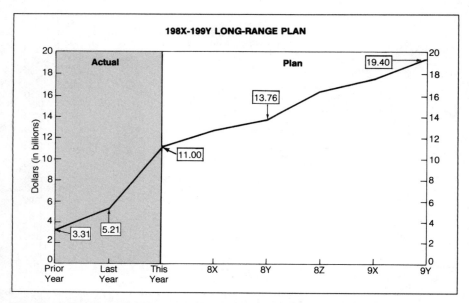

FIG. 13-12 Earnings per Share (Source: James D. Willson, *Budgeting and Profit Planning Manual*, 1984 Supplement (Boston: Warren, Gorham & Lamont, 1984), pp. 1B-9–1B-27. Reprinted by permission.)

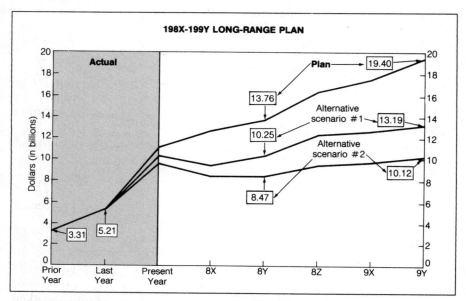

FIG. 13-13 Earnings per Share—Various Scenarios (Source: James D. Willson, *Budgeting and Profit Planning Manual*, 1984 Supplement (Boston: Warren, Gorham & Lamont, 1984), pp. 1B-9–1B-27. Reprinted by permission.)

198X-199Y LONG-RANGE PLAN
(dollars in millions)

	Present Year	198X	198Y	198Z	199X	199Y
Sources of Cash						
Net Income	165	190	210	240	270	300
Depreciation and Amortization	87	115	124	120	117	117
Deferred Taxes, etc.	22	50	33	38	28	12
Subtotal	274	355	367	398	415	429
New Financing	156	—	—	—	—	—
Current Liabilities	66	49	117	212	(34)	(18)
Total Sources	496	404	484	610	381	411
Uses of Cash						
Current Assets	98	53	73	285	91	62
Capital Expenditures	352	285	151	180	180	200
Dividends	33	40	45	55	60	75
Reduction in Long-Term Obligations	13	6	107	62	61	19
Total Uses	496	384	376	582	392	356
Increase (Decrease) in Cash and Cash Items	—	20	108	28	(11)	55
Add: Beginning Cash	55	55	75	183	211	200
Cash at End of Period	55	75	183	211	200	255

FIG. 13-14 Cash Sources and Uses (Source: James D. Willson, *Budgeting and Profit Planning Manual*, 1984 Supplement (Boston: Warren, Gorham & Lamont, 1984), pp. 1B-9–1B-27. Reprinted by permission.)

Earnings per Share

The board of directors and top management usually are interested in the trend of earnings per share, the rate of growth, and reasons therefor. Appropriate comment should be made on these factors and how they relate to the return on equity. (See Figures 13-12 and 13-13.)

Where important changes in strategy have been considered by management, the board may be advised on the impact of other alternative scenarios and the basis upon which the planned strategy was selected. This goes to the heart of long-range planning. The effect of alternative strategies on cash flow, investments, return on shareholders' equity, and other measures may also be presented.

Cash Sources and Uses

Those concerned with guiding the enterprise should be informed about the major sources and uses of cash, especially if any new financing is contemplated. Figure 13-14 provides highly condensed data, with no detail regarding working capital. A tabular presentation was selected as most suitable, although graphs could have been used.

Consolidated Financial Position

It is usually helpful to advise management regarding the asset allocation and level of debt and to assure the group that the financial position is (or is not) satisfactory and will (or will not) continue as such. (See Figures 13-15 and 13-16.) A point of concern for this illustrative company is the very high level of indebtedness—which the company plans to reduce rapidly. Again, data are highly condensed.

Percentage Return on Assets

The rate of return on assets used is an important measure of the effectiveness of management's stewardship. The trend and relative rates for each strategic business unit are depicted in Figure 13-17.

Oral commentary may be needed to discuss the variance in rates and actions being taken to improve performance. Meaningful comparisons with selected competitors may be made. Supplementary data may be provided on turnover rates and net income ratios by segment (return on assets = turnover rate × net income percentage of sales).

Percentage Return on Shareholders' Equity

Return on shareholders' equity (see Figure 13-18) is one of the key measures of management performance. The trend of this relationship is a major determinant in the growth of earnings per share. Since, in the illustrative case, the trend is adverse and the corporate target is not being met, an explanation of what actions are being taken to correct the condition is warranted. Comparisons on this factor may be made with certain competitors on a historical basis.

Ratio of Long-Term Debt to Net Worth

Significant financial relationships should be commented on, and action planned to correct unsatisfactory conditions. In the illustrative company, a major concern is the high level of debt. The planned improvements are graphically shown (see Figure 13-19), together with the comparison to an acceptable ratio (.25:1). Significant deviations from the norm, or standard, should be brought to the board's attention, as well as the impact such an unsatisfactory condition may have on the firm.

Current Ratio

Another vulnerable point of concern in the illustrative company is the relative lack of current liquidity and the danger of being in default of the credit agreement terms. The graph shown in Figure 13-20 addresses the planned improvement.

(continued on page 13-23)

198X-199Y LONG-RANGE PLAN
(dollars in millions)

					Plan		
Assets	Past Year	Present Year	198X	198Y	198Z	199X	199Y
Current Assets							
Cash and Cash Items	55	55	75	183	211	200	255
Receivables	164	216	254	277	388	426	453
Inventories — Net	417	464	479	529	703	757	790
Prepaid Expenses	22	21	21	21	21	20	22
Total	658	756	829	1,010	1,323	1,403	1,520
Property, Plant, and Equipment	1,116	1,468	1,753	1,904	2,084	2,264	2,464
Less: Depreciation and Amortization	309	396	511	635	755	872	989
Net	807	1,072	1,242	1,269	1,329	1,392	1,475
Other Assets	62	61	41	40	39	38	37
Total Assets	1,527	1,889	2,112	2,319	2,691	2,833	3,032

FIG. 13-15 Consolidated Financial Position (Assets) (Source: James D. Willson, *Budgeting and Profit Planning Manual, 1984 Supplement* (Boston: Warren, Gorham & Lamont, 1984), pp. 1B-9–1B-27. Reprinted by permission.)

198X-199Y LONG-RANGE PLAN
(dollars in millions)

Liabilities and Equity	Past Year	Present Year	198X	198Y	Plan 198Z	199X	199Y
Current Liabilities							
Accounts Payable and Accruals	343	360	379	466	668	606	550
Income Taxes	91	140	170	200	210	240	270
Current Maturities Long-Term Obligations	4	4	4	4	4	2	10
Total	438	504	553	670	882	848	830
Long-Term Obligations							
Senior Debt — New	326	482	482	382	326	270	262
Senior Debt — Existing	108	104	100	96	92	90	80
Other Long-Term Obligations	45	36	34	31	29	26	25
Total	479	622	616	509	447	386	367
Deferred Income Taxes and Credits	22	43	72	104	140	167	177
Equity							
Paid-in Capital	117	117	118	118	119	119	120
Retained Earnings	471	603	753	918	1,103	1,313	1,538
Total	588	720	871	1,036	1,222	1,432	1,658
Total Liabilities and Equity	1,527	1,889	2,112	2,319	2,691	2,833	3,032

FIG. 13-16 Consolidated Financial Position (Liabilities and Net Worth) (Source: James D. Willson, *Budgeting and Profit Planning Manual, 1984 Supplement* (Boston: Warren, Gorham & Lamont, 1984), pp. 1B-9–1B-27. Reprinted by permission.)

PRESENTATIONS FOR FINANCIAL MANAGEMENT 13-21

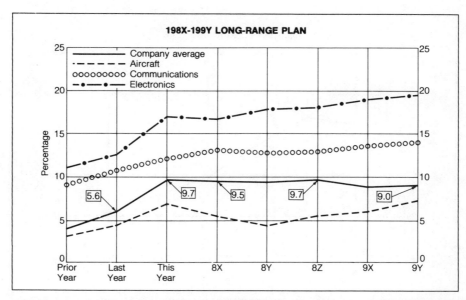

FIG. 13-17 Percentage Return on Average Assets (Source: James D. Willson, *Budgeting and Profit Planning Manual,* 1984 Supplement (Boston: Warren, Gorham & Lamont, 1984), pp. 1B-9–1B-27. Reprinted by permission.)

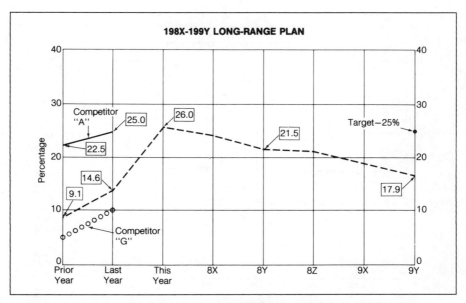

FIG. 13-18 Percentage Return on Average Shareholders' Equity (Source: James D. Willson, *Budgeting and Profit Planning Manual,* 1984 Supplement (Boston: Warren, Gorham & Lamont, 1984), pp. 1B-9–1B-27. Reprinted by permission.)

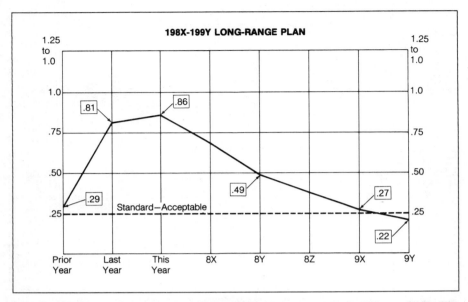

FIG. 13-19 Ratio of Long-Term Debt to Net Worth (Source: James D. Willson, *Budgeting and Profit Planning Manual,* 1984 Supplement (Boston: Warren, Gorham & Lamont, 1984), pp. 1B-9–1B-27. Reprinted by permission.)

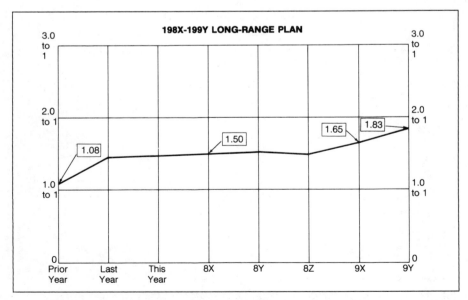

FIG. 13-20 Current Ratio (Source: James D. Willson, *Budgeting and Profit Planning Manual,* 1984 Supplement (Boston: Warren, Gorham & Lamont, 1984), pp. 1B-9–1B-27. Reprinted by permission.)

In summary, the FIS should provide, in simple understandable form, whatever key, long-term financial data are deemed necessary for the attention of management. The CFO should see that the board and top management comprehend how the condition, trends, and impact of the plan will be seen by the financially interested, such as creditors and investors.

THE ANNUAL BUSINESS PLAN

It is by guiding the preparation of the segments of the annual business plan and consolidating, analyzing, and presenting the plan to management that the CFO is especially helpful to the company. One of his tasks is to appraise the plan and ferret out unsatisfactory trends or conditions and, if appropriate, assist in their planned correction. For example, if a bank loan agreement required a minimum current ratio of 1.5:1 at all times, it would be unfortunate if the likelihood of not meeting such a condition did not surface in the month-by-month analysis of the plan while the opportunity to change the plan or loan terms in order to avoid default still existed.

The annual plan may be appraised and evaluated against any number of measures,[3] including:

- The prior year or years
- Management objectives and goals
- Selected competitors' results
- Industry standards

Consequently, the FIS should provide for accumulating the data that are significant in measuring each organizational segment of the enterprise, as well as the firm taken as a whole, and the standards used for comparison (which may continue to change).

In presenting the plan to management, the relevant data should be summarized in a manner that invites reception and covers the plan's significant aspects in a simple way. Although content depends on the important business factors (those that make for success), as well as management style, organizational structure, management interests, existing conditions, and a host of other considerations, a rather complete presentation at the top-management level may include the following elements, perhaps in total and by business segment:

- Basic assumptions for the year or years
- Plan highlights
- Statement of income and expense

---

[3] For a full discussion of appraising or evaluating an annual business plan, see James D. Willson, *Budgeting and Profit Planning Manual* (Boston: Warren, Gorham & Lamont, 1983), chap. 28.

	19X6 Plan	19X5 Indicated Final	Increase (Decrease)	
			Amount	Percentage
New orders received	$1,100.0	$1,106.8	$(6.8)	1%
Order backlog	1,300.5	1,863.7	(563.2)	30
Net sales	1,670.0	1,594.3	75.7	5
Net income				
Amount	71.4	65.7	5.7	9
Percentage of sales	4.3%	4.0		
Earnings per share	5.03	4.77	.26	5
Capital expenditures	42.8	33.0	9.8	30
Dividends	17.1	16.0	1.1	7
Percentage return				
Assets	9.3	10.1		
Equity	25.8	22.9		

CALIFORNIA TECHNOLOGY, INC.
19X6 ANNUAL PLAN HIGHLIGHTS
(dollars in millions, except per share)

FIG. 13-21 Annual Business Plan Highlights

- Sources and uses of cash
- Statement of financial position
- Capital budget
- Significant financial relationships

Some illustrative exhibits used by an advanced technology manufacturing company for its management review are shown in Figures 13-21 through 13-34. It should be remembered that an annual plan is much more specific and detailed than a long-range plan. Yet, management ought not to be flooded with excessive data. The significant information must be distilled and relevant comparisons made. The figures are supported by oral explanations by the CFO. Selected visual aids presented therein are discussed in the following sections.

Annual Business Plan Highlights

The objective is to compare key factors in the business plan for the current (plan) year with the prior year (just about to end). (See Figure 13-21.)

Sales by Business Group

Without providing excessive numbers, the intent of Figure 13-22 is to indicate the growth of each group, the business being organized and managed on a decentralized product basis.

PRESENTATIONS FOR FINANCIAL MANAGEMENT

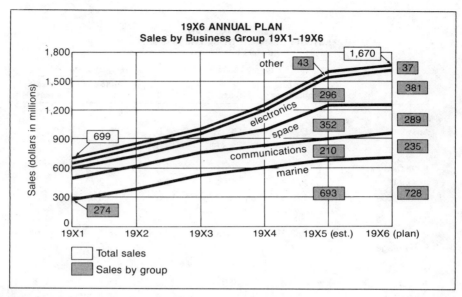

FIG. 13-22 Sales by Business Group

Activity Summary by Business Group

Because new orders, sales, and operating margin are key to group success, the relative performance is summarized in Figure 13-23. In addition, the operating margin for two years is compared to give the sense of direction.

Net Income by Business Group

The intent of the chart shown in Figure 13-24 is to show the net income results of each group vice-president.

Annual Changes in Net Income

The purpose of the table shown in Figure 13-25 is to summarize, in a simple manner, the basic causes of the changes in net income.

Comparative Statement of Planned Income and Expense

Because certain members of the board of directors wish to see the planned operating results in traditional form, the plan is highly summarized and also compared to the year about to end (see Figure 13-26). Because the relationship to sales is significant, this ratio is stated. A comparison could have been made with another year or two.

19X6 ANNUAL PLAN
ACTIVITY SUMMARY BY BUSINESS GROUP
(dollars in millions)

	19X6 Contract Acquisitions	19X6 Sales	Operating Margin 19X6	Operating Margin 19X5 (est.)	Increase (Decrease)
Marine					
Amount	$ 599.6	$ 728.8	$ 54.8	$ 66.9	$(12.1)
Percentage	54.5%	43.6%	48.9%	56.9%	
Communications					
Amount	228.7	235.2	12.6	11.2	1.4
Percentage	20.8	14.1	11.3	9.5	
Space					
Amount	83.2	288.6	17.6	18.2	(.6)
Percentage	7.6	17.3	15.7	15.5	
Electronics					
Amount	133.5	380.5	24.0	16.7	7.3
Percentage	12.1	22.8	21.4	14.2	
Other					
Amount	55.0	36.9	3.0	4.6	(1.6)
Percentage	5.0	2.2	2.7	3.9	
Totals					
Amount	$1,100.0	$1,670.0	$112.0	$117.6	$ (5.6)
Percentage	100.0%	100.0%	100.0%	100.0%	

FIG. 13-23 Activity Summary by Business Group

19X6 ANNUAL PLAN
NET INCOME BY BUSINESS GROUP
(dollars in millions)

	19X6	Percentage	19X5 (est.)	Percentage	Increase (Decrease)
Marine	$51.9	72.7%	$51.1	77.8%	$ .8
Communications	6.3	8.8	4.7	7.2	1.6
Space	2.0	2.8	6.4	9.7	(4.4)
Service	.6	.9	2.8	4.2	(2.2)
Other	10.6	14.8	.7	1.1	9.9
Total	$71.4	100.0%	$65.7	100.0%	$ 5.7

FIG. 13-24 Net Income by Business Group

PRESENTATIONS FOR FINANCIAL MANAGEMENT

19X6 ANNUAL PLAN
CAUSES OF CHANGE IN NET INCOME
(dollars in millions)

Net income, 19X6 plan	$ 71.4
Net income, 19X5 (est.)	65.7
Increase in net income	$ 5.7
Change in operating margins	
Marine	$ (12.1)
Communications	1.4
Space	(.6)
Electronics	7.3
Other	(1.6)
Total	$ (5.6)
Increase in other income	1.3
Decrease in other deductions	5.3
Increase in income before taxes	$ 1.0
Decrease in income taxes	4.7
Increase in net income	$ 5.7

FIG. 13-25 Annual Changes in Net Income

19X6 ANNUAL PLAN
STATEMENT OF INCOME AND EXPENSE
(dollars in millions, except per share)

	19X6		19X5	
	Amount	Percentage Net Sales	Amount	Percentage Net Sales
Net sales	$1,670.0	100.0%	$1,594.3	100.0%
Cost of sales	1,558.0	93.3	1,476.7	92.6
Operating margin	$ 112.0	6.7%	$ 117.6	7.4%
Other income	22.0	1.3	20.7	1.3
Other deductions	(2.1)	(.1)	(7.4)	(.5)
Income before taxes	131.9	7.9	130.9	8.2
Income taxes	60.5	3.6	65.2	4.1
Net income	$ 71.4	4.3%	$ 65.7	4.1%
Earnings per share	5.03		4.77	

FIG. 13-26 Comparative Statement of Planned Income and Expense

19X6 ANNUAL PLAN
CASH SOURCES AND USES
(dollars in millions)

	19X6	19X5 (est.)	Increase (Decrease)
Sources of cash			
Net income	$ 71.4	$ 65.7	$ 5.7
Depreciation and amortization	24.0	22.8	1.2
Total from operations	$ 95.4	$ 88.5	$ 6.9
Income taxes	59.8	79.3	(19.5)
Inventories, net	49.8	(31.5)	81.3
Accounts receivable	5.8	24.7	(18.9)
Total	$210.8	$161.0	$ 49.8
Uses of cash			
Capital expenditures	$ 42.8	$ 33.0	$ 9.0
Accounts payable and accruals	38.5	(46.4)	84.9
Dividends	17.1	16.0	1.1
Long-term obligations	4.9	1.1	3.8
Other	2.7	(16.5)	19.2
Total	$105.2	$ (12.8)	$118.0
Increase in cash and temporary investments	$105.6	$173.8	$ (68.2)

FIG. 13-27 Statement of Planned Sources and Uses of Cash

Statement of Planned Sources and Uses of Cash

The table shown in Figure 13-27 is intended to give management a sense of the planned sources and uses of cash as compared to the current year, as well as the extent of additional financing.

Statement of Consolidated Financial Position

The statement shown in Figure 13-28 is intended to (1) advise management as to the acceptability of the company's financial position, (2) present background data for reviewing the turnover of selected assets in each group, and (3) provide a sense of the further available credit resources (if they exist and might be required if growth is better than expected).

Return on Average Assets by Profit Center

Because resources are allocated in part on relative return on assets, and since this is a factor in executive bonus payments, the comparative performance of the profit centers is shown. (See Figure 13-29.)

19X6 ANNUAL PLAN
STATEMENT OF CONSOLIDATED FINANCIAL POSITION
As at December 31
(dollars in millions)

	19X6	19X5 (est.)
Assets		
Current assets		
Cash	$ 5.0	$ 5.9
Temporary investments	372.7	266.2
Receivables	97.8	103.6
Inventories, net	102.9	152.7
Prepaid expenses	10.0	5.8
Total	$588.4	$534.2
Property, plant and equipment	$328.5	$292.0
Less: Allowances—depreciation and amortization	168.8	147.8
Net	$159.7	$144.2
Other assets	$ 58.0	$ 55.7
Total assets	$806.1	$734.1
Liabilities and equity		
Current liabilities		
Accounts payable	$222.7	$261.2
Income taxes (98.2% deferred)	165.2	105.4
Current maturities, long-term debt/leases	4.6	5.4
Total	$392.5	$372.0
Long-term obligations		
Senior debt	$ 16.0	$ 25.9
Other long-term obligations	39.4	33.6
Total	$ 55.4	$ 59.5
Deferred income taxes and credit	$ 18.2	$ 18.2
Equity		
Common stock	14.1	14.0
Additional paid-in capital	65.4	64.2
Retained earnings	260.5	206.2
Total	$340.0	$284.4
TOTAL LIABILITIES AND EQUITY	$806.1	$734.1

FIG. 13-28 Statement of Consolidated Financial Position

19X6 ANNUAL PLAN
RETURN ON AVERAGE ASSETS BY PROFIT CENTER

Group/Profit Center	19X6 Plan	19X5 Estimate
Marine	29.0	30.1
California	27.4	28.6
Texas	31.6	30.9
New England	16.5	14.3
Communications	5.9	5.3
Washington	7.6	6.4
Chicago	1.3	1.0
Space	4.1	4.6
Florida	3.2	3.5
California	7.4	7.7
Electronics	8.6	8.1
San Jose	9.4	8.9
Europe	6.1	6.0
Consolidated	9.3	10.1

FIG. 13-29 Return on Average Assets by Profit Center

Trend in Operating Results

As a simple operating summary, the trend in net sales, net income, and earnings per share is compared with the planned results for the next year. The compounded growth rate for the five-year period is displayed. (See Figure 13-30.)

Return on Assets—Trend and Composition

In the illustrative company, emphasis is placed on the need for each operating group and profit center to attain a targeted rate of return on assets employed. This may be different for each investment center, but the consolidated target is 10 percent. Because the rate of return is a function of two factors (percentage profit on sales × turnover), the progress on each factor is graphically shown. (See Figure 13-31.)

Comparative Return on Shareholders' Equity

A final test of management's stewardship is the rate of return earned on shareholders' equity. The trend in this important measure is graphed in comparison

PRESENTATIONS FOR FINANCIAL MANAGEMENT 13-31

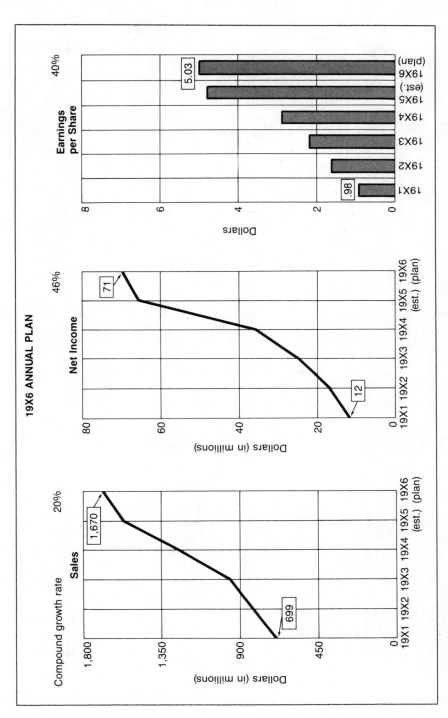

FIG. 13-30 Trends in Operating Results

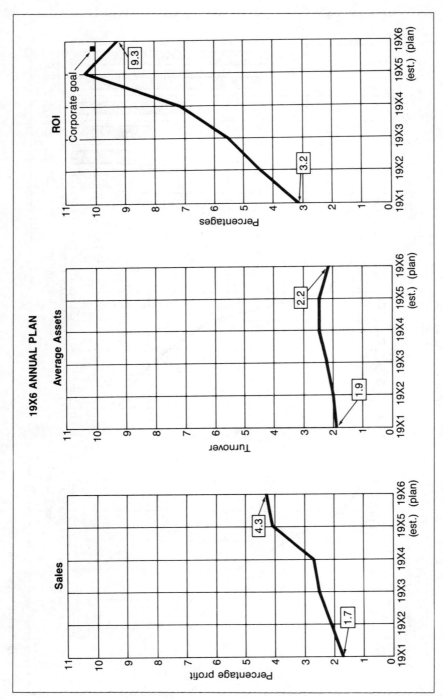

FIG. 13-31 Return on Assets: Trends and Composition

to the performance of selected competitors and an industry average (see Figure 13-32). The corporate goal of 25 percent is identified.

Borrowing Capacity

In any plan presentation, there are certain key issues in which management is interested. In the illustrative company, where a period of rapid growth is foreseen, a point of concern is the ability to handle required increases in current assets. Figure 13-33 illustrates the additional borrowing capacity available under the present bank credit agreement—$291 million, under one test, and $310 million, under another test, by the end of the plan year.

Debt to Equity Ratios

Under prudent financial management both long-term debt and total indebtedness must be maintained within certain limits. Because the illustrative company came quite close to insolvency some years ago, the board of directors continues to monitor the corporate debt. Figure 13-34 reflects the trend of two relationships. The illustration also shows how significant and sensitive relationships may be conveyed very simply.

Other Data

The figures presented illustrate some of the financial data used to plan and manage a large manufacturing company. In the actual case, additional presentations were made showing significant details by each group for such factors as:

- New orders
- Sales by product category and/or program
- Asset turnover rates
- Operating margin by product line
- Capital commitments and expenditures
- Selected ratios

The point to be made is that relatively simple presentations can be made, without excessive figures, to convey the significant aspects of an annual business plan. The data may be prepared by computer or manually, and may be in graphics or tabular form or a combination of the two. It is simply necessary that the required information, to the extent detail is needed, be planned in the FIS.

A comparable format was used for each investment center to the extent applicable. Of course, a basic objective was to convey to appropriate management levels those financial facts and relationships deemed important to the stability and growth of the enterprise.

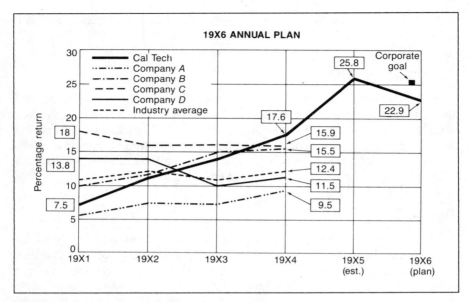

FIG. 13-32 Comparative Return on Shareholders' Equity

19X6 ANNUAL PLAN
BORROWING CAPACITY
(dollars in millions)

	19X6	19X5 (est.)
Tangible net worth		
Allowable debt		
185% of tangible net worth	$629	$526
Less: Actual or expected indebtedness	338	330
Additional borrowing capacity	$291	$196
Senior-funded debt test		
Consolidated tangible net worth	$340	$284
Less: Actual or expected senior-funded indebtedness	30	46
Additional borrowing capacity	$310	$238

FIG. 13-33 Borrowing Capacity

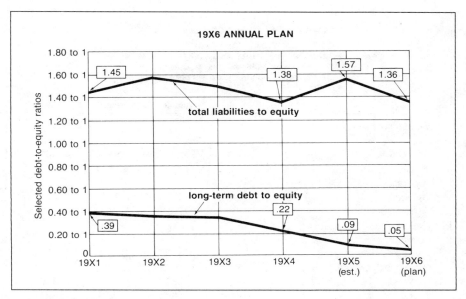

FIG. 13-34 Debt-to-Equity Ratios

COMPANY/SEGMENT OVERALL PERFORMANCE

Some Manufacturing Companies

Whereas the long-range financial plan, or the annual business plan, typically is prepared, analyzed, and presented once a year for the review and approval of the board of directors and top management, a comparison of actual performance and financial position with the plan recurs at this top-management level monthly or quarterly.

The data to be gathered, analyzed, and presented through the FIS must meet the needs of each echelon of management. The extent of information and format varies from company to company depending on the industry, management style, magnitude of difficulties or problems, comprehension, and interests of the directors and officers. The criterion should be whatever is important at the particular level of management. Thus, information and format might extend from a simple two-page report to a rather comprehensive review of each investment or profit center and each major activity thereunder.

A highly condensed report for the board of directors and top management of a manufacturing company, which compares actual and planned results and provides all the significant data thought to be necessary under the circumstances, is illustrated in Figures 13-35 and 13-36. Figure 13-35 presents the overall status and Figure 13-36 reveals the operating performance for each of the profit centers. The figures are accompanied by a brief interpretive commentary. The CFO has sufficient backup data and analyses available to answer the

(continued on page 13-39)

THE NORRIS COMPANY
FINANCIAL REPORT
BOARD OF DIRECTORS AND TOP MANAGEMENT
June 19X6 and Year to Date
(dollars in hundreds, except per share)

	Actual	Plan	Percentage of Plan
Operating results			
Net sales			
Month	$ 4,064	$ 3,900	104%
Year to date	33,129	30,120	110
Operating margin (%)			
Month	12.1%	12.0%	101
Year to date	13.3	13.0	102
Net income			
Month	$ 183	$ 175	105
Year to date	1,756	1,450	121
Earnings per share			
Month	.15	.15	100
Year to date	1.46	1.21	121
Other financial data			
Current assets			
Cash and equivalents	$ 3,855	$ 3,900	
Accounts receivable	5,972	5,750	
Inventories	9,230	9,000	
Other	23	20	
Total	$19,080	$18,670	
Current liabilities	10,042	9,335	
Net working capital	$ 9,038	$ 9,335	
Capital expenditures	$361	$570	
Return on assets (annualized)	7.6%	8.0%	
Return on shareholders' equity (annualized)	13.5	14.0	
Current ratio	1.90:1	2:1	
Book value per share	$21.68	$17.26	

FIG. 13-35 Summary Financial Report for Management

THE NORRIS COMPANY
FINANCIAL REPORT
Summary of Profit Center Operating Performance
(dollars in hundreds)

	Actual	Plan	Percentage of Plan
Net sales			
Western Division			
Month	$ 1,870	$ 1,800	104%
Year to date	14,981	14,000	107
Southwestern Division			
Month	1,412	1,500	94
Year to date	11,967	14,000	85
Southern Division			
Month	882	700	126
Year to date	6,781	4,120	165
Consolidated			
Month	4,064	3,900	104
Year to date	$33,129	$30,120	110%
Net income			
Western Division			
Month	$ 76	$ 72	106%
Year to date	679	600	113
Southwestern Division			
Month	71	75	95
Year to date	657	700	94
Southern Division			
Month	40	35	114
Year to date	439	200	220
Consolidated			
Month	183	175	105
Year to date	$ 1,756	$ 1,450	121%
Return on assets (annualized)			
Western Division	6.1%	6.5%	
Southwestern Division	8.0	8.2	
Southern Division	10.7	9.4	
Consolidated	7.6	8.0	

FIG. 13-36 Summary Performance by Profit Center

THE CHICAGO MANUFACTURING COMPANY
CONSOLIDATED STATEMENT OF INCOME AND EXPENSE
(dollars in hundreds)

	March 19X6		Year to Date	
	Amount	Percentage Net Sales	Amount	Percentage Net Sales
Net sales				
This year	$29,680	100%	$92,746	100%
Plan	30,000	100	95,000	100
Last year	28,413	100	90,812	100
Less: Prime costs (this year)	9,498	32	31,534	34
Gross margin				
This year	20,182	68	61,212	67
Plan	20,700	69	66,500	70
Last year	19,321	68	61,752	68
Operating expenses				
Manufacturing	6,530	22	21,332	23
Research	1,484	5	4,637	5
Marketing	6,530	22	23,187	25
Administrative	1,187	4	2,782	3
Total (this year)	$15,731	53%	$51,938	56%
Plan	16,500	55	52,250	55
Last year	15,911	56	50,855	56
Operating profit (this year)	4,451	15	9,274	11
Other income and (expense)				
This year	1,187	4	3,709	4
Plan	900	3	2,850	3
Last year	852	3	2,724	3
Income before income taxes				
This year	5,639	19	12,983	15
Plan	5,100	17	17,100	18
Last year	4,262	15	13,622	15
Net income				
This year	3,265	11	7,420	8
Plan	3,000	10	9,500	10
Last year	$ 2,273	8%	$ 7,265	8%

FIG. 13-37 Comparative Statement of Income and Expense

more likely questions and provide further information at the board or management meeting.

Quite often, the board of directors and top management are interested in a comparison of operating results not only with plan but also with the prior year. Moreover, there is sometimes a desire to review the entire range of costs and expenses in the traditional income and expense format. The table shown in Figure 13-37 fills this need for a medium-sized manufacturing company. Information is provided on a consolidated basis as well as for each profit center. Moreover, it relates costs and expenses to net sales to provide a sense of relative cost control.

Finally, it may be helpful to illustrate the financial report provided monthly to the executive council of a large advanced technology company located in northern California. (In addition, the board of directors and top management review cash sources and uses and the financial position with financial management.) The corporation operates on a decentralized basis; each group vice-president is responsible for planned net income of his group and a targeted return on assets. The executive council, comprising the central corporate management and the group heads, meets monthly to review operating results. First, the overall results are discussed; then, each group head reviews his operations, using a comparable format (to the extent applicable). The basic content of the report (numbers are fictitious) is shown in Figures 13-38 through 13-51. The following features of the package are worth noting:

1 Actual performance for the month and year to date is compared to plan as well as to prior years. Thus, the principle of comparative reporting is used.

2 Because it is deemed insufficient to compare only actual with planned performance, there is a monthly updating of expected operations for the remainder of the fiscal year. In this way, management is kept continually informed on the prospects for the complete year. Obviously, the FISs must provide for this monthly revision of the expected outlook, as well as analyze the reasons for departure of actual from plan.

3 The top-management report encompasses factors considered key to successful operations in the business, such as:
   - New orders received (contract acquisitions)
   - The order backlog
   - Net sales
   - Operating margin—as a percentage of sales
   - Net income—including percentage of sales
   - Return on assets
   - Return on shareholders' equity

(continued on page 13-54)

CONSOLIDATED TECHNOLOGY, INC.
HIGHLIGHTS OF OPERATIONS
(dollars in millions, except per share)

	March 19X6		Year to Date			Total Year		
	Actual	Over (Under) Plan	Actual	Over (Under) Plan	Prior Year	Indicated Final	Over (Under) Plan	Prior Year
Contract acquisitions	$ 145.7	$(223.9)	$ 820.4	$ 89.1	$ 564.6	$7,300.0	$ 350.0	$2,941.8
Sales backlog			2,865.4	66.5	2,377.6	7,075.2	450.0	2,775.2
Net sales	278.0	16.8	730.2	22.6	493.4	3,000.0	(100.0)	2,472.9
Operating margin	$ (4.8)	$ (.8)	$ 6.5	$ 12.7	$ (35.8)	$ 93.4	$ (98.7)	$ 66.6
Operating margin (percentage of sales)	(1.76)%	(.22)%	.88%	1.76%	(7.26)%	3.11%	(3.09)%	2.6%
Net income	$ (2.0)	$ .9	$ 7.3	$ 11.3	$ (22.3)	$ 70.0	$ (52.7)	$ 63.7
Net income (percentage of sales)	(.74)%	.40%	1.00%	1.57%	(4.51)%	2.3%	(1.63)%	2.60%
Average assets employed	$1,362.8	$ 30.8	$1,348.1	$ 33.4	$1,237.7	$1,473.8	$ 14.2	$1,304.9
Turnover of average assets	2.45	.10	2.17	.02	1.59	2.04	(.08)	1.90
Return on average assets	(1.82)%	.87%	2.16%	3.39%	(7.20)%	4.75%	(3.66)%	4.94%
Return on average equity	(4.95)%	2.37%	5.82%	9.09%	(17.80)%	13.48%	(9.01)%	13.12%
Earnings per share	$(.13)	$.07	$.48	$.75	$(1.48)	$4.60	$(3.48)	$4.21
Average shares outstanding	15,212	25	15,194	13	15,076	15,204	19	15,112
Book value per share			$32.74	$.72	$31.86	$35.83	$(3.50)	$32.60

FIG. 13-38 Summary of Operations

CONSOLIDATED TECHNOLOGY, INC.
ACQUISITIONS
(dollars in thousands)

	March 19X6		Year to Date				Year Projected		Change From Last Month
	Actual	Over (Under) Plan	Actual	Over (Under) Plan	Prior Year	Indicated Final	Over (Under) Plan		Over/(Under)
Space exploration group									
California department	$ 74,368	$(232,439)	$544,871	$35,572	$240,838	$6,158,691	$423,660		$ 1,360
Texas department	4,441	(4,424)	54,903	(1,200)	41,777	195,564	0		0
Eliminations	(920)	(380)	(2,436)	(1,469)	(2,256)	(31,162)	(1,670)		(1,099)
Total	$ 77,889	$(237,243)	$597,338	$32,903	$280,359	$6,323,093	$421,990		$ 261
Computer group									
Main systems	19,470	10,837	98,922	50,768	95,264	235,442	12,474		(5,901)
Microprocessors	14,929	3,463	24,165	3,936	4,593	97,433	(17,319)		(1,931)
Peripherals	2,195	1,253	44,313	3,633	89,043	207,597	(3,213)		(3,213)
European	15,271	7,546	31,539	8,736	26,397	81,400	0		0
South American	12,372	1,875	15,912	2,527	4,136	34,529	0		0
Eliminations	(72)	1,268	(1,390)	1,650	(1,369)	(4,783)	(23)		(81)
Total	$ 64,165	$ 26,242	$213,461	$71,250	$218,064	$ 651,618	$ (8,081)		$(11,126)
Electronics group									
Communications	7,123	(6,095)	11,755	(1,895)	41,357	258,909	2,859		3,000
Service department	(496)	(786)	615	(255)	9,892	134,748	277		(1,261)
Defense	6,528	2,025	9,483	(5,737)	17,180	58,242	0		0
Eliminations	0	0	0	0	6	0	0		0
Total	$ 13,155	$ (4,856)	$ 21,853	$ (7,887)	$ 68,435	$ 451,899	$ 3,136		$ 1,739
Research and technology	637	477	819	(2,076)	511	3,821	76		76
Corporate adjustment	(124)	(124)	(39)	(39)	3,285	(107,953)	(76,619)		533
Eliminations	(9,978)	(8,415)	(13,033)	(5,107)	(6,045)	(22,478)	9,498		8,517
TOTAL	$145,744	$(223,919)	$820,399	$89,044	$564,609	$7,300,000	$350,000		$ 0

FIG. 13-39 Summary of Acquisitions (New Orders) by Organization

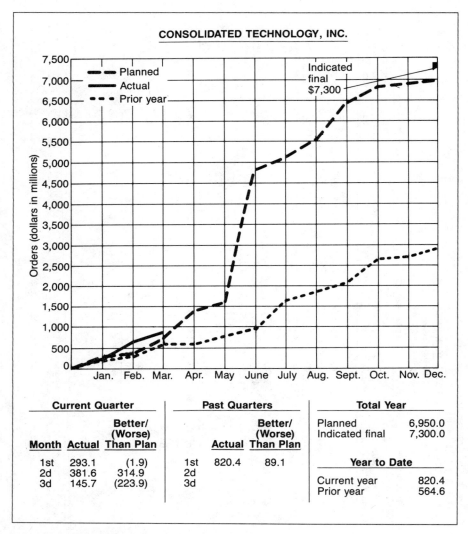

FIG. 13-40 Comparative New Orders Received

	CONSOLIDATED TECHNOLOGY, INC.				
	CONSOLIDATED ACQUISITIONS				
	Three Months Ended March 31, 19X6				
	(dollars in millions)				
	Year to Date			Total Year	
	Actual	Over (Under) Plan	Prior Year	Indicated Final	Over (Under) Plan
On or ahead of plan	$616.5	$50.8	$276.0	$2,509.6	$406.3
Below plan—not significant	67.3	(3.4)	93.0	586.4	3.1
Significant impact					
Main systems	98.9	50.8	95.3	235.4	12.5
Peripherals	44.3	3.6	89.0	204.2	(3.2)
Defense	9.5	(5.7)	17.2	58.2	0
Research and technology	.8	(2.1)	.5	3.8	.1
Corporate adjustment	0	0	3.3	(107.9)	(76.6)
Eliminations	(16.9)	(4.9)	(9.7)	(50.7)	7.8
Total	$820.4	$89.1	$564.6	$3,439.0	$350.0
Space Vehicle	0	0	0	3,861.0	0
Consolidated	$820.4	$89.1	$564.6	$7,300.0	$350.0

Significant impact

- *Main systems*: Ahead of plan through receipt of $67.8 million IBM order not anticipated this year. This was partially offset by slippage of Dutch order ($18.0 million) until next spring.
- *Peripherals*: Indicated final decreased by $5.0 million due to loss of Chicago job, offset by miscellaneous new orders.
- *Space vehicle*: Research program is expected to be awarded in November.
- *Defense*: The service segment has lost the Ft. Revere modification contract ($8.9 million), but did receive the unplanned Catalina contract ($3.0 million). It is anticipated that future change orders in October will fully offset the Ft. Revere loss.
- *Research and technology*: The robot simulation program of $2.1 million has been delayed until June.

FIG. 13-41 Contract Acquisitions—Explanation of Variances

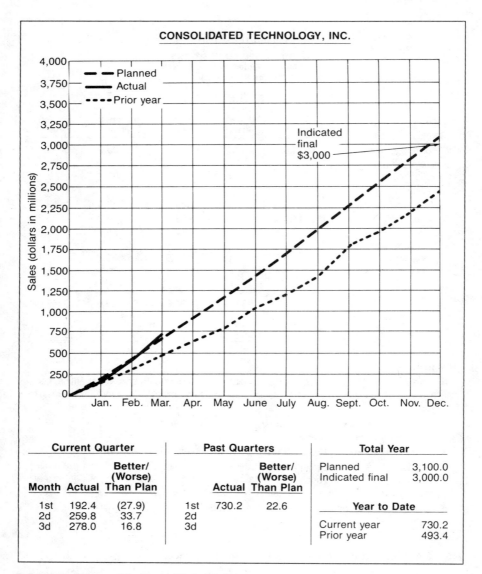

FIG. 13-42 Comparative Consolidated Sales

CONSOLIDATED TECHNOLOGY, INC.
NET SALES
(dollars in thousands)

	March 19X6		Year to Date			Year Projected		
	Actual	Over (Under) Plan	Actual	Over (Under) Plan	Prior Year	Indicated Final	Over (Under) Plan	Change From Last Month Over/(Under)
Space exploration group								
California department	$163,603	$ 5,312	$437,097	$20,194	$205,298	$1,852,985	$ (8,686)	$ (37,369)
Texas department	15,675	2,746	40,316	2,772	31,701	165,867	0	0
Eliminations	(2,275)	179	(6,730)	186	(4,354)	(29,602)	(1,670)	(1,099)
Total	$177,003	$ 8,237	$470,683	$23,152	$232,645	$1,989,250	$(10,356)	$ (38,468)
Computer group								
Main systems	15,113	926	44,332	2,855	52,318	194,363	4,800	4,800
Microcomputers	12,972	500	32,990	(2,868)	19,877	126,079	(6,064)	(455)
Peripherals	19,281	3,304	48,182	3,843	31,480	188,161	2,912	2,912
European	6,365	219	15,564	(2,031)	15,074	82,000	0	0
South American	5,842	597	13,736	37	9,247	54,350	0	0
Eliminations	(866)	(120)	(1,927)	72	(1,424)	(6,944)	(95)	(53)
Total	$ 58,707	$ 5,426	$152,877	$ 1,908	$126,572	$ 638,009	$ 1,553	$ 7,204
Electronics group								
Communications	24,476	3,023	57,102	(1,836)	78,344	259,109	(31,559)	(29,734)
Service department	11,122	352	29,840	67	28,283	129,211	4,649	279
Defense	6,257	319	17,949	1,147	17,504	76,461	0	0
Eliminations	0	0	0	0	(25)	0	0	0
Total	$ 41,855	$ 3,694	$104,891	$ (622)	$124,106	$ 464,781	$(26,910)	$ (29,455)
Research and technology	344	(211)	1,018	(602)	1,105	4,752	(449)	(449)
Corporate adjustment	1,405	(729)	5,406	(1,503)	13,677	(75,945)	(68,726)	(42,105)
Eliminations	(1,237)	386	(4,633)	256	(4,695)	(20,847)	4,888	3,273
TOTAL	$278,077	$16,803	$730,242	$22,589	$493,410	$3,000,000	$(100,000)	$(100,000)

FIG. 13-43 Consolidated Net Sales by Organization

CONSOLIDATED TECHNOLOGY, INC.
CONSOLIDATED NET SALES
Three Months Ended March 31, 19X6
(dollars in millions)

	Year to Date			Total Year	
	Actual	Over (Under) Plan	Prior Year	Indicated Final	Over (Under) Plan
On or ahead of plan	$150.0	$ 7.8	$118.2	$ 609.9	$ 7.6
Below plan—not significant	49.6	(5.5)	36.1	212.7	(6.5)
Significant impact					
California department	437.1	20.2	205.3	1,830.2	60.1
Main systems	44.3	2.9	52.3	194.4	4.8
Communications	57.1	(1.8)	78.3	259.1	(31.6)
Corporate adjustment	5.4	(1.5)	13.7	(75.9)	(68.7)
Eliminations	(13.3)	.5	(10.5)	(53.2)	3.1
Total	$730.2	$22.6	$493.4	$2,977.2	$ (31.2)
Space vehicle	0	0	0	22.8	(68.8)
Consolidated	$730.2	$22.6	$493.4	$3,000.0	$ (100.0)

Significant impact

- *California department*: Indicated final increased by $60.1 million as a result of new spares requirements for delivery this year.
- *Main systems*: The indicated final increase relates to current-year delivery on the new IBM order.
- *Communications*: The change in indicated final is caused by the new delivery schedule on the optic fiber project.
- *Space vehicle*: The $68.8 million under-plan projection for sales results from the deferral of the contract award until November.

FIG. 13-44 Consolidated Net Sales—Explanation of Variances

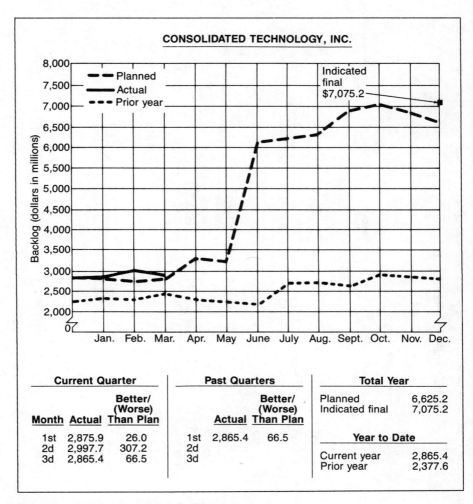

FIG. 13-45 Consolidated Order Backlog

CONSOLIDATED TECHNOLOGY, INC.
SALES BACKLOG
March 19X6
(dollars in thousands)

	Year to Date			Year Projected		
	Actual	Over (Under) Plan	Prior Year	Indicated Final	Over (Under) Plan	Change From Last Month Over/(Under)
Space exploration group						
California department	$1,520,409	$15,378	$1,372,023	$5,718,341	$432,346	$ 38,729
Texas department	170,827	(3,972)	143,210	185,937	0	0
Eliminations	(24,318)	(1,655)	(22,008)	(30,172)	0	0
Total	$1,666,918	$ 9,751	$1,493,225	$5,874,106	$432,346	$ 38,729
Computer group						
Main systems	$ 246,322	$47,913	$ 239,812	$ 232,811	$ 7,674	$(10,701)
Microprocessors	154,084	6,804	179,517	134,263	(11,255)	(1,476)
Peripherals	116,681	(210)	109,691	133,986	(6,125)	(6,125)
European	116,965	10,767	91,939	100,390	0	0
South American	70,272	2,490	77,155	48,275	0	0
Eliminations	(3,778)	1,578	(2,997)	(2,154)	72	(28)
Total	$ 694,546	$69,342	$ 695,117	$ 647,571	$ (9,634)	$(18,330)
Electronics group						
Communications	$ 424,206	$ (59)	$ 72,072	$ 469,353	$ 34,418	$ 32,734
Service department	62,079	(322)	61,306	96,841	(4,372)	(1,540)
Defense	32,105	(6,884)	35,081	22,352	0	0
Eliminations	0	0	0	0	0	0
Total	$ 518,390	$(7,265)	$ 168,459	$ 588,546	$ 30,046	$ 31,194
Research and technology	1,438	(1,474)	4,247	706	525	525
Corporate adjustment	8,185	1,464	35,271	(18,378)	(7,893)	42,638
Eliminations	(24,104)	(5,363)	(18,720)	(17,335)	4,610	5,244
TOTAL	$2,865,373	$66,455	$2,377,599	$7,075,216	$450,000	$100,000

FIG. 13-46 Consolidated Order Backlog by Organization

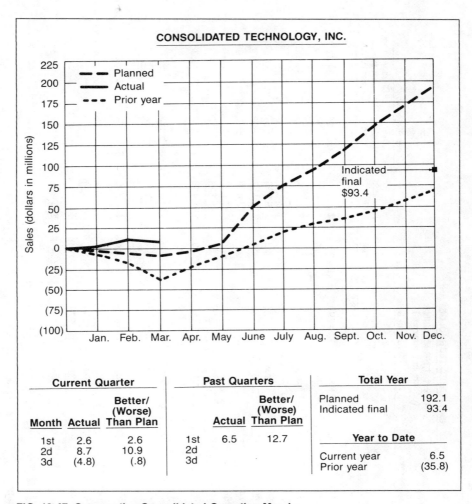

FIG. 13-47 Comparative Consolidated Operating Margin

CONSOLIDATED TECHNOLOGY, INC.
OPERATING MARGIN
(dollars in thousands)

	March 19X6		Year to Date			Year Projected		
	Actual	Over (Under) Plan	Actual	Over (Under) Plan	Prior Year	Indicated Final	Over (Under) Plan	Change From Last Month Over/(Under)
Space exploration group								
California department	$(19,234)	$(7,876)	$(21,847)	$ 5,799	$(64,105)	$ (1,169)	$(93,027)	$(94,832)
Texas department	1,631	531	4,227	120	2,816	17,603	0	0
Total	$(17,603)	$(7,345)	$(17,620)	$ 5,919	$(61,289)	$16,434	$(93,027)	$(94,832)
Computer group								
Main systems	$ 1,259	$ 103	$ 3,869	$ 282	$ 4,990	$16,958	$ 57	$ 57
Microprocessors	2,165	1,266	2,757	3	2,031	10,156	693	1,080
Peripherals	1,474	417	3,447	555	1,601	14,426	618	96
European	862	256	2,227	496	1,427	8,200	0	0
South American	300	219	913	816	150	1,728	0	0
Total	$ 6,060	$ 2,261	$ 13,213	$ 2,152	$ 10,199	$51,468	$ 1,368	$ 1,233
Electronics group								
Communications	$ 6,221	$ 3,870	$ 9,856	$ 3,358	$ 10,763	$33,334	$ 5,082	$ 5,209
Service department	227	(22)	383	(230)	483	2,545	92	5
Defense	305	37	1,084	82	942	4,339	0	0
Total	$ 6,753	$ 3,885	$ 11,323	$ 3,210	$ 12,188	$40,218	$ 5,174	$ 5,214
Research and technology	$ 19	$ 0	$ 62	$ (42)	$ 34	$ 202	$ (88)	$ (88)
Corporate activities	(58)	192	(294)	456	3,188	(5,450)	(2,450)	(2,500)
Corporate adjustment	(60)	139	(233)	978	(164)	(9,451)	(9,666)	(4,510)
TOTAL	$ (4,889)	$ (868)	$ 6,451	$12,673	$(35,844)	$93,421	$(98,689)	$(95,483)

FIG. 13-48 Operating Margin by Organization

CONSOLIDATED TECHNOLOGY, INC.
CONSOLIDATED OPERATING MARGIN
Three Months Ended March 31, 19X6
(dollars in thousands)

	Year to Date			Total Year	
	Actual	Over (Under) Plan	Prior Year	Indicated Final	Over (Under) Plan
On or ahead of plan	$ 18,524	$ 2,354	$ 17,226	$ 73,410	$ 1,368
Below plan—not significant	62	(42)	34	202	(88)
Significant impact					
Communications	9,856	3,358	10,763	33,334	5,082
California department	21,182	(7,172)	5,916	144,931	(2,927)
Services department	383	(230)	483	2,545	92
Corporate activities	(294)	456	3,188	(5,450)	(2,450)
Corporate adjustment	(233)	978	(164)	(9,451)	(9,666)
Total	$ 49,480	$ (298)	$ 37,446	$ 239,521	$ (8,589)
Space vehicle	(43,029)	12,971	(73,290)	(146,100)	(90,100)
Consolidated	$ 6,451	$12,673	$(35,844)	$ 93,421	$(98,689)

Significant Impact

- *Communications*: The improvement of $5.1 million in the indicated final is caused by successful completion of contract negotiation for the Canadian contract.
- *California department*: The degradation in margin is the result of computer chip failures and the need for rework. This may be partially recoverable from the supplier.
- *Services department*: Although relatively small as to overall operations, the severe drop in margin is caused by nonrecoverable start-up costs of the Phoenix plant.
- *Space vehicle*: The research expenditures on this project are running less than planned; hence, the favorable $12.97 million year to date. However, the deferral in the contract award until November will result in a yearly expense of $90.1 million larger than expected. These expenses may not be deferred. However, it is expected that the contract margins ultimately will far offset the present losses.

FIG. 13-49 Consolidated Operating Margin—Explanation of Variances

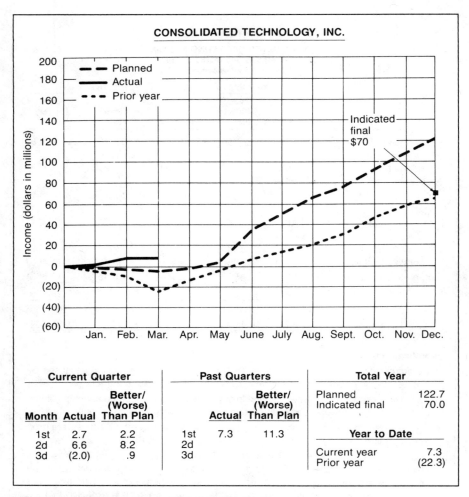

FIG. 13-50 Comparative Consolidated Net Income

CONSOLIDATED TECHNOLOGY, INC.
INCOME AND EXPENSE
Three Months Ended March 31, 19X6
(dollars in millions, except per share)

	March 31, 19X6		Total Year Indicated Final	Prior Year		Total Year
	Year to Date			Year to Date		
	Amount	Percentage Net Sales		Amount	Percentage Net Sales	
Net sales	$730.2	100.0%	$3,000.0	$ 493.4	100.0%	$2,472.9
Cost of sales	723.7	99.1	2,906.6	529.2	107.3	2,406.3
Operating margin	$ 6.5	.9%	$ 93.4	$ (35.8)	(7.3)%	$ 66.6
Interest income	2.3	.3	3.8	7.0	1.4	19.5
Other income	1.5	.2	1.8	1.8	.4	13.5
Interest expense	(1.1)	(.2)	(11.1)	(1.0)	(.2)	(3.1)
Income before taxes	$ 9.2	1.2%	$ 87.9	$ (28.0)	(5.7)%	$ 96.5
Income taxes	1.9	.2	17.9	(5.7)	(1.2)	32.8
Net income	$ 7.3	1.0%	$ 70.0	$ (22.3)	(4.5)%	$ 63.7
Earnings per share	.48		4.60	(1.48)		4.21

FIG. 13-51 Comparative Consolidated Net Income and Expense

4 The principle of interpretive reporting is used, with a brief commentary to explain important variances from plan or conditions requiring attention.

5 Exception reporting is used in that on-plan or acceptable conditions are not detailed but significant departures from plan are highlighted (see Figures 13-4, 13-44, and 13-49).

6 A limited number of simple graphs are included.

A Services Company

The segments of the financial reporting systems illustrated in the preceding section (long-range financial plan, annual business plan, and company/segment overall performance) have been described as those of manufacturing companies. This categorization results from their primary business activities. In reality, the companies' activities comprise both manufacturing and services. The services arms were developed to augment and enlarge the manufacturing functions by way of maintaining the principal manufactured products; this is a trend in U.S. business. In fact, one authority[4] estimates that manufacturing already has declined to about 20 percent of both the U.S. GNP and jobs, and to where, over the next ten years, services will account for six out of seven new jobs.

What effect does that have on the financial reporting system? Very little, in that certain principles should be followed, such as responsibility reporting, exception reporting, summarized reporting (where applicable), interpreted reporting, and comparative reporting. In fact, it is not clear from the examples given whether the company is a manufacturing or service company. The differences become apparent only when reviewing details of items important in a manufacturing business but not usually consequential in a service business (e.g., cost of manufacture, direct labor, direct material, manufacturing overhead, or inventory composition). However, some additional reassurance may be provided if an illustrative segment of a financial report to the top management of a services company is presented. Figures depicting the important parts of the financial report to the board of directors, the top five executives of the firm, and the CEOs of each major subsidiary of a financial services firm follow. Included, with additional supplementary data when deemed necessary, are these statements:

Comparative Condensed Balance Sheet—Figure 13-52

Comparative Income Statement—Figure 13-53

Comparative Statement of Changes in Financial Position—Figure 13-54

Commentary on the Period Earnings by the Chief Financial Officer—
    Figure 13-55

---

[4] Irving D. Canton, "Learning to Love the Service Economy," *Harvard Business Review* (May-June 1984), p. 90.

PARENT COMPANY BALANCE SHEET
September 30,

	19X6 Actual	19X6 Plan	Actual 19X5
Assets			
Investments in subsidiaries	$____	$____	$____
Accounts with subsidiaries	____	____	____
Income taxes receivable	____	____	____
Cash	____	____	____
Other	____	____	____
Liabilities and Shareholders' Equity			
Notes and loans payable	____	____	____
Income taxes payable	____	____	____
Accounts payable	____	____	____
Shareholders' equity			
Common stock	____	____	____
Additional paid-in capital	____	____	____
Retained earnings	____	____	____
Unrealized gain on equity securities*	____	____	____
Foreign currency translation adjustments	____	____	____

*Restated for pooling of interests.
Above amounts are preliminary and subject to change.

FIG. 13-52 Comparative Condensed Balance Sheet

The following explanations may be helpful.

- The statement of financial position is highly condensed, among other reasons, because the company is financially very strong and has no problems in this area.
- The income statement for the nine months is shown, comparing actual with the plan and the prior year. Details of income by subsidiary (each a different line of service) are reflected, together with the significant parent company expenses.
- The statement of changes in financial position is in the usual format.
- The commentary on period earnings reflects the performance of each business line.
  A detailed explanation of how and why each activity compares with plan (not shown) is provided to the management group.

Each management report is tailored to the needs and desires of the principal recipients. In these instances, the data provided are preliminary and are

(continued on page 13-59)

PARENT COMPANY INCOME STATEMENT
Nine Months Ended September 30,

	19X4	19X3	Better (Worse) Amount	Better (Worse) Percentage	Plan	Better (Worse)
Revenues	$___	$___	$___	___%	$___	$___
[*Subdividends*]	___	___	___	___	___	___
	___	___	___	___	___	___
	___	___	___	___	___	___
Other dividends	___	___	___	___	___	___
Miscellaneous	___	___	___	___	___	___
Total	$___	$___	$___	___%	$___	$___
Expenses						
Interest, net	$___	$___	$___	___%	$___	$___
Salaries and benefits	___	___	___	___	___	___
Advertising	___	___	___	___	___	___
Public and employee relations	___	___	___	___	___	___
Shareholder relations	___	___	___	___	___	___
Professional services	___	___	___	___	___	___
Other taxes	___	___	___	___	___	___
Transportation and registration fees	___	___	___	___	___	___
Travel	___	___	___	___	___	___
Building and occupancy	___	___	___	___	___	___
Risk management	___	___	___	___	___	___
Foreign exchange	___	___	___	___	___	___
Other	___	___	___	___	___	___
Pretax income	$___	$___	$___	___%	$___	$___
Federal income tax	___	___	___	___	___	___
State franchise tax	___	___	___	___	___	___
Operating income	$___	$___	$___	___%	$___	$___
Eliminations	___	___	___	___	___	___
Net operating income	$___	$___	$___	___%	$___	$___
Net capital gains	___	___	___	___	___	___
Net Income	$___	$___	$___	___%	$___	$___

FIG. 13-53 Comparative Income Statement

PARENT COMPANY STATEMENT OF CHANGES IN FINANCIAL POSITION		
Nine Months Ended September 30,		
	19X6	**19X5**
Cash provided by operations and retained in the business		
Parent company net profit	$___	$___
Dividends from subsidiaries	___	___
Depreciation	___	___
Net change in other operating items		
Income taxes payable, including related accounts with subsidiaries	___	___
Accounts payable	___	___
Cash provided by operations	___	___
Dividends	___	___
Total	$___	$___
Investments in operations		
Capital contributions to subsidiaries	$___	$___
Sale of	___	___
Other	___	___
Total	$___	$___
Financing transactions		
Proceeds from long-term debt financing	$___	$___
Payment of notes and loans	___	___
Net book value of note receivable prepaid	___	___
Advances to subsidiaries	___	___
Common stock issued	___	___
Increase (decrease) in cash	$___	$___
Cash at beginning of year	___	___
Cash at end of period	$___	$___

Above amounts are preliminary and subject to change.

FIG. 13-54 Comparative Statement of Changes in Financial Position

THIRD-QUARTER EARNINGS

The most significant effect on third-quarter earnings was the large addition to the property insurance reserves, which caused a net loss for that segment of $ . . . . and reduced consolidated operating income to $ . . . . for the quarter.

As a result of the property insurance loss, consolidated operating earnings for the third quarter were $ . . . . , or . . . . . per share, down $ . . . . (. . . . . per share) from the same quarter of last year, and $ . . . . (. . . . . per share) below plan. The property/casualty insurance loss for the quarter included an increase of $ . . . . in loss reserves ($ . . . . after taxes).

Results by major source, compared with last year and plan, are shown in the following table, with dollar amounts in millions.

	Third Quarter			Nine Months		
	19X4	19X3	Plan	19X4	19X3	Plan
Life insurance	$___	$___	$___	$___	$___	$___
Insurance brokerage	___	___	___	___	___	___
Property/casualty insurance	___	___	___	___	___	___
Consumer lending	___	___	___	___	___	___
Title	___	___	___	___	___	___
Manufacturing	___	___	___	___	___	___
Equipment leasing	___	___	___	___	___	___
Travel	___	___	___	___	___	___
Other services	___	___	___	___	___	___
Corporate interest	___	___	___	___	___	___
Corporate expenses	___	___	___	___	___	___
Acquisition costs	___	___	___	___	___	___
Operating income	___	___	___	___	___	___
Other gains	___	___	___	___	___	___
Net income	$___	$___	$___	$___	$___	$___
Earnings per share						
Operating income	___	___	___	___	___	___
Other gains	___	___	___	___	___	___
Total	$___	$___	$___	$___	$___	$___

Comments on this performance for the third quarter and year to date, by item, are contained on the following three pages [*omitted*].

FIG. 13-55 CFO's Commentary on Period Earnings

discussed in the management meetings of both the board of directors and the corporate and subsidiary management.

DAILY CONDITIONS REPORT

During this period of higher growth in some of the new industries—coupled with higher inflation as well as more product obsolescence—maintaining adequate working capital is often a problem for some of the small- to medium-sized companies. Their financial resources often must be stretched to the utmost, and good commercial banking relations are essential. Under those circumstances, close daily control of operations is a necessity. Although some firms have instituted simple manual controls, computer and related communications advances have made the task much easier, even for multiplant operations.

For one such company, the CFO prepares for management use a simple daily report showing the details of working capital (including some estimated elements) and key order, sales, and factory production levels. The format, shown in Figure 13-56, includes these features:

- The active cash balance in the prime lending bank, together with the note payable balance under its credit agreement
- Activity reflected in each of its major current assets (receivables and inventory), together with slow turnover items
- Current payables accumulated and accruals estimated to arrive at approximate working capital
- Orders, net sales, factory, man-hours, and operating expenses closely monitored and compared with the monthly plan and prior year

The normal flow of accounting information should facilitate easy completion of a daily report such as the one illustrated.

OTHER FINANCIAL MANAGEMENT REPORTS

The financial reports illustrated relate primarily to those directed to top management, including the board of directors, corporate top management, or major segment managers. Attention is focused on long-term financial plans, appraisal and reporting on annual plans, overall comparison of actual and planned performance, as well as some simple overall controls. Those areas have been emphasized because (1) a great deal of improvement is possible over present practice and (2) their impact on a business may be much more pervasive than that of lower-level reports.

THE SOFTWARE CORPORATION
DAILY CONDITIONS REPORT
(dollars in thousands)

Work days completed: <u>15</u>
Work days this month: <u>20</u>

Working Capital	Beginning Balance	Additions	Deductions	Ending Balance	Past Due or Slow Moving
Current assets					
Cash					
Security Pacific	$ 1,212	$1,170	$1,482	$ 900	
Other	97			97	
Total	$ 1,309	$1,170	$1,482	$ 997	
Accounts receivable	$ 6,817	$ 306	$ 170	$ 6,953	$290
Inventories					
Raw material	2,520	292	267	2,545	41
Finished goods	4,810	487	306	4,991	87
Total	$ 7,330	779	573	7,536	$128
Other current assets	47			47	
Total current assets	$15,503	$2,055	$2,225	$15,333	
Current liabilities					
Notes payable	$ 4,900	$1,000		$ 5,900	
Accounts payable	3,514	384	$1,410	2,488	
Accruals	2,430	149	72	2,507	
Total current liabilities	$10,844	$1,533	$1,482	$10,895	
Net working capital	$ 4,659	$ 522	$ 743	$ 4,438	

Operations	Today	Month to Date	Plan to Date	Same Period Last Year to Date
Orders received	$ 25	$5,870	$6,000	$5,912
Net sales	306	6,740	6,700	6,408
Factory				
Standard hours (000)	270	5,213		
Actual hours (000)	281	5,410		
Percentage efficiency	96%	96%		
Operating expenses	$212	$4,017	$4,000	$3,871

FIG. 13-56 Daily Conditions Report for Top Management

PRESENTATIONS FOR FINANCIAL MANAGEMENT 13-61

THE JOHNSON COMPANY
WEEKLY CASH REPORT
(dollars in thousands)

	Week Ended 11/23/X6	Month to Date Actual	Month to Date Estimate
Beginning balance	$ 4,819	$ 3,710	$ 3,710
Cash receipts			
Commercial	8,417	20,612	20,600
Government	3,860	4,316	4,100
Bank loans		2,000	2,000
Total	$12,277	$26,928	$26,700
Cash disbursements			
Notes Payable, Current	$ 3,500	3,500	3,500
Accounts payable	2,814	8,970	8,250
Payrolls	3,016	9,402	9,370
Payroll and other taxes	651	2,011	2,000
Income taxes			
Capital expenditures	812	1,416	1,120
Common stock purchases	1,470	1,710	1,500
Total	$12,263	$27,009	$25,740
Ending balance	$ 4,833	$ 3,629	$ 4,670
Estimated month-end cash			$ 4,100

13-57 Weekly Cash Activity

Of course, the FIS must also provide reliable data on activities of the financial department that are the subject of frequent monitoring but that are not necessarily the subject of top-management attention. Financial executives usually know what functions should be covered, including:

- Cash receipts and disbursements as compared to plan or estimate
- Status of temporary investments and related yields
- Aging of accounts receivable
- Status of accounts payable, including past due amounts
- Status and maturities of notes payable (to banks and other creditors)
- Comparison of actual and budgeted operating expenses by department

With a little common sense, acceptable, useful reports may be easily developed, and the typical formats are quite well known. Illustrative reports on cash and temporary investments only are shown in Figures 13-57 and 13-58, respectively.

THE AEROSPACE COMPANY
SUMMARY OF SHORT-TERM INVESTMENTS
As of March 31, 19X6
(dollars in thousands)

	Market Value	Yield	Cost
U.S. government securities			
Repurchase agreements		14.04%	$ 12,430
Treasury bills		16.87	21,010
Treasury notes		13.05	20,000
GNMA certificates		11.06	1,750
Total			$ 55,190
Money market instruments			
Domestic CDs		11.00	$ 82,400
Money market funds		12.40	9,850
Eurodollar CDs		11.90	10,600
Total			$102,860
Other			
Corporate bonds	$ 1,310	16.00	$ 1,000
Municipal bonds	15,400	10.16	14,100
Common stocks	4,900	7.00	3,700
Total	$21,610		$ 18,800
TOTAL			$176,850
Planned investments, year end			$ 50,000

FIG. 13-58 Summary of Short-Term Investments

The general formats for operating expenses of the various financial department activities (e.g., controller's office, treasurer's office, accounting, accounts payable, credit department) are substantially similar to those illustrated by figures in the following chapter.

SPECIAL ANALYSES

The illustrative reports contained in this chapter represent so-called periodic or recurring documents prepared for use by financial management.

However, a review of the information needs of financial management (as outlined in Figure 13-2) include these categories:

- *For the board of directors* — selected financial analyses of problem areas, or fields of special interest

- *For top management* — special analyses showing probable results of alternative scenarios
- *For functional managers* — special analyses to highlight trouble spots

Quite often, these special analyses are the basis for solving problems — that is, making business decisions.

It is impossible to anticipate specifically the analyses that may be required sometime in the future. It is desirable, however, in designing the information system, to consider carefully what studies may be likely, by discussing the range of possibilities with the user — the financial executive. Perhaps only in this manner may conclusions be reached regarding the amount and nature (e.g., extent of detail) to be incorporated in the building blocks that make up a good FIS.

CHAPTER **14**

Financial Reports for Use by Nonfinancial Management

James D. Willson

Introduction	2	Illustrative Report Examples	15
Reports for the Marketing Manager	2	**Reports for the R&D Manager**	29
Marketing Objectives	3	Illustrative Report Examples	29
Typical Reports	3	**General and Administrative Activities**	31
Illustrative Report Examples	5	Illustrative Report Examples	33
Reports for the Manufacturing Manager	15	**Special Analyses**	33

Fig. 14-1 Typical Marketing Management Information Needs	4
Fig. 14-2 Statement of Income and Expense by Territory	6
Fig. 14-3 Statement of Income and Expense (and Contribution Margin) by Product Line	7
Fig. 14-4 Summary Marketing Division Budget	8
Fig. 14-5 Graphic Display—Sales Performance	9
Fig. 14-6 Graph and Table of Net Sales	10
Fig. 14-7 Summary Sales Performance by Division	11
Fig. 14-8 Project Budget Report—Market Research Division	12
Fig. 14-9 Exception Sales Performance Report	13
Fig. 14-10 Sales and Expenses by Salesperson	14
Fig. 14-11 Selling Expenses by District	16
Fig. 14-12 District Selling Expenses by Type of Expenditure	17
Fig. 14-13 Typical Manufacturing Manager's Information Needs	18
Fig. 14-14 Actual vs. Budget Performance by Department	20
Fig. 14-15 Departmental Budget Report	21
Fig. 14-16 Graph of Labor Efficiency Trend	22
Fig. 14-17 Graph of Material Usage Trend	22
Fig. 14-18 Manufacturing Overhead Summary by Department	23
Fig. 14-19 Material Price Variance (Monthly) by Material Classification	24
Fig. 14-20 Daily Excess Material Usage by Type of Material	25

Fig. 14-21 Changes in Unit Material Standard Cost 26
Fig. 14-22 Daily Labor Report 26
Fig. 14-23 Exception Report 27
Fig. 14-24 Capital Budget Status Report—Manufacturing Division 28
Fig. 14-25 R&D Expense Budget by Department 30
Fig. 14-26 R&D Expense Report by Department 31
Fig. 14-27 R&D Project Budget Report 32
Fig. 14-28 Summary of General and Administrative Expense—Planning Budget 34
Fig. 14-29 Budget Summary—Finance Department 35
Fig. 14-30 Budget Performance Report—Administrative Department 36

INTRODUCTION

As noted in Chapter 13, in many management groups the chief financial officer (CFO) is often charged with providing management with the financial and operating data it requires to plan and control properly—that is, manage each member's individual area of responsibility. With the advent of the microcomputer, some aspects of this task may change. The CFO may still have a function related to that activity; conversely, the operational officer may develop his own format. In the real world, the motivated and imaginative CFO works closely with other functional managers to assist them in obtaining the needed financial information in a timely and useful manner, whether from an FIS or another system.

Regardless of technical and/or organizational developments, the CFO has a responsibility either to (1) provide some or all of the financial/operating data for nonfinancial managers or (2) see that the correct data are provided and that the information is properly interpreted or used. For example, problems may be created if a sales manager compares his operating expenses with gross sales in an environment of heavy sales returns and allowances where the realistic measure is net sales.

Some illustrative reports of financial data typically needed by operating managers in nonfinancial functions are presented in this chapter. The principles discussed in Chapters 3 and 13 are applicable here, with the underlying objective being to make sure the report is understood and used. Among other things, reports must be timely, relevant, and comparative; avoid unnecessary detail; and be written in the language of the user. Eye appeal also has many advantages.

REPORTS FOR THE MARKETING MANAGER

A good starting point in developing financial reports for a marketing manager is to discuss with him his recognized needs, preferences, and style of management. The marketing function differs from industry to industry and from company to company. Basically, however, it concerns all activities involved in the

FINANCIAL REPORTS FOR NONFINANCIAL MANAGEMENT 14-3

movement of goods and services from the manufacturing point (or point of origin) to the customer.

Marketing Objectives

The objectives of the marketing manager normally include:

- Selling sufficient products and/or services to meet the sales plans—that is, the annual business plan—but with due regard to long-range implications.
- Obtaining the targeted (planned) sales volume at prices high enough, and in the proper product mix, to attain the planned gross margin, contribution margin, or whatever profit measure is used, perhaps expressed in both absolute monetary units and as a percentage of sales.
- Conducting the marketing effort efficiently and effectively, resulting in sales plans that fall within reasonable (budgeted) cost limits for each functional area (e.g., expenses of selling, advertising and sales promotion, market research, and general marketing administration).

Thus, sales programs must be intelligently conceived, and marketing efforts should be properly planned and executed. Sound planning and adequate control are essential.

Typical Reports

The types of information (largely generated by the FIS) needed by a marketing manager vary from industry to industry, company to company, and manager to manager, depending on specific circumstances such as:

- Important business factors to plan and monitor
- Stage of the business cycle
- Inherent dangers, risks, or opportunities
- Style of management
- Decisions to be made
- Information preferences of the executive

Of course, there are many other considerations, and needs change with time.

It is impractical to list here the particular wants of every marketing manager. These may be gleaned from discussions with him and from understanding the business, product, distribution system, and problems. However, some typical information requirements, segregated into planning and control categories, are illustrated in Figure 14-1. As explained elsewhere, information for the top marketing manager is broader in nature, less detailed in scope, and perhaps covers a greater time span than that needed by the lower-echelon manager.

TYPICAL MARKETING MANAGEMENT INFORMATION NEEDS

PLANNING

Long-term
- Trend of product sales
- Expected growth of market
- Share of market reasonably attainable
- Gross margin trends
  - By product
  - By market
- Marketing expense trends
  - Selling
  - Advertising and sales promotion
  - Unit functional costs
- Facility requirements

Short-term
- Product sales
  Historical, and perhaps projected
  - By product
  - By market or territory
  - By channel of distribution
  - By salesperson
  - By method of sale
  - By customer
  - By size of order
- Distribution costs or selling Expenses
  Historical, and perhaps projected
  - By product
  - By territory
  - By customer
  - By function (e.g., sales calls, shipping, circular mailing, advertising, warehousing, distribution)
- Gross margin or contribution margin analysis
  - By product
  - By territory
  - By channel of distribution
  - By method of sale (e.g., telephone, catalog, personal call)
  - By size of order
  - By salesperson
  - By organizational segment or operating division, etc.
- Impact of alternative decisions (modeling)
  - Volume or mix
  - Product
  - Price
  - Quality
- Plant and equipment requirements (e.g., budget)

FIG. 14-1 Typical Marketing Management Information Needs

FINANCIAL REPORTS FOR NONFINANCIAL MANAGEMENT 14-5

CONTROL

Orders
Receipts and backlog vs. plan

Sales
Comparison of actual and planned
- By organization segment
- By product
- By territory
- By salesperson

Gross Margin
Comparison of actual and planned
- By organization segment
- By product
- By territory

Marketing Expenses
Comparison of actual and budget
- By organization segment (e.g., division, department, district)
- By type of expense (e.g., salaries, traveling expense, advertising)
- Capital commitments and expenditures—actual vs. plan

FIG. 14-1 (cont'd)

Illustrative Report Examples

The FIS should be flexible enough to provide the required segment information for the decision to be made. Moreover, the information should be presented in a format to which the marketing manager is receptive: graphic, tabular, or a combination of both. Certain highly analytical reports may need to be tabular in form to focus on essential points most effectively. Examples of various formats are presented in Figures 14-2 through 14-10.

For planning purposes, a statement of income and expense by territory may be required for selected periods. As shown in Figure 14-2, it is usually essential to identify territorial selling expenses as well as margins by territory.

A decision may require contribution margin date, as well as direct distribution costs, as in the product-line analysis illustrated in Figure 14-3.

When the annual planning process is complete, reports on the approved short-term plan are necessary. An example of the summary budget, by appropriate time period, and compared with the prior year, is shown in Figure 14-4.

Some marketing or sales managers prefer graphic displays. A control graph displaying actual sales by month, as well as plan data and past-year experience, is shown in Figure 14-5. Some managers like graphics data that are supported by,

(continued on page 14-9)

THE PREGO COMPANY
STATEMENT OF INCOME AND EXPENSE BY TERRITORY
For Year Ended December 31, 19X6
(dollars in thousands)

	TOTAL		Middle Atlantic		TERRITORY Midwest		West	
	Amount	Percentage Net Sales	Amount	Percentage Net Sales	Amount	Percentage Net Sales	Amount	Percentage Net Sales
Sales and expenses								
Gross sales	$29,870							
Less: Returns and allowances	4,870							
Net sales	$25,000	100%	$ 5,000	100%	$ 7,500	100%	$12,500	100.00%
Cost of sales	13,750	55	2,900	58	3,975	53	6,875	55.00
Gross margin	$11,250	45%	$ 2,100	42%	$ 3,525	47%	$ 5,625	45.00%
Territorial direct expense	3,000	12	500	10	1,050	14	1,450	11.60
Margin after direct expense	$ 8,250	33%	$ 1,600	32%	$ 2,475	33%	$ 4,175	33.40%
Allocated variable expense	2,500	10	500	10	750	10	1,250	10.00
Margin after variable expense	$ 5,750	23%	$ 1,100	22%	$ 1,725	23%	$ 2,925	23.40%
Allocated expenses	2,000	8	400	8	600	8	1,000	8.00
Income before taxes	$ 3,750	15%	$ 700	14%	$ 1,125	15%	$ 1,925	15.40%
Income taxes (40%)	1,500	6	280	6	450	6	770	6.00
Net income	$ 2,250	9%	$ 420	8%	$ 675	9%	$ 1,155	9.40%
Other data								
Sales potential	$33,500		$ 7,000		$ 9,000		$17,500	
Percentage potential achieved	75%		71%		83%		71%	
Pounds sold	90,990		17,240		28,850		44,900	

FIG. 14-2 Statement of Income and Expense by Territory

THE BEACH CORPORATION, INC.
STATEMENT OF INCOME AND EXPENSE BY PRODUCT LINE
Six Months Ended January 30, 19X6
(dollars in thousands)

	All Products		R		Product Line S		T		U	
	Amount	Percentage Net Sales	Amount	Percentage Net Sales	Amount	Percentage Net Sales	Amount	Percentage Net Sales	Amount	Percentage Net Sales
Sales and expenses										
Gross sales	$49,870		$22,340		$15,930		$6,790		$4,810	
Less: Returns and allowances	9,870		6,340		930		1,790		810	
Net sales	$40,000	100.00%	$16,000	100.00%	$15,000	100.00%	$5,000	100.00%	$4,000	100.00%
Cost of sales, variable	12,000	30.00	7,750	48.40	2,850	19.00	1,000	20.00	400	10.00
Margin after variable manufacturing costs	$28,000	70.00%	$ 8,250	51.60%	$12,150	81.00%	$4,000	80.00%	$3,600	90.00%
Distribution costs, direct	6,820	17.00	3,520	22.00	1,500	10.00	1,000	20.00	800	20.00
Distribution costs, variable semidirect	2,650	6.60	800	5.00	1,200	8.00	250	5.00	400	10.00
Contribution margin	$18,530	46.40%	$ 3,930	24.60%	$ 9,450	63.00%	$2,750	55.00%	$2,400	60.00%
Fixed expenses										
Manufacturing	$ 4,000	10.00%	$ 1,600	10.00%	$ 1,500	10.00%	$ 500	10.00%	$ 400	10.00%
Distribution	2,000	5.00	800	5.00	750	5.00	250	5.00	200	5.00
General	800	2.00	320	2.00	300	2.00	100	2.00	80	2.00
Total fixed expenses	$ 6,800	17.00%	$ 2,720	17.00%	$ 2,550	17.00%	$ 850	17.00%	$ 680	17.00%
Margin before income taxes	$11,730	29.40%	$ 1,210	7.60%	$ 6,900	46.00%	$1,900	38.00%	$1,720	43.00%
Income taxes (40%)	4,692	11.76	484	3.04	2,760	18.40	760	15.20	688	17.20
Net income	$ 7,038	17.64%	$ 726	4.56%	$ 4,140	27.60%	$1,140	22.80%	$1,032	25.80%
Other data										
Sales potential	$58,500		$25,000		17,500		8,000		8,000	
Percentage achieved	68%		64%		86%		63%		50%	

FIG. 14-3 Statement of Income and Expense (and Contribution Margin) by Product Line

THE WEST COAST CORPORATION
MARKETING DIVISION BUDGET
For the Plan Year Ending 12/31/XX
(dollars in thousands)

Department	Type of Budget	Quarter 1	Quarter 2	Quarter 3	Quarter 4	Total	Prior Year	Increase (Decrease)
Direct selling								
East	Administrative	$ 5,310	$ 5,420	$ 5,440	$ 5,530	$ 21,700	$ 20,840	$ 860
Middle West	"	3,100	3,140	3,190	3,220	12,650	11,060	1,590
Far West	"	5,820	5,910	6,180	6,270	24,180	22,810	1,370
Canada	"	1,700	1,770	1,790	1,820	7,080	6,700	380
Total		$15,930	$16,240	$16,600	$16,840	$ 65,610	$ 61,410	$4,200
Advertising and sales promotion	Project	$ 8,820	$ 9,210	$ 9,400	$ 9,610	$ 37,040	$ 35,100	$1,940
Warehousing								
Camden, N.J.	Standard	$ 1,600	$ 1,640	$ 1,730	$ 1,790	$ 6,760	$ 6,300	$ 460
Chicago, Ill.	(fixed	1,120	1,100	1,210	1,240	4,670	4,400	270
Los Angeles, Cal.	and	2,630	2,720	2,540	2,560	10,450	10,300	150
Vancouver, B.C.	variable)	470	480	460	490	1,900	2,000	(100)
Total		$ 5,820	$ 5,940	$ 5,940	$ 6,080	$ 23,780	$ 23,000	$ 780
Administrative								
General and administrative	Administrative	2,100	2,100	2,100	2,210	8,510	8,300	210
Market research	Project	470	490	490	510	1,960	1,900	60
Customer relations	Administrative	100	100	100	110	410	410	—
Branch offices								
New York, N.Y.	Administrative	$ 340	$ 340	$ 350	$ 360	$ 1,390	$ 1,320	$ 70
Chicago, Ill.	"	220	230	230	230	910	880	30
Los Angeles, Cal.		440	440	450	460	1,790	1,700	90
Total		1,000	1,010	1,030	1,050	4,090	3,900	190
Total administrative		3,670	3,700	3,720	3,880	14,970	14,510	460
Grand Total — Division Budget		$34,240	$35,090	$35,660	$36,410	$141,400	$134,020	$7,380
Percentage of net sales						9.6%	9.4%	(.2%)

FIG. 14-4 Summary Marketing Division Budget (Source: James D. Willson, *Budgeting and Profit Planning Manual* (Boston: Warren, Gorham & Lamont), 1983, p. 15-34. Reprinted by permission.)

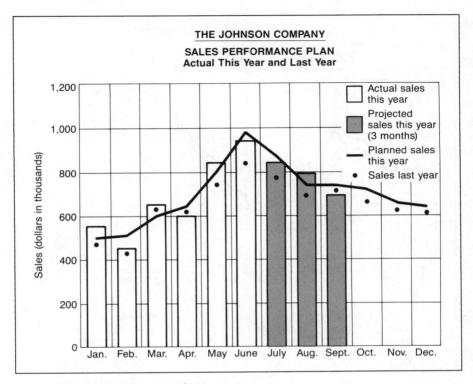

FIG. 14-5 Graphic Display—Sales Performance

or combined with, statistical tabulations. Such a presentation is illustrated in Figure 14-6. Figures 14-5 and 14-6 may both be prepared by computer.

Another kind of representative marketing control report compares actual and planned sales by organization segment (division) for the month and year to date. It also reestimates the total sales for the year and compares this update with the annual plan, by organization segment, as illustrated in Figure 14-7. This summarized report also provides a brief explanation relating to major deviations from plan.

Some phases of marketing activity are best controlled by a project budget format, as presented in Figure 14-8. More comments about project budgets are made elsewhere in this chapter regarding the research and development (R&D) function.

Exception reporting is presented in Figure 14-9, wherein the under-plan sales performance by district is distinct from performances that meet or exceed the plan. The reasons for major departure from plan are also shown.

For lower-echelon marketing managers, actual individual sales and expense performances are compared to quota and budget for each month, as shown in Figure 14-10. Other pertinent data are added as well.

(continued on page 14-15)

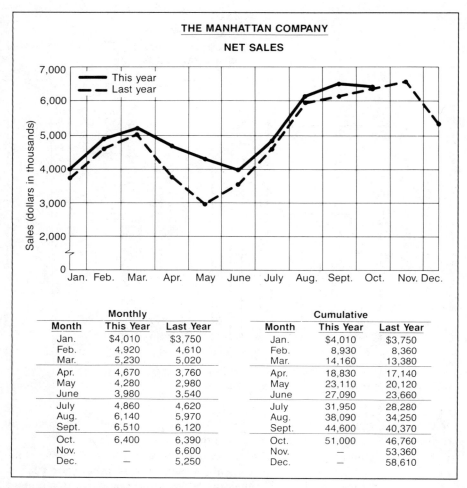

FIG. 14-6 Graph and Table of Net Sales

THE JONES COMPANY
SALES PERFORMANCE BY DIVISION
(dollars in thousands)

	June 19X6			Year to Date			Total Year	
	Actual	Plan	Over/(Under) Plan	Actual	Plan	Over/(Under) Plan	Plan	Indicated Final
Molding	$ 8,412	$ 8,000	$ 412	$ 53,910	$ 51,000	$2,910	$100,000	$105,000
Resins	6,809	7,000	(191)(a)	49,730	46,000	3,730	96,000	96,000
Plastics	4,120	4,000	120	26,340	29,000	(2,660)(c)	64,000	60,000
Adhesives	2,619	1,900	719(b)	17,815	15,000	2,815	25,000	30,000
Total	$21,960	$20,900	$1,060	$147,795	$141,000	$6,795	$285,000	$291,000

(a) The Johnson Company was on strike and could not accept delivery of $200,000 in products.
(b) The Drexell chain was added to the customer list with an estimated volume of $5 million per year and June sales of $430,000.
(c) Our principal competitor, American Cyanamid, has launched a special drive for new customers in the Northwest. We are estimating a loss of $4.5 million in sales as a result of this effort.

FIG. 14-7 Summary Sales Performance by Division

CONSUMER PRODUCTS COMPANY
MARKET RESEARCH DEPARTMENT PROJECT BUDGET REPORT
Month Ended June 30, 19XX
(In hundreds of dollars)

Project		Profes- sional Man- hours	Annual to Date — Actual						Commit- ments	Esti- mated Cost to Com- plete	Indi- cated Total Cost	Project Budget	Indi- cated Under- run (Over- run)
			Salaries and Wages			Con- sult- ants	Other Ex- pense	Total					
No.	Name		Profes- sional	Cleri- cal	Total								
Market Potential Studies													
182	Blender "S"	400	$ 40	$110	$ 150	$ 10	$ 70	$ 230	$ 12	$ 42	$ 284	$ 290	6
183	Portable fan	260	31	20	51	—	22	73	4	12	89	90	1
189	Cordless electric knife	1,410	153	160	313	30	110	453	300	700	1,453	1,500	47
190	Cordless electric toothbrush	800	80	40	120	12	60	192	78	20	290	300	10
192	Remote control color adapter	1,030	214	370	584	51	243	878	400	878	2,156	2,150	(6)
	Total	3,900	$518	$700	$1,218	$103	$505	$1,826	$794	$1,652	$4,272	$4,330	$ 58
Product Acceptance Surveys													
309	New York — "L" Series	170	$ 15	$ 80	$ 95	—	$ 22	$ 117	$ 30	$ 100	$ 247	$ 250	$ 3
310	Chicago — "M" Series	220	20	20	40	$ 3	20	63	10	30	103	100	(3)
311	Los Angeles — "R" Series	60	7	5	12	2	6	20	20	40	80	80	—
312	San Francisco — "A" Series	90	11	19	30	—	15	45	20	20	85	80	(5)
315	Boston — "B" Series	110	13	21	34	7	17	58	30	40	128	130	2
	Total	650	$ 66	$145	$ 211	$ 12	$ 80	$ 303	$110	$ 230	$ 643	$ 640	($ 3)
Other Categories													
802	Salesman's time scheduling	100	9	11	20	—	8	28	5	30	63	65	2
803	Product labels	460	37	17	54	—	27	81	10	20	111	115	4
807	Redesign of call report	70	7	2	9	—	4	13	1	14	28	30	2
808	Credit card promotions	350	43	34	77	—	40	117	40	150	307	250	(57)
	Total	980	$ 96	$ 64	$ 160	—	$ 79	$ 239	$ 56	$ 214	$ 509	$ 460	($ 49)
	Grand Total — Project budgets	5,530	$680	$909	$1,589	$115	$664	$2,368	$960	$2,096	$5,424	$5,430	$ 6

FIG. 14-8 Project Budget Report—Market Research Division (Source: James D. Willson, *Budgeting and Profit Planning Manual* (Boston: Warren, Gorham & Lamont, 1983), p. 15-8. Reprinted by permission.)

THE JONES COMPANY
PLASTICS DIVISION DISTRICT SALES REPORT
(dollars in thousands)

	June 19X6			Year to Date			
	Actual	Plan	Over/(Under) Plan	Actual	Plan	Over/(Under) Plan	Remarks
Under plan for month							
Minneapolis	$ 550	$ 610	$ (60)	$ 3,950	$ 3,600	$ 350	Urea delivered July 1
Cleveland	310	400	(90)	1,970	2,500	(530)	Jellico plant start-up delayed
Detroit	390	470	(80)	2,020	2,800	(780)	Ford refused formula
Total	$1,250	$1,480	$(230)	$ 7,940	$ 8,900	$ (960)	
Better than plan for month							
New York	$1,010	$ 860	$ 150	$ 5,640	$ 6,200	$ (560)	Johnson L.I. doubling sales
Philadelphia	580	540	40	4,410	4,100	310	
Atlanta	250	210	40	1,960	1,800	160	
Houston	120	100	20	720	800	(80)	On plan in September
Seattle	440	420	20	1,350	3,400	(2,050)	Apollo strike just ended
San Francisco	310	250	60	2,850	2,500	350	New branch on stream
Salt Lake City	160	140	20	1,470	1,300	170	
Total	$2,870	$2,520	$ 350	$18,400	$20,100	$(1,700)	
TOTAL	$4,120	$4,000	$ 120	$26,340	$29,000	$(2,660)	

FIG. 14-9 Exception Sales Performance Report

THE DOOR-TO-DOOR CORPORATION
SALES AND EXPENSES, SEATTLE
March, 19X6

Salesperson	Net Sales			Expenses			Number of Calls	New Accounts
	Actual	Quota	Over/(Under) Quota	Actual	Budget	(Over)/Under Budget		
Albross	$ 146,890	$ 150,000	$ (3,110)	$ 10,036	$ 10,500	$ 464	59	1
Barker	228,410	225,000	3,410	11,412	12,000	588	46	2
Davenport	781,205	700,000	81,205	31,608	30,000	(1,608)	53	4
Fischer	486,387	500,000	(13,613)	25,120	25,000	(120)	67	3
Guiliano	510,811	475,000	35,811	28,872	30,000	1,128	49	2
James	74,912	70,000	4,912	5,840	6,000	160	71	
Little	241,305	225,000	16,305	12,968	12,500	(468)	52	1
Total or average	$2,469,920	$2,345,000	$124,920	$125,856	$126,000	$ 144	56.7	13

FIG. 14-10 Sales and Expenses by Salesperson

FINANCIAL REPORTS FOR NONFINANCIAL MANAGEMENT 14-15

A comparison of actual and budgeted selling expenses, by organization segment (the districts making up a division) for the month and year to date are shown in Figure 14-11. Supplemental information relating such expenses to net sales is displayed. Finally, the district summary is supported by a report of actual and budgeted expense, by type of expense, for each district, as illustrated in Figure 14-12. Explanations of important variations are also provided.

In summary, the FIS must provide the needed data, perhaps in several cuts or segments. The user should participate in the design decision, as explained in Chapter 18.

REPORTS FOR THE MANUFACTURING MANAGER

Just as the marketing manager must have sales data to plan the optimum sales mix and cost data to plan and direct marketing efforts intelligently in order to optimize income, so must the manufacturing manager have his special information. Manufacturing costs and related investments must be known for a number of purposes, including these:

- The most profitable use of plant and equipment
- The most profitable or optimum cost mix
- Reduction of costs to the lowest level consistent with maintenance of quality and delivery of products to meet the sales plan.
- Proper valuation of inventories
- Price setting
- The optimum utilization of labor and material

The FIS must provide the right kind of data on a timely basis to permit proper planning and control of the operations. Odd as it seems, the manufacturing manager's information needs often require more detail and are perhaps more varied than those of sales or marketing managers. Again, although it is not practical to list all of a manufacturing or production manager's requirements, some can be discerned from the table shown in Figure 14-13.

Illustrative Report Examples

Typical planning reports for manufacturing include a summary of the planned costs of direct labor, direct material, and manufacturing expenses by appropriate time period (month, quarter, and year) for the annual plan. The analysis, or cut, usually is by organization segment (division, plant, or department) and by type of cost.[1]

(continued on page 14-19)

---

[1] See James D. Willson, *Budgeting and Profit Planning Manual* (Boston: Warren, Gorham & Lamont, Inc., 1983), chs. 11–13, for detailed examples.

THE JONES COMPANY
PLASTICS DIVISION SELLING EXPENSES BY DISTRICT
(dollars in thousands)

	June 19X6			Year to Date			Actual Expenses as Percentage of Sales
	Actual	Budget	(Over)/Under Budget	Actual	Budget	(Over)/Under Budget	
Atlanta	$ 64.00	$ 48.00	$(16.00)	$ 450.80	$ 360.00	$ (90.80)(a)	23%
Cleveland	72.60	80.00	7.40	394.00	500.00	106.00	20
Detroit	101.50	117.50	16.00	525.20	700.00	174.80(b)	26
Houston	21.00	20.00	(1.00)	129.60	164.00	34.40	18
Minneapolis	124.20	134.20	10.00	948.00	720.00	(228.00)(c)	24
New York	159.70	154.80	(4.90)	958.80	1,178.00	219.20(d)	17
Philadelphia	108.00	108.00		882.00	820.00	(62.00)	20
Salt Lake City	27.00	28.00	1.00	279.30	280.00	.70	19
San Francisco	39.00	37.50	(1.50)	427.50	430.00	2.50	15
Seattle	80.60	79.80	(.80)	256.50	646.00	389.50(e)	19
Total	$797.60	$807.80	$ 10.20	$5,251.70	$5,798.00	$ 546.30	20%

(a) Regional industry meeting, unplanned = $72.50.
(b) Commissions on sales not made = $156.00.
(c) Dealer sales meeting in May instead of July = $215.00.
(d) More entertainment needed.
(e) Apollo strike (e.g., no calls).

FIG. 14-11 Selling Expenses by District

THE JONES COMPANY
DISTRICT SELLING EXPENSES, MINNEAPOLIS

	June 19X6			Year to Date		
	Actual	Budget	(Over)/Under Budget	Actual	Budget	(Over)/Under Budget
Salaries and wages	$ 69,300	$ 69,300		$340,000	$340,000	
Commissions	11,000	12,200	$ 1,200	79,000	72,000	$ (7,000)
Payroll taxes and insurance	17,666	17,930	264	92,180	90,640	(1,540)
Fringe benefits	16,060	16,300	240	83,800	82,400	(1,400)
Travel	3,000	5,000	2,000	24,300	30,000	5,700
Entertainment	2,000	6,100	4,100	67,400	40,000	(27,400)[a]
Sales promotion		1,200	1,200	226,590	27,520	(199,070)[b]
Rent	2,500	2,500		15,000	15,000	
Supplies	1,900	2,400	500	14,100	15,000	900
Depreciation	240	240		1,440	1,440	
Miscellaneous	534	1,030	496	4,190	6,000	1,810
Total	$124,200	$134,200	$10,030	$948,000	$720,000	$(228,000)

(a) Expenditures on customer GM = $21,800.
(b) Dealer sales meeting in May = $215,000; July budget = $225,000.

FIG. 14-12 District Selling Expenses by Type of Expenditure

TYPICAL MANUFACTURING MANAGEMENT INFORMATION NEEDS

PLANNING

Long-term
- Manufacturing capacity
- Capital equipment needs
- Unit manufacturing costs, including trends
  - By product
  - By plant
  - Compared to competition

Short-term

Material
- Requirements (usage)
- Purchases
- Inventory levels
- Unit costs, by product
- Price data
- Scrap and spoilage data
- Economical order quantity

Labor
- Requirements (schedule)
  - By department
  - By product
  - By process
- Costs
- Unit costs
  - By operation
  - By department
  - By product
- Rate data

Overhead
- Planning budget
  - By department
  - By type of expense
  - By product or process

Capital budget
- Requirements—commitments and expenditures
- Return on investment

CONTROL

Material
- Inventory levels—actual vs. plan
- Price variance
- Usage variance
- Design change data—costs

FIG. 14-13 Typical Manufacturing Manager's Information Needs

Labor
- Unit costs—actual vs. plan
- Rate variances
  —By responsibility
- Usage variance
  —By responsibility
- [*Other data*]

Expenses
- Actual vs. budget
  —By department
  —By type of expense
- Maintenance (actual vs. budget)
  —By cause
  —[*Other data*]

Capital
- Actual vs. budget
- Planned return vs. experienced

SPECIAL ANALYSES
- Break-even points
  —By plant
  —By product
- Trend of costs and expenses
- Make-or-buy analyses
- Items such as inventory losses and carrying costs
- Comparative scenarios
  —Depreciation methods
  —Maintenance schedules
  —Changed processes or design
- Idle capacity

FIG. 14-13 (*cont'd*)

Typical control reports may compare actual and planned costs by type of cost and by organization segment. Thus, the overall summary may be by plant. This is supported by a comparable, more detailed report for each plant that identifies the actual versus budget performance for each department in each plant, as shown in Figure 14-14. Continuing the responsibility reporting concept is a departmental budget report providing detail by type of expense. Figure 14-15 summarizes the fabrication department's cost performance, with the emphasis on manufacturing expenses.

The manufacturing manager is concerned not only with hourly, daily, weekly, or monthly performance but with trends. Further, his office (or chart room) is likely to contain charts showing performance over a period of time.

(*continued on page 14-23*)

THE METAL STAMPING COMPANY
CLEVELAND PLANT
MONTHLY SUMMARY OF MANUFACTURING COSTS, April 19X6

Department	Direct Labor			Direct Material			Manufacturing Expense			Total		(Over)/Under Budget	
	Budget	Actual	(Over)/Under Budget	Budget	Actual	(Over)/Under Budget	Budget	Actual	(Over)/Under Budget	Budget	Actual	Amount	Percentage
Fabrication	$ 500,000	$ 519,500	$(19,500)	$1,250,000	$1,234,700	$15,300	$ 652,680	$ 654,530	$(1,850)	$2,402,680	$2,408,730	$ (6,050)	0.3%
Subassembly	272,400	259,411	12,989	472,300	470,610	1,690	209,870	216,811	(6,941)	954,570	946,832	7,738	1.0
Assembly	147,900	141,810	6,090	812,500	817,360	(4,860)	113,630	108,212	5,418	1,074,030	1,067,382	6,648	0.1
Polishing	78,300	79,212	(912)	49,800	48,620	1,180	39,810	36,114	3,696	167,910	163,946	3,964	2.0
Grinding	44,610	44,600	10	37,100	36,840	260	29,450	29,410	40	111,160	110,850	310	0.1
Contouring	22,300	20,740	1,560	41,800	42,470	(670)	16,860	17,827	(967)	80,960	81,037	(77)	0.1
Painting	64,380	56,920	7,460	341,300	320,980	20,320	71,300	75,840	(4,540)	476,980	453,740	23,240	5.0
Total	$1,129,890	$1,122,193	$ 7,697	$3,004,800	$2,971,580	$33,220	$1,133,600	$1,138,744	$(5,144)	$5,268,290	$5,232,517	$35,773	.67%

FIG. 14-14 Actual vs. Budget Performance by Department

THE METAL STAMPING COMPANY
FABRICATION DEPARTMENT BUDGET* REPORT

	April 19X6			Year to Date		
	Budget	Actual	(Over)/Under Budget	Budget	Actual	(Over)/Under Budget
Direct labor	$ 500,000	$ 519,500	$(19,500)	$1,940,000	$1,914,700	$ 25,300[a]
Direct material	1,250,000	1,234,700	15,300	4,730,800	4,741,600	(10,800)[b]
Manufacturing expenses						
Supervision	$ 82,000	$ 82,000		$ 328,000	$ 328,000	
Salaries, other	27,000	26,500	$ 500	108,000	105,100	$ 2,900
Payroll taxes and insurance	126,480	131,880	(5,400)	498,960	493,038	5,922
Fringe benefits	182,700	188,400	(5,700)	870,900	868,686	2,214
Repairs and maintenance	75,000	71,300	3,700	250,000	237,412	12,585
Supplies	62,500	57,850	4,650	250,000	234,500	15,500
Power	47,000	46,600	400	192,000	190,100	1,900
Depreciation	50,000	50,000		200,000	200,000	
Total	$ 652,680	$ 654,530	$ (1,850)	$2,697,860	$2,656,836	$ 41,024
TOTAL DEPARTMENTAL COSTS	$2,402,680	$2,408,730	$ (6,050)	$9,368,660	$9,313,136	$ 55,524

* Budget base = 246,000 standard machine-hours
(a) Reflects favorable long run on Model 117
(b) Effect of no incoming inspection in March

FIG. 14-15 Departmental Budget Report

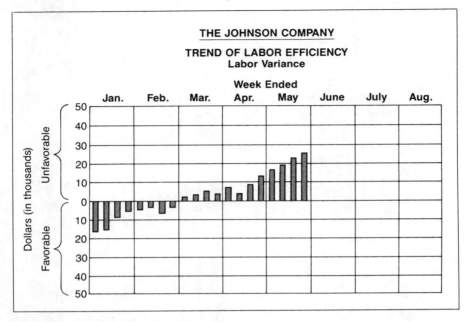

FIG. 14-16 Graph of Labor Efficiency Trend

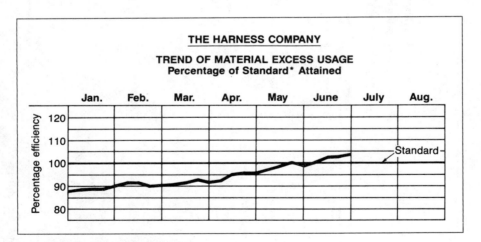

FIG. 14-17 Graph of Material Usage Trend

FINANCIAL REPORTS FOR NONFINANCIAL MANAGEMENT 14-23

THE PLASTICS COMPANY
MANUFACTURING DIVISION EXPENSE SUMMARY
(dollars in thousands)

	March 19X6			Year to Date		
Department	Budget	Actual	(Over)/ Under Budget	Budget	Actual	(Over)/ Under Budget
Manufacturing	$1,670.0	$1,712.5	$(42.5)[a]	$4,840.0	$4,912.3	$(72.3)[a]
Design engineering	220.0	227.4	(7.4)	650.0	649.1	.9
Industrial engineering	155.0	149.7	5.3	450.0	441.4	8.6
Material control	180.0	185.2	(5.2)	520.0	502.6	17.4[b]
Scheduling	59.0	57.0	2.0	170.0	173.8	(3.8)
Quality control	48.0	44.1	3.9	130.0	128.2	1.8
Shipping	81.0	87.3	(6.3)	220.0	230.5	(10.5)
Total	$2,413.0	$2,463.2	$(50.2)	$6,980.0	$7,037.9	$(57.9)

(a) Continuing impact of defective tooling
(b) New system

FIG. 14-18 Manufacturing Overhead Summary by Department

Figures 14-16 and 14-17 illustrate graphs on the trend of labor efficiency and material excess usage, respectively.

Control of manufacturing expenses often is a point of emphasis because of the many difficulties experienced in this area. Figure 14-18 illustrates a summary of manufacturing expenses by department. This summary is usually supported by a department report showing budget performance by type of expense.

Proceeding down the organization chart, middle- and lower-echelon managers usually want reports on their activities in more detailed form, and often more frequently (maybe hourly) than the higher-echelon managers. Illustrated are the following excerpts from a reporting system.

- *Material price variance (monthly) by material classification* — Figure 14-19

- *Daily excess material usage by type of material* — Figure 14-20

- *Changes in the unit material standard cost (monthly)* — Figure 14-21

- *A daily labor report, identifying actual and standard hours, by department* — Figure 14-22 (a representative computer application)

- *An exception report showing off-standard operators and the cause of such performance* — Figure 14-23

(continued on page 14-29)

THE NORRIS MANUFACTURING COMPANY
SUMMARY OF MATERIAL PRICE VARIANCE
March 19XX and Year-to-Date
(dollars in thousands)

Material Classification	Month			Year-to-Date		
	Standard Cost of Receipts	Price Variance	Percentage to Standard	Standard Cost of Receipts	Price Variance	Percentage to Standard
Sheet steel	$1,420	$35.5	2.50%	$ 5,211	$104.2	2.00%
Steel wire	762	5.3	.70	2,406	24.1	1.00
Sheet aluminum	1,946	21.4	1.10	6,712	100.7	1.50
Copper wire	173	(10.4)	(6.00)	541	2.7	.50
Coatings	111	1.1	1.00	210	3.6	1.70
Insulation	243	5.3	2.20	704	21.1	3.00
Paints	710	(24.9)	(3.50)	1,842	(46.1)	(2.50)
Cleaners	86	1.4	1.60	196	2.0	1.00
Miscellaneous	41	.8	.20	97	.9	.90
Total	$5,492	$35.5	.64%	$17,919	$213.2	1.19%

( ) Favorable variance

FIG. 14-19 Material Price Variance (Monthly) by Material Classification (Source: James D. Willson, *Budgeting and Profit Planning Manual* (Boston: Warren, Gorham & Lamont, 1983), ch. 12. Reprinted by permission.)

THE NEW MACHINE SHOP
EXCESS MATERIAL VARIANCES

Date 6/5/19XX

Dept. No. 6
Supervisor _____

Material Used	Quantity of Finished Production	Actual Quantity Material Used	Standard Quantity	Quantity Variance	Unit Cost	Cost Variance	Comments
R	1,240	1,297	1,240	57	$16.00	$ 912	Careless workmanship
S	630	1,342	1,260	82	7.00	574	Machine 12 needs repair
T	900	2,816	2,700	116	1.00	116	Material quality below standard
U	2,100	2,103	2,100	3	3.00	9	
V	310	610	620	(10)	12.00	(120)	Operator Johnson changed speed
Total						$1,491	

FIG. 14-20 Daily Excess Material Usage by Type of Material (Source: James D. Willson, *Budgeting and Profit Planning Manual* (Boston: Warren, Gorham & Lamont, 1983), ch. 12. Reprinted by permission.)

THE ROCKET MFG. CO.
STATEMENT OF UNIT STANDARD MATERIAL COSTS—PRODUCT 4
For the Month of May, 19XX

Item	Standard Cost 4/30/XX	Changes Increases	Changes Decreases	Standard Cost 5/31/XX
Motor	$ 3,840.40	$112.00		$ 3,952.40
Sheet aluminum	876.00	—		876.00
Copper tubing	107.50	—	$ 1.40	106.10
Instruments	8,104.70	57.90		8,162.60
Fasteners	12.70	—		12.70
Electronic gear	1,016.10	70.00		1,086.10
Stabilizer	309.10	15.20		324.30
Composites	201.40	—	17.30	184.10
Small steel parts	81.10	—		81.10
Fuel	119.60	—		119.60
Miscellaneous	41.03	—		41.03
Total	$14,709.63	$255.10	$18.70	$14,946.03

FIG. 14-21 Changes in Unit Material Standard Cost (Source: James D. Willson, *Budgeting and Profit Planning Manual* (Boston: Warren, Gorham & Lamont, 1983), ch. 12. Reprinted by permission.)

DAILY LABOR REPORT, SAN JOSE PLANT
Period Ending 4:00 P.M. May 17, 19X6

Department	Hours Actual	Hours Standard	(Over)/Under Standard	Percentage of Standard
Fabrication	12,816	12,610	(206)	102%
Subassembly	4,704	4,806	102	98
Assembly	4,612	4,507	(105)	102
Polishing	2,097	1,541	(556)	136
Grinding	1,413	1,423	10	99
Contouring	798	847	49	94
Painting	1,736	1,942	206	89
Total or average	28,176	27,676	(501)	102%

FIG. 14-22 Daily Labor Report

THE BEVERLY CENTER
DAILY LABOR REPORT
March 17, 19X6

Center: Contouring
Foreman: Smith

		Labor Cost			
No.	Name	Actual	Standard	Over/(Under) Standard	Reason for Off-Standard Performance
1420	Johnson	$ 161.80	$ 142.30	$ 19.50	Faulty die
1444	Adams	147.30	111.15	36.15	Nonstandard parts
1472	Kamiski	152.19	120.10	32.09	New jig
1481	Wilson	143.12	132.00	11.12	Operator error
1487	Mordy	156.80	125.50	31.30	Waiting time for materials
1491	Okada	162.20	140.20	22.00	Accident
	Total off standard	$ 923.41	$ 771.25	$152.16	
	On standard or better	8,420.62	8,440.20	(19.58)	
	TOTAL	$9,344.03	$9,211.45	$132.58	
		Today	Average Last Week		
	Percentage of standard	101%	103%		

FIG. 14-23 Exception Report

THE MANUFACTURING COMPANY
MANUFACTURING DIVISION CAPITAL BUDGET STATUS REPORT
As of June 30, 19X6

	Work Order Number	Estimated Completion Date	Actual Costs Incurred to Date	Outstanding Commitments	Estimated Cost to Complete	Indicated Final Cost	Original Estimate	(Over)/Under Original Estimate
San Jose plant								
Conveyor system	246	8/14	$ 246,100	45,300	$ 60,000	$ 351,400	$ 350,000	$ (1,400)
Dump trucks	251	7/25	99,000	5,600		104,600	108,000	3,400
Miscellaneous	299		12,360	2,440		14,800	15,000	200
Total			$ 357,460	53,340	$ 60,000	$ 470,800	$ 473,000	$ 2,200
Los Angeles plant								
Quality control lab	407	9/10	396,150	119,430	$ 30,000	$ 545,580	$ 550,000	$ 4,420
Profiling machines	424	7/31	897,800	426,590	112,000	1,436,390	1,500,000	63,610
Welding robots	427	8/15	489,760	310,000	100,000	899,760	890,000	(9,760)
Transportation equipment	430	7/10	107,000	14,350		121,350	110,000	(11,350)
Miscellaneous	499		41,410	10,030		51,440	55,000	3,560
Total			$1,932,120	880,400	$242,000	$3,054,520	$3,105,000	$50,480
TOTAL			$2,289,580	933,740	$302,000	$3,525,320	$3,578,000	$52,680

FIG. 14-24 Capital Budget Status Report—Manufacturing Division

FINANCIAL REPORTS FOR NONFINANCIAL MANAGEMENT 14-29

Aside from operating matters, whether labor, material, or expenses, or machine utilization, the manufacturing manager is concerned with the capital, or plant and equipment, budget for his activities. One illustrative report compares costs incurred to date, plus estimated cost to complete, with the budget authorization for each major piece of equipment (by responsibility, as in each plant). A suggested format is shown in Figure 14-24.

REPORTS FOR THE R&D MANAGER

Another major functional manager who may have a significant impact on the long-term growth of an enterprise is the director or vice-president in charge of R&D activities. To be sure, part of his responsibility is to conduct operations efficiently and within budget. However, an even greater obligation may be to originate R&D in those areas, or on projects, that offer the greatest promise of reward.

Many of his reporting needs are likely to be in subjective areas related to products and processes, competition, or state of the art, and are unrelated to the FIS. There is, however, a need for some limited financial reports. Thus, as in reports for other managers, actual and budgeted expenses must be known by department managers responsible and by types of expenses; but perhaps a more significant report relates to projects. The amounts spent on particular projects or programs must be planned within reasonable bounds, relate to expected rewards (or else why spend funds?), and generally kept within budget.

Illustrative Report Examples

Some of the reports are of the same generic type needed by all major executives. Thus, planning reports provide in reasonable detail, by department, and by type of expense, expenses expected to be incurred during the plan year—as compared to the prior year or other appropriate yardsticks (e.g., percentage of sales). In addition, such plans normally disclose expenditures by project.

With respect to control, budgeted and actual expenses by department are periodically compared. A typical format is that shown in Figure 14-25. Such a summary by department is supported by detailed statements of expenses by type and for each department (with notes regarding the cause of the departure from budget), as illustrated in Figure 14-26. However, a key report is a project status report. Figure 14-27 depicts a project budget report that includes these features:

THE CALIFORNIA COMPANY
R&D EXPENSE SUMMARY BY DEPARTMENT
(dollars in thousands)

	May 19X6			Year to Date		
	Actual	Budget	(Over)/Under Budget	Actual	Budget	(Over)/Under Budget
Research						
Optic fibers	$115.30	$110.60	$ (4.70)	$ 412.70	$ 500.00	$ 87.30
Gas lasers	44.70	49.50	4.80	291.40	275.00	(16.40)
Selenium	22.00	22.30	.30	75.10	75.00	(.10)
Total	$182.00	$182.40	$ .40	$ 779.20	$ 850.00	$ 70.80
Development						
Computer	$272.90	$250.00	$(22.90)	$1,214.30	$1,200.00	$(14.30)
Traveling nave tube	87.00	79.00	(8.00)	261.00	250.00	(11.00)
Heat resistors	57.00	62.00	5.00	164.60	180.00	15.40
Total	$416.90	$391.00	$(25.90)	$1,639.90	$1,630.00	$ (9.90)
Other						
Library	$ 22.30	$ 25.00	$ 2.70	$ 119.00	$ 125.00	$ 6.00
Pilot plant	44.50	50.00	5.50	184.50	200.00	15.50
Underwater lab	94.30	75.00	(19.30)	307.00	300.00	(7.00)
General and administration	93.50	100.00	6.50	379.00	400.00	21.00
Total	$254.60	$250.00	$ (4.60)	$ 989.50	$1,025.00	$ 35.50
TOTAL	$853.50	$823.40	$(30.10)	$3,408.60	$3,505.00	$ 96.40

FIG. 14-25 R&D Expense Budget by Department

- Man-hours spent to date on the project and those required to complete it
- Actual cost recorded to date, by project (with salaries, usually the major component of R&D, identified separately)
- Commitments made and not yet accrued or paid
- Estimated expenses to complete the project
- Updated indicated final project cost as compared with the budget

Such a report may serve as the basis for oral or written commentary on each project—the results to date and prospects for successful conclusion (e.g., new product or process).

THE CALIFORNIA COMPANY
COMPUTER DEPARTMENT R&D BUDGET REPORT
(dollars in thousands)

	May			Year to Date		
	Actual	Budget	(Over)/Under Budget	Actual	Budget	(Over)/Under Budget
Salaries and wages	$ 92.50	$ 90.00	$ (2.50)(a)	$ 380.00	$ 380.00	
Payroll taxes and insurance	20.35	19.80	(.55)	83.60	83.60	
Fringe benefits	27.75	27.00	(.75)	114.00	114.00	
Travel	22.40	17.00	(5.40)(b)	115.20	110.00	$ (5.20)
Seminars	6.35	7.00	.65	37.50	35.00	(2.50)
Supplies	21.30	19.20	(2.10)	109.60	107.00	(2.60)
Postage	14.60	12.00	(2.60)	61.00	60.00	(1.00)
Communications	19.50	15.00	(4.50)(c)	78.40	80.00	1.60
Cartons and containers	15.20	10.40	(4.80)(d)	67.00	65.00	(2.00)
Depreciation	30.00	30.00		150.00	150.00	
Other	2.95	2.60	(.35)	18.00	15.40	(2.60)
Total	$272.90	$250.00	$(22.90)	$1,214.30	$1,200.00	$(14.30)

(a) Overtime on IBM project
(b) Manager's trip to Paris
(c) Largely to Tokyo affiliate
(d) Original plan unacceptable to customers

FIG. 14-26 R&D Expense Report by Department

GENERAL AND ADMINISTRATIVE ACTIVITIES

In most firms, the activities incurring general and administrative expenses relate to the costs of top-management functions that determine the company's mission or purpose, the strategic planning, and the overall direction of current activities. Included are general expenses related to such executives as the CEO, president, CFO, legal officer, public relations officer, industrial relations manager, long-range planning officer, and a host of related management activities.

Each functional group of expenses ordinarily must be planned and controlled on a responsibility basis. The expenses include most departments' normal operating expenses (e.g., salaries and wages, fringe benefits, payroll taxes and insurance, travel and entertainment, supplies, and communications). In addition to these usual expenses are those unique to the various functions, including such items as expenses for:

THE PHENOLIC CORPORATION, INC.
R&D PROJECT STATUS REPORT
Month Ended May 31, 19X6

No.	Project	Man-Hours	Month Salaries	Month Expenses	Month Total	Project Cumulative to Date Man-Hours	Project Cumulative to Date Cost	Open Commitments	Estimate to Complete Man-Hours	Estimate to Complete Cost	Indicated Final Cost	Project Budget	(Over)/Under Budget
New product research													
121	Quick-drying resin	470	$ 23,030	$ 16,121	$ 39,151	819	$ 70,220	$ 2,970	250	17,250	$ 90,440	$ 100,000	$ 9,560
122	Urea filler	932	41,940	30,196	72,136	2,116	163,790	41,220	500	38,700	243,710	240,000	(3,710)
127	Adhesive offset	512	24,064	15,641	39,705	870	67,567	19,800	200	15,510	102,877	80,000	(22,877)
128	"Moon Beam"	1,060	54,060	42,545	96,605	3,410	314,777	262,000	12,500	1,139,210	1,715,987	1,500,000	(215,987)
	Total	2,974	$143,094	$104,503	$247,597	7,215	$616,354	$325,990	13,450	$1,210,670	$2,153,014	$1,920,000	$(233,014)
Product improvement													
156	Alkyd Resin 601	530	$ 22,260	$ 14,469	$ 36,729	612	$ 40,411	$ 650	150	10,400	$ 53,461	$ 60,000	$ 6,539
162	3M Adhesive 419	210	8,400	6,048	14,448	320	22,116	8,150	300	20,700	50,966	50,000	(966)
168	Wet Strength Resin 019	417	17,514	11,384	28,898	871	62,360	14,500	700	50,000	126,860	150,000	23,140
169	Emulsifier 201	615	34,440	25,141	59,581	615	59,581	5,000	900	87,200	151,781	150,000	(1,781)
	Total	1,772	$ 82,614	$ 57,042	$139,656	2,418	$186,468	$ 28,300	2,050	$ 168,300	$ 383,068	$ 410,000	$ 26,932
Other													
310	Manufacturing	210	$ 8,400	$ 5,880	$ 14,280	430	$ 32,410		600	45,200	$ 77,610	$ 80,000	$ 2,390
320	Sales service	340	13,600	8,840	22,440	717	47,322		1,200	80,000	127,322	125,000	(2,322)
	Total	550	$ 22,000	$ 14,720	$ 36,720	1,147	79,732		1,800	$ 125,200	$ 204,932	205,000	68
	TOTAL	5,296	$247,708	$176,265	$423,973	10,780	$882,554	$354,290	17,300	$1,504,170	$2,741,014	$2,535,000	$(206,014)

FIG. 14-27 R&D Project Budget Report

- Litigation
- Charitable contributions
- Incentive payments
- Provision for contingencies
- Annual and quarterly reports to shareholders
- Corporate expenses of registration

The basic tasks for each functional manager are to:

1 Plan the expenses in a reasonable relationship to the tasks to be performed and/or net sales, income before taxes, and prior-year costs.
2 Control such expenses within limits, usually on a budget basis.

These expenses differ from other functional expenses chiefly in that the executives may exercise more latitude in what is spent and the reasonable level is more subjective. The method of planning and control is really not too different from that of the other functions.

Illustrative Report Examples

Planning reports should be prepared on a responsibility basis. One such summary, which indicates the prior-year budget and actual expenses by functional group and the proposed budget, is shown in Figure 14-28. Each line item is supported by departmental or segment breakdown (see Figure 14-29) and by a departmental budget by type of expense.

Control reporting consists principally of comparing actual and budgeted expenses by type of expense, as illustrated in Figure 14-30. It should be noted that, in this example, normal operating costs are segregated from special expenses.

SPECIAL ANALYSES

The reports illustrated in this chapter represent the category of report that may be called recurring. They are issued periodically, whether annually, quarterly, monthly, weekly, or daily. Of course, as problems develop, the frequency may change. The manager may want data formerly received on a monthly basis to be issued on a weekly basis. The timetable may revert to the former schedule when the matter is resolved.

These types of reports cover only some of the needs of functional managers, to whom the CFO is in a position to render valuable assistance by providing special analytical reports. These are required when special problems or conditions develop, or are anticipated. The data useful in decision making simply are not contained in the regular reports.

GENERAL AND ADMINISTRATIVE BUDGET FOR 19XX
Functional Group Summary
(thousands of dollars)

	Prior Year				Proposed Budget		
			Over/(Under) Budget			Increase/(Decrease) From Prior Year Budget	
Group	Budget	Actual	Amount	Percentage	Request	Amount	Percentage
Executive office	$ 8,200	$ 7,700	($ 500)	(6%)	$ 8,500	$ 300	4%
Legal department	3,400	3,300	(100)	(3)	3,500	100	3
Administration and services	5,800	6,200	400	7	7,600	1,800	24
Corporate planning	500	600	100	20	700	200	29
Finance	5,300	4,700	(600)	(11)	5,200	(100)	(2)
Industrial relations	2,800	3,100	300	11	3,700	900	24
Public relations and advertising	3,600	3,400	(200)	6	3,500	(100)	(3)
International marketing	4,900	4,700	(200)	(4)	5,100	200	4
Domestic marketing and technology	5,700	5,400	(300)	(5)	5,300	(400)	(8)
Total	$40,200	$39,100	($1,100)	(3%)	$43,100	$2,900	7%

FIG. 14-28 Summary of General and Administrative Expense—Planning Budget (Source: James D. Willson, *Budgeting and Profit Planning Manual* (Boston: Warren, Gorham & Lamont, 1983), ch. 18. Reprinted by permission.)

GENERAL AND ADMINISTRATIVE BUDGET FOR 19XX
Finance Department Summary
(thousands of dollars)

| | Prior Year | | | | | Proposed Budget | | |
| | | | Over/(Under) Budget | | | | Increase/(Decrease) From Prior Year Budget | |
Unit	Budget	Actual	Amount	Percentage		Request	Amount	Percentage
Vice-president	$ 375	$ 360	($ 15)	(4%)		$ 375	—	—
Controller	1,600	1,260	(340)	(21)		1,500	($100)	(7%)
Treasurer	1,160	940	(220)	(19)		980	(180)	(18)
Tax department	825	850	25	3		910	85	9
Risk management	240	230	(10)	(4)		270	30	11
Internal audit	925	825	(100)	(11)		965	40	4
Business analysis	175	235	60	34		200	25	13
Total	$5,300	$4,700	($600)	(11%)		$5,200	($100)	(2%)

FIG. 14-29 Budget Summary—Finance Department (Source: James D. Willson, *Budgeting and Profit Planning Manual* (Boston: Warren, Gorham & Lamont, 1983), ch. 18. Reprinted by permission.)

THE SERVICE COMPANY
BUDGET REPORT, OFFICE OF THE CORPORATE SECRETARY

	March 19X6			Year to Date		
	Actual	Budget	(Over)/ Under Budget	Actual	Budget	(Over)/ Under Budget
Operating expenses						
Salaries and wages	$110,000	$112,000	$ 2,000	$330,000	$336,000	$ 6,000
Payroll taxes and insurance	24,200	24,640	440	72,600	73,920	1,320
Fringe benefits	33,000	33,600	600	99,000	100,800	1,800
Travel	1,400	2,000	600	7,790	7,000	(790)
Supplies	1,262	1,000	(262)	3,820	4,000	180
Postage	1,870	2,000	130	7,012	6,000	(1,012)
Communications	3,407	2,500	(907)	8,107	7,500	(607)
Miscellaneous	860	1,500	640	3,940	4,000	60
Total	$175,999	$179,240	$ 3,241	$532,269	$539,220	$ 6,951
Special expenses						
Director, fees and expenses	$ 25,000	$ 25,000		$ 25,000	$ 25,000	
Annual report	94,300	90,000	$(4,300)	107,480	100,000	(7,480)
Consultants	4,500	5,000	500	6,000	5,000	(1,000)
Total	$123,800	$120,000	$(3,800)	$138,480	$130,000	$(8,480)
TOTAL	$299,799	$299,240	$ (559)	$670,749	$669,220	$(1,529)

FIG. 14-30 Budget Performance Report—Administrative Department

Examples of subjects that might be covered by these special types of reports include such matters as:

- *Sales returns* — by cause
- *Advertising and sales promotion expense* — trend as related to competition or segment sales (the relevant territory and product)
- *Inventory losses* — by cause
- *Salaries and wages* — trends as related to total costs
- *Conversion costs (labor and overhead)* — as related to price of the product
- *Fringe benefits (vacation, sick pay, holidays, life insurance) costs* — as related to basic compensation

- *Distribution costs* — analyses and subanalyses (other than the usual) related to size of order, method of delivery, and channel of distribution
- *R&D expenses* — as related to competition and to sales and margin of the products developed, as well as other factors

The need for the information arises when special problems occur.

In designing FISs, consideration should be given to the extent of detailed input that should be provided as measured by the probable need or use of the data and the cost of making them available. What building blocks or cuts of data may be required? Not all probable needs can be foreseen. However, discussions with the functional managers may provide important clues. Perhaps information may be provided through the system to a particular level of detail, at which point further added manual analysis may be needed.

CHAPTER **15**

Computer-Based Financial Modeling

Jan Hartman

Definition of Financial Modeling 2

The Need for Financial Modeling 2
Planning and Scheduling Business
   Resources 2
Interrelated Impact of Poor Decisions on
   an Organization 3
External Regulations and Requirements .. 3

**The Process of Designing a Financial
Model** 3
Identify Key Issues to Be Addressed by
   the Model 4
Establish Report and Data Requirements . 4
Develop Model Specifications 4
Select the Appropriate Financial Planning
   Software 5
Develop and Implement the Model 5
Prepare Documentation 6
Execute Model and Analyze Key Factors . 6

**Overview of Selected Modeling
Techniques** 6
"What-If" Analysis 6
Naïve Forecasting 6
Univariate Analysis 9
Multiple Regression 9
Sensitivity Analysis 9
Goal-Seeking Analysis 10
Optimization 10
Risk Analysis 10

**Selection of Financial Modeling Software
Packages** 11

Microcomputer-Based Financial Modeling
   Packages 11
   Micro DSS/F 12
   Lotus 1-2-3 12
   Symphony 12
   Multiplan 13
   Context MBA 13
   Corporate MBA 14
   MicroFCS 14
   IFPS/Personal 14
   Encore! 15
   SuperCalc^3 15
   T/Maker III 15
Mainframe or Minicomputer-Based
   Financial Modeling Packages 16
   FCS-EPS 16
   IFPS (Interactive Financial Planning
     System) 16
   Focus Financial Modeling Language 17
   Impact 17
   MSA/Forecasting and Modeling
     System 17
   Summary 17

**Design and Documentation Guidelines for
Financial Models** 18

**Future Developments for Computer-Based
Financial Modeling** 19

References 19

Fig. 15-1 Modeling Technique Overview 7

DEFINITION OF FINANCIAL MODELING

Financial or corporate modeling is a tool to aid professionals in decision making. It provides management with the information necessary for planning and controlling the organization. Through financial modeling, the decision maker can evaluate a wide variety of alternatives and perform "what-if" scenarios. In our present age of technology, financial modeling is usually considered to be a computer-based program that forecasts the financial performance of an organization or business unit, given selected data.

The equations and mathematical formulas of a model and its associated data are stored in the computer. Some complex models need to be developed by computer programmers using a detailed set of instructions that the computer understands. However, more and more user-friendly financial modeling software packages, or programs, are becoming available to managers and financial planners. Most financial modeling packages are matrix- or spreadsheet-oriented; however, some are structured with English-based commands or instructions that require some programming ability. In addition, many of these financial modeling packages are now available for microcomputers; until recently, they were accessible only through large mainframe or minicomputer environments.

THE NEED FOR FINANCIAL MODELING

Any organization that has established goals and objectives and strives to attain them usually needs planning and decision-making tools. Since the 1970s, management has become more scientific in its dealings with the business environment and less dependent on chance. There are now literally hundreds of financial modeling software packages in the marketplace. These products range from the simplest microcomputer-based spreadsheet packages to the most complex artificial intelligence systems. Many critical decisions that must be addressed by management can be made much more easily and accurately with the results from financial modeling tools.

Planning and Scheduling Business Resources

As the economy becomes more complex, most businesses require greater accuracy in planning and scheduling business resources for short-, medium-, and long-term periods. Financial modeling can be used to (1) assess future economic and business environments and schedule existing resources, (2) plan for the acquisition of additional resources, or (3) determine if and what resources are appropriate. The scheduling of production, transportation, cash, or other material or financing must often be performed before the actual volume or level of demand for that resource is known. To make efficient use of existing

COMPUTER-BASED FINANCIAL MODELING

resources, decision-making tools are necessary for proper planning and scheduling functions.

In addition, planning functions may involve pulling standardized statistical information from large volumes of data. In many cases, organizations must assess a representative value for a large group of data for tax or other financial reporting, requiring statistical functions such as means, medians, modes, standard deviations, or variances. Computerized financial modeling is a useful tool for performing these formerly time-intensive manual functions.

Interrelated Impact of Poor Decisions on an Organization

Because of the complex nature of most businesses and the interrelationship of functions, a poor decision in one department or division may adversely affect the entire organization. Therefore, there is a great interdependency among forecasts from different departments and divisions. As an example, inaccuracies in sales projections may directly affect budget departmental operating plans, cash flows, inventory stock levels, and more. A domino effect occurs as these factors then affect other projections such as funds for product development or the department's or organization's staffing level. Obviously, there is a strong need for accurate planning data at every step of the process.

External Regulations and Requirements

Most corporations are faced with federal and state regulations that also affect corporate decisions or reflect required changes in financial reporting. Promulgations by the Internal Revenue Service, Securities and Exchange Commission, or Federal Trade Commission fall into this category. It is usually in a firm's best interest to use some form of computerized financial modeling for its financial projections. Considering investment tax credit implications is just one example of the need for and positive impact of financial modeling.

THE PROCESS OF DESIGNING A FINANCIAL MODEL

The process of financial modeling involves the following seven steps:

1 Identify key issues to be addressed by the model.
2 Establish report and data requirements.
3 Develop model specifications.
4 Select the appropriate financial planning software.
5 Develop and implement the model.
6 Prepare documentation.
7 Execute the model and analyze key factors.

Identify Key Issues to Be Addressed by the Model

The financial modeler must first evaluate the key issues that need to be addressed by the model and ask, What information is needed and why? This is the most critical step in the process. All necessary planning and scheduling decisions should be considered. Any type of "what-if" analysis that must be performed once the model has been developed should also be evaluated. An example of a typical "what-if" question might be, What will be the impact on net income if sales projections in the Western Region are 25 percent below expected values? Obtaining information on planning decisions to be made and various alternatives ("what-if's") requires interviewing key management and planning executives. Other issues that should be addressed are (1) what is the desired flexibility of the model, (2) who are its ultimate users, and (3) what is its continued use versus one-time application?

Establish Report and Data Requirements

The next step in financial modeling involves defining report and data specifications and procuring the data. The modeler should determine if any special report formats other than the standard financial statements are required. If so, he needs to determine the level of detail required by the report(s). This is based on the user's needs. Top-level decision makers, middle management, or other line managers each have different detail requirements. Once the report specifications have been analyzed and decided upon, the data requirements and specifications should be established. In addition, the data requirements should match all key issues addressed in the first step. The modeler should also determine the format of the data for input (e.g., percentages, millions of dollars) and any conversion efforts that might be necessary. Finally, he should address the requirement of any graphics output.

Once the specifications have been determined, the data should be gathered and adjusted, if necessary, and entered into the computer in its proper format. Any required data verification should be performed at this point. In the case of spreadsheet applications, data input is performed at the time the model is developed.

Develop Model Specifications

Once the key issues have been determined and the data and report requirements developed, the modeler can then develop the model specifications. Any data conversion (for data coming from different sources in incompatible formats) required must be incorporated into the model. Sources of data should be considered (e.g., data needing to be extracted from any corporate or tax databases). If "what-if" analysis is to be performed, the model should be logically structured to accommodate this technique. All necessary calculations also must be determined. A list should be prepared of commonly used functions to be used in the model, such as depreciation, net present value, and internal rate of return.

Select the Appropriate Financial Planning Software

A further step in the financial modeling process is selecting the appropriate financial planning software. Once the report, data, and model specifications have been determined, various features of contending financial software need to be evaluated.

This is a very significant step in the process, since improper selection of software may leave the user with an inadequate or totally inappropriate tool for financial modeling. For example, suppose a planning professional requires a detailed financial model to consolidate financial data from multiple divisions, match that data with divisional and corporate goals, and determine the appropriate associated factors to achieve those desired results. Such a model may be developed with some difficulty by using one of the popular microcomputer-based spreadsheet packages; however, very sophisticated equations and manual consolidation efforts are required. For this type of sophisticated application, a financial modeling package that includes a modeling programming language is much more appropriate. There are languages available for modeling to assist in tailoring a model to the user's specific needs. If the model requires mostly "what-if" analysis with very limited, if any, special report formatting, the modeler may choose one of the popular microcomputer spreadsheet packages. Although inexpensive and valuable for offering many common statistical and financial functions, these packages do not offer the flexibility of complex programming logic. If the model requires more complex program logic or specialized modeling (such as sensitivity analysis or goal seeking), the modeler may want to evaluate a software product that provides a financial modeling language. Other considerations for selecting the appropriate package are the size and location of existing data files to be used in the model if consolidation is to be performed, packages previously used to create similar financial models, cost and availability of the package, and the modeler's computer skills. Many sophisticated financial modeling packages that require large computer environments are available through timesharing.

Develop and Implement the Model

Once all of the appropriate information has been gathered, the model can be developed. In the case of spreadsheet applications, the user will want to obtain a listing of the cell formulas periodically for debugging and documentation purposes. Programming logic will need to be tested.

Prepare Documentation

For larger, more complex modeling, documentation should be prepared at every step of the process where modeling issues or model variables are defined. In addition, the more complex the model, the greater the requirement for complete documentation (see the discussion of design and documentation guidelines for financial models elsewhere in this chapter).

Execute Model and Analyze Key Factors

The final step in designing a financial model involves executing the model and analyzing the results. The modeler can now evaluate the key issues addressed in the first step of the process. Results from a model do not constitute the decisions in themselves; they are only guides or tools for further management evaluation and analysis of these issues. The results presented by the model are only as valid as the model itself. If each step of the process has been followed with care and accuracy, chances are strong that the model will be a useful tool for the organization.

OVERVIEW OF SELECTED MODELING TECHNIQUES

This section discusses several modeling techniques currently used by organizations. Mathematical formulas and procedures are not presented, since the majority of these techniques are preprogrammed into most financial modeling software. Figure 15-1 provides a general overview of each of the techniques described here, as well as an example of their application.

"What-If" Analysis

"What-if" analysis is the capability of changing one or more decision factors or variables in a model and obtaining the recalculated results to the remaining variables. Microcomputer-based spreadsheet applications are perfect for these types of scenarios. The user is provided with a new set of results or outcomes from the model almost instantaneously after a value(s) in the model has been changed. It should be noted that response time—the time needed by the computer to recalculate the equations in the model and return the values to the screen—can vary depending on several factors, such as the size of the model and type of computer processor used.

Naïve Forecasting

Naïve forecasts are obtained through a minimal amount of data manipulation and modeling, and simply use the most recent data available as the future forecast. The data can also be adjusted for seasonality, expected growth, or some other business factor and used as the forecast. An example of naïve forecasting

Technique	Brief Description	Potential Software Available	Manpower Effort to Establish Model	Example
"What-if" analysis	Changing a variable's value and obtaining new results to remaining variables	■ Microprocessor spreadsheet packages ■ IFPS ■ DSS/F ■ FCS-EPS ■ Encore! ■ FOCUS ■ IFPS/Personal ■ Micro DSS/F ■ Micro FCS ■ PC FOCUS	Low–Medium	Changing cost of goods sold on income statement model and viewing effect on net income
Naïve forecasting	Using most recent value as future forecasted value or adjusting this value by some factor	■ All financial modeling packages or most hand calculators	Low	Projecting sales figures for next 5 years, based on 5% annual growth rate
Univariate analysis	Obtaining statistic describing one variable (e.g., mean, median, mode)	■ All financial modeling packages or some programmable calculators	Low	Determining average sales per month for a product
Multiple regression	Determining causal or explanatory relationships to variable of interest	■ IFPS ■ FCS-EPS ■ FOCUS ■ Encore!	Medium	Determining if products' purchasing patterns are based on age and income of consumer

(continued)

FIG. 15-1 Modeling Technique Overview

Technique	Brief Description	Potential Software Available	Manpower Effort to Establish Model	Example
Sensitivity analysis	Determining sensitive variable (variables causing significant changes in variable of interest through slight changes in these variables)—normally used in conjunction with regression or linear programming	■ MicroFCS ■ IFPS/Personal ■ FCS-EPS ■ IFPS ■ Encore!	Medium	Determining if ages and income are sensitive in estimating sales, and, if so, carefully estimating or obtaining values for these variables
Goal seeking	Presetting goal or variable of interest and determining values for all other variables from model	■ Micro DSS/F ■ MicroFCS ■ IFPS/Personal ■ Encore! ■ FOCUS ■ FCS-EPS ■ IFPS	Medium	Desiring net income to be a given value, and letting model solve for all associated values (e.g., sales transportation costs) required to meet this goal
Optimization	A technique to provide the most desirable solution (i.e., largest value if objective is to maximize, or the smallest value for minimization)	■ IFPS/Optimum	Medium	Letting model determine optimum level of net income that can be obtained, given model's constraints
Risk analysis	A technique allowing user to investigate loss potentials on risks associated with various outcomes for actions taken	■ FCS-EPS	Medium–High	Determining whether an oil company should drill for oil or lease the land, given various possible states of nature (e.g., occurrence of dry well or oil-producing well) and considering costs associated with drilling and producing oil from that well

FIG. 15-1 (cont'd)

for sales projections for the upcoming quarter is using last quarter's sales value of $4.5 million, multiplying the value by the expected quarterly growth rate of 5 percent, and adding it to the $4.5 million sales figure to obtain a sales projection of $4.73 million for the upcoming quarter.

Univariate Analysis

Univariate analysis includes any financial or statistical procedure that involves obtaining a representative value for data or observations pertaining to one variable. Examples of univariate statistics are means (also referred to as averages), medians, and modes, because only one variable is used in the calculation of these statistics. Regression is not considered univariate, because two or more variables are required to perform that function.

Multiple Regression

Multiple regression is a forecasting technique that provides results that hope to be causal or explanatory to the application. Therefore, the technique is used mostly for medium- to long-range planning situations. Multiple regression attempts to forecast a desired variable by measuring the effect of two or more different factors on that variable. One benefit of using regression is that it facilitates a better understanding of the environment to be modeled and allows for a study of the impact of multiple variables on the factor being forecasted. Multiple regression assumes a linear or straight-line relationship between the independent variables (factors having an impact on the variable being forecasted) and the variable being forecasted. If that assumption is not correct, the model can provide inaccurate forecasts. It is very often difficult to assess the type of mathematical relationship between the forecasted variable and each additional impacting variable, making accuracy with this model extremely difficult. There are ways to determine what kinds of relationships exist, such as plotting each independent factor or variable with the forecasted variable and fitting each relationship to its closest mathematical form. If those forms are not linear in nature, procedures are available for converting them to linear ones. Statistical procedures are also available for assessing the accuracy of the model. One characteristic of regression is that it allows the modeler to experiment by adding and deleting factors until the model yields satisfactory results.

Sensitivity Analysis

Often, in financial modeling, the factors or variables considered in the model are not previously known, but rather are estimates based on future predicted conditions. These values are often crude "guesstimates" based on existing rule-of-thumb procedures; they can even be values provided by the personnel department that are over- or underestimated to protect its best interests. Therefore, the decision maker should be skeptical about the solutions provided by the model. Sensitivity analysis allows the modeler to investigate the way in which a factor or variable of interest is affected by changing the values of other variables in the model. The sensitive variables are those that, through slight changes in magnitude, cause a significant change in the variable of interest. Once the sensitive variables have been identified, their values should be estimated more carefully, thereby providing a more accurate solution to the model.

Goal-Seeking Analysis

Goal seeking is a modeling technique that allows the decision maker to control the solution of the model. Through this procedure, the modeler forces the goal or factor of interest to take on a desired value. The model must then seek a solution for the other factors or variables in the model. The decision maker should realize that often, with complex models, a nonfeasible solution may result. In other words, given the specified value for the goal or factor of interest, it may not be mathematically possible to solve the model. In addition, solutions may be determined for all variables in the model; however, the values may be totally unrealistic—for example, providing a fractional solution for a departmental head count.

Optimization

Optimization requires the model to provide the most desirable solution for the goal or factor of interest. "Desirable" is defined to mean the largest value for maximizing the objective (e.g., net income) or the smallest value for minimizing it (e.g., cost). Optimization is usually associated with mathematical programming techniques such as linear programming, which strive to obtain the best or most desirable solution given a set of constraints. For example, the president of an automobile manufacturing company may want to know the optimal production mix for three models of cars given the available labor, plant capacity, and supply limitations on material in order to minimize cost. A mathematical programming technique is the appropriate tool for this type of problem. Other examples of optimization through mathematical programming are the assignment of personnel to various tasks, distribution and transportation of materials, and the blending of stocks and bonds in investment portfolios.

Risk Analysis

Risk analysis is a technique that allows the user to investigate the uncertainty of forecasts in a model. Usually, the likelihood of risk is presented through probability distributions. For example, a decision maker may use risk analysis to evaluate the chance of a profit level occurring at a break-even point. The results are presented by probability of occurrence given a specific distribution such as normal or uniform.

SELECTION OF FINANCIAL MODELING SOFTWARE PACKAGES

Computer financial modeling has made great strides since the introduction of the first microcomputer-based spreadsheet product, VisiCalc. With the proliferation of microcomputer-based modeling products on the market, many decision makers favor these products, as they are more flexible, timely, and easier to use than products or customized programs that require the use of mainframe computers. The decision maker faces a tough buying decision regarding the best financial modeling package to suit his needs. He must evaluate, among other things, price versus features and the ease of working the model versus the complexity of the required data. The sheer number of microcomputer-based financial modeling packages on the market, whether for capital investment analysis, sales projections, funds-flow forecasting, budgeting, discounted cash-flow analysis, or general spreadsheet applications, can overwhelm the uninitiated. It almost requires a modeling package to evaluate all of the options! The purpose of the following discussion is to provide an overview of some of the popular financial modeling packages currently available on the market. Information is also provided on locating references for specific financial modeling packages.

Microcomputer-Based Financial Modeling Packages

The financial planning microcomputer-based software packages can be organized into two categories: modeling languages and spreadsheets. Modeling languages are used as a tool to create customized models. Data management features are also sometimes included with commonly used financial and statistical functions. Spreadsheet packages have become very popular over the last few years because of their speed, ease of use, and capability for "what-if" scenarios. To date, at least 1.5 million electronic spreadsheet packages have been sold; the number is still increasing. Many spreadsheet packages offer some program logic capability and many built-in financial, statistical, and mathematical functions. Some common spreadsheet applications in the area of financial modeling are sales and cash-flow projections, consolidations, and product-cost analysis. The requirements of the financial model usually dictate whether a spreadsheet or modeling language is needed. One factor to keep in mind is that all programs require a certain amount of memory to run. Generally speaking, the more complex the program, the greater the memory requirement. Disk-space requirements for the storage of larger financial planning software packages and large financial models must also be considered. The alert user of microcomputer-based financial planning packages needs to consider the appropriate disk capacities and microcomputer memory requirements for the storage and execution of the model. Comments on some of the packages follow.

Micro DSS/F. Addison-Wesley Publishing Company released its microcomputer-based financial modeling package on the marketplace in 1981. Although it has not been modified since that time, many features enable it to retain its standing as a powerful financial modeling tool. Its simple English-language commands make execution of the models possible with very little training of nontechnical individuals. The actual modeling language is structured in a manner similar to mainframe financial modeling packages; therefore, experienced professionals find the modeling logic easy to apply. Micro DSS/F's cell (data field) capacity is 1,919 cells; however, that number can be increased to 32,000 through a command that allocates "virtual" storage on disk. This package performs data manipulation, multiple "what-ifs," and solves simultaneous equations. It also contains a goal-seeking algorithm that allows for the determination of values for selected assumptions about the model, given a required outcome. Many financial functions are available, such as depreciation calculations and paybacks.

Lotus 1-2-3. Shortly after Lotus Development Corporation's announcement of its spreadsheet package, Lotus 1-2-3 rose to the top of the sales charts for microcomputer software. This package is touted for its speed of execution and user friendliness. Given enough memory in the microcomputer, the maximum number of entries is 33,000 (spreadsheet size of 240 columns by 2,048 rows). Lotus 1-2-3 is capable of multiplying "what-if" analysis, basic if-then-else logic, sorting capability, and includes financial, statistical, and database functions. The spreadsheet, however, has no loan, depreciation, or tax functions. It detects simultaneous equations (circular references) when used, but rearranges the calculation order whenever possible to avoid them. Lotus 1-2-3 does not provide for goal seeking, optimization, or risk analysis.

Lotus 1-2-3 provides text, table, and graphics output forms. Formal reports are limited because of difficulties in selecting and reordering rows and columns. Tables, text, and color graphs can be sent to the screen, to random access memory (or RAM) disk or diskette files, to a printer, or to a plotter. The graphics features include pie and bar charts, line graphs (two-dimensional graphs only), and scatter plots.

Lotus is very user friendly, with easy-to-follow instructions for installation and a tutorial diskette. It is able to interface with MS-DOS, VisiCalc, and dBASE III, and can run on twenty-five different microcomputers.

Symphony. Symphony, Lotus Development Corporation's latest software release, integrates an enhanced Lotus 1-2-3 with word processing and telecommunications capability. Lotus 1-2-3 has been enhanced with a new windowing system and an easier procedure for building custom printings. Symphony's enlarged spreadsheet now has a maximum capacity of over 2 million cells (256 columns by 8,192 rows); however, reaching this maximum cell capacity is unrealistic for current microcomputers' size limitations for memory. Its word processing capability includes a form-letter facility and a form-oriented information manager.

Multiplan. Microsoft Corporation has provided the market with an excellent spreadsheet package, but it is perhaps not a strong financial modeler for some planning requirements. The size of the spreadsheet is somewhat smaller than in other popular spreadsheet packages, with a maximum cell capacity of a little over 16,000 cells (63 columns by 255 rows). This may be a limiting factor for many financial modelers. Multiplan has the capability of performing "what-if" analysis, if-then-else logic, and statistical and financial functions. This package does not perform percentage change or goal-seeking algorithms, sensitivity analysis, optimization, or risk analysis.

Multiplan allows for the creation of tables and limited text; however, no graphics capability is available.

The user-friendly nature of this package attracts many modelers. The Multiplan tutorial is excellent, and can be supplemented with plentiful third-party materials. A command menu with full words is always on the screen, and the product provides intelligent suggested answers to its prompts. The reference manual is easy to read and well organized. In addition, on-line help commands are available. Multiplan runs on more than fifty different machines, and is supported under the CP/M and DOS operating systems.

Context MBA. Context Management Systems introduced its package, Context MBA, as direct competition to the spreadsheet packages listed. This product performs "what-if" analysis, if-then-else logic, and has many statistical, logical, and financial functions. Its cell capacity is fairly large (95 columns by 999 rows) given the proper memory requirements of the microcomputer. Context MBA does not perform goal seeking, solve simultaneous equations, or provide loan, depreciation, or tax functions; nor does it offer any other programming logic capability.

This package also contains a database management system with sorting capability and a communications package. Context MBA's response time is not quite as fast as some other spreadsheet packages.

Context MBA allows for text, table, and graphics output. Context was one of the first spreadsheet packages to provide the capability for all three forms of output to reside on the same screen or printout. Graph types include pie and bar charts, line graphs (two-dimensional only), scatter plots, and area diagrams.

As with other spreadsheet packages, Context MBA provides a tutorial and reference manual to facilitate the learning process. An on-line help facility is also available.

Corporate MBA. Corporate MBA is the latest version of Context MBA and contains many new enhancements. A considerably faster package than its predecessor, Corporate MBA provides more sophistication in its word processing and telecommunications capabilities. In addition, four windows are provided in this upgraded version. The package is also functional for custom-forms design, 3270 emulation, and macrocommand programming.

MicroFCS. EPS Inc. has provided decision makers with mainframe-quality planning software for microcomputers. Patterned after the original mainframe-based financial modeling package, FCS-EPS, MicroFCS provides "what-if" and sensitivity analysis, goal-seeking capability, the solution of simultaneous equations, and selected programming functions. Several microcomputers running this product can be integrated into the same network for activities such as consolidation. MicroFCS does not perform any optimization techniques or risk analysis. In addition to the user-defined functions, it provides financial, statistical, and mathematical functions. Tax and depreciation calculations are available in some versions.

Because MicroFCS was patterned after the original mainframe-based financial modeling package, models can be transmitted from the microcomputer to the mainframe EPS packages (or minicomputer-based EPS packages) for execution without adjusting or altering programming commands. MicroFCS includes a full-screen data editor, screen-formatting capability, a report generator, programmable function keys, and user defined functions and commands.

Its reporting capabilities include tables and text and, to a limited extent, graphs. Graphs can only be directed to the screen, since there is no provision for directing graphics to a printer or plotting device.

It has a substantial number of FCS installations, providing many user reference opportunities. EPS has a full-service package that is usually available only to mainframe users. Provided with MicroFCS is extensive systems documentation, such as initial guides, reference manuals, installation instructions, systems notes, and sample model applications. On-line help facilities and a hotline telephone service are also available.

IFPS/Personal. Execucom Systems Corporation has come out with a microcomputer version of its minicomputer- and mainframe-based financial modeling package, Interactive Financial Planning System (IFPS). IFPS/Personal's modeling and command language uses the same commands as IFPS; therefore, given proper memory and disk requirements, it is used in almost the same way as the original mainframe package. IFPS/Personal performs "what-if" analysis, sensitivity anslysis, and goal seeking.

Like MicroFCS, Execucom Systems Corporation provides a full-service package that includes training materials and facilities, documentation, and a hotline telephone service.

Encore! Encore! was introduced to the market in 1983 by Ferox Microsystems Inc., and is one of the most feature-packed packages available for microcomputers. It was designed for professionals who had microcomputer spreadsheet familiarity or previous experience with timesharing or mainframe modeling languages. Encore! has eight interactive sections, which can be used for various decision support needs.

Encore! contains an English-like command language for constructing models, and offers more than fifty commands, including twelve conditional operations and nineteen logic functions. Encore! also provides the executive with a programming language to aid in application development. This interactive section includes special screens with menu option processing.

Encore! provides a spreadsheet containing 500,000 cells and has the capability of multiple windowing. The spreadsheet function includes data-input screen capability and regression and goal-seeking algorithms. It also contains an interactive section that provides a full-screen editor for ease in modifying model logic. Capability for hierarchical consolidation is also provided.

A library of various functions is available to the Encore! user, which includes U.S. tax tables, regression algorithms, loan amortization schedules, various statistical calculations, and various types of depreciation calculations.

Encore! provides report-writing capability to produce formalized, customized reports. A graphics feature is included that provides on-line display capability.

SuperCalc^3. Sorcim Corporation announced SuperCalc^3 as its competition to MS-DOS or PC-DOS operating systems-based packages. Its predecessor, SuperCalc, was solely a CP/M operating-based system. Its spreadsheet capacity of 16,000 cells (63 columns by 254 rows) is somewhat limited as compared to other spreadsheet packages. Also, there has been much criticism from the microcomputer trade press, which contends that SuperCalc^3 should have been structured for a 16-bit processor because of its slow execution time. SuperCalc^3 does provide eight different graphics output forms, which can be displayed on either a monochrome or color monitor, and contains a memo editor and text processor that are very user friendly. SuperCalc^3 has financial, statistical, and logical functions, and contains many of the commands common to the other popular spreadsheet packages.

T/Maker III. T/Maker III, produced and supported by the T/Maker Corporation, was enhanced from the original modeling package, T/Maker, in 1981. Like other spreadsheet packages, it contains twenty logical and financial functions. Like Context MBA, it can integrate text, graphics, and models into one document without combining or merging separate files. Some microcomputer professionals believe that this package has the capability of solving all but the most sophisticated financial models.

Mainframe or Minicomputer-Based Financial Modeling Packages

FCS-EPS. FCS-EPS was designed by business planners at EPS Inc. to provide a flexible modeling language with English-based commands for use by nondata processing management. FCS-EPS has up to 160 built-in financial, statistical, and mathematical functions, including depreciation, net present value, internal rate of return, and loan amortizations. This product also allows the user to define his own customized functions. Planning features include "what-if" analysis, hierarchical consolidation, risk and sensitivity analyses, and goal seeking. Statistical forecasting features are also available; they include moving averages, regression, determining seasonality, and curve fitting.

FCS-EPS provides several methods of data management, including the creation and maintenance of hierarchical and relational databases and flat or sequential files.

One of this package's stronger points is its solid reporting facilities. Over fifty report specifications are available, which allow the user total flexibility. The user also has the ability to transpose rows and columns for printing. In addition, many different graphics forms are available, such as three-dimensional portfolio plots.

IFPS (Interactive Financial Planning System). IFPS, a financial planning language, was developed by Execucom Systems Corporation and provides features for planning, modeling, and decision support. IFPS is structured with English-based commands that allow for ease of comprehension and transportability among different modelers. IFPS performs "what-if" scenarios, goal seeking, and sensitivity analysis. Corporate consolidations may also be performed using this package. IFPS runs on eleven different types of hardware: IBM, Burroughs, CDC, Data General, DEC (Digital Equipment Corporation), Harris, Hewlett-Packard, Honeywell, Prime, Sperry, and Wang VS compatibles. There are over 1,200 installations of IFPS, which create a large user base for reference and future development. As mentioned in the discussion of IFPS/Personal, the service support benefit includes training materials and facilities, systems and reference documentation, and a hotline telephone service.

Execucom Systems Corporation also provides three other systems, all of which interface with the IFPS package—IFPS/ Dataspan, IFPS/Optimum, and IFPS/Sentry. IFPS/Dataspan is a software product designed to extract and interface data from other computer-based files to IFPS. This package also allows the user to store several file management commands into one file for batch execution. Menu creation for data editing is also available in this package.

IFPS/Optimum provides an optimization feature to IFPS. The modeler can identify the factors in the model that can be changed, and the system determines the best or optimum values for them. The system also provides the modeler with the value of trade-offs among the alternatives. Sample business applications for this package are product-mix planning, production scheduling, and inventory planning and control.

IFPS/Sentry is a data entry facility and is used for the input and validation of data into IFPS. Environments requiring periodic input for large volumes of data may find this useful. The data entry feature includes automatic prompting of variables.

FOCUS Financial Modeling Language. Information Builders, Inc., has brought to financial modelers FOCUS Financial Modeling Language, an English command-driven language that allows the user to develop "what-if" scenarios and forecasting. The modeler may develop either row-oriented financial statements or customized matrix-style reports. Financial and statistical functions are available. The FOCUS Basic System must be installed, and runs only on IBM hardware.

Impact. Impact is a financial modeling package that has been developed by MDCR, Inc. In addition to providing a data-entry and verification feature, it allows for consolidation, forecasting, "what-if" analysis, goal seeking, comparative analysis, and the solution of simultaneous equations. It also performs financial and statistical functions. Impact is currently installed in 1,000 locations, and it runs on IBM mainframe or microcomputer hardware.

MSA/Forecasting and Modeling System. MSA (Management Science America, Inc.) has a product that allows for various budgeting, planning, and forecasting models. As with other mainframe-based systems, the Forecasting and Modeling System has been developed with an English-based command language, and provides consolidation features. This package can be integrated with MSA's other popular accounting packages, such as General Ledger, Accounts Payable, Accounts Receivable, and Payroll/Personnel, to allow for common data files. This package requires an IBM mainframe environment.

Summary. The business professional seeking the appropriate decision support package, whether for mainframe, minicomputer-, or microcomputer-based applications, can consult several publications for the name of the package and such additional information as its functionality, cost, name, and the developer's location. One valuable source of information is *Data Sources*, which is published quarterly and contains a separate volume for software information. This publication provides a directory by type or classification of package as well as a small write-up on the package. Cross-referencing is available so that the user can locate the developer's name and the telephone number to call for additional literature.

A second source of information for locating financial planning software is the Datapro subscription. In addition to its previous software planning publications, Datapro has recently released its special report on microcomputers, providing three volumes of information on hardware, software, and telecommunications microcomputer-based systems, as well as various reports on issues in the microcomputer industry.

Finally, several microcomputer trade publications such as *PC World* and *PC Week* occasionally publish comparative studies on financial software. Because computer technology and relative sophistication of software are constantly changing, it is important to look at the most current publications when researching and evaluating available products.

DESIGN AND DOCUMENTATION GUIDELINES FOR FINANCIAL MODELS

The financial modeler should have an organized procedure for file management, data procurement, and storing and retrieving model logic. Following are some general guidelines for designing and documenting financial models. The discussion is geared toward microcomputer-based models; however, these recommendations may apply to mainframe or minicomputer-based systems as well.

File management is a very important factor in the development and ongoing execution of financial models. The developer should maintain a log of all files used in the model, indicating name, diskette(s), a short description of what is contained in the file, date of last change, and the name of the prime developer. File-naming conventions should be established and used throughout the development of the model. Groups of files for a particular project should share the same prefix. Types of files should be identified by descriptive suffixes, such as DATA (data files), LOG (log report files), RPT (report files), WS (worksheet files), and RSLT (result files).

Data handling and procurement are very important functions requiring detailed documentation. Where possible, the modeler should use an input-data worksheet that has been properly labeled with a date, title, subheadings, and column headings. He should also establish an input-data verification worksheet. All text instructions required for the data's input should be included in the data file.

Another critical factor for maintaining financial models is documentation of model logic. The modeler should keep the following points in mind.

1 Keep model logic in the logic files.
2 Do not place growth functions in the data file or store complicated computations in the reporting files.
3 Always spell out row names, rather than keeping them in abbreviated form.
4 Use simple, commonly used functions and/or programming logic where possible.

5 Use comment lines as often as necessary to explain such complex disciplines as logic, subroutines, simultaneity, and probablistic functions.

6 Break the logic into logical groupings or modules for ease of maintenance or modification that any financial modeler can follow.

7 Separate modules with comment lines and a heading.

8 Use parentheses, even where not required, to make functions or logic clear.

9 Keep row numbers in sequential order.

10 Where row numbers are out of order, document the exceptions both at the top of the file and at the place the row is out of order.

11 Break down complex functions, such as the steps in a tax table, into specific, simplified steps.

12 Never reuse row numbers.

FUTURE DEVELOPMENTS FOR COMPUTER-BASED FINANCIAL MODELING

The future promises to provide an even greater variety of feature-packed financial modeling software for business professionals and decision makers. Most software developers continually upgrade their products with more complex modeling features and financial and statistical functions in order to continue to provide managers with more sophisticated and effective decision-making tools. Because of the growing popularity and cost effectiveness of microcomputers, developers will also continue to convert mainframe-based financial modeling software to these computers. However, the modeler should continue to evaluate all financial modeling software with care. The increases in flexibility and complexity of financial modeling software may create new considerations, such as increased processing time or massive amounts of disk-storage requirements, but they also create a greater risk for inaccuracies. Computer-based financial modeling is only a tool, albeit an extremely useful one, in the complex business world. It does not replace the need for astute decision makers.

REFERENCES

"Applications Software," *Data Sources*. New York: Ziff-Davis (Software/1st Quarter 1985), sec. N.

Heckerman, Donald A. "Financial Modeling—A Powerful Tool for Southern Motor Carriers." *Southern Motor Cargo* (June 1980), pp. 96–102.

Hillier, Frederick S., and Gerald J. Lieberman. *Introduction to Operations Research*. San Francisco: Holden-Day, 1980.

Hirsh, Alan T., ed. "All About Electronic Spreadsheets." *Datapro Reports on Microcomputers*. Delran, N.J.: McGraw-Hill (Sept. 1984).

Lampert, Anne. "Expert Systems Get Down to Business." *Computer Decisions* (Jan. 1985), pp. 138–144.

Makridakis, Spyros, and Steven C. Wheelwright. *Forecasting, Methods and Applications*. New York: John Wiley & Sons, 1978.

Perry, Robert. "The Latest Revolution in Financial Modeling Software: Part II." *Computer Decisions* (Nov. 1984), pp. 139–146.

Tucker, Edward G. "Computer-Based Financial Modeling Scaled to Size." *HFM* (Jan. 1983), pp. 24–32.

CHAPTER 16

Design, Development, and Implementation of Decision Support Systems

Allen D. McMillen

Overview and Definition 2
DSS Building Blocks and Applications .. 2

Framework for Designing DSS 3
Three Technology Levels for DSS 4
An Adaptive Approach for Developing a DSS 4
Individual Roles in the Development and Use of DSS 5

Design Objectives for Decision Support .. 7
Types and Levels of Decision Support .. 7
Specific Design Criteria 8
Factors In Design 8

DSS Development 9
The Four Major Components of a DSS 9
Database Management 11
Model Development 11

General Purpose Models 11
Specific DSS Models 12
DSS Model Generators 12
Building DSS Through Interactive Design 12
Levels of Flexibility 13
Development of a Prototype 13

Implementation Strategies 14
Steps Toward DSS Integration 14
Phased Implementation 16
Software Selection Criteria 17

Evaluation of DSS 17

Benefits 18

DSS Today and Tomorrow 18

References 20

Fig. 16-1 DSS Building Blocks 3
Fig. 16-2 The Four Major Components of a DSS 10
Fig. 16-3 Evaluation Criteria for DSS 19
Fig. 16-4 Cited Benefits of a DSS 20

16-1

OVERVIEW AND DEFINITION

The term "Decision Support Systems" (DSS) refers to the general objective of using computer technology to assist the manager, technician, professional, or scientist in making decisions. DSS are appropriate in decision situations that require the use of large databases or extensive or complex calculations and logical algorithms. As such, a DSS may assist in any of the commonly labeled stages of decision making, such as (1) defining the problem, (2) generating solutions, and (3) choosing a solution. DSS are currently in use in business, government, medicine, and education. The purpose of this chapter is to introduce the financial executive to the areas involved with the design, development, and implementation of DSS.

DSS have been used by an increasing number of researchers, practitioners, and managers to define a very different view of computer technology and applications. The concept of DSS represents a well-defined methodology for building information systems for managers that:

- Support them in their planning, problem solving, and judgment in tasks that cannot be routinized (i.e., the computer must support the manager but not replace his judgment or impose methods and solutions).
- Permit ease of access and flexibility of use by providing effective problem-solving that is essentially interactive and is enhanced by a dialogue between man and machine.
- Function as personal tools under the individual's control, which, in most cases, are tailored to his mode of thinking, terminology, and activities.

These concepts are not intended to imply that decision support is needed only at the top levels of management. Rather, decision support is required at all levels of management in an organization where decisions must be made, and are often communicated and coordinated between decision makers across organizational levels as well as at the same level.

DSS Building Blocks and Applications

Recent advances in computer technology provide cheap, powerful, and flexible facilities for decision support. Through the use of interactive terminals, inexpensive access to financial models, information systems, and databases, the decision maker is provided with new opportunities to draw on computer support in making key decisions. Computer technology has become increasingly reliable, and user-oriented languages and applications are widely available.

Peter G.W. Keen and Michael S. Scott Morton, two well-known researchers in the area of decision support, suggest that there are now a tremendous variety of building blocks (see Figure 16-1) and that managers who have a clear

HUMAN
Technical Intermediaries
  Assist in the design process, formalizing of ideas and needs, and evolution of personalized systems.
Staff Intermediaries
  Interface between the manager and the system, translate questions, operate the system, and provide analyses and feedback.

SOFTWARE
Database Management Systems
  Store and retrieve large amounts of data, allow better access to existing data files, allow answers to relatively complex questions.
Specialized Simulation and Application Languages
  Reduce development time, especially for complex models and decision problems.
Application Packages
  Permit off-the-shelf installation of systems especially designed for particular types of applications, thus fitting user's needs, background and skills.

HARDWARE
General Purpose Timesharing Systems
  Permit easy access to substantial computer power and allow faster development of systems.
Graphics Terminals
  Provide effective means for presenting large volumes of data in a meaningful format.
Desk-Top or Microcomputers
  Provide personalized, cheap, and easily transported tools that have allowed DSS to operate in a user-controlled environment.
Telecommunications Networks
  Extend the computer from sophisticated calculations and data processing to message sending and data sharing and provide mutual access to information among decentralized organizational units.

FIG. 16-1 DSS Building Blocks

idea of what they want a DSS to do and how to make use of it can generally obtain a system that accomplishes most of their aims.[1]

FRAMEWORK FOR DESIGNING DSS

A framework is useful in characterizing organizational activities in terms of the kinds and levels of decisions involved. It also has implications for design and implementation. The framework presented in the following section, based largely on the work of Ralph H. Sprague, Jr., and Eric D. Carlson, considers the following topics: (1) three levels of DSS technology; (2) an approach for

---

[1] Peter Keen and M.S. Scott Morton, *Decision Support Systems: An Organizational Perspective* (Reading, Mass.: Addison-Wesley, 1978), pp. 13–14.

developing DSS; and (3) the roles of the individuals responsible in the building and use of DSS.[2]

Three Technology Levels for DSS

Sprague and Carlson have identified three levels of DSS hardware and software used by individuals with different levels of technical capability and decision-making responsibilities. These three levels of technology are (1) specific DSS, (2) DSS generators, and (3) DSS tools.

1 *Specific DSS* — the hardware and software that actually accomplish the work of decision support. Specific DSS provide support for specific decisions and decision makers. Through interaction with the system, the decision makers access and control specific sets of related problems.

2 *DSS generators* — integrated hardware and software facilities used to build specific DSS quickly and easily. Their capabilities include report generation, inquiry, modeling, graphics, and various financial and statistical analysis functions. DSS generators are useful for specific DSS that aid in financial decision-making situations. Two good examples of DSS generators include the Interactive Financial Planning System (IFPS), marketed by Execucom Systems, and EXPRESS, available from Management Decision Systems.

3 *DSS tools* — the last level of DSS technology associated with the development of DSS. These pertain to the hardware and software products that aid in the development of specific DSS applications or DSS generators. In the last few years, there has been a proliferation of products in this area, including high-level and user-friendly languages, improvements in operating systems to support conversational approaches and integration of applications, and a slew of color graphics hardware and supporting software products.

Specific DSS applications may be developed directly from tools. However, since DSS must respond to changes in the ways a user wants to approach a problem, the development and use of DSS generators provide the foundation from which specific DSS applications may be developed and modified with the user's assistance.

An Adaptive Approach for Developing a DSS

DSS require a unique approach to systems analysis and design. This is partly due to the very nature of DSS, whereby the system must support the cognitive

---

[2] R.H. Sprague, Jr., and E.D. Carlson, *Building Effective Decision Support Systems* (Englewood Cliffs, N.J.: Prentice-Hall, 1982), pp. 10–12.

processes of individual decision makers. DSS need to be independent of any imposed process, because each decision maker approaches a problem in a different way, which prevents standardization. Thus, computer support must allow for personalized usage and be flexible.

An interactive design is necessary to make sure that DSS are built with short, rapid feedback from the user. This approach relies on the quick establishment of an initial system to which a user can respond and thus clarify his real needs. After a short period of use, the system is evaluated, modified, and subsequently enhanced. This approach requires a high level of user involvement and participation in design. The functions DSS provide are generally not elaborate; complex systems are evolved from simple components. The final system can be developed only through an adaptive process of learning and evolution.

The adaptive approach of developing DSS ties into Sprague and Carlson's three-level model of a DSS. Specific DSS applications provide the decision maker with interactive problem-solving capabilities to analyze problem areas. The use of the system stimulates learning and new insights that, in turn, stimulate new uses and the need for new functions in the system. Specific DSS applications must evolve in response to new uses through the reconfiguration of elements in the DSS generator. Over a longer period of time, the basic tools evolve to provide the technology needed to facilitate the development of specific DSS by changing the capabilities of the DSS generators.

These views of an approach for developing DSS are not surprisingly new. Most traditional computer systems are adaptive in nature through changes and modifications made during a normal systems life cycle. However, when the length of that life cycle is shortened considerably and costs are reduced, there are significant implications that affect the growth of DSS.

Individual Roles in the Development and Use of DSS

The successful development and operation of a DSS requires a full range of skill requirements in the roles that managers and technicians play. The user of the system is, in effect, the system's designer, who uses and evaluates the system and, in the process, identifies problems and suggests solutions. The user's role requires an understanding that, along with flexibility and responsiveness provided by the system, comes responsibility for the results. The user develops an understanding for, and appreciation of, the specific skills possessed by the analyst or builder. His role includes coordination and communication with other users as well as with the analyst.

The analyst or systems designer/builder constructs successive versions of the system, compromising and resolving conflicts between context and form and a functional knowledge or understanding of the user's responsibilities. The analyst must understand the available technology that can be used to support development of the DSS. He must also identify the entities of interest, some of their attributes, and the relationships among them, as well as those processes essential to the user. Finally, the analyst must relate both data and processes to available databases and models.

Sprague and Carlson define the evolving roles in a DSS as follows:[3]

- *Manager or user* — the person faced with the problems decision; the one who must take action and be responsible for the consequences.

- *Intermediary* — the person who helps the user, perhaps merely as a clerical assistant, to push the terminal's buttons or, perhaps as a more substantial staff assistant, to interact and make suggestions.

- *DSS builder or facilitator* — the person who assembles the necessary capabilities from the DSS generator to configure the specific DSS with which the user/intermediary interacts directly. This person must have some familiarity with the problem area and also be comfortable with the information systems technology components and capabilities.

- *Technical supporter* — the person who develops additional information systems capabilities or components when they are needed as part of the generator. New databases, new analysis models, and additional data display formats are developed by the person filling this role. The role requires a strong familiarity with technology and a minor acquaintance with the problem or application area.

- *Toolsmith* — the person who develops new technology, new languages, and new hardware and software and improves the efficiency of linkage between subsystems.

From the above definitions, it is clear that one person may assume several roles, or more than one person may be required to perform the responsibilities of one role. Generally, the classification of role and responsibility depends on:

- The inherent nature of the problem
- The individual's comfort level with the computer technology, applications, and concepts
- The applicability of the technology (i.e., is it user friendly?)

A few observations about this adaptive framework are appropriate. The framework has specific implications for design and implementation, as follows:

- The people involved in building DSS require specific skills and attitudes.
- The technology required by most DSS must be informal, flexible, and personal.

---

[3] Sprague and Carlson, p. 13.

DECISION SUPPORT SYSTEMS

- Smaller, informal models are required for the support of the financial manager's decisions.
- The process by which DSS are constructed must evolve and be adaptive. The chief financial officer (CFO) must actively participate in the development of the system.

DESIGN OBJECTIVES FOR DECISION SUPPORT

The success of developing effective DSS relies on specific design and implementation strategies needed to support decision making. Effective design depends on the system builder's detailed understanding of financial management decision processes and the financial manager's clear recognition of the criteria for developing useful and effective computer-based decision models.

A manager or user is primarily concerned with what the specific DSS application can do for him. He assesses the DSS in terms of the assistance or support he receives in pursuing various decision-making tasks within the organizational environment.

Types and Levels of Decision Support

The design process should focus on delivering to the financial manager a system that provides most of the following types of support:

- Support for decision making, with emphasis on semistructured and unstructured decisions.
- Decision-making support for users at all levels in the organization. The DSS must often be coordinated and communicated between decision makers across organizational levels as well as on the same level. This need for integration and coordination of decision making is often a requirement for several people dealing with related parts of a larger problem.
- Support for decisions that are interdependent as well as independent.
- Support for all phases of the decision-making process.
- Support for a variety of decision-making processes without being dependent on any one. DSS should help the decision maker use and develop his own styles, skills, and knowledge. The decision maker should be able to personally control what the DSS does to accommodate changes in behavior over time.

Lastly, a DSS should provide ease of use. Generally, this translates into characteristics that provide flexibility and user friendliness.

A DSS can provide a variety of levels of support for the financial manager, the most basic involving simple database operations. Finding relevant information in a large database is not an easy task. A DSS can be useful where a database is so large that the manager has difficulty accessing and making conceptual use of it. Simple DSS routines can be supplemented to provide access to facts or information retrieval.

The next level of support involves adding search and display capabilities to this data retrieval. This provides the CFO with the ability to retrieve information selectively and to give graphic or conceptual meaning to data. The DSS tools available to the CFO include many graphics and display devices used to view data and to communicate the output effectively. A DSS is especially helpful to the CFO because it can graphically display the future financial implications of current trends and patterns.

Another level builds on the first two by adding more sophisticated computational facilities, and it permits the financial manager to ask for such items as simple computations, extrapolations, comparisons, and projections. Thus, the system operates in much the same manner as a sophisticated calculator, preprogrammed to handle some of the manipulations most commonly used by the CFO for such problems.

The final level of support provides useful models to the CFO as well. These models provide structure to the decision process by formulating interrelationships between relevant variables. Thus, processes may be simulated and outcomes from various given events can be evaluated by the decision maker.

Specific Design Criteria

The foregoing definitions and capabilities of a DSS translate into these specific design criteria:

- A flexible development language that allows rapid creation and modification of systems for specific applications
- A systems design and architecture that allow quick and easy extensions and alternatives
- An interface that buffers the user from the computer and allows a dialogue based on the CFO's concepts, vocabulary, and definition of the decision problem
- Communicative display devices and output generators

Factors in Design

The first step in the design of a DSS is to select the right problem to work on by identifying the key decision. The key questions to be asked at the start of the design process are:

- What should the DSS accomplish?
- When is the system complete? (Has it met the design objectives?)

DECISION SUPPORT SYSTEMS

- What are the design priorities and/or sequence of stages?
- Who should be involved?

The first question translates into technical specifications. At this point, the design specification is at best a statement of intent. Objectives are fairly broad, and commitments and expectations are general. These now need to be specifically interpreted into a design specification that focuses on what the DSS is intended to do.

The design of a DSS involves three different areas: (1) the user interface, defined in terms of commands or imperatives; (2) the software interface that links and interprets them; and (3) the database management design. What the system is to do from the user's point of view can be answered best by defining a set of commands or verbs, many of which (FIND, DISPLAY, GRAPH) are common to almost all conversational information systems.

The software interface allows the system to communicate with the user. To the user, the interface is the system. However, behind the user interface are a sophisticated set of complex routines that interpret the user commands for functions such as retrieving data, linking applications, or accessing output devices.

The third aspect of systems design is data management. Data management for DSSs generally requires large databases and complex retrievel facilities with random and infrequent access to most of the data. This, coupled with the necessity of collecting, validating, and maintaining the data needed, is a major effort in DSS design.

Knowing whether design objectives have been met depends primarily on system "usage." By definition, the process by which a DSS is constructed must evolve and be adaptive. In one sense, a DSS is never complete. However, an initial system can be self-contained and operational once the first set of routines are usable. Design specifications may have been met but not necessarily design objectives. Design must be based on usage and what the DSS does. Priorities for routines may be assigned on the basis of either the user's needs or technical feasibility. After a short period of use, the system is evaluated, modified, and subsequently enhanced. Design is complete when the user feels comfortable with the interface and has access to routines to support decision making. The user assesses the DSS in terms of support and assistance. The request for additional routines and support represents the next step in the evolution of the DSS.

DSS DEVELOPMENT

The Four Major Components of a DSS

There are a minimum of four major components in the development of a DSS (see Figure 16-2). The first is a comprehensive database containing some of the data relevant to the decisions supported by the DSS. The database is designed

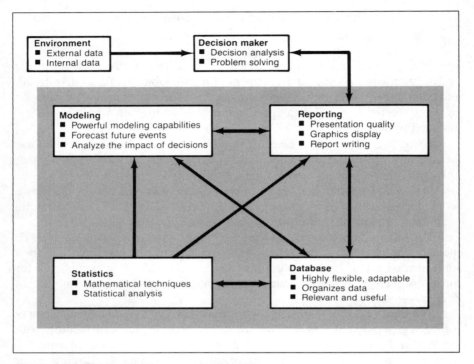

FIG. 16-2 The Four Major Components of a DSS

around the information needs of all users. Thus, the contents of the database must go beyond routine historical data about internal operations and include relevant external data. As such, a database contains data that are maintained by an organization.

Data Base Management Systems (DBMS) provide the functions that make a database useful. DBMS create, maintain, access, update, and protect one or more databases. DBMS provide ready access to, and control of, the database. In short, they organize data in ways that are relevant and useful to financial executives.

The second integral component of a DSS is the ability to model semistructured and unstructured decision processes. Modeling provides the ability to forecast future events, analyze the impact of financial decisions, and evaluate the outcomes of various courses of action (see Chapter 15). Sophisticated financial model building facilitates unlimited "what-if" scenarios. In the past, developing decision models was time consuming and complicated. With new innovations in user-friendly hardware and software, modeling has gained popularity along with structured reports and direct query as decision analysis aids.

Statistical analysis is another component of decision support. Features include a variety of preprogrammed, statistical analysis techniques for data manipulation.

Finally, a DSS provides a range of graphics display and report generator options for purposes of viewing the data and effectively communicating the output of any modeling or analysis.

Database Management

Database management is an important component of a DSS because of the diversity of data that are required for decision making. A database is a mechanism for integrating data from many sources, such as: (1) internal data used for the planning, control, and operation of an organization; (2) external data from outside data vendors and organizations; (3) MIS databases; and (4) data entered on line by executives. The DBMS permits the storage, maintenance, and retrieval of such data. The nature of a DSS requires ease of entering new data and change in the relationships among the data in response to unanticipated user requests.

Model Development

Modeling provides structure to the decision process. Financial executives may reduce uncertainty and evaluate the outcomes from various events by formulating interrelationships between relevant variables. Although the final solution to a problem is left to the decision maker, modeling facilitates good judgment.

There are three approaches to model development: (1) the use of general purpose models, (2) development (or purchase) of in-house specific DSS models, and (3) the use of model generators to develop specific models.[4]

General Purpose Models. General purpose models are purchased software packages. Typical examples include VisiCalc and a range of other spreadsheet compatibles. Electronic spreadsheet models consist of a matrix of cells in rows and columns. Each cell position is a variable, which may be defined as a function of other cells. Any change to the values of key variables causes a ripple effect that recalculates the output values in the spreadsheet. Recalculation and editing features make electronic spreadsheets powerful planning and forecasting tools. Not only are mistakes and omissions able to be corrected effortlessly, but various alternatives to a problem may be examined. Spreadsheet modeling is typically used for sales forecasting, budgeting, and sensitivity analysis.

Integrated software packages such as Lotus Development Corporation's Lotus 1-2-3 and Symphony and Ashton Tate's FRAMEWORK provide sophis-

---

[4] James A. Hall, "Management Information Systems," *Management Accounting* (Dec. 1983), p. 12.

ticated spreadsheet capabilities along with database management, graphics display, word processing, and communications capabilities.

Specific DSS Models. Specific DSS models are designed to support specific decisions, and often are written in procedural languages such as FORTRAN and COBOL.

DSS Model Generators. Model generators are software packages that allow quick and easy development of specific DSS models. In addition to model development, these packages offer additional features to aid financial decision making, such as prewritten functions for depreciation schedules, cost allocation, electronic spreadsheet capabilities, financial graphics display, and database management capabilities. The use of DSS model generators helps to facilitate the quick development of specific DSS models and to adapt easily to shifts in users' needs.

Building DSS Through Interactive Design

It is widely recognized that a DSS must be flexible and adaptive. This is partly due to the very nature of a DSS, whereby the system must support the cognitive processes of individual decision makers, adapt to changes in the environment, and support modification of systems for specific applications and tasks. Keen[5] and his colleagues at the Wharton School, University of Pennsylvania, analyzed about thirty fairly detailed case studies of DSS and their use over the years. These case studies frequently revealed that key factors explaining successful development were (1) a flexible design architecture that permits fast modification and (2) a phased approach to implementation. Flexibility and an adaptive design, according to Keen's research, may be needed for a variety of reasons:

- There is either a lack of knowledge to define the procedures or requirements or a lack of structure intrinsic to the task that limits the user's or builder's ability to specify functional requirements in advance.
- The user often does not know, or is unable to specify, what he wants and needs. By building an initial system or prototype to react to, a user may shape and improve upon the task or decision situation.
- The user's concept of a task is shaped by DSS usage. Use of the system stimulates new learning and new insights that, in turn, stimulate new uses and the need for new functions.

---

[5] Peter G.W. Keen, "Decision Support Systems: A Research Perspective," CISR No. 54, Sloan WP No. 1117-80, (Mar. 1980), pp. 9–10.

- Intended users of the system have sufficient autonomy to handle the task in a variety of ways or to differ in the way they think to a degree that prevents standardization of the process.
- The actual uses of the DSS are almost always different from the intended ones. Case studies indicate that many of the most valued and innovative uses could not have been predicted when the system was designed.[6]

Levels of Flexibility

There are multiple levels of flexibility required for a DSS. The first level of flexibility enables the user to solve different variations of similar problems. It is the user who utilizes this type of flexibility, although an intermediary may assist by pushing buttons or by interacting and making suggestions. A second level of flexibility is the ability to modify the configuration of a specific DSS. This is usually a joint effort by both the user and the builder as they implement additions and deletions of representations, operations, workspace, or choices on a menu. Another level of flexibility is the ability to adapt to changes that take the form of new capabilities in dialogue, data management, and modeling. In this case, it is the builder who is primarily responsible for changes to DSS generators, which allow for the adaptation of a specific DSS. This leads to the fourth level of flexibility, the ability of the system to evolve in response to changes in the technology from which a DSS is built. Here the toolsmith develops new tools that enable the DSS to evolve.

Development of a Prototype

Traditional systems development approaches delay the delivery of tangible information systems capabilities to the user until the last stages of systems development. The drawback here is that shortcomings in systems design do not appear until after systems are developed. Heuristic approaches to information systems development (e.g., prototyping) advocate providing, or at least simulating, user capabilities early in the systems development process. The design step of the traditional development cycle involves defining the systems outputs that financial management requires. The assumption is that management knows what information is needed, and the CFO's cognitive style is seldom considered. At best, the result is often the development of an information system that provides the managers with what was requested and (often) not what is needed. A good reason for this descrepancy is that managers frequently experience difficulty in defining information requirements using traditional systems analysts' tools such as flow charts, file layouts, and report layouts. Financial managers must work with a system to appreciate its strengths and weaknesses. As such,

---

[6] Keen, pp. 9–10.

defining information requirements tends to be a heuristic, or learning, experience.

The adaptive approach to developing a DSS, described elsewhere in this chapter, relies on the quick establishment of an initial system. This initial system or prototype captures the essential features of a later system. A prototype system is to be modified, expanded, enhanced, or supplemented. The prototyping process allows the builder to define the user's information requirements while designing and developing a DSS. This approach provides the financial manager with an opportunity to have tangible, realistic exposure and use of the new system as he learns the capabilities of new technology and refines his information requirements. As a result, systems need to accommodate the individual user while remaining open to change and modification. Therefore, prototyping must be supported by on-line interactive systems, DBMS, high-level query languages, generalized input and output software, and accessible modeling facilities.

IMPLEMENTATION STRATEGIES

Implementation consists of education, installation, and evaluation. Successful implementation requires both process and strategy. The likelihood of success for implementing a DSS depends on the following:

- Top-management support
- A clear, felt need by the user/client
- An immediate, visible problem to work on
- Early commitment by the user and conscious staff involvement
- A well-institutionalized MIS group or data processing department

This translates into an implementation strategy for DSS that requires top-management commitment, appropriate hardware and software, and three other critical factors: (1) the need for interdepartmental cooperation; (2) a specialized support staff; and (3) a phased implementation process.

Steps Toward DSS Integration

The goal for DSS integration is to provide the financial manager with tools he may adopt and combine with his own decision-making and judgment processes by means of whatever software and hardware are suitable and available. Effective implementation involves working through a series of steps for integrating DSS,[7] as follows:

---

[7] Steven L. Alter, *Decision Support Systems: Current Practice and Continuing Challenges* (Reading, Mass.: Addison-Wesley, 1980), pp. 165–169.

1 *Divide the project into manageable components.* Dividing the project into manageable components minimizes the risk of producing a larger system that does not work. The use of prototypes provides for testing concepts before committing significant resources to a massive system. The prototyping process allows the analyst to define the user's information requirements while designing and developing an output system. Prototyping is particularly appropriate for large, expensive systems and in cases where the success of implementation depends on one or more relatively untested conepts or procedures.

   The evolutionary approach should be applied to smaller systems facilitating a number of different functions. This approach relies on the establishment of an initial system to which the user may respond and thus clarify his real needs. The system is incrementally modified to suit the user's needs. This approach requires a high level of user involvement and participation. As a result, user feedback tends to be reasonably accurate.

   Developing a set of tools provides databases and small models that can be created, modified, and discarded. These tools provide the capability of ad hoc analysis.

2 *Keep the solution simple.* To encourage the use of systems and avoid scaring the user away, the solution must be kept simple. Simple solutions encourage user participation and management support, since they are easier to understand, easier to implement, and generally easier to control and modify than complicated solutions. Simple solutions should be used to disguise complexity and avoid change from existing practices. The functions a DSS provides are generally not elaborate; complex systems are evolved from simple components. The final system can be developed only through an adaptive and evolutionary process of learning.

3 *Develop a satisfactory support base.* Successful implementation of a DSS requires top-management commitment, interdepartmental cooperation, and a specialized support staff. Cooperation in gathering data to feed the databases is necessary. User participation includes anything from help in providing data to very active participation in the design of the system. The objectives for user participation include reducing the probability that the final system will be based on misconceptions and misunderstandings and ensuring a firm commitment to the use of the final system.

   DSS must be developed with high levels of user involvement. In order to obtain personal user commitment, management must commit individuals to the project's successful end use. Where participation is mandated, it becomes crucial for the user to feel enthusiasm and commitment toward the implementation process.

Top-management commitment and support are necessary to obtain funding for development and continuation of the project and for ensuring user compliance and usage. Successful implementation requires both management and user support.

4 *Meet user needs and institutionalize the system.* As part of the implementation process, the user's needs must be satisfied. Well thought out training and education programs assist a user who is personally uninvolved in implementation. Implementation includes provision for on-going assistance in using the system, insistance upon mandatory use for those who use the system to help in their individual functions, voluntary use, and the building of systems to accommodate a user's particular capabilities.

Phased Implementation

Phased implementation considers the following four states of DSS growth:

1 Build/familiarize
2 Ad hoc analysis
3 Model structuring
4 Creative usage

The first step toward integration of DSS is to get key data on line. The user manipulates the data with items such as reports, graphs, and models to get a feel for what is happening. Once a financial manager and his staff become familiar with the data, they can begin to visualize how to use it. Very often, new uses are realized as the financial manager learns more about how the system works and as new models and applications are built.

By this time, the financial manager understands the data, has used the system for analysis with various simple models, and is now ready to perform the following:

1 Simulate the future by asking "what-if" questions
2 Develop better financial plans and forecasts
3 Perform financial forecasting and analysis
4 React more frequently to changing financial conditions
5 Become a more effective financial manager

Permitting financial managers to examine more financial issues and conditions in greater depth raises the organization's decision-making effectiveness, because the emphasis is not on performing routine or repetitive tasks more quickly but, rather, on doing a more effective management job with regard to nonroutine tasks and decision analysis.

DECISION SUPPORT SYSTEMS

Software Selection Criteria

Selection criteria for DSS software are more difficult to quantify than are hardware criteria. Ideally, software permits direct access to all the data. Storage costs and access frequently dictate how much is available on line. Powerful software should be matched by powerful hardware to provide fast development. Powerful software with systems building and maintenance features help reduce development time.

Flexibility should not be limited. A system that allows direct access to records and fields offers a significant benefit. An ability to create relationships is an important flexibility feature, as it allows the relationship to change without recreating the database. Because financial systems grow in response to new opportunities and financial conditions, the ability to add new data to a system is also an important flexibility feature. The ideal software allows the user to describe the shape of the data, give the data a name, and add them to the system on line interactively without having to regenerate the entire database.

Another criterion for evaluating DSS software is approachability, the manager/systems interface. This interface should provide a friendly environment for the user, and must be interactive. The ability to extend and customize the system so that the builder can control how it looks to the end user is an important determinant of approachability. Finally, user friendliness is significantly enhanced if maintenance is highly automated. For example, the software should be able to recognize a new feature or product, rearrange the database, and provide storage space automatically.

Finally, comprehensiveness of software should be evaluated. The more tools that can be made available in the same system, the more time will be available to work on productive analysis.

EVALUATION OF DSS

Evaluation is one of the most difficult aspects of DSS development. This is partly because of the evolutionary nature of DSS, in which completion dates may be loosely defined, as well as a reluctance to take the time to review current efforts before moving on to the next stage of development. Evaluation of DSS implementation is key to assessing improvement. A DSS aims at improving decision making.

To evaluate a DSS successfully, an explicit prior plan, formulated in advance of DSS development, should exist, stating what is to be accomplished. As mentioned elsewhere in this chapter, effective implementation involves dividing the project into manageable components. Project length is a major constraint on evaluation. The project phases should be kept to a manageable size, and the elapsed time between phases should be kept short. Effective evaluation of a DSS requires measuring change and decision improvement (i.e., "better" decisions). Figure 16-3 illustrates some evaluation criteria for a DSS.

BENEFITS

In many cases, the justification for the development of a DSS cannot be found by the traditional cost comparison method. Consequently, the benefits realized by DSS development must be expanded to include some quantification of former intangibles, such as competitive advantage, market penetration, and decision quality.

A comparison between traditional systems development techniques and DSS techniques reveals several positive considerations with respect to DSS development.

- The systems appear to be developed over a shorter period of time.
- User participation and commitment are easier to achieve.
- An unusual sense of excitement and anticipation prevails among users during systems development.
- Data processing and MIS personnel appear to develop better communication and rapport with users.
- The determination of user information requirements appears to be resolved with greater precision.
- Users appear to be more pleased with the final product and request fewer modifications.

DSS appear to be less threatening to users, since users have a greater awareness of what is happening and consequently have greater control over what will evolve. Figure 16-4 illustrates some cited benefits of a DSS.

DSS TODAY AND TOMORROW

DSS applications have been fairly successful in making the computer relevant to the financial manager. Excellent tools are available for microcomputers, superminicomputers, and mainframes that can be used directly by the financial managers to assist in decision analysis and problem-solving. The financial manager has access to well-developed and widely accepted tools for financial planning, modeling, and reporting. The most obvious advances for DSS have been in software applications. Fourth-generation end-user languages, microcomputer software products, and computer graphics are well-accepted components of decision support that have allowed DSS to operate in a user controlled environment.

DECISION MAKER
- Performance
- Attitude (before and after)
- Ability to articulate
- Ability to learn
- Role/position, motivation
- Expectations

DEVELOPMENT
- Functional
- Assumptions

Method
- Flexibility

Analyst
- Correctness of analysis
- Skill/knowledge
- Interpersonal skills
- Creativity
- Trust

SYSTEM

Model
- Validity
- Adaptivity
- Credibility

Interface
- Ease of use

- Compatibility
- Credibility

DBMS
- Availability
- Evolvability
- Integrity
- Shareability

DATA
- Completeness
- Accuracy

Content
- Meaningfulness, timeliness

USE
- Frequency, importance, mode, availability
- Who uses
- Involvement, interest, reliability
- Quality of documentation and training

ENVIRONMENT
- Receptivity
- Size, feasibility
- Organizational complexity, stability
- Politics
- Organizational structure

FIG. 16-3 Evaluation Criteria for DSS

In the past few years, there have been considerable improvements of the DSS-user interface. From spreadsheets for microcomputers to sophisticated strategic planning and financial analysis tools on mainframes, the user can understand a DSS without having a technical knowledge of computer software. The user will continue to drive the development and implementation of the DSS.

The future holds several major opportunities for developers of DSS. DSS help the financial manager to plan the future, but rarely provide a means for alerting management to important changes in the business environment. The opportunity exists for designers to develop DSS that provide prediction capabilities so that the user may obtain better information about critical problems

1 Explicit statement of the decision process
- Assumptions
- Constraints
- Objectives
- Alternatives
- Procedure

2 Vehicle for communication
- Superiors
- Subordinates
- Colleagues
- Customers

3 Tool for persuasion

4 Rationale for behavior

5 Faster awareness of problems and opportunities

6 Consistency and accuracy of dcecision procedure

7 Speed of alternative evaluation

8 Ability to consider more alternatives and more complex relationships

9 More time for manager to manage

10 Service to customers

11 General prestige

FIG. 16-4 Cited Benefits of a DSS

that are likely to develop. As such, an early warning system would help the decision maker avoid unsuspected and unpleasant reactions to changes in the marketplace.

Other areas for future growth in DSS include the development of good microcomputer-to-mainframe interfaces, teleconferencing, and the continued support of DSS on local area networks. Whatever the future holds, the goal of DSS remains the same—to provide the financial manager with tools that can be adapted to and combined with his own decision-making and judgment processes by means of whatever software and hardware are suitable and available.

REFERENCES

Alter, S.L. *Decision Support Systems: Current Practice and Continuing Challenges.* Reading, Mass.: Addison-Wesley, 1980, pp. 165–180.

Denise, R.M. "Technology for the Executive Thinker." *Datamation* (June 1983).

Donnelly, R.M. "Keep Up With Decision Support Systems." *Financial Executive* (Aug. 1983).

Hall, J.A. "Management Information Systems." *Management Accounting* (Dec. 1983).

Keen, P.G.W. "Decision Support Systems: A Research Perspective." CISR No. 54, Sloan WP No. 1117-80, March 1980.

Keen, P.G.W., and M.S. Scott Morton. *Decision Support Systems: An Organizational Perspective.* Reading Mass.: Addison-Wesley, 1978.

Lasden, M. "Enriching the Decision-Making Process." *Computer Decisions* (Nov. 1983).

Sprague, R.H., Jr., and E.D. Carlson. *Building Effective Decision Support Systems.* Englewood Cliffs, N.J.: Prentice-Hall, 1982.

Whyte, R. "Data to Fit the Decision." *Chief Executive* (Apr. 1984).

PART IV

Installation and Administration of a Financial Information System

CHAPTER 17

Selection and Implementation of a Financial Information System

Janice M. Roehl

Overview 2	**Cost of the System** 22
Reasons to Buy Software 2	**Final Selection** 23
Defining Systems Requirements 4	**Contract Negotiations** 23
Questionnaires 5	**Implementation Steps** 26
Interviews 5	**Postimplementation Review** 28
Document Reviews 7	
Outside Sources 7	**Appendix 17-1: Hardware Selection Criteria** 31
Preparing the RFP 10	Central Processing Unit 31
Cover Letter 11	Peripherals 31
General Information/Proposal Guidelines 11	Remote Devices 31
Background Material 11	Environmental Considerations 32
Vendor Questionnaire 11	Flexibility and Expandability 32
Vendor Cost Summary 12	Systems Reliability 32
Information Requirements 12	**Appendix 17-2: Vendor Evaluation Criteria** 33
Distribution of the RFP 12	Product Support 33
	Reputation and Stability 33
Review of the Completed RFP 15	Experience 34
Reference Calls 20	Product Availability 34
Site Visits 21	**References** 34

Fig. 17-1 Comparison of Software Packages With Software Developed In House 4
Fig. 17-2 Sample Questionnaire for Defining Systems Requirements 6
Fig. 17-3 Accounts Receivable System Requirements 9
Fig. 17-4 RFP Sections 11

Fig. 17-5 Vendor Cost Summary 13
Fig. 17-6 Accounts Payable System Requirements 14
Fig. 17-7 Completed Accounts Payable System Requirements 14
Fig. 17-8 Guidelines for Rating Application Software 17
Fig. 17-9 Application Software Rating Sheet 17
Fig. 17-10 Scoring for Systems Software 19
Fig. 17-11 Topics to Be Covered During Reference Calls 21
Fig. 17-12 The Implementation Process 29

OVERVIEW

This chapter describes how a company selects and implements an automated FIS, such as a general ledger or accounts payable system. The discussion includes the reasons why software should be purchased instead of developed in house, how to define systems requirements, preparing a Request for Proposal (RFP), how to evaluate software, hardware, and vendors, and how to implement a system. Selection and automation of an FIS are extremely important to an organization. As a result, the company must be willing to devote a substantial amount of time and effort to these activities.

It is assumed that the selection process encompases both computer hardware and software. Many companies have computer hardware in place. However, it is generally recommended that a company select software that best meets its financial information needs instead of being constrained by the hardware in place.

REASONS TO BUY SOFTWARE

The main reasons why it is generally recommended that software packages be purchased, instead of developed in house, to meet the financial information needs of a business include the following:

- *Implementation speed.* In general, packaged software can be installed significantly more quickly than software developed in house, because the software is readily available.

- *Fewer software problems.* Unlike software that is developed in house, packaged software has generally been thoroughly tested and "debugged" before it is sold.

- *Lower overall cost.* Generally, the total cost of packaged software is less than the cost of software developed in house. Software developed in house tends to require a significant investment by companies in terms of human resources.

- *Software vendor assistance.* Most software vendors, especially those in the minicomputer and mainframe market, support their software. This means that the in-house data processing staff can be minimized.

Although software developed in house tends to meet the exact needs of the company more closely, there are some distinct reasons for not recommending this approach.

- *Difficulty of forecasting cost.* The cost of developing software in house is very difficult to forecast because there is generally a significant amount of uncertainty surrounding the entire development process. Also, most companies have little or no information on systems development costs on which to base their cost estimates. Due to the uncertainty and lack of data surrounding the development, most in-house software projects exceed their forecasted costs. In fact, there are many examples of systems development projects that have exceeded their forecasted costs by two to ten times.
- *Delayed implementation.* Just as it is hard to forecast the cost of developing a system in house, it is also very difficult to forecast the time it will take to develop the system. Because of the uncertainty and lack of precise information surrounding a systems development process, it is extremely difficult to predict when a program will be completed. It is not unusual to see deadlines missed by anywhere from one month to two years.
- *Employee turnover.* The data processing industry is known for its extremely high turnover rates. This is due, in part, to the high demand for data processing professionals and the entrepreneurial spirit of many of these professionals. Turnover can wreak havoc with a systems development schedule, especially if the departing individual is a key team member.
- *Reinventing the wheel.* Many systems developed in house duplicate software readily available in the marketplace. This means that the developing company uses its valuable human resources to create a system that may already exist, thereby pushing back the implementation date by a significant amount of time.
- *Poor documentation.* Systems developed in house tend to have poor user, systems, and control documentation. The reason for this is threefold:
  - Programmers often dislike documenting their programs. As a result, the documentation may never be completed unless the orgainzation assigns someone to do it.

ADVANTAGES OF SOFTWARE PACKAGES
- Implementation speed
- Few software problems
- Low overall cost
- Software vendor assistance

DISADVANTAGES OF SOFTWARE DEVELOPED IN HOUSE
- Difficulty of forecasting costs
- Delayed implementation
- Employee turnover
- Reinvention of the wheel
- Poor documentation
- Prevalence of software problems

FIG. 17-1 Comparison of Software Packages With Software Developed In House.

- Organizations frequently fail to make documentation a high priority; therefore, it just doesn't get written.
- When programs are updated, the documentation often is not. Unlike software vendors who have numerous users to satisfy and thus must keep their documentation up-to-date, in-house programmers frequently fail to do so.

- *Prevalence of software problems.* Software vendors normally test their products thoroughly before allowing them to be sold. In addition, packaged software is generally used by numerous users in a variety of ways. Therefore, software problems (i.e., "bugs") are likely to appear early in a package's life cycle. Because of market pressures, the software vendor must correct these bugs as rapidly as possible. This is not necessarily so for systems developed in house, which are generally used only by the developing company. As a result, it may take years before a bug is discovered. Also, once the bug is found, considerable time may pass before the bug is corrected.

Figure 17-1 lists the advantages of packaged software over software developed in house.

DEFINING SYSTEMS REQUIREMENTS

Before software is selected, the requirements for the software system need to be precisely defined. If this is not done, the software selected probably will not meet the organization's needs.

The purposes for developing a Systems Requirement Definition (SRD) are as follows:

- To make sure that the selected software meets the company's current and future needs
- To develop a clear understanding of each application area (e.g., accounts payable and accounts receivable) and how automation can assist in that area
- To prioritize the application areas to be automated

There are a number of methods that may be used to determine the requirements of FISs. These methods include questionnaires, interviews, document reviews, and outside sources.

Questionnaires

Questionnaires may be used to develop a general understanding of an organization, its objectives, and the environment in which it operates. They may also be used to define major financially oriented tasks, analyze transactions, determine major systems interfaces, and assist with the development of requirements.

Before a questionnaire is developed, the individuals preparing it (normally a data processing steering committee or some other such group) needs to make sure that they have top management's support. Without this support, it is doubtful that the questionnaire will be returned on a timely basis and with complete and accurate responses.

The questionnaire should not be so long that it discourages its completion. Alternatively, it should not be so brief that it is useless. Figure 17-2 illustrates the types of questions that should appear in the questionnaire. Note that a cover letter should be attached to the questionnaire, clearly defining its purpose, the date it is to be returned, and the importance of thorough and accurate responses. Also, the cover letter should be signed by someone with authority, such as the vice-president, finance, the executive vice-president, or the director of information services.

Interviews

The purposes of interviews, similar to those of questionnaires, are:

- To develop an understanding of the business—its environment and objectives
- To define major tasks and interfaces
- To analyze transactions
- To determine the adequacy of the current system

QUESTIONNAIRE

1 What functions are you responsible for?

2 What are the primary objectives of your job?

3 What other departments do you interface with?

4 What are your major tasks?

5 What reports do you prepare?

6 What forms do you use? (Please attach a sample of each form.)

7 Where do these forms originate?

8 Where do these forms go when you complete them?

9 What financial information do you receive from other departments?

10 What changes do you predict will occur in your job over the next three years?

11 What additional information could you use?

FIG. 17-2 Sample Questionnaire for Defining Systems Requirements

SELECTION AND IMPLEMENTATION OF AN FIS 17-7

- To identify employees' expectations
- To predict growth areas

Interviews should not be designed to elicit detailed information on systems specifications. Rather, they should help elicit general information systems requirements, transaction volumes, major interfaces, and future needs and concerns.

One group of individuals whose information and reporting needs should be emphasized is the senior management. Too frequently, only the needs of lower management are incorporated into an SRD. The resulting FIS frequently does not provide senior management with the necessary reports for managing the business effectively. Therefore, senior management's information needs must be thoroughly documented.

Interviews, often conducted in conjunction with the issuance of a questionnaire, help to confirm or refute the findings from the questionnaires.

Document Reviews

Another way to define systems requirements is to review input documents and reports. Doing so provides the organization with a listing of its current data elements. Also, the review helps to define the minimum reporting requirements of the proposed FIS.

Audit work papers often contain information that may be used when developing an SRD. The flow charts contained in the work papers frequently provide a clear picture of how an accounting system operates. Also, the work papers often contain volume estimates, such as the number of payroll checks issued and the number of customers in the accounts receivable file.

Outside Sources

A final source of requirements that should be included in an SRD is the environment in which the organization exists. Economic trends, changes in tax laws and industry practices, and revisions to government regulations may all affect the reporting requirements of an FIS, and therefore should be reviewed.

There is a cost involved in collecting the information on systems requirements. As a result, an organization should not spend an excessive amount of time documenting its systems requirements, because it may never get to the point of selecting software.

After the questionnaires and interviews have been completed and the other sources reviewed, it is vital that the existing manual and/or automated financial systems be documented. Included in this documentation should be the following factors:

- The purpose of the system
- Who maintains the system

- The major systems inputs, edits, controls, and outputs
- All systems interfaces and special features
- The volume of transactions handled by the system
- The costs of operating the system

In addition, if the system is automated, it is important to note its hardware, language, age, and the investment involved.

The primary purposes of documenting existing manual and automated systems are:

- To make sure that the SRD contains, at a minimum, the features currently available, if desired
- To identify weaknesses in the current system
- To determine what is currently available and what is missing from the existing systems
- To discuss unnecessary reports
- To highlight procedures that are poorly defined.

After the current financial systems are documented, it is then time to prepare the SRD. The purpose of the SRD, which will generally become part of the RFP, is to communicate to software vendors the systems requirements of the organization and to allow the vendors to identify software products that can meet those requirements.

The SRD should be divided by application area (e.g., general ledger and accounts payable). The application area should be further divided into the following topics:

- General systems narrative
- Processing requirements
- Inquiry requirements
- Reporting requirements

The requirements are stated as a single sentence, and should be divided into the following categories: (1) required (features that must be present) and (2) desired (features that would be nice to have but that are not vital). Figure 17-3 gives a very abbreviated example of these factors for an accounts receivable system.

SRDs may be anywhere from 5 to well over 100 pages long, depending on the number of applications being selected and the level of detail desired. As mentioned elsewhere in this chapter, the preparation of an SRD requires a large commitment of time and money. Therefore, a company should be careful not to overdefine its requirements. Similarly, it should be careful not to make the SRD so general that it allows all software packages to meet its needs.

After completing the SRD for the applications to be automated, the prioritization of the applications should be done. It is vital for an organization to

SELECTION AND IMPLEMENTATION OF AN FIS 17-9

ACME CORPORATION

ACCOUNTS RECEIVABLE SYSTEM NARRATIVE

The accounts receivable system should be designed to handle all of the Acme Corporation's billing, receivable, and collection needs. The system must interface with both the order entry system, to get billing information, and the general ledger system, to post billings, cash receipts, and bad-debt journal entries.

Processing requirements

The accounts receivable system should be able to perform the following functions:

- Post to different revenue accounts depending on the type of service performed.
- Enter nonaccounting data to the customer master file on line.
- Disallow the deletion of customers with an account balance greater than zero.

Inquiry requirements

The accounts receivable system should include the following inquiry features and capabilities:

- On-line review of a customer's billing and payment history
- Inquiry as to the status of a customer's bill using a variety of data elements including:
  —Customer name
  —Customer number
  —Invoice number

Reporting requirements

The accounts receivable system should produce the following reports:

- *Accounts receivable aging report*—a report indicating the amount of time the customer's accounts receivable have been outstanding.

  Frequency: weekly

- *Cash receipts register*—a register containing information on:
  —Date of receipt
  —Check number
  —Customer name and number
  —Amount
  —Invoice applied to
  —General ledger account posted to

  Frequency: daily

FIG. 17-3 Accounts Receivable System Requirements

clearly define each application in the order of importance, to help the organization evaluate the completed RFP and identify the factors upon which the software selection will be decided. Areas to consider when assigning priorities to applications to be automated include:

- *The impact of the system on the organization and its customers.* How many employees will come into contact with the system? Will the system affect relations with customers (as would an accounts receivable system)? How will the system benefit the organization?

- *The costs and benefits of the system.* Will the system impact the organization's net income? Can the system influence its productivity? What are the total direct and indirect costs of the system?

- *The demand for the system.* Are accounting employees demanding a new system? Does senior menagement strongly desire the system? How long will it take to get the system installed?

- *The dependence of the system on other systems.* Will the installation of the purchasing system, for example, have to be delayed until accounts payable is on line?

PREPARING THE RFP

An RFP is used to communicate the FIS's requirements to software and/or hardware vendors in a uniform manner. It is prepared after the SRD, and serves the following purposes:

- To communicate the organization's systems requirements to vendors and to allow them to respond to those requirements.
- To request specific commitments from vendors, such as the system's delivery dates, maintenance provided, costs, and contractual arrangements.
- To serve as a tool for comparing vendors. The RFP should be prepared in a way that allows the organization to easily compare the proposals of various vendors.

Depending on the organization's needs, RFPs may be prepared for software, hardware, or both. However, no matter what the organization selects, the RFP must be well structured and precise in order to elicit a clear and concise response from vendors. A vague and poorly organized RFP is likely to result in proposals that are difficult to compare and that are lacking in many areas.

RFPs are generally organized into the following sections: cover letter; general information/proposal guidelines; background material; vendor questionnaire; vendor cost summary; and information requirements. Figure 17-4 depicts the primary RFP sections.

> **REQUEST FOR PROPOSAL SECTIONS**
> I Cover letter
> II General information/proposal guidelines
> III Background material
> IV Vendor questionnaire
> V Vendor cost summary
> VI Information requirements

FIG. 17-4 RFP Sections

Cover Letter

The cover letter serves to notify the hardware and/or software vendor that the company is requesting a proposal on particular application software and/or hardware. In addition, the cover letter should contain the following information: important deadlines (such as the date the proposal is due) and the projected installation date; the overall purpose of the RFP; the individual within the organization to contact with questions; and the format of the RFP.

General Information/Proposal Guidelines

The general information/proposal guidelines section contains valuable data on how the proposal is to be completed, how the selection process will be performed, and the importance of a concise and timely response. Also included in this section are whether site visits will be made by the organization, the fact that the cost of developing the proposal is entirely the vendor's responsibility, the fact that the organization reserves the right to reject any and all proposals, and the confidentiality of the material contained in the RFP.

Background Material

The background material section contains information about the organization that is of interest to the vendor. Included in this section might be a general description of the organization's business (e.g., retailing, manufacturing, or wholesaling); the company's history; volume statistics (e.g., the number of payroll and accounts payable checks issued per month and the number of general ledger transactions); the current hardware, software, and operating system, if any; and the hours of operation. This information is used by the vendor to determine the size of the FIS needed by the organization.

Vendor Questionnaire

The vendor questionnaire section of the RFP is one of the most important sections. In this section, the vendor is asked to answer a variety of questions on its background, clients, training, and growth; systems reliability, security, and performance; how modifications are handled; how reports are produced; acceptance testing and installation schedule; data control; staffing; R&D; documentation; and hardware proposed, if any. The answers to these questions will determine the vendor ultimately selected by the organization. Therefore, this section must be well constructed and the questions concisely formulated. (See Appendix 17-2 for examples of vendor questions.)

Vendor Cost Summary

In the vendor cost summary section, the vendor is requested to complete a cost schedule delineating the costs of the proposed FIS. Each vendor is asked to provide information on recurring and nonrecurring costs over a five-year period and to provide supplemental schedules to explain the derivation of all costs and what is included in such items as installation and maintenance fees. An example of a vendor cost summary schedule is presented in Figure 17-5.

Information Requirements

The information requirements section sets forth the processing, inquiry, and reporting requirements developed during the systems requirement definition. Each vendor is asked to complete a matrix that has five responses and that contains all systems requirements. The five responses are:

1 Feature exists in the current system.
2 Feature exists in the current system, but is available only for an additional fee.
3 Feature will exist in the system by the projected installation date.
4 Feature will exist in the system by the projected installation date, but only for an additional fee.
5 Not available.

Also, the vendor is asked to make comments, where necessary, and to quote the additional fee when its response falls into either Category 2 or 4. Figure 17-6 illustrates a page from an accounts payable information requirements section. Figure 17-7 shows how a vendor might respond to the requirements listed in Figure 17-6.

DISTRIBUTION OF THE RFP

Once the RFP is completed, the organization must determine the vendors to whom it will be submitted. With over 50,000 software packages available in the

SELECTION AND IMPLEMENTATION OF AN FIS

VENDOR COST SUMMARY

	Year					
	1	2	3	4	5	Total
Recurring costs						
Hardware						
CPU lease	$____	$____	$____	$____	$____	$____
Terminal lease	____	____	____	____	____	____
Printer lease	____	____	____	____	____	____
Other lease	____	____	____	____	____	____
CPU Maintenance	____	____	____	____	____	____
Terminal maintenance	____	____	____	____	____	____
Printer Maintenance	____	____	____	____	____	____
Other maintenance	____	____	____	____	____	____
Software						
Software license	____	____	____	____	____	____
Software maintenance	____	____	____	____	____	____
Other fees	____	____	____	____	____	____
Supplies						
Disks, tapes	____	____	____	____	____	____
Ribbons, paper	____	____	____	____	____	____
Other	____	____	____	____	____	____
Total	$____	$____	$____	$____	$____	$____
Nonrecurring costs						
Hardware						
CPU purchase	$____	$____	$____	$____	$____	$____
Terminal purchase	____	____	____	____	____	____
Printer purchase	____	____	____	____	____	____
Other purchase	____	____	____	____	____	____
Software						
Software purchase	____	____	____	____	____	____
Installation						
Freight	____	____	____	____	____	____
Cabling	____	____	____	____	____	____
Site preparation	____	____	____	____	____	____
Training	____	____	____	____	____	____
Customization	____	____	____	____	____	____
System initialing	____	____	____	____	____	____
Installation	____	____	____	____	____	____
Other	____	____	____	____	____	____
Total	$____	$____	$____	$____	$____	$____
TOTAL	$____	$____	$____	$____	$____	$____

FIG. 17-5 Vendor Cost Summary

	Response					
Requirement	1	2	3	4	5	Comments
1 Enter vendor invoices on line.	☐	☐	☐	☐	☐	....
2 Enter vendor credit memoranda on line and apply credits to future payments.	☐	☐	☐	☐	☐	....
3 Write checks automatically based on invoice date and a predefined pay period (e.g., 30 days from invoice date).	☐	☐	☐	☐	☐	....
4 Automatically process recurring payments.	☐	☐	☐	☐	☐	....
5 Process and post manual checks to correct vendor and general ledger account.	☐	☐	☐	☐	☐	....
6 Automatically interface with general ledger system.	☐	☐	☐	☐	☐	....
7 Edit for duplicate invoice numbers.	☐	☐	☐	☐	☐	....
8 Allow for standard discount terms (e.g., 2/10 net 30).	☐	☐	☐	☐	☐	....

FIG. 17-6 Accounts Payable System Requirements

	Response					
Requirement	1	2	3	4	5	Comments
1 Enter vendor invoices on line.	☒	☐	☐	☐	☐	....
2 Enter vendor credit memoranda on line and apply credits to future payments.	☐	☒	☐	☐	☐	$5,000 additional fee
3 Write checks automatically based on invoice date and a predefined pay period (e.g., 30 days from invoice date).	☒	☐	☐	☐	☐	....
4 Automatically process recurring payments.	☐	☐	☒	☐	☐	....
5 Process and post manual checks to correct vendor and general ledger account.	☒	☐	☐	☐	☐	....
6 Automatically interface with general ledger system.	☒	☐	☐	☐	☐	....
7 Edit for duplicate invoice numbers.	☐	☐	☐	☒	☐	$3,000 additional fee
8 Allow for standard discount terms (e.g., 2/10 net 30).	☐	☐	☐	☐	☒	....

FIG. 17-7 Completed Accounts Payable System Requirements

marketplace, narrowing the field can be a difficult task. However there are some basic factors to consider.

- *Geographic location.* The ability to receive timely support is extremely important. Since many software vendors may not have offices located near the organization, this factor can be used to eliminate many software options.
- *Hardware considerations.* Many software programs run only on certain hardware configurations (e.g., IBM hardware only). Therefore, if the organization owns hardware or has a preference for a certain manufacturer, the software options are significantly reduced.
- *Organization size.* The size of the organization influences the size of the computer system that must be acquired. Software is generally designed to run on either microcomputers, minicomputers, or mainframes. As a result, the software vendors to whom the organization may send the RFP are limited.
- *Organizational preference.* Some organizations prefer to deal with firms who distribute software only. Other organizations prefer to deal with turnkey vendors who supply both a hardware and software solution. The organization's decision in this area will influence the number of vendors to whom the RFP can be sent.
- *Vendor characteristics.* It is frequently possible to prescreen vendors to determine if it is prudent to send them an RFP. This can be accomplished by calling a vendor representative, reviewing vendor literature, or looking at one of the many software reference manuals such as *Datapro* or *Data Decisions*. When prescreening a vendor, the organization should look at such factors as the vendor's stability and related experiences, list prices, and flexibility.

Other means of identifying vendors who should receive the RFP include engaging a consultant experienced in hardware and software selections, reviewing computer-oriented magazines, and contacting hardware vendors for lists of potential software supplies.

In general, the RFP should be sent to between five and twelve vendors; any more that that, and the process becomes cumbersome; any fewer, and the choices become too limited. The vendor must have sufficient time to complete the RFP accurately and thoroughly. Therefore, it should be given three to six weeks to complete the RFP and return it to the organization.

REVIEW OF THE COMPLETED RFP

Three to six weeks after the RFP is issued, the vendors should return it to the soliciting organization. Once all the proposals are received, the organization should review them briefly. This brief review will undoubtedly lead to the elimination of some of the proposals. For example, a vendor may decide not to propose on the systems desired, may not have the on-line capabilities required, or may lack a fully integrated system. Whatever the reason, a brief review eliminates proposals that do not meet the organization's needs.

Most systems decisions are influenced by the software, not the hardware. Therefore, the organization should first review the software proposed by the remaining vendors. The goal of this review is to determine the two or three finalists from whom the organization will eventually select the FIS. (The field should be narrowed to two or three, because any more makes the final selection cumbersome; any fewer leaves the company in a risky situation. For example, if only one finalist vendor is selected and it goes out of business, the organization will have to begin the selection process over again.)

There are two types of software the organization needs to evaluate: application and systems. Application software is the software that performs the functions needed by the user, such as paying invoices, preparing financial statements, and recording cash receipts. It is used to "perform certain specific data processing or computational tasks."[1] Examples of application software include the accounts payable, accounts receivable, and general ledger systems. Systems software is software that makes it possible to "use a computer more conveniently or operate it more efficiently. Included in this broad category are operating systems, data base management systems, report generators, data base compilers, debugging aids, etc."[2]

The information requirements section of the RFP is used to review the application software. As mentioned elsewhere in this chapter, each vendor is asked to respond to each requirement using a number between 1 and 5. The organization should tabulate these responses to determine how well the vendor's software meets the organization's needs. Figures 17-8 and 17-9 describe the scoring process.

In addition, the organization should review the following characteristics of the application software:

- *Flexibility.* Is the software easy to modify? Will it handle the organization's needs five years from installation? Is it easy to debug? Flexibility is also an important factor to consider when reviewing systems software and hardware. According to Myron Karasik, a computer systems consultant:

  Flexibility will be crucial if a vendor does not survive, if it does not continue to service its products, or if the buyer seller relationship breaks down. It is therefore essential to choose products and systems that can be easily upgraded or easily supported by alternative sources as business needs change. If the computer has a standard operating

---

[1] "What to Look for in Software Packages," *Datapro—Software Solutions*, p. AS60-300-002.
[2] "What to Look for in Software Packages," p. AS60-300-002.

SELECTION AND IMPLEMENTATION OF AN FIS

1 Prepare a spreadsheet listing all of the requirements. The spreadsheet should look exactly like the information systems requirement section displayed in Figure 17-6.
2 Determine the number of points a response is worth. For example, Response 1 may be worth 10 points on a required feature but only 6 points on a desired feature. (A sample scoring scheme follows.)
3 Tally the vendor's response.
4 Total the score by application area.
5 Determine the vendor's total score.
6 See Figure 17-9 for a sample of a completed spreadsheet.

RECOMMENDED SCORING SCHEME

Response	Required	Desired
1	10	6
2	10	6
3	6	4
4	6	4
5	0	0

The spreadsheet should look exactly like the information systems requirement displayed in Figure 17-6.

FIG. 17-8 Guidelines for Rating Application Software

Requirement	Required or Desired	Response 1	2	3	4	5	Comments
1 Enter vendor invoices on line.	R	(10)	10	6	6	0	....
2 Enter vendor credit memoranda on line and apply credits to future payments.	R	10	(10)	6	6	0	....
3 Write checks automatically based on invoice date and a predefined pay period (e.g., 30 days from invoice date).	R	(10)	10	6	6	0	....
4 Automatically process recurring payments.	D	6	6	(4)	4	0	....
5 Process and post manual checks to correct vendor and general ledger account.	R	(10)	10	6	6	0	....
6 Automatically interface with general ledger system.	R	(10)	10	6	6	0	....
7 Edit for duplicate invoice numbers.	R	10	10	6	(6)	0	....
8 Allow for standard discount terms (e.g., 2/10 net 30).	D	6	6	4	4	(0)	....
Total Score		40	10	4	6	0	

FIG. 17-9 Application Software Rating Sheet

system and a communication, capability that supports industry standard protocols, you can usually transfer files and programs to other machines.[3]

- *Documentation.* Is it easy to use? Is it accurate and thorough? Is it updated regularly? Does it describe all error messages? Are all screen formats presented? Does it clearly describe recovery procedures? Are terms defined?

- *Controls.* Is a clear audit trail of all transactions available? Are data validated before files are updated? Does password security exist? Are all errors flagged? Is a listing of log-on attempts provided? Are different authorization levels available? Can check digits be used? Are batch and hash totals available?

Analyzing systems software is not as easy as analyzing application software, because it is harder to quantify. However, these guidelines can be useful.

1 *Determine the systems software factors to be evaluated.* For example, it is likely that the organization will want to review the following:
- The operating and database management system
- Multiuser capabilities
- Programming language available
- Compilation speeds
- Systems utilities such as file maintenance programs, backup and restore programs, and sorting and text editors
- Systems support software such as file management processors, password protection, screen formatters, report writers, and print spoolers
- Compatibility of the system with other software products
- Interactive and communications capabilities
- Ease of operation

2 *Once the factors have been determined, prioritize and assign numeric values to them.* For example, the company may need a certain type of operating system, such as PICK. Therefore, this would receive a high priority and thus more points.

3 *Review the vendor's proposal and assign a score to each factor.* Assigning scores is a somewhat subjective process. However, it is important that it be done.

---

[3] Karasik, Myron S., "Selecting a Small Business Computer," *Harvard Business Review* (Jan.-Feb. 1984), p. 27.

SELECTION AND IMPLEMENTATION OF AN FIS

SYSTEMS SOFTWARE

Factor	Points Assigned	Vendor Score
1 Operating system	18	16
2 DBMS	12	12
3 Multiuser capabilities	10	6
4 Programming language	6	6
5 Compilation speed	6	2
6 Systems utilities	8	6
7 Systems support software	10	7
8 Compatability	8	8
9 Interactive and communications capabilities	10	9
10 Ease of operations	12	8
Total	100	80

FIG. 17-10 Scoring for Systems Software

4 *Total the vendor's score in this section.* Figure 17-10 provides an example of how systems software can be prioritized and scored.

As mentioned elsewhere in this chapter, the software decision usually takes precedent over the hardware decision. However, a thorough review of the proposed hardware is extremely important to make sure that the FIS will meet the organization's needs.

The size of the proposed hardware system depends on a number of factors:

1 The volume statistics listed in the background section of the RFP
2 Projected growth rates
3 The vendor's experience with similar clients

Acquiring a system that meets the organization's current and future needs is extremely important. Either an in-house data processing specialist or an experienced data processing consultant must review the capabilities and flexibility of the proposed hardware configuration. (For more details on the hardware factors to evaluate, see Appendix 17-2.)

Other hardware factors to review include:

- Central processing unit (or CPU)
- Peripheral devices (such as disk and tape drives)
- Remote devices (such as communications support equipment)
- Enviromental considerations

- Flexibility and expandability
- Systems reliability

Once the hardware factors to evaluate have been determined, they should be prioritized and assigned a numeric value. (This is similar to the method recommended for reviewing systems software.) Then each vendor's proposal should be reviewed and assigned a score on each factor. The total score on hardware is then determined.

After the hardware and software have been evaluated, the next step is to evaluate the vendor(s). Depending on the system desired, this may involve reviewing a software vendor and a hardware vendor. The primary factors to consider when evaluating a vendor are:

- Product support
- Reputation and stability
- Experience
- Product availability

Once the software, hardware, and vendor have been thoroughly evaluated, the selection of the finalist vendors occurs. These vendors are then analyzed further by means of reference calls and site visits. All relevant factors must be considered when selecting the finalist vendors. Because substantial amounts of time and money are invested in reviewing the finalist vendors, it is vital that the organization choose vendors who can actually provide it with an FIS that meets its needs.

REFERENCE CALLS

One of the most important aspects of the systems selection process is the practice of making reference calls to systems users. Reference calls are a means by which an organization can find out what a vendor may not want them to know. For example, an organization may discover that a vendor's documentation and support are not good as its sales literature claims.

Reference calls should be made with regard to all finalist vendors. The calls should be directed to users with similar hardware and software configurations. If this is not done, the accuracy of the information may be suspect. For example, just because software runs effectively on one hardware model does not mean it will run efficiently on another.

The questions asked during a reference call should be both fact and opinion oriented. The user should be asked to list the software installed and also his overall opinion of the software. Figure 17-11 lists the topics to cover when making a reference call. One important piece of information to elicit are the names of other systems users, as vendors frequently give out only the names of satisfied users. Asking a user for names of other users may lead to one who is not pleased with the system.

SELECTION AND IMPLEMENTATION OF AN FIS 17-21

- Type of Organization
- Volume Statistics
- Software Packages Purchased
- Software Packages Installed
- Ease of Installation
- Operating System
- DBMS
- Hardware Installed
- Hardware Dependability
- Systems Security
- Response Times
- Quality of Reports
- Method of System Selection
- Why Choose the Vendor(s)
- Ease of Operation
- Quality of Training
- Quality of Documentation
- Modifications Made
- Quality of Support
- Vendor Dependability
- Unforseen Costs
- User Group Membership
- Overall Satisfaction
- Names of Other Users

FIG. 17-11 Topics to Be Covered During Reference Calls

SITE VISITS

After the reference calls have been made, the organization should arrange to attend a demonstration of the system at a working installation, not at the vendor's headquarters. The purpose of the site visit is the following:

- To view the system in a real-life environment
- To answer questions that may have arisen during the selection process
- To assist the organization in deciding whether the system will meet its current and future needs
- To help determine the vendor's competence and comfort with the system, as well as its level of interest

The demonstration should take place at a user's place of business and should be on a "live," not "demo," system. The demonstration must take place at a user's site so that the vendor has no opportunity to manipulate the demonstration to its advantage. Although the majority of vendors are extremely honest and ethical, some unscrupulous ones may try to manipulate potential customers.

The individuals present at the demonstration should include in-house data processing personnel; potential systems users, such as the accounts payable supervisor; a vendor representative to answer questions; and a data processing consultant, if one is being used.

In general, the demonstration should take from two to five hours to complete. The organization's representative should come prepared with a set of questions to ask the user. Otherwise, important aspects may not be covered.

If possible, the organization should arrange to see all of the vendor demonstrations during a two-week period. This allows the individuals participating in them to compare the systems more easily. However, an attempt should be made to avoid scheduling two demonstrations on the same day, as confusion and information overload may otherwise result.

COST OF THE SYSTEM

The costs of purchasing hardware and software have not been mentioned up to this point because it is assumed that, if an organization is going through the selection procedure, it has made a commitment to purchase the best system available. In the systems world, as in many other facets of life, "You get what you pay for." Thus, the cost of the system should be a secondary consideration. It is more important to get a system that truly meets the current and future needs of the organization.

According to an article by Edward J. Bride, in *Software News*, which quotes Jerry Weinberg, an information systems consultant, "In the lifetime of a [software] package, a user can expect to spend anywhere between 10 and 100 times the cost of a package in training and other aspects."[4] Therefore, selecting a system that meets an organization's needs is more important than attempting to save a few dollars initially. However, the total cost for the system should play a role in selecting an FIS. It makes no sense to spend more money than is necessary.

The vendor cost summary portion of the RFP may be used to compare the costs of proposed systems. However, other cost factors need to be clarified before comparing the total costs of the proposed systems.

- What will the current proposed enhancements cost?
- How will the cost of future enhancements be determined?
- Is there an additional fee for installation?
- Is there an additional fee for training?
- How much does maintenance cost?
- Is there an additional fee for twenty-four-hour support?
- Is there a charge for systems updates?
- Will the organization receive a discount if it purchases other integrated systems?
- Does the software license allow the use of the software at multiple sites? If not, what is the charge for the other sites?

---

[4] Bride, Edward J., "Think of Software as Being Free," *Software News* (Oct. 1983), p. 5.

- How much does the warranty cost?
- When does the warranty go into effect? (The warranty should go into effect on the date the system is accepted, *not* on the date the system is installed.)
- Does the vendor give a refund if the software does not perform as promised?
- Is the price of documentation included in the total price?
- Can the organization duplicate the documentation, or must it pay for additional copies? If so, what is the cost for additional copies?
- Is the source code included in the system's price? If not, what is the charge for the source code?

FINAL SELECTION

Once the software, hardware, and vendor have been thoroughly reviewed and the reference calls and site visits completed, the organization is prepared to select the system to be purchased. The decision should be sound because of the amount of time and effort spent on it. If the organization has completed the steps outlined in this chapter, it should find itself with an FIS that meets current and future needs. Once the final selection has been made, the organization is in a position to begin contract negotiations.

CONTRACT NEGOTIATIONS

After the software and hardware have been selected, preparation for contract negotiations between the organization and the vendor(s) should ensue. The objectives of contract negotiations are:

- To define the organization's expectations clearly and thereby avoid misunderstandings
- To define precisely what remedies are available if the vendor fails to perform as promised
- To protect the organization against unexpected occurrences, such as the bankruptcy of the vendor
- To ensure the best terms possible for the organization

Negotiating a sales contract can be a long and costly process. However, if done correctly, it may save the organization a lot of time in the long run. When negotiating, there are several points to remember:

1 *Do not accept the vendor's standard contract.* These contracts tend to be one sided in favor of the vendor and to disclaim all responsibility for performance and support.

2 *Negotiate with someone with the authority to bind the vendor.* Negotiating with a vendor representative who has no power is useless, because the promises he makes may be overturned by his superiors.

3 *Never accept oral promises.* When negotiating with hardware and software vendors, everything must be put in writing.

4 *Do not make unreasonable demands.* The organization is responsible for bargaining in good faith.

5 *Obtain advice from a professional experienced in contract negotiations.* The organization should not assume it can negotiate a mutually beneficial contract without the help of a professional (e.g., a lawyer specializing in contract law).

Four specific steps are essential for negotiating a contract effectively that is mutually beneficial:

1 Select a negotiating team to represent the organization. Included on this team should be, at a minimum:

- A data processing specialist
- An individual who will be using the system
- An attorney
- A purchasing department representative

2 Determine the objectives of the negotiations and a plan of action to take if the negotiations fail.

3 Review the standard contract offered by the organization and identify problem areas and points that are missing.

4 Meet with the vendor to negotiate the contract.

Contract negotiations may be a long process. Therefore, the organization should be sure to select a negotiating team it can depend on, one whose members will continue to be with the company in the long run. When the negotiating team reviews the contract, it should have prepared a checklist of items to be included in the contract, as follows:

- The completed RFP that the vendor submitted.
- An implementation plan with specific tasks and dates and assigned responsiblities.
- The penalty for late installation.

SELECTION AND IMPLEMENTATION OF AN FIS 17-25

- The support that will be provided during the implementation process, including the names and qualifications of the individuals who will provide the support.
- The period during which the system is guaranteed. (This period should not begin until the system is fully accepted.)
- A list of agreed-upon modifications and deadlines for their completion.
- The support that will be provided after the system is installed, the times during which the support will be available, and the qualifications of the people who will provide the support.
- The cost basis used to determine the fees for additional support (e.g., $75.00 per hour).
- The amount of training that will be provided and the qualifications of the individuals supplying it.
- The cost of additional training.
- The extent and timing of maintenance (e.g., once a month).
- The steps that will be taken to correct systems bugs found after installation. (There should be no additional cost for correcting bugs.)
- The response time for support (e.g., the vendor may guarantee a one-hour response to systems problems).
- The documentation and the number of copies of that documentation that will be provided. (The organization should also make sure that it has the right to duplicate the documentation without an additional charge.)
- How future modifications will be handled and the pricing method to be used to cost these modifications.
- How updated versions of the system are distributed and priced.
- Performance and operating characteristics guaranteed by the vendor.
- A clear understanding that copies of the source code, if not included in the purchase price, will go into escrow in the event of the software vendor's bankruptcy.
- The criteria to be used to determine systems acceptance.
- The extent to which the organization may modify (or have modified) the software without invalidating the warranty.
- How trade-ins or systems upgrades will be handled.
- The price breaks given for the purchase of other software products.
- The right to use the software at the organization's other facilities.

- Remedies available in the event of a disaster (e.g., alternative processing locations).
- When the software will be delivered and in what form.

The contract should clearly specify the costs for hardware, software, maintenance, installation support, modifications, and upgrades. The organization should be sure it is protected from any price increases without its written consent. The contract should also clearly identify the terms of payment. The organization might hold back a substantial portion of the purchase price (e.g., 10 to 20 percent) until the system is fully operational for a specified period of time and has passed all acceptance tests. Unless that is done, the vendor might not assist the organization with the implementation to the extent needed.

IMPLEMENTATION STEPS

After the hardware and software have been selected and the sales contract negotiated, the organization is ready to begin implementing the system. Implementation is a very time-consuming process. It requires the commitment of a substantial amount of human and monetary resources. Therefore, the organization must make sure that it plans properly for the implementation in order to avoid many of the typical problems that arise. It is estimated that fewer than 10 percent of FISs are installed on time and that between 15 and 20 percent of financially oriented minicomputer systems are currently not operational. For these reasons, the organization must carefully plan and manage the implementation process.

The first step in the implementation process is selecting the implementation team. That team is responsible for managing all aspects of the implementation and making sure they take place on a timely basis and in a cost-effective manner. The team should be made up of data processing professionals, systems users, and representatives from senior management and the hardware and software vendors. In addition, a project manager should be assigned who is responsible for ensuring the ultimate success of the implementation. Each team member should be given an application area (such as accounts payable) for which he is responsible.

After the implementation team has been selected and assigned application areas and responsibilities, it needs to assign priorities to the applications to be implemented. Many organizations make the mistake of trying to implement all of the FISs at once, which often leads to significant problems. To avoid this, the applications must be assigned preferential ratings based on the organization's needs, the resources available, and the ease of implementation.

Once the applications have been rated, the implementation team must develop a schedule containing a detailed work plan with clearly specified responsibilities and target dates. Many software and hardware vendors have developed their own implementation schedules. Therefore, the organization

SELECTION AND IMPLEMENTATION OF AN FIS 17-27

may not need to develop its own from scratch. The implementation plan should take into account the following factors:

- The resources the organization will dedicate to the implementation
- What, if any, outside resources (such as consultants) are needed
- Any projected bottlenecks
- The frequency of status meetings
- Contingency plans
- How communication lines should be established.

One of the most important ingredients of a successful implementation is management support; without it, the implementation is far less likely to succeed. Therefore, the implementation team should enlist the support of top management early in the implementation process.

The team members responsible for a particular application area must thoroughly understand the needs of that area. They should review the requirements detailed in the RFP and make sure that they have not changed in the interim. After this, the team members must design the input forms and output reports to be generated by the system. Software vendors frequently have standardized forms and reports that the team needs to review to decide whether they meet the organization's needs. If they do not, modifications must be made.

A schedule for the completion of software modification, along with the responsibility for the modifications, must be established. The software vendor should be contractually obligated to meet the schedule.

A particular individual or group of individuals should be given the responsibility for interfacing with the hardware vendor on site preparations. Often, a computer room with specialized air conditioning and power supply must be constructed before the hardware can be installed. A schedule delineating specific responsibilities should be established.

One of the most important aspects of the implementation process is training users. Unless the training is done in a timely and thorough manner, the system may never be completely utilized. Many software and hardware vendors provide user training. The implementation team should review the content of this training and make modifications where necessary. Then it should schedule the appropriate personnel for the classes (e.g., end users and data processing professionals). (See Chapter 20 for a complete discussion of training of personnel.)

The implementation team then needs to prepare test data that can be used to check the accuracy of the system. The test data must be as close to live material as possible. The implementation team should then compile the expected results from the test, which will be used later to verify the accuracy of the system.

At this point, the hardware and software are ready for installation. It is normally the responsibility of the hardware and software vendor to actually install the systems. However, the implementation team must monitor the installation to see that it is done on a timely basis.

As soon as the system has been installed, the relevant databases and files, such as the chart of accounts and vendor master file, should be loaded into the system. In some cases, that can be done automatically (e.g., by loading a tape). In other cases, the data must be manually entered.

After the FIS is installed, the implementation team must perform an acceptance test of the system. Using the test data previously prepared, the team should compare the expected results with the actual results. Where differences arise, modification should be made and the test rerun. The team should also make sure that the system meets all of the requirements stated in the RFP.

After the system has been tested, it is ready for parallel testing. Parallel testing means that the new system and the old system are run at the same time (that is, in parallel) to make sure that the new system produces the same results as the old one. Even if the old system is a manual one, a parallel test must be run. Because parallel testing requires that both systems be run simultaneously, it can be very expensive. As a result, the company will not want to run parallel tests for an excessive amount of time; however, parallel systems should be run for at least two months.

After the parallel test has been successfully completed, the organization is ready to begin full operations on the new system. At this time, the old system should be totally phased out of existence.

The implementation process may take anywhere from one month to ten years, depending on the resources committed and the applications to be installed. Figure 17-12 depicts the implementation process.

As mentioned elsewhere in this chapter, many implementations do not succeed. The reasons for the lack of success include:

- Poor planning
- Lack of management involvement
- Lack of user involvement
- Poor communication between implementation team members
- Unrealistic or hidden expectations
- Poorly defined priorities
- Limited commitment of resources
- Unrealistic time schedules

POSTIMPLEMENTATION REVIEW

After a system has been implemented, a postimplementation review (PIR) must be completed. The objectives of a PIR include:

STEPS TO BE TAKEN WHEN IMPLEMENTING THE SYSTEM

1. Select implementation team.
2. Prioritize applications to be implemented.
3. Develop a detailed implementation schedule.
4. Enlist top management's support.
5. Design input forms and output reports.
6. Modify the software.
7. Prepare site for hardware.
8. Train users and data processing personnel.
9. Prepare test data.
10. Install hardware and software.
11. Enter databases and master files.
12. Test system with sample data.
13. Parallel-test system.
14. Begin full operation of system.
15. Perform postimplementation review.

FIG. 17-12 The Implementation Process

- Deciding if the anticipated results of the selection and implementation process have been attained
- Deciding if the original cost vs. budget analysis is still accurate
- Identifying weaknesses in support, documentation, and training
- Reviewing the adequacy of reports and security
- Determining additional systems enhancements that may be required
- Reviewing the timeliness of report preparation

According to one expert,

The best time to perform a postimplementation review is approximately six months after the system is installed. During this period people can become familiar with the new system and can make minor corrections. This time allows significant problems to surface. Earlier review does not allow costs and benefits to stabilize, nor does it allow time for people to give up old habits. Later review may have to deal with larger volumes, law charges, and the like, which tend to distort the scope and intensity of the original process.[5]

The areas to be reviewed during the PIR include documentation, training, output reports, systems security, user satisfaction, and the overall timeliness and accuracy of the system.

Specifically, the PIR must evaluate the following:

- How well the system has been implemented
- The efficiency and effectiveness of the system
- How well the system is being utilized
- If systems features exist that have not been implemented or used
- If users' needs are being met
- If the system is secure enough

The steps to be taken to perform a PIR include:

1 Reviewing the statement of requirements, RFP, and the selected vendor's response to the RFP
2 Interviewing key individuals from the selection committee, implementation team, data processing staff, user group, and internal audit
3 Reviewing the system's implementation, training, documentation, support, security, operations, and reports
4 Analyzing the findings from the PIR and evaluating the implementation process
5 Formulating the findings, conclusions, and recommendation in a report

The benefits of performing a PIR include:

- Detecting problems with the system
- Evaluating the effectiveness of training to see if additional training is required
- Deciding whether additional documentation is needed
- Ascertaining that the expected benefits have been realized
- Recommending improvements to the system in order to maximize its use
- Providing guidance for future systems implementations

---

[5] Dyba, Jerome E., "Post-Implementation System Review," *Auerbach*, sec. 37-01-04, p. 2.

APPENDIX 17-1: HARDWARE SELECTION CRITERIA

The following sections briefly describe some of the factors to review when evaluating a vendor's hardware proposal. The information contained herein is based on Ernst & Whinney's Minicomputer Selection Methodology.

Central Processing Unit

The CPU controls the operations of the computer. The following should be considered when evaluating a CPU:

- Proposed main memory capacity
- Word length
- Data movement rates
- Mathematic instruction times
- Power failure detection capabilities
- Automatic restart features
- Error detection and correction capabilities
- Interrupt handling and prioritization features
- Memory type
- Input/output channels

Peripherals

The following deal with peripheral devices, such as disk and tape drives and printers:

- Transfer rates of disk and tape subsystems, printers, and other devices
- Capacity of peripherals
- Number of disk or tape drives per controller
- Who maintains peripheral devices
- Printer speed
- Printer quality
- Mode of transmission and protocol used
- Magnetic tape specifications
- Peripheral failure rate and recovery time

Remote Devices

This factor deals with remote devices, such as terminals and teleprinters.

- Type of terminals
- Maximum number of terminals supported
- Communications capabilities
- Cabling and connectors supplied by the vendors
- Potential number of remote devices

Environmental Considerations

This factor deals with the physical environment needed to operate the hardware.

- Power supply required
- Temperature tolerance
- Humidity tolerance
- Raised flooring requirement
- Total space required
- Maximum distance between peripheral devices and CPU
- Installation guidelines
- Transportability of equipment

Flexibility and Expandability

These factors are concerned with the ability of the hardware system to grow with the business.

- Maximum number of control slots
- Maximum memory
- Maximum transfer rates
- Other systems available in the same product line
- Devices available for upgrade
- Maximum number of terminals installed at a current user site
- Field upgrades available for the CPU, peripherals, and remote devices
- Networking capability

Systems Reliability

This factor is concerned with the system's failure and repair rate.

- Average number of failures per year

- Average length of those failures
- Automatic error diagnosis
- Error logging capabilities
- Scheduled preventive maintenance
- Number and type of redundant devices proposed
- Availability of remote processing site
- Remote diagnostic capabilities

APPENDIX 17-2: VENDOR EVALUATION CRITERIA

Following are some factors to consider when evaluating vendors.

Product Support

- Location of nearest sales office
- Location of nearest service office
- Size of support staff at nearest service office
- Availability of remote diagnostics
- Availability of twenty-four hour support
- Guaranteed response time
- Preventive maintenance policy
- Problem resolution procedures
- No charge for errors detected
- Availability of programming support
- Training provided
- Availability of installation support
- Existence of user groups
- Existence of complete user documentation
- Frequency of new versions offered

Reputation and Stability

- Number of years in the computer industry
- Number of installations of the particular system still operating
- Sales growth rate of system in question
- Financial condition

CHAPTER **18**

User Participation

Faith Goodland

Introduction 2	**Traditional Role of Users** 17
The User: A Definition 3	Inability of Data Processing to Respond to User Needs 18
Necessity for a User 4	Formal Development Life Cycle 18
	Application Backlog 18
Needs of a User and User Satisfaction .. 5	Programming Languages and Techniques 18
Design Considerations 7	User Documentation 18
Operational Considerations 7	Errors in the System 19
Systems Flexibility Considerations 8	
User Satisfaction 8	**Users vs. Data Processing: The Gap** 19
Systems Dependability 9	
User Training 10	**Current Direction of User Participation** .. 20
User Documentation 10	Use of Decision Support Tools 20
	Applications Built by the End User 21
The Most Common User Complaints ... 11	Evolution of User-Driven Computing ... 21
	Introduction of Fourth-Generation
Main Reasons for Failure of an FIS 12	Languages 21
System Does Not Meet User Needs 13	Use of Information Centers 21
Unrealistic Expectations 13	
Making People Fit the System 13	**How to Resolve and Make User Participation Work** 22
Poor Systems Definition 13	
User Involvement Too Late in the Cycle 14	**What Constitutes a Good User** 23
Implementation Was Poorly Planned, Managed, or Controlled 14	**The Role of Management** 24
Underestimation of Project Manager's Role 14	Goals and Objectives 25
Unrealistic and Rushed Schedules ... 14	Commitment to the Investment 25
Implementing Too Many Systems Together 14	Political Perspective 25
Single-Person Dependency 15	Keeping Informed 26
No Interim Reviews and Approvals .. 15	Policy Statements 26
System Created Negative Impact on the Organization 16	Selection of Key Personnel 26
Resistance to Change 16	**What to Consider When Selecting a Project Manager** 26
Poor-Quality User Involvement 16	Communication Skills 27
Lack of Management Commitment .. 16	Selling Ability 27
Political Environment 16	Decision Making 27
	Good Time and Resource Management .. 27
Then and Now: Different User Roles ... 17	Political Astuteness 27
	Credibility 28
	Open Mindedness 28

What It Takes to Get Users Involved ... 29	Participating in Steering Committees ... 33
User-Friendly Software 29	Preparing or Evaluating Cost/Benefit
Good Training Courses 30	Analysis 33
High-Level User Languages 30	Becoming Project Manager 34
Strong Project Management 30	
	How Users Should Be Involved in Testing
How Users Should Be Involved in the	and Implementation 34
Planning and Development Stages 31	Training 34
Establishing a Design Team 31	Testing 35
Defining Systems Requirements 32	Implementation 35
Validating Systems Requirements and	
Conceptual Design 32	Looking to the Future 36
Attending Structured Walk-Throughs ... 32	
Providing Approval to Proceed 33	References 38

Fig. 18-1 Systems Development Life Cycle 5
Fig. 18-2 User's vs. Data Processing's Concept of Systems Design 6
Fig. 18-3 Quality Factors Researched for the U.S. Department of Defense 8
Fig. 18-4 Project Levels 28

INTRODUCTION

The success of an FIS installation is often directly attributed to the amount and quality of user involvement in all phases of the systems development cycle. One of the reasons for a newly installed system's failure to meet specifications is user apathy, and even user rejection. For many years, there has been increased awareness of the importance of user involvement in installing FISs. Frequently, the initial good intentions quickly fade into oblivion because of other commitments of users, poor communication between data processing and the user, lengthy project life cycles, lack of technical understanding, and many other reasons.

Management has expressed its concerns and initiated the use of user representatives, user review boards, and steering committees. All too often, however, they have deteriorated into partially interested groups who merely act as rubber stamps. When planning the installation of a new FIS, the following questions should be addressed and resolved before the project proceeds:

- To what extent should the user be involved?
- Who should participate from the user community?
- What responsibility does the user have?
- At what points should the user be involved?
- What can be done to ensure user satisfaction?

This chapter addresses these issues and discusses the changing role of the user in the development and installation of FISs. Many of the suggestions made may appear obvious and based on common sense. Unfortunately, there have been too many instances where a disastrous implementation could have been successful with the proper level of user participation.

First, it is essential to establish exactly what is meant by user participation and user satisfaction and why they are necessary. The focus of this chapter is on who the real user is and what he needs. In addition, common user complaints are identified. By examining some of the already known reasons for failure, it is hoped that companies may be able to develop plans for avoiding some of the most frequent pitfalls that have been experienced in the past. Anyone who has experienced a troubled implementation definitely has some specific dos and don'ts for putting in a new system.

Each application that is installed generally has its own separate users. Implementing an integrated FIS presents a significant challenge, as there are generally multiple systems. The FIS is central to all business operations, and the multiple systems feed into each other. Thus, the need for each component to be properly and completely installed in a timely manner increases, as one misfitting part has tremendous repercussions.

It is also important to examine the changing role of the user community. There has been a gradual change away from the traditional approach of little to no user involvement and an increased need for alternative approaches and acceptance to change. User participation is changing; thus, specific ways to allow the user more control of his automation and information needs are given here.

The third main area is a discussion of the specifics of how to complete a project successfully when undertaking a large FIS implementation. The issues of what amount of user participation is required and how to select good users are addressed, and solutions for avoiding known traps in implementing a new integrated system and specific ways for planning user involvement into the project are given. The variety of user involvement in different phases is shown.

The last section presents a look toward the future. Major changes have occurred during the past five to ten years that affect user participation, and these will continue.

THE USER: A DEFINITION

The term "user" has been bandied about for years. Everyone knows what a user is; or do they? The true users of a system can vary; frequently, they are different people at different levels at the same time for the same system. Each user's perception of the system depends on his position and interface with the system.

"To use" is defined in Webster's dictionary as "to put into action or service." Within one context of an FIS, a definition of user that is probably acceptable to most people is "a person who uses information supplied by an automated system." Each potential user has a different perception of the new FIS, and has his own set of expectations from the new system. The perception and expectation of an accounts payable clerk, for example, are very different from those of the controller of a company. Both individuals are users of the system, but to varying degrees and with varying amounts of direct interface.

Being the recipient of a report for budgeting purposes is very different from being the clerk who codes and enters transaction detail.

The user has the most important role in any new FIS. He is the one who uses the information supplied by the different application systems to manage the business on a day-to-day basis and to make management decisions that affect the long-term goals of the company. He uses that information to monitor the business' financial performance and to produce accounts payable checks, justify shareholder dividends, produce statements for legal requirements, and handle credit rejections for overdue customers.

Sometimes problems occur because the true user is not necessarily the person who was perceived to be the user during the design phase. Great care must be taken to make sure that the needs of all levels of user are met. During the initial conceptual phase, it may be best to use a senior-level person in a supervisory or managerial position, but remembering the person who will actually use the system is critical. That person has much valid input to provide to the systems analyst at the detail level. A system must be designed for the person whose hands will actually make it work.

NECESSITY FOR A USER

Once a system is installed, it is easy to see why a user is necessary. However, many data processing departments have operated under the premise that the user should not be involved until after the implementation. They feel that the task of systems selection and implementation is a technical job for which the user is not equipped. A user, in fact, is necessary during all phases of the systems development life cycle. His role varies in each phase, but it is essential that he be involved in the design/construction and implementation phases and not just in the operation/maintenance phases. Figure 18-1 illustrates the systems development life cycle.

Any planning done for a new FIS must be derived from overall business objectives and strategies of an organization. Leaving the task of medium- and long-range information systems planning to the data processing professionals may cause an undesirable detachment between the systems implemented and the functional departments they are supposed to serve.

It is this detachment between data processing and the end user that has been the source of many jokes in the developing computer age. Everyone who has been involved in systems selection and implementation for any length of time probably has his own horror story of an implementation that did not proceed smoothy. There have been many cartoons depicting the user and the technical people on opposite sides of a wall, illustrating the end product of a systems design without good communication. Figure 18-2 shows the system as seen in the eyes of the user versus the system as seen in the eyes of the technician. The systems seldom look like each other.

USER PARTICIPATION

	TIME →
Analysis	XXXX
Conceptual design	XXXXX
Functional design	XXXXX
Detail design	XXXXXXX
Construction	XXXXXXXXXXXX
Testing	XXXXXXXXXXXXX
Training	XXXXXXXXXXXXXXXXXXXXX
Implementation	XXXXXX
Cutover	X
Postimplementation review	X

FIG. 18-1 Systems Development Life Cycle

User participation in all phases of the systems development life cycle enables the end result to resemble the required product and provide the user with what he needs from the system. Without the proper interface between the systems designer and the user and true user commitment, any attempt to design systems is fraught with danger; thus, the potential for failure is almost certain.

NEEDS OF A USER AND USER SATISFACTION

Data processing technicians must know what the user needs, but it is even more important for the user to know what the user needs, which sometimes seems to be far more difficult. Obtaining the right mix of user needs and technical direction best ensures a successful system. The user may have the need, but he is not always able to properly define what he requires from the system.

In many cases, users have defined their systems needs, and the technical people have designed or selected systems that performed exactly as the users requested; but not until the system was implemented and operational did the users discover that what they thought they wanted and got was not really the right system for them.

Defining user needs and requirements for a new system has become almost a separate area of skill. Frequently, companies turn to information systems consultants to help them define their user requirements. Consultants who specialize in this field have found that one of the greatest difficulties a user has is

FIG. 18-2 User's vs. Data Processing's Concept of Systems Design

seeing how an individual system fits into the overall flow of the business. Particularly with a new or updated FIS, the inherent interrelationships between each component require a very clear understanding of how each piece fits together. The impact that changing the general ledger coding structure has on all the feeder systems must be understood—for example, can the necessary extracts still be made to satisfy reporting needs for the budget department?

Before defining user requirements, a clear understanding of what a user really needs in any automated system is essential. The user needs a system that is clear, meaningful, and easy to use. Technical quality is obviously essential. The technical aspects are what make the system work. The user must have confidence in the accuracy of the data being provided. However, just as important as technical quality is the quality as perceived and defined by the user. This is, and should be, the main evaluation criterion in the design and implementation of a new system. That the system is a technical masterpiece is of little consequence to the user. If it does not serve his task needs well, it will be looked upon as a poor system.

There are several separate areas in which quality issues need to be addressed: design considerations, operational considerations, and systems flexibility considerations.

Design Considerations

It makes sense to design what is needed and will be used. More information does not automatically mean a better system. A system that produces fifty reports may be technically advanced, but if only eight of the reports are used on a regular basis, the other forty-two are redundant. Generating the more obscure reports may be what is really needed, as long as it can be done simply by the user. This is where a good report writer feature may be very valuable.

There is a great tendency to design a new system that has every function possible. The designer should keep in mind a design approach where a minimum set of functions are included with alternatives built in. The user can then choose the appropriate options, and does not need all the functions. This is also true in the case of purchasing and implementing packages. Typically, every possible combination of features are available. Of course, they do not all have to be implemented. The message here is to design what is needed but remember to allow for expansion.

The systems designer or selector must be aware of future growth plans and business operations that may affect the proposed system. Too often a system is selected and implemented and, within one to two years, is outgrown or outdated.

Operational Considerations

There are many questions that a good user needs to ask; he must also feel confident with the responses. A user should measure the quality of a system against some of the following criteria:

- Does the processing cycle meet user timing needs, or is the current processing schedule so busy that the new application will have to be run at 3.00 A.M.?
- Is the integrity of the data maintained properly? Can the system be trusted, or are double bookkeeping and cross-checking still necessary?
- Are new reports generated in a reasonable time frame, or does it take weeks for any change?
- Are exceptions to normal processing handled in a fairly straightforward manner?

Factor	Definition
Correctness	Extent to which a program satisfies its specifications and fulfills the user's mission objectives
Reliability	Extent to which a program can be expected to perform its intended function with required precision
Efficiency	The amount of computing resources and code required by a program to perform a function
Integrity	Extent to which access to software or data by unauthorized persons can be controlled
Usability	Effort required to learn, operate, prepare input, and interpret output of a program
Maintainability	Effort required to locate and fix an error in an operational program
Testability	Effort required to test a program to make sure that it performs its intended function
Flexibility	Effort required to modify an operational program
Portability	Effort required to transfer a program from one hardware configuration and/or software systems environment to another
Reusability	Extent to which a program can be used in other applications—related to the packaging and scope of the functions that the programs perform
Interoperability	Effort required to couple one system with another

FIG. 18-3 Quality Factors Researched for the U.S. Department of Defense

Systems Flexibility Considerations

A frequent complaint is the lack of flexibility in an automated system. The lack may be in design flexibility, so that the user does not get exactly what he needs and must tailor his operational procedures to meet the system. It can also be lack of flexibility in incorporating any new user or systems needs that may arise. What appears to the user to be a small change may necessitate a major redesign.

If a user experiences considerable difficulty in any of these areas, he will frequently become dissatisfied and decide that the FIS is not a quality system. Figure 18-3 shows the quality factors researched for the U.S. Department of Defense.

User Satisfaction

User satisfaction is difficult to gauge at the start of a new systems implementation. Resistance to any new system is expected, as it is human nature to be reluctant to accept change. Often, when a system is initially implemented there are a lot of complaints that the system "isn't as good as the old one" or "is difficult to use" or "is too complicated." It is sometimes necessary to withstand these complaints and allow a little time for the user personnel to overcome their initial reluctance to change. Talking to different levels of user (i.e., those in both the managerial and operational ranks) may elicit widely different reactions to new systems. At the clerical level, the system may be a great help in reducing tedious manual tasks; however, at the managerial level, there is no sign of the cost/benefit anticipated. To the person who must recode every general ledger transaction, the new system may be a nightmare; to the CFO and controller, the new reporting code structure may be the exact management tool they have been hoping for since the new system was discussed years earlier.

Thus, different expectations exist at different levels. What needs to be clearly established in any new systems design or selection are the exact objectives and goals of implementing the new system. It is not always possible to please all users to the same degree. There is a tendency for parts of certain systems to routinize jobs and to detract from job satisfaction. That does not mean that the system is not successful. However, goals must be established before the project commences, and unrealistic expectations should be minimized by communicating exactly what information needs must be met.

The goals and objectives of a new user system are often perceived differently by data processing, which tends to want to elevate or increase the technical complexity when designing a new system. However, the FIS needs to meet established goals that serve the user and the company rather than data processing.

A user also needs a system with accurate data. The expression "garbage in, garbage out" is well understood by data processing personnel, but not by user personnel. Systems design is the structure under which data are entered and information is manipulated to produce outputs. The system may be functioning 100 percent to specification; yet user comments indicate that "the system is wrong." It is not always easy for the nontechnical user to understand that the system is only as good as the data entered. Frequently, he needs to be educated about the extreme importance of accurate data input, particularly where dealing with financial or accounting operations.

Systems Dependability

An all too common remark at business facilities these days is "the computer is down." The inability to perform a requested look-up at a given time is a high frustration factor for both users and inquirers. Once a user has become dependent on an on-line terminal, it is crucial to have as little down time as possible. User dissatisfaction rapidly escalates with the amount of down time, which is a very tangible measure of systems dependability. The user is also very interested in whether output can be provided within a scheduled time frame and whether the system will be available when he wants to use it. Some systems require that the on-line portion be brought down before update to certain files can take place. Adequate effective backup and recovery procedures are also essential. However, it is rare for the user to recognize directly the need for these types of systems functions. What the user sees is that he cannot do what is wanted. After a minor processing disaster, all a user knows is that the whole batch of data had to be reentered or that the complete processing cycle had to be rerun, thus missing the all-essential payroll cycle deadline.

Thus, systems dependability is essential to the user, but he relies on the technical expertise of data processing to provide it. Generally, the issue is not discussed with the user, and a gap of knowledge exists, with the user being left at the mercy of DP personnel.

User Training

User training is probably the most frequently mentioned problem area. (See Chapter 20 for complete coverage of this topic.) It is not enough to train the user on the pure mechanics of the system. That leads to myopia regarding the system and how it can be used to serve the needs of the company. Unfortunately, many project schedules and budgets do not include adequate time or money for training the end user. Most users need to have more general training in information systems and to understand the overall system. Management must recognize the need for a commitment to education.

Timing is another very important factor in training. Frequently, people are sent to training classes and then do not get hands-on exposure to the new system until six months later. Most of the value is then lost; all that remains is the expense of the class.

User Documentation

How many times is user documentation prepared by data processing before coding is done? All too few. User documentation is usually an afterthought. It is frequently considered a necessary evil that the technical staff prepares only because it is the last deliverable necessary to obtain implementation sign-off.

There are several advantages to preparing draft-user documentation early in the design process. It helps to ensure completeness of the design specifications and understanding of user needs. It provides a chance for the user to review and to make changes before expensive coding changes are required. It also provides the additional advantage of maintaining user participation during the development stage, instead of the user being left to wait for the product to be built, as is typical.

The format and content of user documentation could be the topic of a complete text. From the user's perspective, at a minimum, the document should be easy to follow, be able to answer user questions, and provide instructions on handling error procedures.

To summarize the issues discussed in this section, user needs include:

- A quality system as defined in user terms

- Information unique to the user's own requirements
- Established goals that serve the user and company rather than data processing
- A minimum system with options/alternatives so the user may select appropriate components based on cost/benefit
- Accuracy of data and an understanding of this need
- Systems dependability in being available and in meeting schedules
- Training in both specific functional use and overall objectives of the system
- User documentation that allows for easy reference

If all these areas are considered during the planning stages for a new FIS, many of the frequent user complaints and implementation mistakes can be averted.

THE MOST COMMON USER COMPLAINTS

The major objectives of user participation are to help make sure that the system designed and implemented meets the user's needs and that the user really knows how to use it. Another objective is to enable the user to assume responsibility for the system and its information from data processing quickly and smoothly. Looking at some of the most common user complaints, whether real or perceived, may highlight areas where extra attention should be paid during the systems development cycle.

Some of the most common user complaints are identified as follows:

1. It will be too long before the system is implemented; data processing has a huge backlog.
2. Data processing never meets its deadlines and always overruns.
3. The cost of a new system is projected to be too high, and data processing chargebacks will not be cost/beneficial.
4. The system does not do what we really need it to do.
5. No one asked what we wanted.
6. The system has no flexibility; we are forced to change everything to suit the system.
7. It's too complicated to use; the old system was better.
8. The training was not helpful, and we had it six months ago.
9. There are no user manuals; the current documentation is out of date and of no help.
10. The error messages are not explicit enough to help us correct errors.

11 The system is always down.

12 Our reports are always late, as we have to wait for the payroll run to be finished.

What the users are expressing in items 1, 2, and 3 is that they are frustrated with data processing and the lengths and costs of the traditional development cycle. In items 4, 5, 6, and 7, the users feel that the system was forced on them and that it was not what was needed; also, they were not involved in the system's specification. In items 8, 9, and 10, the message is that the implementation portion was not properly planned. The level of training and documentation did not meet the users' needs. In items 11 and 12, the users are expressing their frustration and disappointment in systems dependability.

All these user complaints reflect a poorly accepted system, and many are cause for a system to be deemed a failure. It is imperative to realize that, no matter how good a system is technically, if the user does not accept it, the company will be left with a failure.

MAIN REASONS FOR FAILURE OF AN FIS

The failure of a new systems implementation usually results from many mistakes rather than a single factor. Normally, there are indications along the way that something is awry. However, it is not always easy to spot the signs and stop the gradual decline of the project. Experience has shown that a successful systems implementation requires good user participation at all stages of the project. To say that lack of user participation causes failure is to oversimplify the situation.

Leaving the purely technical reasons aside, there are three main reasons why systems fail:

1 *The system does not meet user needs.* The system as designed and implemented does not solve the problem or situation it was intended to solve.

2 *The implementation was poorly planned, managed, or controlled.* The system itself is either too complex or too large for the environment. It is either overwhelming in its implementation or has been improperly or never fully implemented.

3 *The system creates negative impact on the organization.* The implementation of the system in one way or another produces unexpected side effects on the organization.

Almost all the reasons for an unsuccessful implementation may be categorized under one of the three categories.

System Does Not Meet User Needs

Failure of this kind may be attributed to many causes, but they all have the same result: a system that is deemed inappropriate or ineffective by the user. Sometimes, a single factor dominates; mostly, however, there are a combination of individual, but associated, factors.

Unrealistic Expectations. Frequently, a user expects a new system to automatically solve his current problems, and, therefore, he grabs for an apparent solution at the first opportunity. Sometimes, a user is told that the new system will solve those problems. After the system is implemented, the user quickly becomes disillusioned when he finds that the problems still exist. This may happen because of inadequate user involvement in the design/selection phase, lack of understanding of the system and how it operates, or poor communication between data processing and the user. Automation is not a panacea.

Making People Fit the System. Many designers/implementers do not try to install a system to fit the user, but rather, to make the user fit the system. According to an editorial in the *Journal of Association of Systems Managers*, this is a follow on from 2,500 years ago in Greece, where a Greek bandit named Procrustes bedded his guests on a cot of indeterminate size. Guests who were too long were cut down to fit, and those who were too short were stretched to the right size. Many users feel that this is how they have been treated when given a new system. They have been "lopped, chopped, squeezed and stretched to fit the systems and solutions designed for them."[1]

Poor Systems Definition. Poor definition may result from little or no user involvement during the early stages; or it may happen in spite of user involvement. Frequently, the assignment of a user representative is expected to solve the problem, but unless the user representative assigned can supply the needed source of information, his presence on a design team or review board may not have the desired effect. Too often, the representative chosen is not vital to business operations, does not have a good overall perspective of the system and its interfaces, or has no direct authority. Because the representative always attends the meetings, user involvement is assumed; however, that does not constitute participation. Inadequate user involvement is still considered the single most common reason for failure. It is essential that the user representative be able to speak knowledgeably for the user department he represents. He also must have authority and be held responsible for his part in the development process.

---

[1] *Journal of Systems Management* (May 1983).

User Involvement Too Late in the Cycle. Generally the data processing area performs the analysis, prepares design specifications, and codes new systems with very limited communication with the user community. The user is brought into the cycle at the implementation and operational phase, when it is either too late or very difficult and costly to make systems design changes. To avoid this, the user must be involved in the project from its initial inception. Studies have analyzed the impact and cost implications of user changes at different phases of the development cycle. The earlier changes are identified, the more radically their effect is reduced.

Implementation Was Poorly Planned, Managed, or Controlled

Typically, data processing personnel are in charge of project implementation. However, user involvement does not ensure proper planning, management, and control. Poor planning may be caused by unrealistic time frames in an inadequate task/action plan. Poor management may be caused by the wrong project leader. Poor control may arise from an inability to meet the stated budgets and schedules. All three may contribute to failure, whether the project manager comes from data processing or the user community.

Underestimation of Project Manager's Role. The project manager's role in the success of the implementation is often underestimated. The quality of the project is directly related to the quality of the project manager. Some projects succeed in spite of the project manager, but, generally, the stronger the person leading the effort, the higher the success level. Recognizing the key role the selected person plays in the success or failure of the implementation is essential.

Unrealistic and Rushed Schedules. With any new system, once the decision has been made to proceed with the selection or design of a system, it is always wanted yesterday. Frequently, the user has had to wait for a substantial period of time for his particular project to reach top priority of an already overloaded data processing department. A sense of urgency creeps in, and an overambitious implementation schedule is prepared that is unrealistic at best. Usually the planners forget to allow time for many tasks that must be carried out in a predefined order based on processing cycles. Factors such as the impact of month-end/year-end closings and the time to set up new codes and load historical data are not considered.

Implementing Too Many Systems Together. A major problem in implementing a new FIS is that there is a tendency to try to install the many different but interconnecting systems all at the same time. The magnitude of the project becomes overwhelming and all consuming to both data processing and user personnel. The user still has his day-to-day job to perform. He frequently must put in a considerable amount of overtime during the implementation of new systems. Even for the most dedicated employee, it is not possible to maintain a high overtime motivation for extended periods of time.

This is not too difficult at the start of a project, but if the implementation occurs over several years, motivating personnel becomes a real challenge. The best way to minimize interest drop-off is to break the project into phases with measurable milestones. The project teams must continue to feel a sense of achievement and forward movement. Not only does project size affect the project team members but influences how the project is viewed by management and the organization. If discrete systems are implemented and turned over to the user community on a phased basis, management can see that the project is progressing. However, during a typical FIS implementation plan, three or four concurrent systems may be implemented; often some of the same user personnel are required for multiple systems.

Single-Person Dependency. The case of one person becoming the key player in a particular role occurs frequently during implementation; this often becomes even more of a problem during the initial operational phase. Single-person dependency can create bottlenecks in the implementation, as everything waits for the key person to find time to address a particular task. Perhaps only one person is trained in how the application works and everyone relies on this individual. Perhaps a project leader, who is too involved in the details, maintains all the control and does not delegate and manage the project. If he goes on vacation or gets sick, the project comes to a standstill. Also, what happens to the project if this all-important person resigns? If a project development cycle is long, turnover must be anticipated, expected, and planned for.

No Interim Reviews and Approvals. With large or multiple systems implementation, it is even more crucial to make sure that the system being implemented produces the desired results. A milestone approach, where specific tasks and deliverables are identified, assists in a smooth and successful implementation. At each interim review point, there should be a formal approval and sign-off by both the project team and the user department that will be operating the system. This approach enables detection of any deviation from the required operation as early in the cycle as possible and ensures initiation of corrective action. Too often, the implementation has been completed and the system turned over before a major design flaw is detected—one that would have been immediately obvious if a user review and sign-off process had been used. The users must assume the responsibility. It is their system, and they must make it work.

System Created Negative Impact on the Organization

It is often assumed that a system will be rationally and logically accepted by the organization; however, in many cases, the impact of the system was never properly assessed before the project was begun. If the right people are not properly involved or prepared for the new system, failure can ensue. If proper support is not provided during the project's complete life cycle, problems may develop during implementation. Issues relating to jobs, organization structure, communications, and interrelationships must be recognized when assessing the viability of implementing a new system.

Resistance to Change. Resistance to change occurs during every new systems implementation. It is natural for the user to be reluctant to learn a new system, especially if it is the first automated FIS. Healthy skepticism is a good quality when assessing a system's potential, but stubborn resistance is more common. The level of resistance and how it is addressed is a key factor in determining the success/failure potential. If the resistance can be removed, then attitudes can shift. Users often need to be gradually encouraged into new systems, which is a psychological issue more than a technical one. This is where the management of the project requires interpersonal skills more than technical skills. Sometimes, resistance is related to job security, as users are afraid that their jobs will be replaced by a computer.

Poor-Quality User Involvement. A user's lack of awareness of how the proposed system fits into the organization as a whole may lead to tunnel vision. Negative side effects are either not recognized or ignored. Similarly, user involvement that is too low and does not really constitute active participation produces the same result.

Lack of Management Commitment. Without top- and middle-management commitment to a new system, the potential for failure is extremely high. Lack of management commitment takes many forms, from not accepting explainable budget overruns, or time delays, to creating a negative atmosphere within which the motivation of personnel declines and the project falters.

Political Environment. There are certain projects that, when analyzed, make perfect sense for a given organization. However, the political climate may be such that there is no chance for success.

For any or all of the reasons given here, a project that appears to be good for an organization may become another statistic. Political and psychological barriers that may surface and cause the demise of a potentially beneficial system should never be underestimated.

THEN AND NOW: DIFFERENT USER ROLES

In the following sections, the traditional role of the user and how many organizations still operate are discussed, and the new directions becoming prevalent in every industry are addressed.

TRADITIONAL ROLE OF USERS

Consider the following scenario: A user decides that a new accounts receivable system is needed. The request is given to the data processing department, which adds it to a stack of other requests. Perhaps weeks, months, or years later, the request surfaces to the top of the pile. Data processing meets with the user and asks what he needs in the way of an automated accounts receivable system. The user describes what he would like. Data processing then commences either to select or to build an accounts receivable system, intending to follow the formal development life cycle. After the requirements specification document (or RSD) is completed, it may be many more months or years before the user is involved again, at which point it usually time to start training on the new system and take it over from data processing. The user is then left to struggle with a system he does not know or understand, that does not do what he intends, and that may still have gaping flaws or bugs. In these cases, there is rarely good user documentation to provide even the simplest level of answers to the user's questions. The request to data processing to have changes made to correct problems, or simply for assistance, is put back in the request pile. Meanwhile, accounts receivable struggles along doing double duty and keeping the old system going, at the same time trying to make sense of the new system. Management sees the data processing costs incurred and notes that the system is operational and has been turned over to the accounting area. Thus, it assumes that all the past problems with accounts receivable have immediately disappeared, only to find later that this is not the case.

This type of scenario results in high development costs, long development cycles, low user and management satisfaction, and an ever-growing wall between user and application developers. This scenario may appear to be extreme. Unfortunately, it has been the general operating mode of many companies with a medium- to large-sized data processing function.

The traditional role of the user in the development life cycle has been a limited one. Many times, projects have been totally controlled by data processing, with minimal participation by the user community. Data processing has made the majority of the decisions regarding in-house developed versus packaged software, language used, technical hardware issues, and processing considerations. Power and control over new systems have been accorded to the data processing department, and communication between it and the user has been extremely limited. Conversely, data processing has felt that the user does not understand computers or the technical ramifications of new systems, and, in the past, that has generally been true. A user's misunderstandings and unrealistic expectations may quickly mean failure for a new system.

The wall between DP and the user has grown for two reasons: (1) data processing has typically not responded quickly enough to the user's needs; (2) the amount of data processing/user communication has been extremely limited, as has participation.

Inability of Data Processing to Respond to User Needs

Many factors combine to make the traditional approach to systems selection and implementation unacceptable to the user.

Formal Development Life Cycle. The necessity for data processing to follow the prescribed steps for systems development has meant that the formal development life cycle is typically very long. Even for a relatively moderate-sized application, the steps are fairly lengthy. The development methodologies (such as Spectrum and SDM/70[2]) have their place in the data processing world. However, following this formal life cycle does not allow data processing to respond quickly enough to requests from the user community.

Application Backlog. In almost all data processing departments, there is a backlog of user projects that have been requested. Over the past ten years, the desire and need for automation have totally exceeded the capacity of most data processing areas. The result is that the application backlog is now often measured in years rather than months—thus, the current tendency for users not even to ask for a particular project.

Programming Languages and Techniques. Third-generation languages (such as COBOL and PL/1) are not quick to code. Every field and data item must be laboriously specified, and the structure of the language requires long, complex coding statements to describe the operation desired by the programmer.

User Documentation. Documentation is often viewed by data processing as a necessary evil before user sign-off can be given. It is not a popular task for the average programmer/analyst, and it is generally left until the end of the implementation. The document is often lengthy and not in a very helpful format for the user department. While data processing's resources are tied up in documenting systems, they are not available for the next important project.

---

[2] Spectrum and SDM/70 are formalized project development methodologies that can be used to control an entire project development life cycle.

Errors in the System. Errors or bugs in systems design and operation are far from infrequent. Much research has been conducted on the percentage of bugs that emanate as a result of the different phases of analysis, design, coding, and testing. It has been estimated that as high as 60 percent or more of the bugs are caused by analysis and design errors. The earlier in the cycle that the errors were made, the more difficult and time consuming they are to correct. If bugs are caused by an error in analysis, the amount of effort to fix them is generally far greater than that expended on a coding error.

Each of these issues has increased the wall between the user and data processing personnel to such an extent that the low user-satisfaction level has caused the user to resort to other options.

USERS VS. DATA PROCESSING: THE GAP

To enlightened management, the concept of data processing as a service provider is nothing extraordinary. Data processing personnel are sometimes long-term, old-style computer employees. Data processing and the user appear to belong to two different cultures.[3] There are definite differences between the typical data processing employee (or developer) and the user. The common developer-user differences need to be understood to explain why user participation in systems development has typically been low. Users, on the one hand, feel that data processing does not understand the fundamentals of business, while data processing, on the other hand, looks down at the user because he does not understand the technical aspects of data processing. If the user alienates the data processing department, however, it will be reluctant to provide support after the system is operational.

There are surface differences and subtle ones. Surface differences are obvious, such as in education, experience, language, and work interests. They are natural, but both groups need to be aware of them. The language/computer literacy barrier is readily apparent and easily understood. Until recently, the use of computer terminology was exclusive to the data processing professional. The reality of data processing and users having two cultures with two different languages creates a barrier in communication, each side believing its meaning to be clear. A subtle difference is in how users and developers process information. The developer's manner is generally analytic, whereas the user's is heuristic.

Greater mutual understanding is needed, as these differences are not as simple to overcome as it may appear, and the developer can only understand the user by sharing problems and experiences, which takes time and effort.

---

[3] The idea of two cultures was first propounded by C.P. Snow (1969). It concerns the gulf between scientists and the rest of society. Ronald Kintisch and Marvin Weisbord, "Getting Computer People and Users to Understand Each Other," *S.A.M. Advanced Management Journal* (Spring 1977), have adapted that idea to the user/computer-specialist situation, and they provide useful suggestions for closing the gap.

There is, however, a subtle difference between user involvement and user participation. In Webster's Dictionary, "involvement" is defined as "affecting or including," whereas "participation" is defined as "having or taking a share with others." Successful systems require a user who is fully active and committed. There has also been much emphasis in the past on DP's ability to sell the system to the user. If the user has enough responsibility for success of the system, there is no need for this. User/developer teams with mutual commitment are key to the success of the project. The team building approach appears to be more effective than any formal type of user education. If the user shares responsibility for the project and influences the development cycle, the likelihood of a successful outcome is increased.

CURRENT DIRECTION OF USER PARTICIPATION

With the traditional development approach having driven many users to the point of frustration, it was inevitable for a new direction to evolve. The traditional approach is gradually being replaced, out of necessity, by users who are becoming more involved. The advent of microcomputers has eliminated the fear and mystique of computers bringing technology to the nontechnician. The user is gradually becoming computer literate, and computer terminology and understanding are now not solely the province of data processing.

Involvement in development varies from providing the end user with new tools to help him meet his own information needs to assigning full-time user personnel to assist in development and implementation. Current trends in user involvement include:

- Use of decision support tools
- Applications built by end users
- Evolution of user-driven computing
- Introduction of fourth-generation languages
- Use of information center concepts

Use of Decision Support Tools

Once an automated system has been implemented, many of the changes that users request are report format changes, or additional reports with the data sorted in a different order. The concept of decision support tools began by addressing the need for report writer software that could be operated by the user instead of by data processing. In this way, the user could handle minor report changes and sorting requirements quickly and effectively without his having to return to data processing. The growth of decision support tools has gone far beyond this first step, but they are an area that is changing the traditional user/data processing interface. Decision support tools now also include

USER PARTICIPATION

query facilities, graphics languages, application generators, and very high level programming languages.

Applications Built by the End User

With the availability of new software tools and an increased need for automation and problem resolution in an acceptable time frame, the user is beginning to build his own applications. This is possible with products such as Sperry's Mapper and IBM's SQL. The user has grown weary of the inevitable data processing backlog and has begun to branch out and solve his own problems.

Evolution of User-Driven Computing

It is now recognized that there is a difference between the traditional approach of prespecified computing and user-driven computing, where the user creates his own applications and modifies them as needed. The prespecified computing approach is formal and detailed, where requirements analysis, precise specifications, and documentation take many months. There are applications where prespecified computing is essential (e.g., compiler writing, missile guidance, and airline reservations). However, based on today's software, much computing should now be user driven—for example, administrative procedures and information systems where the user develops a version of what he wants and then frequently modifies it.

Introduction of Fourth-Generation Languages

Computer systems started with machine code. When low-level language code (such as Assembler) was invented, it was so radically different that it was called a second-generation language. The progression to high-level languages (such as COBOL and FORTRAN) was considered the third generation; most recently, there have been new language structures that are again so radically different from their predecessors that they are called fourth-generation or nonprocedural languages—for example, Mapper, SQL, and Focus. The advantage of a fourth-generation language is that it is designed for the end user and is relatively easy to use.

Use of Information Centers

Information centers are another route by which the user has become more computer literate. They are typically places within a company where a user may go for training on different software and have his questions answered. Information center consultants interact directly with the end user to assist in developing a particular application. This generally produces fast results.

Having reviewed the weaknesses of the traditional approach, it is not hard to see the advantages of more end-user involvement in solving his own computing needs:

- The user is responsible for his use of automation.
- Applications are operational earlier.
- The user is less-dependent on data processing; that reduces frustration.
- User demands for information are satisfied.
- The traditional development life cycle does not work for user-driven computing.

The development of the user-driven computing concept has also proved to be advantageous and is attracting a growing number of followers. The benefits that have led to adoption of this approach in some organizations have shown the user that, when actively participating in his own systems, he can provide automated applications that work without the time, cost, and frustrations of using the traditional approach. User-driven computing is taking hold for the following reasons:

- It allows applications to work as the user intended.
- It reduces development life cycles.
- It reduces development costs.
- It reduces errors in design.
- It obtains results faster.
- It simplifies ongoing maintenance.
- It increases computer awareness.

Better software tools that further encourage the change in user participation continue to be developed. (Chapter 16 on decision support systems and Chapter 19 on information centers provide additional insight into this fast-growing shift in user computer literacy.)

HOW TO RESOLVE AND MAKE USER PARTICIPATION WORK

The user's role is gradually changing. The slow progression to user-driven computing has developed out of necessity, but it is not yet applicable for all systems. Both traditional and current techniques will continue to coexist. There has been a significant shift in the past ten years to purchasing packaged software instead of developing software in house. This is particularly true of FIS software. All companies require general ledger reporting and financial state-

USER PARTICIPATION

ments; all companies must handle accounts payable and receivable transactions; and all companies need to process payroll. Thus, more than in any other application area, FIS software has been targeted for packaged development by numerous software organizations.

Selecting a package does not automatically solve the problems. There is a huge divergence in the different financial packages available and a bewildering number of alternatives. The key to selecting a new system is to make sure that the user is heavily involved.

WHAT CONSTITUTES A GOOD USER

The success of a new systems implementation is heavily dependent on the amount of user involvement. However, the quality of the user is also very important. Sometimes the user personnel assigned do not have the right skills, enough understanding of the overall system, or enough time to devote to the new systems project. It is therefore important for the team to have users who can really contribute to the project, have positive attitudes, and a high level of motivation.

A good user has the following traits or characteristics:

- *Flexibility.* New automated systems may require significant changes in manual procedures; flexibility is needed to be able to accept change.

- *Good communications skills.* The ability to discuss design concepts with data processing, clearly express user needs, and communicate with both technical and managerial personnel on the appropriate level is essential.

- *Analytical mind.* User involvement at all phases of the project development cycle should include analysis of the impact of the new system, an evaluation of systems requirements and their appropriateness, an assessment of alternatives, cost/benefit analysis, and an evaluation of potential risks.

- *Political awareness.* In most projects, there is a potential for political issues to surface, and the good user is astute enough to recognize those issues.

As the different phases require different levels of expertise, the level of user must be assessed and the type of anticipated involvement defined. Systems specifications are generally developed at three levels: conceptual, functional, and detail design. Not all users are needed at each level. Management involvement is usually at the conceptual level, whereas the detail design issues are more suitable for the hands-on user.

Once the user is identified, his role in the process and why his support is needed must be described. If the user really feels that he is part of the team and that his contribution is important, he will be more highly motivated.

User motivation is a key issue, and rarely is it given enough attention. Because the end product is aimed at the user, it might be expected that he is naturally 100 percent behind the implementation; this is not necessarily true. For the user to remain motivated toward the new system during the almost inevitable lengthy project life cycle, management should understand and consider what motivates or demotivates him and address the following questions:

- Why should he use the system?
- What satisfaction will he get from the system?
- What sense of achievement will he have?
- Is there a positive attitude toward the system's features?
- Does he feel qualified to operate the system?
- Was the user included early on in the process?
- Is it worth the user's effort to be involved?
- Will the system improve his job performance?
- Is the user considered part of the team, or is his inclusion just a token gesture?
- Is user input being considered and acted upon?
- Can the user commit the time needed and still do his job?

Attitudes are formulated during the development stage, not at implementation. User attitudes, and therefore user motivation, may be influenced very early on. It is essential not to alienate the user community, as unfavorable initial expectations may destroy any chance of the systems being successful. Users have their regular jobs to do in addition to their involvement with the new system. That may create conflicts and pressures, and generally it is the system under implementation that suffers.

THE ROLE OF MANAGEMENT

Lack of management commitment has been mentioned elsewhere in this chapter as one of the main reasons for failure of a project. Experience shows that projects with high visibility and a high level of management involvement and commitment have a higher success level. If a project is not deemed important by management, it is hard to expect the user and data processing personnel to be very concerned about the costs, time, or end result achieved. For any company prepared to spend money on a new system, there should be interest and awareness at the management level. Otherwise, user motivation will immediately decline.

Management's ideal role in implementation is somewhat similar to that of a bank manager when handling a large loan. Both functions are concerned that there be a clear objective and that it makes sense to proceed, that the money invested has a payback, that they are kept informed of any major changes, that any specific policies are defined, that the political climate is favorable, and that they provide support and maintain the commitment.

Goals and Objectives

Management should review and challenge the proposed project's stated goals and objectives and monitor its design and implementation to make sure they are being met. Management must be included in the high-level strategy so that any far-reaching implications of implementing the new system are recognized before making the decision to proceed.

Commitment to the Investment

Most new systems software costs more money and takes longer to install than originally predicted. If planning, budgeting, and controlling projects are handled more effectively, that need not be the case. However, management must be realistic and understand the amount of time and money that will be invested and not skimp on the necessary areas of the budget. (This is particularly true with regard to user training.) Once a project is in process, companies often end up pouring additional dollars into the implementation even if it is in trouble, because they have already invested so much. Realistic management expectations and a realistic budget are essential.

Political Perspective

Top management's perspective is generally broader than that of individual department managers. There are always political and organizational issues that have not been shared with all levels of management. The decision to proceed with a new system must be reviewed and approved by top management. That decision should be based on an adequate understanding of the objectives and potential risks—and the implications if the decision to proceed is not made. Political näiveté is fairly common within the framework of automated FISs. Organizational issues may have enormous implications, and management must recognize where these issues can impede a project and deal with them. Many feel that data processing sometimes undertakes the implementation of a complex integrated FIS more for purposes of self-aggrandizement than for the real benefit of the user.

Keeping Informed

Management should make sure that the project life cycle includes regular review sessions so that it may be kept informed on project progress. All too often, management go-ahead is given for a project, and the next time it hears about it is when a request for a budget increase is made or when a time slippage or other major problem is encountered. It is management's responsibility to monitor project progress and insist on periodic reviews. The reviews may be limited to reporting deviations from planned schedule and budget, but that will make sure that no surprises surface long after the problem was first encountered. Management should continue to show its interest and commitment.

Policy Statements

Management must respond to requests for specific policy statements that will almost certainly be necessary during the implementation of an FIS. It must recognize that there will be a need for changes in policy and must provide support in a timely manner to keep the project moving forward.

Selection of Key Personnel

Another major reason for project failure has been attributed to ineffective project management. A great deal of consideration must be given to selecting the appropriate project manager. Management must understand the strengths required to handle a project of the magnitude and complexity of an integrated FIS. If the person selected has a weakness in a particular key area, management must accept the responsibility for his inexperience or underperformance and provide additional support.

Realistic schedules must be set for the project based on rational decisions. Management needs to be wary of potential problems that may result from selecting unrealistic deadlines.

Management's role in the success or failure of a new FIS is more important than is often realized. Top management is ultimately responsible for the outcome of the project. It must be dedicated to the project and believe in the resulting benefits. Top management must accept responsibility for failure and not pass the buck back to the project manager.

WHAT TO CONSIDER WHEN SELECTING A PROJECT MANAGER

Sometimes, a project manager is selected because of seniority or knowledge of a particular area—and, occasionally, simply because of availability. That does not mean that he has the skills necessary for a good project manager. For a project the size of an FIS, communication and leadership skills may be the most critical for success, even more so than knowledge of the subsystems. The project manager is generally responsible for a very large budget, a large number of personnel, and a long project life cycle. The ability to manage and control a large project is a specialized skill that usually comes from experience. The following sections discuss some of the key attributes to look for when selecting a project manager.

Communication Skills

There are presentations to make to management, meetings with company personnel at different levels, and discussions with both technical and user personnel, where good communication skills are crucial.

Selling Ability

There are many occasions during the life of a large project when a new idea must be sold to a group of people. Whether asking for a budget increase from top management or recommending a change in accounting code structure, the ability to present and sell an idea is essential.

Decision Making

There are always varying courses of action available. A project manager must weigh alternatives and decide which one to take. Decision making is not everyone's forte. If a project manager cannot be decisive, the project time schedule may be overrun and create concern among members of the project team.

Good Time and Resource Management

It is extremely important for time and resources to be effectively and efficiently managed. A project manager must be able to allocate resources to the priority tasks and manage within budgetary constraints. A person who frequently misses his own deadlines is not likely to be a good candidate for managing a large project.

Political Astuteness

With a new automated system that affects many areas of an organization, there is a strong need to have a project manager who is politically astute. Someone with an understanding of the political processes underlying decisions and an awareness of issues with potential political implications is of invaluable service on this level.

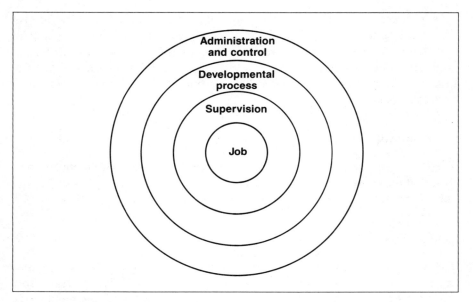

FIG. 18-4 Project Levels

Credibility

The person selected by management to lead a large systems implementation should have credibility within the organization. The quality of the project manager reflects the level of importance that management assigns to the project. If he is not respected or does not have authority, the project will suffer a lack of credibility and the manager will not be effective.

Open Mindedness

A good project manager should be willing to hear all sides of an argument and select the appropriate action without preconceived notions or closed-mindedness inhibiting the decision-making process.

Some of these skills and attributes can be developed by attending courses. Many project management, systems analysis, and leadership courses are available. However, many of the most important attributes cannot be learned in the classroom; they are natural talents that some people have developed to a greater degree than others.

The project manager needs to operate at four levels (see Figure 18-4), as follows:

1 Actual job performance
2 Handling supervisory responsibilities

3 Managing the project development life cycle
4 Providing project control and administration

When selecting a project manager for a system as crucial as a new FIS, top management should be cognizant of the particular strengths and weaknesses of the chosen individual. It should provide support and closer project monitoring in the areas where the skill levels of the project manager are the least strong.

WHAT IT TAKES TO GET USERS INVOLVED

There are different ways that management and data processing can solicit and encourage active user participation. The type of system being implemented has an impact on the amount of user involvement and interest. An FIS is important to all managers in an organization, and is generally very user dependent. That means that the user systems interface is fairly extensive. Interest and knowledge levels of the different users vary, and there are specific aids to assist users in getting involved:

- User-friendly software
- Good training courses
- High-level user languages
- Strong project management

User-Friendly Software

"User-friendly" means different things to different people. What one person needs to understand a system may be overkill for another. A system that allows a user to work at his own pace is the best system to implement. Many on-line systems have menu-driven screens that allow the user to select the appropriate option to be performed. Some force him to go through multiple levels of screen calls for each operation, whereas others provide the flexibility of step-by-step or direct look-up. The latter is more user-friendly, because it accommodates different user levels. The step-by-step route enables the new or unsophisticated user to be walked through each option, whereas the direct look-up allows the experienced user to be more efficient and proceed directly to the operation he desires.

At a James Martin seminar in 1983, the term "user-seductive" was used in place of "user-friendly."[4] This term appears to be more appropriate, as the objective of software design is to seduce the user into using it. User-friendly or user-seductive software raises the level of user interaction with the system. If

---

[4] James Martin, "Seminar for Excellence," Technology Transfer Institute, appears to have coined the phrase "user seductive."

the user must execute complex transaction codes either from memory or reference books, there is a high probability that resistance to using the system will increase. The purpose of software is to attract the user and aid him in his operational tasks, not to bog him down in inefficient and misguided user friendliness.

Good Training Courses

Critical components to a successful implementation are the quality, amount, and timeliness of training. Companies invest a significant amount of money and time in acquiring new FIS software. The benefits can only be achieved if the user knows how to get the most out of the systems. This requires well-planned and well-conducted training courses. (One of the most frequent user complaints is poor-quality training.) To obtain active user involvement, a company must provide the tools to get the job done. If training courses do not address the correct level of audience, the benefits are minimal. Training for top-management users generally requires different programs from those for the hands-on end user. If the user does not know how to operate the system, chances are he will not try to teach himself. There are a growing number of computer-literate users, but that fact should not be relied upon when making the decision to provide training courses.

High-Level User Languages

With the long lead times for data processing support, it is highly advantageous for a user to be able to prepare a new report or revise the format of an existing one, a capability that is put directly into the hands of the user of high-level user languages. Providing this tool is one more way to attract users into becoming more involved. Results can be obtained quickly with fairly simple techniques. These languages give the user control, and provide a great incentive for being more active. However, care must be taken when choosing the high-level languages; the user must be taught how to use them.

Strong Project Management

Getting the user involved at the beginning of a project is not too difficult. Keeping him actively involved during a long implementation while his own job still must be performed is much harder. One of the major roles of the project manager is to coordinate user/data processing efforts and to ensure availability of the right resources for keeping the project on track. The project manager must be strong enough to handle this important task. Sometimes a user needs to be coerced and cajoled into participating; to do this, the project manager requires special skills.

All of the aids mentioned here may help to get and keep a user participating in the new systems implementation. It is essential, however, for data processing and users to feel part of the same team and not to draw up sides for battle. The review/approval cycle may help to promote good working relationships between data processing and the user. It may also contribute toward the development of mutual respect, providing both sides with a true feel for the effort and time required, thus eliminating unrealistic expectations and developing a team-building approach.

HOW USERS SHOULD BE INVOLVED IN THE PLANNING AND DEVELOPMENT STAGES

With new development projects, the extent of user participation normally varies according to the technical nature and complexity of the intended system. When implementing a new FIS, it is especially important for the user to understand the interrelationships of the various systems components and the potential benefits of alternative approaches. The user should be consulted in all phases, including the decision to automate, whether packaged software will be used, or whether custom software is the route for certain applications. The number of users, the appropriate level of user, and amount of user time needed are functions of the particular step being performed.

Some of the areas in which users should be involved during the initial phases of the project's life cycle include:

- Establishing a design team
- Defining systems requirements
- Validating systems requirements and conceptual designs
- Attending structured walk-throughs
- Providing approval to proceed
- Participating in steering committees
- Preparing or evaluating cost/benefit analysis
- Becoming project managers

Establishing a Design Team

Deciding who can best represent the user community requires a broad knowledge of both the company's operations and the functional systems area. Selecting users who meet the need for detailed knowledge of a specific application area and who also have a good comprehension of the overall business perspective is not an easy task. As much care needs to be given to this process as to the selection of the project manager. The role of user representatives on the design team is to serve as an interface. They should be the key contacts after the system becomes operational to make sure that user goals are met.

Defining Systems Requirements

In the past, the user verbally described to a systems analyst what he wanted from a new system. The analyst then immediately started to construct the requested application. There was very little in the way of written specifications—and also very little chance that the end product would look like the system the user had envisioned. Detailed systems requirements, if accurate and complete, can avoid this kind of pitfall. The user should provide information through interviews and questionnaires, as well as help document the reports required and inputs and outputs expected. This phase can be led by users if they have strong analytical and organizational abilities.

Validating Systems Requirements and Conceptual Design

Regardless of who prepares systems requirements, users must be involved in validating the systems requirement definition. The end product is always a system for users; thus, they must be convinced that their requirements will be satisfied. The validation should be at several levels, and address the following questions:

- Is the document complete? Does it cover all major inputs, outputs, and flows?
- Does the proposed specification accurately reflect user needs, and are assumptions identified?
- Does the proposed system fit into the company's overall business perspective?
- Can the system be implemented in the current environment? Will it interface with other applications?

Answering these questions typically requires expertise at both the managerial and staff levels. Users should challenge the original premises and be aware of any assumptions that have been made.

Attending Structured Walk-Throughs

One way to ensure complete specifications is to conduct structured walk-throughs on each new system. At different stages after requirements are defined, or after design/selection, a review meeting should be held. All the users affected by the new system, either directly or because of new interface requirements, should attend a structured walk-through where basic systems concepts and components are described and reviewed. At these meetings, users need to be encouraged to ask questions and challenge the design concepts, as well as given the opportunity to raise objections and discuss interface considerations and other salient issues while all interested parties are in attendance.

USER PARTICIPATION

Every change generally affects someone else. With the heavy interrelationships of FIS, the structured walk-through is particularly critical and may provide an efficient and effective forum for reviewing a new systems specification.

Providing Approval to Proceed

A user often delays and resists providing sign-off, but, by requiring it, management can generally ensure the project's success. Being forced to sign off on each phase or step is probably frustrating and stressful for the user, but the process reduces potential problems and makes the user accept accountability. The result is that the user reviews and analyzes each step in greater detail before signing his name to the sign-off document.

Participating in Steering Committees

The user's perspective is often very narrow, and focuses on his own needs. The role of the steering committee is generally twofold: (1) to monitor the quality of project management; and (2) to ensure the quality of the system being implemented. The steering committee is generally made up of both user and data processing personnel and includes fairly senior level management. These meetings focus on the project management issues of compliance with systems development life cycles, project budgets, and time frames. They act as a status checkpoint where concerns may be addressed before they become major problems. The steering committee's responsibility for ensuring the quality of the system should cover broad issues, such as systems flexibility, maintenance considerations, interface compatibility, and efficiency. The user needs to be part of the steering committee not only to see that his interests are represented but also to learn how the broader issues affect the new system. A successful steering committee chairman does not allow meetings to degenerate to the specific detail levels unless there is an issue requiring a policy decision or general agreement before proceeding. The user's time in the group meeting situation should be minimized. Knowing when to cut discussion and hold a separate meeting for a subset of the steering committee and other personnel is essential to maintain user interest and effectiveness.

Preparing or Evaluating Cost/Benefit Analysis

If users are involved in developing cost/benefit analysis, they will be better able to understand the financial implications. The cost/benefit analysis should always be evaluated by someone other than the preparer. This helps to provide assurance that the data used are accurate and that any assumptions or premises can be supported. If the cost/benefit study is not conducted by users, the validation process should include appropriate user review.

Becoming Project Manager

The responsibility for managing projects used to be given to data processing personnel. However, recently, there has been a gradual move toward user project managers. In many situations, this can be very effective; the role of project manager is by no means the exclusive right of the technical staff. In fact, many of the skills necessary for a good project manager discussed elsewhere in this chapter more often lie with good user personnel. The quality of the project manager generally determines the quality of the resulting implementation.

There are many different ways that the user may and should be involved in the pilot implementation phases. There are also other approaches that some companies have adopted to aid in validating the design. For example, an extra step may be included to simulate systems operation manually by using paper versions of the proposed on-line transactions, in parallel with the existing system. This helps to identify flaws in the design and ensure more certainty of success. However, there is likely to be resistance to the idea because it is time consuming and duplicates effort. Thus, good motivation is essential.

The examples given show how the user may be involved. Not all the examples are necessarily applicable, but consideration should be given to each when a project is undertaken.

HOW USERS SHOULD BE INVOLVED IN TESTING AND IMPLEMENTATION

Even if the user has actively participated in the planning and design phases, it does not automatically follow that the testing and implementation steps will proceed smoothly. The user's involvement must be maintained at each stage. The testing phase generally includes unit and parallel testing. If the user is to assist in testing, user training must already have taken place. Unless the new system has been tested and approved, implementation should not go forward. Thus, three major steps follow the planning and design phases: train, test, and implement.

Training

Training must include a mix of tutorials, documentation, hands-on-experience, and review and feedback sessions. A user cannot be expected to adopt a new system if he does not know how to operate it. Thus, the need for user training. There must also be strong management support and commitment to make sure that users are allowed time to attend appropriate training sessions. (See Chapter 20 for an in-depth analysis of personnel training.)

It is important to note that more than one person needs to be trained on a new system. Training is another area where single-person dependency often occurs. The effect of attrition should not be underestimated. For example, it

USER PARTICIPATION

may seem a remote possibility that the key payroll user/coordinator will resign, but the effect this could have on timely checks is considerable.

Testing

There is a tendency to underestimate the time and effort required to test a new system fully. Often, the size of the effort is forgotten and the time to create and load data is not considered. Creating test data is an unrewarding job that typically falls to the user. Generally, there are two categories of testing: unit testing and parallel testing. Unit testing requires that test data be created, whereas parallel testing uses actual company data to duplicate the existing system. Preparation of good test data is very important, and it is essential to test all cases. Frequently, much emphasis is placed on handling the exception cases, sometimes to the exclusion of more standard situations. The user should be heavily involved in test data generation, as he is the one who confronts different situations on a daily basis.

To obtain good cooperation in testing a new system, the user must feel that he can still affect the design. If he perceives that there is no intention of making any changes, his enthusiasm quickly dwindles. However, there must be a counterbalance. Flexibility and allowing for change is good, but the total impact of the change versus the benefit must always be kept in mind. If the project manager continues to include every user request, the number of changes gets out of hand and the implementation may never end. There must be a cut-off and an awareness of the ramifications of changes made. Some of these modifications may be delayed until the system has been operational for a period of time.

In a multidepartment, multicompany situation, it pays to test the system for a single, or pilot, company and to try to determine and resolve problems that occur. The idea of selecting a pilot company works well, as a group of users first tests a new system and then assists users in other companies with their testing. This eliminates having the same problem found by multiple users, and thus reduces duplication of effort. However, it does require a cooperation between companies and an unselfishness on behalf of the users in the pilot company.

Implementation

This phase overlaps the training and testing phases and includes tasks such as loading historical data, setting up production files and procedures, developing control logs, and defining backup and contingency plans. It should also include finalizing items such as run procedures, documentation and error handling methods, resources and supplies, and timing and operation schedules. Most of these tasks will have previously fallen under the jurisdiction of data processing. However, the user has the most knowledge of historical data and what is really needed. It is he who must resort to secondary backup procedures if the system is nonoperational. The user's function must include establishing these procedures. Ultimately, the system belongs to the user, and the more involved he is in the implementation, the better understanding he will have of the overall system.

Often, companies forget or do not plan for evaluating a system after it has been operational for a period of time. This evaluation, often referred to as postimplementation review (PIR), is a very important step and should generally be conducted four to six months after a system is in operation. It helps the user to determine if the system's goals and objectives have been met and to identify existing problems and weaknesses. It also pinpoints areas where the implementation was not completed, where additional training is required, where different procedures should be adopted, or where other changes are needed. This evaluation process requires objectivity and an ability to differentiate real problems from perceived ones. It also requires an understanding of any external factors that may affect systems performance.

There is a growing trend toward using internal audit or external consultants to perform a PIR on a new system. A user of a new system is rarely considered as having an objective viewpoint. However, a qualified user with analytical skill who has not been too closely involved in the implementation should be considered when a PIR is planned.

LOOKING TO THE FUTURE

From the discussion in this chapter, it should be apparent that the role of the user in the development cycle is gradually changing. The traditional approach is slowly being replaced by more actively involved users and by the introduction of new techniques that encourage user participation.

Two distinct types of applications are evolving. One consists of applications that may be considered true data processing, such as the traditional applications that require involvement in a system's development (e.g., FIS applications). There are also applications that are considered information processing, which manipulate data and are developed by the end users (e.g., spreadsheets and special report writing).

The ability to identify which approach is really needed and when it makes sense is essential. The question should be asked, "Can the existing system be enhanced sufficiently by end-user tools so that there is no need to develop or purchase a new system?" The role of the user is rapidly expanding. With the ever-increasing computer literacy among users and the introduction of microcomputers in most companies, there are now changing situations and, thus, alternatives. Information centers and decision support systems are enhancing user capabilities and awareness. In addition, the introduction of application development without programmers by the user of nonprocedural languages is another contributing factor to the changes taking place.

USER PARTICIPATION

Commitment, involvement, and knowledge of the business, together with frequent technical and managerial reviews, all of which keep a project on track, are key factors critical for success when implementing an FIS. These factors all require user involvement. To reduce potential risks, a user must be confident that he can answer three basic questions:

1 What is the real problem?
2 Will the proposed system provide the correct solution?
3 Can the systems be successfully implemented in the organization as it exists?

A major implementation, such as an FIS, deserves high-quality user involvement. The user must know what he really wants, validate the requirements, and help provide a cost-effective solution. He should ask why the project is being undertaken and whether the correct approach is being adopted. The user should communicate ideas and listen to suggestions without having preconceived notions, and should challenge issues throughout the project's entire life cycle. Communication must be two-way, and design needs must be precisely and correctly interpreted.

There is a growing trend toward professional user-managers who are computer literate. They can often solve their own ad-hoc problems through terminals and personal computers. They can communicate their ideas and needs with data processing and can recognize when technical data processing assistance is required. The gap between data processing and the user is gradually closing, but the essential differences between the two groups must be understood and dealt with.

The user must be involved during the early stages of the project, from helping to develop a good design through implementation planning. He must be aware of his staffing responsibilities during the project and know how much support, personnel, and time is needed, and to what extent. It is much easier for a user to accept a new system from the inside and as part of a team.

Management involvement and commitment is crucial. Top management must provide support and leadership when needed, and the project manager must have the proper mixture of technical, interpersonal, and organizational talents required.

The active involvement of quality user personnel does not automatically assure management that the important systems implementation will succeed. However, if users are involved in all phases, and if the ideas discussed in this chapter are put into operation, the potential for success will be greatly increased. Following these recommendations may also produce another cost saving, as calling in a consultant to help rectify a bad software selection, design, or implementation after the fact will prove unnecessary. The aim of a new FIS is to solve existing problems. If the user is pleased with the system, the implementation may be considered a success.

REFERENCES

Ahituv, Niv, and Seev Neumann. "Controlling the Information System Function." *Journal of Systems Management* (Sept. 1982).

Andrews, Dorine C. "Assessing the Risk for System Failure." *Journal of Systems Management* (Sept. 1982).

Elam, Philip G. "User Defined Information System Quality." *Journal of Systems Management* (Aug. 1979).

Gibson, Cyrus F., and Charles J. Singer. "New Risks for MIS Managers." *Computerworld—Indepth* (Apr. 1982).

Kintisch, Ronald, and Marvin Weisbord. "Getting Computer People and Users to Understand Each Other." *S.A.M. Advanced Management Journal* (Spring 1977).

Martin, James. "Seminar for Excellence." Technology Transfer Institute.

Robey, Daniel. "Perspectives of the User Interface." Proceedings of the Seventeenth Annual Computer Personnel Research Conference, 1980.

CHAPTER **19**

The Information Center

Keith L. Robinett

Introduction	1	Northrop Corporation	4
		Security Pacific National Bank	5
History of the Concept	1	Kidder, Peabody, & Co.	6
		Bechtel Power	6
Growth	2	Exxon	6
Crwth Computer Coursewares		Bank of America	6
Information Center Survey	2	Other Organizations	6
Diebold Survey	3		
INPUT Planning Presentation	3	**Future Status of the Information Center**	7
Information Center Examples	4	**References**	8

Fig. 19-1 Information Center Growth, 1983–1985 3
Fig. 19-2 Typical Information Center Applications 4

INTRODUCTION

One of the trends in systems technology cited in Chapter 2 is the increase in the end user's demand to be more involved in doing his own computing. A concept known as the information center is becoming increasingly popular in response to this demand.

In this chapter, the concept of an information center is defined, and its history and current and projected growth are described, along with several examples. The chapter concludes with a discussion of the dos and don'ts in establishing an information center.

HISTORY OF THE CONCEPT

The information center concept was established by IBM Canada in 1976. The goal was to enhance end-user productivity and to reduce application backlog. In the usual case, the information center provides a walk-in facility where the user can obtain data processing help from a technical staff that is there to train and assist him when he has problems.

In one type of information center, the user finds terminals that are linked to a computer that is dedicated to the exclusive use of the information center. The needed data files are downloaded—that is, the data are transferred electronically to a storage device attached to the dedicated computer—from the primary large processors' databases. The user then may access and operate on these files in an on-line mode. A variety of user-friendly software packages are made available. With these, the user may reformat and manipulate the data to obtain reports or graphics output to meet his unique requirements.

A second type of information center provides microcomputers for the end user. In this case, data entered by the user may be manipulated by the software tools available for the microcomputers. A disadvantage of this approach is that the user is required to enter the data manually.

A third approach is to provide links for the end user to outside timesharing services that provide user-friendly software tools.

In all cases, data files on the primary large processors are protected from inadvertent or deliberate alteration or destruction by the end user.

The information center differs from distributed processing in two fundamental ways:

1 The end user is not given direct access to the large mainframes.

2 The end user can do his own programming.

In most cases (FORTRAN being a notable exception), the end user must rely on professional programmers under the distributed processing scheme of things.

For a number of users in the United States, the information center concept is not new. For years, colleges and universities have made their data processing resources available to their students through this approach. Security Pacific National Bank in Los Angeles has had an information center since 1970.[1]

The accelerating growth trend most likely arises from the increasing computer literacy among end users. Students who come out of the secondary schools and colleges today are usually better schooled in computing than the previous generation. The historically slow process of application software development for mainframe processing taxes their patience. Thus, the information center concept is an attractive solution to their frustrations.

GROWTH

Crwth Computer Coursewares Information Center Survey

Early in 1984, Crwth Computer Coursewares conducted "The Crwth Information Center Survey." This study noted that approximately 1,400 information

---
[1] Laton McCartney, "The New Info Centers," *Datamation* (July 1983), p. 30.

THE INFORMATION CENTER

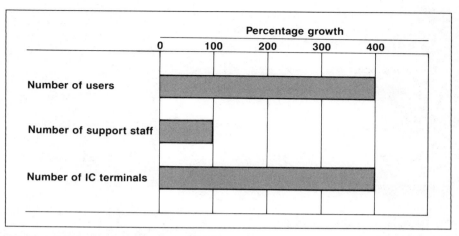

FIG. 19-1 Information Center Growth, 1983–1985

centers were established since the concept was introduced by IBM Canada in 1976.[2]

Other key findings of the survey were as follows:

- Thirty-seven percent of the centers were less than one year old.
- A 50 percent increase was expected by the end of 1984.
- The centers were usually organized within the MIS departments.
- Thirty-six percent of the users were business-oriented analysts.
- Twenty-five percent were clerical and administrative.
- Fifteen percent were supervisory personnel.

Diebold Survey

An earlier survey by the Diebold Group of thirty-two major companies revealed plans for at least two information centers by 1985 in two thirds of the responding companies.

INPUT Planning Presentation

Projections of growth by INPUT (the Information Systems Planning Service) also show phenomenal growth in the information center concept. Figure 19-1 shows a 400 percent growth in users and terminals from 1983 to 1985. Figure 19-2 shows typical information center applications.[3]

---

[2] Patricia Keefe, "Info Center Seen Budding Under Vigilant MIS," *Computerworld* (Mar. 19, 1984), p. 14.

[3] Steve Kerns, "Managing the End-User Revolution," *INPUT Client Presentation* (Nov. 17, 1983), pp. 43, 44.

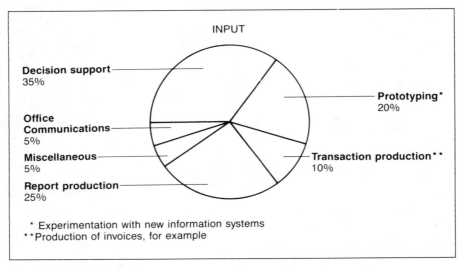

FIG. 19-2 Typical Information Center Applications

INFORMATION CENTER EXAMPLES

Northrop Corporation

Northrop Corporation's information center began as a pilot project late in 1982. With the assistance of an IBM consultant, a user survey was conducted within Northrop's aircraft division. Based on the high level of interest in the information center concept, a center was established to provide initial service to fifty users in the engineering department. The users included administrative and business-oriented personnel as well as engineers. An IBM 4341 was installed as the dedicated processor, and a number of user-friendly software packages were acquired.

At the end of the pilot program's first year, users identified savings of roughly 50 percent over the cost of operating the center. Based on this success, user availability was expanded to all functional areas of the division.

By February 1985, there were more than 450 users. In addition, eleven user groups were able to access the information center computer from twenty different locations. The IBM 4341 had been replaced by the larger IBM 3033 UP. A total of 118 terminals, 25 printers, and 5 IBM PCs were available for use.

Active users by group broke down as follows:

- *Engineering* — 37 percent
- *Finance/administrative services* — 32 percent
- *Information resources* — 10 percent

THE INFORMATION CENTER

- *Human resources* — 9 percent
- *All others* — 12 percent

The information center users were backed by a service-oriented staff that provided support for all of the software packages. In addition, this staff provided for controlled extracts from mainframe databases that were downloaded to the 3033 UP. By February 1985, seventy-one files were being downloaded on a regular basis.

The following software packages were available:

Software	Supplier
APL/DI	IBM
ADRS	IBM
ADRS/BG	IBM
ICU	IBM
PROFS	IBM
PASSTHRU	IBM
SAS	SAS Institute, Inc.
SAS/GRAPH	SAS Institute, Inc.
RAMIS	Mathematica
TELL-A-GRAF	ISSCO
TELL-A-PLAN	ISSCO
DATA CONNECTION	ISSCO
CUECHART	ISSCO
GATEWAY	Software Corporation of America

Although the following were not installed at Northrop, some of the other popular software packages are:

• Focus	Information Builders
• Inquire	Infodata Systems, Inc.
• STAIRS	IBM
• Easytrieve	Panosophic Systems, Inc.

Security Pacific National Bank

At Security Pacific, the information center was established in 1970 as an in-house alternative to outside timesharing services. At the outset, 100 users signed up, and there were 10 to 15 concurrent users. The service proved to be so popular that there are now several thousand internal customers signed up and as many as 250 concurrent users. Since 1983, an Amdahl 5860 has served as the exclusive processor for the information center.

Kidder, Peabody, & Co.

Kidder, Peabody, & Co. selected a Tandem computer for its information center. The Tandem was selected to give growth flexibility in small increments. The center supports more than sixty users using ASCII-compatible terminals. In addition to the Tandem, a user may employ outside databases through a data switch.

Bechtel Power

Bechtel Power in San Francisco tried a different approach. Instead of using its own computer, Bechtel tied into the IBM Information Network. Other suppliers also offer outside timesharing services. Two examples are the National CSS Nomad offering and Sperry's Mapper Executive Information Service Center.

Exxon

Exxon has made widespread use of the information center concept. The first center was operational in March 1982 in the New York corporate headquarters. Its client base includes some 1,200 professionals, managers, and support personnel located in midtown Manhattan, and its staff consists of a secretary and four computer professionals, who complement each other in their breadth of computing and business skills.[4]

By January 1984, Exxon had sixteen information centers, with more planned. Exxon's support staff provides training and consultation to headquarters personnel.

Bank of America

The Bank of America has 84,000 employees, and it is currently developing an information center to support them. Two hundred forty employees at Bank of America now work in end-user computing, which serves 10,000 users worldwide on a dial-up network.[5]

The bank's goal is to make its MIS database available to most users by 1990 on a worldwide basis at any time of day. Its information center is aimed at meeting this goal.

Other Organizations

Other organizations that have implemented the information center concept include:

---

[4] Richard T. Johnson, "The Infocenter Experience," *Datamation* (Jan. 1984), p. 137.

[5] John Desmond, "Bank Develops Info Center to Capitalize on Micro Investment," *Computerworld* (Sept. 10, 1984), p. 20.

THE INFORMATION CENTER

- City of Los Angeles
- E.F. Hutton
- Blue Cross/Blue Shield of Massachusetts
- Atlantic Richfield
- Union Carbide
- Lockheed Corporation
- Chase Manhattan Bank
- North American Philips
- Kelley Services, Detroit
- Merrill Lynch, Pierce, Fenner, & Smith
- Drexel Burnham Lambert
- Shaklee Corporation
- Mervyn's Department Stores
- Household Finance Corporation, Chicago

FUTURE STATUS OF THE INFORMATION CENTER

The information center concept has proved to be a popular and growing response to the end-user revolution. A new generation of computer-literate users are capable of satisfying many of their needs through the availability of user-friendly software packages in the information center. This leaves more time for professional programmers to work on large integrated systems that involve multiple functional organizations.

Although there is no body of set rules to follow in implementing an information center, a number of dos and don'ts were presented at a meeting of the Information Center Management Association in January 1985, in Manhattan Beach, California.

1. DO implement and manage the information center as a service organization, not as a control organization.
2. DO obtain top-management commitment to the concept. Pilot projects are useful for obtaining management support.
3. DO track the costs of the information center and feedback and/or chargeback to the user.
4. DO form a dedicated support staff to work with the end user.
5. DO provide adequate training to the information center staff and the user.
6. DO communicate results, savings, new software, and availability through regular newsletters.
7. DO hold open houses, demonstrate software and hardware, and provide brochures describing the information center.
8. DON'T try to compete with professional programming staffs of large, integrated, sophisticated systems.
9. DON'T open the information center to the user until the start-up problems are ironed out.

10 DON'T expand the number of users faster than the information center staff can handle them.

Based on its rapid growth and the examples of success, it appears that the information center concept is an idea whose time has come.

REFERENCES

Desmond, John. "Bank Develops Info Center to Capitalize on Micro Investment." *Computerworld* (Sept. 10, 1984), p. 20.

Flis, Diane M. "The Route to Information Access." *Computerworld* (Dec. 14, 1983), pp. 40–44.

Johnson, Richard T. "The Infocenter Experience." *Datamation* (Jan. 1984), pp. 137–138, 140, 142.

Karten, Naomi. "Getting There From Here." *Computerworld* (Dec. 14, 1983), pp. 45–47.

Keefe, Patricia. "Info Center Seen Budding Under Vigilant MIS." *Computerworld* (Mar. 19, 1984), p. 14.

McCartney, Laton. "The New Info Centers." *Datamation* (July 1983), pp. 30, 32, 41, 44, 46.

Paul, Lois. "Big Blue Bolsters Info Center Support." *Computerworld* (July 18, 1983), pp. 1, 9.

Rifkin, Glenn. "The Information Center: Oasis or Mirage." *Computerworld* (June 15, 1983), pp. 13–16.

CHAPTER **20**

Training of Personnel

Paul D. McNulty

The Importance of Proper Training	1	When Something Is Old	13
Levels of Training	2	**Effective Training**	14
Advanced User Management Training	3	Location and Layout	14
Operator Training	4	Effective Use of Visual Aids	15
Systems Training	5	Class Session Format	15
User Training	6	Exercises, Examples, and Case Studies	16
Hardware Training	6	Exercises	16
Microcomputer Training	7	Examples	16
		Case Studies	17
Efficient Computer Use: Controls	7	What to Teach, When	17
Methods of Training	8	Beginning Classes	17
Classroom Training	9	Intermediate Classes	18
When to Use Classroom Training	9	Advanced Classes	18
Optimum Classroom Conditions	9		
Programmed Training	11	**Time Spent on Training**	18
In-House Training	11	On-Going Professional Education	18
Internal Training	12	One-Time Training	18
Determining the Time for Training	13	**Effects of Not Training**	19
When Something Is New	13		
Fig. 20-1 Model Classroom			10

THE IMPORTANCE OF PROPER TRAINING

The training phase is one of the most important aspects in the life cycle of a new systems implementation. Even a superior system with extensive and thorough planning will not succeed when implemented if careful thought and adequate preparation are not given to training.

    It is difficult to know the correct way to operate any new system without some prior exposure to the same, or similar, task. Nowhere is this more evident than in the world of data processing. No two programs (even if composed by the same programmer) function exactly alike. No two computer systems (even if both say IBM on the front) function in the same way. There are always very important differences that require the user to achieve a certain level of knowledge before the product can be used effectively.

Training is the fundamental key that unlocks the door to any subject, and computer training is imperative to maintain literacy with the ever-expanding technology. Millions of dollars are spent each year to:

- Advertise classes (from introductory to advanced topics)
- Coordinate class locations, materials, and facilities
- Prepare lectures, hands-on exercises, and case studies
- Pay instructors
- Travel to class locations
- Attend sessions

In 1983, the average U.S. company spent $500 per employee on training. Spending on formal training is expected to rise to about $900 million by 1990, from an estimated $200 million in 1984, according to International Data Corporation, a Framingham, Massachusetts, market researcher. With millions of people in the work force, it soon becomes apparent that training and keeping pace with technological advancements represent a major share of the GNP.

Ever-changing technology requires training and retraining for companies to stay ahead of the competition and keep workers employed. This is especially evident in the DP industry, where systems change daily.

Many professions (including accounting, law, and medicine) require its member professionals to achieve levels of continuing education each year. If the minimum hours are not met, their licenses to practice their vocations can be removed by the body governing their professions' quality control. These governing bodies feel that continuing education is so important that they plan and conduct many classes for their members.

One can imagine what the world would be like today if no one ever attended additional training courses. Many people simply assume they know everything there is to know about a topic. Our society would not have reached its present level of knowledge without dedication to education. Therefore, it is obvious that training and continuing education are necessary in our society.

The discussion in this chapter concerns the various ways to keep computer personnel self-literate and up-to-date on the technical advancements in their field. The benefits of the various methods and how they relate to different individuals and jobs are also analyzed.

Levels of Training

Unsuccessful computer systems installations often can be linked to an unsuccessful training plan. Inadequate user training may lead to improper use of the

TRAINING OF PERSONNEL 20-3

system. Insufficient training of the systems installers may cause hardware problems. Misleading management training on a system's features and benefits may also cause installation failure. At whatever level the problem is discovered, it can often be traced back to some form of training deficiency.

Levels of training required to install a computer system successfully, whether a microcomputer or a mainframe, include the following:

- Advanced user management training
- Operator training
- Systems training
- User training
- Hardware training

Advanced User Management Training. Management should be briefed on understanding a new computer system before it is implemented. This should be done prior to the purchase of a new FIS. Management's advanced educational needs include the following topics:

- Understanding how the system will work in the environment
- What to expect in the way of reports and application process—for example, will the computer properly process invoices and relieve inventory in the same way as the current manual process?
- How it effectively helps the manager
- Time requirements and constraints for processing of information
- Generation of reports and month-end processing
- Manual procedures that must be in place to control computer access and ensure proper use

Management's requirements are significantly different from those of the other various users. For example, the data processing department is not interested in types of reports, but rather is acutely concerned with:

- State-of-the-art technology
- Support for both hardware and software
- Processing speed
- Capacity requirements

While advanced user management training is discussed in this chapter, care should be taken to ensure sufficient advanced training for more than just management, in order to satisfy concerns of all levels of a business that the system being considered will support all of their needs. These individuals include clerks as well as middle management. They perform tasks the detail of which upper management is not aware. These personnel are generally required to gather or "massage" data needed by upper management. If all needs of all levels are not satisfied, the resulting computer system may continue to require a lot of manual effort.

Operator Training. The operator using the equipment must be properly trained to respond to errors or systems failures. When an operator responds properly to a systems error, the problem is resolved and eliminated.

An operator must understand which programs to run and when, in order to achieve the desired results. A system that allows an operator to run programs out of sequence (e.g., run the invoice program before the sales tax calculation on the outstanding items) is an example of a system where this knowledge is crucial. Microcomputer programs are particularly notorious for allowing an operator to execute any program, in any order, without regard for logical operations orders.

Operator training on the proper response to systems inquiries is often overlooked. When the computer asks a question, improper or invalid responses are not always caught by the software, which, months later, may lead to major problems. A classic example of this situation is the month-end update that requests the operator to enter the month-end date. If the month is October and the operator enters November 30, 19XX, several undesirable events can occur. For example:

- The system tries to close November, even though there may be no transactions for November.
- The system does not close October, because it assumes October is already closed.
- No one can enter transactions for November, because that month has been closed.
- Accounts receivable is aged an extra month, which produces an abundance of problems.
- Accounts payable is aged an extra month, which causes most of the outstanding invoices to become due and checks to be generated automatically.

Obviously, this input error can cause serious difficulties. There are many such options, where a computer requests operator input and erroneous responses cannot be detected by a program, that lead to similarly disastrous problems.

TRAINING OF PERSONNEL

Systems Training. Systems personnel (programmers, managers, and operators who actively operate a system) require a different level of training. Systems personnel perform such tasks as:

- Evening batch processing
- Systems backups
- Purges
- Day- and month-end updates

These are the people who are called upon to:

- Train others, or to retrain others (an important topic discussed elsewhere in this chapter)
- Solve problems
- Implement new applications
- Change currently operating applications
- Back up the system
- Restore the system after problems are solved
- Generally be knowledgeable about programs, files, and how to locate information

Major pitfalls in any size of computer system occur where systems management personnel do not fully understand systems operations. Problems arise when update utilities, designed to close accounting periods, move data from one database to another, combine data from two different areas of a database, or are improperly run or run at the wrong time. An example of this would be a distributed system (one utilizing several computers, all speaking to each other and sharing information) that requires update programs to be run to extract data from one computer and place them in the other. If these update programs are not run at the proper time or are run more than once, missing or duplicate data may occur in the master system.

The systems group is generally responsible for setting up and maintaining systems security. Not understanding the availability, levels, or use of the built-in systems security may create problems of data integrity in the future. Protecting the data from unauthorized access is as important as having good data in the system. This segment of training is often put off and considered unimportant until it is too late. Many sophisticated systems require security levels set prior to file and program definition. Once the system is in use, these levels cannot be changed. Careful advanced planning helps to eliminate future problems. (See Chapter 22, which addresses the problem of security.)

Some level of systems knowledge must be maintained by an organization, whether it is a multinational company or a single individual, to ensure some support for problems in the future. Sometimes, training includes knowing whom to call and when and what questions to ask.

User Training. It is hard to say who needs systems training more—user, operator, or manager. Each requires a different type and level of training. The user level is probably the most important, and frequently gets the most attention.

Users are different from operators. Operators typically work in the computer room, run updates, print voluminous reports, process backups, and correct errors created by the users. Users are the people on the front end of the system, and include the following:

- *Clerks at a sales order desk* — who accept telephone orders and enter them into a terminal
- *Accounting personnel* — who process invoices and checks
- *Payroll personnel* — who record time cards
- *Shipping and receiving clerks* — who record inventory levels
- *Managers* — who inquire into financial status and sales reports
- *Marketing directors* — who track salespeople's performance

The users are the heart of the system. They generate the data that the operators process, managers review and respond to, and the results of which customers see. Improper user training causes difficulties or deficiencies, such as:

- Lost revenues because of improper pricing at order entry
- Overstocking of inventory because of improper ordering procedures in the shipping and receiving areas
- Over- or underpayment of employees because of misunderstanding of payroll earnings categories
- Lost charges because of improper coding of orders
- Unhappy vendors because of improper invoice processing and late payment to vendors
- Overpayment to vendors or suppliers
- Improper accounting charges or credits (e.g., expense invoice)
- Inaccurate financial statements

Hardware Training. Not everyone undergoing training should be an expert on computer hardware (the physical equipment, as opposed to software, which is the intangible program that causes the hardware to perform desired

TRAINING OF PERSONNEL

functions). However, a certain degree of hardware knowledge of the computer should be imparted to all users, operators, and members of management. This could include such basics as:

- How to turn the computer on. If the computer is a microcomputer, this is imperative; on large computers, this should be limited to operators.
- How to connect such necessary items as cables, printer, monitor, and disk drive.
- How to determine whether problems are hardware or software related.
- Whom to call to resolve the problems.
- How to correct minor printer problems such as paper misfeed, ribbon change, or forms lineup.

Larger installations should ensure some level of operator competence with hardware. These operators can help the user solve minor hardware-related problems and perform the monthly preventative maintenance (or PM), as well as save the organization money in terms of a hardware maintenance contract.

Microcomputer Training. The typical microcomputer application comes complete with documentation, program diskettes, and a toll-free help line. No formal training is available from the vendor of these packages. In these instances, it is the unfortunate job of the user to try to learn the software by using it, reading a sometimes confusing manual (written by a programmer), and/or calling the hotline.

Before purchasing any form of software, the buyer should be certain that training is available for all personnel mentioned here. The training should be part of the cost of the package. However, in the case of microcomputer programs, the purchaser may have to obtain the proper training from outside sources, such as:

- Retail computer stores
- Consulting and public accounting firms
- Businesses that do nothing except provide training on a variety of microcomputer applications (of which there are many around the country)

EFFICIENT COMPUTER USE: CONTROLS

It may seem that there is only one way to use a computer system, and that is in whatever way the programs allow operation. This is not usually true. With sophisticated programs, it is often possible for the user to have available several different ways of performing the same function. One method may be easier than another, make more sense to the user, or simply be the method the user learned first. An example of different ways to do things may be as simple as how a cursor is moved around in a spreadsheet. Most novice users use the arrow keys, which require one key stroke for each space moved. However, use of the page right/left or page up/down keys allows faster cursor movement and achieves the same goal of getting the cursor from Point A to Point B. In FIS application packages, it is often possible to record a journal entry or process an invoice in more than one way. However, there will always be one way that is the most efficient. That most efficient way to process data is found most quickly through training. People do not modify the way they do something if they have no reason to believe there is a better way. In other words, they usually feel that "if it works, don't fix it."

Controls around the computer are very important. The computer will function as a business tool only if the data entered are controlled properly in advance of input. Training programs on computer applications typically do not address this area, because the computer salesperson and/or programmer knows nothing about the business. The responsible manager should insist that control training be a part of the training package before the user begins to access the system. If the vendor does not offer such a program, one must be developed internally for the business. The controls program normally should include such functions as:

- Batch balancing of invoices prior to data entry
- Reconciliation of journals to the general ledger
- Procedures for reconciling check registers for accounts payable and payroll
- Ways to ensure entry of all invoices and orders into the computer only once
- Methods to ensure proper follow-up of receivables
- Ways to answer certain questions asked by the computer to ensure valid data integrity (i.e., discount percentages, payroll earnings categories, inventory stock numbers)

Without proper controls, users trained in their proper application, and managers trained to monitor them, various reports and totals may be uncontrollably out of balance.

METHODS OF TRAINING

Training may take many different forms. It runs the gamut from formal classes to poorly written self-study documents. Following is a discussion of the more popular methods of training.

Classroom Training

The old standby, and frequently the most productive tutorial method, is classroom training. It is preferred for most initial training for several reasons, paramount among which is environment. Classrooms are designed for learning. Offices, on the other hand, are designed for productive working. Initial classes should not be conducted in an office, where the students will be constantly interrupted by telephone calls, questions, and other work-related problems. This applies to all of the training discussed here.

The classroom environment creates an ambiance of learning. This is always preferable to any other alternative discussed herein.

When to Use Classroom Training. Classrooms can be used for almost any kind of training; however, they are ideal for:

- Topics that require more than casual consideration—that is, where the students will have to put some real thought and creativity into the subject
- Topics that are new to the students as opposed to retraining
- Situations where there are more than a few students—student interaction being a major benefit of classroom training
- Situations in which the nature of the topic lends itself to classroom instruction (Rather vague, but some topics are best studied alone or on the job.)
- Situations in which the subject matter requires at least one full day of training to achieve the desired goals of the course

Optimum Classroom Conditions. As in any other environment, there are certain conditions and features that are especially desirable for classrooms.

- *Comfort.* They should be comfortable, but not so comfortable that students will fall asleep. Hard, straight-backed chairs that do not rock or swivel are best. Temperature should be maintained at a slightly cooler than normal level to keep students at peak levels of consciousness.
- *Small in size.* They should contain a limited number of students per class—ideally about eight or ten per instructor.
- *One terminal for every two students.* This allows hands-on use of the system, builds teamwork, and helps students to learn as they help their partners understand concepts.
- *Breaks.* These should be spaced approximately one and one-half to two hours apart.

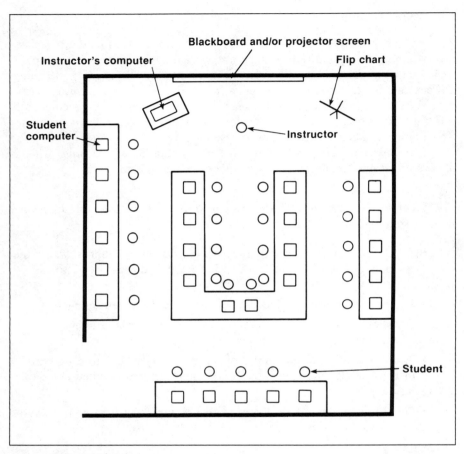

FIG. 20-1 Model Classroom

- *Few or no windows.* This reduces diversion.

- *No telephones.* Telephones should be available only where required to connect the terminals to the main computer system.

- *Location away from workplace.* During a break, classrooms in the office allow students to regress back to work, answer telephone calls, get pulled into meetings, or be lost to the class for some period of time. The result is a student who attends class but does not gain the proper value.

- *Horseshoe formation of tables, with the instructor in the middle and the computer terminals against the wall.* This formation (see Figure 20-1) keeps students from playing with the computer keyboards during the lecture, as their backs are to the terminals.

Classrooms that do not have these features will not be unsuccessful, but they may be less productive. The goal is to create a situation where maximum participation results in maximum learning.

Programmed Training

Programmed training is the art of leading a student, step by step, through a process in a programmed fashion. This method uses instruction, quiz, and proceed tactics. If the student fails the quiz, he must return to the previous instruction section and pass the associated quiz before proceeding to the next instruction section.

Programmed training, using a manual that leads the reader through the process in an understandable fashion, is a very popular method, and requires very little overhead on the part of the training organization. Programmed learning guides have been written for many microcomputer software products. They take the reader through a step-by-step process until he understands the subject. Programmed learning manuals sometimes do not even require the use of a microcomputer or a terminal, because the books show the screens and simulate the activity.

Programmed learning has advanced to the degree that a computer is used in place of a manual as the medium for communicating information. These programs are referred to as tutorials and provide a function similar to programmed learning textbooks. The user places the tutorial diskette into the system and follows the computer's instructions. As in the book version, a user cannot proceed to a new topic without first satisfactorily completing the current one.

Programmed learning guides are ideal for simple applications or as an introduction to new programs, concepts, or techniques. Programmed learning documents should not be considered as replacements for training classes or actual hands-on experience, however.

In-House Training

The in-house training seminar is probably the most popular among budget-conscious companies. This methodology allows training while keeping the students close to the work environment, and it eliminates the costs of travel, facilities, meals, and equipment. It is far from being the most beneficial; for all the reasons that the classroom training method is a most desirable training situation, this method is not.

Traditionally, companies have tried this method to appease employees clamoring for training. It typically results in poorly prepared instructors providing vague information with limited materials (handouts) in a less than adequate facility. The instructor, who is the future user's peer and *not* trained as a teacher, generally cannot be expected to conduct quality programs geared for learning. He usually prepares for the class the night before, and does not use, or even understand, teaching techniques such as:

- Voice inflection
- Blackboards
- Overheads
- Flip charts
- Audiovisuals

Many times, the facility used is the business' conference room, where telephones ring and constant interruptions occur.

In-house training should not be confused with internal training, which does have some very positive applications and appropriate uses.

When confronted with the choice of no training or in-house training, the tendency is to say that some is better than none. Experience shows that this is not always the case. In-house training frequently does not provide up-to-date, correct, or timely information. Nor does it provide a forum conducive to imparting lasting knowledge. It also takes away time from the enlisted instructor that could be put to much better use.

In-house training should be avoided unless a business has quality instructors and facilities. A valuable alternative is internal training.

Internal Training

For purposes of discussion here, internal training has the following qualities, which in-house training does not possess.

- It is conducted by a trained teacher who knows the subject matter and how to convey it.
- It is controlled by the outside trainer, who will not allow interruptions.
- The cost of the outside trainer is greater than for any in-house trainer.
- Materials provided by the trainer are usually more useful, complete, and accurate than those used in in-house training.

Internal training is best suited to circumstances where a business has just purchased software and needs training for those who will use it. When training is conducted using the actual equipment in a firm's own facility, lasting impressions can be made. An inexperienced computer user can relate more easily if the computer and the terminal look exactly like the ones he will have to use on a daily basis.

Another desirable use of internal training is in the case where a business decides to provide general purpose classes (short in duration) for all or many of its employees. Providing a conference room and importing an instructor who is

TRAINING OF PERSONNEL 20-13

trained in the topic is the logical choice. This type of class is usually geared to productivity, sales, motivation, or general computer topics.

Both in-house training and internal training should be short in duration— classes should not last for more than four hours per session.

DETERMINING THE TIME FOR TRAINING

It is time to train when something new is available, when users get sloppy and need "retraining," or when changes occur. There are several distinct types of training and a proper time for each.

When Something Is New

The most common time to train is when something is new. This could apply where any of the following circumstances occur.

- *A new application arises for the existing computer.* In this case, all users need to be oriented to the new product's capabilities.

- *A new employee joins the group.* An individual training plan is needed, unless the situation is such that waiting until there are several new people to train is not disruptive.

- *A new methodology for doing something presents itself.* In this case, several levels of training must occur; user training, supervisor training, and quality control and review training.

These situations present the most common ones for training of personnel. Unfortunately, having training programs available for new employees and in cases of change is too often neglected.

When Something Is Old

Sometimes a business neglects to provide for retraining of its personnel. The most common misuse of computers is not lack of initial education; it is usually caused by lack of forethought, in not understanding that not everything can be absorbed in one initial class. This is why it is important for the computer user to continue taking courses in a subject to make sure that he is using the product to its maximum capabilities.

Generally, six to eight months after a computer system is installed, the user should attend a training update (or be retrained). This update is designed to refresh students on advanced topics and seldom used features of the system. The update should not be used to review everyday material unless there is something new, a better way to use the system and achieve the same goal, or the user is consistently doing something wrong.

Retraining should be conducted outside of the office environment. The preferred format is classroom style. Students should be grouped, when possible, by job function, such as:

- Order entry
- Accounting
- Marketing
- Shipping and receiving
- Systems
- Management

Retraining is important because users develop bad habits over a period of time. Retraining helps to eliminate those habits, and reinforces better techniques for using the computer as a tool.

EFFECTIVE TRAINING

Training is only as useful as the quality of the program. A poor-quality program may have some (or all) of the following features:

- It does not follow the handouts.
- It is taught by an instructor who:
  - Appears not to understand the topic or his notes
  - Is easily confused
  - Cannot field questions from the class
  - Conducts the class in an environment unconducive to education
  - Does not use visual aids
  - Merely reads to the students
  - Teaches with no exercises and has no hands-on experience

A great many training programs leave the student with no more knowledge than when he started. This is due, in part, to the manner in which the programs are conducted.

Location and Layout

The importance of location has already been mentioned. If the facility for training is not conducive to learning, the attendees will learn less. The room should have a classroom structure, complete with such instruction aids as:

- Blackboard (or facsimile)
- Flipchart
- Screen for slides or overhead projections
- Overhead projector

In addition to the foregoing instruction aids, the following are also desirable:

TRAINING OF PERSONNEL 20-15

- *Few or no windows.*
- *Tables set in horseshoe formation* (see Figure 20-1). There should be a ratio of two students to every computer or terminal, thus providing:
  - Plenty of hands-on user experience;
  - Maintaining of student interest; and
  - Pairs of students to interact.
- *Small classrooms.* There should be no more than twenty students to a classroom; having too many students confuses the class, regardless of the teacher/student ratio.

Effective Use of Visual Aids

The instructor should make extensive use of visual aids, including:

- Slides
- Pictures and diagrams drawn on chalkboards
- Films
- Large-screen televisions for videos or that are connected to terminals to demonstrate actual programs
- Flip charts
- Reference manuals
- Handouts

Visual aids can be overused if too much time is spent preparing them during the class. Slides, overhead foils, and the ideas for diagrams drawn on the board must all be prepared prior to the class period. If the instructor spends too much time formulating the idea and not enough time explaining it, the students will drift from the subject.

Using the systems reference manual during the lecture portion and helping students find the answers to questions by using the manual are keys to success in training. If a student does not know how to use the manual or how to find the information during class, chances are that he will not use the manual when a problem arises once away from the class. The reference manual is the most useful tool the instructor has for successfully training the student as a future user of the FIS.

Class Session Format

Experience shows that the format of a successful class session follows this flow:

- *Introduction* — fifteen minutes
- *Lecture* — twenty minutes
- *Hands-on exercise* — thirty minutes
- *Review questions* — five minutes

- *Lecture* — twenty minutes
- *Hands-on exercise* — thirty minutes
- *Review questions* — five minutes
- *Break* — ten minutes

This format is repeated until the course has been completed. It generally allows a break in the morning, lunch, and a break in the afternoon. The ratio of twenty minutes of lecture to thirty-five minutes of hands-on experience and class interaction allows sufficient student participation and limits the amount of information the instructor will try to impart in one session. Stretching a lecture to cover too much information before the student has had the opportunity to understand the subject fully may encourage disappointing results.

During the lecture portion of the class, the instructor usually utilizes the visual aids and handouts. Students should be encouraged either to turn off their computers, dim the screen (so they cannot see what is displayed), or not face the terminal.

The student/teacher ratio of one teacher for every eight to ten students allows the instructor to wander about the room while the students are working on their hands-on exercises. Also, rotating lecturers enhances student attention.

Exercises, Examples, and Case Studies

Exercises, examples, and case studies are vital to the success of a class. Student attention and retention are vastly improved where any or all of these techniques are used.

Exercises. Hands-on exercises, as part of the classroom instruction, should be used to highlight the lecture portion of the course. These exercises must be designed in advance of the class date for use with specific lecture topics. Confusing exercises result where the instructor tries to use too many features of the system at once. Exercises should emphasize the topic being discussed and utilize previous topics as review only. Dwelling on previous topics or introducing new subjects in an exercise are two reasons for exercises failing. New subject matter or exercises that require use of terms, functions, or features not yet discussed must be avoided.

Examples. The use of examples is highly recommended during the lecture portion of the class. They are to be used as often as possible and should be something to which the class can relate. A true story, something that is common to the industry being trained that can be recreated during the exercise portion, or something that occurred during the exercise segment just completed all make good examples.

A good lecturer uses as many examples as possible to try to keep his audience involved and to paint a picture in the student's mind to help him understand the concept and, more importantly, learn what might happen if he does not understand.

Case Studies. Case studies, like exercises, are used to help the student understand the concept being taught. Case studies are ideal as a supplement to class exercises. When a student is slightly ahead of the rest of the class and has completed the current exercise, a case study should be introduced. The case study keeps the accelerated student busy while the balance of the class works on the exercise. This not only keeps everyone occupied, but helps cement understanding and prevents the fast student from bothering other students.

Case studies are typically more involved than exercises. They are frequently real situations presented with facts and goals but no one real answer. The student who attempts a case study has his knowledge and abilities challenged to find a possible solution. A case study may involve knowledge of more of the system than has been discussed in the class.

More time is needed to accomplish the case study; therefore, caution must be exercised to keep the student moving along with the rest of the class, instead of dwelling on the case study from a previous exercise.

An important feature of the case study is the fact that, as the student learns more about the features of the system, he finds new and better ways to solve the case study problem.

What to Teach, When

Choosing the topics to cover in class and their sequence is very important. Students will be lost to the instructor early in the session if the topic becomes too involved too early.

Beginning Classes. Covering the basics is the key to a beginning class. Assume the student knows little. Students with some limited knowledge will appreciate the class more if they know that there are no assumptions. A student who knows he knows nothing will not feel the pressure to compete with knowledgeable students and will be a higher achiever.

The instructor should be keen to watch the students. If it appears that more students understand the topic than do not, he should move on and help the few students who do not understand during the break or the exercise period.

When covering the basics, the instructor must not introduce concepts that require more knowledge than has been provided in class (e.g., discussing database structures when the student does not even know what a file is).

Intermediate Classes. The intermediate-level class should be advertised and conducted as just that. The student is assumed to have a working knowledge of the topic, and the class proceeds from that level. A student without that knowledge should not be allowed to attend—or at least should not be allowed to hold up the rest of the class. Intermediate-level classes start with a brief review of the basics and proceed to the new topics to be presented.

Advanced Classes. Advanced classes present seldom used features. Usually, topics introduce the operator to features that will help him use the system more efficiently but which he does not fully understand or has yet to try.

TIME SPENT ON TRAINING

A very important decision to make is how much time to spend on training and education, keeping in mind that there are two areas of training:

1 On-going professional education
2 One-time training for something new

These two types of training require different levels of effort. In addition, the type of training effects the time requirements and constraints of student and instructor.

On-Going Professional Education

Many organizations have minimum levels of continuing professional education requirements that their members must maintain. Most of those groups require no less than forty hours per year, which can be through classroom training, programmed learning texts, or internal training. Forty hours from a normal work year represents about 2 percent of an individual's available time. This 2 percent is for formal training, and does not mean an individual is learning only 2 percent of the time.

One-Time Training

It is very difficult to say how many hours should be assigned to any one computer product. That varies with:

- The number of users
- The size of the computer system (microcomputer, minicomputer, or mainframe)
- The complexity of the product (e.g., an integrated accounting system vs. Lotus 1-2-3)
- The level of training (manager vs. user)

TRAINING OF PERSONNEL

No computer program, package, or system can be learned in less than one day. The typical number of hours allotted to a multiuser accounting system is forty. (This is generally forty hours per user.) The optimum way to break the forty hours is into twenty-four hours of classroom and sixteen hours of internal training per user. In large businesses, where the user does not know how to access all aspects of the system, this can be reduced slightly to cover only specific areas per user.

The real key is to allot whatever number feels comfortable. Some users are more knowledgeable than others because they have either used computers previously or are more experienced with the manual system than other users.

To ensure adequate training for employees (1) the guidelines discussed should be followed and (2) software should never be purchased without the minimum training available.

EFFECTS OF NOT TRAINING

It cannot be emphasized enough how important all the levels of training are to:

- The individual user who deals daily with the computer
- The successful implementation of the computer within the business
- The software vendor, who would like to use the buyer as a reference and does not want the installation to fail
- Management, who must use the system and who made the decision to purchase the system
- Shareholders of a company, who never see the system but reap either its benefits or losses

The world is full of computers and software packages that are not being used in the manner for which they were intended, in part because of inadequate training. Don't let your system be one of those.

CHAPTER **21**

Office Automation

Philip N. James

Introduction 2	**Key Issues** 19
	People Issues 19
Office Automation Defined 2	Connectivity 19
A Collection of Technologies 4	Revisability 19
Support for Intellectual Work 5	Support Infrastructure 20
Support for Both Group and Individual	Ease of Access to Information 20
Work 6	Systems Availability, Reliability,
Communication Among Groups and	Usability 20
Individuals 7	Security and Privacy 21
The Competitive Edge 7	
	Cost Justification for Office Systems . . . 21
Office Productivity 8	
Strategic Planning 9	**Common Pitfalls of Office Automation**
Systems Engineering 9	**Implementation** 22
Nominal Group Technique 10	Failing to Plan 22
The Sociotechnical Approach 11	Waiting to Plan 25
	Office Automation as a Political Issue . . 27
Kinds of Office Technologies 11	Failure to Sell Office Automation to Top
Word Processing 11	Management 27
Electronic Filing and Retrieval 12	Picking the Wrong Client for a Pilot . . . 29
Administrative Augmentation 13	Automating Production Personnel 31
Telecommunications 14	Focusing on Features 31
Electronic Mail 14	Insisting on Hard-Dollar Savings 32
Voice Mail 15	Equating Office Automation With Word
Teleconferencing 15	Processing 33
Public Databases 17	Ignoring Other Office Disciplines 34
Telecommuting 18	
Personal Computing 18	**References** 35

Fig. 21-1 Graph of Investment vs. Productivity 2
Fig. 21-2 Human Resources Investments 3
Fig. 21-3 Pilot Project Planning Questions 25
Fig. 21-4 Sample Strategic Objectives 26
Fig. 21-5 Taxonomy of People Issues 28
Fig. 21-6 Office Technologies 33
Fig. 21-7 Office Disciplines 35

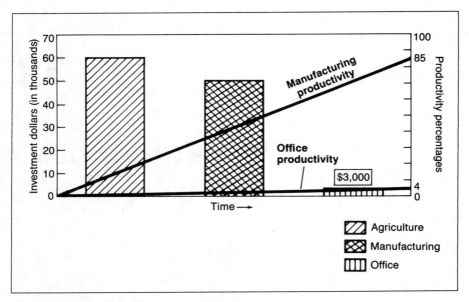

FIG. 21-1 Graph of Investment vs. Productivity

INTRODUCTION

Today's managers are inundated with information and misinformation about office automation. The purpose of this chapter is to sort out the important aspects of office automation information and provide insights that may help managers realize the full promise of office automation.

First is a discussion of what office automation is and, more importantly, what it is not. The second section deals with the issue of office productivity and its relationship to office automation. The third section introduces several different kinds of office technologies. The fourth and fifth sections explore key issues and identify some common pitfalls, with recommendations about how to avoid them.

OFFICE AUTOMATION DEFINED

Office automation is generally touted as a solution to the office productivity problem, much as factory automation was a solution to the factory productivity problem. This is usually supported by charts such as the one shown in Figure 21-1, which compares the growth of productivity as a function of capital investments in farm workers, factory workers, and office workers. The implication is that office productivity is low because investments for office workers have lagged behind those for other workers and that increased investments for office workers will improve their productivity.

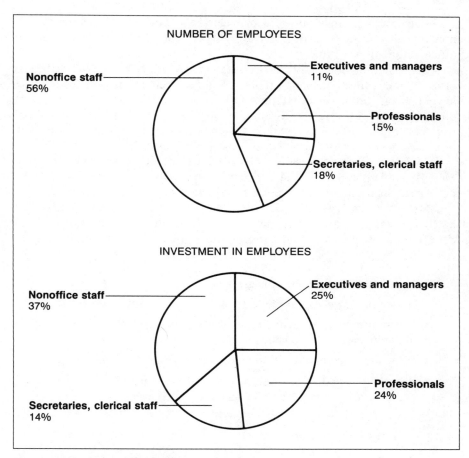

FIG. 21-2 Human Resources Investments

Early efforts in office automation seem to bear this out. Word processing has enabled production typists to turn out more and better work. People realized, however, that typing represents only a small fraction of office work. A classic multiclient study by Booz, Allen & Hamilton in 1978[1] revealed that productivity improvement efforts should be focused on managers and professionals. Although they constitute a relatively small portion of the work force in numbers, their aggregate compensation represents a high significant annual investment (see Figure 21-2). Furthermore, managers and professionals have more influence on a corporation's success than any other group. If they can be provided with tools that allow them to be more productive or more effective, then the company benefits enormously.

---

[1] Harvey L. Poppel, "Who Needs the Office of the Future?" *Harvard Business Review,* Vol. 60, No. 6 (Nov.-Dec. 1982), pp. 146–155.

But how is productivity of a manager or a professional measured? And how can they be automated? These are serious issues, and show a new facet of office automation.

Office automation is not usually automated at all. Nor is it confined to the office. Some office jobs are production jobs, such as processing invoices, keypunching, and production typing. Office automation tools can improve productivity in these areas just as automation has done in the factory. Indeed, business data processing is based on the premise that automating clerical functions save money, which cost/benefit analyses confirm.

Managerial and professional jobs are not at all like those production jobs. How is the daily ouput of a manager measured—Decisions per hour? Reports per week? Such questions prompt a new look at office productivity.

So far we have described what office automation is not. There is no general agreement about what it is, as each office systems professional has a different definition. Most people would agree, however, that office automation has the following characteristics:

- It is a collection of technologies.
- It supports intellectual work.
- It supports work by individuals or, more importantly, by groups of individuals working together.
- It facilitates communication among these individuals and groups.
- When supported by a strategic vision, it helps people move an organization toward a better competitive position.

A Collection of Technologies

Office technologies include such functions as word processing, electronic mail, copying, facsimile transmission (fax), teleconferencing, and electronic filing and retrieval. At present, most office technologies support the management of documents. An obvious exception is video teleconferencing, unless it is used in unusual ways.

The basic operations on a document are:

- Create; revise.
- Store.
- Send.
- File.
- Retrieve.

Filing differs from storage in that a stored document can be retrieved by name only; there are many ways to locate and retrieve a filed document.

A document is usually thought of as something similar to a report or a letter. However, the world of office automation has produced the compound document, which has been described as consisting of the following:

- Text
- Data
- Graphics
- Image
- Audio

Graphics are images generated by mathematical relationships. Other types of images are similar to traditional artwork—company logos on letterheads, photographs, handwiring or drawings, and signatures.

Few people have any difficulty envisioning a document that contains the first four elements. Even a simple letter usually contains text and image information, the latter in the logo and the signature. Often, letters contain tables of data; occasionally, they also include graphs. Most other kinds of documents are readily perceived as composed of these elements.

However, modern office technology allows voice messages to be captured, as well as stored and forwarded. This is possible even in the crude form of a telephone answering machine; but some equipment allows for voice annotation of a text document, where the voice message actually becomes part of the document and is played when the document is displayed at the proper point.

It is a small step from a document containing text, data, graphics, and image information with voice annotations to a videotape record as a compound document. Thus, it is possible to create, store, file, retrieve, and transmit the information on the videotape. Revising such a document presents problems, but even they can be overcome.

Consequently, office automation may be defined as a collection of technologies that work together, and a significant portion of office automation involves the management of documents.

Support for Intellectual Work

By taking such a broad definition of "document" and looking at the basic operations, it is possible to imagine the power and potential that office automation can bring. The use of these mutliple technologies in doing one's work becomes clearer. Most important, although the complexity of using these technologies in combination with one another may seem awesome at first, clever applications may be devised by creative people at all levels in an organization. All that are necessary for the release of this creativity are:

- Training and support to develop fluency with the tools

- A supportive environment that encourages their creative use
- A strategic vision toward which their creative use is encouraged

Office technologies, therefore, are power tools that support the intellect in much the same way that physical power tools support physical work or scientific instruments support research and development. For the first time in history, power tools may be used creatively and productively by ordinary people to perform ordinary office jobs.

However, there is another, more important outcome. These power tools provide the ability to do the following:

- Eliminate work that must be done because there is no better way.
- Devise new ways of doing work that were never before possible.

When these concepts are internalized by an organization, that organization begins to become more efficient and effective. This requires leadership and investment, but usually the payoff is enormous.

Continuing this concept, William Zachmann, Vice-President of International Data Corporation, has coined the term "mindware" to describe systems that augment individual human mental activity "rather like a bulldozer or a backhoe [augments] individual human physical activity."[2] Mindware augments that portion of a person's mental activity that cannot be delegated to someone else.

Adding rows and columns of figures, typing letters, sorting lists, summarizing results, etc., do not have this quality. These can be delegated. But solving problems, thinking up new ideas, learning something new, getting better at something, gaining a better understanding of something, becoming aware of additional alternatives—*these* are the kinds of things which cannot be delegated.[3] Mindware supports the kind of work that benefits the person using it, much as food provides nutrition. Its use cannot be delegated any more than can a "kiss be sent by messenger."[4]

Support for Both Group and Individual Work

Douglas Englebart of Tymshare is a pioneer in the use of computers to support work by both individuals and groups.[5] He invented the mouse, and was among the first to use CRTs, reverse video displays, icons, and many other tools now

---

[2] William F. Zachmann, "Mindware," *Office of Technology Assessment Occasional Paper,* Vol. 2, No. 7 (Framingham Mass.: International Data Corporation, 1984).

[3] Zachmann.

[4] Zachmann.

[5] Englebart's pioneering word and its fruits in the marketplace were reviewed in a session entitled "Augment, Lisa, Star . . . : Progeny of an Idea," held at the AFIPS Office Automation Conference, Los Angeles (Feb. 20–22, 1984).

becoming common. Descendents of his fertile mind include the Xerox Star, the Apple Lisa and Macintosh, and Tymshare's Augment.

In the mid-1960s, with the limited computer equipment then in place, Englebart had working models of computer systems with many of these features. Users could share the same information on different screens and manipulate it together. This kind of collaboration was made possible because Englebart clearly saw the value of collaboration among brilliant people who are geographically distant from one another. He deliberately set about to build tools that would support this kind of collaboration. Further, he recognized that most people would not be computer specialists, and developed some pioneering interfaces with the information, of which the mouse is an example.

One team that is beginning to be recognized by office automation vendors is the manager/secretary dyad,[6] as Rand Corporation calls it. Many of the systems on the market explicity support that team. This is somewhat ironic, since the one-secretary-per-manager rule is going out of vogue, largely through the influence of office automation, and secretaries' roles are changing drastically.

Communication Among Groups and Individuals

The networking of terminals, personal computers, and other workstations realizes the full potential of these devices. This is the beginning of the fulfillment of Englebart's dream. Most vendors have not yet seriously addressed the issue of more than one worker sharing the same information on more than one screen and allowing them to modify it; however, this is necessary before the full potential can be realized.

It is important to distinguish among several facets of communications. There is the technical facet, embodying both voice and data communication, the broadcast media, and other technologies. More important is the human facet of exchanging information. The best information exchanges occur where people work face to face, often with a chalkboard or pad and pencil to sketch out ideas. This is a sharing of space. Telecommunications technologies all work toward the creation of that same sense of shared space among users who are geographically distant. Each new technology introduces its improvements and its problems, and research on the effects of the new technologies, is seeking to improve understanding of effective communications among poeople.

The Competitive Edge

With the advent of office automation and personal computing, power tools are being put in the hands of people who can make them incredibly effective if they work together imaginatively. If the strategic vision placed before them is cutting costs, much will be accomplished. However, if asked to work toward a

---

[6] T.K. Bikson and B.A. Gutek, "Advanced Office Systems: An Empirical Look at Utilization and Satisfaction," Rand Note N-1970-NSF (Feb. 1983).

competitive edge, a different result will occur. There may be a repetition of the stories of American Hospital Supply and McKesson,[7] who extended the boundaries of their business to include the customer and so lock him into their way of doing business that a competitor could not break in. However, bringing in new business, finding new ways of doing business, and working on the revenue-generating side of the house will substantially increase the competitiveness so necessary in today's world.

OFFICE PRODUCTIVITY

"Office productivity" is an elusive term. At one level, it is obvious that a production word processing department that turns out 600 pages a day is more productive than one of the same size that turns out 500 pages a day.

A shop that turns out 600 widgets a day really is more productive than the shop of the same size that turns out only 500. However, each widget produced goes into a product that is sold. The value of that product, and of all of the parts that comprise it, is determined by the marketplace. Each widget, therefore, has a definite value. So do the inputs of raw materials and labor that produce it.

Does each page produced by the word processing shop have value? In a publishing company where the page is part of a book or magazine, the answer is yes, because a value can be assigned to the page based on the value of the book. Most typing, however, is for internal consumption or correspondence, and there is no easy way to assign a value to it. Nor is it any easier to evaluate the input to the page.

Is a manager who used to produce a report for his boss once a month and now, with word processing, can produce it once a week four times as productive? His boss now has to read four times as many reports. What has happened to his productivity? Situations like these make the measurement of office productivity difficult.

There are many ways to make an office productive besides introducing technology, such as cleaning up procedures or eliminating unnecessary work. If the office is a mess, it is important to clean it up before automating.

Many experts feel that office productivity is simply the result of good management.[8] In this context, good management includes doing the right things and doing things right. Further, a top-down view of the whole organization is necessary in order to identify the right things to do. The doubling of one department's productivity achieves nothing if the department using its output does not need twice as much of the product. Achieving a balanced organization

---

[7] These cases were discussed at a seminar held jointly by Index Systems, Inc., and Hammer and Co., both of Cambridge, Mass. (July 1984). More detailed information can be obtained from these firms.

[8] Robert M. Ranftl, *R&D Productivity,* 2d ed. (Culver City, Cal.: Hughes Aircraft Co., 1978).

is an art called organizational design, which is usually much more conducive to improved office productivity than any form of automation that may be introduced.

It is also necessary to distinguish between productivity and effectiveness. Sometimes, this takes the form of "working hard versus working smart." Again, a top-down view is important, for many unproductive people are just doing the job they were hired to do. They may have no way of knowing that the job is unnecessary. An example is the general manager who visited the factory floor and saw his planning analysts swarming over the equipment taking measurements and talking to the operators. They were really busy, and their productivity had improved as they learned how to apply their analytical techniques in manufacturing more effectively. However, the manager realized that the factory itself had shown only marginal gains since the productivity improvement program was begun.

He then wandered through the research department, where he saw one of the researchers sitting with his feet up on the desk staring into space. "Why is he wasting time like that?" the manager wondered. Then he remembered that six of the last ten new products, and the four that contributed most to the bottom line, had been invented by that researcher.

The best approaches for implementing an office productivity program are discussed in the following sections.

Strategic Planning

The first step in implementing a productivity program is strategic planning. What is the nature of the business? What is its mission? Who are its customers, and what do they need? Who are its competitors and how are *they* meeting customers' needs? What are the company's strengths and weaknesses, and what are its competitors'? Finally, what are the opportunities and threats in the environment?

Systems Engineering

Once the basic parameters of the business are established, the next step is organizational design. In most companies, planning is, or should be, a continuous process; also, there is usually an organization already in place. Organizational design then becomes a process of causing appropriate organizational changes in response to changes discovered in the business environment through the planning process. Because these processes are often out of phase, it is necessary periodically to do a more thorough job of assessing whether the tasks performed by the organization are still relevant to its business, and whether the organization is properly structured to carry them out.

Systems engineering is helpful here. By taking a top-down view based on the planning results, it can document the as-is information flows in the organization. These must be tested continually against the views of those who actually carry out the work to make sure they are correct and complete. Any of the common structured analysis methodologies can be used here.[9]

Once the as-is situation is documented and supported as correct, one can begin to look for ways to improve it. There is no better source for such ideas than the people who do the work. In order to help them think creatively, several preconditions must be in place.

- Everyone must realize that the object of the program is to improve productivity of the entire enterprise—not people, machines, or departments.
- Any effort must have the active cooperation and support of those affected or it will fail.
- Those affected should share in whatever gains are realized.
- A system of job security should be introduced to offset the fear of job loss from productivity improvements.
- Continuing training and retraining is an absolute requirement in the work world.

These principles resulted from the deliberations of the White House Conference on Productivity held in 1983.[10]

Nominal Group Technique

The American Productivity Center in Houston, Texas, has refined a technique called the nominal group technique for deriving from a work group the ideas necessary to improve its own productivity.[11] In using this technique, the group first reviews the documented as-is situation in a context conducive to improvement. Then the individuals in the group spend some time writing their ideas for improvement. These are then shared in a structured discussion session, and additions and improvements are made to them. Through continued discussion, the detailed structure of the to-be situation evolves and is documented, embodying the ideas. Then productivity measures are identified—collections of measures are generally better in the office than individual measures—and the group sets productivity goals they feel they can meet. Competition between departments in meeting their goals should be encouraged. Most people respond well

---

[9] For a collection of papers describing such methodologies, see *IBM Systems Journal*, Vol. 21, No. 1 (1982).

[10] John J. Connell, "White House Conference on Productivity," remarks before the 12th meeting of the Office Technology Research Group (OTRG). Copies may be obtained by writing to OTRG at Box 65, Pasadena, Cal., 91102.

[11] Information about one current implementation of the nominal group technique may be obtained from the American Productivity Center, Houston, Tex., 77024.

to this kind of competition, which is why the commitment to people is such an important first step.

It should be noticed that, so far, office technology has not been mentioned. Office productivity is achieved by a process something like the one described, and basically results from good management. Many things can be done to improve office productivity. These will surface if a process such as the one described is carried out well. Where other conditions are met—for example, tasks are needed and technologies make them more effective or faster—the use of these technologies can be a major contributor to office productivity. However, it should be considered at the end of the process, not as a substitute for it.

The Sociotechnical Approach

Most real systems in organizations consist of a people component and a technology component. Paper and pencils, typewriters, file cabinets, and modern office technologies are all part of the technology component. To work well, an organization must make sure that both components work well together. The achievement of this objective is the domain of sociotechnical engineering.[12]

Most commonly, a documented understanding of the as-is and to-be systems described earlier is created with explicit attention to how people technology, and each component are organized and work both within themselves and with the other components. A body of literature in this field is developing, and there are consultants who offer services in this type of organizational design.

KINDS OF OFFICE TECHNOLOGIES

Normally, office technologies encompass those computer-assisted applications associated with text management. In fact, many office technologies date back many years. The typewriter, the telephone, and the copier are all office technologies, and all have had a significant effect on how an office functions. The newer technologies will have a much greater effect, partly because they are so much more versatile than anything that previously existed. The objective and responsibility of managers is to see that these effects are positive, both for the organizations of which they are a part and for the people entrusted to their care.

Word Processing

As a stand-alone technology, word processing transformed typing into a much less frustrating activity, allowed documents to be generated much more rapidly, and allowed successive drafts to be clean, not subject to the cut-and-paste or

---

[12] For information with references about the sociotechnical approach, see *EDP Analyzer* (May 1982 and April, May 1983).

markup processes formerly used. Most managers found they turned out better documents, that the typing backlog was reduced, and that their secretaries had time to do other things. Typing pools became word processing centers, and the skill levels of those in the word processing centers increased. The result was certainly more paper, and very often better paper. Many people have mixed emotions about the benefits of this technology.

As office automation progressed, word processors began to communicate with one another and with the data processing computers. This allowed the exchange of information among people. It allowed the blending of text and data into documents. Soon it was recognized that word processing was the data entry function of office automation. There is a necessary step of converting information to machine-readable form, and the word processor is the preferred vehicle for this task where text is concerned. Once the information is machine readable, it can participate in many of the other office technologies. Through them, it can begin to become the major resource that it should be in organizations.

Word processing, direct or through optical character readers, will continue to be the primary method for converting information to machine-readable form for some time to come. Devices that recognize continuous speech and convert it to text (dictation devices without the need for manual transcription) began appearing on the market in early 1985. It is doubtful, however, that they will dominate the information-to-text field during the 1980s.

Electronic Filing and Retrieval

In its simplest form, electronic filing and retrieval means storing a document under a given name and retrieving it from storage using the same name. Where a central storage facility with locations for each user is available, this is a simple process, provided the name given to the document can be recalled. With many word processors and personal computers, the documents are stored on floppy disks. If there are very many of them, the management of the floppy disks becomes a significant administrative chore. But if it is remembered which disk contains the necessary document and its name, there is usually no retrieval problem.

Newcomers to the field often wonder why remembering a document's name is such a problem. If the name given suggests the document's content, it should be easy to identify. Most systems, however, restrict the name to a few characters—usually eight. Formulating a meaningful name for each of several hundred documents can become a chore.

Electronic filing and retrieval systems are much more sophisticated, and much easier to use, than the simple system of filing under document name. Many of them extract key words from the document itself. For example, if the document is identified as a memorandum, the system knows where to find the author, the addressee, those designated to receive copies, the date, and the subject, and indexes these to make retrieval on them easy. Usually, such systems also allow search terms to be added, based on the subjects covered in the document. Some systems also allow documents to be filed in electronic folders and file drawers, again with the objective of organizing the file in order to make it easy to obtain any document of interest.

The most sophisticated systems make use of what is called full-text search and retrieval methods. There are several of these, some more efficient in their use of machine resources than others. Under this system, a search strategy is developed, which simply means that the user decides which terms the document should contain and how they should relate to each other. For example, the user might want all documents that referred to apples and oranges—or, conversely, apples but not oranges. Taking advantage of the fact that the full text of the documents in the file are in machine-readable form, such a search method reads them all through and tells the user which ones contain the desired information.

With some systems, compound documents may be stored and retrieved by name. A few allow search of the text portion of compound documents. Usually, once they have been assembled, none of the parts of a compound document can be further edited. This is a limitation that will disappear over time. A video recording is a form of compound document, and may be handled in the same way. Special equipment is required, of course, but video recordings are not used in many offices.

Administrative Augmentation

Many routine functions are necessary in order for managers to organize and manage their time and work. Some of them may be helped by computer-assisted systems, including managing the calendar, completing tasks, assigning priorities, and reminding themselves of scheduled tasks as they become due. Other factors are the people they must work with, both inside and outside of the company, and the resources they must live with or secure more of. A few systems on the market can assist with many of these tasks. Further, creative use of such general purpose tools as word processing and records management systems can support many of these functions. Successful time and task management with computer-based tools is largely a function of the ingenuity of the individual.

Some systems provide great benefits beyond those to the individual. Calendaring systems, for example, allow a secretary to determine when a group of people have free time for a meeting, and can even schedule the use of an appropriate meeting room and projection facilities. The scheduling of meetings, including the facilities and other resources to support them, is a major time consumer for most secretaries. Further, even though there is no personal satisfaction involved, the job must be done well, or the consequences are substantial. Calendaring systems are effective in supporting this activity.

Telecommunications

As noted elsewhere in this chapter, telecommunications is the glue that ties all of these new capabilities together and allows people who are geographically separated in a building, city, nation, or the world to work together. There are many telecommunications technologies in current use, and many more will evolve. Some of the more popular ones are discussed in the following sections.

Electronic Mail. Electronic mail means many things to many people. Early electronic mail systems include telegraph, teletype, TWX, and fax. The term is now more commonly applied to computer-based message systems (CBMS).

CBMS also come in many forms. Most of the public packet switched networks (e.g., Telenet, Tymnet) provide the service, and some vendors of the new private packet switched networks (e.g., BBN) are offering it as well. Most office automation systems have some type of CBMS incorporated, but the capabilities of these systems vary widely.

Perhaps the oldest and most heavily used CBMS is that on the ARPAnet, an early packet switched network still in use. The original intent of ARPAnet was to permit defense contractors to run computer programs wherever they might reside. Thus, if a user wanted to run a special type of numerical analysis available only on the computer at a particular university, he could do so. Electronic mail was originally on this system simply to facilitate communication about how to do this. People began to communicate other messages through the network, however, because it was much faster than more conventional means. The ARPAnet has tied together many groups of collaborators over the years, and it continues to do so.

A good CBMS provides many assists to make it easy for a user to send and receive mail. Each user has a "mailbox" into which messages and documents are deposited. Each piece of mail is logged into a mailbox log that usually shows whom the message is from, the subject, the time of arrival, and often other information about the message. A series of commands allows access to the message, and further commands allow various means of disposition. Most commonly, the user wants to reply to the message; this can be done without addressing the sender. The system retains the sender's address and automatically sends the reply, which is a great convenience.

Other options available are the ability to forward a document to someone else for action with a note attached, to file it, and to throw it away. The latter function, sometimes referred to as the wastebasket function, is often implemented to permit retrieval of the discarded document for as much as a week after it was discarded to be sure it really was not needed.

Electronic mail systems always include text editing capabilities to permit the creation of documents, but these editors are not nearly up to conventional word processing standards. To create long documents, it is usually preferable to use a conventional word processor, then deposit the finished document in an electronic file where the electronic mail system can pick it up. The document or message can be sent to a single individual, with or without electronic carbons. It can also be sent to a group of almost unlimited size (e.g., a distribution list that can be stored for later use). Each electronic mail system has a different mix of features, so several should be compared before picking one. Electronic mail will become an increasingly important part of the electronic office.

Voice Mail. There is a special case of electronic mail called voice mail. A user may digitize, store, and retrieve a compound document, of which audio is one possible component. This means that the user may speak a message and name, store, and retrieve it just as he would a text document. At this point, it cannot easily be edited or its text searched for key words, but even that will come in time. The fact that a voice message can be stored and retrieved means that the user can store it in a person's mailbox and retrieve it so long as he has the right equipment. Furthermore, a data processing terminal or personal computer (PC) is not needed to use a voice mail system; any telephone, anywhere in the world, will do.

With voice mail, most of the options under other types of electronic mail are available. The user can be sent to a distribution list, forward with his own voice message attached, and respond without entering the address of the sender.

The real value of voice mail is that it reduces telephone tag. One study showed that only 37 percent of telephone calls made were completed.[13] Further, voice mail allows users to communicate across time zones, when working different shifts, when secretaries are away from their desks making copies, and in any other instance where there is a time-synchronization problem. Another study showed that people voluntarily extend the work day when they have voice mail available.[14] Salespeople, in particular, use normal working hours to make calls in person and use the time after work to return calls and set appointments for the future. Buyers can send messages to all relevant vendors for a bid on an item with a single phone call. Voice mail is seen as natural for executives and managers, because they tend to communicate verbally and the telephone is their most used office tool.

Many PBX vendors are beginning to incorporate voice mail features in their devices. The technology will grow in use as it becomes more readily available and more of a user's community of interest have mailboxes.

Teleconferencing. A great deal of attention is being given to full motion color video teleconferencing because it has an appealing show business element. It also has a show business price, and there are many alternatives for

---

[13] VMX, Inc., private communication.
[14] VMX, Inc.

accomplishing nearly the same objectives. The major objective is to reduce travel without reducing people's ability to collaborate.

- *Audio teleconferencing.* One of the most cost effective teleconferencing methods has been around for years, yet most people take little advantage of it—audio teleconferencing, the old-fashioned conference call. Modern telephone equipment is making the conference call easier; many office telephone systems allow the user to place a three-way conference call without the aid of an operator. Very often, this teleconferencing method accomplishes as much or more than the more elaborate methods at a fraction of the cost.

- *Computer teleconferencing.* It is only a small extension from an electronic mail system to a computer teleconferencing system. Many software packages make this possible. Many electronic mail systems have special mailboxes called public bulletin boards, which are accessible to anyone on the system. Access can be restricted to particular groups of people as well. Anyone can post a message on the bulletin board for others to read, and the message can be any kind one wants. In fact it is possible to create a special bulletin board around a specific topic and to invite participants to enter relevant papers. The other participants post their comments on the papers, the authors reply, and the dialog is joined. A computer teleconference must have a moderator who is generally familiar with the subject matter and with computer teleconferencing. The success of the conference depends substantially on his effectiveness.

  There are many books on the subject, any one of which is a good introduction to the technique.[15]

- *Video teleconferencing.* Full motion color video teleconferencing is certainly the most visible form for obvious reasons. It commands attention because it is spectacular, as is its price tag. Successes are fewer than failures in implementing this technology, however, because its success depends so much on the human factors involved and so little on the technology. People must be well prepared for what this technology will and will not do. Generally, their expectations are too high, and they come away from their first teleconference extremely disappointed. There are many consultants eager to help large corporations implement video teleconferencing, but here, especially, care must be taken that the user has demonstrated success elsewhere and that he understands the human factor issues thoroughly.

  Certain versions of video teleconferencing are relatively inexpensive and highly effective in certain situations. One of the least expensive

---

[15] A good introduction is provided in Rebert Johansen and Christine Bullen, "Teleconferencing," *Harvard Business Review*, Vol. 62, No. 2 (Mar.-Apr. 1984), pp. 164–174.

forms is the so-called stop motion video. This technique allows a slow scan video camera to sweep the subject matter, generating a picture. The recipient sees a new still picture appear on the screen every few seconds. This is ample for presentations involving Vugraphs, the review of engineering drawings or photographs, and use in similar situations. The audio in such situations is usually handled by speakerphone. What this amounts to is augmented audio teleconferencing, but the augmentation vastly enhances the effectiveness of the conference. Other forms of augmented audio teleconferencing include the use of fax and the electronic blackboard.

Video teleconferencing involves a large number of intermediate technologies in between these two extremes; however, the subject is too large in scope to be covered in depth in this Manual.

Public Databases. In the first decade after the inception of computers, service bureaus provided data processing services for organizations that could not or did not wish to acquire a computer. These have evolved over the years, offering a changing mix of services as the market and technology have changed. Now, service bureaus are usually connected on line to terminals on their customers' premises.

Along with the growth and development of service bureaus came the development of the public packet switched networks such as Telenet and Tymnet. Many service bureaus made their offerings available through these public value added networks (VANs). Indeed, many of the VANs were developed by service bureaus. An example is General Electric's Information Services Company, which has a worldwide network and a large number of data processing options available to customers through the network.

As data processing concepts moved from the technology to the information handled by the technology, many information professionals began to realize new possibilities. Librarians, for example, looked for ways to provide library services on line. Indexing companies such as Chemical Abstracts realized the help a computer could be in literature searching. Early efforts were directed toward improving indexes (e.g., the KWIC (key word in context) index). Soon, it was realized that the computer allowed searching the full text of articles and abstracts for otherwise buried references. A few hundred indexing services are now available on line.

Creative people saw that not just access to articles containing data but access to the data themselves was valuable; therefore, they put their data compilations on line. Nearly 2,000 public databases are now available from the home computer or office terminal on nearly any subject imaginable. There are probably hundreds of databases containing economic time series data for the world and its various subdivisions—for example, the Official Airline Guide is on line; major newspaper indices are on line; databases covering restaurants by type of food and location, plays in New York theaters, and many others are on line. Several directories for these on-line databases are available, and the reference librarian of any large library can locate them.[16] The majority of the databases available contain statistical data of economic and financial interest.

Telecommuting. Technology makes it possible to use files without the user being in the office; this makes it possible for him to work at home. In telecommuting, messages travel to the files and information from the files travel to the user, wherever he may be. When this concept becomes popular, it will have an enormous effect on the use of energy, design of buildings, need for highways and telecommunications networks, urban planning, and many other aspects of the way we live.

Many factors stand in the way of greater use of telecommuting, including costs of various kinds and concern for the security of information. Probably the greatest barrier, however, is management. Many managers ask, "How can I know what my employees are doing if I can't see them?" The University of Southern California's Jack M. Nilles, a pioneer in telecommuting and author of the seminal book [17] in the field, responds, "How do you know when you *can* see them?" Humor aside, there are some serious management issues for which there are no readily available solutions. For example, does telecommuting reinstate the concept of piecework? If not, how does a manager keep track of an employee's time, and how does he assure himself that the time spent is productive? If a telecommuter suffers an injury at home, is that an industrial accident? These and many other questions are under active discussion in many quarters.

There is no doubt that telecommuting will become a way of life in the information age. Its exact shape will evolve and may surprise us all, but it will become the usual way of working, not an isolated phenomenon as it is today. With the proliferation of robotics and other forms of factory automation, it may pervade the factory as well.

Personal Computing

Personal computing involves much more than the use of PCs. Personal computing is the use of computer-based tools to accomplish intellectual work. The qualification of intellectual work separates personal computing from the use of terminals for data entry and other nonintellectual tasks.

Personal computing encompasses the use of spreadsheets, word processing, and database managers on a PC. It also encompasses the use of large mainframe-based software programs (e.g., NASTRAN) by engineers. Its most distinguishing characteristic is its use of computer-based power tools along the lines discussed elsewhere in this chapter. Most office automation professionals

---

[16] One that is easy to use is *Directory of On-Line Databases,* (Santa Monica, Cal.: Cuadra Associates, Inc.). This directory is updated quarterly.

[17] Jack M. Nilles et al., *The Telecommunication-Transportation Tradeoff: Options for Tomorrow* (Melbourne, Fla.: Krieger, 1978).

OFFICE AUTOMATION

see the use of the power tools for securing a strategic competitive advantage by a company's leaders and its most creative people as the most important use of office automation with the highest payoff.

KEY ISSUES

The range of technologies discussed in the preceding sections are generally considered to fall under the umbrella of office automation. New technologies and new combinations of existing technologies whose synergistic interactions almost constitute new technologies are emerging daily. The most serious set of key issues are "people" issues.

People Issues

The success of office technologies will be almost totally governed by managers' effectiveness with regard to the people issues associated with their use. Excellent technologies have failed to live up to their potential because people stopped them. They were seen as threats, attempts to control, or as otherwise dehumanizing; no technology can succeed against a concerted effort by people to cripple it.

This is one reason why the basic paradigms that govern the use of these emerging technologies must be examined closely. Managers must place their faith in people, treat people as an asset and manage them that way, take human resource accounting seriously, and use the technologies as tools to enhance the contribution people can make. The day of considering people as tools to be used while they fit and discard thereafter is over. Failure to recognize and act on this premise is a surefire formula for failure to realize the potential these technologies can provide.

There are many other issues that are important as well, as discussed in the following sections.

Connectivity

The value of office automation is in its ability to enhance communication among people. If that value is to be realized, no technical roadblocks can stand in the way of connecting all of the devices in the network together.

Revisability

The ability to ship an electronic document from one workstation to another and continually revise it is crucial to the concept of collaboration, which applies to the manager-secretary dyad, to the proposal team, and to many other working groups in organizations. People know about this problem, and know that solutions are emerging; but they are not emerging rapidly enough.

Because the issue of text revisability looms so large, it is often forgotten that there are similar revisability problems beyond text. The ability to continue revising graphic and other images and the ability to revise audio data sets at all will become more important as solutions to the text revisability issue improve.

Support Infrastructure

The nature and extent of the support infrastructure probably says more about the people-based orientation of an enterprise than any other single factor. The success of these technologies, and of their creative use to achieve a competitive edge, is crucially dependent on an effective support infrastructure. This infrastructure includes training and support—some visible, much invisible. Good training in varieties that recognize different optimal learning modes, good training materials, and good reference materials for use when a user is generally skilled are important with any equipment. The more user friendly the equipment, the less critical this component of the infrastructure becomes; however, it never vanishes. Further, excellence in this arena compensates effectively for many shortcomings in the technology itself.

Once training is complete, the remaining visible infrastructure comes into play. This includes daily visits to those using the technology to help with problems, suggest new techniques, provide encouragement, and generally keep the technology sold and the learning of it active. It includes a responsive hot line with enough visible and invisible support to respond quickly to even the most trivial problems. It includes user groups, newsletters, study teams, and many other vehicles for keeping users' skills in the use of the equipment growing and focused on the competitive advantage or whatever other strategic vision may be appropriate.

Ease of Access to Information

Employees need information to perform their jobs. Sometimes the information is in computerized form, sometimes not. Sometimes the information comes from within the company, sometimes from outside. Part of the function of the visible support infrastructure and management is to keep visible each worker's need for information. Part of the invisible support infrastructure's function is to find ways to provide the information needed in the form required, regardless of its source.

Systems Availability, Reliability, Usability

The new pervasiveness of the computer for all work will require finding ways to keep that work available when needed. If the chief executive officer needs a document, he may have to exercise patience if the computer is down; information professionals will have to find ways to keep it up or expect to be replaced. The situation is complicated by the fact that the whole system, including the network, will require significantly greater expectations than have heretofore surfaced in the data processing world.

Usability refers to user friendliness. As one expert, Floyd Kvamme, once said, "A computer system should be as natural to use as a car is to drive."[18] He saw the Apple approach (as in Macintosh and Lisa) as meeting that criterion. His point is well taken; but the marketplace is a long way from that ideal. The culture change that is now in progress as students learn about computers in school is also essential. The criterion of usability for the majority of systems users should certainly be incorporated, and it should be evaluated as a touchstone in various implementation decisions.

Security and Privacy

These are extremely complex issues with international ramifications. Transborder data flows are sensitive issues for multinational corporations and the countries in which they operate. The protection of individual rights and the privacy of personal information are key elements in those corporations' discussions.

Privacy refers to the right of individuals to be sure that no personal information about them is disclosed to another without their permission, even inadvertently, and raises a series of technical and management issues. Security is related to privacy and raises an even broader set of technical and management issues.

Security can be physical or logical. Physical security is breached when a data center is bombed or its key parts are otherwise destroyed. Logical security is breached when information is obtained or destroyed without permission (e.g., by a hacker) while the physical vessels that handle that information remain intact. Security and privacy must be considered at all levels from the individual worker to the corporation as a whole when office automation is implemented. The literature now provides many in-depth looks at this subject.[19]

COST JUSTIFICATION FOR OFFICE SYSTEMS

Production office systems (e.g., power word processing, data entry, transaction processing) can be cost justified in the same way as factory automation or traditional data processing applications: More work per person means either fewer people for the same work load (cost savings) or the ability to handle an increased work load without a corresponding increase in staff (cost avoidance).

---

[18] Remarks before the International Data Corporation Spring Executive Conference, Phoenix, Ariz. (1984).

[19] One is *Data Security Management*, one of several manuals in the Auerbach Information Management Series (Pennsauken, N.J.: Auerbach).

For other office jobs, especially those of executives and managers, the same kinds of analyses are much more difficult to apply. Productivity measures that emerge from the nominal group technique described earlier may offer some help. Unless there is an actual reduction in staff or a significant increase in work load, however, there is likely to be no *real* change in costs/benefits, reallocation of work to higher priority activities notwithstanding.

Nevertheless, reallocating work to higher priority activities is certainly valuable. In some cases, successful cost justification has been achieved by computing the amount of such value needed to pass the hurdle for project acceptance. Management is asked subjectively to judge whether the "soft" benefits claimed are worth at least that amount. Of course, if, over time, greater effectiveness achieved through office technologies can be tied to increases in business (through better proposals, better negotiations, and greater customer responsiveness), then such data make a good business case.

Paul Strassman of Xerox Corporation has been working on a value added approach to making a business case and tracking it.[20] Very simply, his method deducts from both costs and revenues those items actually acquired for a fixed price, primarily purchases of materials and services, plus unskilled and semi-skilled labor. What is left on the cost side are largely managerial and professional efforts, and the excess of revenues over costs is the value added by those efforts. If that value added increases over time in rough proportion to the investment in office technologies, then there is at least an inferential case that the investment is paying off.

Despite all this, however, some of the highest potential values derive from technologies that require large investments and cannot be cost justified readily. Implementation of a corporationwide telecommunications architecture and network is an example. Here, it may be necessary to rely on persuading a senior executive that the opportunity is worth the risk and to let his instincts sell the system to his colleagues.

COMMON PITFALLS OF OFFICE AUTOMATION IMPLEMENTATION

Failing to Plan

Office automation will cause more organizational change than has been caused by any prior use of the computer. Plans for introducing the technology, managing it, and training users are essential.[21]

---

[20] Strassmann's work has been carried out largely in concert with the Strategic Planning Institute, Cambridge, Mass., which has also conducted additional studies in this area. Further information can be obtained from the Institute.

[21] This section is adapted from "Ten Pitfalls in Office Automation Implementation," Portfolio 1-05-14, General Management section, *Data Processing Management*, Auerbach Information Series (Pennsauken, N.J.: Auerbach).

Some organizations try to build a comprehensive strategic plan for office automation that provides for the systematic testing and introduction of the technologies over a span of years. At the present state of the art of office automation, such a plan is probably unnecessary, and may even be counterproductive. Office technologies are evolving so rapidly that flexibility is needed to take advantage of opportunities that new technologies make available. A comprehensive plan rarely provides such flexibility in practice.

The sort of planning that should take place depends on many factors, the most important being the characteristics of the organization. A mom-and-pop store needs very different solutions from a major multinational corporation; governments and universities have still different needs. Some key planning questions are as follows.

1. *How much risk can the organization manage?* The greater the organization's risk tolerance, the more likely it is to pioneer newer technologies. Done effectively, this can provide it with significant competitive advantages. But the vendors likely to offer the newer technologies are also more likely to be out of business when help is needed. Therefore, costs associated with converting to alternatives may occur more frequently if this strategy is adopted; nevertheless, the alternatives will probably be more advanced.

    If the risk level is low, it is better to stay with vendors who have a good track record and prognosis, and with systems from them that have been effective with many users. Such a low-risk strategy limits the organization's options significantly in this explosive field. The options available can be effectively utilized, as many major corporations have demonstrated.

2. *How large and complex is the organization?* A large multinational corporation that wants to provide an integrated electronic office worldwide is severely limited in the options from which it can choose. Those who are willing to allow company elements to adopt different approaches have more options, but they must consider the complex problems of providing gateways for the transfer of documents, messages, and other communications among the several systems chosen. Allowing local independence without gateways limits the potential benefits of office automation for the corporation as a whole because one principal value of office automation is improved companywide communications.

    The smaller, more coherent, and independent the organization, the more options it can review. The mom-and-pop store can probably meet its needs with a single personal computer. Such needs may even include on-line relationships with its suppliers and/or customers.

    Those who work in small units of large corporations often wish to go it alone, because they do not expect to interact much with the rest of the corporation. Experience has shown that these people come to realize the value of interconnection as they become increasingly familiar with what their equipment can do. This is referred to as organizational learning. If a company can effectively manage the redeployment of its equipment, it may find it better to start users with the limited equipment they want and to replace it when the need for interconnection is clear.

3 *How entrepreneurial is the organization?* This is related to the question of risk. Entrepreneurialship may further limit the options in a company that can tolerate some risk, or it may open some options in a company that probably should not tolerate any. The entrepreneurial environment may influence any company's choice of options substantially. If the decision maker cannot afford to fail, he is going to look at the safest options and forgo some of the benefits.

4 *What technology should be introduced where?* A requirements analysis is the usual starting place for most office automation initiatives. A few office automation advisers feel, however, that the answers to the first three questions must be known and understood before the requirements study begins. This way, the company may focus on the real options available as requirements are developed.

A requirements study documents the company's mode of doing business and quantifies the flow of information among its units. Its principal objective is to find high payoff applications of office technology and to assess their prospects for success. Often some individual has enough knowledge of the company to simplify or eliminate a comprehensive requirements study and to direct the focus to two or three obvious areas. If document creation is the issue, word processing may suffice. If heavy travel is the issue, teleconferencing may suffice. If telephone tag is the issue, voice mail may suffice. If a vendor performs the requirements study, then the problems he finds are likely to be ones his system will solve.

An important element here is to find a reasonably localized application. "Localized" means local with respect to organizational variables. A worldwide marketing organization is local in this sense. Pilot projects that span organizational boundaries are less likely to be successful than those that operate within a single manager's sphere of influence.

5 *How should the technology be introduced?* Most office automation advisers favor a pilot project or prototype approach, although there are some cases where an organizationwide go-for-broke approach is reasonable.

OFFICE AUTOMATION   21-25

---

1 Overview: Why is the pilot project being conducted, and what results are expected?

2 How will the pilot project change the nature of the work in the target organization?
  - What benefits will participants realize? What should they *not* expect?
  - What problems might occur? How will they be handled?
  - What should participants do if they encounter anything unexpected?
  - What records should participants keep? How should they share their experiences with each other and with the pilot project management?

3 What training will be provided? What feedback is desired on the effectiveness of the training?

4 What support will be provided during the pilot: hotline, consulting, individual assistance, user group?

5 What is the time frame of the pilot?

6 When the pilot is over, how will it be evaluated? What role will the participants have in the evaluation?

7 How will the results of the pilot be made available?

8 What role will the participants have in disseminating the pilot results to other departments?

9 How will the results of the pilot be institutionalized in the target organization?

10 How will the target organization cause the systems introduced in the pilot to evolve as the organization evolves during its use?

FIG. 21-3 Pilot Project Planning Questions

6 *How should the pilot project or prototype be supported?* The word "supported" is used instead of "conducted" because support is the key to a project's success. The organization conducting the pilot, be it in data processing, office automation, or records management, must understand the technology being introduced well enough to anticipate the kinds of problems likely to occur. The pilot should be well planned, and the planning should be done in full partnership with the user. Elements of the plan should address the questions listed in Figure 21-3.

If the planning outlined in this section is done, there are good chances for success in introducing office technology. If less planning is done, the organization should prepare to deal with unexpected problems.

Waiting to Plan

It is important to understand the needs of the potential user and to guess how the technology will evolve. It is equally important to get the technology in use, and to learn from its use.

> Priorities are in the following order:
>
> **1** Implement an electronic mail system that is compatible with the market leaders in data and word processing terminals.
>
> **2** Add data or word processing terminals until 60 percent of the executives, managers, professionals, and secretaries are within 100 feet of one that is convenient to use.
>
> **3** [*Additional priorities*]
>
> Select equipment only from vendors who:
> - Have been in business profitably for at least five years
> - Have captured at least 10 percent of the market for the technology in question
> - Have a good track record for introducing innovative approaches
> - Had sales of under $25 million last year but a business plan that shows them at more than $100 million next year
> - Have an excellent financing portfolio

FIG. 21-4 Sample Strategic Objectives

As discussed elsewhere in this chapter, office automation will cause more organizational change than has been caused by any prior use of the computer, and the field is explosively dynamic. Careful long-range planning is not possible in this environment. It should be possible to establish a few strategic directions but not a detailed plan. Some examples of strategic objectives are shown in Figure 21-4.

Peters and Waterman, *In Search of Excellence*,[22] stress the need for action and experimentation. It is not possible, they feel, to anticipate all of the key business effects of an idea without trying it out. Too many companies suffer from "paralysis by analysis."[23] The excellent companies try things out, and they learn from the results, whether successful or not.

Planning at too detailed a level can cause missed opportunities in this dynamic field. Planning to take advantage of a particular mix of features companywide, for example, may cause the company to overlook a successor technology that does the real job better. This underscores the need to keep in mind what the real job is, however. As mentioned in the previous discussion, formal requirements analysis is only one way of discovering this.

Perhaps the most important reason for avoiding too much planning is organizational learning. Organizations absorb change slowly, and the introduction of too much technology too quickly will cause stresses that may be difficult to relieve. The job of making the organization office technology literate takes

---

[22] Thomas J. Peters and Robert H. Waterman, Jr., *In Search of Excellence* (New York: Harper & Row, 1982).

[23] Peters and Waterman.

time, and it never begins until some technology is introduced. Growth in understanding based on actual experience is essential in moving toward the office of the future.

Office Automation as a Political Issue

"People" issues are the most important issues in the implementation of office technology. Although there have been technical failures in the office automation world, by far the most dramatic failures have taken place because the organization was not ready to accept the technology. Among the many reasons for this have been unrealistic expectations, inadequate training, and a weak support infrastructure. Some of these problems can be minimized by proper implementation of a pilot project plan.

However, even if all the proper guidelines are followed, implementation (or, more importantly, proliferation of a successful pilot) often fails to take place because the people it could help do not want it. The real reasons are many, and are rarely articulated. Any reasons explicitly stated are likely to be misleading. Sometimes office technology makes a department unnecessary. Clearly, that department will use any tool at its disposal to keep the technology out. Sometimes an individual is important because everyone has to go to him to get certain information. When the information is available instantly to everyone, he is no longer important. He will fight automation even if it clearly simplifies his job and makes it more interesting.

Figure 21-5 gives a brief taxonomy of "people" issues that need to be understood and addressed in order to introduce office technology, or indeed to bring about nearly any kind of organizational change.

Systems that cross organizational lines have been difficult to introduce in the data processing department. Office technology must cross many organizational lines if it is to be fully effective for a corporation. Where some organizations embrace and others resist office automation, there can be major political fights. Often, only top management can resolve them. For all of these reasons, the key element in introducing office automation is not technology but politics. The most important skill needed is skill in the management of organizational change.

Failure to Sell Office Automation to Top Management

Without the understanding and support of top management, an organization is not likely to capture the major benefits of office automation. Worse, powerful opponents may be able to shoot the program down.

The problems that office automation can solve are not usually visible in a corporation, especially at the top. Therefore, senior executives often fail to see the strategic significance of this set of tools. Furthermore, they are frequently

Securing top-management support for office automation
- Office not a hot button.
- Office automation seen as junior staff responsibility.
- No real appreciation of:
  - Potential benefits
  - Organizational evolution problems
- Assures support of business plan.
- Surfaces strategic organizational/operational issues.
- Supports information resource management.
- Resolves corporationwide compatibility/divisional autonomy conflict.
- Orders backlog priorities.
- Defuses fatal politics.
- Enables entrepreneurial decisions.

Integrating office disciplines

Ergonomics
- Man-machine interface.
- Working environment.

Power within and among organizations
- Power based on differential access to information.
- Power based on ownership or control of information.
- Power based on ownership of the means of processing information.
- Power migration upward in the organization.
- Power migration toward the organization's centers of technical expertise.

Attitudes about human resources
- People are assets; we should invest in them.
- People are expenses; we should control them.
- The tools we provide enhance the value of the people asset.
- The tools we provide control the people expense.
- The tools enable new ways to do work never before possible.
- These new ways to do work require new approaches to career planning and management by individuals, with effective support by the company.

Productivity
- Turning out more work in one department may create more work for others and *reduce* productivity of the organization as a whole.
- Productivity of managers and professionals, and of the organization as a whole: effectiveness.
- Attitudes about human resources affect attitudes about productivity:
  - Definitions/measurement of productivity
  - Productivity rewards and consequences
- Conversion of text/data to machine-readable form.

Organizational culture
- Entrepreneurial or bureaucratic?
- Aggressive or conservative?
- At the frontiers of technology or well behind the leaders?
- Centralized or decentralized?
- Coherent business area or a diverse conglomerate?
- Is the industry stable or volatile?
- Will managers keyboard, or is that beneath them?
- Planned or reactive?
- Long- or short term perspective?

FIG. 21-5 Taxonomy of People Issues

OFFICE AUTOMATION

unaware of the significant organizational dislocations that proliferation of office automation is likely to cause.

Bringing office automation's strategic potential to the effective attention of top management is a major responsibility. Its understanding and personal involvement is necessary (see Figure 21-5).

Leading-edge users of office automation tend to be quicker on their feet than their competitors. The involvement of an informed upper management undoubtedly encouraged the use of these new technologies, because the executives recognized the competitive edge the tools could provide. It is this kind of understanding that must be brought to those who lead our corporations.

Picking the Wrong Client for a Pilot

It is important to pick an enthusiast who will make the system work and who will help sell it. In most organizations, there are many people knowledgeable about office technology who are demanding support. Managers with office automation implementation responsibilities should become well acquainted with these individuals. Often they can be organized into an office automation steering committee whose enthusiastic support of these technologies can be most helpful.

Too often, office automation managers pay closer attention to the results of a requirements study than to the political realities of their organizations. The departments of managers who enthusiastically seek automation are better candidates for pilot projects than those for whom the benefits seem most obvious. Even here, some caution is in order. There are many ways for a project to fail and few for it to succeed. Failure can result for any of the following reasons:

- Lack of real commitment by the manager
- Lack of interest, active resistance, fear, or insufficient skills of the department members despite the manager's enthusiasm
- Use of a technology inappropriate for the job
- Use of a brand of technology different from the brand that excited the department manager without demonstrating how they compare
- Inadequate preparation of the department for the technology (e.g., understanding and describing the changes they will experience and training)
- Several departments who support the project in different ways
- Unforeseen events such as a key person's vacation or personal emergency at a critical point in the project
- Inadequate evaluation methodologies
- Excessive expectations

Selection for pilot projects from among an enthusiastic group of departments should be based on the following factors:

- Probability of success
- Willingness of the manager to provide resources to ensure success
- Willingness of the manager to work constructively with the implementation team in problem-solving
- Whether the manager is an opinion leader in the organization
- Ease of cost justification for the project
- Transportability of a successful pilot to a significant number of other departments
- Enthusiasm of those in the department who will actually use the technology
- Adequate resources (money, people, facilities) to succeed

Enthusiastic managers are an office automation manager's best friends; collectively, they constitute a precious resource. It is vital to know them and their operations well, however. Some may be good candidates for word processing, others for electronic mail or voice mail, still others for teleconferencing or telecommuting. The technology should match the need and also the organizational style. For example, it does no good to initiate a telecommuting pilot project, even if all other conditions seem right, if the manager is not secure managing a distant work force.

Finally, the key objective of a successful pilot is proliferation. If the technology works, is cost effective, and improves productivity, then those benefits ought to be realized wherever in the organization the technology is appropriate. If more than one department meets the criteria established for selection, then the one whose manager will be most effective during the proliferation phase should be chosen. His enthusiastic presentations about his successes to his peers and to upper management will be far more persuasive than any presentation an office automation manager could make.

Sufficient involvement with enthusiastic departments and their managers will lead, formally or intuitively, to a ranking of them in terms of prospects for pilot projects. When a technology becomes available, the office automation manager will know right away whom to contact. When a pilot is successful, an office systems automation manager will know which department is the best candidate for the next implementation. He will probably have a chain of stepwise implementations well in mind before the pilot begins; the experiences during the pilot may well modify the chain.

In the last analysis, implementation of office automation is hard enough; the easiest pathway possible should be chosen. The only way to know what pathway is easiest is to know one's organization well enough, and especially to know the office automation enthusiasts very well indeed.

Automating Production Personnel

The major opportunities for profitability lie in providing power tools to enhance the productivity of professionals and managers, especially at the higher levels.

It is relatively easy to justify word processing on the basis that it allows fewer people to accomplish more work, and these benefits can be quantified. As word processing moves to a shared environment and becomes used by people at higher levels, the benefits become harder to quantify and more difficult to justify. Consideration of the organization's pattern of investment in people, not the numbers (see Figure 21-5), shows that a much higher order of cost effectiveness can be realized if key people—executives, managers, professionals—can be made more effective through the use of power tools. Further support for this conclusion comes from other considerations. Conventional wisdom says that people at higher levels will make effective use of time saved through automation and that the effect on organizational efficiency of a better decision by an executive will be much larger than any savings that could result from further substitution of automation for human labor.

The difficulty of this approach for traditional cost/benefit analysis is that there are no really effective methods for quantifying the output of principals and, therefore, for measuring productivity improvements. Further, many believe that effectiveness, not productivity, is the issue. Better methods for evaluating the effectiveness that automation brings to upper management must be high on the agenda for office automation professionals.

Focusing on Features

Choosing a vendor with good future prospects is more important than choosing a system with clever features. Features are what vendors use to distinguish their products from one another. In copy machines, facsimile transmission devices, telephone switches, and PCs, the advertiser stresses features. Features are the new capabilities vendors add that advance the state of the art.

In most technologies, however, certain features become virtual necessities, and most vendors provide them. This list grows continually as the state of the art evolves. As features are put into the market and found useful, vendors adopt them.

Lists of necessary features grow because many people find them useful. Features reach the "necessary" list when their availability, or lack thereof, begins to change customers' brand loyalties.

People do have special needs, however, and there are useful features that do not appear on the "necessary" lists. However, the two sometimes coincide, and when they do, the user may insist on a particular piece of equipment. Sometimes, choosing it is the right decision.

More often, however, other considerations dominate, such as the frequency of need for the feature, a need to participate in an electronic mail system, or generation of the need to justify acquiring the device, by either the user or the advising vendor. Special needs should be understood and addressed, not simply satisfied. In addressing them, strategic questions should be kept in mind.

Insisting on Hard-Dollar Savings

Although a cost/benefit analysis is important, most benefits occur in ways that are hard to estimate and to demonstrate. The work done by executives, managers, and professionals is rarely measured by assessing productivity changes. Good quantitative measurements for the overall, continuing effectiveness of these principals do not exist. However, certain studies have been conducted that demonstrate significant improvements in productivity. For example, a study was made by Booz, Allen & Hamilton of a government office that produced several large documents similar in structure (although not in content) each year.[24] At that office, professionals and clerks worked together to produce these documents. About thirty-three person-weeks of effort were required. By introducing automation, nearly six person-weeks of professional time per document were saved, whereas the amount of clerical work remained the same. Where an office or department produces a product on a regular basis, the kind of detailed work analysis used in this case can quantify savings opportunities and measure their attainment. However, the cost of such an analysis is significant, so it may be better to make an entrepreneurial decision based on analogy with such a study than to go through the analysis.

Similar studies have shown savings attributable to the introduction of electronic mail. For large corporations, some of these studies show savings of over $500,000 per month. Again, the level of detail necessary for an effective study may make its cost enough to wipe out most of the savings.

In none of these cases was any study effort reported that treated effectiveness. Did producing seven instead of six documents per year increase the total organization's effectiveness, or was the use of the added document downstream enough to offset the improvement in this department? Was the total volume of mail necessary, or would more savings have occurred by finding ways to reduce the volume?

These are the kinds of questions that make any reasonable quantitative estimate of cost effectiveness subject to challenge. Attention to this issue is necessary to be sure that a reasonable business case can be stated and that the

---

[24] Presented by Ira Cotton of Booz, Allen & Hamilton at the International Data Corporation's Spring Executive Conference, Boca Raton, Fla. (1981).

OFFICE AUTOMATION

Word processing

Electronic filing and retrieval
—companywide

Electronic mail
- Telegraph
- Teletype
- Fax
- Computer-based message switching
- Electronic document distribution
- Voice mail

Personal computing
- Personal computers

- Information service centers
- Nonprocedural languages
- Decision support
- Executive information support

Public databases

Teleconferencing
- Audio (conference calls)
- Video, monochrome and color
  —Full motion
  —Differential motion
  —Freeze frame
- Computer

Telecommuting

FIG. 21-6 Office Technologies

case relates to the use of the technology to support a business objective. The requirement for a business case is necessary in order to identify frivolous requests, to help in setting priorities and to encourage new analytical approaches to cost/benefit analyses in this area.

Equating Office Automation With Word Processing

The major benefits of office automation derive from improved communications throughout a company; word processing benefits derive from a faster rate of document production. Because word processing was the first real introduction of the computer into the office for other than well-structured tasks—the first significant computer-based office automation—word processing and office automation are often considered to be synonymous. This human phenomenon is not new. There was time when every camera was a Kodak, every color movie in Technicolor, and every copy a Xerox. The first product on the marketplace gets all the attention; the rest must fight for it.

Office automation is comprised of many technologies, most of them communications related. Figure 21-6 lists these communications technologies, all of which help to overcome such time wasters as mail delay and telephone tag.

The following example of a geographically diverse proposal effort may help in the understanding of why word processing provides only a fraction of the benefits of office automation.

The proposal team meets face to face to refine concepts and establish a plan. Typically, the proposal is then parceled out to the team's members each of whom prepares a section. As each section is drafted, it is sent to the other members for review. A substantial amount of time is lost in transit, and rewriting certain sections based on the contents of other sections causes more time loss. When it is all together, the proposal is sent to one location for final review. Any changes resulting from this effort are then incorporated into the final version, and the proposal is submitted.

Word processors at each location would speed up text preparation. However, without communications, documents (or diskettes if the devices are compatible) would still have to be mailed. The mail delays and telephone tag would eat into the narrow window available for the creative work of the proposal. (If coordination is performed through successive meetings, a large travel bill would be incurred.) Thus, even with word processing, there would still be a substantial need for more effective communications.

To compress the time required for the physical work of producing the proposal and freeing up time for a better job of developing its creative content, the following could be implemented.

1 *Hold meetings via teleconferencing.* Many more meetings can occur this way, so that sticky issues that surface may be resolved before they become large.

2 *Exchange draft proposals instantly.* This way, the document remains intact all during the process.

3 *Implement a single electronic filing and retrieval location with appropriate configuration management of the various parts of the proposal.* All versions, including the latest, are then available for everyone at all times.

4 *Handle communications for simple questions and answers by computer-based message systems or voice mail.* This avoids time-zone incompatibilities resulting from geographic diversity.

5 *Utilize fax or slow-scan videoconferencing.* This is appropriate if drawings or other images are involved.

6 *Handle some of the draft review work by voice annotation.* This can be accessed by the authors for revision.

Word processing speeds up the production process significantly except where drawings are involved. However, most gains in effectiveness are produced by other technologies, mostly communications based, which allow a document to evolve effectively under the continual care of the proposal team.

Ignoring Other Office Disciplines

Most office disciplines support the office more effectively than data processing and office automation, and each makes a key contribution.

Figure 21-7 lists several of the office disciplines that need to work together to create the office of the future. Each discipline has a long history of support-

> - Word processing
> - Data processing
> - Micrographics
> - Reproduction
> - Telephone management
> - Records management
> - Filing and retrieval
> - Office management
> - Policy/procedure/methods management

FIG. 21-7 Office Disciplines

ing businesses effectively. To varying degrees, each is recognized as necessary and helpful. Most have been around far longer than data processing and other computer-based disciplines. More important, most have been at work right in the office.

Ways have been found to enable these disciplines to draw upon the computer's power to do their job more effectively. Proponents of each have a clear sense of their own mission and of the office they support. Because data processing personnel have been in the back room so long, they lack this perspective.

Each proponent sees his discipline as the leader in office support. There have been rivalries among the disciplines for decades, and they continue still. However, there is agreement on a few things, and one of them is that no one wants data processing invading his territory.

The fact is, data processing threatens nearly everybody. Doing things faster and better helps only a few, and most people worry about job displacement, disappearing departments, slave-driving controls, and all manner of other evils. If the desire to be the primary drivers of office automation is submerged and if proponents of each discipline recognize that all share a common interest in a successful result, that each has something necessary to contribute, and, even more, that those who use the technologies have good ideas about how they might fit together, then progress certainly could be better served.

REFERENCES

Barcomb, David. *Office Automation—Survey of Tools and Technology*. Bedford, Mass.: Digital, 1981.

Chorafas, Dimitris N. *Office Automation—The Productivity Challenge*. Englewood Cliffs, N.J.: Prentice-Hall, 1982.

Lieberman, Mark, et al. *Office Automation—A Manager's Guide to Productivity*. New York: John Wiley & Sons, 1982.

McWilliams, Peter A. *The Personal Computer Book*. New York: Ballantine, 1983.

_____. *The Word Processing Book*. New York: Ballantine, 1983.

It is often valuable to contact professional associations in the local area to determine if good individual consultants exist. A local office automation council or the local chapter of information-related professional societies are good prospects for this kind of inquiry. Consultants can be an enormously valuable source of help in solving office automation problems, but the selection and management of consultants is not a trivial task.

CHAPTER **22**

Security Implications for On-Line Financial Information Systems

Dwight Catherwood

Introduction	1	Authorization Maintenance	8
Computer Security	2		
		Surveillance	9
Controlling Systems Access	3	Real-Time Surveillance Functions	9
User Identification and Accountability	3	Detection	9
Terminal Identification	4	Security Response	10
User Authentication	4	Reporting and Logging	10
Something the User Has	4	Contents of a Security Audit Log	10
Something the User Knows	4	User's Role in Surveillance	11
Something Known About the User	5		
Password Guidelines	5	**On-Line Security Physical Checkup**	12
Confidentiality	5	User Identification and Accountability	12
Password Content and Origination	6	Authentication	12
Frequency of Change	6	Authorization and Data Access	13
Authorization and Data Access	7	Surveillance	13
Defining Systems Resources	7		
Defining User Capability	8	**References**	14

INTRODUCTION

Not too many years ago, computer security meant locking the computer-room door, putting the magnetic tapes in a fireproof vault, and making sure that there was adequate fire protection in the computer area. However, rapidly advancing technology has changed all of that. On-line systems, distributed processing, and remote computing have altered the ground rules significantly. Computer security is no longer just a problem for the data processing (DP) department; the issue extends to every department and user who has access to terminals.

The purpose of this chapter is to familiarize the financial manager with the principles of computer security for on-line systems. On-line systems are analyzed because (1) they offer the greatest exposure to accidental or intentional compromise and (2) the financial manager must bear much of the responsibility for proper administration of security in the on-line processing environment. Typically, the DP department is responsible for providing the tools with which to implement proper security. However, the degree to which the tools are utilized rests heavily on the commitment of the user department to administer and enforce security safeguards.

Computer Security

Computer security is a system of safeguards designed to protect computer systems from unauthorized destruction, modification, or disclosure and to ensure sustained, reliable operation of the system. Leonard Krauss, a noted security specialist, further defines the risks and exposures encountered in computer security as the "SIX D's."

- *Disclosure* of sensitive data, programs, and documentation
- *Dishonesty* of people both within and outside the organization who potentially have access to on-line financial information
- *Dysfunction* of the computer systems resulting from malfunctions and undetected errors
- *Disruption* of computer operations and of the operations of an organization
- *Destruction* of sensitive data, programs, and computer equipment
- *Deception* or misrepresentation accomplished through manipulation of computer data or programs[1]

Most of these exposures and risks may rise accidentally or willfully. Sometimes, weaknesses in the on-line security system present opportunities to commit unethical or dishonest acts.

Following are the key characteristics of an effective system of on-line security.

- *Prevention* — taking active steps to forestall the accidental or willful occurrences of exposures and risks.

- *Determent* — discouraging attempts at circumventing security safeguards by implementing surveillance features, which will tend to ensure accountability for their actions by individuals attempting such acts.

---

[1] Krauss, Leonard I., and MacGahan, Aileen, *Computer Fraud and Countermeasures* (Englewood Cliffs, N.J.: Prentice-Hall, 1979).

- *Detection* — providing for discovery and early warning of accidental or willful attempts to circumvent controls.

- *Recoverability* — providing the capability to restore data and programs to their proper value or condition and to maintain continuity of critical computer functions in the event of a disaster.

- *Accountability* — identifying the individuals who performed specific actions, or in whose name actions were performed, and holding those individuals responsible for their actions.

- *Auditability* — providing (1) an audit trail of all events that take place so that, should an incident occur, it can be investigated thoroughly and (2) evidence regarding the existence of compliance with security policies and procedures.

No one security feature typically addresses all these characteristics for a given exposure. Therefore, in building an effective system of security, there must be multiple lines of defense, with a realization that 100 percent security is impossible. A balance must be struck between manual and automated controls in designing the multiple lines of defense.

No one can guarantee that fraud, natural disasters, or accidental errors will not occur, but reducing risk by providing a reasonable level of protection for on-line systems is rational and prudent.

CONTROLLING SYSTEMS ACCESS

The primary security objective is to restrict systems access to authorized users from authorized locations and terminals, which is best accomplished by a combination of the controls, as discussed in the following sections.

User Identification and Accountability

Every user of the system should be assigned a unique user identification (user ID). The user ID becomes the cornerstone of the access control system. Establishing a unique identification for each user is important for three reasons: (1) it provides a basis to authenticate positively that a user is who he says he is; (2) it provides a way to associate the user with specific functions he may perform; and (3) it provides a means to establish individual accountability for the actions taken by the user on the system. Individual accountability is the cornerstone of on-line security control. Without it, the security objectives described elsewhere in this chapter cannot be achieved.

User IDs can be alpha or numeric. The user ID is public information used to identify a user by name. It may be an employee number, payroll number, an arbitrarily assigned code, or any other convenient coding system that identifies systems users.

Terminal Identification

A terminal identification code (terminal ID), when used in conjunction with a user ID, provides an additional safeguard against unauthorized access to the system. It verifies a user's presence at an authorized location (e.g., by limiting payroll clerks to terminals located in the payroll area).

Terminal IDs are also very useful in providing an additional level of control over special transactions that must be restricted to a small set of users. Examples are security maintenance functions or systems maintenance functions that should be performed from designated master terminals.

User Authentication

In establishing sound on-line access controls, it is essential to authenticate a user's identity prior to allowing him any further access to systems resources. There are three commonly used ways to authenticate a user: (1) by something he has; (2) by something he knows; or (3) by something known about him.

Something the User Has. A user can be authenticated by something he physically has in his possession, such as a magnetically encoded card, badge, or key. Many terminals offer an optional card reader; some offer versions that can be locked with a key. The advantages of these authentication schemes are that they are simple to implement and do not require the user to remember anything. The magnetically encoded card key may also carry additional information, such as the user's name, account number, or department.

The major disadvantage of this type of authentication method is that cards and keys can be lost, stolen, or easily shared among users. The user may also forget to remove the card or key at the end of an on-line session. A further disadvantage is the added cost of card readers and cards.

Something the User Knows. Another method of authentication is the use of secret passwords, information supposedly known only to the user (e.g., mother's maiden name), or some other predefined list of questions or algorithms known only to the user and the computer.

The advantages of this type of authentication scheme are that it is fairly inexpensive to install and maintain and can be made reasonably secure if properly installed and maintained. In addition, most commercially available on-line systems provide some facility for password use.

The disadvantages of password schemes are that they (1) require administrative overhead to maintain the systems and (2) can be easily compromised if not properly administered. One need only read any one of the number of accounts of "hackers" compromising on-line networks to understand the potential problems associated with password schemes.

Something Known About the User. A third method of authentication is the use of fingerprints, handprints, or voiceprints. A great deal of research is being conducted on these various schemes. Prototype systems are commercially available; however, they are not in widespread use because of their high cost and relatively high error rates. One problem with virtually all of these systems is their tendency to reject valid users.

The computer industry should be encouraged to support research into these authentication schemes. The perfection of a low-cost, effective authentication device will be a major breakthrough in preventing unauthorized access to on-line systems. Until physical characteristics systems are perfected, passwords remain the most common and practical method of authenticating a user and controlling systems access for most commercial on-line applications.

Password Guidelines

Because of the widespread use of passwords and their importance in controlling systems access, an understanding of the key issues in administering a password scheme is paramount to the success of any security program. Mismanagement of passwords not only creates a dangerous exposure, but often leads to a false sense of security just because passwords are being used. The key issues in password administration are (1) confidentiality, (2) content and origination, and (3) frequency of change.

Confidentiality. A main factor in the effectiveness of passwords is maintaining their confidentiality. The underlying premise of a password is that only the user and the computer know the correct password. Preserving this confidentiality is no easy task. Two opposing forces are at work: (1) creating a password that cannot be easily deciphered or guessed and (2) keeping the password so simple that the user will not be tempted to write it down and thus compromise its confidentiality. Short passwords are easy to remember, but also easy to guess.

Studies have shown that for most commercial on-line systems, a password length of five characters is most effective. Shorter passwords are susceptible to guessing, and longer passwords are difficult to remember.

Other precautions are also advisable to make sure that a user does not inadvertently disclose his password to others.

1 Never display passwords on the terminals.

2 Advise the user of the importance of maintaining the confidentiality of his password.

3 Ask each user to sign a statement indicating that he understands his responsibility for protecting his password.

4 Never allow passwords to be shared.

5 Give each user his own unique user ID and password.

6 Store all passwords in the computer in a manner that protects their secrecy (which usually means storing them in encrypted form in protected files).

Password Content and Origination. Ideally, passwords should be randomly generated to reduce the possibility of guessing or deciphering. However, ensuring randomness usually requires that passwords be centrally or computer generated, since a user cannot be counted on always to select a random password. The debate over how passwords should be generated is a lively one; indeed, there is no one perfect solution.

If the user is allowed to choose his own password, there is a high probability that he will pick one that is easy to remember. This drastically reduces the work factor in guessing systems passwords. This problem can be overcome to some extent by such techniques as disallowing the use of vowels or requiring the password to contain one or more special characters or numerals. The main advantages of allowing a user to select his own password are that (1) the administrative overhead is low and (2) this method keeps passwords fairly confidential. No one but the user and the computer need know the password. If the password is stored in an encrypted form and the user keeps his code a secret, confidentiality remains high.

An alternative is for a central authority, such as a security administrator, to control the generation and distribution of passwords. This helps guarantee randomness, since computer programs can be used to generate random characters, but the disadvantage is that the password must then be distributed to the user by some means (such as a sealed mailer). This opens up the opportunity for compromise from the point of generation until the password reaches the user's hands.

Frequency of Change. No matter how good the password generation system, the longer a password is in use, the more likely it is to be compromised. Many studies have been conducted on the proper duration of password use. The studies consider such things as the time required to break a password scheme or guess a valid password—sometimes referred to as the work factor or safe time—and more subjective considerations, such as risk of being compromised over time due to loss or being written down, shared, or accidently viewed by a third party.

There is no sure solution to this dilemma. However, it is generally accepted that passwords should be changed periodically. Intervals of from 60 to 180 days appear appropriate for most commercial on-line systems. Passwords should also be changed any time a compromise is suspected or reported by a user.

Another related issue regarding passwords is what to do with the user who enters an incorrect one. Legitimate mistakes do occur, but repeated attempts to enter a password should not be allowed, as they may indicate that someone is trying to guess his way onto the system. A user should be allowed two or three chances to enter the correct password; then a record should be written to a security log, and the user should be signed off. Further repeated attempts should result in the user ID being locked out until reinstated by the appropriate security authority. This procedure is absolutely essential to thwart trial-and-error attempts to gain unauthorized access to the system.

Authorization and Data Access

Once an authorized user has gained access to the system and has been properly authenticated, he should be allowed access only to those programs, transactions, and data required to perform his job. This can be accomplished in a number of different ways. Often, the method selected is dictated by the authorization control capability of the operating system or teleprocessing control program in use.

Regardless of the approach utilized to implement the authorization function, certain basic principles always apply.

- The user should be limited to the least set of privileges, activities, or functions required to perform his job.
- The authorization function must be capable of identifying the individual user or requestor of resources and be capable of enforcing access to systems resources based on access rules established by user management. Although this appears obvious, many commercial systems are not capable of protecting systems resources to this degree without supplemental security software or a separate commercially available access control package.
- The authorization or access control software must be capable of protecting itself and its access tables from unauthorized access.
- The access control software should grant access based on an explicit authorization to perform a function or access a resource. In other words, the system should keep track of what a user is allowed to do, as opposed to what a user is not allowed to do.
- User access must be monitored, and the user must be held individually accountable for his actions.

Defining Systems Resources. Systems resources are the objects in the system that a user must access and/or utilize in performing his job. Resources include such things as transactions, programs, files, records, and data. There are a number of ways to restrict access. Following are some of the more common.

- Limit access to specific records in a file (e.g., expense records pertaining to a certain department).
- Limit access to specific data elements in a file (e.g., labor hours but not labor rates or salaries).
- Specify transactions or groups of transactions that a user may invoke.
- Limit access to certain application programs or groups of programs.

Defining User Capability. Defining the resources that a user may access is only half of the authorization function. The capabilities that the user is allowed to perform on the resource must also be defined. Capabilities may be granted to a user in one or more of the following categories:

- *Read access* — also defined as inquiry capability. This limits the user to viewing data without modifying it.
- *Write access* — also defined as update capability. This allows the user not only to view data but also to write to files or add, change, or delete records or data fields within records. Sometimes, the ability to add or delete records is further restricted from the function of modifying existing records.
- *Execute only access* — allowing a user to execute a program or invoke a transaction without altering the program code.
- *Data entry only* — restricting data entry clerks to input only functions.
- *Time-of-day restrictions* — limiting a user to capabilities only for certain days of the week or times of day (e.g., restricting access to payroll files to the normal working hours of the payroll department).
- *Location restrictions by terminal location* — for example, limiting payroll transactions to terminals in the payroll department.
- *Range restrictions* — for example, allowing access to invoices under $1,000.

Authorization Maintenance. The responsibility for administering the rules and circumstances of authorization and data access is an extremely important function. This function can be the responsibility of user management, a data administrator, or a computer security administrator. Often the responsibility is shared among all three. The security administrator ensures the availability of proper tools for establishing access controls and helps to train the user. The data administrator establishes data classifications, names conventions, compiles data dictionaries, and defines resources. User management controls the user's explicit access to defined resources.

SURVEILLANCE

Security surveillance of a computer system concerns the maintenance of continual control over the security state of the system. Although security surveillance does not, in itself, constitute a protection mechanism for the on-line system, it supports the responsible security officials and management personnel in their tasks of making sure that (1) security controls are in effect and functioning as intended and (2) exceptions are receiving appropriate response. In addition, security surveillance can act as a deterrent to unauthorized access when the user knows his activities are being monitored.

In order to support the security officials adequately, the surveillance mechanisms must fulfill the following three objectives:

1 Provide timely, systems-generated responses to suspected security violations or systems tampering.
2 Provide adequate monitoring and security maintenance functions to allow the security administrator to know what is happening in the system.
3 Provide an audit trail of all significant events, including actions on or by the system that might affect security.

Real-Time Surveillance Functions

It is vital that certain attempted security violations be detected and responded to in real time. Three aspects of real-time surveillance work together to deter unauthorized activity: detection, response, and reporting.

Detection. Any exception to the normal operation of a computer system must be considered a potential security exception and initially treated as such. Exceptions fall into two categories: (1) systems malfunctions and (2) unauthorized user actions. Systems malfunctions include such things as input/output errors, data transfer errors, and hardware and software failures.

Systems errors are usually detected by the systems or application software, and are handled as part of the normal error-handling routines designed into on-line systems.

The detection of unauthorized user activity is dependent on the security controls designed into the system and the decision rules that have been established for systems and data access. The basic requirement is that every control mechanism must have a denial path, whereby the software prevents the user from further processing, stores pertinent information about the user and the reason for denial of access, and activates the appropriate surveillance software. This might involve setting warning flags in the system or directing transfer to the appropriate response software for immediate action.

Security Response. The response software must decide what action to take based on the type of potential security violation detected. The first step is to try to separate potential violations from honest errors. Since all users make errors, some allowance must be made before a user is branded as a security violator. Examples of such errors include entry errors in typing user IDs or passwords and the use of incorrect transaction codes or file names. This separation of bunglers from "burglars" is usually done by counting the occurrences of certain classes of errors and, when the number of errors reaches a predetermined value, changing the status of the user from bungler to burglar and responding accordingly.

Typically, a system can do one of four things with these exception conditions: (1) ignore them; (2) retry the process; (3) abort the process; or (4) hold the process in abeyance and ask someone what to do. All four depend on the operating characteristics and decision rules established for an individual system and are, therefore, systems dependent. However every system should be capable of:

- Determining the security significance of each detected exception
- Invoking a proper response to prevent violations
- Maintaining systems integrity (preventing the burglar from creating further problems once detected)

Reporting and Logging. Once the system has detected and responded to an exception condition, reporting techniques are needed that consolidate the information about the event and present it to an individual(s) responsible for monitoring the system, such as a security administrator, console operator, or network operator.

In addition to real-time reporting of certain security events, the system should maintain a nonperishable systems log or journal that contains security-related information necessary for review, damage assessment, and post facto analysis of systems activity.

The ability to provide off-line processing of systems logs is extremely important where one log may be used for multiple purposes (e.g., message journaling, checkpoint information, performance statistics, and security audit entries). Unless the security data can be extracted, the results are useful only for restart and archiving.

Contents of a Security Audit Log

Determining what should be included in the security audit log is not easy to do in the abstract. Some events, such as access denials, obviously should be reported to the security administrator and recorded in the systems log. Recording other events, such as operator interactions, may cause excessive overhead;

SECURITY IMPLICATIONS FOR THE ON-LINE FIS 22-11

records of such events can usually be extracted from the console log. As a minimum, the following guidelines are suggested:

1 Record all systems and user exceptions detected by the automated surveillance function as potential violations. This includes invalid passwords, attempts to access unauthorized files, or attempts to perform unauthorized transactions.

2 Record all security administration interactions to monitor users, alter security profiles, or otherwise change the security system's status. Examples include adding new users to the system, changing user access privileges, and changing the number of attempts users are allowed to sign on successfully.

3 Record user sign-on and sign-off information to allow reconstruction of who was on the system at any point in time.

4 Record access and/or updates to sensitive files, such as updates to a vendor payment file.

5 Record abnormal terminations to production programs.

Obviously, these suggestions are intended to provide examples of the kinds of events that may have security implications, and are therefore not all inclusive. The exact makeup of the security audit log depends on the type of system, the nature and amount of the information available, and the amount of systems overhead involved in maintaining the systems log. The final objective is always to be able to reconstruct systems events and establish accountability for every significant action.

User's Role in Surveillance

In dealing with computer security, it is often necessary to concentrate on worst-case situations related to possible use of the system by unauthorized individuals or authorized individuals trying to overstep their bounds. Normally, there are reliable, friendly, and authorized users on the system who can be a valuable source of information in determining whether it is running as intended.

Adequate procedures should be established for reporting abnormal conditions to the security administrator. Such reports, along with audit log information, can be analyzed to determine the nature and extent of a malfunction and whether the security systems controls are functioning properly.

In addition, the financial system's user typically performs a number of balancing and reconciling procedures for the on-line financial applications. Although these controls are usually considered to be outside the on-line security system, they are nonetheless important compensating controls, and should be encouraged. The user should be alert to the security, as well as the financial, implications of an out-of-balance condition.

The significant security features of on-line systems therefore include:

1 *Identification* — features used to establish the identification of a specific user or terminal attempting to access the on-line system.

2 *Authentication* — features used to verify that a user is who he says he is prior to allowing him access to any systems resources.

3 *Authorization* — features in place to limit and control a user's capabilities only to those functions required to carry out his job. Access may be restricted by user ID and terminal ID.

4 *Surveillance* — features used for real-time and post facto review of security violations.

The actual security features used involve technical, administrative, and physical safeguards appropriate to the risks and exposures present in a specific on-line environment. The features used are also influenced by the hardware, systems software, and application systems in use. Regardless of the environment, however, incorporating the security principles described herein into a business' on-line financial system leads to a more secure environment with reduced risk and exposure to unauthorized activity.

ON-LINE SECURITY PHYSICAL CHECKUP

The following questions are intended to give the financial manager a reasonable indication of where the company's system stands regarding on-line security. This is not intended as an exhaustive security checklist, but rather should serve as a diagnostic tool in determining if major exposure areas exist in the system.

User Identification and Accountability

1 Is a discrete sign-on required to access the system for each terminal session?

2 Does the system recognize repeated illegal attempts to sign on?

3 Are repeated illegal attempts to sign on logged and reported?

4 Is every user uniquely identifiable to the system—that is, does every user have his own user ID?

Authentication

1 Is the user required to authenticate his user ID through an appropriate validation routine (e.g., passwords, magnetic cards)?

2 If passwords are used:

- Are they randomly generated or, if user generated, are precautions taken to make sure that the user is not picking easily guessable words?
- Are the passwords at least four characters in length?
- Is the password suppressed on terminal entry?
- Is the user given a limited number of attempts to enter a correct password?
- Are repeated failures logged and the user signed off or locked out?
- Are password files stored in protected, preferably encrypted, files?
- Is the user required to sign a statement indicating his understanding of the confidentiality of his password?
- If passwords are centrally generated and delivered to the user, is this process highly controlled, preferably through the use of sealed mailers?
- Are passwords changed at least once every nine months?

Authorization and Data Access

1 Is authorization explicitly keyed to need-to-know or need-to-use?
2 Are authorizations established by user management and/or systems owners?
3 Are access and authorization requests submitted in writing?
4 Is appropriate access control software in place to restrict the user to a predefined set of systems resources?
5 Is access to systems resources further controlled on the basis of the functions a user may perform (e.g., inquiry, update, time-of-day)?

Surveillance

1 Does the surveillance system recognize and log the following security-related events:
   - User sign-on and/or sign-offs?
   - Illegal sign-on attempts?
   - Illegal password attempts?
   - Illegal access authorization attempts?
   - Authorized accesses to critical or sensitive files or functions (e.g., updates to the access tables themselves)?
2 Can the system recognize certain security violations in real time and take appropriate action to report the attempt immediately and/or stop the user from further action—for example, print a message at a monitored systems console, lock out the user, lock out the terminal?

3 Are violation reports printed from logs of security events?

4 Is someone specifically designated to review security logs and follow-up on security violations?

If the answer to the majority of the above questions is yes, then the organization is probably well on its way to a reasonable system of on-line security safeguards. However, constant monitoring of the security system along with periodic security audits is required to ensure compliance with established security procedures.

If the answer to the majority of the questions is no, the organization may be facing serious risks and exposures in its on-line financial system. We recommend seeking the assistance of qualified security advisors to help in determining the extent of the exposure and in developing a plan of action for taking corrective measures.

REFERENCES

Krauss, Leonard I., and Aileen MacGahan. *Computer Fraud and Countermeasures.* Englewood Cliffs, N.J.: Prentice-Hall, 1979.

Martin, James. *Security, Accuracy, and Privacy in Computer Systems.* Englewood Cliffs, N.J.: Prentice-Hall, 1973.

————. *Data Security Management.* Pennsauken, N.J.: Auerbach Publishing, 1984.

CHAPTER **23**

Disaster Recovery

William O'Malley and Faith Goodland

Introduction 2	Task 2: Define the Minimum Operating Requirements for Each Critical Application 13
Background on Disaster Recovery 2	Task 3: Develop Operating Requirements 13
Why Disaster Recovery Is Important . . . 4	Task 4: Identify Scheduling Requirements 13
Objectives of Disaster Recovery and Contingency Planning 5	Task 5: Prepare Step 3 Project Summary 13
Disaster Recovery Methodology 7	Step 4: Analyzing Risks and Alternatives 14
Step 1: Getting Started 9	Task 1: Analyze Risk and Rank Resources 14
Task 1: Establish the Contingency Planning Team 9	Task 2: Identify Data Processing Resource-Loss Situations 14
Task 2: Develop the Detailed Work Plan and Schedule 9	Task 3: Identify Recovery Alternatives 14
Task 3: Evaluate Existing Backup Procedures and Insurance Provisions 9	Task 4: Evaluate Recovery Alternatives 14
Task 4: Identify Short-Term Recovery Options 10	Task 5: Prepare Step 4 Summary . . . 15
Step 2: Establishing Priorities 10	Step 5: Developing the Plan 15
Task 1: Interview Selected Company Personnel 10	Salvage Team 16
Task 2: Develop Evaluation Criteria 11	Facilities Administration Team 17
Task 3: Prioritize and Select Critical Applications 11	Systems Software Team 17
Task 4: Prepare Step 1 and 2 Project Summary 11	Application Software Team 18
Step 3: Determining the Resources Required 12	Operations Team 18
Task 1: Define Operating Requirements for Each Critical Application 12	Hardware Team 19
	Communications Team 19
	Logistics Team 19
	Data Preparation Team 20
	Data Control Team 20
	Step 6: Making Sure the Plan Works . . . 21
	Step 7: Training Personnel 22
	References 23

23-1

INTRODUCTION

Can a company's key management personnel be assured that the user of the various financial application operating units will know what to do in the event of the interruption or loss of data processing (DP) services? How would its daily operations be affected by a total loss or interruption in the availability of the FISs, and how would that loss affect the company? How long of a delay in the availability of these business systems can occur before the company is inconvenienced or suffers a monetary loss? How much hardship can be accepted if these automated business systems are unavailable for an extended period of time?

The discussion in this chapter focuses on the objectives of and an approach to disaster recovery (systems contingency) planning, and address such basic systems contingency planning issues as:

- How to determine which applications are critical enough to need continued computer support
- How to identify the processing requirements for those applications
- How to select an approach to the recovery of normal operations on the basis of cost effectiveness
- How to prepare and validate a contingency plan
- How to train company personnel to use the plan

Much of the material presented herein may be of assistance in the development, documentation, and testing of a disaster recovery or systems contingency plan for both DP and critical financial application user departments.

Disaster recovery encompasses both contingency response planning and emergency operations management. In this chapter, we provide material that serves as a starting point for contingency planning efforts. By providing information about a workable and proved approach to contingency planning, the guidelines outlined may be used to streamline the time and effort required to protect the company's financial applications.

BACKGROUND OF DISASTER RECOVERY

Computers are increasingly being used in operational support of business. Early computer systems were batch oriented, with weekly, biweekly, or monthly processing cycles for systems being common, and daily cycles rather unusual. The increase in user sophistication, the decrease in hardware prices, and the competitive demands of business have provided the basic motivation for increasing use of on-line and real-time FISs. Direct operational support to the activities of a business organization is now provided by computer systems.

DISASTER RECOVERY

When such on-line systems have been in use over a reasonably long period of time, systems reliability increases to the point where revisions to a manual mode become infrequent or are completely abandoned. Such circumstances usually develop over a period of years. The result is that business operations cannot be continued without computer support.

The risks faced in operating a data center are many. Any one of the following events can cause serious disruptions to the normal mode of operations of a data center:

- Fire
- Flood/water damage
- Natural disasters
  - Hurricanes
  - Tornadoes
  - Earthquakes
- Vandalism, sabotage, and riot
- Environmental failures
  - Power
  - Air conditioning
  - Building integrity
- Nonavailability of personnel
  - Strike
  - Disruption of transportation

A risk analysis of computer centers takes into account some of these factors and provides remedies. For instance, fire suppression systems may be installed to fight fire, or cross-training of employees may be used to continue operations in the absence of key personnel. These remedies, however, provide a reasonable sense of assurance only, and do not afford complete protection. For example, the fire suppression system may be able to localize and contain fires originating in the computer room, but if the fire originates elsewhere in the building and is already out of control by the time it reaches the computer room, the local fire suppression system will be totally ineffective. Similarly, cross-training of personnel may provide for the unscheduled absence of a few employees, but job actions such as strikes may deprive the data center of all employees. A flood or other natural disaster may disrupt communications and affect a substantial portion of a distributed DP system. In view of the dependency of critical business operations on computer support, it is necessary to plan ahead for such potentially disruptive situations. That is the focus of disaster recovery planning.

WHY DISASTER RECOVERY IS IMPORTANT

It is not uncommon to pick up a newspaper or journal and read about a disaster. Following are two such cases. The first, written in February 1983, describes a disaster that occurred at the Northwestern National Bank Building in Minneapolis.

> A wooden table in the corporation boardroom was charred beyond recognition. In some offices, no chairs or desks remained and metal cabinets melted. The chief executive officer's suite was reduced to rubble and ash.
> In what was perhaps the worst fire in Minneapolis' history, a blaze that began in a vacant department store quickly rose six stories, spread across the street, and engulfed two wings of the Northwestern National Bank Building last Thanksgiving Day.
> All 17 floors of the 53-year-old concrete bank building were rendered useless. The first six levels, occupied by the bank, were damaged by smoke and water. Above levels, which housed a subsidiary mortgage company, bank corporate headquarters and a law firm, varied in degree of destruction. Offices facing the department store were completely destroyed.[1]

As the article goes on to explain, Northwestern National Bank had a disaster recovery plan.

> Despite the devastation, the Northwestern Bank Corp., an interstate firm with 86 affiliates, was operating at 75 percent of capacity on the Monday after Thanksgiving. Bank officials attribute the amazing recovery to a recently revised disaster plan and a little bit of luck.
> "Because we had all the directives on paper, all the key elements right there in a binder, no one panicked. No one was shouting out suggestions, changing their mind, or unsure about who should make decisions," said Virgil Dissmeyer, vice president of operations. "Having the plan in front of us provided stability. It gave everyone confidence that we could pull through this."[2]

Another example is the disaster that occurred at the Suffolk County Federal Savings and Loan Company.

> It was the end of a bitter cold three-day weekend on Long Island when Augustus Weaver, information services manager at Suffolk County Federal Savings and Loan, received an emergency call. He arrived at the computer center shortly after 1 A.M. and opened the door to a data processing manager's nightmare.
> Water poured from the ceiling tiles forming a miniature Niagara Falls above the company's SPERRY UNIVAC 90/60 mainframe. Chunks of

---

[1] Kerngon Lydon, "Investing in Disaster Plans," *Security World* (Feb. 1983).
[2] Lydon.

ceiling tile, papers, forms and supplies floated in the pooled water of the basement floor.

Fortunately, the company had a disaster recovery plan and calls could immediately be placed to the local Univac branch. Within an hour, four Univac field engineers were on-site, and shortly thereafter, the field engineering group manager was making contacts at corporate headquarters in Blue Bell, Penn.

The water had run for two days, after a heating pipe on the second floor of the building burst. Pumps in the baseboard heating system continued to circulate until eventually the hot water that was created tripped the fire alarm. The problem was further compounded by the anti-corrosive chemicals used in the heating system. During normal operations, the chemicals kept the boilers from rusting. When the water came out of the sealed system, however, the chemicals worked in the opposite fashion, causing corrosion. As a result the staff at Suffolk County Federal actually watched pieces of equipment rust before their eyes.

With the water finally stopped and the room pumped dry, Weaver and the Univac representatives began assessing what could and could not be salvaged. Once the field engineers were able to inspect the 90/60, it was clear that all power supplies were completely soaked. Although they could attempt to dry out the power supplies, they ran the risk of a possible explosion if they were not thoroughly dry.

The mainframe, as well as a number of peripheral devices were scrapped.[3]

These two excerpts describe disasters that actually occurred. Based on extensive research, it is concurred that the risks of fire and water damage have the two highest probabilities of happening.

Everyone has a tendency to say, "This will not happen to us so why should we plan for a disaster?" The passages excerpted describe two cases where fire and water caused disaster situations. The question is, Would your company be ready to deal with these situations?

OBJECTIVES OF DISASTER RECOVERY AND CONTINGENCY PLANNING

As mentioned earlier, DP has assumed an important operational role in many organizations. In industries such as banking and retailing, DP is critical to the point where the survival of the organization is threatened if data processing support is disrupted for an extended period of time. This importance of DP to business operations is in contrast to EDP expenditures. Typically, these expenditures range from 2 to 7 percent of the organization's total spending. In comparison with the start-up cost of a new project or manufacturing facility, data processing costs seem insignificant; yet data processing plays a more

---

[3] Charlotte K. Lowie, "Disaster Recovery," *Unisphere Magazine*.

important role in support of operational activities than is commonly recognized.

This misperception of the significance of the role of DP has led to a serious flaw in the operational aspects of a DP facility. Generally speaking, there is no alternative way to support computerized applications if a loss of some portion of the DP facility occurs. Failures typically arise from hardware/software malfunctions that are corrected in a matter of hours or that require only that the affected portion of the equipment be taken out of commission. That has encouraged the belief that all emergencies can be handled in a similar manner and no detailed plans are needed to cope with other types of outages and emergencies.

That belief is held despite the widespread reporting of the destruction of data centers by agents such as fire, flood, hurricanes, and bombing; the loss of major communications networks due to natural disasters; the loss of manpower due to strikes; and the magnitude of effort required to bring DP services to normal.

Disaster recovery or contingency planning has developed in response to the vulnerabilities of data centers observed during internal evaluations of computer controls and data systems security reviews, as well as to the concerns of enlightened executives regarding the hardships associated with any extended outage of computer equipment.[4] A comprehensive and consistent approach to designing and implementing a DP contingency plan is needed.

The objective of the disaster recovery or contingency planning process is to provide the plans and procedures required to cope with a major emergency in the data center. The approach presented herein is as follows:

1 Determine the applications that are critical enough to need continued computer support.
2 Identify the processing requirements for those applications.
3 Select an approach to the recovery of normal operations on the basis of cost effectiveness.
4 Prepare and validate a contingency plan.
5 Train personnel in the use of the plan.

An installation using a minicomputer for monthly batch reports does not have problems similar to an installation using an identical minicomputer for on-line DP if an emergency arises. Nor does a minicomputer installation pose problems comparable to those found in a large-scale computer installation. A minicomputer installation with monthly batch reports may need no more than a list of vendors (including vendors in the resale market) who will be able to supply the needed equipment if data and program files have been safeguarded.

---

[4] Ernst & Whinney, *EDP Contingency Planning Guidelines*.

DISASTER RECOVERY

However, the solution cannot be reduced to this minimum in preparing a contingency plan for a medium- or large-scale installation. Thus, the objectives and scope of the effort vary significantly from company to company.

A major reason for developing such a plan before emergencies occur is the need for speed in restoring critical services and applications. Dollar losses and hardships build up rapidly as recovery time increases. A ready-to-use contingency plan provides the following advantages in coping with emergency situations:

- Limits financial losses and hardships.
- Minimizes the extent of interruption to routine business operations.
- Limits the severity of disruption, damage, and hazards to employee welfare and safety.
- Defines alternatives for accomplishing critical EDP services.
- Provides trained personnel to handle emergency conditions and recovery operations.
- Establishes a means for orderly restoration of services.

DISASTER RECOVERY METHODOLOGY

There are many companies that have worked on disaster recovery methodologies. The following is a disaster recovery methodology that has been tried and tested.

Seven steps of the approach serve the following critical contingency planning objectives.

- *Step 1* — organizes the effort and evaluates any existing backup or contingency plan.
- *Steps 2, 3, and 4* — determines critical applications, identifies resources needed for critical processing, and specifies means of recovery.
- *Steps 5, 6, and 7* — develops emergency procedures and recovery plans, tests them, and provides appropriate initial training for company personnel.

To develop a workable plan, management must have a clear understanding of priorities. Critical systems applications and functions must be identified. Cost-of-recovery features must be weighed against the costs of hardships incurred in the absence of these features. The extent to which in-house personnel may be relied upon and the need for outside services must be determined; these costs must also be weighed against the benefits.

This seven-step methodology provides a sound basis and some valuable insights for making these decisions. Equally important, the methodology enables the decisions to be carried out step by step in a systematic and controlled manner.

A key feature in EDP contingency planning is the ability to restore service for critical applications much faster than would be possible without planning. It is easy to see that dollar losses and hardships can build up very rapidly as recovery time increases. For example, one company figured that, without a plan, there would be lost motion, mistakes, and guesswork of such a nature as to make the recovery time several times as long as with a plan. In dollars alone, this time difference would mean multimillion-dollar losses versus a loss of a few hundred thousand dollars.

This seven-step methodology allows companies to overcome some serious problems that have been experienced in EDP contingency planning. In positive terms, they are:

- Integrating user and top-management views into the overall planning process.
- Understanding, in the beginning, the major steps and determinations that must be made.
- Recognizing that EDP contingency planning must give serious consideration to economic realities.
- Related to the above point, making decisions about how much to spend on EDP contingency planning based on reasonable information about potential dollar losses and hardships that could be experienced.
- Incorporating provisions to monitor progress and control the expense of the contingency planning project as well as the cost of the problem solutions that are developed as a result of the project.
- Realizing that procedures and plans, if they are to have any chance of working when needed, must be based on specifics.

The following sections discuss these seven steps:

- *Step 1:* Getting started
- *Step 2:* Establishing priorities
- *Step 3:* Determining the resources required
- *Step 4:* Analyzing risks and alternatives
- *Step 5:* Developing the plan
- *Step 6:* Making sure the plan works
- *Step 7:* Training personnel

DISASTER RECOVERY

Step 1: Getting Started

Step 1 establishes the framework for performing the contingency planning project. It defines the contingency planning team, provides data collection techniques, outlines the interview format, and describes the specific tasks to be performed in the remaining steps. It also includes the preparation of a corporate information systems plan summary, a master application list, the evaluation of existing backup plans, and a preliminary assessment of applications.

After establishing a contingency planning team and initiating the project, interviews are scheduled and performed with selected executive management, user, and EDP personnel. The purpose of these interviews is to determine corporate goals and objectives, information systems plans, applications and functions performed, and their associated loss-impact and dollar-loss amounts.

At the conclusion of this step, the project responsibilities have been clearly defined, a summary of the corporation information systems plan's elements has been prepared, and a master application list has been culled.

Step 1 establishes the scope of the effort and the framework for performing the detailed tasks required throughout the project through the completion of the following tasks.

Task 1: Establish the Contingency Planning Team. Task 1 identifies the personnel assigned to the contingency planning team and establishes the organizational and reporting procedures to ensure the effective cooperation and coordination of the various team members. An orientation seminar should be conducted for all members of the team and other interested company personnel to explain the contingency planning objectives and methodology and establish a common basis for the work in each of the remaining steps.

Task 2: Develop the Detailed Work Plan and Schedule. The development of a contingency plan is a long and complex procedure involving personnel from different areas of the company. In order to ensure the performance of all important activities and to make sure that the end product is a practical and workable plan, a detailed work plan defining what needs to be accomplished must be developed. The plan should also include who is to perform the work, how much time is required to complete each task, and what specific output is to be produced during each step.

Task 3: Evaluate Existing Backup Procedures and Insurance Provisions. Next, a review and evaluation of all provisions for data backup that presently exist is incorporated into the final contingency plan. As a part of the review of backup procedures, it is imperative to examine any insurance coverage for business interruption that may currently be in force to determine what funds would be available for contingency operations in the event of a disaster situation. A master application list to identify all the applications that need to be considered in the course of the project must be prepared.

Task 4: Identify Short-Term Recovery Options. As a part of this step, a limited operations appraisal survey to determine what can be done to reduce the risk of a significant power outage situation that might occur during the contingency planning project must be conducted. Next, the short-term recovery option existing in the time span between the initiation of the contingency planning project and the implementation of the appropriate recovery alternative must be identified.

At the conclusion of this task, the short-term recovery options that are available for immediate or near-term implementation should have been identified.

Step 2: Establishing Priorities

Step 2 verifies the results of the preliminary assessment and to select a critical application set for which contingency plans are required.

Priority analysis uses information on application interrelationships. Loss-impact and dollar-loss-amount data previously collected is evaluated (taking into account application interrelationships) and verified for correctness.

Priority analysis is performed according to analysis criteria developed as the first part of the step.

After applications are ranked by dollar-loss amount, a dollar-loss-amount cutoff determination is made. Critical applications are those exceeding the cutoff value, or alternatively, those identified by management as being critical applications regardless of the dollar-loss amount.

The first step toward establishing priorities is to gather information on applications processed by the company and on the potential economic loss associated with each important application. The criticality of each application should be assessed, selecting those for which a contingency plan is required. The current applications and all planned applications in the next three to five years should be considered in this process so that the contingency plan reflects the actual environment of the company when it is implemented. This step involves extensive data gathering through interviews and related group information analysis techniques.

Task 1: Interview Selected Company Personnel. The need for a contingency plan is based on the value of information to the firm. The process of determining the value of information involves both an objective and subjective analysis. In order to arrive at these, it is first necessary to go through a process of establishing the corporate goals and objectives that need to be addressed by the contingency plan. These need to be further refined into information systems goals and objectives, which can be used to define the importance and value of application systems.

To gather the required information, selected executives and management, user, and information systems personnel should be interviewed. Questions relating to corporate goals and objectives, information systems goals and objectives, and specific functions and applications currently performed or planned within the organization should be asked. To ensure uniformity in the collection of data and to aid in the analysis of critical applications, standard interview guides and data collection forms should be developed.

A key element of the interviews should be estimation of the potential dollar loss in the event that data, on-line inquiry, reports, or other functions or information resources are unavailable for an extended period of time. Emphasis should be on quantifying the value of automated functions and applications performed in the organization by estimating the dollar losses that might be incurred in their absence.

Task 2: Develop Evaluation Criteria. The purpose of this task is to develop the quantitative and qualitative criteria to be used in determining the priority of critical applications.

Task 3: Prioritize and Select Critical Applications. The process of ranking the applications considered to be most critical establishes the scope of the contingency plan required for the organization. The criteria developed in the previous task—the estimates of economic loss and management's assessment—should be used to select the critical applications.

Task 4: Prepare Step 1 and 2 Project Summary. At the conclusion of Steps 1 and 2, a report summarizing the interim project results should be prepared and submitted to top management for review and specific recommendations. At all times, it is necessary to obtain management's approval to proceed.

The following major items should be discussed in the summary:

1 *Corporate and information systems goals and objectives.* This information provides the basis for assessment of alternatives chosen for the contingency plan. It also establishes the basis for future activities. These should be stated in strategic terms. A full corporate plan or an information systems plan should not be developed for this summary.

2 *Short-term recovery options.* This summary provides the firm with immediate or short-term recovery options that can be implemented to reduce the risk of a disaster situation crippling the company during the contingency planning project.

3 *Master application list.* This should identify all major applications either existing, under development, or planned for further development. This ensures, as the contingency plan is developed, consideration of the most current applications in the plan.

4 *Potential economic loss summary.* This analyzes by major applications the financial impact of losing DP resources for various significant outage periods. This analysis should be subsequently used to justify economically the level of contingency recovery preparedness required.

5 *Critical application list.* This lists the existing and planned applications that have been found to be the most critical to the company based on their value to the organization. This list should define the target group addressed by the contingency plan.

6 *Step 3–Step 7 work plan.* This provides a detailed list of tasks to be performed in the remaining steps of contingency planning.

Step 3: Determining the Resources Required

Step 3 identifies and documents the operating requirements of the critical set of applications.

In this step, operating requirements information for all identified critical applications are collected. This includes hardware, software, data, telecommunications, power, documentation, personnel, and installation requirements. The analysis is supplemented by information on scheduling requirements and timing constraints placed by the user on the information systems functions.

Once the information is collected, it is analyzed and used to identify a minimum-operating-requirements configuration for each critical application.

Scheduling and timing information is also collected from systems analysts and users. It should be used to identify significant scheduling and timing constraints and to develop an operating schedule based on the minimum-operating-requirements configuration.

This step, which is concerned with DP resource losses, results in a definition of the minimum operating requirements for each critical operating and planned application. The type of information collected in this step should be more detailed and technically oriented than that collected in Steps 1 and 2. Key tasks are as follows.

Task 1: Define Operating Requirements for Each Critical Application. Working with DP personnel, a list of the current and projected operating requirements for each critical application must be prepared. Each application's operating requirements should be defined in terms of its critical resources, such as hardware, software, telecommunications facilities, and personnel.

DISASTER RECOVERY

Task 2: Define the Minimum Operating Requirements for Each Critical Application. The purpose of this task is to analyze the resources required for each application and determine the minimum resources that can be used to support it.

Telecommunications resources should (if applicable) be considered in great detail, taking into account any planned future growth or increased reliance on this resource. Analysis of the minimum operating requirements for on-line applications should consider such items as processing capacity requirements, minimum number of on-line devices, response-time constraints, and possible alternate procedures.

Task 3: Develop Operating Requirements. During the performance of this task, each critical application's minimum operating requirements and the minimum operating specifications to handle the processing of all critical applications should be reviewed and evaluated, taking application interrelationships into consideration. This specification should be independent of any specific recovery alternative.

Task 4: Identify Scheduling Requirements. The ability of the processing requirements and timing constraints of the critical applications to be met by the environment defined in the minimum operating requirements must be verified.

The next activity is to develop a schedule for processing the critical applications during a contingency situation. This schedule is needed to make sure that everything that needs to be done in a contingency situation can be accomplished with the defined minimum operating resource requirements.

Task 5: Prepare Step 3 Project Summary. The final task is to prepare, at the conclusion of Step 3, an interim summary for management that includes the following major items:

- *Critical application minimum operating requirements* — minimum requirements for hardware, software, data, documentation, personnel, facilities, and telecommunications.

- *Minimum operating resource requirements* — consolidated operating requirements that define the resources necessary to process all of the critical applications in a contingency situation, irrespective of the selected recovery alternative.

- *Critical application operating schedule* — identification of the time frame required to process the critical applications and perform the critical functions.

Step 4: Analyzing Risks and Alternatives

Step 4 identifies critical resource-loss situations and selects backup and recovery alternatives for each situation.

The emphasis is on identifying resource-loss situations rather than on enumerating the causes of resource losses ("loss of computer processing for one week" rather than "electrical fire"). The recovery alternatives analysis similarly emphasizes recovery from resource-loss situations, not causes.

Risk and recovery alternatives analysis begins with the identification of information on resource-loss situations and their associated costs and information on backup and recovery alternatives for each resource-loss situation.

The resource-loss information is used to select critical resource-loss situations based on identified cost-of-outage figures. Then, once the critical resource-loss situations are identified, backup and recovery alternatives can be developed for each situation. The backup and recovery alternatives are analyzed, and the best alternatives are selected based on the minimum operating requirements data and the cost to implement. Key tasks in this step are discussed in the following sections.

Task 1: Analyze Risk and Rank Resources. All resources associated with the critical applications are evaluated, and should be ranked in order of significance.

Task 2: Identify Data Processing Resource-Loss Situations. The importance of individual DP resources should be examined. Concentration on resource-loss situations rather than on identification of potential disaster situations emphasizes the most important resources and the need to recover from the loss of those resources.

Task 3: Identify Recovery Alternatives. Investigation of alternatives should concentrate on developing recovery alternatives for all critical applications based on the identified minimum operating requirements and the resource-recovery options. It is important to document such alternatives as use of service bureaus, vendor recovery operations centers, mutual assistance agreements, a second existing company operations center, multiple existing company operations centers, manual procedures, and other alternatives identified during the course of the project.

Task 4: Evaluate Recovery Alternatives. Each recovery alternative identified should then be examined in detail using comparable criteria and analysis techniques. A comparison of benefits and a financial analysis of one-time, on-going, and contingency-event costs associated with each alternative should be performed. It is also wise to visit vendor sites to assist in the evaluation of alternatives.

DISASTER RECOVERY

Task 5: Prepare Step 4 Summary. At the conclusion of this step, a management summary report is issued. The following major items should be included:

- *Critical resource-loss situations.* This identifies the DP resources that are subject to the greatest risk and the recovery options that are available for each of these resources.

- *Recovery alternatives.* This gives a detailed analysis of alternatives available for processing all of the critical applications, along with the basis for selecting the alternative, the associated cost estimates for the implementation of that alternative, and additional information, including benefits to be gained. The most appropriate alternatives should be presented to management.

Step 5: Developing the Plan

Step 5 develops and documents a contingency plan in the form of an emergency procedures manual and a recovery operations manual.

In this step, the results of prior steps are used to develop procedures for the notification of personnel, the protection of resources, and the recovery of DP operations. The contingency plan is developed and documented using appropriate documentation formats. Determination is made of the tasks necessary to implement the selected recovery alternative.

Contingency plan development makes use of the list of critical applications, the minimum operating requirements for each critical application, a master critical application operating schedule, and a list of critical resource-loss situations with appropriate recovery alternatives for each situation.

The contingency plan has two major aspects: (1) development of the procedures to be carried out and (2) the assignment of responsibilities for carrying out the procedures to persons who have certain authority and responsibility. The procedures to be defined in the contingency plan may be logically compartmentalized into the activities required to be carried out by several teams, each responsible for dealing with one or more aspects of the disaster. Suggested teams include:

- Salvage
- Facilities administration
- Systems software
- Application software
- Operations
- Hardware
- Communications
- Logistics
- Data preparation
- Data control

The number of separate teams needed depends on the size and complexity of the individual operation. In smaller companies, several teams may be consolidated into one.

Emergency procedures should be carried out by these teams under the leadership of a contingency management team. The contingency management team must take the lead in actively managing the efforts that follow a disaster. It is its responsibility to assess the extent of disruption to normal operations, determine the efforts needed to normalize operations, and decide on staffing levels for the different functions involved. Emergency mode operations may involve initiation of service at an outside commercial facility. The start-up cost and the daily operations charges should be planned for.

It is also the contingency management team's responsibility to determine the appropriate response according to the magnitude of the problem. This leads to the activation of only those teams that will be involved in a limited-scope disaster; the rest of the contingency plan need not be invoked.

The functions of the contingency management team are managerial in nature, calling for the exercise of judgment and prudence. The exact course of action for this team cannot be completely prescribed in a contingency plan, but the members of the contingency management team can and should be identified and their responsibilities defined.

The emergency procedures manual must contain procedures for notifying one or more members of the contingency management committee at all hours of the day.

The suggested teams and their functions and responsibilities are discussed in the following sections.

Salvage Team. The objective of the salvage team is to appraise the damage, minimize further losses, and salvage what can be saved.

During the contingency planning step, this team should establish contacts with outside contractors, the insurance company, and with security personnel. After the disaster, this team is responsible for:

- Reporting to the contingency management team on the extent of damage
- Reducing danger to personnel in the damaged facilities
- Identifying materials to be salvaged
- Preventing further damage
- Initiating insurance claims and maintaining liaison with insurance company personnel
- Arranging insurance for the new site and equipment
- Arranging crews for salvage and cleanup
- Establishing security at the destroyed facility
- Establishing security at the new site

DISASTER RECOVERY

Facilities Administration Team. The objective of this team is to provide a facility where backup-mode operations can be performed and to provide the administrative support required by all personnel engaged in the disaster recovery effort. During the planning step, this team is responsible for:

- Preparing a short list of backup sites
- Obtaining power and air conditioning
- Drawing up tentative floor plans for the backup sites
- Identifying requirements for furniture, telephones, and office equipment (e.g., copiers, typewriters)
- Preparing a list of suppliers and contact persons
- Preparing a list of consumable supplies (e.g., forms, cards)
- Maintaining an off-site emergency stockpile of supplies
- Preparing a list of suppliers and establishing a contact person with each supplier

After the disaster, this team is responsible for:

- Obtaining decisions on site from the contingency management team
- Checking out power and air conditioning
- Arranging furniture and office equipment
- Installing telephones for voice and data communications (the latter in conjunction with the communications team)
- Preparing the site for occupation
- Distributing an emergency stockpile of supplies
- Ordering replacement supplies
- Providing administrative and secretarial support
- Setting up internal mail
- Providing authorization for expenditures by other teams
- Recording and controlling extraordinary costs and expenditures
- Arranging for catering
- Arranging for cleaning and janitorial services

Systems Software Team. The objective of this team is to maintain a working version of the operating system and related systems software and to install it at the backup site.

During the planning step, this team is responsible for arranging the maintenance of an off-site copy of the systems control program. The version maintained off site must have associated parameters that define the backup computer configuration. The team is also responsible for periodic testing of the backup version and keeping it up with modifications made to the version in use at the regular facilities.

During a disaster, this team is responsible for generating the new control program at the backup site and for debugging and resolving any errors that may occur in the systems software.

Application Software Team. The objective of this team is to supply working versions of all critical application systems and most current versions of the associated data files.

During the planning step, this team is responsible for establishing procedures to maintain off-site copies of programs and data files and updating them to match the updates to production libraries at the main site. During the emergency, this team is responsible for:

- Accessing off-site storage, obtaining backup copies, making new backup copies, and transferring them to the backup site
- Reestablishing software and procedure libraries at the backup site
- Restoring user disk packs and tapes
- Supervising resumption of critical processing
- Resolving any errors in the application programs

Operations Team. The objective of this team is to operate the computers at the backup site to meet critical processing requirements. During the planning step, this team is responsible for:

- Establishing requirements for programs, data files, and procedures and operations manuals in conjunction with the application software team
- Defining requirements for supplies and consumables to the facilities and administration team
- Obtaining a list of senior operations staff and their home telephone numbers

During the emergency, this team is responsible for:

- Establishing the processing schedule at the backup site
- Bringing up systems in the required sequence
- Operating the backup computer equipment
- Maintaining a liaison with maintenance engineers to keep the backup equipment in good working order

DISASTER RECOVERY 23-19

Hardware Team. The objective of this team is to obtain hardware to meet minimum processing needs and to obtain new hardware for a new data center. During the planning step, this team is responsible for:

- Defining the minimum configuration needed to support the critical applications
- Advising the systems software team of this configuration
- Establishing contact with hardware vendors, brokers, dealers, and rental organizations

During the emergency, the team is responsible for:

- Locating new hardware
- Ordering new hardware, including computer equipment, data entry equipment, paper-handling equipment, and microfilming equipment
- Arranging with the facilities and administration team for floor plans
- Supervising hardware installation and testing
- Handing over the replacement site to operations

Communications Team. The objective of this team is to reestablish the teleprocessing network and supply communications facilities to the backup site. During the planning step, this team is responsible for:

- Establishing minimum requirements for communications lines and terminal equipment (including modems)
- Installing a basic set of lines to the backup site

During the emergency, this team is responsible for:

- Ordering needed telecommunications equipment
- Assisting with installation
- Supervising testing and commissioning
- Arranging for communications equipment for other teams as needed

Logistics Team. The objective of this team is to provide for transportation of material and personnel between the old and new sites.

During the planning step, this team should prepare transportation arrangements. During the emergency, this team is responsible for:

- Arranging for transportation of equipment and backup files and supplies
- Arranging courier schedules
- Arranging for hotel or other temporary accommodations

Data Preparation Team. The objective of this team is to meet data preparation requirements for computer usage.

During the planning step, this team should identify data preparation equipment needed, suppliers of such equipment, telephone numbers of contact persons, list of sites that may be willing to share equipment, data entry/preparation service organizations, and organizations that can supply temporary employees. During the emergency, this team is responsible for:

- Identifying resources available
- Preparing revised data preparation schedules—to be done in association with the operations team so that the data preparation schedules are compatible with computer-run schedules
- Supervising physical transportation of data
- Supervising and providing data preparation support

Data Control Team. The objective of the data control team is to establish the data control function at the backup site for the critical applications. During the planning step, this team is responsible for:

- Preparing a user list of emergency numbers
- Establishing procedures for contacting data control staff at all times of the day
- Off-site storage of data control procedure manuals

During the emergency, this team is responsible for:

- Notifying the data control staff to report to alternate locations
- Notifying users of new locations
- Establishing liaison with the data preparation team
- Resuming input and output control functions

Where the critical applications' processing requirements are small, several teams may be composed of one person each, or they may share personnel. On the other hand, a very large DP installation needs several people on each team. The project team should consider the functions outlined in these guidelines, determine what other functions may be appropriate in the company's environment, and define detailed procedures for them.

An additional consideration in this task is the implementation of modifications to critical systems to enable reduction in resource requirements. The following modifications may be required:

- Change data input from on-line mode to batch mode or vice versa.

- Change processing priorities, sequences, or frequencies.
- Change output dissemination techniques.

Step 6: Making Sure the Plan Works

The most significant task in contingency planning is testing and validating the plan. Most of the work of the project has been planning in nature and does not consider the many problems likely to occur. Nevertheless, it is unwise to rely upon the plan in the absence of a concerted effort to identify any potential problems that inadvertently may have been overlooked. If the plan has been drawn up by several subgroups, it is quite possible that certain key problems have not been identified and that others have fallen through the cracks, because each group assumes that responsibility for resolving the problem belongs to another group. A few tests under controlled conditions may be carried out without seriously disrupting normal computer operations to identify such problems so that the plan may be corrected. The plan can then be relied upon to provide an effective course of action during an actual emergency.

In Step 6, the contingency plan is given a walk-through and/or a live test in order to confirm its procedures. At the same time, maintenance procedures for keeping the contingency plan current are also developed.

The validation process makes use of the contingency plan manuals. A validation group develops a schedule for the walk-through and the live testing. This schedule is used to initiate testing and as a guide to policing, observing, and monitoring the test environment. Once the test is completed, the contingency plan is corrected or modified as necessary.

In order to test the plan effectively, it is necessary to hold these tests without prior announcement. However, such a course of action assumes that the plan is perfect if disruptions to normal operations are minimized. Since initially the project team is unsure of the validity of the contingency plan, it is best to hold one or more preannounced tests in so-called dry runs before running a live test.

In order to minimize costs and disruptions to normal operations, dry runs should simulate limited-scope disasters rather than full-scale disasters. Individual limited-scope emergencies, simulated to cover each component of a DP facility, add up to the simulation of a full-scale facility loss; thus, testing all aspects of the plan through a full-scale loss is likely to cause greater confusion and disruption.

To derive the greatest benefits from the tests and to minimize disruption, it is necessary to orient and train the test team. If the tests simulate partial loss of facilities, then some of the additional teams previously identified may be necessary. For instance, a loss of communication lines requires the participation of the communications team and potentially the data preparation and data control teams.

The tests must be planned so that every aspect of the contingency plan is exercised. During at least one of the tests, the total loss of one or more individual components of the DP facility must be simulated in order for the tests to be exhaustive. The project team should document, for its own use, the procedures in the contingency plan that will be followed for each one of these test disasters.

In the dry run, a written scenario of the disaster should be distributed to employees along with a description of the impact. The disaster can be simulated by shutting down affected components. The project team should observe and log all actions taken by test participants. When the test has been completed, normal operations can be resumed.

The log of actions taken during the test should be compared against the ideal sequence as conceived by the project team. Discrepancies between the two should be examined carefully to identify potential areas of improvement in the contingency plan. In addition, issues that arise during the test but that are not covered in the model test implementation must be reviewed carefully to identify potential gaps in the contingency plan. On the basis of this review, the contingency plan must be revised. The announced tests should be repeated until each aspect of the contingency plan is tested.

The next activity is to hold a live test. The test is not preannounced and may simulate a partial or total disaster. Again, the project team should prepare a model implementation plan prior to the test. The team observes and logs all action taken, compares it against the model implementation plan, and resolves any discrepancies. The test results are discussed among the project staff and with company personnel to identify parts of the contingency plan that need modification. A report is then prepared for the contingency planning committee on the validity of plan.

Step 7: Training Personnel

The purpose of Step 7 is to develop and implement training programs for management, data processing, and user group personnel.

The training requirements for key personnel identified in the development of the contingency plan are used to define the objective and scope of the training programs and to develop the detailed programs.

A simulated resource-loss situation should be part of the training program and used both to update the training programs and the contingency plan itself and to test personnel on their understanding of the plan.

The next task is the development of training programs to train other personnel in the use of the contingency plan. The objectives of training vary with the level of personnel involved because of their varying levels of responsibilities. It is thus necessary to establish initially the responsibilities for each level along the management chain. Careful consideration should be given to the requirements of cross-training so that employee absences do not affect the implementation of the plan. Based on the responsibilities assigned to each level of personnel, training objectives must be developed for each level. Training manuals must be prepared that deal with:

- Terminology
- Personnel responsibilities
- Use of the contingency plan.

Regular and alternate communication channels must be explained, in view of the possible use of a contingency management team that supersedes normal organizational boundaries.

The training procedures and manuals need to be submitted to management for approval. There may be a need to revise the manuals on the basis of management comments.

Training sessions should be observed by a member of the project team to determine the program's effectiveness. The observers should discuss their impressions with the instructors and with the project team so that the training programs can be updated as needed.

As a last step, a report to management should be prepared on the effectiveness of the training programs and on the preparedness of employees to meet emergencies.

REFERENCES

Ernst & Whinney. "EDP Contingency Planning Guide." *System Security Standards for Electronic Data Processing*, rev. ed. The City of New York Department of Investigation, May 1983.

Back-up Resource Pool. DPCS Data Planning Control Systems.

Klein, Ralph L. "Disasters Prevention." *Journal of Systems Management* (Mar. 1983).

Devlin, Edward S. Devlin Associates, Inc. "Developing the Disaster Recovery Plan."

Index

[*Chapter numbers are boldface and are followed by a colon; lightface numbers after the colon refer to pages within the chapter; italic numbers after the colon refer to figures.*]

A

Access
  to computers, types of, **22**:8
  controlling, re computers, **22**:3–8
  to data, **5**:15–16
  data security, **5**:15–16, **22**:7–8
Accountability
  in computer access, **22**:3
  controls, elements, **10**:11–12
  control techniques, **10**:29–30
Accounting
  packaged programs, **7**:13–15
  responsibility, defined, **12**:12–13
Accounting control
  defined, **10**:4–5
  principles, **12**:12–13
Accounting information system (AIS), **1**:7–8
Accounting packages
  assistance sources, **7**:13–14
  features, desirable, **7**:14–15
Accounting standards, of FCPA, **10**:8–9
Accounting systems, **6**:1–31
  See also Financial accounting system
Accounts payable system, **6**:18–32
  check reconciliation, **6**:21
  integration with purchasing and receiving, **6**:20–21
  major files, **6**:20
  packages, features of, **7**:14
  purpose, **6**:18
  reports, **6**:21–22
  system features, **6**:21–22
Accounts receivable system, **6**:22–25
  balance forward system, **6**:23
  balance only system, **6**:23
  features, **6**:25
  interfaces, **6**:24

  open item system, **6**:23–24
  packages, features of, **7**:14
  purpose, **6**:22–23
  reporting, **6**:24–25
  types, **6**:23–24
Accuracy
  in data, **5**:9–10
  plan requirements, **12**:6
Activity measures for determining variable costs, **12**:15
Actual costs, defined, **12**:8
Administrative control, defined, **10**:4
Advanced materials technology, **2**:4
AIS. *See* Accounting information system
Allin Industries, DBMS, example, **8**:6–8
American Institute of Certified Public Accountants (AICPA), controls, definitions of, **10**:4–6
American Telephone & Telegraph Company, **9**:3
Annual business plan
  See also Annual plan
  measures of acceptability, **13**:23
  actual vs. planned performance, **13**:35–62
  reports on contents, **13**:23
  and FISs, **13**:23–35
Annual plan
  cash plan, **13**:28
  changes in income, reasons for, **13**:25–27
  financial position plan, **13**:28–29
  purpose, **12**:2–3
  reports, subjects to discuss, **13**:33
  strategic plan re, **12**:5
Application projects in LRSP, **11**:11–16
Applications, widening, and FISs, **2**:13, **18**:36–37

I-1

I-2   INDEX

[*Chapter numbers are boldface and are followed by a colon; lightface numbers after the colon refer to pages within the chapter; italic numbers after the colon refer to figures.*]

Application software
  See also Software
  features needed, **17**:16–17
  guidelines for selecting, **17**:18–19
  RFP, review of, **17**:16–19
Application software team for disaster recovery, **23**:18
Application technology, **2**:5
Assumptions as report content, **13**:9–10
Audio teleconferencing, **21**:16
Auditability
  concept, **10**:14
  defined, **10**:6
Audits, security, need for, **22**:14
Audit trails
  re computer security, **22**:9
  in GLS, **6**:10–11
  requirements for, **8**:33
Authorization
  concept, **10**:10–11
  techniques to assure, **10**:25–26
Automation, office. *See* Office automation

B

Babbage, Charles, role in FISs, **2**:6
Backup features for security, **8**:32–33
Backup system, defined, **7**:20
Balance sheet, applicability of budgeting, **12**:31, 35–38
Baseband signalling schemes, **9**:15
Board of directors
  annual plan, report on, **13**:*23–32, 34, 35,* **13**:23–35
  function, **7**:8–9
  long-range plan, report on, **13**:8–24, **13**:*11*
Borrowing capacity
  annual plan, report contained in, **13**:33–34
Broadband signalling schemes, **9**:15
Budgeting
  See also Budgets
  defined, **12**:25–26

determining semivariable costs, **12**:15–24
  GLS application, **6**:13–16
Budgets
  administrative type, **12**:28
  applicability to financial position, **12**:31, 35–38
  extraordinary costs, treatment of, **12**:24
  fixed type, **12**:28–30
  flexible, **12**:28–34
  project type, **12**:26–28
  re standard costs, **12**:25
  types of, **12**:26
  variable, **12**:28–34
Bulletin boards, electronic, **5**:3
Business factors
  for success
    reported on, **8**:6, **13**.39–54
    use in models, **5**:4
Business management
  See also Management
  microcomputers, impact on, **7**:2–3
  success factors, **8**:6
  use of FISs, **3**:1–25
Business, nature of, as factor in DP organization structure, **4**:10–12
Business model
  See also Model
  critical success factors, role in, **5**:4
Business organization structure, influence of on DP organization, **4**:11
Business plans, system of, **12**:2–3
Business purpose, **3**:2
Business success
  information quality as factor, **1**:12
  management factor, **1**:12–15
Byte, defined, **7**:5

C

CAATs. *See* Computer-assisted audit techniques
Calendaring systems, **21**:13
Cash flow, systems output, **6**:25
Cash reports
  annual business plan, **13**:28

INDEX

I-3

[*Chapter numbers are boldface and are followed by a colon; lightface numbers after the colon refer to pages within the chapter; italic numbers after the colon refer to figures.*]

control type, **13:**57, 61
long-range financial plan, **13:**17
Cathode ray tube (CRT). *See* Microcomputers, monitors
Centralized data processing
  described, **2:**8–9
  organization structure, **4:**3–6
CFO. *See* Chief financial officer
Changes, impact of on FISs, **1:**15–17
Chart of accounts, structuring, **6:**6–8
Chief financial officer (CFO)
  See also Financial executive; Financial manager
  basic functions, **13:**3
  CIO, **4:**9–10
  DSS, types for support of, **16:**8
  DSS development, role in, **16:**7
  duties and responsibilities, **13:**3–5
  FIS responsibilities, **5:**1–2, **13:**3–5
  functional outline, **13:**3–5
  groups needing data from, **13:**6–8
  reports for
    accounts receivable budget, **12:**36
    cash budget, **12:**35
  service function to management, **13:**3
Chief information officer (CIO)
  CFO re, **4:**9–10
  functions, **4:**8–9
  LRSP, role in, **11:**5
  systems technology, 2:17–18
CIO. *See* Chief information officer
Class training
  optimum conditions, **20:**9–11
  types of, **20:**17–18
Communications
  computers, use in, **21:**7–8
  evolution of, **9:**8–10
Communications systems
  networking, **9:**1–23
  planning steps, **9:**11–12
Communications team for disaster recovery, **23:**19
Comparative reporting, **13:***39–53*
Complaints, common re FISs, **18:**11–12
Components technologies, **2:**3–5
Computer application controls, **10:**5

Computer-assisted audit techniques (CAATs), **10:**38
Computer-based financial modeling, **15:**1–20
  See also Financial modeling; Model
Computer-based message systems, **21:**14–15
Computer-based telephone, advantages, **9:**9
Computer contingency planning
  See also Contingency planning
  benefits, **23:**8
Computer general controls, **10:**5
Computer illiteracy, **2:**11
Computer operations, disaster recovery, **23:**1–23
Computers
  controls, importance of, **20:**7–8
  support for group work, **21:**6–7
Computer science, defined, **2:**2–3
Computer security, **7:**19–20
  characteristics desired, **22:**2–3
  checklist, **22:**12–14
  controlling access, **22:**3–8
  defined, **22:**2
  log, **22:**10–11
  maintenance authorization, **22:**8
  for on-line systems, **22:**1–14
  passwords, **22:**5–7
  principal features, **22:**11–12
  response to violations, **22:**10
  "Six O's," **22:**2
  surveillance objectives, **22:**9
  terminal identification, **22:**4
  user identification, **22:**4–5
  user IDs, **22:**3–7
Computer security administrator, duties, **22:**8
Computer technology for DSS, **16:**2
Computer teleconferencing, **21:**16
Consultants, for performing PIR, **18:**36
Context MBA, **15:**13
Contingency planning
  See also Disaster recovery
  disaster recovery, **23:**1–23
  team organization, **23:**15–21

I-4   INDEX

[*Chapter numbers are boldface and are followed by a colon; lightface numbers after the colon refer to pages within the chapter; italic numbers after the colon refer to figures.*]

Contracts
  negotiating team for FISs, **17**:24
Contract terms for FISs, **17**:23–26
Contribution margin, defined, significance, **12**:10–11
Control
  See also Controls
  computer access, **23**:3–14
  cost classifications for, **12**:11–14
  DBMS, role in, **8**:4
  defined, **3**:6
  information needs for, **3**:7–8
  information systems, overview of, **10**:2–3
  version, described, **5**:16–17
Controls
  for accountability, **10**:11–12
  computer, importance of, **20**:7–8
  for computer processing, **10**:5
  for database integrity, **8**:27–28
  for data processing, **10**:12, 15–16
  EDP type, **10**:5–6, 15–16
  FCPA, applicability, **10**:6–9
Control systems, variability of, **10**:9–15
Coordinating, defined, **3**:5
Core financial systems
  See also Financial accounting system
  interface problems, **6**:30–31
  planning vs. control, **12**:2
  purpose, **6**:2–4
Corporate goals, examples, **11**:10
Corporate MBA, package described, **15**:14
Corporate mission, example, **11**:9–10
Corporate strategic plan
  LRSP re, **11**:14–15
  segments of, **11**:9–10
Cost accounting, GLS application, **6**:16–17
Cost allocation on GLS, **6**:15–17
Cost/benefit analysis, user participation, **18**:33–34
Cost classifications for planning, **12**:8
Cost components, graphic determination, **12**:22–24
Costs
  See also various costs
  automation, office, justification for, **21**:21–22
  for control purposes, **12**:11–14
  of database software, **8**:20–21
  of an FIS, **17**:22–23
  for planning purposes, **12**:8–9
  segregation into components, **12**:14–25
  semivariable, determining, **12**:15–24
  types of, determining, **12**:6–8, 14–25
  volume re, **12**:9–10
Current ratio, report on, **13**:18, 22

D

Data
  See also Databas
  access guidelines, **22**:7–8
  access restrictions, **5**:15–16
  accuracy, relevance, **5**:9–10
  defined, **8**:9
  organization of, **5**:7–9
  protection of, **5**:17–18
  relevance re organization level, **5**:6
  sources for, **5**:7
  timeliness, importance of, **5**:19–20
Database
  categories of data needed, **13**:3
  classifications of, **8**:15–19
  defined, **5**:5–6, **7**:11, **8**:8
  design
    basic concepts, **8**:12–13
    desirable characteristics, **8**:14–15
    LRSP re, **8**:13–14
    organization for, **8**:14–15
  entry, **6**:8–10
  environment, elements of, **8**:10–12
    fourth-generation languages re, **8**:19–20
    GLS, **6**:4–6
    general ledger updating, **6**:8–10
    hierarchical, **8**:15–16
    integrity, maintaining management responsibility for, **8**:29
    machines, defined, **8**:26
    maintenance, **5**:10
Data base administrator (DBA), defined, **8**:10
Database management, **8**:1–35
  See also Data Base Management System

INDEX

I-5

[*Chapter numbers are boldface and are followed by a colon; lightface numbers after the colon refer to pages within the chapter; italic numbers after the colon refer to figures.*]

advantages, **8**:3–5
benefits, **8**:3–5
components, **8**:2
disadvantages, **8**:5–6
distribution (of data) management,
    5:18–20
evolution of, **8**:2–3
future trends, **8**:33–34
illustrative system, **8**:6–8
need for, **2**:12, **5**:7–9
programs, **7**:11–13
relational method, **5**:8–9
Data Base Management System (DBMS)
    defined, **8**:8
    disadvantages, **8**:5–6
    DSS, relationship to, **16**:9–11
    functions included, **8**:8
    need for, **2**:12
    productivity, role in, **8**:4–5
    security re operating system, **8**:29–30
Database networks
    advantages, **8**:16–17
    disadvantages, **8**:17
Database organization, functions of,
    8:10–12
Databases
    public, examples of, **21**:17–18
    relational, defined, **8**:17–19
    security, **8**:29–33
    software
        classifications of, **8**:20–24
        costs, relative, **8**:20–21
        selection, factors in, **8**:24–26
        systems, **8**:20–24
    version control, **5**:16–17
Data center, risks, **23**:2–4
Data communications
    networks, benefits of, **9**:10
    overview, **9**:1–3
Data control team for disaster recovery,
    23:20
Data definition language, defined, **8**:8–9
Data dictionary, defined, **8**:9
Data distribution
    means of, **5**:19
    selection of data, **5**:18–19
    timeliness, **5**:19–20
Data element, defined, **8**:9
Data management

accuracy, relevance, **5**:9–10
base maintenance, **5**:10
data sources, **5**:7
DSS design, factors in, **16**:9
need for, **5**:5
organization as factor, **5**:7–8
overview, **5**:5–10
relevant data, **5**:5–6
security element, **5**:14–18
Data organization methods, **8**:2–3
Data preparation team for disaster
    recovery, **23**:20
Data processing, disaster recovery,
    23:1–23
    DP personnel vs. user, **18**:18–20
    security system elements, **10**:12–13
    steering committee, role in LRSP, **11**:5
    user relationships, barrier to, **18**:18–19
Data processing department
    administrative group, **4**:17
    centralized structure, **4**:3
    CIO, role of, **4**:8–10
    component groupings, **4**:15–18
    decentralized structure, **4**:4–6
    distributed structure, **4**:4–7
    factors influencing structure, **4**:10–15
    federated structure, **4**:7–8
    importance of, **23**:5–6
    internal organization structure, **4**:15–18
    operations group, **4**:16–17
    organization concepts, **4**:2
    organization structures
        alternative, **4**:3–8
        for, **4**:1–18
    scientific programming group, **4**:18
    structures, organization, **4**:1–18
        cultural factors, **4**:13–14
        development factors, **4**:12
        economic factors, **4**:13
        people location factor, **4**:11–12
        political factors, **4**:13–14
        senior-management factor, **4**:12
Data security
    See also Security
    security program, **5**:15–18
DBMS. *See* Data Base Management
    System
Decentralized data processing, **4**:4–6

[*Chapter numbers are boldface and are followed by a colon; lightface numbers after the colon refer to pages within the chapter; italic numbers after the colon refer to figures.*]

Decision makers, knowledge needed by, **1**:2–3
Decision making
 steps in process, **3**:6–7
 use of models, **15**:3
Decision support systems (DSS), **16**:1–21
 benefits of, **16**:18–20
 building blocks for, **16**:2–3
 components, major, **16**:9–11
 database re, **16**:9–10
 defined, **16**:2
 design, **16**:1–9
  areas for, **16**:9
  criteria, **16**:8–9
  objectives, **16**:7–9
 development, **16**:9–14
 evaluation, **16**:17–19
 facilitator, defined, **16**:6
 flexibility levels, **16**:13
 function, **16**:2
 generators, described, **16**:4
 implementation
  general discussion, **16**:14–17
  phased, **16**:16
 integration, steps in, **16**:14–17
 interactive design, need for, **16**:5, 12–13
 manager, role of, **16**:5–6
 model generators, **16**:12
 modeling re, **16**:10
 prototypes for, **16**:13–14
 requirements of, **16**:7–8
 software, criteria for, **16**:17–19
 support, **16**:7–8
 technicians, role of, **16**:5–6
 technology levels, **16**:4
 tools, **16**:4
 trends, **16**:18–20
Depreciation, fixed asset system, **6**:29
Design team, user representatives, **18**:31–32
Detection re computer security, **22**:9
Developments in financial modeling, **15**:19
Direct costs, defined, **12**:7
Directing, defined, **3**:6

Disaster recovery, **23**:1–23
 See also Contingency planning
 analyzing risks, **12**:14–15
 application software team, **23**:18
 communications team, **23**:19
 data control team, **23**:20
 data preparation team, **23**:20
 determining resources, **23**:12–13
 developing plan, **23**:15–21
 facilities administration team, **23**:17
 getting started, **23**:9–10
 hardware team, **23**:19
 importance of, reasons for, **23**:2–5
 logistics team, **23**:19
 methodology, **23**:7–8
 objectives, **23**:5–7
 operations team, **23**:18
 organization structure, **23**:15–21
 planning, steps in, **23**:7–8
 priorities, establishing, **23**:10–12
 salvage team, **23**:16
 scope of discussions, **23**:2
 steps in plan, **23**:6
 systems software team, **23**:17
 testing the plan, **23**:21–22
 training personnel, **23**:22–23
Diskettes, function of, **7**:5
Disk storage, **7**:5
Disk-storage technology, **2**:4
Distributed data processing, **4**:4–7
Distribution management of data, **5**:18–20
Division managers, information needs, **13**:7
Documents
 basic operation, **21**:4–5
 elements of, **21**:5
 financial models for, **15**:6
 management of, **21**:4–5
 systems in use, **17**:8
 user, **18**:10
Downloading, defined, **19**:2
DP. *See* Data processing
DSS. *See* Decision support systems

INDEX

I-7

[*Chapter numbers are boldface and are followed by a colon; lightface numbers after the colon refer to pages within the chapter; italic numbers after the colon refer to figures.*]

E

Earnings per share, reports on various scenarios, **13**:16–17
Economics, factor in DP department structure, **4**:13
Electronic bulletin boards, **21**:16
EDP. *See* Electronic data processing
EDP department, impact of technology on, **2**:15–16
EDP steering committee
 function, **2**:17–18
 systems technology, impact on, **2**:17–18
Electronic data processing (EDP)
 auditing
  growth, **10**:33–34
  types, **10**:33–38
 contingency planning method, **23**:8
 controls, applicability, **10**:6
 internal control environment, **10**:15–16
 organization growth, **10**:2–4
 security
  objectives, **10**:30
  risks, **10**:16–22
Electronic filing, **21**:12–13
Electronic mail, **21**:14–15
 mailbox, **21**:14
 wastebasket function, **21**:14
Embedded audit routine, **10**:35–37
Encore! package, **15**:15
ENIAC (Electronic Numerical Integrator & Computer), **2**:6
Environment, current, and FISs, **1**:10–15
Enterprise model. *See* Model
Ernst & Whinney, LAN case study, **9**:18–23
Evolution
 forces of, re FISs, **1**:9–10, **1**:*12–15*
 impact of on MIS department, **2**:6–7, 16–17
Exception reports
 audit trail, **6**:10–11, **6**:*11*
 defined, **3**:17, **3**:*19*, **5**:13–14
Executive information system, **7**:*18*
Executive support system, defined, **5**:5

Expert system, role, **5**:5
Extraordinary costs, budget for, **12**:24

F

Facilitator (DSS), defined, **16**:6
Facilities administration team for disaster recovery, **23**:17
Failure of systems, reasons for, **18**:12–17
FCPA. *See* Foreign Corrupt Practices Act
FCS-EPS modeling package, **15**:16
Federated data processing, **4**:7–8
Feedback reporting
 See also Reports
 essential elements, **5**:11–13
 precautions, **5**:10–8
Fiber optics technology, **2**:4
File, defined, **8**:9
Financial accounting system
 accounts payable, **6**:18–22
 accounts receivable, **6**:22–25
 basic systems, **6**:2–4
 core systems, **6**:2–4
 developments, current, **6**:30–31
 fixed assets, **6**:27–30
 general ledger, **6**:1–31
 interface problems, **6**:30–31
 payroll, **6**:25–27
 reevaluation process, **6**:31
 software programs, **7**:13
 subsidiary ledger, **6**:2
Financial condition
 annual plan, report on, **13**:28–29
 daily report on, **13**:59–60
 long-range plan, report on, **13**:18–20
Financial database, content, **8**:8
 See also Database
Financial executive
 See also Financial manager
 database areas to manage, **8**:27–29
 FIS
  knowledge required re, **1**:2–3
  responsibility for, **5**:1–2
 systems evolution, impact on, **2**:16–17
Financial information system (FIS)
 See also specific subject headings

[*Chapter numbers are boldface and are followed by a colon; lightface numbers after the colon refer to pages within the chapter; italic numbers after the colon refer to figures.*]

Financial information system (FIS) (*cont'd*)
  defined, **1:**6–7, **7:**15
  failure, reasons for, **18:**12–17
  groups needing, **13:**6–8
  integration, need for, **2:**11–12
  key ingredients, **5:**1–20
  knowledge required for, **1:**2–3
  overview, **1:**1–18
  perspective, **1:**8–15
  selection and implementation, **17:**1–34
  trends, **2:**14–15
  types, **18:**36–37
Financial manager
  LANs, knowledge needed re, **9:**17–18
  reports for, **13:**1–63
    cash, weekly, **13:**61
    expense summaries by department, **14:**35
    short-term investments, **13:**62
    special analyses, **13:**62–63
    subjects for, **13:**59–62
    time, use of re, **9:**8–9
Financial modeling, **15:**1–20
  application of, **15:**2–3
  developing, **15:**5–6
  developments, future, **15:**19
  documentation needs, **15:**6
  guidelines for designing, **15:**18–19
  key issues in, **15:**4
  need for, **15:**2
  packages for minicomputers or mainframes, **15:**16–18
  process, steps in, **15:**3–6
  report requirements, establishing, **15:**4
  software selection, **15:**5
  software packages, **15:**11–15
  specifications, developing, **15:**4–5
  techniques, **15:**6–10
  uses of, **15:**2–3
Financial planning
  See also Planning
  microcomputer software packages, **15:**11–18
Financial position
  See also Financial condition
  applicability of budgeting, **12:**31, 35–38

  reports
    annual plan, **13:**29
    re long-range, **13:**18–20
Financial reports
  See also Reports
  evolution in, **1:**12–14
FIS. *See* Financial information system
Fixed assets system, **6:**27–30
  features, **6:**27–31
  process flow, **6:**27–28
  purposes, **6:**27–28
Fixed costs
  defined, **12:**7
  method of determining, **12:**14
Flash report, defined, **3:**22, **3:***22*
Flexible budget, **12:***30–34*
  See also Variable budget
  advantages, **12:**30–31
  defined, **12:**28–31
FOCUS, modeling package, **15:***17*
Foreign Corrupt Practices Act (FCPA)
  accounting standards, **10:**8–9
  controls, applicability, **10:**6–9
Fourth-generation language
  database re, **8:**19–20
  DBMS, role in, **8:**4
Full-text search technique, **21:**13
Function, factor in information needs, **3:**7–9
Functional organization, information needs as factor in, **3:**15

G

General and administrative management
  See also Board of directors
  reports for
    budget summary
      by department, **3:**18
      by function, **14:**34
    expense summary
      by department, **14:**35
      by type, **14:**36
General ledger systems (GLS), **6:**3–18
  audit trails, **6:**10–11
  budgeting applications, **6:**13–16
  chart of accounts, **6:**6–8

INDEX

I-9

[Chapter numbers are boldface and are followed by a colon; lightface numbers after the colon refer to pages within the chapter; italic numbers after the colon refer to figures.]

cost accounting, **6:**16–17
cost allocations, **6:**15–17
database, **6:**4–6
data entry, **6:**8–10
data update, **6:**8–10
features, **6:**19
journal entries, **6:**8–10
on-line access, **6:**6
overlapping reporting, **6:**7–8
packages, desirable features, **7:**15
processing flow, **6:**4–6
reports, types, **6:**11–13
systems security, **6:**17–18
GLS. *See* general ledger systems
Goals
   directing to meet, **3:**6
   organizing to meet, **3:**5
Graphic determination, fixed and variable costs, **12:**22–24
Graphs, use of in calculating cost elements, **12:**22–24
Growth, impact of on FISs, **1:**9–15, **2:**2
Guidelines
   financial modeling, **15:**18–19
   password security, **22:**5–7
   for RFP, **17:**11

H

Hardware
   contract negotiations, **17:**23–26
   defined, **7:**3–4
   site visits, **17:**21–22
   vendor evaluation, **17:**21–22
Hardware team for disaster recovery, **23:**19
Hierarchical databases, defined, **8:**15–16
Highlights
   annual business plan content, **13:**24
   long-range financial plan content, **13:**10
Historical perspective of FISs, **1:**8–15
Hollerith, Herman, role in FISs, **2:**6
Human resource investments, scope, **21:**3

I

IFPS (Interactive Financial Planning System), **15:**16–17
IFDS/Personal, **15:**14
Implementation
   See also Systems implementation of FISs
   failure, reasons for, **17:**28
   steps in, **17:**29
   user participation in, **18:**34–35
Incremental costs, defined, **12:**7
Indicators, key, role in business, **5:**4
Indirect costs, defined, **12:**7
Information
   as factor in business success, **1:**10–12
   key properties, **3:**12–13
   quality of as success factor, **1:**12
   relevance, **3:**12
   timeliness, **3:**12
Information centers, **19:**1–8
   applications, **19:**3–4
   database software, **8:**20
   defined, **18:**21–22, **19:**1–2
   dos and don'ts, **19:**7–8
   examples, **19:**4–7
   future status, **19:**7
   growth in, **19:**2–3
   types, **19:**2
Information flows
   See also Information networks
   formal, **3:**11–12
   horizontal, **3:**9–12
   informal, **3:**9–11
   networks, types of, **3:**9–12
   vertical, **3:**9–11
Information needs
   board of directors, **13:**7
   control for, **3:**7–8
   criteria for, **3:**12–13
   DBMs and changes, **8:**3
   division managers, **13:**7
   financial groups, **13:**6–8
   financial managers, **13:**1–63
   functional managers, **13:**7–8
   influences
      function as factor, **3:**7–9
      managerial activity as factor, **3:**15
      managerial level as factor, **3:**7, **13:**13–14

[*Chapter numbers are boldface and are followed by a colon; lightface numbers after the colon refer to pages within the chapter; italic numbers after the colon refer to figures.*]

Information needs *(cont'd)*
 influences *(cont'd)*
  organization structure as factor, **3**:14–15
  nature of function as factor, **3**:15
  nature of problem, **3**:7
  resource type as factor, **3**:7–9
 management
  lower, **13**:8
  top, **13**:7
 manufacturing manager, **14**:15, 18–19
 marketing manager, **14**:3–5
 planning for, **3**:7–8
 plans, for different types of, **12**:3–6
 properties, key, **3**:12–13
 types of, **3**:12–13
Information networks, **9**:1-23
 See also Information flows
 types, **3**:9–12
Information officer. *See* Chief information officer
Information overload, defined, **5**:7, 13
Information sources, for planning, **12**:5
Information systems (IS)
 See also Data processing department
 auditability and control, **10**:1–41
 auditing of, **10**:33–37
 components of LRSP, **11**:6
 contingency planning, **23**:1–23
 control objectives, **10**:23–40
 controls, reasons for absence of, **10**:2–4
 control techniques, **10**:26–33
 costs of not planning, **11**:2–3
 defined, **1**:4, 6
 defining hardware and communications architecture, **11**:21–23
 laws, **10**:20–21
 LRSP, **11**:1–33
 management's queries re, **10**:21–22
 planning, benefits of, **11**:3–4
 projects, defining, **11**:20–21
 security, control techniques, **10**:30–33
Input for different plans, **12**:3–6
Integrated programs, **7**:12
Integration technology, **2**:3–4
 large-scale (LSI), defined, **2**:3–4
 very large scale (VLSI), defined, **2**:3–4

Integrity of database, maintaining, **8**:26–33
Interactive design, **16**:12–13
Interfaces in DSS design, **16**:9
 man-machine in LRSP, **11**:19–20
Internal auditing, **10**:33–37
 application auditing, **10**:35
 CAATs, **10**:37
 concurrent auditing, **10**:35–36
 control techniques for PCs, **10**:37–40
 developing systems, **10**:35
 embedded audit routines, **10**:37–39
 PIRs, **18**:36
Internal control
 authorization techniques, **10**:25–26
 defined, **10**:4
 EDP environment, special features, **10**:15–16
 reasonable assurance, **10**:13–14
Interviews for Systems Requirement Definition, **17**:5–7
Inventory packages, desirable features, **7**:14–15
IS. *See* Information systems

J

Journal entries, types, **6**:8–10

K

Keyboards, function, **7**:5–6
Key indicators, role in business, **5**:4

L

LANs. *See* Local area networks
Large-scale development software, **8**:22–23
Least squares method for determining cost behavior, **12**:24
Local area networks (LANs), **7**:16–17
 access methods, **9**:16–17
 advantages, **9**:14, 18
 applicability, **7**:17
 baseband signalling scheme, **9**:15

INDEX

I-11

[*Chapter numbers are boldface and are followed by a colon; lightface numbers after the colon refer to pages within the chapter; italic numbers after the colon refer to figures.*]

broadband signalling scheme, **9:**15
carrier sense, multiple access/collision detection access method (CSMA/C), **9:**16–17
case study by Ernst & Whinney's National Systems Group, **9:**18–23
characteristics, **9:**14
components, **9:**13
configurations, **9:**15–16
defined, **2:**4
features, **9:**14
and FISs, **7:**16–17
functions, **7:**16–17
installation, typical, **7:**16
overview, **9:**12–13
planning for, **9:**17–18
signalling schemes, **9:**15
token passing access method, **9:**16
topologies, **9:**15–16
Log, security, contents, **22:**10–11
Logistics team for disaster recovery, **23:**19
Long-range financial plan
assumptions, **13:**9–10
content, report, **13:**8–9
highlights, **13:***10–11*
report, **13:**8–24, **13:***11*
sales data, **13:**10–14
Long-range systems plan (LRSP), **11:**1–33
See also Information systems planning
application, defining projects, **11:**11–16
beginning, **11:**8–9
benefits of, **11:**32
communications architecture, defining, **11:**21–23
components of, **11:**6
contents of plan, **11:**8
corporate strategic plan re, **11:**9–10, 14–15
criteria for use, **11:**3–4
development, steps in, **11:**6–30
hardware, defining, **11:**21–23
implementation plan, developing, **11:**26–28
implementing, **11:**30–31
man-machine interface, **11:**19–20
not planning, impact, **11:**2–3
organization for, **11:**4–5

planning horizon, **11:**5–6
personnel, defining, **11:**23–24
projects, defining, **11:**20–21
revision of, **11:**31–32
software architecture, **11:**15–17
Long-term debt, report on (LRP), **13:**18, 22
Lotus 1-2-3
function, **7:**11
spreadsheet package described, **15:**12
LRSP. See Long-range systems plan

M

Mainframes in FISs, **7:**17–18
Maintenance of FISs, **2:**10–11
Management
See also Information needs
activity as factor in information needs, **3:**13–14
database integrity, responsibility of for, **8:**29
decisions, types of, **3:**6–9
DSS development, role in, **16:**5–6
FISs, role and functions re, **3:**1–25, **5:**10–14, **18:**24–26
information needs, **3:**7–10
involvement needed, **18:**37, **21:**3
knowledge required, **1:**2–3
levels, impact on information needs, **3:**7–8
MISs
defined, **1:**3–4
impact of on, **2:**15–18
nonfinancial, use of financial reports, **14:**1–37
personnel, selection of, **18:**26
reports
income and expense, **13:**52–54
long-range financial plan, **13:***8–24*
performance, by group, **13:**25–26
performance summary, **13:***39–54*, **13:**40
return on assets, **13:***18, 21*
return on shareholders' equity, **13:***18, 21*
role of, **18:**24–26
support needed, **17:**27, **21:**27–28
task, **3:**2–3

[*Chapter numbers are boldface and are followed by a colon; lightface numbers after the colon refer to pages within the chapter; italic numbers after the colon refer to figures.*]

Management *(cont'd)*
  training in computer use, **20**:3–4
  use of FISs, **3**:1–25
Management information system (MIS),
    defined, **1**:3–4
Manufacturing manager, reports for
  capital budget, **14**:29
  costs, departmental vs. budget, **3**:19,
      14:21
  cost summary by department, **14**:20
  exception, **3**:*19*
  exception, labor, **14**:*23*
  expenses, budget, **12**:18–19
  expense summary by department,
      14:23
  information needs, **14**:15, 18–19
  labor, daily
    by department, **14**:26
    exception, **14**:23
  labor efficiency, trend, **14**:22
  material
    excess, **14**:25
    unit standard cost changes, **14**:26
  material inventory vs. budget, **12**:3
  material price variance, **14**:24
  material usage trend, **14**:22
Margin, contribution and significance,
    12:10–11
Marginal costs, defined, **12**:7
Marginal income, **12**:*11*
Marketing management
  information needs, **14**:3–5
  marketing objectives, **14**:3
  reports for
    acquisitions, **13**:*43*
    advertising and sales promotion
        budget, **12**:27
    division summary, **12**:34
    exception, **13**:*46, 51*
    expense
      summary budget, **12**:29
      by type, **12**:30
    financial types for, **14**:2–17
    flexible budget, **12**:32
    marginal income by product line,
        12:11
    market research project budget, **14**:8
    needs, **14**:3–5
    operating income by product line,
        12:11
    by organization, budget, **14**:8
    product-line expense, **14**:7
    sales
      annual plan, **13**:44–45
      long-range, **13**:10–14
    sales backlog, **13**:*14, 47–48*
    sales performance
      by division, **14**:11
      exception, **14**:13
      graphic, **14**:9
    by salesperson, sales and expenses,
        14:14
    sales summary, **3**:*21*
    selling expenses
      by district, **14**:16
      by type, **14**:17
    territorial income and expense, **14**:6
Marketing objectives, **14**:3
Measurement
  defined, **3**:6
  problems to avoid, **12**:13–14
Memory technology, **2**:4
Microcomputers
  See also Software
  boards, **7**:8–9
  business
    impact on, **7**:2–3
    role in, **7**:1–22
  disks, **7**:5
  re FISs, **7**:15–19
  hardware, **7**:3–4
  keyboards, **7**:5–6
  manufacturers, **7**:3–4
  monitors, **7**:6
  vs. personal computers, **7**:2
  printers, **7**:6–8
  small business, impact on, **7**:2
  software, **7**:9–10
    application software, **7**:11–13
    packages for modeling, **15**:11–18
    systems, **7**:10–11
  training, **7**:21–22
Micro DSS/F, **15**:12
Micro FCS, **15**:14
Microprocessor
  defined, **7**:4–5
  technologies, **2**:3

INDEX

I-13

[Chapter numbers are boldface and are followed by a colon; lightface numbers after the colon refer to pages within the chapter; italic numbers after the colon refer to figures.]

Mindware, defined, **21**:6
MIS. *See* Management information system
Model
  business, components of, **5**:2–5
  critical success factor, **5**:4
  culture as factor in, **5**:3
  defined, **5**:2
  development, methods, **16**:11–12
  DSS, specific for, **16**:12
  enterprise, components of, **5**:2–5
  expert system, role of, **5**:5
  general purpose, **16**:11
  organization as factor, **5**:3
  policies and procedures as factors, **5**:3
  software, **15**:5
  training, **20**:10
Model generators (for DSS), defined, **16**:12
Modeling
  DSS re, **16**:10–11
  languages, software packages, **15**:11
  techniques
    goal-seeking analysis, **15**:10
    multiple regression, **15**:9
    naïve forecasting, **15**:6–7
    optimizing, **15**:10
    overview, **15**:7–8
    risk analysis, **15**:10
    sensitivity analysis, **15**:9–10
    univariate analysis, **15**:9
    "what-if" analysis, **15**:6
MSA/Forecasting and Modeling system, **15**:17
Multiplan, **15**:13
Multiple regression in financial modeling, **15**:7, 9

N

Naïve forecasting modeling technique, **15**:6–7
Networks
  database, **8**:15–17
  technology, **2**:4
Nonprocedural language. *See* Fourth-generation language

Northrop Corporation, information center, **19**:4–5
Northwestern National Bank Building, disaster plan, **23**:4

O

Objectives
  in design of DSS, **16**:7–9
  FIS, management review of, **18**:25
Occurrence as factor in report design, **3**:*16*, 19
Office automation, **21**:1–35
  See also Automation, office; Office technologies
  access, **21**:20
  advantages, **9**:10
  availability, **21**:20–21
  calendaring systems, **21**:13
  characteristics, **21**:2–8
  as competitive edge, **21**:7–8
  connectivity, **21**:19
  consultants, source of, **21**:35
  cost justification, **21**:21–22
  defined, **9**:7 **21**:2–8
  disciplines involved, **21**:34
  documents, compound, **21**:5
  elements, **21**:8–11
  failure to plan, **21**:22–23
  issues, key, **21**:19–21
  justification, value added approach, **21**:22
  "people" issues, **21**:19, 27–29
  personal computing, **21**:18–19
  pilot project, selecting, **21**:25, 29–30
  pitfalls, **21**:22–34
  planning, key questions, **21**:23–25
  political issues, **21**:27–32
  privacy, defined, **21**:21
  productivity re, **21**:2–4
  productivity applications, **21**:31
  proliferation as factor, **21**:30
  revisability, **21**:19–20
  scope of, **21**:33
  security, defined, **21**:31
  steering committee, composition, **21**:29
  strategic objectives, **21**:26
  support infrastructure, **21**:20
  technologies involved, **9**:7, **21**:4–5, 32

[*Chapter numbers are boldface and are followed by a colon; lightface numbers after the colon refer to pages within the chapter; italic numbers after the colon refer to figures.*]

Office automation *(cont'd)*
  telecommunications, **21**:14–19
  telecommuting, **21**:18
  teleconferencing, **21**:15–17
  trends, **21**:19–20
  usability, **21**:21
  vendor selection, **21**:31–32
  voice mail, **21**:15
"Office of the future," segments, **9**:9–12
Office technologies
  components, **21**:32
  defined, **21**:11
  electronic filing, **21**:12–13
  electronic mail, **21**:14–15
  as power tool, **21**:6
  support for intellectual work, **21**:5–6
  telecommunications, **21**:14–19
  telecommuting, **21**:18
  teleconferencing, **21**:15–17
  types, **21**:11–19
  voice mail, **21**:15
  word processing for, **21**:11–12
Operations team for disaster recovery, **23**:18
Opportunity costs, defined, **12**:8
Optimization in financial modeling, **15**:8–10
Organization
  common characteristics, **3**:5
  and data relevance, **5**:6
  data structure, impact on, **5**:7–9
  design and productivity, **21**:8–10
  for disaster recovery, **23**:15–21
  EDP evaluation, **10**:2–3
  FISs, impact on, **1**:15–17
  model, element of, **5**:3
Organization structures
  See also Organization
  for data processing, **4**:1–18
  FISs, impact, **2**:15–18
  information needs, factor in, **3**:14–15
  for internal data processing, **4**:15–18
  IS, long-range plan, **11**:4–5
  IS department, **4**:1–18
  MISs, effect on, **2**:15–18
Organizing, defined **3**:5

P

Packaged software, defined, **6**:2
Packages
  accounts payable, **7**:14
  accounts receivable, **7**:14
  assistance sources, **7**:13–14
  general ledger, **7**:15
  inventory, **7**:14–15
  payroll, **7**:14
  security, **8**:30–32
Parallel testing, defined, **17**:28
Pascal, Blaise, role in FISs, **2**:6
Passwords
  change, frequency of, **22**:6
  for computer security, **22**:5–7
  confidentiality, ensuring, **22**:5–6
  content, **22**:6
  origination, **22**:6
  precautions in use, **22**:5–6
Payroll
  data, evolution in requirements, **1**:14–15
  packages, features of, **7**:14
  processing
    files, **6**:26
    steps in, **6**:24–26
  systems, **6**:24–27
    features, **6**:26–27
    labor distribution, **6**:26–27
    multistate capabilities, **6**:27
    personnel data, **6**:27
    purpose, **6**:25
People, issues of in office automation, **21**:27–29
Performance criteria, **5**:11
Period costs, defined, **12**:7
Personal computers
  See also Microcomputers
  control techniques for, **10**:37–40
Personal computing, content and scope, **21**:18–19
Personnel
  See also Training
  involved in DSS, **16**:6–7
  steering committee, **18**:33
  training
    for disaster recovery, **23**:22–23

INDEX

I-15

[Chapter numbers are boldface and are followed by a colon; lightface numbers after the colon refer to pages within the chapter; italic numbers after the colon refer to figures.]

    importance, **20:**1–2
PIR. *See* Postimplementation review
Planning
    accuracy requirements, **12:**6
    controlling to meet, **3:**6
    cost classifications, **12:**8–9
    defined, **3:**3–5
    for disaster recovery, **23:**1–23
    financial model, use of, **15:**2–3
    horizon for LRSP, **11:**5–6
    information sources, **12:**5
    LANs, **9:**17–18
    need for re FISs, **9:**2–3
    office automation, **9:**11–12, 21–25
    for report types, **3:**16–17
    strategic information needs, **3:**7
    tactical information needs, **3:**7–8
    time horizons, **12:**5
    types of, **12:**2–3
Policies and procedures, as factor in enterprise model, **5:**3
Politics as factor in DP structuring, **4:**13–14
Postimplementation review (PIR), **17:**28–31
    purpose, **17:**28–29
    steps in, **17:**30
    time needed to perform, **17:**29
Printers
    categories, **7:**6–7
    dot matrix, **7:**7
    function, **7:**6–7
    laser, **7:**7–8
    letter quality, **7:**7–8
    near letter quality, **7:**7–8
Privacy as an issue, **21:**21
Private branch exchange (PBX) systems available, **9:**6–7
Problem-solving apparatus, **3:**7–9
Processing (data) inefficiencies, **2:**9
Procurement of an FIS, contract negotiations for, **17:**23–26
Productivity, office
    database management, role in, **8:**4–5
    elements of, **21:**8–11
    and fourth-generation language, **8:**19–20

    nominal group technique to increase, **21:**10–11
    vs. office automation, **21:**2–4
    sociotechnical method to increase, **21:**11
Programmed costs, defined, **12:**7
Programs
    See also Packages
    accounting package, **7:**13–15
    integrated, **7:**12
    software security, **7:**20–21
Project budgets, characteristics of, **12:**26–28
Project manager of FIS
    qualifications, **18:**26–28
    levels of performance, **18:**28–29
Purpose as factor in report design, **3:**16–17

Q

Questionnaires
    for systems requirements design, **17:**5–6
    vendor for RFP, **17:**11–12

R

Reasonable assurance on data center protection, **23:**3
Relational database, defined, **8:**17–19
Relevant data, **3:**12, **5:**5–6
Replacement cost, **12:**8
Reporting, updating probable performance, **13:**39–54
Reporting facility, purpose, **6:**12–13
Reporting principles, **3:**20–22
    See also Reports
Reporting systems, **3:**23
    elements, **5:**10–14
    financial structure for, **13:**7–8
    responsibility report flow, **3:**23–25
Reports
    accounts payable, **6:**21–22
    accounts receivable, **6:**24–25
    acquisitions (orders), **13:***42*

I-16   INDEX

[Chapter numbers are boldface and are followed by a colon; lightface numbers after the colon refer to pages within the chapter; italic numbers after the colon refer to figures.]

Reports *(cont'd)*
  on annual business plan,
    borrowing capacity, **13**:33–34
    cash sources and uses, **13**:28
    complete report, **13**:23–35
    content, **13**:23–24
    financial position, **13**:28–29
    highlights, **13**:24
    net income, comparative, **13**:27
    operating results, trend of, **13**:30–31
    return on assets, **13**:30, 32
    return on shareholders' equity, **13**:33–34
  assets, return on, **13**:18, 21
  assumptions to be disclosed, **13**:9–10
  audit trails, **6**:10–11
  board of directors, summary picture, **13**:7, 8–23, 24–35
  capital budget, **14**:29
  cash
    weekly, **13**:61
    sources and uses of, long-range, **13**:17
  cash flow, **6**:25
  changes in financial position, **13**:57
  classification, **3**:15–25
  conciseness as a factor, **3**:17–19
  control type, **3**:*18*
  current ratio, **13**:18, 22
  earnings per share, **13**:16–17
  elements, essential, **5**:10–14
  event-triggered, **3**:16, 19
  exception, **3**:*19,* **13**:*43, 46*
    audit trail, **6**:10–11
    defined, **5**:13–14
  on financial activities, **13**:61–62
  financial condition, daily, **13**:59–60
  financial management, **13**:6–8
    accounts receivable, **12**:36
    cash budget, **12**:35
    budget summary, by department, **14**:35
    examples, **13**:1–63
    marginal income, by product line, **12**:11
    responsibility of to nonfinancial executives, **14**:2
    suggested subjects for, **13**:61–62
  financial position, **13**:18–20
  flash, **3**:*22*

  flexible budget, **12**:32
  formats, **3**:16, 20–21
  general and administrative management
    expenses by department by type, **14**:36
    expense summaries, **3**:18, **14**:34–35
  GLS output
    custom, **6**:11–13
    semicustom, **6**:11–13
    standard, **6**:11–13
  group performance, **13**:25–26
  highlights, **13**:10–11
  income and expense, **13**:52–54
  informational, **3**:16–17
  interpretive, **3**:*20,* **13**:*43, 58–59*
  legal compliance, **3**:16–17
  long-range financial plan
    assets, return on, **13**:18, 21
    assumptions, **13**:9–10
    cash sources and uses, **13**:17
    content, **13**:8–9
    current ratio, **13**:18, 22
    earnings per share, **13**:17
    financial position, **13**:18–20
    highlights, **13**:11
    long-term debt, **13**:18, 22
    net income, **13**:14–15
    objectives, **13**:9
    operating results by group, **13**:12, 14
    orders, **13**:14
    sales, **13**:10, 12–14
    shareholders' equity, return on, **13**:18, 21
  to or about management, top,
    earnings per share, **13**:16–17
    operating margin, **13**:*49–51*
    overall performance, **13**:*39–54,* **13**:40
    performance by segment, overall, **13**:35–59
    sales, **13**:10–14
  manufacturing manager
    capital budget, **14**:29
    comprehensive selection, **13**:35–54
    costs, departmental vs. budget, **14**:21
    cost summary by department, **14**:20
    departmental costs, **3**:19
    exception report, labor, **14**:23
    expense summary by department, **14**:23

INDEX

I-17

[Chapter numbers are boldface and are followed by a colon; lightface numbers after the colon refer to pages within the chapter; italic numbers after the colon refer to figures.]

information needs, **14**:15
labor
   daily, exception, **14**:23
   vs. standard, **14**:26
labor efficiency trends, **14**:22
manufacturing expense at varying activity levels, **12**:18–19
material, inventory budget, **12**:37
material standard cost, changes, **14**:26
material price variance, **14**:24
material usage
   graphic trend, **14**:22
   by type, **14**:25
marginal income, **12**:11
marketing manager
   advertising and sales promotion budget, **12**:27
   comprehensive examples, **14**:2–17
   department budget by type, **12**:30
   division budget, **14**:8
   exception report, sales, **14**:13
   expense, summary budget, **12**:29
   factors influencing content, **14**:3
   flexible budget, **12**:32
   information requirements, **14**:3–5
   marginal income by product line, **12**:11
   market research project budget, **14**:8
   new orders, **13**:41–42
   occurrence as design factor, **3**:*16*, 19
   product-line income and expense, **14**:7
   sales, long-range plan, **13**:10–14
   sales backlog, **13**:14
   sales performance, **14**:*9–10*
     by division, **14**:11
     exception, **14**:13
     by salesperson, sales and expenses, **14**:14
   selling expenses
     by district, **14**:16–17
     by organization, **14**:16
   simplified, **3**:*21*
   summary budget, **12**:34
   by territory, income and expense, **14**:6
multipurpose, **3**:17
net income, **13**:14–15
for nonfinancial management, **14**:1–37

occurrence as design factor, **3**:*16*, 19
operating margin, **13**:*49–51*
on performance, **13**:35–59
performance
   vs. plan, **13**:35–62
   summary, **13**:37
plant and equipment budget, **14**:29
principles, **3**:20–22
profit center performance, **13**:37
purpose, classification by, **3**:16–17
ratios, long-term debt to worth, **13**:18, 22
responsibility, **3**:23–25
research and development management,
   department expenses vs. budget, **14**:31
   expenses
     vs. budget, **14**:31
     by department, **14**:30
   information needs, **14**:25
   project budgets, **14**:28–32
sales, **13**:*44–45*
sales, by organization, **13**:24–25, 45
sales backlog, **13**:*47–48*
selected structure, **13**:6–8
service company, **13**:*54–59*
shareholders' equity, return on, **13**:18, 21
short-term investments, **13**:62
simplified, **3**:*21*
special analyses, **13**:62–63, **14**:33, 36–37
stewardship, **3**:16–17
summary, **3**:16, 17–18
types, **3**:15–25
writer-facility, **6**:12
Request for Proposal (RFP)
   contents, **17**:10–12
   distribution, **17**:12, 15
   mailing, factors in, **17**:12, 15
   purpose, **17**:10
   review of completed form, **17**:15–20
   software, review of, **17**:15–19
Resources
   information needs, factor in, **3**:7–9
   planning, use of model, **15**:2–3
Responsibility accounting, defined, **3**:23–25, **12**:12–13

[*Chapter numbers are boldface and are followed by a colon; lightface numbers after the colon refer to pages within the chapter; italic numbers after the colon refer to figures.*]

Responsibility reporting
  described, **3:**23–25, **12:**12–13
  problems to avoid, **12:**13–14
Return on assets
  comparative performance, **13:**30, 32
  long-range, reported, **13:**18, 21
  short-term, **13:**30
Return on Investment (ROI) evolution, **1:**12–13
Return on shareholders' equity
  annual business plan, report on, **13:**33–34
  long-term, report on, **13:**18, 21
RFP. *See* Request for Proposal
Risk analysis
  in EDP, **10:**16–19
  in financial modeling, **15:**8–10
Risks, **2:**13
  See also Security
  in data center operation, **23:**2–4
  in EDP
    external, **10:**18
    internal, **10:**18
  reducing, **2:**13–14
"Rules of the game," enterprise model as factor, **5:**3

S

Sales management. *See* Marketing management
Salvage team for disaster recovery, **23:**16
Schema, defined, **8:**8–9
Screen. *See* Microcomputers, monitors
Security
  audit log, contents, **22:**10–11
  audits, need for, **22:**14
  backup system, **7:**20
  of database, **8:**29–33
  in database management, **5:**14–18
  EDP
    risks in, **10:**16–22
    elements of system, **10:**12–13
  in GLS, **6:**17–18
  lapses in, **2:**10–11
  management of, **7:**19–20
  re on-line applications, **22:**1–14

on-line checklist, **22:**12–14
  for on-line FISs, **22:**1–14
  packaged, available types, **8:**30–32
  physical, **7:**19–20
  response to violations, **22:**10
  technology, **2:**5
  training personnel, **20:**5
Semivariable costs
  budget, **12:***16–20*
  components, segregation into, **12:**20–24
  defined, **12:**7, 15
  determining level, **12:**15–24
  graphic determination, **12:**22–24
Senior management
  See also Management
  DP departmental structure, factor in, **4:**12
Sensitivity analysis in modeling, **15:**8–9
Short-term investments, report on, **13:**62
Short-term plan. *See* Annual business plan
Site visits for evaluation, **17:**21–22
Software
  application review of RFP, **17:**16–19
  applications, **7:**11–13
  contract negotiations, **17:**23–26
  cost factors, **17:**22
  criteria for DSS, **16:**17–19
  database
    available systems, **8:**20–24
    factors in selecting, **8:**24–26
  database management programs, **7:**11–13
  defined, **7:**9–11
  defining requirements, **17:**4–10
  favorite programs, **7:**12–13
  for FISs, **17:**1–34
  in-house development, disadvantages, **17:**3–4
  for LAN technology, **9:**13
  packages for financial modeling, **15:**11–18
  popular programs, **7:**12–13
  purchasing, advantages of, **17:**2–4
  programmer productivity, **8:**23–24
  RFP, review of, **17:**15–19
  security, **7:**20–21
  selecting model requirements, **15:**5
  site visits, **17:**21–22

INDEX

I-19

[Chapter numbers are boldface and are followed by a colon; lightface numbers after the colon refer to pages within the chapter; italic numbers after the colon refer to figures.]

spreadsheet programs, **7:**11
systems
  general discussion, **7:**10–11
  review of RFP, **17:**16–19
  user-friendly, defined, **18:**29–30
  user-seductive, defined, **18:**29–30
  vendor evaluation, **27:**30–34
Special costs, budget treatment, **12:**26
Spoolers, defined, **9:**13
Spreadsheets, **15:**11
Stand-alone applications, **2:**8
Standard costs
  re budget, **12:**25
  defined, **12:**8
Steering committee in user participation, **18:**33
Strategic planning
  for office automation, **21:**23–25
  and office productivity, **21:**9
  purpose, **12:**2–3
Success factors in business, **1:**12–15
Suffolk County Federal Savings & Loan Co., disaster plan, **23:**4–5
Sunk costs, defined, **12:**7
SuperCalc, **7:**11
SuperCalc^3, **15:**15
Surveillance
  See also Security
  functions, elements of, **22:**9–10
  re computer security, **22:**9–12
  logs, **22:**10
  responses, **22:**10
  user's role in, **22:**11–12
  violations, reporting, **22:**10
Symphony, **15:**12–13
Systems
  See also Control systems; Financial accounting systems; General ledger system; Information systems; specific systems
  auditability and control, **10:**1–40
  backup, **7:**20, **8:**32–22
  characteristics of new FISs, **2:**9–15
  control, objectives, **10:**23–40
  DBMS, **8:**1–35
  definition as factor in failure of, **18:**13–14

dependability as responsibility of DP personnel, **18:**9–10
development, life cycle, **18:**4–5
engineering, in office productivity, **21:**9–10
evaluation, need for, **18:**36
failure, reasons for, **18:**12–17
implementation
  milestones, need for, **18:**15
  negative impact of, factors in, **18:**16–17
  poor performance, impact of, **18:**14–16
  training of personnel, **20:**1–2
integration, **2:**11–12
maintenance, costs of, **2:**9–10
planning for LANS, **9:**17–18
recovery, **8:**32–33
software
  examples of projects, **11:**17–18
  projects for LRSP, **11:**16–17
software team for disaster recovery, **23:**17
Systems Requirement Definition
  for accounts receivable, **17:***9*
  document reviews, **17:**7
  features, desirable, **17:**8–10
  interviews, use of in, **17:**5–7
  methods, **17:**5–10
  outside sources, use of in, **17:**7–10
  purposes of, **17:**5, 8
  questionnaire, use of in, **17:**5–6
technology **1:**15–16
  changes, impact of on, **1:**15–17
  CIO, role of in, **2:**17–18
  components, **2:**2–5
  defined, **2:**2–3, 5–6
  evolution, **2:**6–7
  finance function, impact of on, **2:**16–17
  FISs, common characteristics, **2:**8–16
  management structure, impact of on, **2:**17–18
  overview, **2:**2
  social impact, **2:**8
  trends, **2:**1–19
Systems validation, user participation, **18:**32
Systems expert, defined, **5:**5

I-20   INDEX

[*Chapter numbers are boldface and are followed by a colon; lightface numbers after the colon refer to pages within the chapter; italic numbers after the colon refer to figures.*]

Systems software, defined, **17**:6
Systems technology, defined, **12**:2–3, 5–6

T

Team
   implementation, for FISs, **17**:26–28
   negotiating, for FISs, **17**:24
   user representative in design, **18**:31–32
Technical support (for DSS), defined, **16**:6
Techniques, modeling **15**:6–10
Technologies
   advanced materials, **2**:4
   disk storage, **2**:4
   fiber optics, **2**:4
   integration, **2**:3–4
   memory, **2**:4
   microprocessor, **2**:3
   network, **2**:4
   office automation, **21**:4–5
   security, **2**:5
   telecommunications, **9**:1–23
Technology, DSS levels, **16**:4
Telecommunications
   general discussion, **9**:1–23
   need for long-range planning, **9**:2–3
Telecommuting, **21**:18
Teleconferencing, **21**:15–17
   audio, **21**:16
   computer, **21**:16
   as part of office automation, **21**:15–17
   types, **21**:16–17
   video, **21**:16–17
Telephone, computer-based features, **9**:9
Testing, **18**:34–35
   parallel, defined, **18**:35
   unit, defined, **18**:35
Time horizons for planning, **12**:5
Timeliness of information, **3**:12
T/Maker III, **15**:15–16
Token passing, LAN access method, **9**:16
Toolsmith, defined, **16**:6
Training, **7**:21–22, **20**:1–19
   aids, **20**:14–15
   case studies, **20**:16–17

   changing technology and, **20**:2
   classroom, **20**:9, 15–16
   for clerks, **20**:4
   re computer controls, **20**:7–8
   for disaster recovery, **23**:22–23
   effective, **20**:14–18
   examples, **20**:16–17
   for hardware use, **20**:6–7
   improper, results of, **20**:6
   in-house
      general discussion, **20**:11–12
      vs. internal, **21**:12–13
   instruction aids, **20**:14–15
   internal, **20**:12–13
   levels of, **20**:3–7
   management, **20**:3–4
   methods, **20**:8–13
   for microcomputer users, **20**:7
   new systems, **20**:13
   operators, **20**:4
   programmed, **20**:11
   retraining, **20**:13–14
   for security, **20**:5
   systems personnel, **20**:5
   time spent, **20**:18–19
   timing of, **20**:13–14
   topics covered, **20**:17–18
   tutorial, **20**:11
   types, **7**:21–22
   users, **8**:28–29, **17**:27, **18**:34–35, **20**:6
   visual aids, **20**:15
Transaction audits, desirable systems features, **8**:32–22
Trends in database management, **8**:33–34
Tutorials as training method, **20**:11

U

Univirate analysis in modeling, **15**:7, 9
User
   access, permitted, defined, **22**:8
   authentication, methods, **22**:4–5
   changing role, **18**:36–37
   complaints, common, **18**:11–12
   defined, **18**:3–4
   vs. DP personnel, **18**:18–20
   -driven computing, popularity, **18**:21–22
   identification of types, **22**:3–7

INDEX

[Chapter numbers are boldface and are followed by a colon; lightface numbers after the colon refer to pages within the chapter; italic numbers after the colon refer to figures.]

levels of, **18**:3–4, 23
motivating, **18**:24
needs
  defining, **18**:5–11
  dependability of system, **18**:9–10
  design considerations, **18**:7
  documentation, **18**:10
  DP, lack of response from, **18**:18–19
  flexibility, **18**:8
  general discussion, **18**:5–11
  operational considerations, **18**:7
  participation, **18**:1–18
  quality issue, **18**:7–11
  summarized, **18**:10–11
  training, **18**:10
participation, **18**:1–18
  in cost/benefit analysis, **18**:33–34
  current trends, **18**:20–22
  factors improving, **18**:20–22
  functions, **18**:31–34
  importance of, **18**:2–3
  involvement, need for, **18**:4–5
  role of, **18**:17–22
  vs. user involvement, **18**:20
resource access, defined, **22**:7–8
satisfaction subjectivity, **18**:5–11
testing, types, **18**:35
training, **8**:28–29
  need for, **18**:10
  types of, **18**:34–35
traits of good, **18**:23–24
weaknesses, characteristic, **2**:8–11
User-friendly software, defined, **18**:29–30

V

Value added networks (VANs), **9**:3–6
  examples, **21**:17
  vendors, **9**:5–6

VANs. *See* Value added networks
Variable budget
  See also Flexible budget
  defined, **12**:28–29
Variable costs
  defined, **12**:7
  measures of activity, **12**:15
Vendor
  cost summary for RFP, **17**:12, 13
  evaluation, **17**:20–23, 33–34
  hardware proposal, evaluation, **17**:31–33
  reference calls, **17**:20–21
  VANs, **9**:5–6
Version control, elements, **5**:16–17
Video display tube. *See* Microcomputers, monitors
Video teleconferencing
  described, **21**:16–17
  stop motion video, **21**:16–17
VisiCalc, function, **7**:11
Visual aids for training, **20**:15
Voice mail, **21**:15
Voice messaging, features, **9**:9–10
Volume relative to costs, **12**:9–10

W

Word processing, function, **21**:11–12
"What-if" analysis in modeling, **15**:6–7